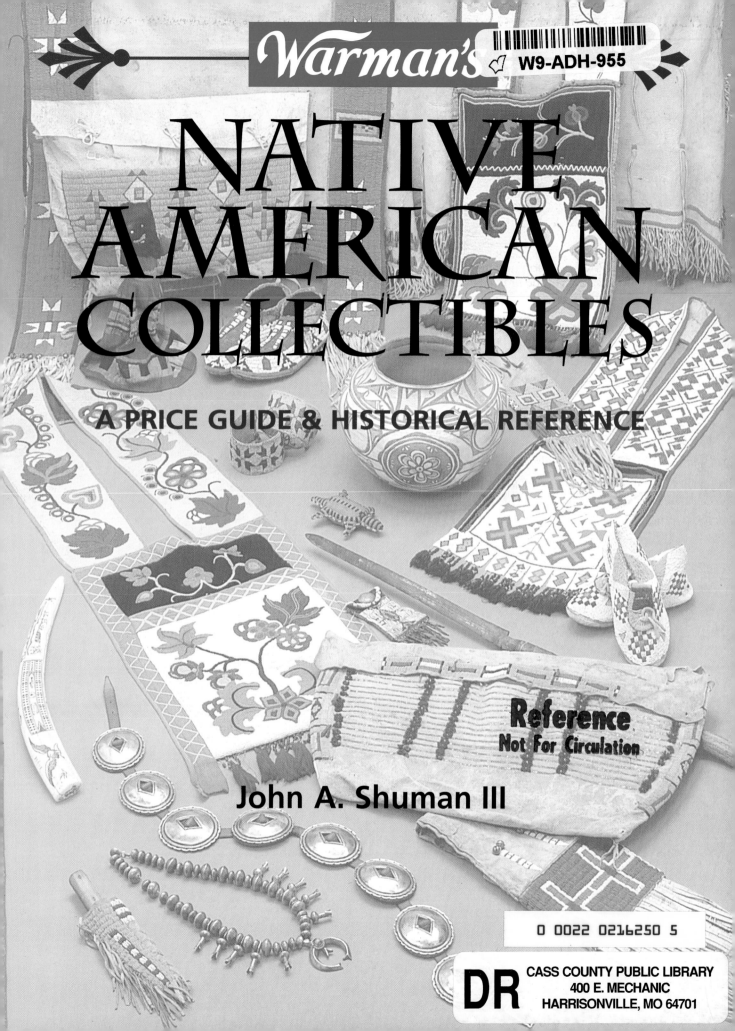

Warman's
NATIVE AMERICAN COLLECTIBLES

W9-ADH-955

A PRICE GUIDE & HISTORICAL REFERENCE

John A. Shuman III

Published by

**krause
publications**

700 East State Street, Iola, WI 54990-0001

Please, call or write us for our free catalog of antiques and collectibles publications. To place an order or receive our free catalog, call 800-258-0929. For editorial comment and further information, use our regular business telephone at (715) 445-2214.

Library of Congress Catalog Number: 97-80613
ISBN: 0-87069-767-6
Printed in the United States of America

Front cover photo: courtesy of Dunning's

Back cover photos: clockwise from top right, Pomo basket, courtesy of Bowers Museum Collections; Sioux shirt, courtesy of Midwest Auctions; doll from Ruby, Alaska, courtesy of Midwest Auctions; jar, courtesy of Bowers Museum Collections; and wooden "Booger" face mask, from Elwood Brunt Collection.

TABLE OF CONTENTS ━━━━━━━━━━━━━━ ✦

DEDICATION: ELWOOD BRUNT

Warman's Native American Collectibles: A Pictorial Price Guide & Historical Reference is dedicated to Elwood Brunt, owner of the Lenape Indian Museum and Trading Post, 2159 Weber Rd., Lansdale, PA 19446. Call (610) 584-6761 for an appointment; admission is by donation. In addition to the many local elementary school children and other groups from the United States who visit the museum, there are people from all over the world who take the tour, including those from Canada, the European countries, Asia and Africa.

Mr. Brunt and I met some years ago at the Kutztown Extravaganza in Pennsylvania. I was attracted to his booth by the primitives and Indian arts and crafts that he offered. We met and talked many times, and I have found Mr. Brunt to be cordial, honest, straight-forward, courteous and intelligent. In short he is both a scholar and collector, along with his travel and love of the Native Americans. On Sept. 22, 1996, the first day of autumn at 1:00 PM, the following interview was granted by Mr. Brunt:

Q: How old are you and how did you get started in collecting?

A: I will be 81 years old in December 1996 and I began collecting when I was 12, thus I have been at it for 68 years. I joined the Boy Scouts when I was 12, and the Scoutmaster picked up an arrowhead. That Friday night, he came to the meeting with a cigar box of arrowheads. Well, that intrigued me so much that I decided that I would search until I found something. Along the Wissahickon Creek, I found my first arrowhead and I have been walking the fields ever since.

Q: I've heard that many of the Indians are leaving the reservations to work at something other than making turquoise/silver jewelry in the Southwest. [I've heard] that there are 153 gambling casinos nationwide run by the Indians. Do your agree?

A: Ya, I would say so, most of the early good old trades are gone. A lot of the weaving and other arts are being made in Mexico and elsewhere.

Q: Is it too late to go out in the field and collect?

A: Most good articles have been collected and only come out of collections about every 35 years. Then they are offered usually at high-priced catalog auctions. I know of two young collectors who got together over 200 pieces which they found up above Williamsport.

Q: People dig and they follow the plows to discover stone artifacts?

A: People used to follow the horse plows in the spring, when they harrowed and planted corn; a few weeks later, they would cultivate the corn and the top soil was stirred up. Now they never cultivate the corn. In the fall, the corn would be in the shock and the ground would be bare. I often found arrowheads with a shotgun over my shoulder, when there weren't any rabbits to shoot at. Today modern machines grind up the soil, so unless you're digging, you would not discover an ax head, for example.

Q: What about the interest in Native Americans in the 1990s?

A: There has been the movie, "Dances With Wolves" and the TV series called "The West." Also, the Smithsonian will have a separate building to contain their collection ready in the year 2002. One of the things that amazes me is the interest that foreigners have in Indians. I have sold objects that have been shipped all over the world to museums and collectors.

Q: Where could one go to see many of George Catlin's original paintings?

A: If you ever get out to the Buffalo Bill Museum in Cody, Wyoming, they have a lot of his paintings.

Q: What did William Penn have to say about the Indian and the white man?

A: "He invites me in out of the rain, he gives me food, he gives me drink, he warms me at his fireplace. The white man invites me to his home and says give me money."

Q: How did the different tribes of Indians communicate since there were so many different dialects?

A. The tribes devised a method of symbols—hand and facial gestures that all could understand. These symbols and pictures were carried over to their teepees, clothing and buffalo robes. I have been fortunate over the years to have picked up six buffalo robes at farm sales—no one wanted them. The first one I paid $1.50 for. The backing was torn, so I removed the cloth to discover a date of 1840 along with the drawings. I sold two to a man in Oklahoma back in the 1960s for $40 each. Five of the robes were attributed to Western Indians; the one presently in the museum has been attributed to Eastern Indians by the Smithsonian.

Q: What about the origin of Indians and their characteristics?

A: They were the first people in America who immigrated across the Bering Strait to Alaska when land bridges existed. As wandering hunters some 30,000 years ago, they sought ice free lands and hunting grounds. As they spread across North and South America, they learned to adapt to the climates. Most were tall with broad cheekbones, sloping foreheads, bold jaws and muscular bodies. Their skins were cinnamon to copper colored. Indian farmers were the first to grow tobacco, squash, pumpkin, wild rice, tomato, pineapple, sweet potato, avocado, gourd, bean and peanut. Other products that were Indian gifts to the Americas were rubber, quinine, coca, cashew nut, maple sugar, the toboggan, pipe, turkey, the kayak, moccasin and parka.

Q: What did the white man learn from the Indian and vice versa?

A: *Indians learned not to trust whites, that they broke over 400 treaties, that they destroyed their homes, families, gave them smallpox and other diseases, destroyed the buffalo and moved them to reservations. The Indians learned from whites about guns, rifles, alcohol, beads and numerous other articles of trade. The whites have learned to look at the history of the Native Americans with great awe and respect. Today their arts and crafts are admired and collected with enthusiasm.*

Q: What do modern Indians know about their heritage?

A: *Very little, they buy arrowheads and other Indian articles at flea markets. In Gallup, New Mexico, there are at least two or three hock-shops in every block, filled with turquoise, jewelry, saddles and guns. The first of the month, they get their checks and go in to get their stuff out of hock. Drugs and alcohol are still big problems. For many Indians, their diets are poor as they live on junk foods.*

Q: Do any of the Indians wear the old-fashioned garb today?

A: *No, only for special occasions, such as talks, rallies and powwows.*

Q: What were some of the key factors that proved to be the undoing of the Indians?

A: *The poor attitudes that whites had toward them, the Westward Movement, the transcontinental railroad, killing off the buffalo, the discovery of gold at Sutter's Mill and the spreading of white man's diseases.*

Q: Where would one go to find Indian pieces?

A: *No matter what you collect, there is more to he found in Pennsylvania, New York and Ohio, than anywhere else. Perhaps it's because our history goes back to the founding of Philadelphia, plus the wealth in the area.*

Q: Who started the process of scalping?

A: *From my reading it was the government who offered soldiers up to $50 per scalp. Only the round central crown was taken and many whites lived to tell about the harrowing experiences.*

Q: What do you think about the recent movement and the right of ownership as brought out by law, lawyers, whites and Native Americans?

A: *Many Indians today do not know about the ancient customs and practices or what was sacred. Museums and dealers must be ready to verify and state the province and situations under which articles were acquired. The government will only legally permit Native Americans to own eagle feathers.*

Q: Tell us about the Cliff Dwellers?

A: *I was able to climb into Montezuma's Castle in 1972—it has since caved in. But I was able to look across to Montezuma's Well and I could see the roadway that they used to water their corn.*

Q: What about the variety in museums?

A: *Each one is different. In recent diggings, more respect has been shown for burial sites. Many museums have great quantities in storage that are only show on occasion. Some feature beaded items, others focus on pottery, baskets, clothing and war articles. Some articles over the years were donated through wills to museums.*

Q: What sites locally [Pennsylvania] were important in the development of the Indians and their interaction with the whites?

A: *Bethlehem for the Moravians, William Penn and his treaty with the Indians, Conestoga, near Lancaster where the "Prairie Wagon," or Conestoga wagon was built. Also Baumstown near Reading, where Daniel Boone was born and lived until 16. Then he took his Kentucky rifle, made in the Lancaster area, and moved with his family to North Carolina. He fought in many wars and also helped to defend several forts.*

Q: Site an interesting and unusual happening during your travels?

A: *We were in Pendleton, Oregon, in 1976 and a parade was coming down the street with horseback riders and Conestoga Wagons, and we found out that they were going to Valley Forge, PA. The state park was given over to the government as a national park during the short presidency of Gerald Ford.*

Q: What about the Indian's general longevity?

A: *The incidents of death among infants was very high. Only the really strong survived. Smallpox and cholera killed large groups. In Paducah, we viewed a skull in the museum with seven drill holes and the person lived.*

Q: How did European beads revolutionize the Indian's mode of dress?

A: *Previous to this there was a whole range of shells: cardium, conus, glycemeris, olivella, conch shells, whelks, columella, marginella, cowrie and dentalium of all colors and shapes. They were used for rings, pendants, fetishes, trumpets, drinking, tools, as money, belts and decoration on mantles, headdresses, girdles and anklets. During the 16th and 17th centuries, beads were sold made by glassblowers in Spain, France, England, Holland, Sweden and Murano in Venice. Today beaded examples are highly coveted by collectors.*

INTRODUCTION

Vision Quest

The vision quest took us back thousands of years. It was a chance to ponder our dreams and reinforce a spirit of freedom and independence, to commune with the spirits and get to know nature again as a friend, to communicate and coexist in a disciplined and harmonious way. This was long before the white man arrived on our grounds.

We had crossed over the Bering Strait land bridge from Asia and entered a new land, rich in plants, animals, one that provided everything. As we continued to migrate, we adapted tools and learned how to live off the land.

There were hot and cold regions, mountains and valleys, arid deserts, refreshing thirst quenching streams and lakes, plains and forested areas. We learned how to cure with roots and herbs, plant, hunt, fish, trap and harvest.

Our own kind found nourishment from growing corn, pleasure from weaving baskets and rugs. Needs were fulfilled through our pottery and other arts, plus irrigation, house construction, storage pits and burial sites.

As a unified people we established cultural traits, mannerisms, beliefs, styles that became evident in our arts and crafts. Creations were both functional and beautiful and we traveled and traded with other tribes. Through our contact we continued to learn and grow. We knew nothing yet of the Europeans—their men, animals, diseases. That was all yet to come.

We were dependent upon and lived in harmony with nature. It was our source of life and death, of reward and punishment. Man was a part of nature, not apart from it!

Our thinking was derived from our parents at an early age. We did not know self-inflicted whips, threats, punishments. Children grew in an adult world and were indulged and quietly supported. Our mothers gave us much attention; they were affectionate, nursed and taught us cleanliness and how to walk and talk. Young males were being instructed in survival, how to hunt, use the bow and arrow and the knife.

Our word was sacred; it was the law. We knew honor, dignity and trust. A critical part of our behavior was to know the true nature of a person we came in contact with and remain silent until the relationship was evident.

We did not have written laws, but established codes of conduct among each other, within the family and the tribe. The Indian knew what was expected of him in every situation. Revenge or retribution for crimes were dealt with according to tribal customs and sanctions.

As whites began arriving, we initially were friendly and provided for their every need. Our Indian generosity implied similar generosity in return when it was needed. Thus the term "Indian giver," properly understood, suggested a barter system, a psychological equivalent, both a diplomatic and human response. This attitude toward goods was also carried through with the transfer of lands.

More and more ships arrived and the quest for power began. There was the age old question as to who owned the land. As a collective people the white culture was very materialistic. From the beginning there were gifts and countergifts, ceremonial trade, speeches and feasts.

We Indians favored receiving mirrors, European cloth, liquor, beads, brass thimbles, copper, sword blades, steel files and guns. In return we offered furs, harvested crops, tobacco, meats, blankets, pottery, jewelry and baskets. But, that was not enough.

Whites altered our valued environment with trade, enslavement, war, alcohol, diseases and expulsion. There was intense competition for hunting and fishing; whites possessed finer firearms, metal knives, fishhooks, iron cooking pots. Being naive, we were cheated when trading goods, morals were reduced through lust and liquor, many diseases began to take their toll and choice lands were surrendered by way of negotiations, grants and treaties.

Forts were built, towns established. The Conestoga wagon, rifle and horse opened the doors wide for travel. Disagreement arose between Indians and whites and between one tribe and another. One treaty was broken, then another. White men "spoke with forked tongues."

Generous gifts cemented relationships; inadequate gifts caused alliances to deteriorate. In wartime we could be supportive. The generosity of one colony toward a tribe could exceed that of another and soon trouble was brewing.

Then came Lewis and Clark charting 2,000 unknown miles. Their bribes were the peace medals. In 1827 Governor Lew Cass "made tribal leaders" among the Menominees. The principal chief looked upon the medal as a "token of Friendship," a "badge of power," a "trophy of renown."

Religious missions became prevalent throughout the U.S. There was the "belief that the heathen should be converted." Our Indian society had not drawn the line between politics and religion. Thus, thousands were converted, some unfortunately through threats and punishments.

Then came the Indian Wars brought on by unreasonable white demands and English authority unwilling to concede to Indian nations. There was resentment, massacre; colonists, soldiers and we died in great numbers. At the end of the 17th century, our Atlantic coastal tribes were either destroyed, dispersed or subjected to European control.

The American Revolution became the turning point in American Indian history; the character of Indian-white relationships was changed forever. Articles of peace were signed after the war, in Paris on Nov. 30, 1782. The British ceded lands that we held, but no provisions were made for us. Individual tribes were selling lands to the confederacy. The 1830s saw the removal—voluntary, induced and forced of the Seminoles, Choctaw, Cherokee and Creek. The forced marches to forlorn lands across the Mississippi had begun. After the War of 1812, John C. Calhoun, President Monroe's Secretary of War, established the Bureau of Indian Affairs.

Andrew Jackson became president in 1830 and the tides were turned forever as he enacted the Indian Removal Act to the Trans-Mississippi West. There was a brief remission during the Civil War, but from 1830-1890 the destruction of our way of life was brought to a remorseless and rapid conclusion. The army, economic greed, cultural blindness and political advantage were our undoing.

First confronted by the Europeans were the Northeast and the Atlantic seaboard; then the Great Lakes and the North; the Southeast and Florida; California; the Northwest coast; the Great Basin; and finally the Plains.

The Medicine Lodge Treaty of 1876 was to grant the principal tribes of the Plains reservations. This like over 400 other treaties was broken by white man. Between 1870-1874, 100 million buffalo were slaughtered to feed the eastern market with hides, tallow and buttons. A white hunter with his big "buffalo gun" killed 200 in one day.

Chief Red Cloud, an Oglala Sioux in 1865 detained an army detachment sent to watch the Bozman Trail through Montana. The army ignored warnings and entered Powder River, WY. Red Cloud's War in 1866 killed 80 soldiers outside Fort Laramie. Two years later the garrisons were removed and the forts were dismantled. Red Cloud was the only Indian to win a war against the United States.

General Sheridan in charge of the War Department sent General George Custer to fight the Hunkpapa and Oglala Sioux and the Cheyenne at the battle of Little Big Horn on June 25, 1876. In less than an hour Custer and 224 men of the Seventh Cavalry were dead. News of the disaster roused and angered white Americans. They sought justice.

The last scene in the drama was with Chief Joseph and the Nez Perce who had lived in Oregon and Idaho on lands awarded by treaty. Gold was discovered on the reservation and we Indians were asked to leave our fertile Wallowa Valley. Violence broke out, as we were preparing to move, whites died and troops were beaten at the battle of White Bird Canyon. Eighteen other skirmishes followed; and then came the two day battle at Kamiah, ID, against General Howard and his 600 men. Chief Joseph decided to flee, rather than surrender. With his 200 warriors and 600 women and children he traveled 2,000 miles seeking asylum in Canada. His trip was cut short by only 30 miles and on Oct. 7, 1877, Joseph's lament and surrender conveyed for later generations the utter and crushing defeat we experienced.

In the early 1880s the Nations held 138 million acres. The Dawes Severalty Act of 1887 and the Burke Act of 1907 reduced our holdings to 52 million acres. In the Dawes Act, 30 million acres were allotted to each of us individually; in 1934, 29 of the 30 million acres ended up in the hands of whites. We were losing about 4,500 acres per day.

Our former good fortunes had reached their lowest point. The Plains were no longer filled with the thundering dust and brownish haze of millions of buffalo causing iron horses to halt for hours.

Tribal villages were gone with smoke eddying heavenward through the niches in the teepee tops; many tribal cultures had been completely wiped out by fighting and diseases. White power now confined us to the reservation system with specific boundaries.

A reversal occurred under President Harding who had appointed Albert B. Fall, Secretary of the Interior. Fall and his friends declared by executive order that oil reserves found at Teapot Dome, WY, and Elk Hills, CA, both on reservations, belonged to the government. With Harding's sudden death, Calvin Coolidge became the 30th President on Aug. 2, 1923. He appointed lawyers to prosecute those involved in the oil scandals One Supreme Court Judge from Chester County, PA, was Owen J. Roberts; he successfully placed the guilty in jail.

In 1933 President Roosevelt appointed John Collier, Commissioner of Indian Affairs. The Indian Reorganization Bill of 1934 gradually revolutionized the way whites thought about our culture. Bans were lifted on ceremonials, folkways and the wearing of Indian dress. Our people were beginning to acquire a sense of dignity and self-respect.

Today there are 317 reservations in 26 states. Our Indian populations are on the increase, estimated at around 800,000. Over half of the population work on and half off the reservations.

A major event occurred in Washington, DC, in July 1978, when several hundred Native Americans walked for five months from San Francisco. This "Longest Walk" symbolized our forced removal from our original homelands. The "Walk" was spiritual and peaceful.

Much work still needs to be accomplished! Forgiving is required by both sides, along with truthful conversation, restitutions and settlements of lands and mineral rights.

Native Americans are alive and well and being highly acclaimed and accepted in the areas of arts, crafts and collectibles. There are contemporary examples in literature and fine arts; marble and stone; metal and wood; quality pottery and baskets; jewelry and clothing; and the like. And of course, there are the cherished items of antiquity that show off our power and beauty through a specific art. Today museums, galleries, historical societies, collectors and dealers, seek examples of merit and excellence to include: baskets and pottery; jewelry and textiles; clothing and skinwork; appliqué, quill and beadwork; wood and stonework; metals and shellworks; plus objects fabricated in bone, antler and horn. Prices continue to escalate and quality items are becoming very scarce.

Here are areas in which you might want to focus a collection:
• Memorabilia from TV shows, miniseries, motion pictures
• Postage stamps, coins, paper currency
• Limited editions: lithographs, oils, temperas, prints, jewelry
• Logos on fruit crates, cigar bands, cigar boxes, other brand name products
• Blankets, rugs, felt pennants, puzzles, early cigarette flags
• Popular records, tapes, sheet music, plays
• Vintage and contemporary busts and statues: chalk, plaster, bronze, china, clay, porcelain, pottery, glass
• Postcards, books, magazine articles, newspapers, maps, calendars, trade agreements, treaties, land deeds, letters
• Clothing, beadwork, baskets, pottery, jewelry, war accouterments, arrowheads, projectile points, axes, chipped artifacts, banners, stones, weights, pendants, gorgets, birdstones, effigies
• Circus-related items
• Indian dolls: plastic, wood, wax, clay, material, hide, bisque, porcelain, china
• Hardwood carved and decorated objects, totems, carved cigar store Indians and princesses, birch bark items
• Quillwork, clay and cast pipes, toys and games
• Paintings (all media): sand, oil, animal and vegetable pigments
• Whirligigs, weathervanes, dance masks, hide and ledger drawings
• Patent medicine containers and their original advertisements
• Broadsides, steel engravings (hand-colored examples)
• Bookends, doorstops, slot machines, letter openers, lead Indian play sets, figurines, match safes, metal Tiffany objects
• Banks, buttons, calendar plates, cookie jars, Gone with the Wind lamps, lunch boxes, plastic figurine sets, chess sets, Masonic pieces, tin and iron toys, wind-up and battery-operated toys, automotive emblems
• Bauer Pottery, Rookwood Pottery, Flow Blue, Indian Tree China, Nippon porcelains, Mosaic Tile Company, North Dakota School of Mines, Overbeck Pottery, Roseville Pottery, Sleepy Eye Stoneware, Frankoma Pottery, Clifton Pottery, Heisey Wampum Pattern Glass, Majolica, Weller, Van Briggle Pottery
• Bottle openers, carousel pieces, Christmas lights and ornaments, folk art figures, Halloween Indian costumes, paper dolls, glass and wooden tomahawks

ACKNOWLEDGMENTS

Creating a book from beginning to end requires patience, understanding, stamina, disappointments and hard work. It is an act of love and giving birth, in order to inform the reading audience about a particular area of collecting. Ideas must be generated and put into motion. Personal photo sessions take days and weeks with lighting, setting up, tearing down, measuring, describing and pricing. Letters and telephone calls take time. Acquiring transparencies and slides on loan requires focus and dedication. All of this information must be processed and arranged logically in the text. Then there are proofreading, retyping, rearranging, additions and subtractions. The entire process requires complete discipline and drive to see a task satisfactorily through to its completion.

The facts volunteered are based upon research. Prices are from a variety of sources: private collectors, dealers, auction houses and museums. The prices shown are simply a guide, they do not indicate that you could buy or sell an artifact for the same money. In some instances, no prices are given at the request of the individual to honor their privacy. Certainly a book of this nature can offer a limited amount of information and illustrations. Generally the examples shown are available to the museum and collector. Hopefully this volume will serve you well and enable you to have a clearer picture of Native Americans.

I would like to thank the following organizations, companies and individuals for their help.

Alderfer's Auction Company: Hatfield, PA

George Batman: 226 Hanley Pl., Reading, PA 19611

Bookworm: 742 Main St., Phoenixville, PA 19460

The Bowers Museum of Cultural Art: 2002 N. Main St., Santa Ana, CA, Armand J. Labbe, director of research and collections/chief curator and Jackie Bryant, visual coordinator

Christie's: 502 Park Ave., New York, NY, Stacy Marcus Chidekel, consultant

CML Books: The Market Place, Morgantown, PA 19543

Cottone Auctions and Appraisals: 15 Genesee St., Mt. Morris, NY 14510, Samuel J. Cottone, owner

Elizabeth R. Davidson: West Chester, PA

Desert Winds: Rt. 282 and Marshall Road, Glenmoore, PA 19343

Dunning's: 755 Church Rd., Elgin, IL 60123, Shawn Dunning, advertising and public relations

John A. Eastman: 858 N. Woodstock St., Philadelphia, PA 19130

Lenape Indian Museum and Trading Post: 2159 Weber Rd., Lansdale, PA 19446, Elwood Brunt, owner

Merritt's Museum of Childhood: Rt. 422, P.O. Box 277, Douglassville, PA 19518, Anne Darrah

Midwest Auctions, Inc.: 13594 500th Ave., Miles, IA 52064, Phil Russo and Frank Henagan Collections, Mr. and Mrs. Hayward, owners

National Museum of the American Indian: Smithsonian Institution, One Bowling Green, New York, NY, Laura Nash

The Philbrook Museum of Art: 2727 S. Rockford Rd., Tulsa, OK, David B. Gabel, registrar

Pioneer Auction Gallery: 158 SW First Ave., Canby, OR 97013

Portland Art Museum: 1219 SW Park Ave., Portland, OR, Ann Eichelberg, assistant registrar

Rankokus Indian Reservation: Burlington County, NJ

Sheldon Jackson Museum: 104 College Dr., Sitka, AK, Peter L. Corey, curator

Howard Szmolko: antique dealer, Lahaska, PA

"Unexplained Mysteries": aired locally on channel 39, Oct. 16, 1996, 8 p.m.; host: Robert Stack, "An Albino Buffalo Calf"

United American Indians of the Delaware Valley: 225 Chestnut St., Philadelphia, PA 19106, Michel T. Leonard

Note: Objects pictured without prices are at the request of the museums.

The Merritt's Museum of Indian Art and Relics, a 33-year collection, was sold on Monday, Nov. 17, 1997, 4:00 PM by the Conestoga Auction Company, 768 Graystone Rd., Manheim, PA 17545. Prices reflect the selling value plus a 10% buyer's premium. Buyers attended from 25 states and Canada.

ABOUT THE AUTHOR

John A. Shuman III—a lifelong resident of Pennsylvania—taught secondary English for 35 years, plus a variety of adult courses. He avidly buys and sells, refinishes, lectures on and appraises antiques. He enjoys photography and attending flea markets and antique shows. Shuman takes great pleasure in traveling and researching glass, china, primitives, arts and crafts, collectibles and assorted antiques. His memberships include: Smithsonian Associates, Nature Conservancy, Pennsylvania State Antiques Association, Antique Appraisal Association of America, Mount Washington Art Glass Society and The National Early American Glass Club.

He is a graduate of Bloomsburg High School, Wyoming Seminary, Bloomsburg University and Pennsylvania State University. He has visited renowned museums, galleries and historical societies both in the United States and Europe. His travels have taken him to the British Isles and 16 European counties on seven occasions.

Over three decades, he has written more than 1,000 articles for the following publications: *Collector News, The New York Antique Almanac, The Antique Trader Weekly, Antiques Journal, The Antique Trader Price Guide to Antiques, The Historical Review of Berks County* and *Glass Collector's Digest*. He created two videos on American and European Art Glass for Award Video and Film Distributors (Sarasota, Florida) in 1993. As a feature writer, his weekly column on general antiques has appeared in the Sunday edition of the *West Chester Daily Local* since 1988.

Warman's Native American Collectibles is Shuman's fifth book; his other titles are *Art Glass Sampler, The Collector's Encyclopedia of American Art Glass, Lion Pattern Glass* and *The Collector's Encyclopedia of Gaudy Dutch and Welsh*.

CHAPTER 1

ART &
ARTISTS

Arrowhead display: left, 10" spear head and knives; right, drills, gorgets, flute points, small bird points—$400. (Elwood Brunt Collection)

An Introspective Look into Native North American Visual Arts

The diverse Native North American arts have a history of some 25,000 years. They are part of a living cultural tradition which is deeply rooted in the past and shows much promise for the future. Since the 1960s, there has been a renewed interest in Native North American arts. Awareness has been brought about through art historians, books, TV programs, archaeologists and ethnohistorians. North American art is complex, unique and indigenous to the soil of the United States.

Native arts fall into four categories:

1. Traditional arts forms used by the community

2. Tourist art forms sold for years to both travelers and collectors

3. Contemporary arts sold in galleries which includes crafts, prints and carvings

4. Mainstream art which is now in major provincial, state and national museums and historical societies

North American art dates somewhere between 25,000 B.C. to 1800 A.D. Works have been uncovered by bulldozers, through digging and by farmers plowing their fields. Much of an early era was lost due to the fact that art forms were perishable: hide, wood, vegetable and animal fibers. Best preserved are works of stone, clay, antler and bone.

"Rock art" includes pictographs and engravings accomplished on flat bedrock surfaces, vertical cliffs, on boulders and rock shelters. Many are impossible to date accurately; cave art dates back 30,000 years in France and Spain. Many contemporary Native artists have been inspired by these works.

Native societies set down through "oral tradition" embroidery, paintings and incisions on hides and bark of their art and culture. Colonists dated such happenings between 1500 A.D. and 1900 (first in the 16th century in the Southwest and the 17th century in the Great Lakes). Examples were gathered by traders, explorers, missionaries and government agencies. Some are housed in museums in Spain, Germany, Russia, Canada, the United States, Great Britain and other sites.

Colonial period Native art is called "post-contact." For more than 300 years, examples were sketched, collected and studied by scholars, artists and other factions of the society.

Tourist or souvenir examples were created to satisfy the need of the Euro-American market. The Haida of British Columbia carved the small wooden totems; Pueblo women made pottery to be sold; the Hopi and Zuni created Kachina dolls; the Southwest fabricated Navajo blankets; and there was beadwork and embroidery for the tourists from the Niagara Falls area. Unfortunately. booming business has created trade of arts and crafts

Arrowhead mixture of western and Pennsylvania types; in the center is a huge spear point—$400. (Elwood Brunt Collection)

Arrowheads, copper and glass beads, elk teeth beads—$225. (Elwood Brunt Collection)

by workers in Korea, Canada, Japan and Taiwan.

On the Canadian Northwest Coast, the law of 1884 banned important ritual rites, called the "potlatch." Now that Bill 87 has been repealed, carvers and painters create totems and masks and totems are being raised along the coast in Native villages. Art works are for sale to include bowls, masks, rattles and boxes. Other workers produce prints, paintings, bronzes, soapstone, ivory and bone carvings. There are also silk-screens, engravings and etchings to be collected.

Noteworthy to the Southwest are the Zuni Pueblo, Hopi, San Ildefonso and Navajo peoples producing silver jewelry, hand-woven textiles, painted pottery and baskets. Maria Martinez, who died in 1980, inspired all and instructed and motivated such potters as Elizabeth Naranjo and Juan Tafoya.

Indian music and dance occurs throughout North America and on the reservations. No Indian dance exists without music; today women are taking larger roles in these ceremonies. Dances are performed to entertain, for religious reasons, as a way of life , to renew the world and to keep it in balance. The U.S. government banned the Sun Dance and the Ghost Dance in the late 19th century. Missionaries in many instances changed and exterminated many Native practices so that the heritage was lost forever.

Since the 19th century, scholars (both Indian and non-Indian) have tried to preserve the Indian way of life: customs, languages, stories, dance, music, history, folklore, linguistics and anthropology. Younger Indians have recorded traditional music and dance plus rituals, oral histories, narratives and stories.

Voice is important to Indian music accompanied by drums and rattles. Singers create solos, choruses and multi-part songs. Both water and soft hide covered drums are used. Rattles are created from gourds, coconut shells, turtle shells, buffalo tails, carved wood, baskets, bark, rawhide, clay, moose feet and metal shakers. Other instruments include flutes, whistles, fiddles, clap sticks, rasps, scrapers and bullroarers. Indian composers and singers play a major role in both creating and passing on Indian music through oral tradition.

Dances are tied to life cycles and seasonal events; they are regional and tribal by nature and the singers perform in native languages. Solo dances are few but there are many group events. Small steps are taken to conserve energy, while the head and torso are filled with movement. Dancers move in both clockwise and counterclockwise fashion, dance in place, move forward or backward in groups and repeat to cover all four directions in their proper order.

Games of the North American Indians are played using both dance and music. Popular games include stick games and handgames. Each team has experienced guessers and lucky songs. Men and women have separate games and gender-specific songs.

Eskimos in Alaska and Canada gather in midwinter in large community houses for dance and music. Male and female dancers act out daily activities, hunting and fishing. Fiddle guitar music and shallow drums made from the bladders of large sea animals are the custom.

The Northwest Coast area has multi-part singing, rituals and elaborate painted screens. Honors to music and dancing include honoring families, installing a totem or recognizing a new chief. Washington State Indians concen-

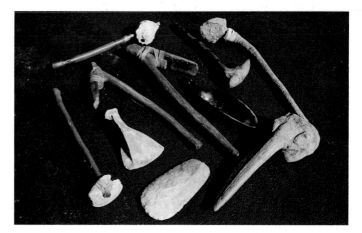

Shown clockwise are a variety of work tools: conch shell, clam shell, Arizona beef jerky mallet, Pennsylvania hoes and axes—$100 each. In the center is a horn dipper, trowel and a polished stone—$100 each. (Elwood Brunt Collection)

Trade axes. Top left: hoe with twisted handle; right, hand forged hoe; along with a grouping of other examples— $250 each. (Elwood Brunt Collection)

A cottonwood branch showing how its interior fibers were braided and fluffed—$35. (Elwood Brunt Collection)

1-11. An early type of "Indian corn" believed to be like that grown by Native Americans. Note how each kernel is sheathed separately—$15. (Elwood Brunt Collection)

1-12. A grouping of clubs: Mohawk tree root; New York Mohawk burl; Plains variety with a stone head; and carved Penobscot club with Indian face. $150 each. (Elwood Brunt Collection)

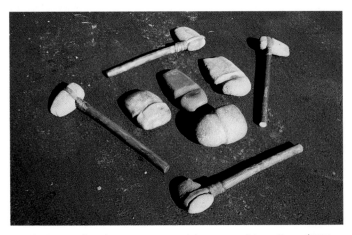

1-13. Pennsylvania stone axes with restored handles—$300 each; center stones—$300-$400 each. (Elwood Brunt Collection)

trate on ritual healing with the ringing of bells. Northwest California Indians center their dance and music around world renewal and healing.

In California, vocals are relaxed using rattles. Both men and women play double whistles, dance and sing and use split-stick clappers for healing rituals and social dances. Music and dance are common at funerals and fiestas. Bird songs are the main repertoire.

Masks, decorative textiles and body painting have always been important in the Pueblo Indian arts. Important instruments include gourd rattles, wooden drums and deer hoofs, turtle shell and marine shell rattles worn by the dancers. Ceremonies are seasonal, many are called feast days where friends and relatives are expected to accept their hospitality. Apaches and Navajos use music and dance to cure rituals and prepare girls for puberty ceremonies.

The Plains area stretches from Texas to Canada, and this great variety of peoples has made popular the intertribal powwow. Flutes were used for courting and love songs. Small hand-held drums were played by a group of men in unison.

Both sexes perform music in the Eastern Woodlands, the Southeast and the Northeast. Songs and dances include shouts, animal cries and responsorial songs. Dancing is counterclockwise, nasal and high pitched singing. Hand-held and leg rattles and water drums are the instruments of choice.

Some innovations include guitars and fiddles among many groups. Church "sings" have incorporated the piano, organ, guitar and bass fiddle. Since the 1990s, singers have incorporated electronic keyboards, synthesizers and tape recordings. Powwows are very popular and Indians are also discovered performing at tourist attractions, graduations, fairs, receptions, political rallies, colleges, museum programs and national Indian conference. Many young and old have learned about the Indian way of life through study programs, community organizations and Indian powwows.

The Native peoples of North America created art that reflected their environment. Cedar trunks 40-feet long were fabricated by the Northwest Coast peoples into totems, masks, dance rattles, storage boxes and feasting bowls. Fish, game and fruit were popular foodstuffs.

The arts of the Pacific Northwest, the mid section of the United States and the prairies of Canada were small and portable during the 18th and 19th centuries. Plains peoples lived in tipis and the women quickly put them up and took them down. The seasonal migrations of the buffalo herds were followed and relied upon heavily for meat, fur, sinew, bones and the like. There were painted shields, hide clothing with paint, articles beaded with quills and hair, beaded moccasins and fur and feather headgear. Buffalo horn was used for carved utensils and jewelry.

Due to the severe weather, the Arctic region of Alaska and Canada had the peoples become dependent upon walrus, whale, seal, caribou, polar bear and salmon. The women made the animal skins into warm clothing. Fishing and hunting implements, knives, buttons and toggles were created by the men from whale bones, caribou antlers and walrus tusks.

Peoples of the southwestern area of Arizona and New Mexico have been permanent farmers for 1,500 years. Their communal multi-story apartment compounds are constructed from brick and stone. The interiors are plastered with clay and then painted. The tradition of clay pottery taken from Mother Earth dates back more than 1,000 years. Clothing is created from plant materials to include cotton fibers. Shell and turquoise jewelry set in silver remains as a powerful art form.

Native arts are for use in daily life, but the processes involved often reveal a deeper and more spiritual nature as they are being created. Individual objects have power as they are incorporated into the whole: feathers adorn carved and painted figures, paintings are made of sand and crushed materials and painted bowls are created to hold cornmeal. Paintings on war accouterments bestow both power and protection in battle.

For the Navajo, rug-making is a sacred activity. Their stories tell that the universe was woven on a giant loom by a sacred ancestor, Spider Woman, who employed natural worldly materials as she wove. All were woven together to create the world: sunrays, clouds, lightning and rainbows. As the Navajo women weave, they think of Spider Woman and combine the sheep's wool, plant dyes and human creativity.

One can only learn about a culture and their ideas by learning about that social group, striving to know the techniques involved, plus the spiritual and social processes that have been incorporated.

Designs reflect cultures and rights: the Sioux painted his exploits upon the tipi where he lived and upon his buffalo robe. A Cheyenne woman ornamented the family's clothes with dyed porcupine quills. Power, prestige and honor came about through these efforts. The Iroquois of upper New York State used tobacco and a carved "False Face" spirit mask to get rid of diseases.

One myth states that an artist may lose his/her art by abusing such creative power. Too much attention to the art implies that the artist is not living a balanced life; over involvement, isolation from the community and withholding knowledge lead to their downfall.

All tribes and all peoples may be considered to be fairly artistic. Experience becomes the best teacher-watch, learn and help, learning at an early age and by making mistakes. Often the artist worked under the direction of an expert or master, starting as an apprentice. As the apprentice proved him- or herself doing menial chores, he or she gradually worked up to becoming an artist.

Northwest Coastal societies created payment schemes and contracts with an art specialist. A public feast might be held to agree orally to the contract between the artist and the patron. Many works of exceeding beauty came about through dreams: complex designs, patterns, facial expressions, colors, and innovative quill and beadwork.

Native American life in the 20th century and beyond shows some living like their ancestors; others are college and university educated. Much of their art today has its roots in traditions 1,000 years old. Other art has also emerged through the study of world art history. Many artists have toyed and played with cultural mixtures. Thus Native American artists have and will continue to use a diversity of materials and make strong and different statements about their personal artistry and Native identity.

Painted totems: left, carved wood—$300; right, a fiberglass circus prop from the Barnum and Bailey Circus—$700. (Elwood Brunt Collection)

Fur trapping group: beaver skin on a frame and deer skin—$100 and $75; trapper's basket—$150; scraping tools—$100; antler knife—$200; Southwest deer teeth—$25. (Elwood Brunt Collection)

Horsehair group: Southwest rope—$75; Navajo halter—$300; Southwest belt—$35. (Elwood Brunt Collection)

Basket grouping: left, burden basket—$200; middle, pine-pitch covered Apache water jug—$300; tall woven Apache basket—$300. Front left, Hupa hat—$300; northern California winnowing tray—$200; covered basket—$200. (Elwood Brunt Collection)

Pacific Northwest cedar bark and spruce root basket grouping, Tsimshian—$200-$400 each. (Elwood Brunt Collection)

Woven group: Three open bowls and two lidded baskets. All Hopi except front row left, possibly Yavapai—$325 each. (Elwood Brunt Collection)

A Look at Artist George Catlin

George Catlin was a most extraordinary man of the 19th century. He was born in Wilkes-Barre, PA, on July 26, 1796, one of 14 children to Polly Sutton and Putnam Catlin, a gentleman farmer and lawyer. George attended law school at Reeves and Gould, Litchfield, Connecticut. Returning upon graduation to Luzerne County, he practiced law with mediocre success from 1820 to 1823. "During this time another and stronger passion was getting the advantage of me, that of painting, to which all of my pleading soon gave way; and after having covered nearly every inch of the lawyer's table with penknife, pen and ink and pencil sketches of judges, jurors and culprits, I very deliberately resolved to convert my law library into paint pots and brushes and to pursue painting as my future and apparently more agreeable profession."

By 1821 he had gained some reputation as an amateur portrait painter. With no formal training in art, meager funds and determination, he went to Philadelphia in 1823 to pursue painting as his life's craft. He met and knew distinguished Philadelphia artists Rembrandt Peale, John Neagle, Tomas Sully and Charles Willson. There was also a mutual respect among prominent and intellectual statesmen and scientists of the period.

Catlin was the first artist of stature who traveled to the Western Plains to document 48 different Indian tribes in painted portraits, sketched and painted scenes of village life and with detailed notes. He amassed a fine collection of decorated skin garments, ceremonial paraphernalia, artifacts and other ethnological materials. This whole process had been set in motion when Catlin met a delegation of tribal chieftains visiting Philadelphia, on their way to Washington, D.C.

In 1830, Catlin settled in Saint Louis, leaving his young wife, Clara, behind in the East. He traveled into an unknown and difficult land, by boat, horse and foot. His is the most comprehensive picture we have of these people in their natural habitat-warriors, portraits of their most notable chieftains, medicine men and women, religious and tribal dances and ceremonies, various activities and the pursuits of games, amusements, warfare and hunting.

Catlin in his own time was accused of being sentimental toward the Indians with his life-long crusade on their behalf. In August 1882, General Sherman attempted to justify his destruction of the red man, "They are…wasteful and hostile occupants of millions of acres of valuable agricultural, pasture and mineral lands."

The artist declared his opinions about the Great Plains Indians of the West. "I love a people who have always made me welcome to the best they had…who are honest without laws, who have no jails and no poor house…who never take the name of God in vain…who worship God without a Bible and I believe that God loves them also…who are free from religious animosities…who have never raised a hand against me or stolen my property, where there was no law to punish either…who never fought a battle with white men except on their own ground…and oh! how I love a people who don't live for the love of money."

For generations, the art of George Catlin has been the subject of much controversy. Some critics praise, other condemn. One says his work is romantic, another too realistic and another too primitive. This confusion was brought about when critics did not seem to realize that Catlin's goal was to be truthful and meticulous and portray the Indians in their original environment; this was the reason for the paintings.

Some of those who would not support and praise, much less understand, were in high offices. Even Congress refused to appropriate the funds for the collection, when Catlin returned East in 1836. Honorable Henry Clay commented: "Mr. George Catlin…has been engaged many years among the various Indian tribes who inhabit this continent and collected a mass of valuable information touching the habits, usages and laws and the state of society among them, surpassing that which was probably ever possessed by any man or what is to be found in any books." Again before the Senate in 1849, the Honorable Daniel Webster paid tribute to Catlin's work: "Their (the Indians) likenesses, manners and customs are portrayed with more accuracy and truth in this collection by Catlin than all the other drawings and representations on the face of the earth…I look upon it as a thing more important to us than ascertaining the South Pole or anything that can be discovered in the Dead Sea or the River Jordan."

General Lewis Cass praised Catlin's work in a letter dated December 8, 1841: "Your collection (of paintings of the Indians) will preserve them as far as Indian art can do and will form the most perfect monument of an extinguished race that the world has ever seen. In a similar manner, Joseph Henry, Smithsonian Institution Director on December 13, 1873, said about Catlin's works: "They will grow in importance with advancing years and when the race of which they are the representation shall have entirely disappeared, their value will be inestimable."

Catlin's life with the Indians had been a remarkable one. Following this period, he carried his thesis to the entire world. The "Indian Gallery" appeared in the East, New York, Washington and then went on to Europe. Similar lectures and exhibitions were set up in Paris, London and throughout Europe. Patrons included the King and Queen of Belgium, Queen Victoria, the Czar of Russia and King Louis Philippe. The entire collection was shown in the Louvre, Paris.

George Catlin weighed about 135 pounds, was 5-feet 8-inches tall, had dark hair and complexion which gave him the appearance that he might have Indian blood in his veins. His eyes were blue and a long scar on his left cheek was a reminder of a boyhood playmate who, while playing Indians, threw a tomahawk at a tree that glanced off and hit Catlin. The artist was moral, religious, outspoken, but also warm and charming. His modesty, charity and complete abandonment from all matters stands out most clearly in the story of his career. While in Paris, his wife and son died; Catlin went bankrupt and was forced to sell the entire collection. From 1852 to 1858, he wandered to Brazil searching for gold and painting Indians. He became deaf at 50; later, in 1870, Catlin returned to the United States. He died on December 23, 1872, at the venerable age of 77. After his death, his works were installed in the Smithsonian Institution, the American Museum of Natural History, the New York Public Library, New York Historical Society, Chicago Newberry Library and others.

Perhaps no artist who has made such a monumental contribution and had a vast impact upon Western art, literature and history, has waited such a lengthy time for just recognition as has George Catlin.

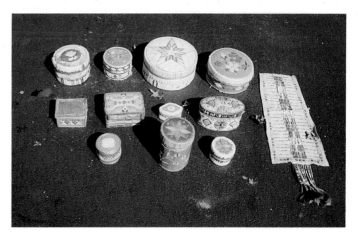

Eleven assorted birchbark containers with decorative quill work—$250 each; on the left is a porcupine decorated Plains breastplate—$650. (Elwood Brunt Collection)

Eight covered boxes with designs, Pacific Northwest, Haida and Wakashan—$250 each; Wakashan bag with handle shows whale and eagle—$500. Row two, first example on the left, Shoshonean (Panamint?) bowl. (Elwood Brunt Collection)

Southwest coarsely woven basket grouping—$150 each, all Papago except back row middle, Apache—$350. (Elwood Brunt Collection)

Top two miniature horsehair plates—$35 each; grouping of snuff boxes in leather, wood and born. Some decorated, others with dovetailing—$175-$225 each. (Elwood Brunt Collection)

Birchbark group: back row, left to right, moose horn—$150; two open containers—$200 each; decorated cradle board—$400. Front row, left to right, additional open containers and holders with tops—$150 each. (Elwood Brunt Collection)

Traps: front, wooden bird snare with horsehair noose—$100; back, splint woven eel trap with fitted lid—$150. (Elwood Brunt Collection)

Paul Apodaca (1951-): Navajo artist and community organizer. Actively involved in the arts at both the state and national levels. Professor at Chapman University, lectured at the University of California-Irvine. Associated with the Bowers Museum, California, works as a consultant for the Smithsonian Institution National Museum of the American Indian. Illustrates, reviews and has been honored with many awards and grants.

Michael Chiago (1946-): Tohono O'Odham (Papago) dancer and illustrator. Served in Vietnam and Okinawa, does surrealistic painting using water colors covered with a special glaze which gives depth. A powwow dancer who has toured the East Coast and danced in Nevada, California and Arizona. Has pieces of his art in the permanent collection of the Heard Museum.

Luisa Keyser (1835?-1925): Washo basketmaker, using 36 stitches per inch. Datsolalee produced about 300 fine baskets in her lifetime; some 120 were purchased by Abraham Cohn, a Carson City merchant. Her baskets are very valuable today.

Charles Edenshaw (1839-1924): Haida artist, member of the Eagle clan. A skilled carver of wood and slate, he showed talent at an early age. He was equally talented as a gold and silversmith. Museums and art collectors purchased his carvings, drawings, sketches and model totem poles.

Harry Fonseca (1946-): He is best known for his depictions of coyote in ultra-modern clothing or awkward situations. His subject matter is based upon Maidu mythology. He continues to explore new techniques in painting and print making.

Carl N. Gorman (1907-): A member of the Black Sheep clan who served in the U.S. marines during World War II as a famous Navajo Code Talker. His native tongue confused the Japanese in the Pacific. Taught Indian art at the University of California and worked as a technical illustrator for Douglas Aircraft; he established his own silk-screen design company.

R.C. Gorman (1932-): The son of Carl Nelson Gorman, he made his first drawings at age 3, tracing in the mud with his fingers. Probably the most honored of all contemporary Indian artists, he was included in the "Masterworks of the Museum of the American Indian," held in New York City at the Metropolitan.

Allen Houser (1914-): Internationally recognized sculptor and painter. He has worked as a muralist, pipe-fitter, carved in wood and stone and done sculptures in bronze. Awarded a fellowship from the Guggenheim in 1949. Taught at the Institute of American Indian Arts, Santa Fe, NM, from 1962 until retiring in 1975.

Oscar Howe (1915-1983): Yankton Sioux graphic artist (Mazuha Koshina). Had special training in mural painting at the U.S. Indian Center, Fort Sill, OK. Had a bachelor's and a master of fine arts degrees from Dakota Wesleyan University and the University of Oklahoma. Had taught on both the high school and college levels.

Kevin Locke (1954-): Lakota dancer and musician. He is a traditional flute player and a hoop dancer. He has traveled all over the world to ensure that his culture survives. His storytelling incorporated 28 hoops. He performed at the Kennedy Center, Washington, DC, in 1982 playing the seven notes of his flute which "gives voice to the beauty of the land." Awarded a National Heritage Fellowship in 1990.

Charles Loloma (1921-1991): Hopi artist with original jewelry designs that are among the most unique in the world. Incorporated gold and diamonds with turquoise. Painted murals for the Federal Building on Treasure Island in San Francisco Bay. Painted murals for the Museum of Modern Art in New York. In the army he worked as a camouflage expert in the Aleutian Islands off Alaska's coast. Received a Whitney Foundation Fellowship to study the clays of the Hopi area. His unusual personal style in jewelry has been widely imitated.

Linda Lomahaftewa (1947-): Choctaw-Hopi educator and painter. A teacher, assistant professor and instructor from 1971 to 1976. During the 1970s, her paintings were in more than 40 exhibitions. She has been listed in two editions of *Who's Who in American Indian Arts*, 1976 and 1978.

Solomon McCombs (1913-): Creek Nation/Oklahoma painter using traditional Native American themes. Won the Grand and Grand Masters Awards in 1965, 1970, 1973 and 1977. He has had exhibits and lectures in Burma, India, Africa and the Middle East, sponsored by the U.S. Department of State. He is a member of NCAI and the Five Civilized Tribes Council.

Norval Morrisseau (1932-): He combines rock painting with European easel painting; his work has been described as "legend art." Uses bold and brilliant colors and lines; incorporates figures within figures and shows the interior and exterior of animals and humans. His work shows a deep commitment to spiritual and religious values.

R. Carlos Nakai (1946-): Navajo composer and musician born in Flagstaff, AZ; his instrument of choice is the Native flute. Records for the Canyon label and has released a number of offerings.

Nampeyo (1860-1942): World recognized Hopi-Tewa potter; has brought about a revival of traditional Native American ceramics. She used shards of dug pottery to study and base her style and designs on. The Smithsonian purchased her pottery and now it is sought by many collectors throughout the world.

Daphne Odjig (1919-): She is a well known and influential Native Canadian Potawatomi artist. Her father and mother were both artists; she lived on Manitoulin Island in Lake Huron, Ontario, moved to British Columbia, then Manitoba. Opened a museum in Winnipeg and has exhibited in Canada, Europe, Japan and Israel.

Kevin Redstar (1942-): Crow-Northern Plains artist who draws heavily upon his culture for designs that exhibit life forces beyond the surface decoration. Also does etchings, lithography and serigraphs. Helped form the Crow-Cheyenne Fine-Arts Alliance. He is recognized as one of the masters among Indian artists.

William Ronald "Bill" Reid (1920-): Renowned Haida sculptor, known around the world for his monumental sculptures. Studied jewelry, engraving and was a broadcaster for the Canadian Broadcasting Company. His best known example is a 4-1/2-ton cedar sculpture entitled "Raven and the First Humans," on display in the University of British

An assortment: spoons, ladles, cups and combs, made from bone and horn—$75-$100 each. (Elwood Brunt Collection)

A combination of nine pipes and bowls: two beaver, Plains Catalinite bowl with pewter inlay, beaded; large stone; Red Lake, Minnesota stone pipe; Catlinite Sioux, North Dakota; soapstone bird effigy; wooden Eskimo pipe with ivory bowl and tip; polished bowl—$100-400 each based on size and quality. (Elwood Brunt Collection)

Grouping of Eskimo tools in bone, metal, wood, slate and reindeer antler, 1917. Pictured are awls, scrapers and knives—$75-100 each. (Elwood Brunt Collection)

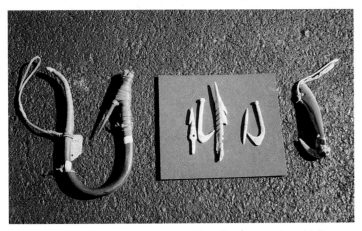

Fishhook grouping: left, shell and hook—$75 each; middle, small bone hooks—$35 each; right, large halibut hook, Tinglit—$200. (Elwood Brunt Collection)

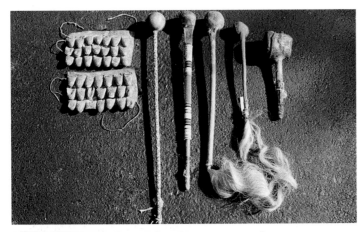

Club grouping. Left to right: Sioux, two Apache Poppamoggins with pony tails, two beaded clubs and leg rattles from cocoons—$150-$300 each. (Elwood Brunt Collection)

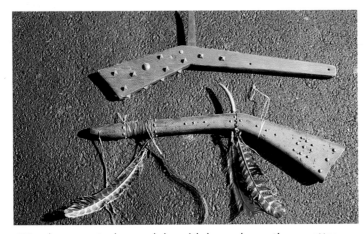

Wooden gun stock war clubs with brass decorative rosettes, protruding knife blade, lower example is completed with feathers and sharpened antler spike—$300 each. (Elwood Brunt Collection)

Columbia School of Anthropology. He also works in other media and has illustrated and worked on numerous books. Received an honorary doctorate in 1976 from the University of British Columbia.

Buffy Sainte-Marie (1942-): Well known folk singer and Academy Award winning songwriter. Sang in Greenwich Village, played the guitar, has written songs since she was 16. Records for Vanguard Records; her songs give a sense of purpose relating to Indian concerns and their culture, reflecting both backwards and forwards. She is author of a children's book set on an Indian reservation, *Nokosis and the Magic Hat.*

Fritz Scholder (1937-): Luiseno artist born in Breckenridge, MN. Has a master of fine arts degree from the University of Arizona; for five years instructed in advanced painting and art history at the Institute of American Indian Arts. His works often combine Native American mysticism and surrealist pop imagery. He is controversial and addresses such subjects as alcoholism, degradation and assimilation into mainstream U.S. society. His largest work is a lithograph 40 inches by 60 inches called "Indian Contemplating Columbus."

Diosa Summers Fitzgerald (1945-1989): Mississippi Choctaw educator and artist. Earned a bachelor's from State University College at Buffalo and a master's from Harvard University. The author of Indian museum brochures; worked as an instructor, tribal coordinator, artist-in-residence and artist.

Gerald Tailfeathers (1925-1975): Native Canadian Blackfoot artist, had his first exhibition when he was not yet 20. Worked as a technical draftsman for an oil company. His style is nostalgic and pictorial. Revealed in his paintings are the Indians living in the 19th century, engaging in ceremonies, hunting buffalo and setting up camp.

Roger Tsabetsye (1941-): Zuni Pueblo artist who majored in silver and metal processing. He helped to develop the philosophy and curriculum for the Institute of American Indian Arts School. Roger works in silver, ceramics and painting. In 1968, he was asked by President Lyndon Johnson to create a squash blossom for the president of Costa Rica. He also helped to initiate President Johnson's War on Poverty. He is a retailer and wholesaler on Zuni jewelry, the founder and owner of Tsabetsye Enterprises.

Pablita Velarde (1918-): Santa Clara Pueblo painter, her childhood eye disorder when restored gave her new insight into the appreciation of the visual perception. Her unique painting technique combines ground colored rocks mixed with other painting materials. One of her most renowned works is a series of paintings showing the daily life of the Rio Grande Pueblos.

Baubles, Bangles and Beads

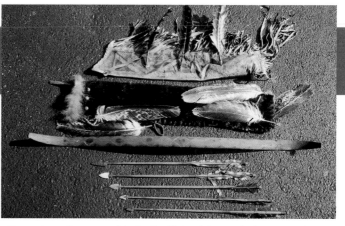

Prior to 1900 Indian jewelry was fabricated in the Southwest by melting silver coins and casting them into ingots. Silver softens easily with heat, thus it was beaten into sheets and cut into bracelets, buckles and brooches. By hammering the sheet silver into an iron or wooden form, halves of beads and buttons were created along with plates for belt buckles.

Molds for casting were cut into sandstone and pumice. Casting was probably learned from both the Europeans and/or Mexicans. After a capstone was put into place, the molten silver was poured and permitted to cool. Then the mold was reopened and the rough form had to be shaped through filing. Polishing was accomplished with sand and ashes and examples previous to 1900 will reveal the stone polishing marks.

Prehistoric North American Indians did little work with silver. Iroquois and other Northeast tribes were creating ornaments by 1800. Then the craft spread to the Plains, Prairie and Lakes groups. All of these had an influence upon the Navajo. In the Southeast, Seminole and Creek worked in silver; on the Northwest Coast, the Tlingit and the Haida became accomplished silversmiths. Much jewelry sold as Indian is garish and too shiny and the stones are inferior and merely dyed to appear real. Let the "buyer beware" of imported objects coming from Taiwan and the Philippines.

The practice of pawning began in the 1870s at the trading posts. Indians traded jewelry, expendable pieces, for money to get through the winter. In the spring the articles were redeemed with the shearing of the sheep.

Jewelry not retrieved within the time limit was sold by the dealer for 10% over the original price paid, a regulation imposed by the Bureau of Indian Affairs. Today pawn jewelry is expensive and limited in supply. Again watch for reproductions!

Hollow silver beads are created by machine-one looks like the next. Others were conceived on a bench by hand. Beads made by hand will have flaws and no two will be exactly the same size.

Most early artists did not sign their work, since they believed that quality and design spoke of the creator. By the 1930s this practice of hand stamping and using hallmarks was supported by both the Hopi Silvercraft Guild and the Museum of Northern Arizona, Flagstaff. Before 1900 broken turquoise stones were repaired not replaced by having the crack or hole closed with a silver spike. Check examples with a 10X loop so you do not invest in a broken stone.

Use of a black light helps to determine the real turquoise from the spurious. Plasticized turquoise looks fluorescent. A hot needle to the stone causes slight charring, not melting the genuine. Real turquoise can also be scratched with a knife. Quality silver always has a nice weight. Generally as the years ticked by, Navajo silver became lighter, thus examples from the 1870s to 1880s are lighter than those designed from earlier 1800s.

Like most collectibles, silver workmanship speaks to you. Each repetitive unit will be slightly different from the last. This of course is not possible with machine-created objects. Jewelry should also possess genuine signs of wear,

Grouping: decorated baby buffalo skin made into a quiver case, sewn with sinew, feathers and fringes; quiver case, painted leather; decorated bow and five arrows—$400 each. (Elwood Brunt Collection)

Silver razor used to pull hair, with conch shell decoration— $150. (Elwood Brunt Collection)

Three decorated hand held drums, skin stretched over a wooden frame—$300-$400 each. (Elwood Brunt Collection)

Miniature kayak of leather, sinew sewn, over a wooden frame, with doll—$250. (Elwood Brunt Collection)

Bear claw and beaded Indian chief's necklace, Onondaga, Jamesville, NY— $350. (Elwood Brunt Collection)

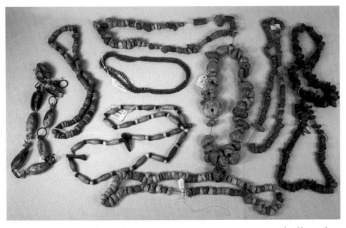

Necklaces: beaded, shell, vertebrae, stone, oyster shell and fossilized plant stem—$150 each. (Elwood Brunt Collection)

slight scratches, dents, thinner portions, missing pieces and a nice even patina.

The Anasazi were the earliest of the jewelry makers; turquoise and shells were mounted and drilled, pendants were in animal shapes. Hopi work for many years was similar to the Navajo and Zuni. By 1930 the Hopi used designs on their textiles, baskets and pottery and incorporated them into the jewelry. In 1949 the Hopi Silvercraft Guild was founded under the GI Bill. The guild was located in New Oraibi and the craftsmen developed both new techniques and designs. Some Hopi jewelry will incorporate shells, red coral and turquoise, but there are many exceptions. Look for cut-out styles, darkened overlays with chisel marks and decorative repoussé patterns.

Work began among the Iroquois around 1800; coins and ingots were hammered into sheets and then ornated with stamped designs. Popular items were dangling earrings, brooches. Common designs in the brooches included curved and double hearts, crowns, Masonic emblems and both round and square sunbursts. Heart with crown signified "Guardian of the Night," and the double heart was the "Iroquois National Badge."

Menominee in the Great Lakes region made silverwork that was much simpler than the Iroquois. Their jewelry included stamped and engraved designs on earrings, combs and bracelets. Mandan jewelry relied upon antlers to produce bracelets. The antlers were soaked, cut into strips, bent and engraved.

Navajo jewelry is some of the most beautiful in the world. During the 1850s Navajos worked in copper and brass ornaments and also learned to work in iron from the Mexicans. By 1870 silver bracelets and earrings were a first and American silver dollars were hammered and used by 1875. In 1890 steel dies copied from Mexican leather workers were used to create stamped effects. The Mexican peso also was turned into jewelry; by 1900 great quantities of commissioned silver was for sale to tourists.

"Squash blossom" necklaces were copied from the Spanish and the Mexican pomegranate. Among the ornaments created were rings, flasks, buttons, buckles, brooches, pendants and bowguards worn around the wrist.

Northwest Indians include the Tlingits and the Haida tribes. In 1865 silverworkers began using trade silver coin creations, including thin and narrow bracelets with animal designs and finely engraved lines, semi-circular and drop earrings, rings and nose rings, hair ornaments and spoons and napkin rings. Long before the white man, these Indians worked in copper. They achieved rather interesting results using stone anvils and hammers. The Tlingits also worked in iron; most proficient in silver were the Haida. Popular designs are the geometric Haida eagle, the realistic Tlingit eagle and the distinctive Tlingit flipper whale format. Haida silversmith, Charles Edenshaw had a career that spanned 50 years. He went from the dogfish style to a "classic style" in 1880. His work is fluid, with less angular form lines and carefully planned negative spaces.

Plains silverwork commenced in 1805 and was used until brass, tin and German silver became the vogue in 1850.

Metal was filed, hammered and stamped into graduated circular hair plates, stamped buckles, broad armbands, crosses, silver mount halters, breastplates and headbands.

The Seminoles carried European watch chains as jewelry and wore necklaces, earrings, pendants and brooches. Coin necklaces in the early 1900s circled the entire neck, made up of Liberty quarters and Mercury dimes.

Zuni silverworkers created large bracelets, earrings, necklaces, brooches and bracelets. Up until 1930 their works were for personal use, then they began creating for the tourists. Tools like fine pliers, emery wheels and draw plates from deer scapulae made it possible to draw out fine wire and make thin silver sheets. For hundreds of years the Zuni have created jewelry from jet, shell, inlayed turquoise and mosaics on bone, stone, wood and shell. Theirs is the oldest and best known of the Pueblo silverworkers. Fanciful designs have been made in mosaic fashion depicting the Knife Wing God, dragonflies and kachinas.

Here are some notable Indian jewelry makers:

Andy Abeita: Isleta Pueblo, fetishes and jewelry including semiprecious which he inlays.

Florence Aguilar: San Domingo Pueblo, uses mosaic designs.

Vidal Aragon: Santo Domingo, fine overlay silver since the 1940s.

Ralph Atencio: first Santo Domino jeweler, learned from the Navajos in 1893.

Abraham Begay: Navajo, master silversmith using innovative, modern and traditional designs.

Mike Bird: San Juan Pueblo, self taught, has won numerous prizes, with a necklace in the Millicent Rogers Museum, Taos, NM. Creates petroglyph figural pins, carves animals and fish, incorporates the heart and cross in his works.

Cippy Crazy Horse: Cochiti, a disabling accident brought him to do silverwork. He has been awarded many prizes, the 1987 Indian Market George C. West Memorial Award and first place for a concha belt in "Traditional Jewelry without Stones" area. Works with both handmade and modern tools.

Joseph Jojolla: takes custom orders for squash blossom necklaces, necklaces, belts, rings, watchbands and buckles. His grouping of unusual tools encompasses a plastic hammer, wooden baseball bat, dentist items, some old objects and a washing machine motor for polishing the silver.

Jake Livingston: mixed Zuni and Navajo blood, 1988 IACA "Artist of the Year," earned three Purple Hearts in the Marines, awarded "Best of Show" in 1974 at Gallup, won again the next year with a four-sided gold necklace that brought $60,000.

Charles Loloma: Hopi painter, potter and silversmith, creator of the first modern jewelry, has a generous following of artists who use gold and semiprecious stones, other than coral and turquoise. His gold bracelet with coral and lapis lazuli was on the cover of the American Craft Museum; it sold for $10,000.

Anthony Lovata: Santo Domingo, awarded the Salem

Plains breastplate, bone hairpipes, blue and white beads, sinew and deer toes—$600, approximately 16" x 10". (Elwood Brunt Collection)

Eskimo doll driving a jaw bone sled, with a black baleen interior from a whale—$600. On the right is a small doll—$150. (Elwood Brunt Collection)

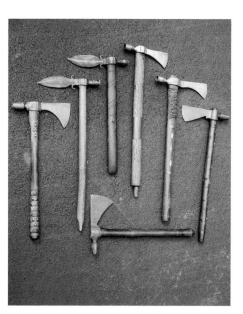

Grouping of seven tomahawks, brass and steel heads, carved, inlayed and brass studded handles, some are peace pipes—$900-$1,200 each. (Elwood Brunt Collection)

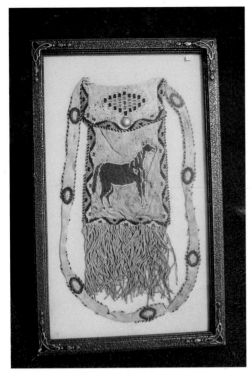

Fellowship in 1992, uses traditional tufa and sand casting methods which have been passed down.

Preston Mononcye (1927-1987): Hopi, learned smithing at age 9 from his uncle, attended college, served during the Korean War. Known both in the U.S. and internationally with over 700 awards to his credit. His works are prized by collectors.

Gibson Nez: Navajo-Apache, learned the jewelry art in 1973, also was a rodeo bronc rider and is listed in the Indian Cowboy Association Hall of Fame. His works bring up to $20,000 and are in such collections as Hal Ketchum and Dale Robertson. He has won many awards and his creations are sold by a variety of galleries.

Angie Reano Owen: Santo Domingo, parents, five brothers and two sisters all create jewelry. Her works are shown in Western and New York galleries, Santa Fe Indian Market and Eight Northern Indian Pueblo Artist and Craftsman Show. Designs based on Hohokam and Anasazi ancestors; her work is in the Heard Museum, Phoenix.

Joseph and Jerry Quintana: Cochiti brothers whose works are well known, with numerous awards to their credit.

Howard J. Sice: Hopi/Laguna, in 1992 won the Pueblo Grande Museum Auxiliary Fellowship, creates silver bowls, engraved and inlayed pins, bracelets and earrings. Works with silver, exotic metals, gold, turquoise, coral and rare earth.

Robert Sorrell: Navajo, casts silver, won Dorothy and Robert Walker Fellowship in 1992.

Alan Wallace: lives in Taos, NM, designs mosaic rings, necklaces and bracelets.

Beaded tobacco/pipe bag with strap, on buckskin, Sioux—$3,500. (Elwood Brunt Collection)

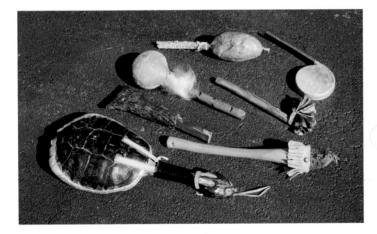

Seven assorted rattles: top to bottom, original bladder—$200; raw hide—$100; fish skin—$200; deer claw—$100; elm bark—$100; snapping turtle claw—$125; and tortoise shell—$300. (Elwood Brunt Collection)

Grouping of Southeastern Pennsylvania wooden mortars and pestles from hollowed trunks. Back three—$200 each; front—$75. (Elwood Brunt Collection)

The Art Of Basketry

Beaded and colorful umbilical cord fetishes: $400 each. (Elwood Brunt Collection)

Tribal baskets were created from the geographic materials available. Colors depended upon the objects being harvested in addition to natural dyes. Symbols were incorporated into the three basic types of weaving. Coiled baskets are stitched or sewn; twined baskets interweave the flexible weft with the vertical warp; plaited baskets have the warp and weft placed at right angles.

Quality baskets have a tight weave. Pomo Indian baskets, the finest in the world, have 60 stitches per inch. An artistic basket will have 28 stitches to the inch; a finely woven basket will show 15 stitches per inch. When investing consider breaks, holes, weakly woven areas and dryness. These are all red flag areas, telltale signs not to consider these objects for purchase.

Collectors seek attractive and well made examples of tribal art. Check the colors, originality, unusual features, aesthetic appeal, age, size, rarity, workmanship, weave, function, design and documentation. Most baskets filled a working role for a variety of uses. The list includes carrying a baby, fruit, grains, beans. Others were for cooking, eating, mixing and trading. Baskets played a part in ceremonies and came into gambling usage. There were fishing and eel weirs and baskets, those for sifting the grains from the chaff and storage baskets to hold clothing, belongings and trinkets. Some basket-like jars were water tight and transported liquids.

Left and center: beaded bags with beaded fringes—$350 each; right, Sioux beaded pouch with metal tinklers and dyed horse hair—$1,000. (Elwood Brunt Collection)

Basket periods of Native Americans include: Early, Classic, Transitional, Hiatus and Contemporary. The Early period includes the first baskets with European influences. Classic are those that were created before Europeans influenced their art. Between 1775 and 1875 the transitionals were made and the Hiatus occurs during the late 19th and early 20th centuries. Contemporary baskets have been fabricated since the early 20th century.

Learn about baskets by attending shows and visiting museums. Also, travel to flea markets and craft cooperatives. Look and study closely, as a profusion of baskets have flooded the market that have some resemblances to Native American styles and techniques.

Major basket areas of the U.S comprise 11 areas: Plains-Upper Missouri, Southeast, Northeast, Northwest Coast, Cascades, Coast Columbia, Northern California, Central California, Southern California Desert, Southwest and the Basin. Twining and coiling were Western techniques; plaiting was Eastern. Most tribes employed plaiting and twining for utilitarian objects.

Some materials for making baskets include spruce and tule root, squaw weed, slough grass, sisal willow, cat's claw, sumac shoots, unicorn plant, yucca roots, amole, dog wool, mountain goat fur, corn husks, wild hemp, plus yucca and fine grass. In addition, split corn husks, tender roots, shoots, fibers, inner bark of the red and yellow cedar, cattail stems, wild cherry tree bark, fern stems, duck down,

Group of nine Northwest totems, nicely carved, brightly polychromed; large, 3 feet—$1,000 each; small, 6" to 12"—$350 each. (Elwood Brunt Collection)

Painting of an Indian Princess on leather— $225. (Elwood Brunt Collection)

Grouping of Plains Indian beadwork, left to right: knife sheath—$600; awl cover—$350; Apache pouch sewn on buckskin—$400; pouch—$400; knife sheath—$600. (Elwood Brunt Collection)

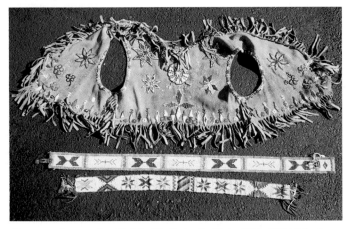

Rare vest worn by Maide Walls in Buffalo Bill's Wild West Show, 1895—$3,000; two beaded belts from the show—$400 each. (Elwood Brunt Collection)

woodpecker feathers, quail feathers, beads, yucca leaves and rush stems.

Colors in baskets are usually symbolic: red is sacred, white for peace and happiness, black signifies death, blue suggests trouble and so forth. Colors were evolved using aniline dyes; by soaking in water; using charcoal paste, dirt and ashes; deriving colors from nuts, barks and plants; and utilizing plants, flowers and roots as dyes.

Here is a list of basketmaking tribes:

Aleut: delicate, fine, woven with bird feathers and embroidered in silk, wool and grass.

Algonkian: Materials used include hardwood splints, cedar bark, sweet grass, willow and basswood. Forms comprise handled butt baskets, rectangular and square baskets and round covered boxes. Plaited baskets are of hardwood splints with double rim hoops, others have curlicue work, dyed splints, painted designs and potato stamping.

Anasazi: Prehistoric, ancestors of the Pueblos, twined bag types.

Apache: Water jugs are of sumac or strawberry twigs woven and filled in with red ocher and juniper leaves. Waterproofed with pinon pitch. Burden baskets of wild mulberry, cottonwood and willow, decorated with buckskin strips and metal tinklers. Common to the Apache is the whirling logs or swastika design. The Jicarilla make three- and five-bundle baskets sewn with sumac and colored with native and aniline dyes. Mescaleros rely upon the three rod-stacked coiling process. Use yucca fibers stitched with green and tan yucca splints. Western Apache baskets are hard and stiff, produced with three-rod bunches; decorations include figures of men and animals, whirls and stars. They are willow stitched with red yucca and black devil's claw materials.

California Missions: Under the control of Spanish religious leaders, they used deer grass, jungus grass and sumac. Some baskets were decorated with feathers; other materials consisted of redbud bark, bulrush root, willow and sedge root. Designs include the rattlesnake up to 1920, quail, lizard, mice, rat, butterfly, fish, camel, burro and dove. Finely woven in all sizes and shapes with 18 to 30 wrappings per inch.

Chemeheuvi: three-rod coiling turning clockwise, stitched with willow and devil's claw, designs of animal tracks, animals and butterflies.

Cherokee: North Carolina materials include sugar maple, river cane and white oak splints; hickory bark is used to bind rims; plaiting is with oak splints; twill plaiting with river cane. Diamond patterns are common along with geometrics; forms consist of melon and butt baskets, miniature and nesting baskets, sieves and fish baskets, processing and gathering baskets, trays, bottlenecks and handled baskets.

Chickasaw: Created winnowing and wall baskets, "elbow" and "cow nose" shapes of fine twill-plaited cane. Made in Mississippi, Oklahoma and Louisiana. Geometric patterns are in red and yellow.

Chitimacha: Baskets with square bases and round

sides in black, red, orange, yellow and dark purple. Other objects include trinket baskets with finialed lids, flat trays, sieves, and winnowing baskets and lidded baskets. Bundles of coiled pine needles were thread-stitched during the contemporary period. Baskets are of narrow cane splints, rims have a double-spiral twist.

Choctaw: Baskets are fabricated from narrow cane splints and oak splints, backgrounds are natural with decorative red and black splints. Twin and double twill-plaited makers lived in Mississippi and Oklahoma. Their work consists of storage, egg, laundry, miniature and rimmed burden baskets. Like the Chickasaw, they also made "elbow," "cow nose," winnowing and wall baskets.

Creek: Common colors are orange and brown using hickory splints, split cane and stem splints. Plaited twill geometrics end in false braids. Production included trays, sieves, the "cow nose," and the "elbow" handled baskets.

Haidas: Their wares include wallets, mats, plaited bags and a variety of hats. Designs are often brightly painted on the objects. Bear grass was incorporated in their false embroidery. Baskets are twined of Sitka spruce and plaited of western red cedar bark. Colors include red, green and black.

Havasupai: Their basket types include bottles, bowls, trays, burden baskets in black geometrics and concentric circles. Materials implemented were sumac, devil's claw, willow, acacia and shrub strawberry. Dyes were in black, yellow, gold and red. Their baskets used three-rod coiling, finely closed with diagonal twining. Coiled rims are overcast, others have a "herringbone" false braid.

Hidatsa: Created baskets, burden baskets and coiled gambling trays from box elder, black willow and willow bark. Weaving was accomplished using black willow, box elder and twill plaiting. Willow splints were coiled and four ash saplings shaped the framework for twill burden baskets.

Hopi: Considered to be the greatest basket producers of the Pueblos. Their basket shapes displayed great variety and incorporate the three styles of weaving. For a time, 1880 to 1900, they incorporated aniline dyes; by 1906 they went back to natural forms to create color. Coils were reduced by the 1930s with improvement in overall designs. Materials used include yucca and galleta grass with geometric and sunbursts, clouds with and without rain and kachinas. Forms are plaques, bowls, round and rectangular trays and baskets. There is much symbolism associated with the ways plaques are made; they are given at births, weddings and displayed at a person's death. Baskets are formed from sumac warps and types of rabbit brush for wefts. Designs on baskets are kachinas, eagles, butterflies, rain clouds and lightning symbols.

Hupa: This tribe created sifts, mats, caps, dippers and assorted baskets to include utility, wood, cooking, storage, serving, burden and fish, plus openwork cradles. Their fabrication materials were lowland spruce roots, willow, alder, hazel, cottonwood, wild grape and digger and yellow pine. Their decorations are geometric with a horizontal dividing line and half-twist overlays in black, white, red

A group of items worn by troupe member in Buffalo Bill's Wild West Show, cow hide chaps—$1,500; belt—$300; moccasins—$2,000; jump rope—$250; child's boots with wooden pegs in the soles—$300. (Elwood Brunt Collection)

Moccasin tops, Mohawk, for ceremonial dance, dyed moosehair on birchbark—$1,000. (Elwood Brunt Collection)

Clockwise: buffalo skull—$100; Western Navajo decorated baby buffalo skin gathering bag—$350; buffalo horn rattle with deer leg handle, Plains, 1875—$300; Turtle shell mask—$250. (Elwood Brunt Collection)

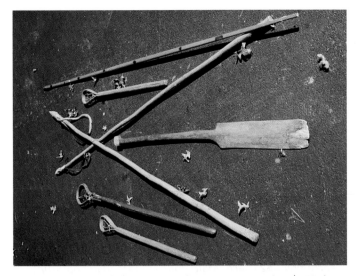

Wood grouping: left, snow snake spear, Iroquois—$250, has burned measuring marks; three Southeastern lacrosse sticks, sinew webbing, varied lengths—$200 each; crossed wooden shafts with arrowhead spears—$150 each; hand-carved canoe oar—$150, probably Ottawa. (Elwood Brunt Collection)

Finely painted and carved wooden "Booger" face mask, intertwined snake head band, Cherokee, North Carolina, ca. 1900—$500-$700. (Elwood Brunt Collection)

Three buckskin dolls for children with beading, two with cloth faces; center red-colored example is Crow from Montana—$225 each. (Elwood Brunt Collection)

and yellow.

Iroquois: Most widely used are black ash splints, birch bark embroidered with dyed moose hair and corn husks. Forms include corn washer baskets, pack baskets, berry pickers, sieves, salt and tobacco bottles and ceremonial medicine masks.

Jamez: Yucca is the main construction material with sumac being used on the rim of a ring basket. Men and women plait baskets for winnowing, shelling corn and washing wheat. There are also square woven mats and rings for transporting jars of water on the head.

Navajo: Baskets are coiled with two rods and a fiber bundle traditionally and today in three- and five-rod examples. Designs include radiating starbursts and outlined steps. Their water bottles are very portable and wedding ceremonial baskets are highly collectible.

Northwest Coast: Some baskets were woven and twined upside down, others were coiled and sewn. Their output included basketry cradles, hats, capes, robes and containers. Prized weaving materials were dog hair and mountain goat wool, yellow cedar bark, bird down and cotton pappus from plants. Decorations comprised bleached and dyed grasses and splints of black fern stems in geometrics. Common weaving techniques were twining and plain twining.

Paiutes: Baskets are created from martynia, yucca and aromatic sumac. Their production featured large cone-pack baskets, open twined hooded cradles, seed and water bottles, parching and winnowing trays and open-twined paddle-shaped beaters. The diagonal whip stitch border-herringbone-is highly sought of all Paiute baskets.

Papago: Contemporary basket makers are very prolific to include trays, coiled shallow bowls, twill-plaited mats, jars, miniature and trinket baskets, head rings, lidded and open baskets. Construction is with yucca leaves, bear grass, yule stem and willow splints. Baskets are pounded between stones to make them smooth. Waterproof bowls were created to brew cactus wine and early sturdy trays parched corn using live coals. Popular are effigy figures and human and plant designs.

Pima: Shapes include assorted sized bowls, rectangular covered baskets and museum miniatures which take up to three months to create. Designs are whirlwind, swastika, star, fret, butterfly and zigzags. Forward and backward stitches are employed as a border stitch.

Pomo: Baskets produced by this tribe are supreme works of art. Between 1880-1920, nine weaves were employed. Weave indicates purpose: loosely woven were gathering baskets; a fine weave served to gather seeds; a very fine weave was to serve as a water basket. Ovid baskets held trinkets, sugar or clothing; conical baskets were hung on the headband in front of the carrier to carry objects. Ceremonial baskets were globular, constructed of slough grass roots covered with quail and red-headed woodpecker feathers and beads. Other feathers used were lark, mallard, jay, golden eagle, oriole and blackbird.

Tlingit: The raven and the wolf are symbolic to this clan and these are incorporated into trays, cradles, hat forms and shaman double baskets. Baskets are fabricated from split spruce root soaked in water. Native pigments used from designs are (black) sulfur spring mud and iron, (white) natural grasses, (brown) Sitka spruce root, (purple) maidenhair fern, (blue-green) copper oxide and hemlock bark, (red) alder bark and sea urchin juice and (yellow) wolf moss or lichen.

Yavapai: Three coiled from willow twigs and split willow and devil's claw sewn. Items include deep jars, trays, plaques and bowls. The baskets are strong, have food cooked in them and resemble Apache ones in designs and techniques.

Zuni: Used willow and sumac rods bundled with yucca to create their baskets. Objects were both for everyday and ceremonial usage. Their baskets were both wicker and plaited. Little decoration appears and examples of wares include coiled water bottles, openwork wicker bowls and shallow ring baskets.

Here are some known basket makers (seldom are examples signed):

Maria Antonio: Diegueno, in 1898 designed the first rattlesnake basket.

Joseppa Beatty: noted central Pomo basket maker; in 1892, lived on the Yokayo Rancheria, CA.

Clara Dardin: Chitimacha who lived in Bayou Teche, LA, worked from the late 1800s to the early 1900s. She incorporated the double-twill plaited technique with river cane splints. Colors worked into designs were called "something around," "eyes of cattle" and "cross marks."

Dat-So-La-Li: also spelled Datsolalee, Washo basketmaker, known for large globular willow baskets, three-rod coiled, 30 stitches per inch, incorporated the elongated triangles called "birds migrating."

Molly Hatchett: Pautatuck Indian, Connecticut, died in 1829. Used block-stamp decoration and red-painted splints.

Caroline Masta: Abenaki Indian from Pierreville, Canada, who worked in a shop at Belmar, NJ. Her materials were black ash and sweet grass sent to her ready for the last step in creating checker-work baskets.

Mercedes Nolasquez: Mission Agua Caliente, bundle coiled baskets of grasses stitched with black martynia and sumac (California).

Peggy: Miwok or Wappo, Spanish Flats, Placerville, CA.

Mary Snyder: Chemeheuvi Indian, known in Arizona for baskets and designs that resemble Southern California workers.

Susie-Pima: prior to 1940 she had woven 140 miniature baskets.

Tootsy Dick Sam: Washo, representational and geometric designs, lived in Great Basin, NV, died in 1928.

Mary Walker: Chemehuevi, Great Basin, NV.

Agnes L. Welch: Cherokee, North Carolina, native basket maker worked in the 1980s. Created pieces from white oak splints and those dyed red and dark brown.

Collection of assorted Seminole doll sizes, Florida, with very colorful outfits: large—$100 each; medium—$75 each; small—$50 each; tiny—$25 each. Male dolls are rare. (Elwood Brunt Collection)

In the foreground and to the left are a variety of Skookum dolls, prices range from $75 to $300 depending upon size and complexity. The center shows an Eskimo doll driving the jawbone on a whale as a sled with a black baleen center—$350. On the right are varying hues of painted wooden Kachinas—$600 each; and clay Hopi dolls in the foreground—$250 each. (Elwood Brunt Collection)

Mortar and pestle grouping: left and right, Southeastern Pennsylvania; middle example, lava from the Southwest; $75 each. (Elwood Brunt Collection)

Mortars and pestles: back row, left to right, Southwest lava—$100; Southwest petroglyph—$125. Front row, left, Boone County, MO, bell pestle—$150; middle, paint pot with turtle effigy—$500; right, Red Hill, Montgomery County, PA, double faced—$200. (Elwood Brunt Collection)

Mask grouping: numbers 1, 3 and 4 are Cherokee; number 2 is from the Northwest Coast—$500-$700 each. (Elwood Brunt Collection)

Rare decorated buffalo hide with the "rising Sun" decoration. Acquired at a farm sale in the 1960s for less than $5. The Smithsonian attributed it to an Eastern Coast tribe. The decoration was not known until the owner removed the cloth backing—$6,000. (Elwood Brunt Collection)

Creating Pottery

North American pottery making dates in the East to about 2000 BC and in the Southwest to around 500 BC. Excavated pieces and shards help in dating ancient cultures since they last indefinitely. Most pottery was for cooking and general use, although much of it was decorated. The main recognized pottery regions are the Southwest where the tribes were separated, Central and Northeastern, Gulf and Southeast. Wood, bark and baskets took the place of pottery in California, the Lakes Region and the Northwest Coast.

None of the potters used the wheel, however, it had been known since the ancients in the Old World. Clay was the basic ingredient, along with techniques and creativity. Shapes and designs varied from one group to the next. Clay was first gathered from choice deposits. The potter crushed and made a dust like consistency with a stone or wooden club. In the Southwest the clay is ground with a metate and mano. Winnowing baskets were employed where the clay is thrown into the air. A blanket downwind catches the fine clay and the basket holds lumps and pebbles which will be discarded. The dry clay is stored until pottery making begins.

To prepare the clay water is added so it gains a dough-like consistency. This is done with the hands on a stone slab as tempering materials are added: plant fibers, sand, limestone, shell, shards. Just the proper additions prevent pots from cracking when fired and dried. A surplus of tempering will make the clay very difficult to work.

Coiling/modeling and paddling are the two basic pottery making techniques. With wet hands, the potter sets a pancake of clay inside a bowl or basket to form the bottom of the pot. Then snakelike coils are rolled out and placed one on top of the next around the rim of the pancake. The layers are pinched together so that they are firm. As the coils spiral upwards, the pot is formed. The coils must be thinned to their final thickness both on the inside and outside of the vessel. All the cracks are smoothed so that they are no longer noticeable.

Several pots are shaped at the same time, as the walls must dry as they are curved. The left hand is held inside the wall as the right hand curves the outside wall with curved pieces of shell or gourd. One small example is shaped at one sitting, while larger jars must harden before tops can be added.

Eastern tribes and the Cherokee employed the modeling and paddling process. In Arizona, the Yuma and Papago still use this technique. An inverted jar serves as the mold to which a pancake of clay is placed over the bottom. The clay is thinned evenly with a smooth flat stone or a curved wooden paddle. After the clay has been spread over one-third of the jar, a shape begins to unfold. Placed on a fiber ring, the potter uses an anvil stone to smooth and thin the walls.

To finish a water jug or deep bowl requires many additional coils. Surfaces are worked with an anvil and paddle to remove the coil marks. Once the jar has dried in the sun for several days, smoothing begins. Cracks and holes are repaired with wet clay and the surfaces smoothed with sandstone or a dry corncob. Then the entire surface is wet with a cloth. A flint chip, piece of bone or knife is used as a scraper. Again the wet cloth is used to wipe the pot and then it is fired.

If an example is to receive decoration, it must have slip applied. A creamy mixture of water and colored clay is applied in several coats, with a rabbit tail or a cloth. After each coat, the pot must dry. Slip gives the example smoothness and covers all imperfections. Slip was also applied on edges and inside surfaces. Firing and smudging requires half an hour to several hours. Large examples must be fired alone. Smaller pots are fired in groups. They are inverted on a support: a rock, can or metal grill. Sheep and cow dung are piled over the pots so that the burn occurs slowly and evenly. The manure rests on top of shards or galvanized iron which protects them from being stained.

To create smudging requires damp manure and a fire with little draft. Consequently a dense smoke is created which covers the pots with a shiny, black finish.

An open fire permits air to the pots. This in turn creates a paint red clay which is permanent. Wiping is accomplished after the pots have cooled. The secret is knowing when to remove them, so there are not uneven spots, flaking or discolorations. Good results are achieved by rubbing with a greasy cloth or chamois.

Decorations are achieved by many techniques and with numerous designs. A feather or a brush of yucca is employed by the Pueblo, while the Papago paint with a stick. Ground minerals and boiled plant juices are applied free-hand. The designs are retained in the potter's head. A potter will chew the ends of a split yucca leaf and then trim it to size before using. Negative designs are created by painting the background black and permitting the natural color to show. This was popular in northern Arizona; patterns are contrasting geometrics.

A resist-painting method coats the outlined areas with wax, then slip is applied. The design is then scraped through the wax to reveal the design. Then the article is painted black and the slip sticks to the bowl to create a design. The residual wax is then removed. Corrugation was created by permitting the ridges of the coils to show on the outside of the pot. Pinching of the coils gave a very nice scalloped effect. Additional designs came about through incising and pressing other designs into the coiled surfaces.

Eastern tribes like to create designs in wet clay with their nails, cord, net, shells and reeds. Fabric markings, scallops and "bearpaws" were also impressed. Creek, Shawnee and Caddo used the incising method; designs were scratched into the soft clay with a wood or bone tool. Engraving encompassed complex designs found on the hard surfaces of fired black pots. Also known as sgraffito, this art was used by the prehistoric Southeast and modern Pueblos.

Stamping was a form of impressing in the soft clay. Designs included whirls, parallel grooves, overlappings, concentric circles and diamonds. They were accomplished with both paddles and stamps. Effigy modeling existed among prehistoric Central Region tribes. There were all forms of vessels with humans, animals and birds. Others had bears, fish, animals and human heads on their rims.

Cochiti Pueblo paint figures and create storytellers. Modeled doll figures, painted birds, serpents in relief and

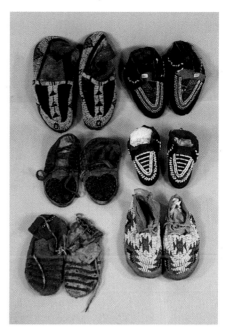

Grouping of children's moccasins: a combination of Plains and Mohawk tribes—$200 pair. (Elwood Brunt Collection)

Colorful moccasin grouping: $350 per pair. (Elwood Brunt Collection)

Two pair of ornate Pueblo leggings with colorful beadwork—$300 a pair. (Elwood Brunt Collection)

Seven beaded Mohawk bags, ca. 1880-1910, done on black velvet and then trimmed in red—$250 each; a beaded pouch on tanned leather—$75; and a beaded bird ornament—$75. (Elwood Brunt Collection)

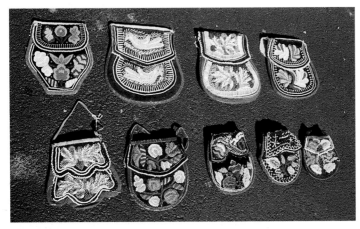

Nine colorful Mohawk bags in a variety of beaded patterns—$250 each. (Elwood Brunt Collection)

other small animals are created by the Zuni, Yuma and Mohave. The Iroquois were noted for their effigy-faced pipes.

Native American pottery, especially that created by the New Mexico pueblos, is very adaptable to a variety of decorating styles. Its bold black, red and cream colors go well with Country, Primitives, and the Arts and Crafts period.

Many American dealers no longer specialize, but display a number of good designs from numerous cultures. Alongside quilts and folk art will be the Pueblo culture pottery, Navajo rugs, Apache baskets and Plains Indian beadwork.

Many fine collections are on the East Coast waiting to be discovered. Early Pennsylvania collectors traveled to the West by rail. They had the time, money and interest to preserve what was even then beginning to vanish.

Pottery from the early cliff dwelling Anasazi cultures on the Southwest dates to 1000 AD. Religious pots were buried with the dead and these along with utilitarian examples attract collectors. The early prehistoric figural pottery from the Mimbres culture commands thousands of dollars per item at auction. Some examples are placed on the market that have been acquired through illegal excavations.

The most valuable pottery examples are from the Historic

Period, with Spanish explorers arriving in the Southwest. Such pieces date from the 1600s through the 19th century.

As the West was inundated with tourists in the 1880s, a new phase of pottery making began. Such objects were intended for sale and not for use within the pueblos. Later examples from the 1920s to 1950s even command five figures when sold. Pottery prices are governed by the maker's name, size, condition, age and degree of rarity. Certain periods also demand higher prices. When buying seek knowledgeable dealers who will guarantee both age and authenticity. Consider potential growth and objects with artistic merit.

Here are some notable potters;

Karen Abeita (1961-): Hopi, left the reservation to study, returned home to Polacca in 1984, comes from a long line of potters. She learned potting from people her age, she and her husband Darryl Daw, also collect; her works are inspired by prehistoric pieces.

Delores Aragon (1969-): Acoma, learned the art from her mother and mother-in-law and her husband, Marvis Aragon Jr. Created small clay animals at an early age, uses customary materials, techniques.

Karen Kahe Charley: started creating pottery in 1983, Hopi, uses a secret red orange hue to color her pottery.

Cordero Family: George (1944-), Tim (1963-), Duffy (1969-) and Kevin Peshalakai (1964-) all make storytellers.

Tony Da: grandson of Maria Martinez, great innovator, had an accident, no longer pots, does paint. Prices are high for his work.

Tony Dallas (1956-): Hopi, introduced to creating mudhead storytellers by his mother-in-law.

Marie Juanico: Acoma, learned to pot at four years of age, digs and mixes her own clay, employs both traditional and complex designs.

Lucy Lewis: Acoma, born during the 1890s, her work was influenced by Helice Vallo, her great-aunt. Dr. Ken Chapman, New Mexico Museum Art Director, showed her ancient pottery which aided in her development. Her Mimbres designs have received worldwide recognition.

Charles Loloma (1921-): Hopi, painter, potter and silversmith, studied ceramics at Alfred University.

Maria Montoya Martinez (1887-1980): San Ildefonso potter, taught by her aunt Nicolasa at an early age. She learned to dig clay, mix it with ash and construct with the coil method. In 1904 she married Julian and also debuted at the World's Fair. At an archaeological dig they found Anasazi shards. Later, the designs were copied and the husband and wife team learned how to blacken pots. Ten years passed before the trademark black on black was perfected. Julian created the puname (feather) and the avanyu. As a janitor at the Museum of New Mexico, Julian and his wife studied the old forms. Maria made and polished the pottery and her husband painted the designs. Maria's sister also worked to make a trio. Maria started to sign her work in 1923 and Julian in 1925. Throughout their careers seven signatures were used. Their first works sold for 75 cents to $1.25; by 1930 the price was up to $2 for a medium pot. Julian died in 1943 and Maria's daughter-in-law decorated for her as did Maria's son, Popovi Da. He assembled a great collection of her pottery. By 1971 Maria's eyesight had failed and Popovi died. During Maria's life she worked at world's fairs from 1904 until her death. She met many celebrities, received numerous awards and also got two honorary doctorates, 1971-New Mexico State University and 1977-Columbia College. She is one of the greats and her works are shown in museums throughout the world.

Nampeyo (1856-1942): called the "Old Lady," lived on the Hopi First Mesa. Three miles from her home the prehistoric village of Sikyatki was discovered and her husband a worker there, brought home shards. Nampeyo got permission to recreate ancient designs on her pottery. Her work has brought about new artistic expression.

Christina Naranjo: worked in the 1970s with Mary Cain her daughter, both signed the pieces. Linda, Mary's daughter, has works in many galleries. Her daughter, Teresita, carves and polishes black examples; large bowls sell for $6,000 in shows and at galleries.

Louis and Virginia Naranjo: Cochiti husband-and-wife team, known for their storytellers and nativities.

Joy Navasie: called "Frog Woman," paints pots on almost pure-white slip, uses Sikyatki styles.

Rose Pecos (1956-) and Sun Rhodes: Jamez storytellers, husband and wife, figures are Navajo-styled.

Margaret Quintana: Cheyenne/Arapaho, creates Cochita-styled storytellers in red clay with the addition of mica.

Dextra Quotskuyva (1928-): Hopi who learned from her mother, started later (age 39), follows age-old uses of yucca brush, polishing stone and mineral/organic paints.

Ada Suina (1930-): Cochiti Pueblo, works in fine details creating drummers, story-tellers and nativities; her four daughters are also working in clay.

Camilio Tafoya: Serafina's son, creates contemporary miniatures, his children, Grace Medicine Flower and Joseph Lonewolf, are also potters, as is Rosemary, Lonewolf's daughter.

Serafina Tafoya (1863-1949): was the initial potter in the family, children (Camilio, Margaret and Christina) and grandchildren have followed in Serafina's tradition.

Margaret Tafoya: Santa Clara, polished blackware with bear paws, water serpents, rain clouds and buffalo horns. When working she thanks Mother Clay and Mother Earth. The secret to her work, she claims, is in polishing stones retained in the family. Four generations of this family have contributed to classic pottery.

Mary E. Toya (1934-): Jamez Pueblo, worked six months to make the largest storyteller, with 115 children. She also creates tiny examples of this type; her seven daughters also work in clay.

Yellowbird: San Ildefonso, sells animal forms made by hand, which are dried, slip-painted, polished and fired.

Tlingit flannel shirt, edged with swansdown, design outlined with pearl buttons, inverted face below and floral border design—$9,000. (photo by Ernest Manewal, Sheldon Jackson Museum)

Rattle cover spruce root basket with porcupine quills, 6-1/2" high, 6-7/8" diameter. The basket shows zoomorphic and Chilkat blanket-like designs in false embroidery; the design field shows a killer whale and the Chilkat face—$2,000. (photo by Steve Henrickson, Sheldon Jackson Museum)

Haida dish, carved of slate or argillite, possibly repre-sents a bear with a human face between the hind legs; in each paw there is a human face carved in bone, 9-3/4" long, 5-3/4" wide, 2-1/2" high—$2,000. (photo by Ernest Manewal, Sheldon Jackson Museum)

Left, Nampeyo early Hopi polychrome jar, finely painted black hatched feather design on creamy orange slip, 7-1/4" x 11", estimated value—$7,500-$9,500. Right, Nampeyo pottery polychrome vase, painted bird pattern on creamy orange slip, 9-1/4" x 4-1/2", estimated value—$3,500-$5,000. (Dunning's)

Navajo pictorial weaving Teec Nos Pos, hand-woven, vertical center row of stylized eagles, flanked by chevrons with arrows and double zigzag with triangle encasing feathers with arrows, double border of stacked chevrons and outside border of double-hook motif, 85-1/2" x 50", estimated value—$5,000-$7,000. (Dunning's)

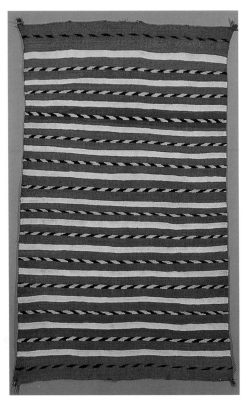

Navajo man's wearing blanket, hand-spun wool in aniline orange, mustard, indigo yellow, indigo blue and natural ivory with alternating band design, 78" x 46", estimated value— $7,500-$9,000. (Dunning's)

Oil on canvas, Leonard Reedy, "Wagon Train," signed lower right, 21-1/2" x 27-1/2"—$2,990. (Dunning's)

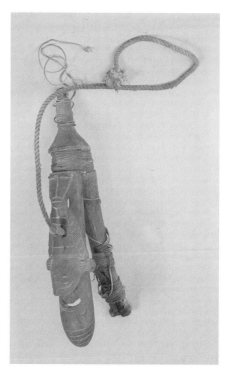

Tlingit headdress with frontlet and trailer, 7" high, upper edge set with sea lion's whiskers and woodpecker feathers—$6,000. (photo by Alice R. Hoveman, Sheldon Jackson Museum)

Tlingit octopus finger bag, 21-3/4" long, 13" wide—$1,200. (photo by Ernest Manewal, Sheldon Jackson Museum)

Tlingit halibut hook, alder, cedar, bone or metal and spruce root, 12" long; shows a figure of a man holding a flat fish—$1,500. (photo by Ernest Manewal, Sheldon Jackson Museum)

Tlingit large cylindrical basket, spruce root and grass, 11-1/2" high, 13" diameter—$850 (photo by Ernest Manewal, Sheldon Jackson Museum)

Tlingit women's work basket, rattles in top of cover, spruce root, grass and stems of maidenhair fern, 3-1/2" high, 6-1/2" diameter—$1,700. (photo by Ernest Manewal, Sheldon Jackson Museum)

Portrait headdress frontlet, collected Southeast Alaska, carved in close-grained hard wood, 7" long, 6-3/16" wide, abalone shell, red, black and blue paint—$12,000. (photo by Steve Henrickson, Sheldon Jackson Museum)

A great diversity of materials were required to complete an artifact. The human was required to find, discover, trade, hunt, kill, mine and create through his many talents. The finished example might be a piece of pottery, jewelry, tool, weapon, clothing, rug, basket and the like.

Each example was created for utilitarian as well as symbolic, ceremonial and aesthetic purposes. Thus through the craft the art was evolved. The artifact displayed quality workmanship, design, detail and expressiveness. "Fine art" is a term applied to contemporary works where traditional techniques are employed to achieve an aesthetic purpose. Crafts displayed at powwows and festivals are now considered fine art. Some fine arts include painting, drawing, sculpture, dance, drama, architecture, literature and music.

Alabaster: Both dense and fine grained; a variety of calcite, often white and translucent. This was quarried and carved by North American Indians; gypsum was a whitener for both feathers and leather.

Amber: Fossilized resin discovered in alluvial soils; orange or brownish yellow, translucent and able to take a high polish. Valued for beads and other ornaments.

Annealing: Heating metal, tempering it and then cooling. Silver may be quenched quickly in water. Copper and other metals require that they be cooled slowly. The process toughens the metal and reduces brittleness.

Anthropomorphism: An artwork is which human figural elements are given to nonhuman objects.

Appliqué: An embroidery technique in which one material is attached to another. Quillwork and ribbonwork are examples. This practice is also used on pottery surfaces and to inlay designs in wood.

Articulate mask: A typical mask of the Northwest Coast Indians that has movable portions. Sometimes the sections are controlled with strings.

Baleen: A horny growth from certain whales, from 2 feet to 12 feet in length, usually black, strong, light and flexible. The whale used the baleen to strain plankton and other foods from the sea. Also found in white and green, the Native Americans used it to create tools and ceremonial objects.

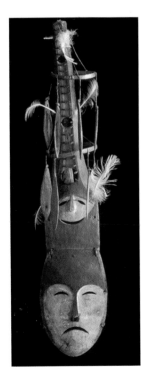

Mask, human face, two beads in the septum, tattooing, red and blue paint, two hoops of willow on the board, each trimmed with paddles, 29" high—$5,000. (photo by Sam Kimura, Sheldon Jackson Museum)

Ceremonial mask, the face surrounded with small carvings, a blue face with a red edge, 9-3/4" high, 12-1/4" wide—$4,000. (photo by Ernest Manewal, Sheldon Jackson Museum)

Basalt: Black or dark gray, hard, dense, igneous and relied upon for tools and utensils. Such outcroppings in the West are termed lava beds.

Bas-relief: A low relief sculptural projection.

Bast: Used to make cords and baskets; numerous strong woody fibers such as flax, hemp and the inner barks of trees.

Bayeta: A flannel of English origin, traded to the Indians by the Spanish. The Southwest Indians unraveled this material and used the yarn with their native wools for weaving. This bayeta weaving was carried on by the Navajo from 1800-1880.

Blackware: Pertains to shiny and matte-finished pottery which is made from red clay while the blackening occurs through low oxygen in the firing and also low temperatures. Typical to the Santa Clara and San Ildefonso Pueblos.

Blade and core: A percussion flaking technique used to create a long, narrow flake with parallel sides.

Bonework: Bone carving was used to create tools and ceremonial pieces. Similar carving was accomplished on teeth, antlers, tusks, hoofs and beaks.

Braidwork: Weaving with three or more strands; also called braiding when referring to hairstyles. This term is also used when discussing the sewed and bound edge on the rim of a basket.

Buffalo robe: Typical of the Plains Indians and often embroidered by women and worn by men. Also, men painted the skin side to show totems and deeds.

Buffalo skull: A bleached skull was painted symbolically and stuffed with prairie grass. These sacred objects were used during the Sun Dance of the Plains Indians.

Ceramic: A product resulting from firing to include pottery, glass, brick, enamel and cements.

Chalcedony: Translucent to transparent varieties of quartz with a waxy luster and black impurities. Included are jasper, agate, bloodstone, onyx, flint and chert.

Checkboard: A simple over one and under one pattern used in making baskets.

Chert: A favored stone for flaking into arrow points, tools and spears. A fibrous chalcedony; glassy and dense, often purplish in color.

Chip: Called a flake; a small piece of waste stone in flaking.

Cire Perdue: Metal can be cast through the lost wax method. A clay model is wax covered, then coated on the outside with clay and charcoal. When heated, the wax melts forming a space between the two ceramic layers. Molten metal is poured into this opening. Upon drying, the clay is removed. Solid objects require a wax model covered with

Armor made of rib bone plates, laced with rawhide, three tiers of bones, collected at Cape Prince of Wales, 17" wide, 13" long—$5,000. (photo by Sam Kimura, Sheldon Jackson Museum)

Hunting hat, collected at Anvik, walrus head in the center with two long bird beaks on the sides, two large pieces of carved ivory on the sides, with black Jaeger feathers, 12-1/2" long, 9" deep—$7,500. (photo by Sam Kimura, Sheldon Jackson Museum)

Lower Yukon salmon skin bag, 12-1/2" high, bottom 13-1/4" across—$1,500. (photo by Ernest Manewal, Sheldon Jackson Museum)

Point Hope smooth carved mask, 10-1/2" high, 6-1/4" wide—$4,000. (photo by Sam Kimura, Sheldon Jackson Museum)

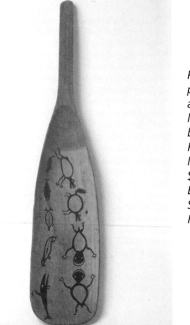

Paddle-like ladle, painted mythical animal figure out lined and painted black, originated at Kuskokwim, 21-5/8" long, 4-3/8" wide—$3,000. (photo by Ernest Manewal, Sheldon Jackson Museum)

clay; thus the hot metal takes the place of the wax core.

Coiling: Used in making baskets and pottery. Rope-like clay coils are built from the bottom of the pot and the irregularities are smoothed on the inside and outside walls. With baskets, the coils are spiraled upward and sewn together with a flexible weft.

Cold-hammering: Shaping metals without heating.

Cone: Conical polished stone artifacts created from hematite. Prehistoric and generally discovered east of the Mississippi River. They were perhaps part of the shaman's wares.

Copper: A malleable and ductile metal of reddish coloration. Near Lake Superior, copper nuggets were found. The Indians learned to hammer these nuggets into ornaments, weapons, tools and copper sheets. The Northwest Coast Indians thought of copper as "the light of heaven and the wealth of the sea."

Cordage: Used to secure frameworks and boat riggings. Made from plant fiber, animal hides into rope, string and cords.

Cord-marked pottery: Designs are created on the exterior of the pottery by pressing or stamping with a cord wrapped paddle before firing.

Corn cob: Central to the ear of corn on which the kernels grow. The cob served as fuel, to smoke meat and hides and as a scrubbing brush or scratcher. Also used as a stopper in the neck of containers, on the ends of dance wands and for the bodies of dolls.

Corn husk: The dry outer covering of the corn highly valued by the Native Americans for kindling, to wrap food for cooking, for mats, bedding, cordage, pouches, quivers, rattles, moccasins, dolls, masks, balls, ankle bands and others.

Crazing: A pottery term where cracks occur in the slip or the glaze; this results from uneven shrinkage of the clay during the firing process.

Cross: A symbol showing two intersecting straight lines. A common design in the Indian arts. May also represent the cardinal points: north, south, east and west. The Sioux called them the "Four Directions" and the "Four Winds." The Cheyenne thought that "Four Sacred Persons" guarded the four directions.

Deerskin: Known as buckskin, a leather made from deerhide. This skin was used for clothing, fringed jackets and shirts.

Woman's work box from Sfaganuk, painted reddish brown, carved bottom and cover, ivory handle and six ivory bands, 14-1/2" long, 6-1/2" wide, 6-1/2" deep—$2,500. (photo by Sam Kimura, Sheldon Jackson Museum)

Dentalium: A slender univalve shellfish found on the west coasts of Queen Charlotte Islands and Vancouver Island. Sometimes called the money tooth shell. Northwest Coast Indians used the shell for commerce; the practice became widespread in western North America.

Driftwood: Employed by the Inuits for carving masks and tent poles. It was any wood found floating or washed ashore by the water.

Duck tablet: Probably ceremonial objects; a prehistoric artifact of wood, copper or bone in the stylized shape of a duck; especially found in the southeast.

Effigy: Applies to sculptured images in stone to painted and drawn images, free standing and carved monuments, images on pottery, on pipes and doll figures.

Elm bark: The Iroquois used the elm bark slabs for the wall and roof coverings on their long houses. The Algonquin groups used elm bark to cover their wigwams. Iroquois used the bark to cover their canoes. Other tribes shaped the elm bark into containers, rattles and toboggans. Inner bark was also woven into coverings for doors, floors and beds. The slippery elm was used medicinally to aid bleeding lungs.

Embroidery: Creating designs with needle and thread on cloth or leather. The embroidery was a means of pictorial expression among native peoples.

Engraving: The cutting or scratching into a material such as bark, stone, wood, antler, ivory, pottery, silver, copper and gold. American Indians carved abstract designs as well as pictographs.

Etching: Creating a design on glass or metal with acid. The Hohokams covered shells with acid-resist pitch from trees, carved through the pitch, then soaked the shells in acid made from the saguaro, a giant cactus grown in the Southwest and in northern Mexico.

Excising: A pottery technique where deep grooves are carved into the surface to create recessed designs.

Featherwork: Bird feathers used on arrows, for ceremonials, as exploit feathers, in prayer feathers and prayer sticks. Birds such as the eagle, turkey and quetzal were considered sacred. Highly valued were the wings of the eagle and the tails of the turkey and quetzal. Bird skins and feathers were woven into clothing, blankets and some baskets.

Fiber craft: American Indians used plant tissue, stems, leaves and inner bark to create clothing, furniture and other artifacts.

Figurine: A small statuette or sculpture usually of a human figure, made out of pottery.

Firing: Exposing pottery to intense heat to harden it. Pots are protected with pottery fragments and scrap metal and then surrounded with dung chips, which are set ablaze.

Footprint sculpture: A representation in pictographs or soft materials such as sandstone. The image may be human, animal or legendary.

Fresco: Painting on wet plaster using pigments ground and dissolved in water.

Fur: Thick pelts were used for many types of clothing.

German silver: A mixture of zinc, nickel and copper used by the Plains Indians to make jewelry in the 19th century.

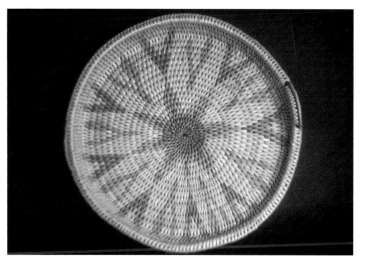

Twined grass basket with cover, decorated with wool yarn and false embroidery, designs in blue, red, pink, yellow and green, 10" high, 7-1/2" diameter—$1,500. (photo by Alice Postell, Sheldon Jackson Museum)

Fully dressed doll, from Ruby, Alaska, made by Altona Brown. Complete with wolf fur, wolverine ruff, flannel underclothing, knitted socks, trimmed mukluks, 16-1/2" high—$1,000. (photo by Ernest Manewal, Sheldon Jackson Museum)

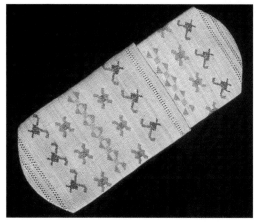

Flat basket tray, from Shageluk, handles on opposite sides, made from willow, one rod coiling technique. The red and green star is from dyes, the blossoms of the strawberry spinach are used to create the red—$1,500. (photo by Ernest Manewal, Sheldon Jackson Museum)

Plaster of Paris bust, 28" high, wearing a turban and bear claw necklace, marked "Sitting Bull"—$750; image is really Tecumseh. (Howard Szmolko)

Indian chief, Plaster of Paris, 22" high—$350, wearing a war bonnet, coin necklace and tomahawk. (Howard Szmolko)

Glaze: A coating of minerals painted on pottery before firing which melts at high temperatures to create a vitreous surface.

Glue: A substance that yields holding powers used extensively by Native Americans on canoes, arrowheads, etc. These adhesives were from tree resins, fish glands, animal neck muscles and horns.

Grasswork: American Indians employed numerous grasses with narrow leaves and hollow jointed stems for baskets, mats, rope, brushes, bedding, house coverings, igniting fires and other applications.

Hair pipe: Also called a shell hair pipe made of shell, bone, copper and stone. The hair pipes were suspended from clothing and used in the making of breastplates. The shell variety was a tubular bead that was hollow and cylindrical and more than 1-1/2 inches long.

Hairwork: Human and animal hairs (bison, horse, dog, deer, etc.) were used for weaving, stuffing, wigs for masks and dolls, roach hair pieces and so on.

Heartline: A pottery motif showing animals, especially deer, painted with a line from the mouth to an arrowhead in the chest. Prevalent on Hopi, Zuni and Keres pottery from the mid-1800s.

Hemisphere: A small (usually polished) stone object in the shape of a half sphere; possibly used in ceremonies.

Heshi: Typical beadwork of the Pueblo Indians drilled and strung and then rolled against a harsh surface to give them uniformity. Semiprecious stones were used, as well as shells, coral, bone and turquoise.

Hide: The term designates larger animals such as the buffalo and deer, while skin refers to smaller reptiles, mammals, birds and fish. A skin may be raw or dressed. Hidework is the artifact.

Horn and antler work: A horn, when heated, could be made into different shapes and two pieces could be joined together. Horn was steamed and boiled to create combs, spoons, dippers, ladles, dishes and drinking utensils. The complete horn plugged at both ends served later to carry gunpowder. Harder antlers were utilized as hoes, bows, awls, knives and flakers.

Iron: The Europeans brought iron tools to America, thus the Native Americans' ideas about technology were revolutionized. Out of trading and learning came extensive native ironwork.

Ivory work: Beautiful objects created from imported elephant ivory, mammoths and mastodons. The Inuits are praised for their elaborate ivory and walrus tusks carvings and also from sperm whale teeth.

Kiln: Modern kilns used ovens in which the pottery is fired by gas and electricity.

Ledger art: Drawings often in pencil or crayon showing incidents from the lives of imprisoned Indians, especially Kiowas, Cheyennes and Comanches. These ledgers were obtained from soldiers and white traders.

Mat: A coarse fabric created from animal hair, rushes, husks, straw and similar plant materials. Used for coverings of dwellings and bedding.

Metalwork: The art and science of extracting metals from ores. These processes include smelting, casting, hammering, embossing, engraving, annealing, sheathing, welding and soldering.

Mica: Crystalline mineral silicates which can be separated into translucent and thin layers. Used by the Native Peoples for ornaments and mirrors.

Mining: A process to derive metals, salts or minerals from the earth. A mine is a dug tunnel; a quarry is an open pit. Silver, gold and copper were mined by the Native Americans. The Spanish forced the Indian populations into the mining operations.

Mound ware: Pottery, effigy figures and other artifacts found at the site of a mound.

Negative painting: A resist process employed on pottery surfaces. First the surface is partly covered with wax or gum before the slip is applied. Firing only yields colors where the slip was. When the gum is removed, there is a design.

Netting: Created from roots, stems, bark, leaves, hair, wool, hide, sinew and intestines. A material may be woven, knotted or twisted threads formed into openwork meshes and used for fishing and hunting nets, clothing, baskets, lacing on snowshoes, lacrosse sticks and travois.

Ocher: Used as a pigment; a variety of natural earths consisting of sand, clay and mineral oxides of iron. There is also red and yellow ocher.

Ornament: A decoration, embellishment or adornment. Something usually worn or carried; it also may be a design.

Paddling: A pottery decorating technique in which a wooden paddle (either flat or curved) is pressed against the wet clay; there may be a carved or stamped design or a cord may be wrapped around it.

Paint: Coloring agents derived from minerals, berries, nuts, leaves, flowers, bark, animal blood and the yellow substance found in the gall bladder of the buffalo.

Painting: The process of applying paint with the fingers; by spraying with the mouth; with chalk, clay and charcoal; with the softened ends of reeds, bark and wood; with the spongy knee joint from the buffalo, etc. Many items were painted–humans, horses, weapons, masks, pottery, bags, dwellings and totem poles. Body and face painting was accomplished before ceremonies. Body paint was also worn into battle. Contemporary artists of Native American heritage have achieved international and national fame in the fine arts.

Pecking: To strike and shape with a hard and pointed implement.

Pelt: The skin of an undressed animal still having its hair attached.

Perforated stone: Any stone artifact with holes; especially the pendant, sinker, spade-stone, bar-gorget and ringstone.

Pigment: Any substance used for coloring.

Pipestone: A famous quarry in Minnesota in the 1830s; also called "Catlinite" since frontier painter George Catlin wrote about it. Its substance is a compacted clay, dark red to pale grayish red and sometimes mottled. Native Americans carved and inlayed this material making creative and beautiful pipes.

Pitch: Tree resin, asphalt and bitumen in a variety of mixtures to seal birch-bark canoes and waterproof baskets.

Plaiting: Used to weave cloth and baskets in which two different elements cross each other. Four types of plaiting are: hexagonal, wicker, twilling and checkerboard.

Polishing implement: A small, hard, smooth stone for polishing pottery. Also, any tool, hide, clay, shell, bone, stone or wood used to smooth and shine artifacts by means of friction.

Pony beads: Known as trade beads, they were small glass beads introduced to Native Americans by European traders in the early 1800s. The original varieties were black and white; later there were numerous colors coming from Italy and other European countries.

Positive painting: To paint the design directly on the surface with pigments.

Pottery: A widespread skill highly refined by the Southwest and Southeast cultures. The clay objects are fired and include such items as bowls, cups, utensils, toys, effigy figures and more. Most pots originally were made by women and were coiled, not thrown on a wheel.

Redware: Typical pottery of the Pueblo Indians, especially the groups known as Santa Clara and San Ildefonso. Made from red clay, the pottery stays red after firing.

Ribbonwork: Typical of the Seminoles where silk ribbons are sewn in strips on a dress. Known also as ribbon appliqué, silk appliqué, appliqué and patch-work.

Rock art: Found in the West and also among the Chumash Indians in California. Pictographs deal with drawings on rocks, boulders, on overhangs, in rock shelters and in caves. Petroglyphs are designs that are carved, pecked or abraded. Painting constitutes rock painting.

Scrimshaw: Originally applied to whalers carving various forms of ivory and then rubbing ink or pigments into the incised lines to bring out the details

Buckskin quiver, 50" long, with red flannel trim, probably Apache, with arrows from different tribes, lengths vary from 22" to 25"—$85 each. Also shown is a Blackfoot war club, ca. 1890, polished stone, handle is wrapped with interlocking hoops of horsehair, a symbol of tribal unity—$450. (Howard Szmolko)

Left, beaded pipe bag, 1880, Cheyenne, 32" buckskin—$1,800; top right, Eastern Woodland, 1910, colorful beaded floral pattern, wall pocket accessory—$350; beading on buckskin flint/steel bag, Apache, 1880—$650. (Howard Szmolko)

Covered basket, imbricated overlay, Northern and Western sub-area, British Columbia or Washington State, 8-1/2" high—$550. (Howard Szmolko)

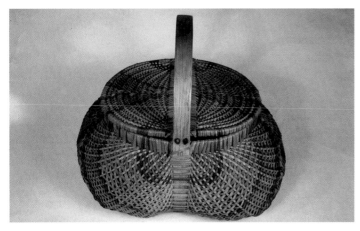

Cherokee lidded rib basket, Southeastern North Carolina, ca. 1943, oak with dyed splints and hinged lid, 14" across, 12-1/2" from top of the handle—$375. (Howard Szmolko)

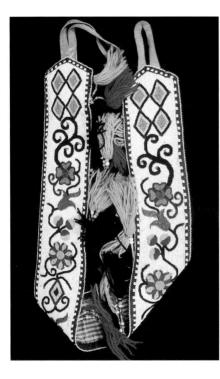

Floral beaded papoose burden strap, Canadian, 1920s, trade cotton cloth underneath, multi-colored tassels and beads—$1,200. (Howard Szmolko)

when cleaned with a cloth. The Inuits worked with bone, ivory and shells.

Sculpture: Any Native American figurines and other ceremonial objects; also included are pieces with strong aesthetics such as woodwork, bonework, stonework and shellwork.

Shellwork: Artifacts created from shellfish to include beadwork, wampum, tools, ornaments and ceremonial objects. Some shells were enhanced by polishing, trimming, grinding, drilling and cutting.

Skin dressing: A process to prepare a skin or hide for use. Varieties of tools were used for fleshing, dehairing and soaking. Soaking formulas were soaking in grease, soaking in tannin and covering with cooked brains and liver.

Slate: Used by Eastern Indians and the Haida Indians on Queen Charlotte Islands of British Columbia. This rock is fine grained, dense and varies in color from gray to black, green, blue and purple. Slate takes a polish, may be carved and is made into ornaments and tools.

Soapstone: A steatite and a variety of talc. It has a soapy texture, may be carved with stone tools, is resistant to fire and darkens with polishing and handling. The Iroquois worked with this material as did many tribes; popular with contemporary Native American sculptors. Shades from gray to green and brown.

Spirit break: A ceremonial or line break in the design circling a piece of pottery. The Navajo and Pueblo Indians use this break in the pattern.

Splint: A strip of split wood or vegetable fiber used for making baskets. A favorite was black ash since it is elastic, tough and splits easily.

Swastika: A symbol and design common to numerous tribes; known in Navajo sandpaintings. It is a cross with bent arms at right angles, each the same length and each extended in the same direction. Its symbolism is the cyclical nature of time and its movement is counterclockwise. Nazi Germany's symbol a version of the Swastika moved clockwise. Its meaning is derived from Sanskrit, svasti, "good luck."

Textile: Usually cloth and clothing; woven material, also broadly referring to weaving, beadwork, basketry, quillwork, featherwork and embroidery.

Tie-dye: Typical coloring method of the Southwest Indians where material is crushed, folded and tied and then dyed. The dye does not penetrate the folded areas and varieties of unusual patterns and colors evolve.

Tourist pot: Pottery and tradewares crafted for sale to tourists as curios and souvenirs; low priced and not traditional.

Trade goods: Objects made or gathered in intertribal trade and intended to be bartered or sold to whites. These were also used to obtain goods made in Europe; most notably the fur trade. They took the place of money and became a medium of exchange.

Turquoise: Valued for its beauty and used by the Southwest Indians combined with silver in jewelry making. An aluminum phosphate mineral with some copper; it is blue, blue green and green gray. Treated turquoise may be darkened with a chemical hardener.

Twilling: Weaving used for baskets and textiles where the weft is over one or two threads of the warp and then under two or more, creating diagonal lines.

Utilitary ware: Practical pottery with little decoration used for storage, eating and cooking. Not intended to be ceremonial or aesthetic.

Wattle: A group of stakes or poles twined with vines, branches and twigs to construct houses.

Weaving: The interlacing of plant materials and animal hair to create baskets and textiles. Finger weaving was subscribed to by some tribes; others used true looms, frames, suspended materials from trees or staked them to the ground.

Weft and warp: Weft in weaving is a horizontal thread woven at right angles, over and under the warp. The warp threads are vertical or lengthwise, attached to the bottom and top of the loom and are the foundation before over and under weft threads are added at right angles.

Wooden Indian: A carved likeness of Indian chiefs and princesses from blocks of wood which are painted and usually placed upon a base with rollers. They were placed outside tobacco and snuff stores as advertising; the custom began in 1600 in England and the sculptures became popular in North American after the 1700s. The association began since the Indians were the first to plant and cultivate tobacco.

Woodwork: The carving of objects from wood popular with American Indians and used to make boats, tools, houses, weapons, containers and ceremonial objects. Stone tools were used first, followed by iron tools. The art evolved to a high art form with the Northwest Coast Indians who made plank houses, masks, chests and totem poles. The False Face Society of the Iroquois carved wooden masks from living trees to frighten away spirits that caused illness. Known as the "faces of the forest," these masks were cut out of the trees during prayer ceremonies and the offering of tobacco.

Sioux headdress with matching feathers, beaded front band and side hanging ribbons—$6,000. (Howard Szmolko)

Spanish colonial bit and bridle, Navajo silver—$1,800. (Howard Szmolko)

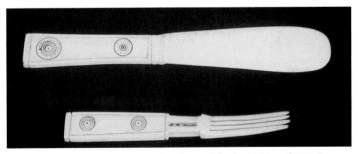

Eskimo etched marine ivory knife and fork, 1920s—$150 for the set. Note the trapped carved balls within the fork's tine. (Howard Szmolko)

Foreground, Illinois clay pipe, Mound Builder period, 18th century—$750; background, Acoma pottery pot, 1910—$250. (Howard Szmolko)

Rocks Used by Indians in Everyday Life

- **Agate:** Chips were used as points for spears and arrows.
- **Chrysocolla:** Used in jewelry-making and sandstone painting.
- **Granite:** Used as mortars and pestles to grind corn into meal.
- **Obsidian:** The rock's sharp edge proved suitable for knife blades.
- **Pyrite:** Fool's gold for jewelry inlays.
- **Quartz:** Produced sparks for starting a fire when struck together.
- **Salt:** Aided in food storage and the tanning of animal skins.
- **Sandstone:** Valuable as a tool to create molds for casting silver.
- **Serpentine:** Chips were carved into tiny fetishes to aid herdsmen in protecting their flocks.
- **Staurolite:** A talisman of good luck, also called the "Fairy Stone" or "Fairy Cross" said to be the crystallized tears of fairies, formed when the fairies heard about the death of Christ. Pocahontas, daughter of Chief Powhatan, wore staurolite crystals and presented Capt. John Smith with one of these to protect him from harm.
- **Sulfur:** Used by medicine men to captain spells. Directed to the four cardinal directions as an offering, it dissipated darkness and cleansed the Earth of corruption.
- **Terra Cotta:** For creating pottery.
- **Turquoise:** The principal rock for jewelry-making.

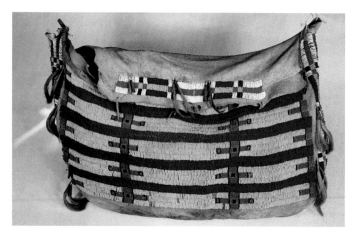

Sioux teepee or possible bag, beaded on skin, 1880s, 21-1/2" wide, 14" long—$2,500. (Howard Szmolko)

Two beaded belts: top, Blackfoot, 35" long, beads and studs—$500; bottom, flags indicating a power symbol, 39" long, possibly Sioux, 1880s—$200. (Howard Szmolko)

Papago basket, 1880s, 12" high, as is—$200. (Howard Szmolko)

Child's wooden doll with movable legs, 1880s, nice patina—$650. (Howard Szmolko)

Maple canoe paddles, decorated, 1860s, Delaware—$1,200 pair. (Howard Szmolko)

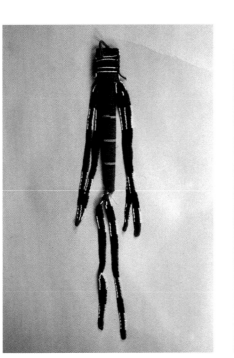

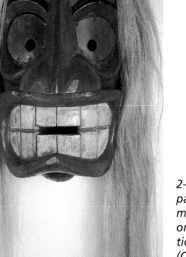

Beaded awl case, 1880s, possibly Crow—$350. (Howard Szmolko)

2-38. Carved and painted false face mask, excellent original condition—$2,400 (Cottone's).

Left to right: Indian basket, 4" high, excellent—$175; beaded moccasins 10" long, excellent—$770; Apache basket, some rim breaks, 13" diameter—$1,760; carved and painted Eskimo mask, original condition—$550; covered basket, 5" high, excellent—$190 (Cottone's)

Acoma decorated pottery, 8-1/2" high x 11" diameter—$1,400; Hopi decorated bowl, some scratches, 10-1/2" diameter—$250; Kachina doll, 6" high, all original—$200; beaded knife sheath, 11", excellent—$1,870 (Cottone's)

Indian basket, 2" high x 5-1/2" diameter, excellent; Indian basket, 3" high x 6-1/2" diameter, excellent; carved effigy spoon, 7" long, excellent; Northwest Coast carved spoon, top broken; 13" long; quill work doll cradle, Northeast, 9" long, excellent condition. Top basket—$350; bottom basket—$800; spoon—$40; Northwest spoon—$720; cradle—$2,100. (Cottone's)

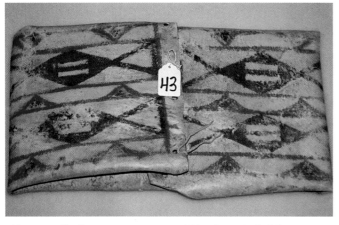

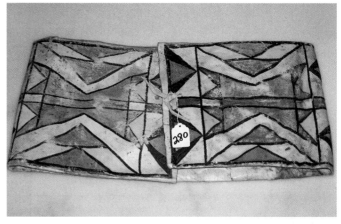

Sioux parfleche, 11" x 20", ca. 1880—$1,250. (Midwest Auctions)

Plateau parfleche, 1880, 13" x 27"—$1,700. (Midwest Auctions)

Sioux shirt, 19th century beaded strips on later commercial tanned hide, red ochre painted, buffalo hair tassels—$4,000. (Midwest Auctions)

Pair Sioux leggings, 19th century beadwork on later commercially tanned hide—$850. (Midwest Auctions)

Glass tube fully beaded cape, bell and Indian head penny drops, early 20th century—$750. (Midwest Auctions)

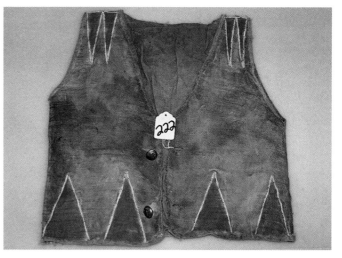

Plain's bird quilted vest, red ochre painting, replaced military buttons, ca. 1850-1870—$850. (Midwest Auctions)

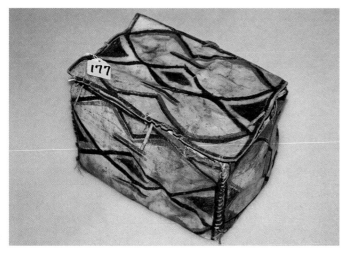

Sioux parfleche box, 8" x 12" 1880—$2,600. (Midwest Auctions)

Show Low prehistoric polychrome bowl, 4-1/2" x 9-1/2"— $625. (Midwest Auctions)

San Idlefonzo polychrome jar, 1930s, 10" high x 11" wide—$1,500. (Midwest Auctions)

Prehistoric Pinto polychrome bowl, 3-1/2" x 6"—$600. (Midwest Auctions)

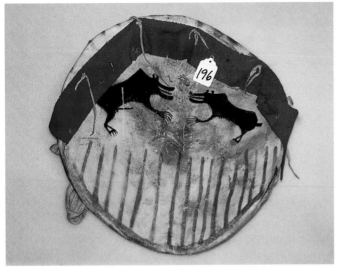

Plains buffalo hide shield, 1870-1890, ochre painted bears on 1920 or earlier hide cover—museum quality. (Midwest Auctions)

Pueblo drum created from a barrel, replaced rope, 1900—$75. (Midwest Auctions)

Pueblo drum, 6" x 9", 19th century—$700. (Midwest Auctions)

Pair Blackfoot floral beaded moccasins, 1890—$400. (Midwest Auctions)

Pair Cheyenne beaded moccasins, 1890—$800. (Midwest Auctions)

Pair Arapaho fully beaded moccasins, 1880s—$1,500. (Midwest Auctions)

Fully beaded on one side, Sioux knife sheath, 1900, 8"—$600. (Midwest Auctions)

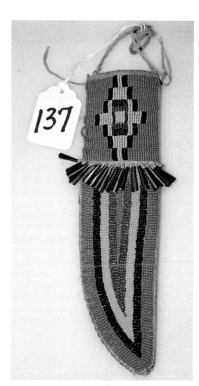

Sioux fully beaded on one side, knife sheath with cone drops, 1890—$850. (Midwest Auctions)

Sioux fully beaded one side knife sheath with knife, 1890—$700. (Midwest Auctions)

Pima basket, 1900, 4-1/2" x 14-3/4"—$1,000. (Midwest Auctions)

Pima basket, 3" x 12-3/4", 1900—$750. (Midwest Auctions)

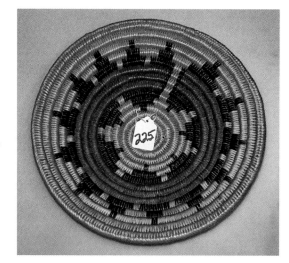

Navajo wedding basket, ca. 1920, 3" x 15"—$300. (Midwest Auctions)

Chapter 2

MEDIA

George Burdeau (1944-): Blackfeet producer, screenwriter, director. Over 20 films and TV credits. Director of the Communication Arts Department at the Institute of American Indian Arts. Did one-hour special for ABC-TV in 1986, *"Color Us California."*

Gil Cardinal (1950-): Cree/Metis filmmaker. Director, editor, writer, producer, working with camera for 20 years. Numerous projects dealing with legal, ethics, alcohol and suicide. Joined Canada's National Film Board in 1980.

Tantoo Cardinal (1950-): Cree/Metis actress, one of Canada's most renowned Native film actresses. Best known for her supporting role as the wife of a Lakota man in *"Dances with Wolves."* Received the best actress award at the American Indian Film Festival.

Gary Dale Farmer (1953-): Cayuga activist, actor, producer. Born on the Six Nations Reserve in Ontario, Canada. Has many acting credits in radio, TV and theater. Lectures throughout the U.S. and Canada, plus at Dartmouth and Cornell Universities. Won the best actor award in *" Powwow Highway"* in 1988.

Carol Geddes (1945-): Tlingit writer and filmmaker. Born in the village of Teslin in the Yukon, Geddes introduced the successful Montreal Native Friendship Centre. She compiled a report on The Native Community, for the National Film Board of Canada. In 1990, she became the first appointed producer of the National Film Board's Studio One, Edmonton, Alberta.

Haney Geiogamah (1945-): Delaware/Kiowa teacher, director and playwright. Artistic director of the Native American Theater Ensemble in New York City from 1972 to 1976. Also the artistic director of Native Americans in Arts in New York City between 1980-1982. Technical advisor for *"The Dark Wind,"* produced by Wildwood Production and Robert Redford. He has received numerous honors and awards and grants to promote NATE and NAPAF.

Dan George (1899-1981): Born on the Burrard Indian Reservation near Vancouver, British Columbia. He is best known for his portrayal of Old Lodge, a Cheyenne elder, in the film, *"Little Big Man."* Chief of the Squamish band on Burrard Inlet, British Columbia, from 1951 to 1963. Worked in film, theater and TV and also authored two books.

Graham Greene (1950-): Oneida actor born on the Six Nations Reserve in southwest Ontario. Worked a number of different jobs, lived in Britain, and portrayed Kicking Bird, an elder, in *"Dances with Wolves."* Also active on the Toronto theater scene.

Tomson Highway (1951-): Cree playwright who created his first play *"The Rex Sisters"* in December 1986. It toured to sold out audiences throughout Canada. He has won the Dora Mavor Moore award on four occasions.

Jane Lind: Aleut actress, choreographer and director. Taught drama in rural Alaska communities, has also held a variety of roles in famous theater. In the 1970s, she founded the Native American Theater Ensemble. She has sung, directed and acted in productions both in Europe and the U.S.

Phil Lucas: Choctaw director and producer. Develops projects for TV and motion picture; owns the independent film company, Phil Lucas Productions. Has worked for the Public Broadcasting Corporation series, *"Images of Indians."* Completed in 1989 a 15-part series called *"Native Indians: Images of Reality."*

Alanis Obomsawin (1932-): Abenaki filmmaker raised on the Odonak Reserve in Quebec. She is one of the country's leading documentary filmmakers. Awarded Canada's highest government award, the Order of Canada in 1983. Recorded a record album *"Bush Lady,"* featuring her songs in French, English and Abenaki.

Gary Robinson (1950-): Cherokee writer, producer and director/Mississippi Choctaw. Twenty years experience with a master's degree in film and TV. Produced educational media programs and trained teachers in the use of AV and video equipment. Worked for the Creek Nation of Oklahoma from 1981 to 1990, directing, producing and writing video programs. Co-founded American Indian Media Services in 1990. Has directed more than 50 films. Won Best Documentary awards at the American Indian Film Festival and the Red Earth Film Festival.

Will Sampson (1934-1987): Creek actor, best known as the Indian chief feigning muteness in *"One Flew Over the Cuckoo's Nest."* Came to acting late in life; was also a professional artist, cowboy, forest ranger. Studied and researched an acting role "thoroughly." Nominated for an Academy Award as best supporting actor. Acted in a number of films.

Jay Silverheels (1912-1980): Mohawk actor best known as Tonto, the Indian partner of the Lone Ranger. His real name was Harold J. Smith born in Canada and a member of the 1938 Canadian national lacrosse team. In the 1960s, he founded the Indian Actors Workshop in Hollywood. In 1979, he became the first Native American awarded a star on Hollywood's Walk of Fame.

Chris Spotted Eagle: Houma director and producer. Worked as project manager and field producer at Twin Cities Public TV, KTCA, Minneapolis. Independent film producer, staff director for the American Indian Center, Minneapolis. A veteran of the U.S. Army and the Air Force.

Eskimo basket, 1930, 2-3/4" x 7-3/4"—$175. (Midwest Auctions)

Hopi 12" wicker tray with eagle, 1900, minor rim damage—$250. (Midwest Auctions)

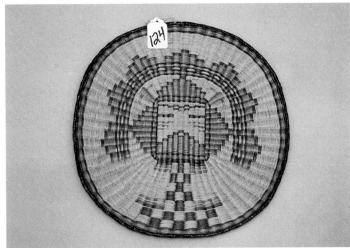

Hopi 14-1/2" wicker tray with kachina, 1920—$550. (Midwest Auctions)

Notable Films With a Native American Theme

Hiawatha (1907)
Pocahontas (1908)
The Redman and the Child (1908)
Leather Stocking (1909)
The Mended Lute (1909)
Ramona (1910)
Red Eagle's Love Affair (1910)
A Squaw's Love (1911)
The Heart of the Indian (1913)
The Battle at Elderbush Gulch (1914)
In the Land of the War Canoes (1914)
The Squaw Man (1914)
The Red Woman (1917)
Wild and Wooly (1917)
The Iron Horse (1924)
Braveheart (1925)
The Vanishing American (1925)
The Big Trail (1930)
The Silent Enemy (1930)
The Squaw Man (1931)
The Last of the Mohicans (1932)
Laughing Boy (1934)
Behold My Wife! (1934)
The Miracle Rider (1935)
The Plainsman (1936)
The Lone Ranger (1938)
Drums Along the Mohawk (1939)
Stagecoach (1939)
Northwest Mounted Police (1940)
They Died with Their Boots On (1941)
She Wore a Yellow Ribbon (1948)
Broken Arrow (1950)
The Last Hunt (1955)
Run of the Arrow (1956)
The Searchers (1956)
Flaming Star (1960)
The Outsider (1961)
A Man Called Horse (1970)
Soldier Blue (1970)
Little Big Man (1971)
Ulzana's Raid (1972)
Harry and Tonto (1974)
One Flew Over the Cuckoo's Nest (1975)
I Will Fight No More Forever (1975)
Return of a Man Called Horse (1976)
Manitou (1978)
Nightwing (1979)
Windwalker (1980)
Legend of the Lone Ranger (1981)
Return of the Country (1982)
Harold of Orange (1983)
Triumphs of a Man Called Horse (1984)
Our Sacred Land (1984)
Powwow Highway (1988)
Dances with Wolves (1990)
Starting Fire with Gunpowder (1991)
Thunderheart (1992)
The West-directed by Ken Rums, a 12, half-hour series (1996)
500 Nations-a series, (1996)
Keeping the Promise-a two-hour TV special, CBS (1997)

Native American Print Media: Newspapers

Ak-Chin O'dham Runner: 42507 Peters and Nall, Maricopa, AZ 85239.

Akwesasne Notes: Mohawk Nation, P.O. Box 196, Rooseveltown, NY 13683-0196.

Bichinik: P.O. Box 1210, Durant, OK 74702-1210.

Char-Koosta News: P.O. Box 278, Pablo, MT 59855.

Cherokee Advocate: P.O. Box 498, Tahlequah, OK 74465.

Cherokee One Feather: P.O. Box 501, Cherokee, NC 28719.

Chickasaw Times: P.O. Box 1543, Ada, OK 74820.

Choctaw Community News: P.O. Box 6010, Philadelphia, MS 39350.

The Circle: 1530 E. Franklin Ave., Minneapolis, MN 55404.

Coeur D'Alene Council Fires: Plummer, Idaho 83851.

The Council: 122 First Ave., Fairbanks, AK 99701.

De-Bah-Ji-Mon: P.O. Box 100, Cass Lake, MN 56633.

Fort Apache Scout: P.O. Box 898, Whiteriver, AZ 85941-0898.

Hopi Tutu-Veh-Ni: P.O. Box 123, Kykotsmovi, AZ 86039.

Ho-Chunk Wo-Lduk: P.O. Box 667, Black River Falls, WI 54615.

How-Ni-Kan: 1901 Gordon Cooper Dr., Shawnee, OK 74801

Indian Time: P.O. Box 196, Rooseveltown, NY 13683-0196.

Kahtou: 203 540 Burrard St., Vancouver, British Columbia V6C 2K1.

Lakota Times: P.O. Box 2180, Rapid City, SD 57709.

Mandan Hidatsa Arikara Times: P.O. Box 1, New Town, ND 58763.

Muscogee Nation News: P.O. Box 580, Okmulgee, OK 74447.

Navajo Times: P.O. Box 310, Window Rock Navajo Nation, AZ 86515-0310.

New Breed Journal: Saskatchewan Native Bay 202 173 Second Ave., South Saskatoon, Saskatchewan S7K 1K6.

News from Indian Country: Rt. 2, Box 2900-A, Hayward, WI 54843.

News from Native California: P.O. Box 9145, Berkeley, CA 94709.

Ourselves: Ni-Mah-Mi-Kwa-Zoo-Min: Minnesota Chippewa Tribe, Cass Lake, MN 56633.

Press Independent: 5120 49th St., Yellowknife, Northwest Territories X1A 1P8.

Sac and Fox News: P.O. Box 246, Stroud, OK 74079

Secwepemc News: 345 Yellowhead Hwy., Kamloops, British Columbia V2H 1H1.

Seminole Tribune: 6333 Northwest 30th St., Hollywood, FL 33024.

Sho-Ban News: P.O. Box 900, Fort Hall, ID 83203.

Spilya Tymoo: P.O. Box 870, Warm Springs, OR 97761.

Treaty Council News: 710 Clayton St., No. 1, San Francisco, CA 94117.

Treaty Seven News: P.O. Box 106, Standoff, Alberta TOL 1YO.

Tribal Tribune: P.O. Box 150, Nespelem, WA 99155.

Wind River News: P.O. Box 900 Lande, WY 82520.

Wind Speaker: 15001 112 Ave., Edmonton, Alberta T5M 2V6.

Hohokom prehistoric scoop, 10" x 5" x 5"—$650. (Midwest Auctions)

Navajo squash blossom necklace with earrings, early pawn—$750. (Midwest Auctions)

Navajo claw and turquoise squash blossom necklace—$900. (Midwest Auctions)

Navajo rug, 51" x 77" plus fringe, 1940—$250. (Midwest Auctions)

Magazines

American Indian Art Magazine: 7314 E. Osborne Dr., Scottsdale, AZ 85251.

Cowboys and Indians: P.O. Box 2441, Cupertino, CA 95015-2441.

Indian Artist: P.O. Box 5465, Santa Fe, NM 87502-5465.

Journal of Alaska Native Arts: P.O. Box 80583, Fairbanks, AK 99708.

Native Nations: P.O. Box 1201, Radio City Station, NY 10101-1201.

Native People: P.O. Box 36820, Phoenix, AZ 85067-6820.

Sierra: 85 Second St., San Francisco, CA 94105-3441.

Turtle Quarterly: 25 Rainbow Mall, Niagara Falls, NY 14303.

Wild West: 300 N. Zeeb Rd., Ann Arbor, MI 48106.

Winds of Change: 1630 30th St., Ste. 301 Boulder, CO 80301.

Navajo second Phase weaving, 46" x 60" ethnographic wear, frayed edges, 1880s—$1,500. (Midwest Auctions)

American Writers Writing About Native Americans

Frank Applegate: *Native Tales of New Mexico and Indian Stories* from the Pueblos, 1932 and 1929 respectively.

Mary Austin: *One Smoke Stories*, 1934.

George Boyce: *Some People Are Indians*, an anthology.

Dee Brown: *Bury My Heart at Wounded Knee*, 1971.

Joseph Bruchac: Abenaki publisher, poet and storyteller. Four-hundred magazines and anthologies have published his poetry and stories. His books include *Thirteen Moons on Turtle's Back: A Native American Year of Moons*, 1992; *Keepers of the Earth: Native American Stories and Environmental Activities for Children*.

Robert Conley: Cherokee who wrote *Indian Voice*.

Adelina Defender: Pueblo who wrote *An American Indian Anthology*. Included in this series was "No Time for Tears," a mission woman's account of harsh treatment, which forced her to return to her Indian ways, 1971.

Charles A. Eastman: A Santee Sioux writer who has been published in *Ladies' Home Journal*, *Harper's*, *Old Indian Days*, *Sunset* and *Craftsman*. His realistic stories were compiled in the early 1900s.

Alexander Ewen: Editor of *Native Nations* which began publishing in 1990.

William Faulkner (1897-1962): Wrote many outstanding novels. His short stories about the Native Americans appeared in *The Saturday Evening Post*.

Hamlin Garland (1860-1940): Many of his American Indian stories were published in 1927 in *The Book of the American Indian*, along with *Western Story* and *Prairie Son*.

Richard Green: An Oneida Indian who wrote for the *Indian Voice* in the 1970s.

George Grinnell: Wrote about mythology and Indians for *Harper's* in the early 1900s.

Ernest Hemingway (1899-1961): Created tales of Indian lore in his short stories "Indian Camp," "Fathers and

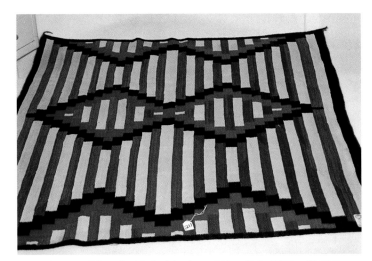

Navajo transitional Chief's blanket, 65" x 68", 1920—$2,250. (Midwest Auctions)

Sons," and "Ten Indians."

Dorothy M. Johnson: Created the short story *"A Man Called Horse"* in 1953. Later Richard Harris starred in the movie.

Martha Kosanke: Published *Indian Romances of the Western Frontier* in 1954.

Jack London (1876-1916): Writes of the Northwest territory; his collections comprise *The Best Short Stories of Jack London*.

N. Scott Momaday: Won the Pulitzer Prize for *House Made of Dawn*, 1968, about a World War II Tanoan Indian veteran reentering society. Also wrote *The Way to Rainy Mountain*, 1969, his memoir, two volumes of poetry and the coffee table book, *Colorado: Summer, Fall, Winter, Spring*, 1973.

Simon J. Ortz: Acoma writer who deals with modern Indian problems. Published in the late 1970s in *Howbah Indians* and *The Man to Send Pain Clouds: Contemporary Stories by American Indians*.

Mary Summer Rain: She is of Shoshone descent and the last apprentice to No Eyes, Chippewa visionary. Her books include *Spirit Song, Phoenix Rising, Daybreak, Soul Sounds, Phantoms Afoot* and *Dreamwalker*.

Verner Z. Reed: Wrote at the turn of the century for anthologies: *Tales of the Sunland*, 1897 and *Adobeland Stories*, 1898.

Frederic Remington (1861-1909): In addition to his art and wonderful bronzes, he created short stories dealing usually with half-breeds for *Harper's*.

Leslie Siko: Published for Viking in 1974, the title story in *The Man to Send Pain Clouds: Contemporary Stories by American Indians*.

William Joseph Snelling: Wrote anonymously in the early 1800s in *Tales of the Northwest: Or, Sketches of Indian Life and Character*.

John Steinbeck (1902-1968): Created stories which appeared in *The Long Valley*, 1938.

Little Steven: Publisher of the magazine *Native Peoples*, which started in 1991.

Cy Warman: His stories deal with half-breeds and their relations with French-Canadians. Featured in periodicals and anthologies his titles include *Frontier Stories*, 1918 and *Weiga of Temagami and Other Indian Tales*, 1908.

Frank Waters (1902-): Celebrated his 95th birthday on June 26, 1993, which Governor Bruce King of New Mexico declared "Frank Waters Day." He has written 22 books to include *The Man Who Killed Deer, Flight from Fiesta, Pumpkin Seed Point, Masked Gods* and *Fever Pitch*. His most recent book is *Brave Are My People: Indian Heroes Not Forgotten*.

Crying Wind: A Navajo woman who has written *Crying Wind* and *My Searching Heart*. She is an artist, lecturer and freelance writer. Her paintings have been shown at museums and art shows; she also received the "Distinguished Christian Service in the Highest Tradition of the American Indian" award.

Beverly Hungry Wolf: Has written the history of her tribe, the Blackfoot, in her book *The Ways of My Grandmothers*.

Southwest cloth saddle bags, possibly Apache, stained, 16" x 80" fringed, 1890-1920—$300. (Midwest Auctions)

Carved 30" wood puzzle pipe stem, bead and tack decorated, minor bead loss—$675. (Midwest Auctions)

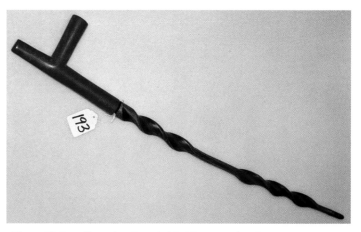

Sioux 8" Cataline pipe bowl, 28-1/2" wood twist stem, 1880—$2,100. (Midwest Auctions)

Large Sioux "T" pipe, early 20th century stem, pipe 1860-1880—$1,100. (Midwest Auctions)

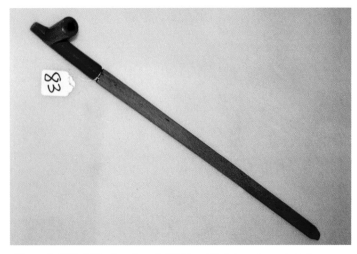

Sioux 4-3/4" "T" pipe bowl, 1870, with later stem, total length 26-1/2"—$700. (Midwest Auctions)

Sioux fully beaded blanket strip, 1890—$2,700. (Midwest Auctions)

Early photographers have preserved for the viewer a variety of Indian tribes. Working from 1850-1900, the list includes: Robert Vance, John Mix Stanley, Jean-Jaques Rousseau and John Wesley Jones. It took some educating to explain the photographic process to Indians who were hesitant to use their sacred sun to record images that neither spoke or moved.

Then came the government photographers who surveyed the land and made a visual record. This group consisted of Tim O'Sullivan, William Henry Jackson and Jack Hillers. Images were created for the military by army photographers Ben Wittick and Will Soule. Indian delegations to Washington were recorded on film by Zeno Schindler and Alexander Gardner.

Deterioration and communication existed between 1885 and 1900. The Amerind was safely portrayed through romanticized views, not real tribal poses. Dimestore novels and the Wild West shows reduced Indians to degraded and distant circus figures. Europeans who had become Americans wanted little to do with Native American heritage.

Photographer Biographies

Edward S. Curtis (1868-1952): Created 20 volumes of Native American photographs. In 1991 a complete set at Sotheby's brought $79,200. Curtis traveled with, had a respect for and learned the Indians' ways. His poses reflect dignity and power.

Adam Clark Vroman: Worked during the late 1890s recording with empathy the harsh lives of various tribes to include the Zuni, Taos, Navajo and Hopi. His art shows religious conviction and deep character and strong beliefs.

Julius Vannerson: Managed a studio in Washington, DC, in 1858. Photographed Indian groups for the American government.

Shan Goshorn: Cherokee woman born in Baltimore, MD, majored in photography at the Cleveland Institute of Art. Many of her works have appeared in the Southern Plains Indian Museum.

Timothy O'Sullivan: Recorded a documentary of the American West from 1871-1873, which were assembled in 1875. O'Sullivan's works included Apache territory, the Grand Canyon and Death Valley. He had served as an apprentice for Matthew Brady and photographed during the Civil War, but received little recognition for his efforts. O'Sullivan surveyed in 1873 the Zuni Indians and their ancient pueblo.

William Bell: In 1872 he photographed the Colorado River, portions of Utah and Nevada and areas around the Grand Canyon. Lieutenant George Montague Wheeler headed the Army Corps of Engineers that Bell and O'Sullivan worked with. Photos were gathered as an aid to exterminate the tribes living in the Southwest: Navajo, Zuni, Apache and Paiute. Bell came from Philadelphia and used a dry photographic process.

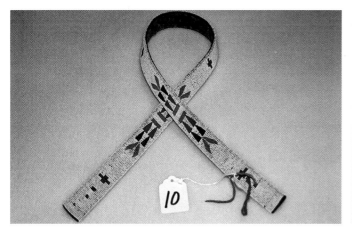

Plains Cree fully beaded belt, 1880—$450. (Midwest Auctions)

French or English trade ax, 14", 19th century or earlier—$250. (Midwest Auctions)

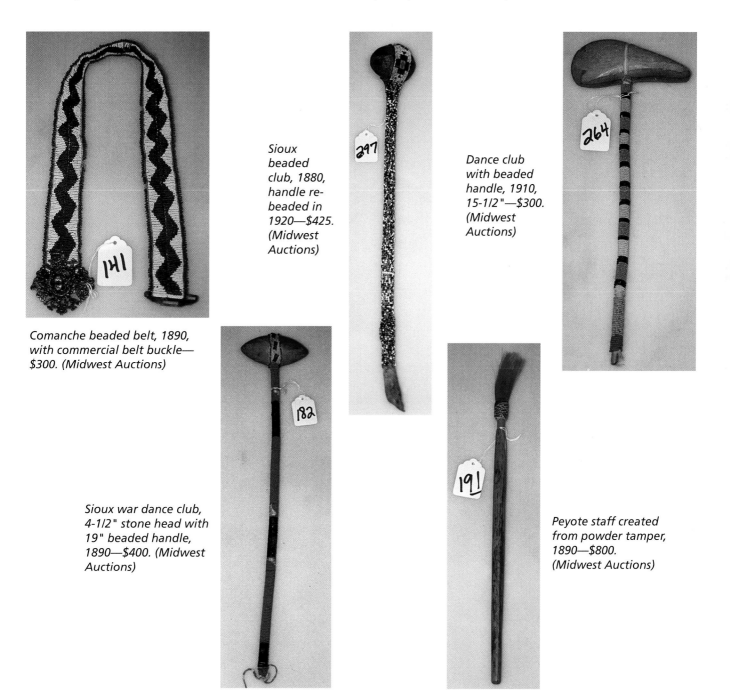

Comanche beaded belt, 1890, with commercial belt buckle—$300. (Midwest Auctions)

Sioux beaded club, 1880, handle re-beaded in 1920—$425. (Midwest Auctions)

Dance club with beaded handle, 1910, 15-1/2"—$300. (Midwest Auctions)

Sioux war dance club, 4-1/2" stone head with 19" beaded handle, 1890—$400. (Midwest Auctions)

Peyote staff created from powder tamper, 1890—$800. (Midwest Auctions)

Plains club, beaded stone head, wooden handle, quilted drops, 1880—$750. (Midwest Auctions)

Beaded buffalo horn ornament, minor bead loss, 1890—$400. (Midwest Auctions)

Reworked buffalo horn headdress, 19th century beadwork on later cloth with turkey feather drops—$425. (Midwest Auctions)

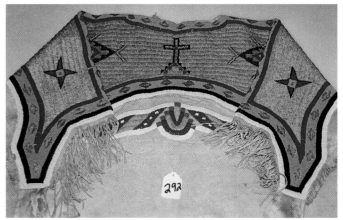

Sioux beaded ceremonial dress, fully beaded yoke, elk hide with fringe, 1910—$7,000. (Midwest Auctions)

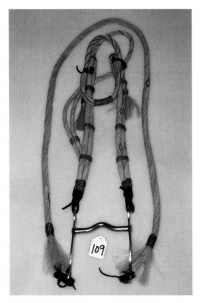

Horsehair bridle with bit, Montana State Prison—$425. (Midwest Auctions)

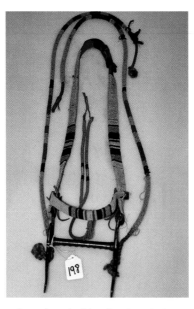

Plains beaded bridle, beaded reins with bit, 1900—$700. (Midwest Auctions)

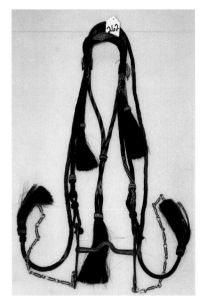

Wala Wala Prison horsehair bridle and reins—$725. (Midwest Auctions)

Sioux beaded child's vest, front and back, 1890—$2,200.
(Midwest Auctions)

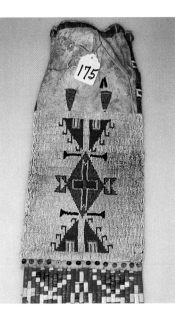

Sioux tobacco bag, beaded and quilted on both sides, 7-1/2" x 29" with fringe, 1910—$2,600. (Midwest Auctions)

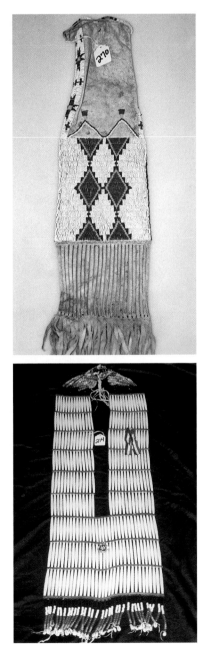

The front and back of a Sioux pipe bag, beaded both sides, parfleche slats, 1890, 7" x 36" with fringe—$3,750. (Midwest Auctions)

Sioux partially beaded and quilted (both sides) pipe bag, 6" x 32" with fringe, ca. 1900—$1,800. (Midwest Auctions)

Hair pipe collar, early 20th century, 13" x 46"—$1,600. (Midwest Auctions)

Sioux bandoleer bag, beaded, 1900—$600. (Midwest Auctions)

Chapter 3

FACTS

Indian Cultures: United States, Canada and Alaska

Arctic: Defined as the region north of the treeline; the mean 10 degrees C (50 degrees F.) in July is the other.

Arctic tribes: Siberian Eskimo, St. Lawrence Island Eskimo, Nauivak Eskimo, Aleut, Pacific Eskimo, Mainland Southwest Alaska Eskimo, Bering Strait Inuit, Kotzebue Sound Inuit, Interior North Alaska Inuit, North Alaska Coast Inuit, Mackenzie Delta Inuit, Copper Inuit, Netsilik, Caribou Inuit, Sallirmiut, Iglulik, Baffinland Inuit, Polar Eskimo, East Greenland Eskimo, West Greenland Eskimo, Labrador Coast Inuit and Inuit of Quebec.

California: Nearly 1,200 miles of coastline, from Death Valley (the continent's low point) to the peaks of the Sierras.

California tribes: Tolowa, Karok, Yurok, Shasta, Hupa, Chilula, Whilkut, Wiyot, Chimariko, Wintu, Mattole, Nongati, Sinkyone, Lassik, Wailaki, Cahto, Yuki, Northern Pomo, Northeastern Pomo, Eastern Pomo, Southeastern Pomo, Central Pomo, Southern Pomo, Kashaya, Nomlaki, Achumawi, Atsugewi, Maidu, Yana, Konkow, Nisenan, Patwin, Lake Miwok, Wappo, Coast Miwok, Miwok, Northern Valley Yokuts, Costanoan, Esselen, Monache, Foothill Yokuts, Southern Valley Yokuts, Tubatulabai, Salinan, Chumash, Kitanemuk, Tavaviam, Serrano, Gabrielino, Luiseno, Cahuilla, Cupeno and Diegueno.

Northeast: New England States, southern Canada, New York, Pennsylvania, New Jersey, Delaware, Ohio, Indiana, Illinois, Wisconsin, Minnesota, Michigan, Virginia, West Virginia, Kentucky and Tennessee.

Northeast Tribes: Chippewa (Ojibwa), Menominee, Winnebago, Illinois, Potawatomi, Sauk, Fox, Mascouten, Miami, Shawnee, Kickapoo, Algonquin, Nipissing, Huron, Ottawa, Petun, Neutral, Wenro, Erie, Seneca, Cayuga, Onondaga, Oneida, Mohawk, Mahican, Delaware, Susquehannock, Nanticoke and neighbors, Virginia Algonquins, Virginia and North Carolina Iroquoians, North Carolina Algonquins, St. Lawrence Iroquoians, Western Abenaki, Eastern Abenaki, Maliseet Passamaquoddy, Micmac, Southern New England and Eastern Long Island Algonquins.

Northwest Coast: Washington, Alaskan panhandle and Vancouver Island, plus Alaska.

Northwest Coast tribes: Eyak, Tlingit, Haida, Nishga, Gitsan, Tsimshian, Haisla, Haihais, Bella Bella, Bella Coola, Oowekeeno, Kwakiutl, Northern Coast Salish, Nootkans, Central Coast Salish, Makah, Southern Coast Salish, Quileute, Chemakum, Southwestern Coast Salish, Kwalhioqua, Chinookans, Clatskanie, Tillamook, Alseans, Siuslawans, Kalapuyans, Coosans, Athapaskans and Takelma.

Plains: From the North Saskatchewan River in Canada south to the Rio Grande almost in Mexico; east-west boundaries are the Mississippi-Missouri valleys and the foothills

Crow bag, fully beaded (one side), 5" x 16" with red ochre fringe, 1920—$700. (Midwest Auctions)

Sioux beaded "strike-a-lite" bag, 1900, 4"—$250. (Midwest Auctions)

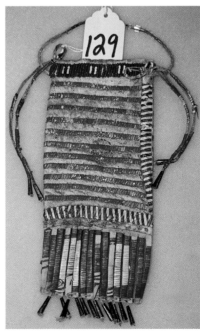

Sioux quilted both sides pouch with cone drops, minor quill loss, 1890, 3-3/4" x 8"—$800. (Midwest Auctions)

Fully beaded Plains medicine/token pouch, 1900, 3-3/8"—$250. (Midwest Auctions)

Shoshone "strike-a-lite" bag with cone drops, 1890, 2-3/4" x 7"—$500. (Midwest Auctions)

Sioux hair drop, beaded on parfleche, with cone drops, 1890, 2-3/8" x 13"—$950. (Midwest Auctions)

of the Rocky Mountains. States included are North and South Dakota, Nebraska, Montana and Kansas.

Plains tribes: Sarcee, Plains Cree, Blackfeet, Gros Verde, Assiniboin, Plains Ojibwa, Crow, Teton Sioux, Hidatsa, Mandan, Arikara, Yanktonai Sioux, Santee Sioux, Cheyenne, Ponca, Omaha, Yankton Sioux, Iowa, Oto, Pawnee, Arapaho, Kansa, Missouri, Kiowa, Kiowa Apache, Osage, Comanche, Wichita, Quapaw, Tonkawa and Kitsai.

Plateau and Basin: From central British Columbia, south across the U.S. border, eastern Oregon, Washington, the northern half of Idaho and northwestern Montana.

Plateau tribes: Lilooet, Shuswap, Thompson, Nicola, Okanagan, Lakes, Kutenai, Kalispel, Sanpoil, Columbia Salish, Yakima, Spokane, Palus, Coeur d'Alene, Flathead, Nez Perce, Wall Wall, Cayuse, Umatilla, Klikitat, Wishram, Tenino, Molala, Klamath and Modoc.

Basin tribes: Eastern Shoshoni, Northern Shoshoni, Bannock, Northern Paiute, Washoe, Western Shoshoni, Ute, Southern Paiute, Owens Valley Paiute and Kawaiisu.

Southeast: The Atlantic Plain, Appalachian Highlands, Florida Plain, Gulf Plain and the Coastal Plains. Includes Florida, Georgia, South Carolina, Alabama, Mississippi, Louisiana, Arkansas and Eastern Texas.

Southeast tribes: Ais, Alabama, Apalachee, Atakapa, Biloxi, Caddo, Calusa, Catawba, Chakchiuma, Chatot, Cherokee, Chickasaw, Chitimacha, Choctaw, Creek, Cusabo, Hitchiti, Houma, Keys, Koasati, Lumbee, Mikasuki, Muskogee, Natchez, Ofo, Seminole, Tekesta, Timucua, Tocobaga, Tohome, Mobile, Tunica, Tutelo, Yamasee and Yuchi.

Southwest: Arizona, New Mexico, Sonora and parts of Chihuahua in Mexico, plus portions of Utah, Texas and Colorado.

Southwest tribes: Acaxee, Acoma, Apache, Chiricahua Apache, Cochimi, Cocopa, Concho, Cuechan, Eudeve, Grande Keresans, Groups of the Gulf Coastal Plain and Interior, Guarijio, Guasave, Guaycura, Halchidhoma, Havasupai, Hopi, Jano, Jemez, Jicarilla Apache, Jocome, Jova, Jumano, Karankawa, Kiliwa, Laguna, Lower Pima, Maricopa, Mayo, Mescalero Apache, Mohave, N. Tiwa, Navajo, Opata, Paipai, Pame, Papago, Pecos, Pericu, Pima, Piro, Quechan, S. Tiwa, Seri, Suma, Tahue, Tano, Tarahumara, Tepehuan, Tewa, Toboso, Tompiro, Tubar, Walapai, Western Apache, Western Zuni, Xixime, Yaqui, Yavapai and Zacatec.

Subarctic: An area of 2 million square miles covering the entire North American continent from the Labrador peninsula in the east, including Newfoundland, to the south of Hudson Bay, then west to Alaska.

Subarctic tribes: Holikachuk, Ingalik, Kolchan, Tanaina, Koyukon, Kutchin, Tanana, Ahtna, Han, Tutchone, Hare, Mountain Indians, Tagish, Inland Tlingit, Kaska, Tahitan, Tsetsaut, Sekani, Slavey, Beaver, Carrier, Chilcotin, Dogrib, Yellowknife, Chipewyan, Western Woods Cree, West Main Cree, Northern Ojibwa, Lake Winnipeg Saulteaux, Naskapi, East Cree, Atti Kamek, Montagnais and Beothuk.

The Wild West Show

William Frederick Cody was born February 26, 1846, in Le Claire, Scott County, IA. He was the fourth of eight children and was usually called Will by his family. His death came at noon on January 10, 1917, at his sister's home. May Cody Decker lived in Denver at 2932 Lafayette St. Burial took place on June 3, 1917, when Buffalo Bill, also known as Pahaska, was laid to rest. Brigadier General William F. Cody was placed in a tomb on the crest of Lookout Mountain above Denver. "It was the most impressive, the most notable funeral ever witnessed in America." At his demise he became immortalized as the Great American Hero; 25,000 citizens were in attendance to pay their last respects.

Everyone in America knew Buffalo Bill: he had hunted buffalo for the railroad crews, served as a Pony Express rider, scouted for the U.S. Cavalry and was a professional actor for 11 years. All before age 37! In 1883 Nebraskans in Omaha were treated to the grand opening of his show which would reign for 30 years. An admission of 50 cents permitted you to see the famous star as cowboys dazzled with their stunt riding, clever roping and accurate marksmanship. Bill hit dozens of colored glass balls thrown into the air, while riding his horse at full speed. The crowd and the press loved the performance and a decision was made to take the show on tour. At its peak, the Wild West Show employed over 500, toured all of the U.S., England and Europe. In 1884, 41,448 saw a single performance in Chicago; the year before he had played to 6 million in Chicago. In London, 83,000 bought tickets for one show.

Many celebrities saw Buffalo Bill's Wild West Show: New York Governor David B. Hill, Mark Twain, Prince Dom Augusta of Brazil and English actor Henry Irving. Other participants were Mr. and Mrs. Oliver Belmont, Henry Ward Beecher, General William Tecumseh Sherman and Queen Victoria and her court. Additional visitors to the show were the Prince and Princess of Wales, Pope Leo XIII, King Ludwig III of Bavaria and his daughters, Kaiser Wilhelm II and President Cleveland.

In 1894 the Wild West played Ambrose Park, Brooklyn, from May 12 to October 6, excluding Sundays. After that 126-day run, a series of one-night stands commenced through America and Europe for the next 20 years. In 1895 there were 321 performances; Cody didn't miss one. The train, in three sections, traveled 8,980 miles in 195 days. This record was beaten in 1899 with 11,111 miles logged in a 200-day season.

Troubles often plagued the tours: winter rehearsals and organizing, quarrels among the groups, wet and cold weather and high winds and fire. Forty-two fine horses had to be shot due to disease, there were also the deaths and injuries of participants, broken flat-car axles and even the collapse of a pavilion under the great weight.

The quality of his troupe always improved. Star bill-

Left and right: Paiute open twined cradles—$522.50 each; center, laced buckskin and basketry—$300. (Merritt's Museum of Childhood)

Left, birchbark covered box with floral quill work—$200; birchbark food container with lid, leaf decor, Eastern Algonquin—$250. Right, birchbark syrup basket—$175. (Merritt's Museum of Childhood)

Desirable Pomo gift basket decorated with redheaded woodpecker feathers—$990. (Merritt's Museum of Childhood)

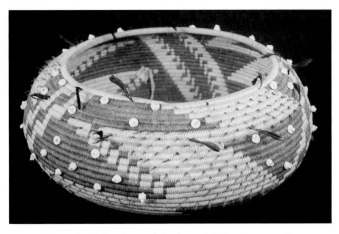

Large Pomo gift basket, globular with feathers and shells—$6,600. (Merritt's Museum of Childhood)

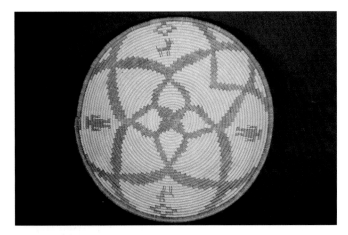

Apache basket, radiating star rosettes enclosing deer and men—$2,310. (Merritt's Museum of Childhood)

Grouping of five Hopi examples: three bowls—$350 each; tall vase with stylized Parrot design—$275; and double-spout water jar—$500. (Merritt's Museum of Childhood)

ing was given to "Little Sure Shot," Mrs. Phoebe Ann Butler, known as Annie Oakley. During his European tours he recruited the best horsemen in Europe for the "Rough Riders of the World." Sitting Bull, the Sioux chieftain, agreed to sign on in 1885 for $50 a week plus $125 bonus. He signed and sold his photographs by the hundreds. The chief called Cody by an Indian name, Pahaska, "Long Hair," and their affection for each other was sincere and genuine. At the end of the tour Sitting Bull was given a horse that performed when a gun was fired. Back on the reservation, a group of government Indian recruits came to arrest the chief. Sitting Bull refused to leave his people; in a skirmish, he was shot and killed. The trick horse reared and pawed the air at the cue of gunfire. The Indians believed that the fallen chief's spirit had entered the horse's body. Unharmed, the horse was returned to Buffalo Bill to perform again in the Wild West show.

The acts were filled with a variety of nationalities: Americans, English, Germans, Mexicans, Cossacks, Arabs, Cubans, Hawaiians and Filipinos. Native Americans comprised Sioux and other tribes. In addition to Sitting Bull, the list included Short Man, Has-No-Horse, High Heron, Willie-Spotted-Horse, Chief Red Cloud, Chief American Horse, Red Shirt, Iron Tail, Black Fox, Growlers and Iron Cloud. Also part of the crowd were Spotted Weasel, Good Horse, Comes Out Holy, Flying Horse, John Kills Brave, Standing Soldier, White Bird, Little Bull, Comes Last, Comes Out Bear, Richard Lip, Spotted Horse Flight, White Bonnet and Kills in Loge. Others in the troop were Holy Bear, Comes Killing, Kill Enemy, Mary Kills Enemy, Jennie Spotted Horse, White Cow, Sam Stabber, White Belly, Eagle Fox, Pluck Porcupine, Jacob Iron Eagle, Red Calf, Charging Thunder, Dreamer, Wounded, Loud Thunder, Frank Meat, Albert Thunder Hawk, Ed Porcupine Knee, Sam Lone Bear, Mounted Sheep and Whirlwind Horse.

Cody was denounced for showing Indians as savages, but he gave them employment when opportunities were few. Many learned that there was a world beyond the village. By using the buffalo in his show, the species was kept from extinction. His historic aspects of the cowboy and Indian West were exhibited well by this famous showman. His fame ranks with Wild Bill Hickok, Jim Bridger, Kit Carson, Davy Crockett and Daniel Boone.

The Buffalo: An All-Purpose Plains Beast

Every portion of the buffalo was used; the most versatile was the animal's hide. Thickness and uses varied according to the age and the sex of the animal. Old bulls had the thickest skins and these became soles for winter moccasins and shields. Berry bags were created from thin unborn calves' skins. The intermediary cowskin was fashioned into a great number of items. Cowhide was made rainproof by grease and smoke; untreated skin was tough and stiff and called rawhide; after tanning, the skin became soft. The woman's chemical treatment included flexing, stretching and squeezing on the brains, fat and liver. Winter garments had the hair on the hides.

Clothing: hide with hair-robes, caps with ear flaps, mittens, coats and capes; hide-moccasins, leggings, shirts, dresses and breech cloths; bull rawhide-moccasin soles, belts; calf hide-

underclothes; hair, horns-headdress ornaments.

Tipi and furnishings: cowhide-tipi covers, door flaps, linings; rawhide-medicine cases, cache pit covers, trunks; hide with hair-bedcovers; hair, tail-tipi ornaments.

Ceremonial objects: skull-sun dance altars; hoofs, rawhide-rattles; hide, horn-horse masks; hide winding sheets for the dead.

Recreation: ribs-ice sled runners; bone-dice; hair-ball stuffing; calfskin-ball coverings; rawhide-lacrosse hoop netting.

Weapons: bull sinew-bow backings, bowstrings; bone-arrowheads; sinew-arrowheads, feather wrappings; rawhide-knife sheaths, cover and hefting of war clubs; hair, beard-club ornaments; horn-powder flasks; rawhide from bull's neck-shields.

Riding and transportation: hide-burden straps, pad saddle coverings, saddle blankets, horse blankets; rawhide-frame saddle coverings, saddle rigging straps, stirrup coverings, cruppers, parfleches, saddlebags, hackmores, lariats, picket ropes, hobbles, travois hitches, pole hitches, snowshoes, horseshoes, horse troughs; hide of an unborn calf-berry bags; calfhide-tobacco pouches.

Tools and utensils: horn-quill flatteners, cups, ladles, spoons; hump-arrow straighteners; rawhide-mauls' hefting, meat and berry pounders; tibia and femur-fleshing tool; shoulder blade-hoes, paint brushes; paunch-cooking vessels, water buckets; bone-knives, sewing awls, hide scrapers; dung-fuel; rough side of the tongue-hairbrushes; hooves, hide-glue; brains, fat, liver-tanning agents.

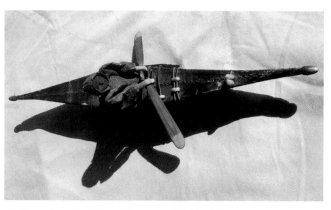

Eskimo kayak of wood covered with skin, 16-1/2" long, wooden oars, bone trimmings—$550. (Merritt's Museum of Childhood)

Rawhide and beaded cradleboard with doll and carrying handle, 12" long, 1880s—$715. (Merritt's Museum of Childhood)

White Man's Reliance Upon Native Americans

The white man was influenced and his destiny shaped through an Indian's existence to include arts and crafts, economics, trade, mythology, religion, government and agriculture.

● Indians supplied the Europeans with many new aspects: foods, methods of planting, hunting and fishing, watercraft, as guides over wilderness trails, plus implements and tools and clothing and utensils. Styles were revolutionized as a result of the fur trade.

● More than half the crops grown were first domesticated by American Indians. These include potatoes, corn, rice, wheat, manioc and sweet potatoes. Others are tobacco, cotton, peppers, tomatoes, squash, peanuts, chicle, cacao, pineapples, pumpkins, avocados, numerous beans and many other fruits and vegetables.

● Indian devices used today are hammocks, parkas, dog sleds, kayaks, canoes, snowshoes, moccasins, smoking pipes, ponchos, toboggans, rubber syringes, the rubber ball and the game of lacrosse.

● Many English terms were adopted from the Indians such as the names for cities, geographical sites, rivers, lakes, mountains and states.

Northeast beaded picture frame showing Indians, multi-colored dangling beads—$200. (Merritt's Museum of Childhood)

Three Chippewa beaded headbands—$100 each; beaded Plains ration ticket pouch, used on the reservations so they could obtain supplies, Crow design—$247.50. (Merritt's Museum of Childhood)

Finely beaded examples from left to right—$137 each; Cheyenne/Arapaho red and white beaded necklace, Canadian River, Oklahoma—$250; in the center is a decorated leather pouch with flap, beads and cowry shells are implemented in the design—$650. (Merritt's Museum of Childhood)

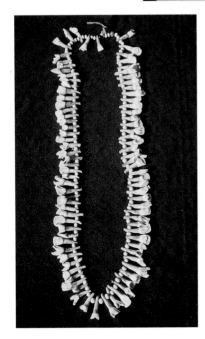

Navajo necklace, 36" long, mustang teeth spaced with light green beads, ca. 1880—$300. (Merritt's Museum of Childhood)

● Indian contributions to English include skunk, terrapin, chigger, jaguar, puma, cougar, manatee, barracuda, chipmunk, opossum, raccoon, caribou and moose. Some trees, plants and foods also have Indian names such as saguaro, yucca, mesquite, maypop, mangrove, mahogany, persimmon, pecan, hickory, maize, squash, hominy, avocado, manioc, pemmican, papaya, cassava, pawpaw, tapioca, succotash and scuppernong.

● Other common expressions derived from the Indian language are war paint, happy hunting ground, Indian summer, big chief, warpath, bury the hatchet, paleface and Indian file.

● Some other crossover words are bayou, savanna, pampas, muskeg, pocosin, podunk, hurricane, Chinook, pogonip and blizzard.

● Additional American words from Native American are wigwam, wickiup, teepee, igloo, hogan, jacal, moccasin, mukluk, parka, toboggan, tumpline, Yankee, okay, honky-tonk, wampum, kachinast squaw, papoose, mugwump, powwow, potlatch.

● The international Boy and Girl Scout movements were inspired partly by the lives of Indians.

● Secretary of the Interior, Stewart Udall, wrote in his 1963 book *The Quiet Crisis*, "It is ironical that today the conservations movement finds itself turning back to ancient Indian land ideas, to the Indian understanding that we are not outside of nature, but of it."

● TV, motion pictures, dance and drama, art, music and literature to some extent reflect the Indian influence. Most times, the interpretations have not been accurate.

● Early white pioneers often relied upon Indian shamans. Their cures have been acclaimed in the Midwest and in New England.

● Later the drugs and herbs were exploited as worthless elixirs created under such labels as "Kickapoo Juice," and "Seneca Oil."

● Recently, studies have been made concerning psychiatry and psychosomatic medicines. It has been discovered that the Indian curers sought to treat mental health by bringing the body back into harmony with the universe.

● Child psychologists are studying the Indian practices used to raise, educate and discipline youths.

● Government poverty programs and self-helps are learning by studying Indian-directed group activities.

● The League of the Iroquois influenced the thinking of Benjamin Franklin as he worked toward the union of Colonies at Albany in 1754. He stated: "It would be a strange thing if Six Nations of ignorant savages should be capable of forming a scheme for such a union and be able to execute it in such a manner as that it subsisted ages and appears indissoluble; and yet that a like union should be impracticable for ten or a dozen English colonies, to whom it is more necessary and must be more advantageous and who cannot be supposed to want an equal understanding of their interests."

● Compromise sessions in the House and Senate after 1789 show a marked resemblance to the ways that the Iroquois League operated.

● Indians were described as living in a Golden Age of virtue and innocence as described by Peter Martyr in the 16th century. He noted: "men lived simply and innocently without enforcement of laws, without quarrels, judges, libels, content only to satisfy nature, without further vexation for knowledge of things to come."

● European masques and balls played at being happy like the innocent American Indians.

● Montaigne and Rousseau wrote of the state of Europeans who were living in want under various forms of tyranny. Rousseau wrote, "man is free and everywhere he is in chains." Through their philosophy, revolutions occurred that changed the world.

● Indian societies observed freedom and dignity for the individual. It took a unanimous council to make a decision, rather than a majority. Thus, Native Americans in numerous ways shaped the way colonists thought and acted. These new sets of values turned Europeans into "freedom-loving Americans."

● Twenty six states have North American Indian names. Translations of state names vary:

Alabama: A tribe of the Creek confederacy.
Alaska: Aleutian meaning "mainland."
Arizona: Papago suggesting "place of the small spring."
Arkansas: A Sioux tribal name.
Connecticut: Algonquin for "the place of the long river."
Idaho: Kiowa-Apache name for the Comanche.
Illinois: Algonquin tribal name meaning "men."
Indiana: commemorates the Indians.
Iowa: Sioux tribal name.
Kansas: Sioux tribal name.
Kentucky: Perhaps Iroquois for "meadow land."
Massachusetts: Algonquin for "at the place of large bills."
Michigan: Algonquin for "big lake."
Minnesota: Sioux meaning "water cloudy."
Mississippi: Algonquin for "big river."
Missouri: Algonquin tribal name.
Nebraska: Sioux meaning "flat water."
North Dakota: Sioux tribal name.
Ohio: Iroquois for "water fine."
Oklahoma: Muskogean for "people red," derived by a Choctaw chief.
Oregon: Indian-specific origin disputed.
South Dakota: Sioux tribal name.
Tennessee: Name of a Cherokee town.
Texas: Caddo and other Indian for "friends."
Utah: From tribal name, Ute.
Wisconsin: Possibly Algonquin for "big-long-at" (river).
Wyoming: Algonquin for "big-flats-at."

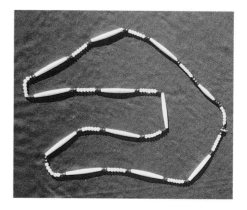

Bone and glass bead necklace, Cheyenne, Canadian River, Oklahoma—$137. (Merritt's Museum of Childhood)

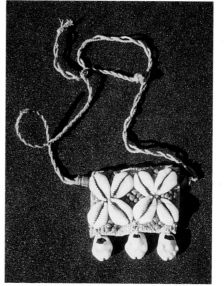

Miniature woven grass bag with carrying strap, designed with beads and cowry shells—$100. (Merritt's Museum of Childhood)

Six engraved stone pendants—$75 each. (Merritt's Museum of Childhood)

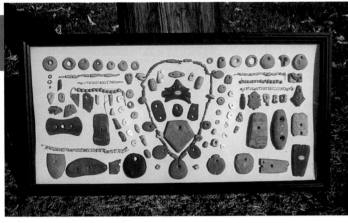

A framed assortment of shells, beads, gorgets, pendants—$450. (Merritt's Museum of Childhood)

Seven rows of stone objects mounted on a wooden arrowhead board: hatchet—$150; three celts—$100 each; toma-hawk—$200; three pestles—$100 each; three bow string stones—$75 each; two paint mortars—$75 each; three gun flints—$25 each. (Merritt's Museum of Childhood)

A great variety of common and treaty arrows (board mounted). To the left are prehistoric, leaf, bleeding, stunning game, stemmed, edge barbed, square blade, bird points, fish tail and saw tooth. Those to the right include: fish, serrated, curved, smooth face, tribe marked, shark tooth, sandstone, New Jersey rotary, barbed iron, treaty, unfinished, combi-nation, vein, drill point, bird dart, ceremonial—$1,000 framed. (Merritt's Museum of Childhood)

Place Your Bets!

The list provided includes Native American Casinos operating in various states:

Arizona

Apache Gold, P.O. Box 1210, San Carlos 85550

Blue Water, 119 W. Riverside Dr., Parker 85344

Bucky's, 530 E. Merritt, Prescott 86301

Casino of the Sun, 7406 S. Camino De Oeste, Tucson 85746

Cliff Castle, P.O. Box 4677, Camp Verde 86322

Cocopah, 15136 S. Avenue B, Somerton 85350

Desert Diamond, 7350 S. Old Nogales Hwy., Tucson 85734

Fort McDowell, P.O. Box 18359, Fountain Hills 85269

Gila River, Lone Butte, 1201 S. 56th St., Chandler 85226

Gila River, Wild Horse, 5512 W. Wild Horse Pass, Chandler 85226

Harrah's Phoenix Ak Chin, 15406 Maricopa Rd., Maricopa 85239

Hon Dah, P.O. Box 3250, Pinetop 85935

Mazatzal, P.O. Box 1820, Payson 85547

Paradise, 540 Quechan Dr., Yuma 85364

Pipe Spring Resort & Casino, HC 65, Box 3, Fredonia 86022

Spring Mountain, 8555 S. Highway 95, Mohave Valley 86440

Yavapai Gaming Center, 1505 E. Hwy. 69, Prescott 86301

California

Black Bart, P.O. Box 1177, Willits 95490

Cache Creek Indian Bingo & Casino, 14455 Hwy. 16, Brooks 95606

Casino Morongo, 49750 Seminole Dr., Cabazon 92230

Cher-Ae Heights, P.O. Box 635, Trinidad 95570

Chicken Ranch Bingo, 16929 Chicken Ranch Rd., Jamestown 95327

Chumash, 3400 Highway 246, Santa Ynez 93460

Colusa Casino & Bingo, P.O. Box 1267, Colusa 95932

Elk Valley, 2500 Howland Hill Rd., Cresent City 95531

Fantasy Springs, 82-245 Indio Springs Dr., Indio 92203

Havasu Landing Casino & Resort, P.O. Box 1976, Havasu Lake 92363

Jackson Indian Bingo & Casino, 12222 New York Ranch Rd., Jackson 95642

Palace Indian Gaming Center, P.O. Box 308, Lemoore 93245

Robinson Rancheria Bingo & Casino, 1545 E. Hwy. 20, Nice 95464

San Manuel Indian Bingo & Casino, 5797 N. Victoria Ave., San Bernardino 92346

Soboba, 2333 Soboba Rd., San Jacinto 92583

Spa, 140 N. Indian Canyon Dr., Palm Springs 92262

Spotlight 29, 46200 Harrison Place, Coachella 92236

Sycuan Gaming Center, 5469 Dehesa Rd., El Cajon 92019

Table Mountain, 8184 Table Mountain Rd., Friant 93626

Viejas Casino & Turf Club, 5000 Willows Rd., Alpine 91901

Win-River, 2100 Redding Rancheria Rd., Redding 96001

Colorado

Sky Ute Lodge & Casino, Hwy. 172 North, Ignacio 81137

Ute Mountain, 3 Weeminuche Dr., Towaoc 81334

Connecticut

Foxwoods Resort (largest Indian casino in U.S.), Rt. 2, Ledyard 06339

Mohegan Sun, Mohegan Sun Blvd., Uncasville 06382

Florida

Miccosukee Indian Gambling, 500 S.W. 177 Ave., Miami 33194

Seminole Poker, 4150 N. State Rd. 7, Hollywood 33021

Seminole Indian, 5223 N. Orient Rd., Tampa 33610

Seminole Indian, 506 South 1st St., Imokalee 33934

Iowa

Casino Omaha, Blackbird Bend, Onawa 51040

Mesquaki Bingo & Casino, 1504 305th St., Tama 52339

Winnavegas, 330th St., Sloan 51055

Kansas

Golden Eagle, Rt. 1, Box 149, Horton 66439

Prairie Band Potawatomi Bingo, Rt. 2, Mayetta 66509

Sac and Fox, P.O. Box 11, Hiawatha 66434

Louisiana

Cypress Bayou, P.O. Box 519, Charenton 70523

Grand Casino Avoyelles, 711 Grand Blvd., Marksville 71351

Grand Casino Coushatta, 777 Coushatta Dr., Kinder 70648

Michigan

Bay Mills Resort & Casino, Lakeshore Dr., Box 249, Brimley 49715

Chip-In, P.O. Box 351, Harris 49845

Kewadin, 102 Candy Cane Ln., Christmas 49862

Kewadin, 3 Mile Rd., Hessel 49745

Kewadin, Rt. 1, Box 15330, U.S. 2, Manistique 49854

Kewadin, 2186 Shunk Rd., Sault Ste. Marie 49783

Kewadin, 3039 Mackinaw Trail, St. Ignace 49781

Kings Club, Rt. 1, Box 313, Brimley 49715

Lac Vieux Desert, 446 Watersmeet, Watersmeet 49969

Leelanau Sands, 2521 N.W. Bayshore Dr., Sutton's Bay 49682

Ojibwa, Rt. 1, Box 284 A, Baraga 49908

Soaring Eagle, 2395 S. Leaton Rd., Mt. Pleasant 48858

Minnesota

Black Bear Casino & Hotel, 1789 Hwy. 210, Carlton 55718

Firefly Creek, Rt. 2, Box 96, Granite Falls 56241

Fond-du-Luth, 129 E. Superior St., Duluth 55802

Fortune Bay, 1430 Bois Forte Rd., Tower 55790

Grand Casino Hinckley, 777 Lady Luck Dr., Hinckley 55037

Rawhide apron with shells and beads—$250. (Merritt's Museum of Childhood)

Oyster shell ornaments, Maidu Mound, Hallister Ranch, CA— $385 each. (Merritt's Museum of Childhood)

Two war clubs: top, stone head and rawhide bound, 30" long, dyed horsehair and beading—$350; bottom, round stone rawhide covered, beaded— $450. (Merritt's Museum of Child-hood)

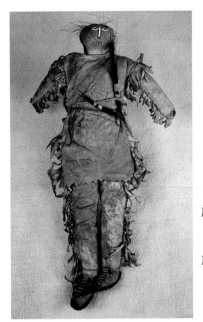

Buckskin Plains doll, beaded face and moccasins, horsehair wig—$1,650. (Merritt's Museum of Childhood)

Grand Casino Mille Lacs, 777 Grand Ave., Onamia 56359
Grand Portage Lodge & Casino, P.O. Box 233, Grand Portage 55605
Jackpot Junction Casino Hotel, P.O. Box 420, Morton 56270
Lake of the Woods Casino & Bingo, 1012 E. Lake St., Warroad 56763
Mystic Lake Casino Hotel, 2400 Mystic Lake Blvd., Prior Lake 55372
Northern Lights, HCR73, Box 1003, Walker 56484
The Palace Bingo & Casino, RR #3, Box 221, Cass Lake 56633
Red Lake Casino & Bingo, Hwy. 1 East, Red Lake 56671
River Rd. Casino & Bingo, RR 43, Box 168A, Thief River Falls 56701
Shooting Star Casino Hotel, 777 Casino Blvd., Mahnomen 56557
Treasure Island, 5734 Sturgeon Lake Rd., Welch 55089

Mississippi

Silver Star Hotel & Casino, Hwy. 16 West, Philadelphia 39350

Montana

4 C's Cafe & Casino, Rocky Boy Route, Box 544, Box Elder 59521
Little Big Horn, P.O. Box 580, Crow Agency 59022
Northern Cheyenne, P.O. Box 128, Lame Deer 59043
Silver Wolf, P.O. Box 726, Wolf Point 59201

Nevada

Avi Hotel & Casino, 10000 Aha Macao Pkwy., Laughlin 89029

New Mexico

Apache Nugget, P.O. Box 650, Dulce 87528
Camel Rock, Rt. 11, Box 3A, Santa Fe 87501
Casino Apache, P.O. Box 269, Mescalero 88340
Cities of Gold, Rt. 11, Box 21-B, Santa Fe 87501
Isleta Gaming Palace, 11000 Broadway S.E. Albuquerque 87022
Ohkay, P.O. Box 1270, San Juan Pueblo 87566
Sandia, P.O. Box 10188, Albuquerque 87184
San Felipe Casino Hollywood, 25 Hagan Rd., Algodones 87001
Santa Ana Star, 54 Jemez Dam Canyon Rd., Bernalillo 87004
Sky City, P.O. Box 519, San Fidel 87049
Taos Slot Room, P.O. Box 1477, Taos 87571

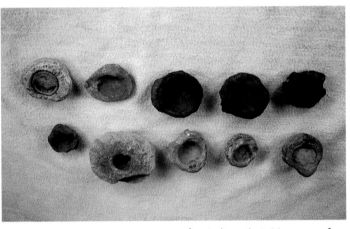

Nine large and small paint pots—$100. (Merritt's Museum of Childhood)

New York

Mohawk Bingo Palace, St. Regis Indian Reservation, Rt. 35, Hogansburg 13655
Turning Stone, Patrick Rd., Verona 13478

North Dakota

Four Bears Casino & Lodge, P.O. Box 579, New Town 58763
Prairie Knights Casino & Lodge, HC 1, Box 26-A, Fort Yates 58538
Spirit Lake, Hwy. 57, Spirit Lake 58370
Wild Rose, P.O. Box 1449, Hwy. 5 West, Belcourt 58316

Oregon

Chinook Winds Gaming Center, 1777 N.W. 44th St., Lincoln City 97367
Indian Head Gaming Center, P.O. Box 720, Warm Springs 97761
Klamath Tribe, P.O. Box 436, Chiloquin 97624

Sioux horn decorated dance club with fur and beaded handle—$440. (Merritt's Museum of Childhood)

The Mill, 3201 Tremont St., North Bend 97459
Seven Feathers Hotel & Resort, 146 Chief Miwaleta Ln., Canyonville 97417
Spirit Mountain, P.O. Box 39, Grand Ronde 97347
Wild Horse Gaming Resort, 72777 Hwy. 331, Pendleton 97801

South Dakota

Dakota Sioux, Rt. 1, Box 107, Watertown 57201
Fort Randall, West Hwy. 46, Wagner 57380
Golden Buffalo, P.O. Box 204, Lower Brule 57548
Grand River, P.O. Box 639, Mobridge 57601
Lode Star, P.O. Box 140, Fort Thompson 57339
Prairie Wind, HC 49, Box 10, Pine Ridge 57770
Rosebud, P.O. Box 21, Mission 57555
Royal River Casino & Bingo, Veterans St., Box 326, Flandreau 57028

Washington

Coulee Dam, 515 Birch St., Coulee Dam 99155
Clearwater, 15347 Suquamish Way N.E. Suquamish 98392
Double Eagle, 2539 Smith Rd., Chewwlah 99109
Harrah's Skagit Valley, 590 Dark Ln., Bow 98232
Little Creek, West 91, Hwy. 108, Shelton 98584
Lucky Eagle, 12888 188th Rd. S.W., Rochester 98579
Lummi, 2559 Lummi View Dr., Bellingham 98226
Mill Bay, 455 E. Wapato Lake Rd., Manson 98831
Muckleshoot, 2402 Auburn Way South, Auburn 98002
Nooksack River, 5048 Mt. Baker Hwy., Deming 98244
Okanogan Bingo and Casino, 41 Appleway Rd., Okanogan 98840
Seven Cedars, 270796 Hwy. 101, Sequim 98382
Swinomish Casino & Bingo, 837 Swinomish Casino Dr., Anacortes 98221
Tulalip, 6410 33rd Ave. N.E., Maryville 98271
Two Rivers, 6828-B Hwy. 25 South, Davenport 99122

Wisconsin

Bad River Bingo & Casino, P.O. Box 39, Odanah 54861
Grand Royale, Hwy. 55, Mole Lake 54520
Ho Chunk, S3214A Hwy. 12, Baraboo 53913
Hole in the Wall, P.O. Box 98, Danbury 54830
Isla Vista, Hwy. 13 North, Bayfield 54814
Lac Courte Oreilles, Rt. 5, Hayward 54843
Lake of the Torches, 567 Peace Pipe Rd., Lac du Flambeau 54538
Majestic Pines, Hwy. 54, Black River Falls 54615
Menominee, P.O. Box 760, Hwy. 47 & 55, Keshena 54135
Mohican North Star, W12180A County Rd. A, Bowler 54416
Northern Lights, P.O. Box 140, Hwy. 32, Carter 54566
Oneida Bingo & Casino, 2100 Airport Dr., Green Bay 54313
Potawatomi Bingo, 1721 W. Canal St., Milwaukee 53233
Rainbow, 494 County Rd. G, Nekoosa 54457
Regency Resort, Hwy. 55, Mole Lake 54520
St. Croix Casino & Hotel, 777 U.S. Hwy. 8, Turtle Lake 54889

Two Penobscot wooden birch war clubs with carved faces, Penobscot River, ME—$577.50 pair. (Merritt's Museum of Childhood)

Unusual and lethal wooden war club with 11 inset flint arrows—$300. (Merritt's Museum of Childhood)

Two wooden handled tomahawks with carved stone heads, bound by rawhide—$350 each. (Merritt's Museum of Childhood)

Seven-color floral beaded bag, Flathead, bound on cloth with rawhide hand straps— $412.50. (Merritt's Museum of Childhood)

Ute beaded pouch, steer and florals on the front, marked "Anna" in beads on the back, trimmed with beads and leather streamers—$495. (Merritt's Museum of Childhood)

Ute beaded pouch, deer and florals on the front, trimmed with red velvet, black felt backing, marked "KAT" on the front in the upper left corner—$522.50. (Merritt's Museum of Childhood)

Did You Know?

● Before Europeans entered the New World, Indians had learned how to adapt to the flora, fauna and climates of many different geographic areas.

● Television and motion pictures have generally stereotyped Native Americans making them into something fierce, feared and savage.

● Indian tribes today are rediscovering their old traditions and ceremonies and trying to deal with such problems as alcohol, drugs, poverty and environment.

● Museums are holding 600,000 Indian skeletons according to the Smithsonian Institution.

● Works of art in museums are considered sacred to Indian tribes who believed that they should be returned and taken care of by spiritual leaders. Numerous court cases are pending.

● More than 400 treaties between Indians and whites have been broken. The Council of Energy Resource Tribes states that large portions of this nation's resources (coal, oil and uranium) are on Indian grounds.

● Aleut kayakers of Alaska admire the playful and intelligent black and silver coated sea otter. They had two close calls with extinction during the 17th century over hunting by Russian fur traders and oil spills during the 1980s.

● Arctic people have their own TV stations and the Inuvialuit Communications Society provides native language programs by satellite.

● W. Richard West Jr., born in 1943, is the founding director of the National Museum of the American Indian, part of the Smithsonian.

● Archaeologists do not agree as to when the first people (PaleoIndians) arrived in the Arctic. One belief is that the Aleut and Inuit were one of the last peoples who migrated from Asia about 10,000 years ago. Arctic peoples disagree with the theory and say that they were much earlier.

● It was not until the 1800s that Indians learned about paper and ink. Previous to that date, personal symbols and illustrated histories were recorded on animal hides with plant dyes and earth.

● In the 16th century, before horses, the Plains Indians relied upon dogs to pull their loads by means of travois.

● During the 19th and 20th centuries, mission and government schools were established to educate Indians: they could not follow tribal customs, worship their own religion or speak their own languages.

● During the California gold rush of 1848, miners and settlers killed more than 50,000 Indians. By 1872, some tribes were extinct and the Indian population in California was a mere 30,000.

● Blow guns were used by the Catawha of South Carolina and other Southeastern tribes when hunting rabbits, squirrels and birds.

- The Cayuga of the Iroquois Confederacy were influenced in their silverwork by Scottish designs of the late 18th and 19th centuries.

- Sequoya, a Cherokee scholar (1770-1848) starting in 1809, spent 12 years creating an 86-character alphabet, for the people so that they could write their language.

- Wilma Mankiller, born 1945, was the first woman chief elected in 1987. Her birth was at Tahlequah, OK.

- Chores were dictated by gender among the Cheyenne. Women cooked, did crafts, raised the children and put up and took down the tipi poles. Men kept the tribe safe, hunted, fished and went to war.

- Ben Nighthorse Campbell, Cheyenne, born 1933, is the only American Indian in the U.S. Senate, representing Colorado. In the 1990s, he had the name changed from Custer National Monument to the Little Bighorn National Monument. His jewelry designs have won more than 200 awards and he was also captain of the U.S. Olympic Judo Team in 1964.

- Linda Hogan, born 1947, has a Chickasaw father and a white mother. She has published several collections of her poems and they also have been included in several anthologies.

- Chipewyan Indians from the Northwest territories designed oval-shaped snowshoes with wooden frames and caribou hide.

- Allen Wright, Choctaw, named Kiliahote (1825-1885), went to New York City, became a minister and returned to his people to translate their laws into English. He prepared a Choctaw dictionary and came up with the name Oklahoma, which means "Red People."

- The Chumash one of the largest California tribes at one time had over 40 villages which were reached with canoes.

- The prehistoric Anasazi lived in the Mesa Verde pueblo, a village of clay houses in southwestern Colorado. This site was not discovered by whites until 1888; no one knows why the Anasazi left the area and disappeared.

- Chief Seattle (Sealth), 1786-1866, led the Duwamish and Suquamish along the coasts of Washington and British Columbia. Whites were guided by him and traded with the Hudson Bay Company. Seattle was also named after him; in 1854, the government pushed his people off the land. The chief in his refusal to sign a land treaty commented: "How can you buy or sell the sky? The land? The earth does not belong to man, man belongs to the earth."

- Salish baskets had geometric designs, were fabricated from spruce root and coiled dyed cedar bark in shades of black, red and yellow. Cooking baskets were watertight; hot stones were dropped into a basket filled with water and food.

- Sherman Alexie became a major Native American writer at 21. His books include: *The Lone Ranger and Tonto, Fistfight in Heaven* and *Reservation Blues*. He was born in 1967 on the Spokan-Coeur d'Alene reservation in Wellpinit, Washington.

Typical Iroquois beaded floral bag on black velvet, Great Lakes, ca. 1875—$247.50. (Merritt's Museum of Childhood)

"Caroline" beaded Plateau bag— $357.50, 10" x 12" floral. (Merritt's Museum of Childhood)

Plains beaded pouches: left, geometric designs in red and blues ($632.50); right, cross on white, two shades of blue and yellow. Pouch has overlapping flap and a profusion of tinklers—$1,155. (Merritt's Museum of Childhood)

"Strike-a-lite" flint and steel beaded bag, shades of light and dark blue, green, yellow and russet, diamond and cross motifs, plus tin tinklers, 6" long, 1880s—$1,155. (Merritt's Museum of Childhood)

Colorful cloth bandoleer bag with shoulder strap, beads and tinklers trim the edges, stitched floral designs, Menominee, 1870s—$1,100. (Merritt's Museum of Childhood)

Child's possible tanned hide bag, beautifully bordered in multicolored beading, squares, rectangles and crosses— $550. (Merritt's Museum of Childhood)

- LaDonna Harris, born 1931, is from Oklahoma. As a Comanche she has been involved in Indian self-help government, civil rights and social welfare programs. She became president of the Americans for Indian Opportunity.

- The Cree from Quebec and Montana create moccasins decorated with dyed porcupine quill embroidery. The hides are made from caribou and moose hide and the work is accomplished by women.

- Joy Hargo a Creek poet born in 1951 is from Tulsa, OK. Her poetry has won numerous awards and she taught at the University of New Mexico. Now she resides in Santa Fe, NM, writes poetry and plays saxophone in a band called Poetic Justice.

- Dean Bear Claw is a Crow film maker who created The Film and Video Center of the American Indian, New York City, in the early 1980s. His works include: "Native Visions, Native Voice" and "Warrior Chiefs in a New Age."

- John Trudell, Dakota musician, was national chairman of the American Indian Movement (AIM) from 1974 to 1980. He mixes traditional and contemporary music with political conscious lyrics.

- Jim Thorpe in 1934 was cast in Sylvia Sidney's film "Behold My Wife."

- Nathan Chasing His Horse is a Lakota who appeared in "Dances with Wolves" in the role Smiles A Lot.

- Flathead children in Montana learned to ride horses soon after they learned to walk. Both the horse and the rider were highly decorated.

- Flathead D'Arcy McNickle (1904-1977) was an early activist for Indian self-government. As a writer of poetry books and an anthropologist, he earned the title father of Native American literature.

- Ancient Indian medicine wheels measure up to 80 feet in diameter and are typically made of rocks and boulders that form a central ring with radiating spokes.

- Writer James Welch, born in 1940, is part Gros Ventre and part Blackfeet. He has written a poetry book, Riding the Earthboy and novels with such titles as Fools Crow, The Death of Jim Loney and Winter in the Blood.

- Haida clan names include Raven, Eagle, Beaver, Bear and Frog. Their home includes Alaska, Washington and British Columbia.

- Robert Davidson is a Haida sculptor whose contemporary totems are carved from cedar using traditional materials and tribal subjects.

- Carlos White Shirt, Hidatsa, had a role in the 1992 film, "The Broken Chain," an Iroquois Confederacy story.

- Central to Hopi spiritual life is the kachina; they take the forms of humans, plant, birds and animals. Most are friendly and some are Hopi law enforcers; over 250 bring continued health, rain and ensure productive crops.

- Hopi girls wear their hair in butterfly whorls; this implies that they are old enough to marry.

- Hupa David Risling, born 1921, has worked for accuracy in teaching Native American history in schools. He was the co-founder of the first Indian-run college and he also designed the first Native American Studies program in the country.

- Huron of Oklahoma and Quebec decorated jewelry and clothing with dyed moosehair embroidery. Floral designs came about from the French and Dutch who came in the 17th century.

- In the 1880s, teams of three or more Husky dogs pulled Inuit families across the tundra with their loaded sleds. Today snowmobiles are very much in vogue; however, the dogs are still trained for dog sled racing.

- The Yup'ik, who live on Alaska's Pacific Coast, celebrate a Halloween-type of event at the end of October. Two men dressed in rags and funny masks beg food from the women. Then they feast with other men.

- Susan Aglukark, born 1967, was the first Inuit to sign a musical contract with a major recording company.

- Bear claws were always difficult if not dangerous to get. They became so prized and valuable that they were typically made into chiefs' necklaces.

- Four clans are common to all Iroquois nations: Snipe, Wolf, Bear and Deer. Membership is inherited from the mother's family. Clan mothers serve as teachers and guardians.

- Cradleboards were favorites with Native American women who strapped their children to the decorative backpacks, as they went about their chores. Each tribe had beautiful decorations, some were very elaborate with beadwork.

- N. Scott Momaday, born 1934, has a Cherokee mother and a Kiowa father. He has been awarded the Pulitzer Prize for fiction and the Guggenheim fellowship and is a professor of English at Stanford University.

- Lakota women in North and South Dakota decorated their deerskin dresses with marine cowrie shells.

- Mary Crow Dog is a Lakota writer, born in 1953 on the Rosebud Sioux Reservation. Previous to marriage her name was Mary Brave Bird. Two of her books are *Lakota Woman* and *Ohitaka Woman*.

- Small medicines wheels are often carried in a car or placed in the home. Their function is for prayers and vision quests.

- The Walam Olum, carved on reeds, is the sacred record of the Lenape. In the beginning was the sun and stars and then the tribe's great migration over the frozen sea. "Wolf Man was the chief when all were friends."

- In 1937, California Congressman Harry R. Sheppard sponsored a bill that gave Luiseno Indians greater access in federal courts concerning land claim suits.

Chippewa child's dyed skin moccasins, russet ground, nice floral beading, 1890—$275. (Merritt's Museum of Childhood)

Carved wooden dagger and sheath, early 20th century, marked "J.F. Suser, Indian School," squirrel and seal decor—$125. (Merritt's Museum of Childhood)

Drilled shell necklace on woven reed, 26" long—$100. (Merritt's Museum of Childhood)

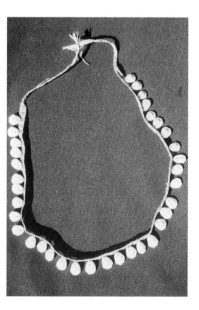

Six plummets, assorted shapes, made from carved stone: top—$85 each; bottom—$100 each. (Merritt's Museum of Childhood)

A counting stone discovered on Dr. Abbott Farm, Trenton, NJ—$175. (Merritt's Museum of Childhood)

Carved wooden bird club with attached wings, deer antler beak—$800. (Merritt's Museum of Childhood)

● Maidu of California along with many other tribes honor the bear and perform bear dances to guard this splendid animal, a powerful guardian spirit.

● The Mandans of North Dakota lived in lodges constructed from logs, clay, branches and grass. Horses and animals were kept in the home. Both domesticated animals and the lodges were property of the women.

● Menominee families in Wisconsin had villages of bark cabins before the Europeans arrived. Hide lodges served as temporary homes while hunting and traveling.

● In 1993, Menominee Ada Deer, born 1935, became the first woman assistant secretary of the Interior, Bureau of Indian Affairs. She and others created (DRUMS) Determination of Rights and Unity for Menominee Shareholders.

● Little Turtle Miami war leader opposed expansion beyond the Ohio River. With British guns he led Algonquin warriors killing 1,400 soldiers in the battle against General Arthur St. Clair, 1791. The Indians celebrated the victory by stuffing soldiers' mouths full of earth; this was to symbolize the whites' greed for land.

● Micmac film maker Catherine Anne Martin, living in Nova Scotia, made a documentary about Micmac parenting entitled "Mi'kmaq Family."

● French Catholics and English Protestants settled in the Northeast of North America; Spanish Catholic missions were established in Mexico, the Southwest, California and Florida.

● Today there are around 250 ministers and Indian priests. Many Native Americans curious about Jesus and his miracles adapted Christianity to their own beliefs.

● Greg Sarris is chief of the California Coast Miwok tribes and also a professor of English at UCLA. He authored *Grand Avenue.*

● Michael Dorris, a Modoc on his father's side, wrote about fetal alcohol syndrome in his 1989 book *The Broken Cord.* He and his wife have written many fiction works. His wife, Louise Erdrich is an Ojibwa.

● The Mojave of California, Arizona and Nevada suffered like many Indian tribes from terrible living conditions and malnutrition. In 1907, 90% of all Mojave deaths were due to tuberculosis.

● In Chillicothe, Ohio, is the Great Serpent Mound, a quarter-mile long, showing a giant uncurling snake with an egg in its mouth. The Mound Builders were a succession of similar cultures in the U.S. (1400 BC to 1450 AD).

● Newfoundland Naskapi Indians constructed bows and arrows from dried juniper wood. Blunt headed arrows were used to kill birds and small animals.

● The Natchez, who lived in the Southeast, called upon the power of the sun by smoking tobacco in special pipes. During dancing and chanting, they asked for peace, good health, rain and the destruction of their enemies.

- The Navajo loom design is based upon a 300 year old type. Some of the blankets are woven so tight that they are waterproof.

- Originally Navajo participated in two days of healing through singing and sand paintings. These were from colored sand and pollen arranged on the ground to illustrate spirits and legends. Tourist sand painting are accomplished on pieces of stone and other materials by gluing the designs in place.

- Hattie Kauffman, a Nez Perce, in 1990 became a national correspondent for *CBS this Morning*.

- Nootka of British Columbia wear basketry hats as a sign of high social rank. These are woven of waterproof cedar bark, shed the rain and display intricate and colorful designs.

- Iroquois and Algonquin clans were based on the mother's or father's family. Clans were represented by such symbols as the Eagle, Butterfly, Deer and vegetables such as the potato. Each clan had a legend as to it's origin with responsibilities and special powers.

- Wampum carved beads were actually shells from the Atlantic beaches. Predominately white and purple, they were strung together as money and jewelry and woven into belts. The belts could be long and elaborate with woven in patterns that had special meanings. Some wampum belts attested as legal documents and records of the tribes histories.

- Northeast Indians smoked stone pipes carved into shapes with wooden stems. The turtle was hero to Northeast creation stories.

- Prior to 1800, Northwest Coastal Indians numbered more than 500,000, speaking 45 different languages.

- Northwest Coast totem poles show various designs based upon artistic and tribal styles. Typical Haida characters that interlock in the carving are frog, beaver, raven and eagle. The poles are carved from cedar logs and when completed, raised in a prominent location.

- Gerald Vizenor of French and Ojibwa ancestors, teaches American Indian Studies at the University of Minnesota. He has also written several books dealing with the Anishinabe and Ojibwa-Chippewa cultures.

- Ojibwa artisans have created some of the most astonishing, elaborate and beautiful beadwork ever made. Their patterns and designs are usually those of their ancestors.

- Louise Erdrich, born 1951, has an Ojibwa mother and a German-American father. Her writings include: *The Bingo Palace, Tracks, Bove Medicine* and *The Beet Queen*.

- The Omaha of Nebraska are said to have created the modern powwow. Their annual celebration called the Dance of Thanksgiving, is the oldest gathering of its kind.

- Oil was discovered on the Osage reservation in Oklahoma in 1896. By 1920 this tribe was called "the wealthiest nation in the world."

Two Canadian decorated antler knives—$250 each. (Merritt's Museum of Childhood)

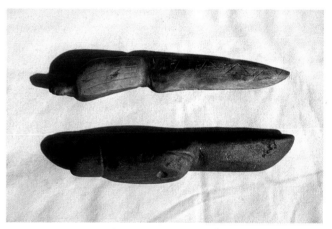

Two stone knives—$400 each. (Merritt's Museum of Childhood)

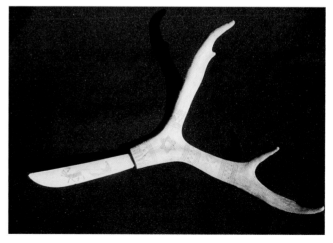

Canadian decorated antler knife, shows etched reindeer pulling a sled—$1,000. (Merritt's Museum of Childhood)

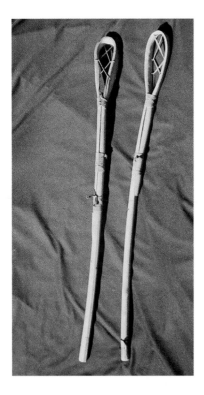

Creek Indian crosses or lacrosse sticks, sinew netting—$330 pair. (Merritt's Museum of Childhood)

Felt bat with braided wicker handle on wood, four stone game balls; bat—$200; each ball—$50. (Merritt's Museum of Childhood)

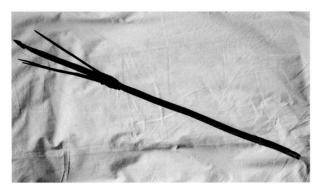

Wooden two piece, three-pronged fishing spear—$250. (Merritt's Museum of Childhood)

- Paiutes living in Utah, Arizona, Oregon, Nevada and California followed seasonal food supplies. Their small wickiups were made from willow poles and brush reeds.

- Pawnee Larry EchoHawk became attorney general of Idaho in 1994; he is the first Native American to hold that office. He was also the first to lead the Idaho delegation to the Democratic National Convention in 1992.

- The Peoria have moved numerous times until now they live in Oklahoma. Their warriors honored bird skins in all-night ceremonies and also carried the skins into battle. When attacking, warriors gave bird cries and when victorious there was an Eagle Dance.

- The Foxwood Casino opened in Connecticut in 1992. Owned by the Pequots, it quickly became the most profitable casino in the Western Hemisphere. Profits go toward educating Pequot children and helping to preserve Native American Indian culture.

- Painted buffalo skulls are still at the center of Plains altars even today. People continue to lift the skulls in prayer, since to the Indians the buffalo was part of their great nation, closely related to the creator.

- Plains lodges were based upon available materials: in the south wickiups were of grass, northern nomads carried hide tipis and northern farmers built earthlodges.

- All Plains tribes blended everyday life with religion; although languages were different, customs were similar.

- Plains ceremonies utilize powerful eagle feather fans; these are sacred to all Indians since they represent messages from the creator.

- Before the Europeans arrived, around 60 million buffalo roamed the Plains. The U.S. military destroyed buffalo herds to weaken the power of Plains Indians.

- One of the worst disasters of the Plains Indians was the 1864 Sand Creek Massacre. Colonel John Chivington ordered 700 soldiers to attack a peaceful southern Cheyenne and Arapaho camp in eastern Colorado. Bayonets were fixed and cannons fired as 200 Cheyenne men, women and children died.

- Pomo basketmakers are internationally known for their traditional designs and brightly woven feathers also placed in the designs. One of these basketmakers is Susan Billy who uses her baskets to connect with "all the grandmothers who have gone before me."

- Pueblo Indians still practice the tradition of baking bread in outdoor ovens called hornos. The ovens are constructed from dried earth and straw.

- Pueblo in Spanish means "town," and is used to describe both the towns they built and the Pueblo people. Most Pueblos are descended from the Anasazi Cliff Dwellers.

- Pueblo author, Leslie Marmon Silko has written *Almanac of the Dead*, *Ceremony* and *Storyteller*.

- Gambling is illegal in South Dakota, except on the reservation where people attend the Dakota Sioux Casino at Watertown.

- Most Indians do not live on reservations today.

- The Sarcee, a nomadic group from Alberta, only carried essential items when on the move. Their buffalo hide jackets were painted and quite beautiful; they also protected the wearer from the extreme cold on the north Plains.

- The Seminole in the Florida swamps hunted alligators by pushing a log down their throat and then turned them over and killed them with a club.

- Vine Deloria Jr., born 1933 is an author of numerous books including: *Behind the Trail of Broken Treaties* and *Custer Died for Your Sins*. He is the son of an Episcopal priest, grandson of a Yankton Nakota Sioux chief and was executive director of the National Congress of American Indians. Vine also teaches at the University of Colorado at Boulder.

- Black Indians descended from runaway slaves and Native Americans of Texas and the Southeast; there, tribes bordered on slave plantations.

- Famous Black Indians were Nat Love also known as Deadwood Dick, an excellent range rider and marksman; Cherokee Bill famed outlaw, robber of banks and con artist; James Beckwourth was a fur trapper who married the daughter of a Crow ruler and became chief of the Crow in the 1850s.

- In the Southeast, the greatest ceremony was the Green Corn Dance, a celebration commencing in early summer. There was fasting, prayers, renewal and thanksgiving. Women broke all cooking pots, cleaned the house and put out hearth fires. Men painted the buildings and settled old quarrels. All participants wore white and painted their bodies red. With the beating of drums and the Green Corn Dance, a new and sacred fire was lit. Coals from this fire were carried to each home to light their fires. After bathing in the stream there was a feast.

- Exquisite natural settings of the Southwest are the Painted Desert, Grand Canyon, Sangre de Cristo Mountains, the sculpted pinnacles and the plateaus of Monument Valley.

- Susquehannocks from Pennsylvania made finely carved combs from deer antlers.

- William Penn, a Quaker, came from England to America and founded Pennsylvania. He was friendly with the Lenape Indians and guaranteed them land rights and freedom to worship in a treaty signed in 1682.

- Alfrus Hewitt fought for the North in the Civil War, was wounded twice and was a Tuscarora Indian.

- 150 years ago there were 30 million buffalo roaming the plains. Today that number has been significantly reduced to 130,000 which are mostly on ranches.

- In Janesville, Wisconsin, on August 20, 1994, David and Valerie Heider were blessed with the birth of an albino buffalo calf. The odds of this happening are 1 in 10 million. This prediction had been known in legends for the last 600 years. With the birth of "Miracle," the Lakota Sioux prophecy commenced and told of the healing of the Earth and of the Indian nations. People visited the ranch from all over the world in a "wave that never ended." The prediction for the next five

Stone canoe anchor, discovered at Montico, NJ—$150. (Merritt's Museum of Childhood)

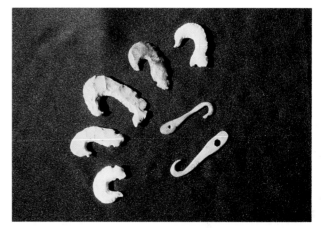

An assortment of seven stone fish hooks—$100 for the set. (Merritt's Museum of Childhood)

Haida fish hooks, Vancouver Island, British Columbia—$143 pair. (Merritt's Museum of Childhood)

Stone fish net sinker, Raven Rock, NJ—$125. (Merritt's Museum of Childhood)

Woven spruce root Nootka hat, for the wealthy, painted on two sides; this view is the Painted Raven, Vancouver Island, British Columbia—$3,300. (Merritt's Museum of Childhood)

Nootka common work Spruce root hat, used in canoe travel, British Columbia, Vancouver Island—$715. (Merritt's Museum of Childhood)

years is "evil killing evil," and then a spiritual awakening with peace and harmony. Miracle has grown and lost his white coat; as he has matured his coat has changed from white to black to red to yellow.

● Sweetgrass was used by the Iroquois to create baskets. It grows along the marshes from Canada into the Rockies and is considered to he sacred for its ability to protect and purify. Found in medicine bundles, the leaves when lit smoke. Ceremonial uses are to clear objects, places and people. Sweetgrass is also braided and hung in the home to create a pleasing fragrance. The braid may be held over heat; as smoke escapes, a person or object may be fanned to attract positive energies.

● As of November 3, 1996, the Nez Perce have developed a horse breeding program which so far has cost $500,000, financed by the U.S. government's Department of Health and Human Services, the Nez Perce and a nonprofit group called the First Nations Development Institute. The new breed is named the Nez Perce and in Lapwai, Idaho, the first foal crop of 24 horses was born last spring. These unusual horses are a cross between an appaloosa and a rare Central Asian breed called Akhal-teke. Rudy Shehala, a Navajo Indian, runs the breeding program; he is married to a Nez Perce. The Akhal-tekes are thought to he similar to the original Spanish horses brought to North America. These slim and elegant horses of Turkmenistan will be bred with the appaloosa's "blanket" rump and blocky, muscular traits.

● In 1623, Miles Standish arrived at Merry Mount to discover Thomas Morton enticing Indian maidens to dance around the maypole; he arrested Morton for fraternizing with the Indians.

● Ben Franklin chose the wild turkey over the bald eagle to represent our country. "The turkey is...respectable... a true native."

● The misinterpretation of language meaning between whites and Indians continues. Sensitivities are cooled to some degree by using a dual name. In the 1980s, Alaska's most popular park was renamed Denali National Park and Preserve. Members of the Devils Lake Sioux Tribe have voted to change their name to Spirit Lake Dakota Nation.

● Less than 60 adult panthers are believed to be living in the subtropical swamps and forest lands of Southern Florida.

● Devils Tower National Monument in the northeastern corner of Wyoming is 600 feet high. It was named by Colonel Richard Dodge during an 1875 scientific expedition. More than 20 tribes use it in their creation story. The Lakota call it Bear's Lodge, where a boy was as the legend goes, transformed into a bear. He chased his seven sisters, who hid on the stump. Their prayers were answered and the stump grew; the bear raked the sides with his claws, creating the tower's unusual columns.

● Winona LaDuke is founder of the White Earth Recovery Project and the Indigenous Women's Network. She was the Green Party's vice-presidential candidate in the 1996 presidential elections.

● Worldwatch Institute states that 317 reservations in the U.S. are threatened by environmental hazards.

- Nationally, 77 sacred sites have been desecrated through development and resource extraction.

- There are 80 million acres offshore lands in Alaska, near Native coastal villages, that have oil leases.

- On Dine land, over 1,000 uranium mines sit abandoned and leaking radioactive materials into the air and water.

- In the last 45 years, more than 700 atomic explosions have taken place in Nevada, on Western Shoshone lands.

- The Indigenous Environmental Network was founded in 1990 at the Dine village, Dilkon, Arizona. In the summer of 1996, an annual Protecting Mother Earth Gathering was held at the Cherokee Nation, North Carolina.

- Henry David Thoreau on trips in the Maine woods, learned from Indian guides the names of birds, plants and places. By learning the Penobscot and Abenaki names he noted in his journal: "In proportion as I understood the language, I saw them from a new point of view... A dictionary of the Indian language reveals another and wholly new life to us."

- Sioux mothers were trained in silence from infancy and passed this lesson on to their children; thus they could travel safely through tribal territories.

- Brave Cheyenne warriors took as their role model the quick and clever fox; his swiftness was respected in the chase and his fierceness when cornered.

- People of the Northern Plains knew the bull elk as the crooner, He-Ha-Ka. His solo call pierced the cool, early morning air, as it echoed from the canyons and the ridges.

- Vern Jackson head of Manhattan-based Frontier Buffalo Company claims that there are at least 200,000 buffalo in North America and every 4 years the herds double. Chefs of upscale restaurants are familiarizing customers with buffalo, as a possible American dietary mainstay. Containing less fat and cholesterol than chicken and turkey, this ultra lean meat can be served numerous ways. There is roast tenderloin, marinated cut eye of the round and buffalo flank with macadamia-chili paste. Rates per person for a buffalo dinner are $60.

- The Okehocking Indians part of the Leni-Lenape tribes lived a life of planting, fishing and trapping. Every winter they traveled from Delaware County, Pennsylvania, to their ancestral hunting grounds in northern Pennsylvania. Here they had sugar maple family run camps. Okehocking chiefs Muttagoopa, Sepopawny and Pokhais in 1701 asked William Penn to set aside 500 acres by issuing a writ. The vacant land took 10 months to survey. In 1703 the Indians received the area free since a first deed (patent) was never issued. The document stated that the Indians could not "give, grant, sell, or attempt to sell or any way dispose of any of the said 500 acres..." The diamond-shaped tract is part of 1,100 acres of a tract placed on the National Register of Historic Places. The ground is situated between West Chester Pike on the South, Goshen Road on the North, Plumsock Road on the East and Garrette Mill Road on the West.

- Governor Kieft of New Amsterdam is credited with offering the first bounty for Indian scalps.

A Nootka Makah shaman's hat with colorful woven design; done in Spruce root, the cylindrical top is a mark of distinction—$770. (Merritt's Museum of Childhood)

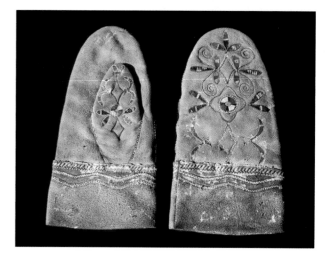

Tanned hide Eastern Sioux-Metis mittens with floral quill work, both sides are shown—$7,480 pair. (Merritt's Museum of Childhood)

Two Eskimo bone dippers—$50 each. (Merritt's Museum of Childhood)

Child's leather-bound cradle with primitive carved wooden doll—$200. (Merritt's Museum of Childhood)

Horn scoop with beaded handle, tin tinklers, horsehair tufts—$275. (Merritt's Museum of Childhood)

A cluster of 6 Navajo silver bracelets, stamped with inset turquoise— $85-110 each. (Merritt's Museum of Childhood)

• Governor Lewis Cass of Michigan Territory and Governor William Henry Harrison of Indiana Territory hired fighting men from friendly tribes; $1 a day for chiefs and 60 cents for mounted warriors.

• Congress, in 1953, removed the ban of liquor sales both on and off the reservations.

• The Gibson girl style at the turn of the century inspired pompadour hair and long dresses on Seminole women.

• Indian police were expected to wear white man's clothes, cut their hair, practice monogamy, take an allotment and determine if a fellow tribesman was working to gain his ration of coffee, sugar and tobacco.

• Black Beaver was one of the most accomplished Indian scouts working with the Army as they dealt with the Wichita, Comanche and Kiowa Indians. On the side of the Union, he guided wagon trains west, worked 10 years for the American Fur Company. He and 169 other Delawares volunteered for service in 1862. In addition, Black Beaver used Plains Indian sign language, knew eight different Indian languages and spoke English, French and Spanish. On May 31, 1861, he completed as guide a 500-mile march with Confederate prisoners to Fort Leavenworth in northern Kansas. In charge was Colonel William H. Emory.

• Other Civil War groups were the Union Oneidas and the Cherokee of the Confederacy's Thomas Legion. Union Company K of the First Michigan Sharpshooters were trapped on July 30, 1864, in a giant crater; death tolls were high as the Confederates surrounded the men in Petersburg, Virginia. Most of the men were Ottawas.

• Other groups who fought in the Civil War included Catawas, Pequots and Iroquois. A famous Iroquois was Ely Samuel Parker, Union secretary under Lieutenant General Ulysses S. Grant. Being 5-feet, 8 inches tall and weighing 230 pounds, he was referred to in camp as "Falstaff," "Big Indian," and "Grant's Indian." Parker acted as scribe at the surrender of Lee's army at Appomattox Court House, Virginia. Grant was Parker's best man at his wedding in 1867 and in 1869 Parker became the first Indian to hold the job of commissioner of Indian Affairs.

• Stand Watie, a Cherokee planter and slaveholder, was the best known and highest ranking Indian of the Civil War. On May 10, 1864, he was commissioned brigadier general; the only Indian to achieve such a rank during the Civil War. His troops were all Indians and consisted of Osages, Creeks, Cherokees and Seminoles.

• The Great Sioux Uprising took place in August 1862 in Minnesota. Santee Sioux attack the German settlement at New Ulm, in rebellion for the growing numbers of white settlers. The Indians were defeated, but they also killed over 800 whites. Thirty-eight Sioux leaders were found guilty and all hanged at once on a giant scaffold. It was the largest Indian hanging ever!

• Washington, Pennsylvania, is one of the richest historical sites on the East Coast, according to Joe Baker, archaeologist for the Pennsylvania Historical and Museum Commission. In 1995 the law was changed concerning artifact searches. Taxpayers must foot the bill and there is a time limit for state searches.

Developers want to move ahead. Often clues of a past civilization are being buried that could reveal mortality rates, dietary practices and sexual habits.

● Brucellosis is a disease carried by buffalo which is not harmful to humans, but causes cattle to miscarry their young. Once on the brink of extinction, the buffalo now roam Yellowstone National Park, Wyoming. Across the border, the State of Montana has filed a lawsuit to keep the animals from crossing the northern border and entering Montana, where private cattle ranches exist. Some 3,500 bison are in Yellowstone, but in January 1997 animals headed for the border were slaughtered and given to nearby Indian tribes.

● In the early 1970s, 11 cemeteries of the Kaw Indians were ordered to be relocated in Oklahoma. Then the U.S. Army Corps of Engineers built a dam on the Arkansas River creating Kaw Lake, with 168 miles of shoreline in northern Oklahoma. Totals for those buried included 669 at the Washunga Cemetery and 495 at the Oak Grove Cemetery. Erosion of the lake bank in 1996 has turned up pieces of tombstones, casket fragments and human bones. In August 1996, the Kaw Nation stepped in at the Washunga site. The 1990 Native American Graves Protection and Repatriation Act gives American Indians increased authority over human remains and sacred objects found on federal lands.

● The site of Fort Amsterdam built in 1626 was at the southern tip of Manhattan Island. The Lenape stood on Menatay (Manhattan) and watched the tall ships sail into New York Harbor. Nearby is Wall Street, a street named for a wall which defended European settlers from attacks by "northern Indians."

● Plains Indians created a yellow body paint from a mixture of roots, moss, clay, bullberries and buffalo gallstones.

● Apache boys were taught the laws of survival and endurance; adults are known to have run 70 miles in one day.

● The Dog Men of the Arapaho, a warrior society, refused to retreat from an enemy in battle. They drove a stake or lance through their sashes into the ground.

● Plains Indians considered the pronghorn antelope more succulent to the taste than buffalo.

● Human handprints on an Indian's horse told the enemy of those killed in battle.

● Oglala Sioux leader, Crazy Horse, prepared for battle by painting a lightning streak on his face and hailstones on his chest. Pinned in his hair was a stuffed red-backed hawk; he tied a small stone behind one ear.

● Indian tribes ate the raw heart of the grizzly bear, believing that this act would bestow upon them the strength and power of the animal.

● The horse was prized by the Plains Indians and became known as "Holy Dog," "Medicine Dog" and "Spirit Dog."

● When butchering slain buffalo cows, Blackfeet examined the unborn calves for hair; this signified the approach of spring.

● The Blackfeet diapered their children with moss and wrapped them in soft animal skins.

Fine Mohegan, Northeast woven basket, 24" high, has ring handles and ring lid, in the "Twist Weave" or "Porcupine Twist"—$200. (Merritt's Museum of Childhood)

Bark drum with bound rawhide, 12-1/2" diameter, painted chief and Thunderbird— $400. (Merritt's Museum of Childhood)

Tom-Tom of bark and rawhide, 16" diameter, Tesuque, near Tesuque River, NM—$412.50. (Merritt's Museum of Childhood)

Arapaho rawhide moccasins with beading in green, white, blue and yellow—$1,210. (Merritt's Museum of Childhood)

Iroquois colorful branched floral moccasins, red felt trim on the high tops—$550. (Merritt's Museum of Childhood)

Leather Iroquois moccasins with delicate and many hued beaded leaves—$650. (Merritt's Museum of Childhood)

● Geronimo became a Christian, joined the Dutch Reformed Church and was at the inauguration of President Theodore Roosevelt.

● Between 1866 and 1891, according to U.S. Army records, there were 1,065 combat engagements between Western Indians and the U.S.

● Soldiers fighting Indians of the West seldom kept their bayonet or saber; they were left behind on the march.

● General George Armstrong Custer had many nicknames during his life including "Curly," "Fanny," "Cinnamon," "Autie" and "Iron Butt." Indians called him "Long Hair" and "Son of the Morning Star."

● Elizabeth Bacon Custer, widow of George A. Custer, died at 91 in her apartment at 71 Park Ave., New York City, at 5:30 p.m., on April 4, 1933. She is buried beside him at West Point.

● Custer carried the following weapons into the battle at Little Big Horn: two British-made revolvers, a hunting knife and a Remington .50 caliber Sporting Rifle.

● In the 1940 Western, "*The Santa Fe Trail*," Ronald Reagan played the role of young George Armstrong Custer.

● Jeff Chandler was the Apache leader Cochise in the 1950 film, "*Broken Arrow.*"

● The first feature film to use Indian dialogue was the 1930 Western, "*The Indians are Coming,*" which included Sioux language.

● In the 1941 film, "*They Died with Their Boots On,*" Custer was portrayed by Errol Flynn and Anthony Quinn was Crazy Horse.

● For the 1924 silent epic, "*The Iron Horse,*" director John Ford employed 800 Indians and 3,000 railroad workers. There was a full cavalry regiment, 10,000 cattle and 1,300 buffalo.

● Elvis Presley was a persecuted Indian youth in the 1960 film, "*Flaming Star.*"

● In the 1970 Western, "*A Man Called Horse,*" Richard Harris was a rich British sportsman captured by Western Indians.

● Washington Irving suggested renaming the nation the United States of Appalachia or Alleghania.

● An act of Congress in 1991 changed the eastern Montana battlefield known as Custer's Last Stand to Little Bighorn Battlefield National Monument.

● In March 1997, John R. Collins, a Philadelphia architect and Penn State graduate was awarded a $30,000 check as winner for his design of the Little Bighorn Battlefield monument. He beat out more than 550 other entries. Collins' memorial will be built on Custer Hill just 225 feet from the Seventh Cavalry Monument which is a 19th century obelisk listing the approximate 220 troops and their Indian scouts who died on June 25, 1876, along with Lieutenant Colonel George Armstrong Custer. The Seventh had expected to fight 800, instead their were greeted by 2,000 fighting men. The memorial is a grass covered berm 8 feet high and 32 feet wide. The inside walls are rough, unmortared rock. Spirit tracings, flat sculptures of warriors on horseback, stand in a cut away section of the wall. The design is to be low key, rising gently from the earth, but still meant to make a strong statement. Collins' inspirations were drawn from burial or religious mounds built by many ancient people (if not specifically the nomadic Plains Indians).

Finely beaded on rawhide Sioux Plains moccasins, sinew ties, white, green, yellow and russet—$825. (Merritt's Museum of Childhood)

Two pair of Arapaho moccasins, Wind River, WY—$440 each. (Merritt's Museum of Childhood)

Children's Iroquois beaded moccasins— $880. (Merritt's Museum of Childhood)

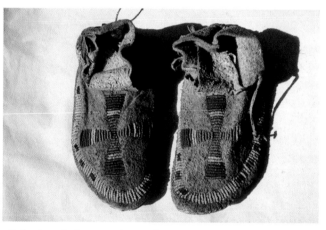

Baby beaded moccasins, yellow dyed skins, maltese cross, 7" long—$385. (Merritt's Museum of Childhood)

Buckskin uppers, rawhide soles, children's or women's knee-high moccasins with beading and brass rosettes, Kiowa, Washita River, OK, 12-1/2" high—$4,290. (Merritt's Museum of Childhood)

Cheyenne/Arapaho tall deerskin boots, beaded with leather tassels, brass rosettes, Canadian River, OK, 15" high—$5,500. (Merritt's Museum of Childhood)

Sioux girl's beaded dress on rawhide— $9,750. (Merritt's Museum of Childhood)

Interesting stone-lasts to create moccasins—$200. (Merritt's Museum of Childhood)

Beaded pouch on rawhide with beaded rawhide tassels— $3,300. (Merritt's Museum of Childhood)

Exquisite and heavy woman's beaded yoke of skin, Sioux, trimmed with a profusion of brass thimbles which serve as resonant tinklers—$5,500. (Merritt's Museum of Childhood)

Ute beaded arm bands, geometric stars and arrows, ribbons— $412.50. (Merritt's Museum of Childhood)

Beaded band, geometric diamonds, hues in white, green, yellow and black—$275. (Merritt's Museum of Childhood)

Beaded Sioux belt on rawhide, beads in white, yellow and russet—$275. (Merritt's Museum of Childhood)

Sioux necklace, shades of white, green and black, Upper Mississippi River, North Dakota—$150. (Merritt's Museum of Childhood)

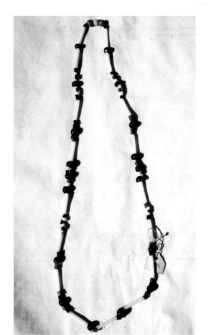

Finely beaded leg bands, possibly Sioux—$770. (Merritt's Museum of Childhood)

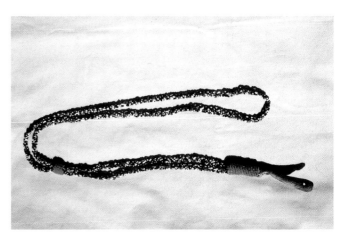

Finely beaded multi-colored necklace—$100. (Merritt's Museum of Childhood)

Beaded black, red, white and blue arm band with brass tinklers—$300. (Merritt's Museum of Childhood)

Grouping of three Sioux necklaces: left, all blue; right, red and black; bottom, red, yellow and white, Upper Missouri River, ND—$200 each. (Merritt's Museum of Childhood)

Chapter 4

QUOTABLE

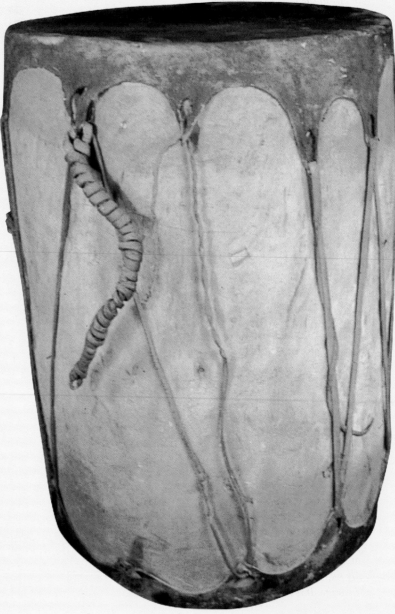

Native Americans Sharing Their Thoughts

Unusual Arapaho Indian marriage charm, two large pendants (mother and father), 2 small pendants (children), ca. 1876, French Trade beads—$250. (Merritt's Museum of Childhood)

Chariot, Flathead chief, in an 1876 speech after resisting white man's advances into the Bitterroot Aalley, Montana. After 30 years, he was forced to cross the borders into Canada: *Since our forefathers once beheld the white man, more than seven times ten winters have snowed and melted. He has filled graves with our bones. His course is destruction. He spoils what the Spirit of this country made beautiful and clean…What is he? Who sent him here? We were happy when he first came. We thought he came from the light. But now he comes like the dusk of the evening, not like the dawn of the morning. He comes like a day that has passed and night enters our future with him…He comes more and more often. He seizes more and more. And he dirties what he does not take.*

A **Taos Pueblo** chief speaking on white man noted the following: *See how cruel the whites look. Their lips are thin, their noses sharp, their faces furrowed and distorted by folds. Their eyes have a staring expression; they are always seeking something. What are they seeking? The whites always want something; they are always uneasy and restless. We do not know what they want. We do not understand them. We think that they are mad.*

Portion of a prayer by **Black Elk** in 1930: *Grandfather, Great Spirit, you have been always and before you no one has been. There is no other to pray to but you. You yourself, everything that you see, everything has been made by you. The star nations all over the universe you have finished. The day and in that day, everything you have finished. Grandfather, Great Spirit, lean close to the earth, a relative to all that is! Give me the eyes to see and the strength to understand, that I may be like you…*

Little Warrior, a Pawnee scout, 1879, accompanied the U.S. forces and gave this advice to a Ute leader: *My friend, you and I have the same skin and what I tell you is for your good. I speak to you as a friend and what I say to you now is so that you may save your women and children. It is of no use for you to try to fight the white people. I have been among them and I know how many they are. They are like the grass…If you try to fight them they will hunt you like a ghost. Wherever you go they will follow after you and you will get no rest. The soldiers will be continually on your tracks. Even if you were to go up on top of a high mountain…the soldiers would follow you and wait, even for fifty years…There is one white man who is chief of all this country and what he says must be done. It is no use to fight him.*

Speech of Black Hawk, Sauk-Fox leader, concluding the "Black Hawk War," in 1832: *You have taken me prisoner with all my warriors. I am much grieved, for I expected, if I did not defeat you, to hold out much longer and give you more trouble before I surrendered. I tried hard to bring you into ambush, but*

Beaded Iroquois bag on black velvet, red felt trimming, green cloth strap—$247.50. (Merritt's Museum of Childhood)

Seed beads on rawhide baby moccasins—$880. (Merritt's Museum of Childhood)

Grouping of assorted Hupa baskets, Trinity River, CA; back right, dated 1875, large, top left—$2,035; large, top middle—$770; small—$600 each. (Merritt's Museum of Childhood)

Five colorful Chitimacha baskets, located near Grand Lake, LA—$850 each. (Merritt's Museum of Childhood)

Two California covered and decorated baskets, plus a round place mat—$300 each for baskets;—$150 mat. (Merritt's Museum of Childhood)

your last general understands Indian fighting. The first one was not so wise. When I saw that I could not beat you by Indian fighting, I determined to rush on you and fight you face to face. I fought hard. But your guns were well aimed. The bullets flew like birds in the air and whizzed by our ears like the wind through the trees in the winter. My warriors fell around me; it began to look dismal. I saw my evil day at hand.

Black Hawk, 1830: *No indiscretion can banish a woman from her parental lodge: no difference how many children she may bring home, she is always welcome: the kettle is over the fire to feed them.*

Black Hawk, 1830: *We always had plenty; our children never cried from hunger, neither were our people in want…our village was healthy and there was no place in the country possessing such advantages, nor hunting grounds better than those we had in possession. If a prophet had come to our village in those days and told us that the things were to take place which have since come to pass, none of our people would have believed him.*

Tecumseh, Shawnee, 1795: *Hear me! A single twig breaks, but the bundle of twigs is strong.*

Tecumseh's speech to Governor W.H. Harrison, August 12, 1810, Vincennes. Given in part, the contents repudiate the alleged fraud in purchasing Indian land: *The way and the only way, to check and to stop this evil, is for all the Redmen to unite in claiming a common and equal right in the land, as it was at first and should be yet; for it was never divided, but belongs to all for the use of each. That no part has a right to sell, even to each other, much less to strangers: those who want all and will not do with less. The White people have no right to take the land from the Indians, because they had it first, it is theirs. They may sell, but all must join. Any sale not made by all, is not valid. The late sale is bad. It requires all to make a bargain for all. All Redmen have equal rights to the unoccupied land. The right to occupancy is as good in one place as in another. There cannot be two occupations in the same place.*

Chief Curly, a Pawnee, relating early contact with Anglo-Americans in 1800-1820: *I heard that long ago there was a time when there were no people in this country except Indians. After that the people began to hear of men that had white skins; they had been seen far to the east. Before I was born they came out to our country and visited us. The man who came was from the Government. He wanted to make a treaty with us and to give us presents, blankets and guns and flint and steel and knives…You see, my brother, that the Ruler has given us all that we need, the buffalo for food and clothing, the corn to eat with our dried meat; bows, arrows, knives and hoes; all the implements which we need for killing meat or for cultivating the ground. Now go back to the country from whence you came. We do not want your presents and do not want you to come into our country.*

Black Elk talking about the massacre of Wounded Knee,

on December 29, 1890: *We followed down the dry gulch and what we saw was terrible. Dead and wounded (Indians) women and children and little babies were scattered all along where they had been trying to run away. The soldiers had followed along the gulch, as they ran and murdered them in there. Sometimes they were in heaps because they had huddled together and some were scattered all along. Sometimes bunches of them had been killed and torn to pieces where the wagon guns hit them. I saw a little baby trying to suck its mother, but she was bloody and dead.*

Black Elk, Oglala Sioux holy man, speaks on the circle:…*everything an Indian does is in a circle…because the Power of the World always works in circles and everything tries to be round…The sky is round and I have heard that the earth is round like a ball and so are all the stars. The wind, in its greatest power, whirls. Birds make their nests in circles, for theirs is the same religion as ours…Even the seasons form a great circle in their changing and always come back again to where they were. The life of a man is a circle from childhood and so it is in everything where power moves.*

Black Elk: *The life of an Indian is like the wings of the air. That is why you notice the hawk knows how to get his prey. The Indian is like that. The hawk swoops down on its prey; so does the Indian…The eagle is the same. That is why the Indian is always feathered up; he is a relative to the wings of the air.*

Seattle, Suquamish chief: *There is no death. Only a change of worlds.*

Lone Man, Teton Sioux:…*I have seen that in any great undertaking it is not enough for a man to depend simply upon himself.*

George Copway, Ojibwa chief: *Among the Indians there have been no written laws. Customs handed down from generation to generation have been the only laws to guide them…This fear of the Nation's censure acted as a mighty band, binding all in one social, honorable compact.*

Wooden Leg, Cheyenne, late 1800s: *"To make medicine" is to engage upon a special period of fasting, thanksgiving, prayer and self denial, even of self-torture. The bodily abstinence and the mental concentration upon lofty thoughts cleanses both the body and the soul and puts them into or keeps them in health…the individual mind gets closer toward conformity with the mind of the Great Medicine above us.*

Brave Buffalo, Teton Sioux medicine man: *I have noticed in my life that all men have a liking for some special animal, tree, plant or spot of earth. If men would pay more attention to these preferences and seek what is best to do in order to make themselves worthy of that toward which they are so attracted, they might have dreams which would purify their lives.*

Geronimo, Chiricahua Apache chief: *We had no churches, no religious organizations, no sabbath day, no holidays and yet*

Seed gathering baskets, Lake Tribes, left, Washo—$330 each. (Merritt's Museum of Childhood)

Papago "dog" design basket with handles—$467.50. (Merritt's Museum of Childhood)

Chiricahua-Apache basket with thongs, made near Elk Creek, NM—$412.50. (Merritt's Museum of Childhood)

Covered Thompson River basket, near Thompson River, British Columbia, Nitlakapamuk Tribe—$357.50. (Merritt's Museum of Childhood)

Large and small Pomo baskets, Clear Lake, CA—$800 pair. (Merritt's Museum of Childhood)

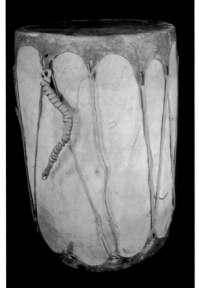

Hollow log drum, skin covered with sinew—$715. (Merritt's Museum of Childhood)

we worshiped. Sometimes the whole tribe would assemble and sing and pray; sometimes a smaller number, perhaps only two or three. The songs had a few words, but were not formal. The singer would occasionally put in such words as he wished…

Geronimo, 1886: *There is one God looking down on us all. We are all children of the one God. God is listening to me. The sun, the darkness, the winds, are all listening to what we now say.*

Eagle Chief, Pawnee: *In the beginning of all things, wisdom and knowledge were with the animals, for Tirawa, the One Above, did not speak directly to man. He sent certain animals to tell men that he showed himself through the beasts and that from them and from the stars and the sun and the moon should man learn…*

Sarah Winnemucca, Paiute: *The traditions of our people are handed down from father to son. The chief is considered to be the most learned and the leader of the tribe. The doctor, however, is thought to have more inspiration. He is supposed to be in communion with spirits…He cures the sick by the laying on of hands and prayers and incantations and heavenly songs…*

Sarah Winnemucca: *We do not call him a medicine man because he gives medicine to the sick, as your doctors do. Our medicine man cures the sick by laying on of hands and we have doctresses as well as doctors. We believe that our doctors can communicate with holy spirits from heaven. We call heaven the Spirit Land.*

Big Thunder, Wabanaki Algonquin: *The Great Spirit is our father, but the earth is our mother. She nourishes us; that which we put into the ground she returns to us…*

Shooter, Teton Sioux: *All birds, even those of the same species, are not alike and it is the same with animals and with human beings. The reason Wakantanka does not make two birds or animals or human beings exactly alike is because each is placed here by Wakantanka to be an independent individuality and to rely upon itself.*

Mourning Dove, Salish: *When a child carried water for the home, an elder would give compliments, pretending to taste meat in water carried by a boy or berries in that of a girl. The child was encouraged not to be lazy and to grow straight like a sapling.*

Luther Standing Bear, Oglala Sioux chief: *Silence was meaningful with the Lakota and his granting a space of silence to the speech-maker and his own moment of silence before talking was done in the practice of true politeness.*

Luther Standing Bear: *The man who sat on the ground in his tipi meditating on life and its meaning, accepting the kinship of all creatures and acknowledging unity with the universe of things was infusing into his being the true essence of civilization.*

Wolf Chief, Hidatsa Sioux: *Somewhat past ten years of age, my father took me with him to watch the horses out on the prairie. We watered the herd and about the middle of the day came home for dinner…while we sat watching the herd my father said: "These horses are godlike or mystery beings."*

Brave Buffalo, Teton Sioux medicine man: *A horse is the Indian's most valuable piece of property. If an Indian wishes to gain something, he promises his horse that if the horse will help him he will paint it with native dye, that all may see that help has come to him through the aid of his horse.*

Wooden Leg, Cheyenne, late 1800s: *The idea of full dress in preparation for a battle comes not from a belief that it will add to the fighting ability. The preparation is for death, in case that should be the result of the conflict. Every Indian wants to look his best when he goes to meet the great Spirit…*

N. Scott Momaday, Kiowa, 1974: *From the time the Indian first set foot upon this continent, he centered his life in the natural world. He is deeply vested in the earth, committed to it both in his consciousness and in his instinct. To him the sense of place is paramount. Only in reference to the earth can he persist in his true identity.*

Tecumseh, Shawnee, 1800: *Touch not the poisonous fire-water that makes wise men turn fools and robs the spirit of its vision.*

Don Talayesva, Hopi, 1940: *Don't be afraid to cry. It will free your mind of sorrowful thoughts.*

Luther Standing Bear, Lakota, 1933: *No longer should the Indian be dehumanized in order to make material for lurid and cheap fiction to embellish streetstands. Rather, a fair and correct history of the Native American should he incorporated in the curriculum of the public school.*

Indian Chief to the Governor of Pennsylvania, 1796: *We love quiet; we suffer the mouse to play; when the woods are rustled by the wind, we fear not.*

Tachnecdorus (Logan), Mingo chief, 1774: *I appeal to any white man to say if he ever entered Logan's cabin hungry and he gave him not meat; if he ever came cold and naked and be clothed him not. During the course of the last long and bloody war, Logan remained idle in his cabin, an advocate for peace. Such was my love for the whites that my countrymen pointed as I passed and said, "Logan is a friend of the white man."*

Anonymous, Kwakiutl, 1886: *It is a strict law that bids us dance. It is a strict law that bids us distribute our property among our friends and neighbors. It is a good law. Let the white man observe his law, we shall observe ours.*

Walking Buffalo, Stoney, 1958: *Hills are always more beautiful than stone buildings, you know. Living in a city is an*

Top, bear claw necklace on leather with over 175 claws—$250; left, clam shell dipper—$150; right, tortoise dipper which also serves as a rattle—$175. (Merritt's Museum of Childhood)

Two pottery water jugs, Cochiti Pueblo Indians, left, bird effigy; right, two closures for a carrying strap—$825 and $440. (Merritt's Museum of Childhood)

Apache pottery bowl with bird decor—$1,000. (Merritt's Museum of Childhood)

Apache woven trays—$121 pair. (Merritt's Museum of Childhood)

Loom woven Navajo Indian blanket, 74" long x 43" wide, central medallion of 10 diamonds bordered by 54 smaller diamonds, light brown, white and black, early 20th century—$450. (Merritt's Museum of Childhood)

Larger than life-size cast metal Indian chief in his regalia, on wheels, restored in 1955—$15,000. (Merritt's Museum of Childhood)

artificial existence. Lots of people hardly ever feel real soil under their feet, see plants grow except in flower pots or get far enough beyond the street light to catch the enchantment of a night sky studded with stars.

Dr. Charles Eastman, Santee Sioux, 1911: *Each soul must meet the morning sun, the new sweet earth and the Great Silence alone!*

Dr. Charles Eastman: *Our native women gathered all the wild rice, roots, berries and fruits which formed an important part of our food. Grandmother understood these matters perfectly and it became a kind of instinct with her to know just where to look for each variety and at what season of the year.*

Black Thunder, Fox, 1860: *When this pipe touches your lip, may it operate as a blessing upon all my tribe. May the smoke rise like a cloud and carry away with it all the animosities which have risen between us.*

Don Jose Matsuwa, Huichol, 1989: *The teachings are for all, not just for Indians…The white people never wanted to learn before. They thought we were savages. Now they have a different understanding and they do want to learn. We are all children of God. The tradition is open to anyone who wants to learn.*

Sitting Bull, Hunkpapa Lakota, 1885: *What treaty that the whites have kept has the Red Man broken? Not one. What treaty that the white man ever made with us have they kept? Not one. When I was a boy the Sioux owned the world; the sun rose and set on their land; they sent ten thousand men to battle. Where are the warriors today? Who slew them? Where are our lands? Who owns them? What white man can ever say I ever stole his land or a penny of his money? Yet, they say I am a thief. What white woman, however lonely, was ever captive or insulted by me? Yet they say I am a bad Indian. What white man has ever seen me drunk? Who has ever come to me hungry or unfed? Who has ever seen me beat my wives or abuse my children? What law have I broken? Is it wrong for me to love my own? Is it wicked for me because my skin is red? Because I am a Sioux; because I was born where my father lived; because I would die for my people and my country?*

Sitting Bull, 1887: *What does it matter how I pray, so long as my prayers are answered?*

Red Jacket, Seneca, 1820: *Brother, if you white men murdered the Son of the Great Spirit, we Indians had nothing to do with it and it is none of our affair. If he had come among us, we would not have killed him; we would have treated him well. You must make amends for that crime yourselves.*

Pontiac, Odowa, 1763: *My children, you have forgotten the customs and traditions of your forefathers. Why do you not clothe yourselves in skins, as they did, use bows and arrows and the stone pointed lances, which they used? You have bought guns, knives, kettles and blankets from the white man until you* can no longer do without them; and what is worse you have drunk the poison firewater, which turns you into fools. Fling all these things away; live as your forefathers did before you.

Buffalo Bird Woman, Hidatsa, 1926: *I am an old woman now. The buffaloes and black-tail deer are gone and our Indian ways are almost gone. Sometimes I find it hard to believe that I ever lived them. But for me I cannot forget our old ways I seem again to see our Indian village, with smoke curling upward from the earth lodges; and in the river's roar I hear the yells of the warriors, the laughter of little children as of old…It is but an old woman's dream. Our Indian life, I know, is gone forever.*

Pretty Shield, Crow, 1925: *My people were tough in those days…if in winter a person fell into icy water, he got out, took off his wet clothes and rolled in the snow, rubbing his body with it and got warm. Then, after squeezing out the water, be put on his clothes and forgot about getting wet…the buffalo-runners rubbed their hands with snow and sand, so that their fingers would be nimble at handling the bow and arrows. Now my people wear gloves and too many clothes. We are soft as mud.*

Words from a wedding ceremony, Navajo, date unknown: *Now you have lit a fire and that fire should not go out. The two of you now have a fire that represents love, understanding and a philosophy of life. It will give you heat, food, warmth and happiness. This new fire represents a new beginning: a new life and a new family. The fire should keep burning; you should stay together. You have lit the fire for life, until old age separates you.*

Sweet Medicine, Cheyenne, undated: *There is a special magic and holiness about the girl and woman. They are the bringers of life to the people and the teachers of the little children.*

He Dog, Oglala, Lakota, 1900: *It is well to be good to women in the strength of our manhood because we must sit under their hands at both ends of our lives.*

Black Elk, Oglala Lakota, 1932: *You know, in the old days, it was not so very easy to get a girl when you wanted to be married. Sometimes it was hard work for a young man and he had to stand a great deal.*

Black Elk, 1949: *The hearts of little children are pure and therefore, the Great Spirit may show to them many things which older people miss.*

Lakota proverb: *See how the boy is with his sister and the other ones of his home lodge and you can know how the man will be with your daughter.*

Social tradition, Assiniboine: *Good acts done for the love of children become stories good for the ears of people from other bands, they become as coveted things and are placed side by side with the stories of war achievements.*

Skookum doll grouping, all eyes right: left and right, mothers with children—$150 each; center—$100. (Merritt's Museum of Childhood)

Contemporary brushed-velvet Navajo dolls: left and right—$60 pair; center—$30. (Merritt's Museum of Childhood)

Buckskin Cheyenne doll, ca. 1860s, 24" high, fine bead work in black, white and mustard, split hide and metal tinklers serve as the fringe—$1,500. (Merritt's Museum of Childhood)

Unusual adult pair of apple-faced dolls with child; note the war bonnet and bead work, $1,500 pair. (Merritt's Museum of Childhood)

Wooden folk art doll, possibly Indian, carved, jointed arms and legs, 17-1/2" high—$600. (Merritt's Museum of Childhood)

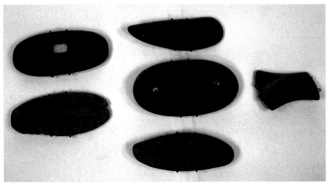

Six assorted stone gorgets—$50 each. (Merritt's Museum of Childhood)

Canassatego, Onondaga, 1744: *You who are so wise must know the different nations have different conceptions of things; and you will therefore not take it amiss, if our ideas of this kind of education happens not to be the same with yours. We have had some experience of it. Several of our young people were formerly brought up in the Colleges of the Northern Provinces; they were instructed in all your sciences; but, when they came back to us, they were bad runners, ignorant of every means of living in the woods, unable to bear either cold or hunger, knew neither how to build a cabin, take a deer or kill an enemy, spoke our language imperfectly, were therefore neither fit for hunters, warriors, nor councilors; they were totally good for nothing…*

Red Cloud, Oglala Lakota, 1870: *We do not want riches, but we want to train our children right. Riches would do us no good. We could not take them with us to the other world. We do not want riches, we want peace and love.*

John (Fire) Lame Deer, Rosebud Lakota, 1972: *Indians chase the vision, white men chase the dollar.*

Northern Blackfeet Chief, 19th century: *Our land is more valuable than your money. It will last forever. It will not perish by the flames of fire. As long as the sun shines and the waters flow this land will be here to give life to men and animals. We cannot sell the lives of men and animals; therefore we cannot sell this land…You can count your money and burn it within the nod of a buffalo's head, but only the Great Spirit can count the grains of sand and the blades of grass of these plains. As a present to you, we will give you anything we have that you can take with you, but the land, never.*

Mangas, Coloradas, Apache, 1851: *Money cannot buy affection.*

Santanta, Kiowa, 1867: *I don't want to settle. I love to roam over the prairies. There I feel free and happy, but when we settle down we grow pale and die.*

Pontiac, Odawa, 1762: *We are not your slaves. These lakes, these woods and mountains were left us by our ancestors. They are our inheritance; and we will part with them to none. Your nation supposes that we, like the white people, cannot live without bread and pork and beer. But you ought to know that He, the Great Spirit and Master of Life, has provided food for us in these spacious lakes and on these woody mountains.*

Oral tradition, Hopi: *Argument doesn't pay: you don't come home happy.*

Wilma Mankiller, Cherokee, 1987: *Crisis changes people and turns ordinary people into wiser or more responsible ones.*

Chief Ouray, Ute, 1868: *Agreements the Indian makes with the government are like the agreement a buffalo makes with the hunter after it has been pierced by many arrows. All it can do is lie down and give in.*

Chief Joseph, Nez Perce, 1877: *Let me be a free man: free to travel, free to stop, free to work, free to trade where I choose, free to choose my own teachers, free to follow the religion of my fathers, free to think and talk and act for myself: and I will obey every law or submit to the penalty.*

Chief Joseph, 1879: *Treat all men alike. Give them all the same law. Give them all an even chance to live and grow. All men were made by the same Great spirit Chief. They are all brothers. The earth is the mother of all people and all people shall have equal rights upon it. You might as well expect the rivers to run backward as that any man who was born a free man should be contented penned up and denied liberty to go where he pleases.*

Edward Ahenakew, Cree, 1920: *We are as well behaved as you and you would think so if you knew us better.*

Spotted Tail, Sicangu Lakota, 1880: *White men have education and books and ought to know exactly what to do, but hardly any two of them agree on what should be done.*

The Peace Maker, Iroquois oral tradition: *We do now crown you with the sacred emblem of the antlers, the sign of your lordship. You shall now become a mentor of the people of the Five Nations. The thickness of your skin will be seven parts, for you will be proof against anger, offensive action and criticism. With endless patience you shall carry out your duty and your firmness shall be tempered with calm deliberation. In all your official acts, self-interest shall be cast aside. You shall look and listen to the welfare of the whole people and have always in view, not only the present but the coming generations: the unborn of the future Nation.*

Osceola, Seminole, 1838: *They could not capture me except under a white flag. They cannot hold me except with a chain.*

Crazy Horse, Oglala Lakota, 1877: *We preferred our own way of living. We were no expense to the government. All we wanted was peace and to be left alone.*

John Mohawk, Seneca, 1992: *Christopher Columbus is a symbol, not of a man, but of imperialism…Imperialism and colonialism are not something that happened decades ago or generations ago, but they are still happening now with the exploitation of people…The kind of thing that took place long ago in which people were dispossessed from their land and forced out of subsistence economies and into market economies: those processes are still happening today.*

Polingaysi Qoyawayma, Hopi, 1964: *We, who are clay blended by the Master Potter, come from the kiln of Creation in many hues. How can people say one skin is colored, when each has its own coloration? What should it matter that one bowl is dark and the other pale, if each is of good design and serves its purpose well?*

Clyde Bellecourt, Ojibway, 1978: *We want to change the image that has been portrayed by John Wayne, the media and the*

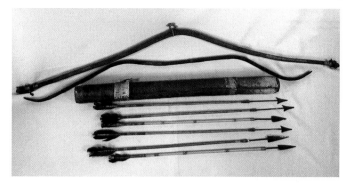

Two bent wooden bows, pony skin quiver, six arrows with assorted steel shafts and points—$1,500 set. (Merritt's Museum of Childhood)

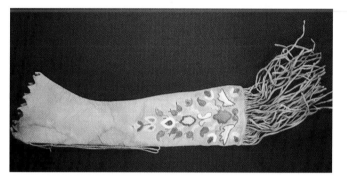

Colorful beaded Sioux pipe bag—25" long, $2,970. (Merritt's Museum of Childhood)

Top, red covered box, bird points—$650; bottom, arrowheads collected by E.D. Zimmerman, Montgomery County, PA, May 4, 1919, mostly from California, Oregon and Washington—$797. (Merritt's Museum of Childhood)

Model birch bark canoe with colorful porcupine quills used to create vines and flowers—$1,017.50. (Merritt's Museum of Childhood)

Cone-shaped Modoc basket, Klamath, OR, near Upper Klamath Lake—$302.50. (Merritt's Museum of Childhood)

Funnel-shaped basket, Archomiwal, Pit River, CA—14" high, $1,320. (Merritt's Museum of Childhood)

history books. We want to portray the truth. We, the Indian people, the Red Man of the Western Hemisphere, are the truth of the Western Hemisphere!

Dennis Sun Rhodes, Arapahoe, 1993: *The tipi encloses a circular space that has no end…whereas the log cabin formed a square with exact dimensions marking the ends of walls. The design of this log cabin reflects the non-Indians' way of life, exemplified by a need to find exact distances, time increments, philosophical definitions and finite answers to scientific riddles in a materialistic world filled with the implements of technology. The tipi is the Plains Indians' contribution to the architecture of the Americas. The tipi taught the tribal members to recycle a space for many uses and the communal space of the tipi helped develop the tribe's interpersonal relationship norms.*

Chiksika, Shawnee: *When a white army battles with Indians and wins, it is called a great victory, but if they lose it is called a massacre.*

Florida chief, 1539: *I have long since learned who you Castilians are…To me you are professional vagabonds who wander from place to place, gaining your livelihood by robbing, sacking and murdering people who have given no offense.*

Corn Tassel, Cherokee, 1785: *You say: Why do not the Indians till the ground and live as we do? May we not ask, why the white people do not hunt and live as we do? The great God of Nature has given each their lands…he has stocked yours with cows, ours with buffalo; yours with hog, ours with bear; yours with sheep, ours with deer. He has indeed given you an advantage, in that your cattle are tame and domestic while ours are wild and demand not only a larger space for range, but art to hunt and kill them.*

Zuni saying: *The landscape is our church, a cathedral. It is like a sacred building to us.*

Joe S. Sando, Jemez Pueblo: *The Pueblo have no word that translates as "religion." The knowledge of a spiritual life is part of the person 24 hours a day, every day of the year. Religious belief permeates every aspect of life; it determines man's relation with the natural world and with his fellow man. The secret of the Pueblo's success was simple. They came face to face with nature but did not exploit it.*

Allan Houser, Apache: *They had war dances at night before battle…keeping time with the drum, ducking down and moving with their shield…and people would say you could hardly see them because they did it so fast.*

Thayendanegea (Joseph Brant), Mohawk, 1776: *The Mohawks have on all occasions shown their zeal and loyalty to the Great King; yet they have been very badly treated by his people. Indeed it is very hard, when we have let the king's subjects have so much of our lands for so little value. We are tired out in making complaints and getting no redress.*

Chief Joseph's Surrender Speech

I am weary of fighting. our chiefs are killed. Looking Glass is dead. Toohoolhoolzote is dead. The old men are all dead. It is now the young men who say "yea" or "nay," and he who used to lead them, my brother Olicut, is dead. It is cold. We have no blankets. The children are freezing. Some of my people have taken to the hills and have no covering and no food. No one knows where they are. Perhaps they too are freezing. I want to look for them and try to find them. Perhaps they are dead.

Hear me, my chiefs. I am tired. My heart is sick and sad. From where the sun now stands. I will fight no more forever.

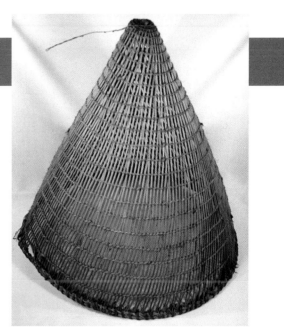

Hupa winnowing tray, California—$385. (Merritt's Museum of Childhood)

Left, vase-shaped Apache basket—$1,925; right, rare water-proof grass bottle, pitch-lined, Utah—$400. (Merritt's Museum of Childhood)

Sweet grass basket, Canadian Indians—$200. (Merritt's Museum of Childhood)

Rare Papago basket, Robles Pass, AZ—$495. (Merritt's Museum of Childhood)

Basket, Frazer River Indians, British Columbia—$680. (Merritt's Museum of Childhood)

Quiniault basket, Washington—$450. (Merritt's Museum of Childhood)

Western Apache figural flat tray—$2,750. (Merritt's Museum of Childhood)

Double-tube pipe monitor, Union County, SC—$82.50. (Merritt's Museum of Childhood)

Fish-head pipe bowl—$200. (Merritt's Museum of Childhood)

Catlinite pipe bowl; eagle claw decor—$330. (Merritt's Museum of Childhood)

Side view, Eastern Sioux Catlinite pipe bowl, carved frog and buffalo symbols—$825. (Merritt's Museum of Childhood)

Snake pipe stem, Catlinite—$200. (Merritt's Museum of Childhood)

Two plain Catlinite pipe bowls—$100 each. (Merritt's Museum of Childhood)

Pennsylvania smoked stone, effigy bird pipe bowl—$200. (Merritt's Museum of Childhood)

Clay eagle effigy pipe bowl, etched with two pony heads, U.S. and two shields with a flag—$300. (Merritt's Museum of Childhood)

Carved pipe bowl showing a child with crossed arms— $175. (Merritt's Museum of Childhood)

Etched and carved effigy bear pipe bowl—$200. (Merritt's Museum of Childhood)

Cherokee figural face pipe bowl—$825. (Merritt's Museum of Childhood)

Clay pipe with a curl, New Jersey, $104.50. (Merritt's Museum of Childhood)

Etched pipe bowl, submarine-shaped—$192.50. (Merritt's Museum of Childhood)

Pipe with three etched grooves showing European influence—$150. (Merritt's Museum of Childhood)

Type of Eastern trade pipe, 22" long, carved wooden stem with feather—$150. (Merritt's Museum of Childhood)

Three extra large pipe bowls, one with designs, another with a face—$200, $175 and $150. (Merritt's Museum of Childhood)

Iroquois snow shoes, bent wood and braided sinew, 42-1/2" long x 14" wide, St. Lawrence River, Canada—$220. (Merritt's Museum of Childhood)

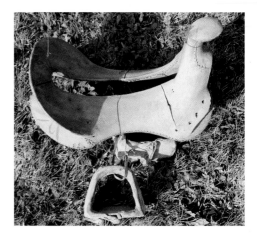

Hand-sewn Western saddle, all leather with stirrups—$275. (Merritt's Museum of Childhood)

Chippewa birch bark canoe, 49" long, near Leech Lake, Northern Minnesota—$412.50. (Merritt's Museum of Childhood)

Hand-carved canoe, painted black, 35" long, Fort Rupert, British Columbia—$412.50. (Merritt's Museum of Childhood)

Sioux war clubs, White River, South Dakota, 26", 21" and 21" in length. The largest weighs approximately 10 pounds—$440; 21" clubs are $300 each. (Merritt's Museum of Childhood)

Sioux war clubs, 21" and 23"—left, $300; right $55. (Merritt's Museum of Childhood)

Chapter 5

NATIVE AMERICAN HISTORY: STATE BY STATE

SHOTTED WOLF.

Top to bottom: Arrow in a tree—$35; red Arapaho leather bag—$50; buffalo horn ladle—$100; Comanche beaded leather bag—$150. (Merritt's Museum of Childhood)

Alabama

1540: De Soto crosses Alabama and fights Indians near Choctaw Bluff at Mauvila.

1629: Charles I includes Alabama area in Carolina grant.

1699: A colony is founded near Biloxi, MS, by Pierre le Moyne, sieur d'Iberville; as a portion of Louisiana, Alabama is governed from there.

1702: Fort Louis is constructed on the Mobile River by Jean Baptiste le Moyne; the capital is moved from Biloxi to the fort.

1711: Fort Louis is moved to the present site of Mobile.

1763: Alabama is given by France to England in the Treaty of Paris.

1798: The Mississippi Territory is created and includes Alabama.

1803: The U.S. claims Mobile as part of the Louisiana Purchase.

1805: Choctaw, Cherokee and Chickasaw give a portion of Alabama land claims to the U.S.

1813: Colonists massacred at Fort Mims by Creek Indians. The Creeks are defeated by General Andrew Jackson at the battle of Horseshoe Bend in 1814.

1817: Congress creates Alabama Territory; capital is St. Stevens.

1819: Becomes 22nd state; capital Huntsville.

1820: Capital moved to Cahaba.

1846: Legislature moves to have state capital in Montgomery.

1861: Alabama leaves the Union; Montgomery Confederate government formed; Jefferson Davis is the Confederate president.

1868: Alabama readmitted to the Union.

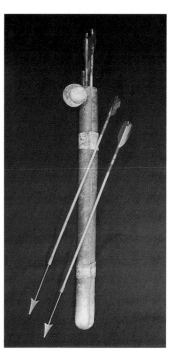

Pony hide quiver with two steel-pointed arrows—$300. (Merritt's Museum of Childhood)

Alaska

1728: Vitrus Bering proves that North America and Asia are separate.

1774-1792: Spanish groups explore the southeast coast.

1778: The Alaskan coast is surveyed by British Captain James Cook.

1784: Russian settle at Three Saints Bay, Kodiak Island.

1791: British navigator, Captain George Vancouver, charts the southeast corner of Alaska.

1799: Sitka is founded; American-Russian Company chartered by Russia for trade.

1823: Work begins among the Aleuts by Russian missionary, Father Ivan Veniaminov.

1867: Secretary of State William H. Seward purchases Alaska from Russia for $7.2 million.

1884: District of Alaska created; capital is Sitka.

1891: Reindeer introduced to aid the Eskimos by Reverend Sheldon Jackson, Presbyterian missionary.

1896: Gold discovered at Nome in the Klondike Basin of Canadian Yukon.

1900: Capital moved to Juneau.

Ancient copper Indian arrows, $75 set. (Merritt's Museum of Childhood)

Eight assorted sizes obsidian spear points—$25-$50 each. (Merritt's Museum of Childhood)

Poison cup with arrow—$150. (Merritt's Museum of Childhood)

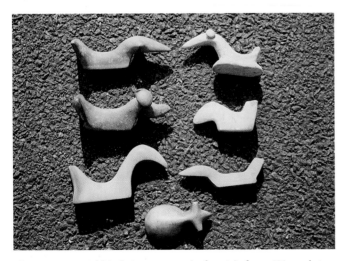

Seven assorted bird stones, one in front is from Wyandot County, OH—$200 each. (Merritt's Museum of Childhood)

1912: Alaska Territory created; Juneau capital.

Arizona

1200: Oraibi the oldest Indian community in the U.S. is founded.

1528: Wrecked off the Gulf of Mexico coast, Cabeza de Vaca wanders to Arizona and Mexico.

1539: Black companion to De Vaca, Estevan, takes Friar Marcos de Niza to Zuni villages; the region is claimed for Spain.

1540: Coronado reaches the Zuni River; a detachment under Garci Lopez de Cardenas discover the Grand Canyon.

1582: Antonio de Espejo finds silver near Prescott.

1680: The Hopi Indians rise up against the Spanish priests.

1692: Father Eusebio Kino begins his missionary work with the Pima Indians; founds the Guevavi Mission.

1696: The Tumacacori Mission is founded.

1700: Mission at San Xavier del Bac.

1751: Pima and Papago revolt.

1771: Missionary work begun by Father Francisco Garces.

1781: The Yuma kill Garces; Spanish retaliate in 1782.

1821: Mexico becomes independent of Spain.

1824: New Mexico Territory is created; American traders enter the area.

1848: Mexico gives Arizona region north of the Gila River to U.S. New Mexico Territory.

1853: Railroad survey made by Lieutenant A.W. Whipple.

1854: First copper mine at Ajo.

1857: Stagecoach established.

1861: Arizona declared Confederate territory.

1863: Congress creates Arizona territory; capital at Fort Whipple.

1864: Capital moved to Prescott; in 1867 to Tucson; 1877 to Prescott; and 1889 to Phoenix.

1869: Major John Wesley Powell explores the Grand Canyon.

1878: Southern Pacific reaches Yuma; to Tucson in 1880.

1886: Chief Geronimo, Apache leader, surrenders.

1912: Becomes 48th state.

Arkansas

1541-1542: De Soto explores the area.

1682: La Salle claims the Mississippi valley for France.

1686: Arkansas Post built by Henri de Toni; first white settlement in the lower Mississippi Valley.

1762: Arkansas ceded by France to Spain; in 1800 Spain secretly returns it.

1800: Cotton first grown commercially.

1803: Becomes part of the U.S., through the Louisiana Purchase.

1805: Louisiana Territory created.

1808: Osage Indians clash with the Cherokee.

1817: Cherokee granted land in western Arkansas.

1818: Quapaw cede a large area to the U.S.

1820: Homesteaders enter the area. Choctaw granted land in western Arkansas.

1825: Choctaw give land to the U.S.

1828: Cherokee agree to leave the area.

1836: Becomes 25th state; capital is Little Rock.

1849: Fort Smith (1817) becomes an outfitting point for California gold seekers.

1861: Arkansas cedes from the Union.

1868: Arkansas readmitted to the Union.

California

1542: San Diego Bay entered by Juan Rodriguez.

1579: New Albion is claimed by Sir Francis Drake for England.

1602: The coast is mapped by Sebastian Vizcaino.

1697: Jesuit mission founded at Loreto, Baja California.

1701: Father Eusebio Kino works with Indians at Alta California.

1767: Jesuits ordered out of California by King Charles III; missionary work assigned to Franciscans.

1769: Mission founded at San Diego by Father Junipero and Don Gaspar; first of 21 missions built by 1823.

1777: San Jose becomes the first town.

1812: Russians build Fort Ross north of San Francisco.

1822: California is granted freedom from Spain.

1825: Mexico claims California.

1839: Captain John Sutter settles at present Sacramento.

1848: Mexico cedes California to the U.S. Gold discovered at Sutter's sawmill.

1849: California gold rush.

1850: Becomes 31st state; in 1854 Sacramento named capital.

1861: Telegraph links the East Coast to California.

1863: Work commences on the Central Pacific Railroad.

1969: American Indians occupy Alcatraz Island.

Colorado

1541: Coronado crosses Colorado returning to Mexico.

1706: The land claimed by Juan de Ulibarri for Spain.

1762: France gives to Spain land west of the Mississippi River; secretly regains it in 1800.

1803: Colorado becomes a part of the Louisiana Purchase.

1842-1853: John C. Fremont explores Colorado.

1848: Mexico gives western Colorado to the U.S.

1851: First permanent settlement at San Luis.

1854: Ute Indians massacre settlers at Fort Pueblo.

1858: Gold discovered at Denver.

1859: Pikes Peak gold rush.

1861: Colorado Territory created; capital Colorado City.

1862: First oil found at Florence; Golden become territorial capital.

1864: Indians are attacked by U.S. troops at Sand Creek.

1868: Cheyenne Indians defeated at the battle of Beecher Island.

1870: Denver Pacific Railway link Denver with Union Pacific at Cheyenne, WY.

1876: Becomes the 38th state; capital at Denver.

1877: Lead and silver boom at Leadville.

1879: Utes attack settlers at White River Agency.

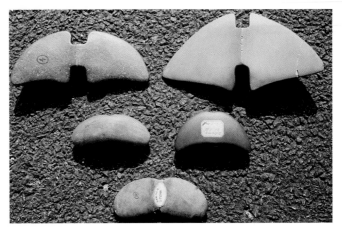

Five winged banner stones, Adams County, Illinois and Indiana—large, $450 each, small, $200 each. (Merritt's Museum of Childhood)

Three treaty stones with etchings—$300 each. (Merritt's Museum of Childhood)

Catlinite pipe tomahawk, two parts, 16-1/2" long, etched with arrow carving on the handle—$660. (Merritt's Museum of Childhood)

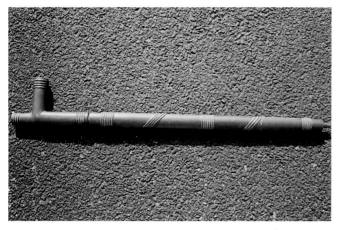

Two-piece Catlinite pipe with carved grooving—$742.50. (Merritt's Museum of Childhood)

Catlinite Chippewa twist stem pipe—$8,800. (Merritt's Museum of Childhood)

Eastern Sioux Catlinite tomahawk pipe, round grooved stem, unusually shaped head with interesting florals—12-1/2 long, $467.50. (Merritt's Museum of Childhood)

1891: Great gold field at Cripple Creek.

Connecticut

1614: Dutch navigator, Adriaen Block, explores Connecticut.

1632: Plymouth Colony explores the region.

1633: Dutch build Fort Good Hope at Hartford; post is established at Windsor.

1635: Massachusetts Bay colonists settle at Windsor, Hartford, and Wethersfield. John Winthrop Jr. constructs a fort at Saybrook.

1637: Pequot Indians massacre settlers at Wethersfield; colonists defeat them in the Pequot War.

1687: Andros is named governor of New England in 1686, demands a Connecticut charter; document is hidden in the Hartford Charter Oak.

1788: Connecticut is the 5th state to ratify the U.S. Constitution on January 9.

1875: Hartford becomes the state capital.

Delaware

1609: Henry Hudson discovers the Delaware River and Bay.

1631: Dutch colony of Zwaanendael established near Lewes; Indians massacre the settlers.

1638: First permanent settlement by Swedish colonists, called New Sweden.

1651: Governor of Dutch New Amsterdam, Peter Stuyvesant, builds Fort Casimir at New Castle; Swedish capture the fort in 1654 and call it Fort Trinity; recaptured in 1655 by Stuyvesant, also takes Fort Christina.

1682: Duke of York grants Three Lower Counties (present Delaware) to William Penn as part of the Pennsylvania Province.

1787: Delaware is the 1st state to ratify the U.S. Constitution on December 7.

Florida

1513: Ponce de Leon seeks the Fountain of Youth, lands near St. Augustine, calls area Florida, claims it for Spain.

1539: De Soto lands at Tampa Bay; proceeds north.

1565: First permanent white settlement in the U.S. a fort erected by Pedro Menendez de Aviles.

1586: St. Augustine is looted and burned by Sir Francis, Drake.

1704: English destroy Spanish mission.

1750: Creek Indians from Georgia migrate to Florida.

1768: New Smyrna with 1,500 colonists led by Andrew Turnbull is established; the project fails in 1776.

1779: Spanish attack West Florida; occupy it in 1781.

1783: British return Florida to Spain.

1822: Florida Territory created; in 1824 Tallahassee is the capital.

1835: Seminole resist removal to Indian Territory; seven-year Seminole War started by Dade Massacre.

1845: Becomes 27th state; capital is Tallahassee.

1861: Florida secedes from the Union.

1868: State readmitted to the Union.

Georgia

1540: De Soto marches through Georgia.

1566: Fort is constructed on St. Catherines Island by Pedro Menendez de Aviles.

1721: English build Fort King George.

1733: General James Oglethorpe founds Savannah. Creek Indians sign land treaty with Oglethorpe.

1736: John and Charles Wesley come to Savannah to preach Methodism.

1754: Georgia becomes a royal province.

1777: First state constitution ratified in Savannah.

1786: Augusta becomes the temporary state capital.

1788: Georgia is the 4th state to ratify the U.S. Constitution on January 2.

1828: Gold is discovered in Cherokee territory, conflicts follow, Cherokee Indians are removed from the state by 1838.

1861: Georgia cedes from the Union.

1870: Georgia readmitted to the Union.

Hawaii

About 1000: Islands settled by Polynesians believed to have come from Tahiti.

1555: Spaniard, Juan Gaetano, may have visited the islands.

1778: English explorer, Captain John Cook, visits the island; killed by Hawaiians in 1779.

1794: Captain George Vancouver visits the islands three times.

1819: First American whaler calls at Honolulu; whaling peaks in 1858.

1820: New England missionaries arrive.

1894: Republic of Hawaii created.

1959: August 21, becomes 50th state.

Idaho

1805: Lewis and Clark enter Idaho on their way to the Pacific.

1809: North West Company fur trading post is established near Hope, by David Thompson.

1810: Missouri Fur Company builds Fort Henry near St. Anthony.

1811: John Jacob Astor's fur trading expedition reaches Idaho.

1834: Hudson Bay Company builds Fort Boise; buys Fort Hall in 1836.

1836: First mission on the Lapwai Creek is established by Henry Spalding.

1843: John C. Fremont explores the Oregon Trail area.

1848: Jesuits found Sacred Heart Mission at Cataldo.

1855: Mormon mission built in Lemhi Valley.

1860: Mormons settle at Franklin. Gold is discovered at Orofino Creek by Captain E.D. Pierce.

1861: Gold strikes on Boise and Salmon Rivers.

1863: Idaho Territory created; temporary capital, Lewiston.

1864: Capital moved to Boise.

1877: Nez Perce War.

1965: Nez Perce National Historic Park established.

Two-piece Catlinite pipe, carved square stem, blade has a floral decor—$2,000. (Merritt's Museum of Childhood)

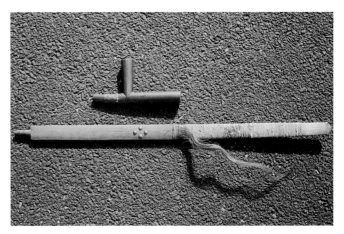

Catlinite pipe bowl with lead inlay, wooden stem with brass rivets, wrapped with dyed porcupine quills, tuft of decorative dyed horsehair—$2,340. (Merritt's Museum of Childhood)

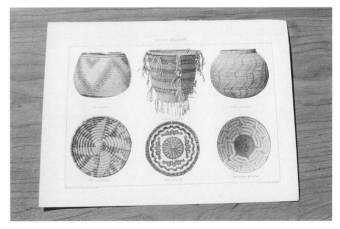

Indian baskets top row, left to right, California, Arizona Apache and Pima from Arizona. Bottom, left to right, Hopi, Arizona, Hopi, Arizona and Maricopa, Arizona. — $15 each. (Merritt's Museum of Childhood)

Postcard showing the cigar store Indian collection at Merritt's, some in carved wood, others cast in metal—$3,000 to $8,000 each, depending upon rarity. (Merritt's Museum of Childhood)

Three Southern Alaska totem poles. —$15. (Merritt's Museum of Childhood)

Illinois

1673: Marquette and Joliet return to Wisconsin via Illinois River and Lake Michigan.

1675: Mission of Immaculate Conception founded by Marquette near Starved Rock.

1763: Illinois ceded by the French to the British after the French and Indian War.

1804: Fox and Sauk Indians cede to the U.S. lands east of the Mississippi River.

1812: Indians massacre troops at Fort Dearborn.

1818: Becomes 21st state on December 3.

1820: State capital is moved from Kaskaskia to Vandalia.

1832: Black Hawk War drives the Fox and Sauk from Illinois. Potawatomi and Winnebago cede lands.

1837: Springfield is chosen as the state capital.

1933-1934: Century of Progress World's Fair held in Chicago.

Indiana

1679: La Salle explores St. Joseph River to its south bend; returns in 1681; meets Indians under Council Oak.

1763: Pontiac Conspiracy, Indians destroy settlements and Forts Miami and Ouiatenon.

1794: "Mad Anthony" Wayne defeats Indians at the battle of Fallen Timbers, OH.

1800: Indiana Territory created; capital, Vincennes.

1809: Treaty of Fort Wayne made by Governor Harrison and the Indians.

1811: General Harrison defeats the Indians at Tippecanoe.

1812: Renewed Indian attacks stopped.

1813: Tecumseh killed.

1816: December 11, Indiana became the 19th state.

1818: Indians sell central Indiana in a treaty.

1837: Remaining Potawatomi driven out.

As part of the ongoing research for this book, the author attended a juried American Indian Arts Festival held on October 12-14, 1995, at the Rankokus Indian Reservation, Rancocas, NJ. This was the 13th annual Burlington County event, the largest juried art festival on the East Coast. Represented were 50 tribal nations—150 artists and entertainers. Featured were Eagle Dancers, Aztec Dancers, Hoop Dancers, storytellers, alligator wrestling, clothing and crafts. Also on display were wolves, bison, a bird aviary, American Indian cuisine and handmade jewelry. Additional demonstrations showed doll and bow making, pipe stone carving, horse-painting, bareback riding and stories by the wisdom keepers. A spectacular 100-foot Aztec pole ceremony featured a flute player and six performers who hung by their ankles and spun slowly to the ground as the pole turned. Shown here are varied samples of contemporary silver/turquoise jewelry, ranging from $40 to several hundred per item. (Rankokus)

Iowa

1673: Juliet and Marquette become the first whites in Iowa.

1682: La Salle claims the Mississippi Valley for France; named Louisiana for Louis XIV.

1788: First white settler, Julien Dubuque, given permission by the Indians to mine lead near Dubuque.

1805: Zebulon M. Pike explores the Mississippi bluffs.

1808: Fort Madison built as a defense against the Indians.

1812: War of 1812.

1813: Indians burn Fort Madison.

1824: Half-breeds granted lands in southeastern Iowa.

1832: Indians defeated in the Black Hawk War; Chief Black Hawk of the Sauk surrendered eastern Iowa.

1838: Iowa becomes a territory; Burlington, temporary capital.

1842: Sauk and Fox Indians give up remaining lands.

1846: December 28th, becomes 29th state.

1857: Sioux Indians attack settlers in Spirit Lake Massacre. State constitution adopted, capital moved to Des Moines.

Kansas

1541: Coronado searching for Quivira, arrives in central Kansas.

1804: Lewis and Clark enter Kansas.

1806: Zebulon M. Pike explores the Republican River.

1812: Missouri Territory created.

1824: Presbyterian mission founded on the Neosho River.

1825: Kansa (Kaw) and Osage Indians cede lands.

1827: Daniel Morgan Boone founds Indian school, Jefferson County.

1830: Shawnee Methodist Mission for Indians established near Turner; moved near Shawnee in 1839.

1849: California seekers of gold follow the Kansas trails.

1853: Fort Riley established.

1854: Kansas Territory created; temporary capital, Fort Leavenworth.

1860: Pony Express crosses Kansas en route to the West.

1861: Becomes 34th state on January 29; capital, Topeka.

1867: First herd of Texas cattle driven to Kansas.

1874: Mennonites introduce Turkey Red wheat to the U.S.

1878: Cheyenne Indian raid is the last in the state.

Kentucky

1750: Cumberland Gap discovered by Doctor Thomas Walker.

1751: Christopher Gist explores along the Ohio River.

1763: France cedes Kentucky to Britain.

1769: Daniel Boone and John Finley explore Kentucky.

1774: Building of Harrodstown commences; Indians force the settlers out; they return in 1775.

1775: Indians give Richard Henderson land between the Ohio and Cumberland Rivers. Boone creates the Wilderness Road; Boonesboro is founded.

1778: Indian siege of Boonesboro repulsed.

1792: Becomes 15th state on June 1; capital, Lexington.

1794: General "Mad Anthony" Wayne's victory at Fallen Timbers, OH, ends Kentucky Indian attacks.

1796: Wilderness Road opened to wagons.

Contemporary silver/turquoise jewelry—$40 to several hundred per item. (Rankokus)

Contemporary silver/turquoise jewelry—$40 to several hundred per item. (Rankokus)

Possibilities demonstrated with feather art. (Rankokus)

Full-length deerskin dress made by the Shenandoah Family. Note the fringes, beading and matching shoulder bag. (Rankokus)

A variety of porcupine quill objects, small pieces were $250; larger examples were priced at $3,000. Shenandoah Trading Post, Oneida, NY. (Rankokus)

A wide range of colorful Penobscot baskets—$100-$300 each. (Rankokus)

Louisiana

1541: De Soto explores northern Louisiana.

1682: La Salle names the territory Louisiana.

1717: A mission is established by the Spaniards near Natchitoches.

1762: Louis XV gives all of Louisiana west of the Mississippi River plus "island of New Orleans" to Spain.

1795: Boundary between West Florida and Louisiana set at the 31st parallel.

1800: Spain ceded Louisiana Territory to France.

1803: U.S. purchases Louisiana from France.

1812: Becomes 18th state on April 30; capital, New Orleans.

1835: Caddo Indians give up lands in Louisiana.

1861: Louisiana secedes from the Union.

1868: Louisiana readmitted to the Union.

Maine

1497-1499: John and Sebastian Cabot visit the Maine coast.

1606: Plymouth Company granted a charter.

1607: Popham Colony founded; abandoned in 1608.

1614: Captain John Smith charts the Maine coast.

1630: Plymouth English Council grants large Maine tract to Thomas Leverett and John Beauchamp.

1635: Council for New England surrenders it charter.

1639: England grants Governor William Gorges, charter to territory called Maine.

1652: Massachusetts Bay Colony agrees to govern Maine.

1675-1678: Indians attack settlers in King Philip's war.

1739: Boundaries fixed between Maine and New Hampshire.

1759: The fall of Quebec, final peace with the French and Indians.

1820: Becomes 23rd state on March 15; capital, Portland.

1827: Augusta chosen state capital.

Maryland

1608: Captain John Smith charts the Chesapeake Bay.

1631: Trading post is established by William Claiborne on Kent Island.

1634: St. Mary's City is founded by Leonard Calvert.

1649: First act of religious toleration in the colonies passed.

1652: Peace treaty is made with the Susquehanna Indians.

1692: Maryland becomes a royal colony.

1763: Mason and Dixon survey the Pennsylvania boundary.

1783: Congress meets at Annapolis under the Articles of Confederation; George Washington resigns as commander in chief.

1784: Treaty of Paris is ratified.

1788: Maryland becomes the 7th state to ratify the U.S. Constitution on April 28.

1814: Francis Scott Key writes "The Star-Spangled Banner" as the British bombard Fort McHenry.

1844: First telegraph line in the U.S. joins Baltimore and Washington, DC.

Massachusetts

1602: Coast explored by Bartholomew Gosnold.

1614: Captain John Smith charts the coast.

1620: Plymouth Company reorganized as the Council for New England. The Pilgrims land at Plymouth; found Plymouth; elect as governor John Carver. About 100 men, women and children landed (December 21).

1621: The Plymouth settlers join with the Indians in celebrating their first Thanksgiving.

1629: Massachusetts Bay Company chartered.

1639: Cambridge is the site of the first English printing press in North America.

1643: The New England Confederation is formed by the Puritan colonies to oppose Indian and Dutch attacks.

1675: King Philip's War prompts Indian attacks on the settlers.

1692: Witchcraft trials begin in Salem.

1773: Boston colonists disguised as Indians dump £15,000 of tea overboard, saying "King George will never collect a tax on this tea."

1788: Massachusetts becomes the 6th state to ratify the U.S. Constitution on February 6.

Michigan

1634: Samuel de Champlain explores Green Bay and the Straits of Mackinac.

1668: Marquette opens a mission at Sault Ste. Marie, first permanent settlement.

1671: St. Ignace Mission established at Marquette. Simon Daumont, sieur de St. Lusson, claims the Great Lakes region for France. Algonquin tribes greet Europeans to the Great Lakes.

1763: Pontiac lays siege to Detroit.

1764: The Indians are defeated.

1787: The Northwest Territory is created, includes Michigan.

1794: General Wayne's defeat of the Indians at Fallen Timbers, OH, open Michigan to settlement.

1805: Michigan Territory organized; capital, Detroit. Capital is destroyed by fire.

1807: Indians give southeastern Michigan to the U.S.

1812: War of 1812, Detroit surrenders to the British; Indians join the British.

1819: Treaty of Saginaw, Indians cede central Michigan.

1821: Treaty of Chicago, Indians cede southern Michigan.

1837: On January 26. becomes 26th state.

Minnesota

1654-1660: French fur traders make two expeditions to Minnesota.

1679: Daniel Greysolon, sieu du Lhut, meets Chippewa and Sioux near Duluth; area claimed for France at Mille Lacs Lake.

1727: Mission founded on Lake Pepin by Father Guignas.

1762: France cedes to Spain lands west of the Mississippi; Spain secretly returns the lands in 1800.

1763: England wins eastern Minnesota from France

1783: England cedes eastern Minnesota to the U.S.;

Three birch bark containers and a canoe—$75-$150 each. (Rankokus)

A young girl weaving on a loom. She noted that this size would take about 2 weeks to complete and sell for $75. (Rankokus)

An actor portraying an Indian about to demonstrate the art of horse painting. (Rankokus)

An actor wearing typical Indian garb as he lectured. (Rankokus)

Colorful replicas of Indian teepees. (Rankokus)

Another replica of an Indian teepee. (Rankokus)

North West Company begins fur trading in Minnesota.

1805: Zebulon M. Pike picks site for Fort St. Anthony.

1816: John Jacob Astor's American Fur Company takes over the fur trade.

1819: Work begins on Fort St. Anthony; renamed Fort Snelling in 1825.

1835: Mission work begun with the Sioux by the Pond brothers.

1837: Indian treaties open eastern Minnesota to whites.

1849: Minnesota Territory created; capital, St. Paul.

1851: Sioux treaties open land west of the Mississippi.

1858: Becomes 32nd state on May 11; capital, St. Paul.1861: State is the first to offer Civil War troops; followed by Indian uprisings.

1862: Sioux massacre many settlers.

Mississippi

1540: De Soto becomes the first European to explore the Mississippi.

1682: The French claim the Mississippi Valley under La Salle.

1699: Fort Maurepas is built by Pierre le Moyne, sieur d'Iberville, at Ocean Springs.

1716: Fort Rosalie is founded at Natchez by Jean Baptiste le Moyne, sieur de Bienville.

1763: Treaty of Paris awards Britain West Florida east of the Mississippi River, south of the 31st parallel.

1798: Mississippi Territory organized; capital, Natchez.

1801: Chickasaw Indians give U.S. Natchez Trace right-of-way.

1802: Territorial capital moved to Washington.

1806: Improved Mexican cotton introduced.

1817: Becomes 20th state on December 10; capital, Washington.

1820: Treaty of Doak's Stand has the Choctaw cede land.

1822: Jackson becomes the state capital.

1830: Choctaw in the Treaty of Dancing Rabbit Creek cede remaining lands and move to Oklahoma.

1832: Chickasaw cede land.

1861: Mississippi secedes from the Union; Jefferson Davis becomes the president of the Confederate States of America.

1862: Union troops invade the state.

1870: Mississippi readmitted to the Union.

Missouri

1673: Marquette and Joliet discover the mouth of the Missouri River.

1682: La Salle claims the Mississippi Valley for France.

1700: Jesuit mission established at St. Louis, abandoned in 1703.

1735: First permanent white settlement founded by the French at Ste. Genevieve.

1762: France cedes to Spain area west of the Mississippi; Spain secretly cedes it back to France in 1800.

1764: Settlement is built at St. Louis by Pierre Laclede.

1803: Louisiana Purchase makes Missouri a U.S. territory.

1804: Lewis and Clark depart St. Louis on trip through Missouri to the Northwest. Upper Louisiana is formally transferred to U.S. at a ceremony held in St. Louis.

1805: Missouri becomes a portion of Louisiana Territory.

1812: Missouri Territory organized; capital, St. Louis.

1821: Missouri admitted to the Union as a slave state, becomes 24th state on August 10; capital, St. Charles.

1826: Capital moved to Jefferson City.

1837: Platte Purchase ends Indian claims to Missouri.

1860: Pony Express begins from St. Joseph to California.

Montana

1762: France gives Montana east of the Rockies to Spain; Spain returns it in 1800.

1803: Through the Louisiana Purchase, eastern Montana becomes a portion of the U.S.

1805: Lewis and Clark assisted by Indians as they cross Montana on their way to the Pacific. The Indians called this vast land where the bison roamed the Land of Shining Mountains. Chief tribes of the eastern plains were Crow and Blackfeet. Others were Arapaho, Shoshoni, Cheyenne, Sioux and Assiniboin. In western Montana were the Flathead (Salish) and Kutenai tribes.

1807: Fort Manuel is built by Manuel Lisa on the Bighorn.

1810: Blackfeet drive out those living on a trading post near Three Forks.

1822: Fort Henry constructed on the Yellowstone River by the Rocky Mountain Fur Company.

1823-1835: Other fur trading posts built.

1841: The first mission is founded at St. Mary's by Jesuit, Pierre Jean de Smet.

1853: John Grant starts the first beef herd, Deer Lodge Valley.

1854: St. Ignatius Mission established in Mission Valley.

1857: First sheep ranching begins in Bitterroot Valley.

1858: Gold found at Gold Creek.

1858-1862: Mullgan wagon road built over the Rockies.

1864: Montana Territory created; capital, Bannack.

1865: Virginia City become the territorial capital.

1867: Indians attack Fort C.F. Smith, established on Bighorn in 1866; area declared a reservation in 1868.

1876: Lieutenant Colonel George A. Custer and his troops are wiped out in the battle of Little Bighorn.

1877: Nez Perce defeated in the Bear Paw Mountains.

1889: Becomes 41st state on November 8; capital, Helena.

Nebraska

1682: La Salle lays claim to the Mississippi Valley for France.

1720: Spanish expedition led to the Platte River by Pedro de Villasur; killed by the Pawnee Indians.

1803: Louisiana Purchase includes Nebraska.

1804: Lewis and Clark visit Nebraska, make a treaty with the Nebraska Indians including the Pawnee, Oto, Missouri, Omaha, Ponca. The Winnebage arrived in the middle 1800s; Western Nebraska was hunted by the Cheyenne, Sioux and Arapaho.

1832: First wagon train is led along the Platte Valley-

A domed hut being constructed from tied branches and grasses. (Rankokus)

A wickiup as it would have appeared. (Rankokus)

A contemporary log canoe on display. (Rankokus)

113

Three buffalo grazing. (Rankokus)

Nelson Tsosie, Navajo Arizona Indian sculptor. (Rankokus)

Indian painter at work. (Rankokus)

South Pass route west by Captain B.L.E. Bonneville.

1833: Missionary, Moses Merrill, arrives at Bellevue.

1838: Roman Catholic missionary work commences among the Nebraska Indians, Father Pierre Jean de Smet.

1842: John C. Fremont explores the Platte River area; Oregon Trail mass migrations begin.

1854: Kansas-Nebraska Act creates Nebraska Territory; Omaha made capital.

1863: Homestead Act of 1862 permits Daniel Freeman in Gage County to secure the first homestead.

1865: Union Pacific Railroad lays tracks and runs them across Nebraska by 1867.

1867: Becomes 37th state on March 1; capital, Lancaster.

1874-1877: Chief Crazy Horse surrenders as a Sioux at Fort Robinson; this marks the end of Indian Wars in Nebraska.

Nevada

1830: Led by William Wolfskill, traders cross Nevada to California via Old Spanish Trail.

1843-1845: John C. Fremont explores the area and his reports arouse interest.

1848: Nevada given by Mexico to the U.S. in Treaty of Guadalupe-Hidalgo.

1849: Forty-niners cross Nevada on their way to the gold fields of California.

1850: Utah Territory created which includes Nevada.

1857: Brigham Young asks Nevada Mormons to defend the Salt Lake area from threatened U.S. army attacks.

1859: Comstock Lode of gold and silver discovered; Virginia City is founded.

1860: Settlers battle the Indians near Pyramid Lake; Fort Churchill is built. The Pony Express between California and Missouri crosses Nevada.

1861: Transcontinental telegraph line completed; Nevada Territory created, capital, Carson City.

1862: Indians attack in the east; Fort Ruby constructed.

1864: Becomes 36th state on October 31; capital, Carson City.

1868: Central Pacific Railroad reaches Reno; joins the Union Pacific Railroad in Utah to finalized the first transcontinental route in 1869.

New Hampshire

1603: Piscataqua River explored by Martin Pring.

1605: Samuel de Champlain lands at Piscataqua Bay.

1614: Captain John Smith sails along the coast.

1622: New England Council grants land between the Merrimack and Kennebec Rivers to Sir Ferdinando Gorges and Captain John Mason.

1629: Mason names the area New Hampshire.

1635: Mason's death leaves land claim in doubt.

1638-1639: Hampton and Exeter founded.

1641: Four towns place themselves under the rule of Massachusetts' government.

1689-1697: Indian raids and King William's War.

1697: Indian captors killed near Penacook by Hannah Dustin.

1702-1713: Indian attacks and Queen Anne's War.

1740: Boundary dispute between Massachusetts-New Hampshire settled by royal decree.

1744-1748: King George's War brings fighting about with the French and Indians.

1788: New Hampshire is the 9th state to ratify the U.S. Constitution on June 21.

1808: Concord becomes the permanent capital.

New Jersey

1524: Giovanni da Verrazzano explores the shore.

1609: Henry Hudson ascends the Hudson River.

1618: Dutch trading post created at Bergen.

1623: Fort Nassau built by Captain Cornelius Mey.

1638: Swedish settlers build forts on the east bank of the Delaware.

1664: England grants the area to Sir George Carteret and Lord Berkeley.

1674: Berkeley's western New Jersey interest purchased by Quakers, John Fenwick and Edward Byllynge.

1676: Colony divided into East and West Jersey.

1774: Provincial Congress meets at New Brunswick and adopts the Constitution in 1776.

1776: General George Washington retreats to Pennsylvania, then re-crosses the Delaware River to take Trenton.

1777: Americans defeat the British at Princeton.

1779-1780: Washington and his Army winter at Morristown.

1783: Princeton is the national capital from June 30 to November 4; Trenton from November 1 to December 24, 1784. Washington gives his farewell address to the Army at Rocky Hill.

1787: New Jersey is the 3rd state to ratify the U.S. Constitution on December 18.

1790: Trenton becomes the state capital.

New Mexico

1536: Cabeza de Vaca enters New Mexico from Texas.

1540: Coronado begins his conquest of New Mexico.

1598: Juan de Onate claims New Mexico for Spain; founds church and settlement.

1680: Pueblo Indians revolt and drive the Spanish out.

1692-1696: Governor Diego de Vargas reconquers New Mexico.

1776: Franciscan friars open the first leg of the Old Spanish Trail.

1787: Pedro Vial opens St. Louis to Santa Fe trail.

1821: Mexico wins its independence from Spain; New Mexico becomes a Mexican province.

1833: First gold lode west of the Mississippi River discovered at Sierra del Oro.

1846: U.S. declares war on Mexico.

1848: Guadalupe-Hidalgo Treaty cedes New Mexico and California to the U.S.

1849: Stage line begins: Santa Fe to Independence, MO.

1850: Territory of New Mexico created; capital, Santa Fe.

1851: First English language school founded at Santa Fe.

1864: Colonel Kit Carson defeats the Navajo.

1912: Becomes 47th state on January 6; capital, Santa Fe.

Navajo silver-maker, Arizona. (Rankokus)

A vast array of Navajo sand paintings—Nelson and Judy Lewis. (Rankokus)

A monumental eagle sculpture by Chip Isaacs, Oneida, NY. (Rankokus)

Lumbee pottery by Karl A. Hunt, Lumbee, NC. (Rankokus)

Indian war bonnet with beading—$285, also a decorated drum. (Rankokus)

Contemporary bows and arrows for sale. (Rankokus)

New York

1609: Hudson River explored by Henry Hudson. Samuel de Champlain enters New York from Quebec.

1614: The Dutch build Fort Nassau on Castle Island.

1625: Dutch establish New Amsterdam on Manhattan.

1626: Peter Minuit, director general of the colony, bought permission from the Wappinger Confederacy to occupy Manhattan Island.

1629: Dutch West India Company establishes a patroon system.

1653: Early city government called burgher (borough) granted to New Amsterdam.

1664: English capture New Netherlands and change its name to New York.

1693: First printing press set up by William Bradford.

1735: John Peter Zenger acquitted in freedom of press trial.

1775: Ethan Allen captures Fort Ticonderoga from the British.

1777: First state constitution adopted at Kingston.

1783: British leave New York City. General George Washington makes his Farewell Address to his officers.

1788: New York becomes the 11th state to ratify the U.S. Constitution on July 26.

1797: Capital moved from New York City to Albany.

North Carolina

1584: Sir Walter Raleigh granted the right to colonize America by Queen Elizabeth I.

1585: Raleigh's second expedition establishes first English colony in America on Roanoke Island.

1586: Raleigh's settlement abandoned.

1587: Virginia Dare, granddaughter of Governor John White, is the first child of English parents born in America.

1629: Charles I grants territory 31 to 36 degrees North latitude to Sir Robert Heath; he names it "Carolina."

1705: First school opened in Pasquotank County. Bath is the first incorporated town in the state.

1711: Tuscarora War, Indians massacre settlers.

1729: Lands sold by seven lords to George II.

1774: Provincial congress set up at New Bern.

1775: First declaration of independence issued by citizens of Mecklenburg County.

1776: North Carolina is the first colony directing delegates to vote for independence at Continental Congress.

1789: North Carolina is the 12th state to ratify the U.S. Constitution on November 21.

1790: North Carolina cedes western lands to the U.S.

1792: Raleigh named permanent capital.

1861: May 20, North Carolina cedes from the Union.

1865: Washington Duke packs tobacco near Durham. James B. Duke founds the American Tobacco Company in 1890.

1868: North Carolina readmitted to the Union.

North Dakota

1682: The Mississippi Valley is claimed by La Salle for France.

1738: Fur trading rights granted by France in the Northwest to Pierre Gaultier de Varennes, sieur de la Verendrye; he and his sons visit the Mandan Indians in North Dakota.

1762: France gives lands claimed by La Salle to Spain; lands are secretly returned in 1800.

1763: The Treaty of Paris gives a portion of North Dakota to England.

1797: Charles Chaboillez establishes the Fur-trading North West Company at Pembina.

1800: North West Company post built at Park River; moved to Pembina in 1801.

1804-1805: Lewis and Clark winter near Stanton; Charbonneau, French fur trader, permits his Indian wife, Sacagawea, to guide them to the Pacific; Fort Mandan built.

1812: Colonists from Canada build the first white settlement at Pembina.

1818: England cedes eastern Dakota to the U.S.

1829: American Fur Company builds Fort Union on the Yellowstone River.

1831: Fort Clark erected on the Missouri River.

1853: Major I.I. Stevens surveys a railroad route.

1861: Dakota Territory organized.

1863: Upper Missouri Valley opened for homesteading.

1868: First homestead in northwestern Red River Valley by Joseph Rolette; Sioux reservations established, descendants include Wahpeton, Sisseton and Yanktonai.

1872: Northern Pacific Railway reaches Fargo; by 1873 to Bismarck; and to the West coast in 1883.

1873: Fort Abraham Lincoln built near Bismarck.

1876: Lieutenant Colonel George A. Custer departs Fort Lincoln on Indian fighting expedition to Little Bighorn River, MT.

1889: Becomes 39th state on November 2; capital, Bismarck.

Ohio

1748: Virginians create the Ohio Land Company.

1749: Land claimed for France by Pierre Joseph Celoron de Blainville.

1763: France gives Ohio country to England in the Treaty of Paris. Settlers defeat Indians led by Chief Pontiac.

1772: Moravian Indian mission founded at Schoenbrunn by David Zeisberger.

1773: First school west of the Allegheny Mountains opened.

1788: Marietta founded, first permanent white settlement in Ohio, by Rufus Putnam.

1794: General "Mad Anthony" Wayne defeats the British Indian confederation at Fallen Timbers.

1795: Treaty of Greenville opens Ohio to settlement.

1803: Becomes 17th state on March 1; capital, Chillicothe.

1809: Capital moved to Zanesville; in 1812 to Chillicothe; and in 1816 to Columbus.

Oklahoma

1541: Coronado claims land for Spain.

1682: La Salle claims all lands drained by the Mississippi

Beautifully beaded knife sheath, pipe bolder and beaded bag, by Woody Richards, Lakota-Oglala Sioux, NC. The artist gave it beaded eyes and a brain and feet—bells to restore the voice and the tail is backwards to show that the animals is in the spirit world. (Rankokus)

Skull with mandala (painted), beaded knife sheath and pony stick. (Rankokus)

Lumbee painting, first prize winner, by Karl A. Hunt, Lumbee, NC— $1,200. (Rankokus)

Top, Indian decal; center, Squaw brand canned peas label; bottom, left, Tru-Type Indian River fruit label; right, Bushkill Falls decal—$5 each. (Privately owned)

Famous Indian chiefs in color by James L. Vlasati. Top, left to right: Quanah Parker, Comanche (1845-1911); Sitting Bull, Sioux (1834-1890); Black Hawk, Sauk and Fox (1767-1838). Bottom, left to right: Geronimo, Apache (1834-1909); Tecumseh, Shawnee (1768-1813); and Osceola, Seminole (1803-1838). Set of 12—$50, 12" x 10". (Privately owned)

Six felt tourists' pennants with Indian logos—$25 set, largest is 26" long. (Privately owned)

River for France.

1762: Region ceded by France to Spain; returned to France in 1800.

1802: Frenchman, Pierre Chouteau Jr., establishes a fur trading post at Salina.

1820: Treaty of Doak's Stand gives Choctaw Indians Oklahoma lands; land occupied in 1830.

1821: Sequoyah, after 12 years of work, devises the Cherokee alphabet; moves to Oklahoma in 1828.

1824: Fort Gibson built near Neosho.

1830: Indian Removal Act passed by Congress; eastern Indians moved to Oklahoma; journey (1830-1840) known as "trail of tears."

1842: Fort Washita established on the river.

1850: Texas cedes U.S. land defining the southern boundary of the Oklahoma panhandle, north of 36 degrees 30 minutes.

1854: Border fixed at 37th parallel between Kansas and Oklahoma.

1861: Numerous Oklahoma Indians side with the Confederacy in the Civil War; fierce local skirmishes.

1866: Five Civilized Tribes free their slaves; western Oklahoma is given for settlement by other Indians.1867: Cattle drives from Texas through Oklahoma Indian Territory to Kansas railroads.

1868: Fort Sill (Camp Wichita) founded.

1889: First "run" by Homesteaders into Oklahoma.

1890: Congress creates western Oklahoma territorial government; capital, Guthrie. Panhandle added.

1893: Cherokee Outlet opened; greatest run of white settlers to claim lands.

1901: Last reservations of the Kiowa-Comanche and Wichita opened to white settlement.

1905: Five Civilized Tribes fail at Muskogee to create new state called Sequoyah.

1906: Platt National Park created. Delegates from Oklahoma and Indian territories meet at Guthrie to draft state constitution.

1907: Becomes 46th state on November 16; capital, Guthrie.

1910: Capital moved to Oklahoma City.

1920: Osage County produces oil; Osage Nation Indians become wealthy.

1940: Pensacola Dam on the Grand River forms the Lake o' the Cherokees.

1965: Western Heritage Center and Cowboy Hall of Fame (National) is dedicated at Oklahoma City.

Oregon

1775: Land claimed for Spain by Bruno Heceta.

1778: James Cook and first Americans visit Oregon.

1792: Robert Gray discovers and names the Columbia.

1805: Lewis and Clark journey to the mouth of the Columbia River; winter at Fort Clatsop.

1811: John Jacob Astor's Pacific Fur Company builds the Astoria trading post near the Columbia.

1813: Fort Astoria sold to British fur traders; renamed Fort George.

1818: British and U.S. occupy Oregon jointly.

1819: Spain renounces their claim north of 42 degrees North latitude.

1824: Russia gives up its claim south of 54 degrees and 40 minutes; Fort Vancouver built.

1834: Fort William built by Nathaniel Wyeth.

1835: Mission school established by Jason and Daniel Lee in Willamette Valley.

1843: Great migration of about 900 arrives over the Oregon Trail.

1845: Portland is founded.

1846: Treaty with England gives U.S. Oregon country.

1847: Indians massacre missionaries Marcus Whitman and his wife.

1859: On February 14, becomes 33rd state; capital, Salem.

1872-1873: Modoc War.

1878-1880: Bannock and Paiute Indians terrorize settlers in eastern and central Oregon.

1884: Railroad links Oregon with the East.

Pennsylvania

1609: Henry Hudson enters the Delaware Bay.

1638: New Sweden established by the Swedes on the Delaware River.

1651: Peter Stuyvesant builds Fort Casimir on New Castle, Delaware site.

1654: Swedes seize Fort Casimir.

1655: Stuyvesant and the Dutch recapture Fort Casimir.

1664: Duke of York's rule established.

1681: King Charles II grants Pennsylvania to William Penn; Duke of York leases Three Lower Counties to Penn in 1682.

1682: Philadelphia laid out by Penn; becomes capital in 1685. Penn deals favorably with the Delaware Indians (Lenni-Lenape), signs several treaties of friendship.

1683: June 23, by the treaty signed at Shackamaxon, the Indians grant land to Penn. Colonists and Indians would "live in love as long as the sun gave light." Quakers and Mennonites found Germantown.

1701: Penn grants Charter of Privileges to the colony.

1755: French and Indians defeat British in battle on the Monongahela River; Indians terrorize the area.

1758: Indians make peace with the colonists at Easton.

1763: Pontiac War with Indians breaks out. Charles Mason and Jeremiah Dixon survey Pennsylvania-Maryland boundary.

1768: Treaty of Fort Stanwix settles some Indian problems.

1774: First Continental Congress meets in Philadelphia.

1775: Second Continental Congress meets.

1776: Declaration of Independence signed at Philadelphia.

1777: British defeat the Americans at Brandywine; occupy Philadelphia. General George Washington is defeated at Germantown; camps at Valley Forge.

1778: British leave Philadelphia; Congress returns. Tories and Iroquois Indians attack the town of Wyoming and massacre men, women, and children.

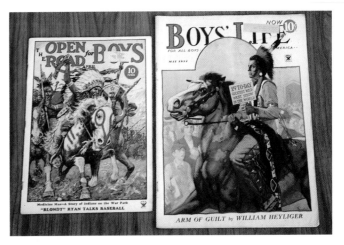

Maganize covers. Left, The Open Road for Boys, April 1934—$3; right, Boys' Life, May 1934, artist William Reusswig—$5. (Privately owned)

Colored illustration by M.L. Kirk, from The Story of Hiawatha, 1910, "Pleasant Was the Journey Home," one of 12 in the series—$75 for the complete book, 9-1/2" x 7" wide. (Privately owned)

A grouping of four felt-printed Indian/cigarette premium banners—$5 each, 8-1/8" long x 5-3/4" wide. (Privately owned)

Birch bark grouping: top, Chippewa calling horn, bark stripped designs of leaves, flying geese and moose—$125; bottom, left, covered container trimmed in black string and sweet grass, Northeast, Chippewa—$85; Indian tourist canoe with Skookum doll—$75. (Privately owned)

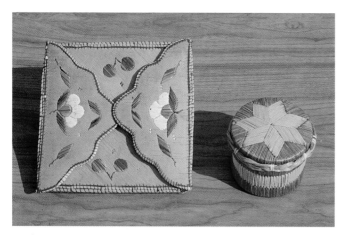

Left to right, birch bark hanky box, 7-1/2" square, Micmac, dyed porcupine quills with a floral design—$85; cylindrical lidded Chippewa container, 2-3/4" high, beautifully decorated in porcupine quills, stamped "Joe and Libby Meuse"—$125. (Privately owned)

Hardwood hinged box, 4-1/2" diameter x 3" high, Indian litho marked "Nomans Heart." The interior of the lid states in black ink, "Souvenir–117th Time The Round Up–Dec - 20 - 1907–Broadway Theatre," red felt lining—$125. (Privately owned)

1787: On December 12, becomes 2nd state to ratify the U.S. Constitution.

1790: Philadelphia becomes U.S. capital.

1799: State capital moved to Lancaster; and to Harrisburg in 1812.

1800: National capital moved to Washington, D.C.

Rhode Island

1636: Roger Williams flees Massachusetts; founds Providence.

1638: Narraganset Chief Canonicus deeds land to Williams.

1639: John Clarke and William Coddington found Newport. First Baptist church in America formed at Providence.

1642: Warwick (Shawomet) is sold by the Indians to Samuel Gorton.

1644: Aquidneck Island renamed Rhode Island.

1647: Four original towns form the first General Assembly.

1675: Power of the Narraganset Indians broken by Great Swamp Fight in King Philip's War.

1708: Triangular Trade of rum, slaves and molasses begins.

1727: First printing press set up at Newport.

1776: Rhode Island is the first colony to declare independence.

1778: Articles of Confederation adopted by Rhode Island.

1790: Rhode Island is the 13th state to ratify the U.S. Constitution.

South Carolina

1562: Jean Ribaut founds Port Royal as a French colony.

1566: Spanish build Fort San Felipe on Parris Island.

1629: King Charles I grants 31 to 36 degrees North latitude to Sir Robert Heath.

1665: King Charles II grants to eight lords Carolina charter, 29 degrees to 36 degrees and 30 minutes North latitude.

1670: Charles Town, first permanent English settlement in Carolina.

1680: Madagascar rice introduced.

1715: Yamasee attack settlers; subdued by 1716.

1760: Cherokee attack settlers; fighting ends in 1761.

1783: Charles Town renamed Charleston.

1786: Capital moved to Columbia.

1788: On May 23, South Carolina is the 8th state to ratify the U.S. Constitution.

South Dakota

1743: Francois and Louis Joseph Verendrye claim land for Spain; place lead plate in the ground near Fort Pierre; recovered in 1913.

1785: Pierre Dorion establishes home along the James River.

1804: Lewis and Clark travel the Missouri River on their way to the Pacific.

1807: U.S. troops and Indians fight near Grand River.

1812: Fur traders build Fort Manuael near present Kenel.

1813: Indians destroy Fort Manuel; Manuel Lisa constructs new post near Big Bend.

1817: Fort Pierre is the first permanent white settlement erected by Joseph La Framboise.

1822: Columbia Fur Company rebuilds post as Fort Tecumseh.

1823: Ree Indians attack General William Ashley and his party near Grand River; attack avenged by Colonel Henry Leavenworth.

1832: American Fur Company rebuilds Fort Tecumseh as Fort Pierre.

1856: Indians and General W.S Harney hold council at Fort Pierre; Fort Randall is constructed on the Missouri River.

1858: Sioux give lands from the Missouri River to Big Sioux River.

1861: Dakota Territory organized; capital, Yankton.

1862: War of the Outbreak, Sioux rise in Minnesota; kill settlers near Sioux Falls, the rest are evacuated.

1866: Grasshopper plague; severe again 1874-1877. Chief Red Cloud resists Montana road survey.

1868: End of Red Cloud War; Sioux Reservation set up west of Missouri River in Dakota area.

1874: Expedition led by Custer finds gold in Black Hills.

1876: Indians attack illegal settlers in the Black Hills. Sioux turn over the Black Hills to the U.S.; Homestake gold lode found.

1883: Bismarck is the territorial capital.

1889: On November 2, becomes 40th state.

1890: State's last Indian trouble, Messiah War; Sitting Bull killed near Little Eagle; Wounded Knee Indian massacre.

1910: Pierre becomes the state capital.

1973: American Indian Movement members occupy town of Wounded Knee for 70 days.

Tennessee

1541: De Soto camps near Memphis site.

1665: English charter to Carolina Company includes Tennessee.

1682: La Salle claims the Mississippi Valley for France; Fort Prudhomme built at Memphis.

1757: Fort Loudoun completed; captured by the Cherokees in 1760.

1760: Daniel Boone explores eastern Tennessee.

1763: France gives area east of the Mississippi River, including Tennessee, to England.

1769: First permanent white settler, William Bean, builds a cabin near Watauga River.

1775: Transylvania Land Company purchases Cherokee lands.

1786: Davy Crockett born at Limestone.

1796: On June 1, becomes 16th state.

1813: General Andrew Jackson begins Creek War.

1818: U.S. purchases western Tennessee from the Chickasaw Indians.

1843: Nashville becomes the state capital.

1861: Tennessee is the last state to cede from the Union.

1866: First state to be readmitted to the Union.

Original framed print of an Indian maiden, Minneota, in canoe with bow and arrow—$45. In the background, a 1930-1950s Navajo blanket—$75, 8-1/2" high x 6-1/4" wide. (Privately owned)

Top, framed Indian print, a lesson in weaving—$65; bottom, Indian, "The Great Spirit," 9" high x 7" wide, lifting his spirit in prayer—$45. (Privately owned)

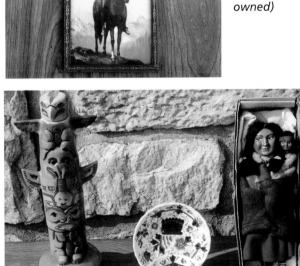

Left to right, Ezra Brook liquor totem, 1972, Heritage China—$25; Gaudy Welsh War Bonnet cup and saucer—$135; Skookum doll in its original box, box is 12-1/2" long, rare and mint—$225. (Privately owned)

Collectible Indian Barbie series: 1992, first edition—$50;
1993, second edition—$30; 1994, third edition—$25.
(Privately owned)

Custom designed and dressed 30" female Indian doll, 1996, limited edition, by John Eastman—$350. Called "Sunflower," the doll took one month to complete. (Privately owned)

Pipe tomahawk, brass head with nice patina, original hardwood handle—$800, 16" long, deacquisition number C 8559. (Privately owned)

Texas

1519: Coast explored by Alonso de Pineda.

1541: Coronado crosses the Panhandle.

1685: La Salle founds Fort St. Louis on Garcitas Creek.

1691: Texas becomes a Spanish dominion; first mission is built, San Franciso de los.

1803: France sells Louisiana to the U.S.

1823: Stephen F. Austin founds San Felipe de Austin.

1836: Texas declares its independence. Alamo falls to Santa Anna. General Sam Houston captures Santa Anna in San Jacinto battle. Houston made president of the Republic of Texas; capital, Columbia.

1837: U.S. recognizes the independence of Texas; Houston is capital from 1837-1839.

1839: Austin is capital from 1839-1842; Cherokee expelled.

1845: Becomes 28th state on December 29; capital, Austin.

1866-1885: Cattle driven to Northern markets on trails.

1870: Texas readmitted to the Union.

1881: Southern Pacific joins Texas and California.

Utah

1540: Garcia L. de Cardenas and his men sight Utah.

1776: Fathers Francisco Dominguez and Silvestre de Escalante explore Utah seeking a route from New Mexico to California.

1821: Mexico claims Utah.

1824: Jim Bridger discovers the Great Salt Lake.

1826: First overland expedition to California led by Jedediah Smith.

1832: Uinta Basin trading post built by Antoine Robidou.

1841: First wagon trains are led by Captain John Bartleson from Utah to California.

1844-1845: Fort Buenaventura built by Miles Goodyear.

1847: First Mormons arrive in the area of Great Salt Lake; communal irrigation.

1848: Mexico gives Utah to the U.S. in Treaty of Guadalupe-Hidalgo.

1849: State of Deseret organized by the Mormons; capital, Salt Lake City.

1852: Mormons permit plural marriages as church rule.

1853: Walker War with the Ute Indians begins over Indian slavery; settled in 1854.

1868: Ute-Black Hawk War ends major Indian conflicts in Utah.

1896: January 4, becomes 45th state; capital, Salt Lake City.

Vermont

1609: Samuel de Champlain discovers lake which is named for him.

1666: French build Fort St. Anne on Isle La Motte.

1724: Fort Drummer built by Massachusetts colonists to fight the French and Indians; first permanent white settlement in Vermont.

1759: During the French and Indian Wars the British drive the French from the Lake Champlain region.

1763: France gives the area to England.

1791: On March 4, becomes 14th state.

1805: Montpelier chosen as state capital.

Virginia

1606: Two companies chartered to colonize Virginia under King James I.

1607: Jamestown founded; first permanent English settlement in North America; John Smith leads the colony.

1610: Colonists leave Jamestown.

1612: Cultivation of tobacco begins under John Rolfe.

1622: Indians massacre many colonists.

1699: Capital moved from Jamestown to Williamsburg.

1716: First theater built in the U.S. at Williamsburg.

1776: Virginia declares independence.

1779: Richmond becomes the state capital.

1784: Virginia cedes its northwestern lands to the U.S.

1788: June 26, becomes 10th state.

1861: Virginia leaves the Union.

1865: Lee surrenders to Grant near Appomattox to end the Civil War.

1870: Virginia readmitted to the Union.

1926: John D. Rockefeller Jr., restores Williamsburg.

Washington

1579: Francis Drake names the area New Albion.

1774: Juan Perez visits Washington coast.

1775: Washington area is claimed for Spain by Bruno Heceta.

1788: Trading post named Mount Olympus is built on Vancouver Island by Captain John Meares.

1811: Pacific Fur Company establishes Fort Okanogan.

1813: Britain buys Pacific Fur trading posts.

1825: Fort Vancouver is built for the Hudson Bay Company on the Columbia River by John McLoughlin.

1834: Mission on the Willamette River founded by Jason Lee.

1836: Waiilatpu Mission built near Walla Walla by Marcus Whitman.

1846: Britain cedes to U.S. all claims south of 49 degrees latitude.

1847: Whitman family massacred by the Cayuse Indians.

1848: Oregon Territory created including Washington.

1853: Washington Territory capital, Olympia.

1854-1855: Indian treaties negotiated with Governor Isaac I. Stevens; Indian Wars begin and end in 1858.

1883: Northern Pacific ties Washington to the East.

1889: November 11, becomes 42nd state.

1893: Great Northern Railroad completed to Seattle.

West Virginia

1609: Area granted by English king to the Virginia colony.

1725: Fur traders enter the area west of the Appalachians.

1768: Iroquois give land north of Little Kanawha River to the British in the Treaty of Fort Stanwix.

1774: Indians defeated in Lord Dunmore's War.

1776: Fort Fincastle renamed Fort Henry.

1782: Indians and the British attack Fort Henry.

1788: Virginia becomes part of the U.S.

China plates: left to right, Wedgwood 1982 calendar with 12 panels, 10" diameter—$35; Americus Hotel, Allentown, Indian logo, manufactured by Maddock, England, 9" diameter—$25. (Privately owned)

Left to right, Jamestown's 350 Anniversary plate (1607-1957), Homer Laughlin—$35; rare Indian plate, Spotted Wolf, by Haynes, Baltimore, Chesapeake Pottery, 1879-1910, 13" diameter—$250. (Privately owned)

Left to right, china Frankoma trivet showing the "Seals of Five Civilized Tribes of Indians in Oklahoma"—$25; Van Briggle, Colorado Springs, matte green Indian woman kneading dough—$200; tired warrior stand and plaque, from blended clay and Mount St. Helen's ash—$50. (Privately owned)

Plaster of Paris group: left, 10-1/2" bust of Hiawatha—$75; center, 20-1/2" bust, Arapahoe—$200; 15" chief—$125. (Privately owned)

Carnival chalkware painted and glittered Indian on horse, 10-1/2" high—$45; center, hollow plaster Indian, 4-1/4" high—$20; detailed plaster Indian wall plaque, 14" high—$100. (Privately owned)

Grouping of four sterling silver rings with turquoise settings, Southwest, bear claw—$250; others—$100 each. (Privately owned)

1794: Indian attacks into West Virginia halted by Wayne's victory at Fallen Timbers, OH.

1853: Baltimore and Ohio Railroad reaches Wheeling.

1863: June 20, becomes 35th state; capital, Wheeling

1896: First rural free delivery in the U.S. begins

Wisconsin

1634: Jean Nicolet of France, emissary of Samuel de Champlain, lands near Green Bay.

1661: First Wisconsin missionary, Father Rene Menard visits Chequamegon Bay.

1665: Permanent mission is founded at Chequamegon Bay, by Father Claude Allouez.

1763: France gives Wisconsin to the British.

1783: British give Wisconsin to the U.S.

1814: Fort Shelby built.

1816: Fort Crawford and Fort Howard erected.

1832: Sauk Indians defeated in Black Hawk War.

1836: Wisconsin Territory organized; capital, Madison.

1848: May 29, becomes 30th state.

1856: First U.S. kindergarten opens in Watertown.

1864: First cheese factory opens at Ladoga.

1868: Christopher Sholes invents the typewriter in Milwaukee.

1918: Wisconsin is the first state to use numbers on highways.

Wyoming

1807: John Colter discovers the Yellowstone area.

1822: Trading post established on Yellowstone River by General William Ashley.

1834: Fort William is the first permanent Wyoming trading post; later it will be called Fort Laramie.

1836: First women to cross the Continental Divide are Mrs. H.H. Spalding and Mrs. Marcus Whitman accompanying their missionary husbands.

1843: Jim Bridger founds Fort Bridger in Uinta County.

1847: Brigham Young leads the Mormons across Wyoming.

1860: Express Companies include: Pikes Peak, California, Overland and Central. Pony Express crosses Wyoming until 1861.

1865: Fort Reno established after the Indians attack settlers on the Platte River.

1867: Cheyenne is founded.

1868: Wyoming Territory is created; Cheyenne becomes the capital in 1869. Indian peace treaty signed at Fort Laramie.

1869: The Union Pacific joins Wyoming with the East and West coasts.

1872: Yellowstone National Park created.

1876: Stage Lines join Black Hills and Cheyenne.

1890: On July 10, becomes 44th state; capital,

Heavily beaded museum-quality Sioux moccasins, 1880-1900, thick soles—$1,600, 11-1/2" long. (Privately owned)

Beaded examples on soft hides: left, elaborate five-color, drawstring pouch, 6-1/2" long, signed in ink on the inside, "Made by Daisy Star in Kingfisher, Oklahoma, June 1917"—$350; child's embroidered Canadian moccasins,2-1/2" x 5-1/2"—$150. (Privately owned)

Rare land deed from the Choctaw-Chickasaw Nations, 80 acres in Oklahoma to David G. Williams for $132.50, dated, stamped and signed, Feb. 15, 1918 and Nov. 18 and 20, 1918—$400. (Privately owned)

Elaborately beaded trinket tourist boot, beaver, fox and leaves, 11" high—$175. (Privately owned)

Beaded tourist canoe on heavy canvas, ca. 1930, "From Niagara Falls," 7" long—$95. (Privately owned)

Left to right, glass Masonic mug, Indian painted face, silver Syrian sword handle, raised lettering "Saratoga," acid-etched "Pittsburgh 1903," 3-1/4" high—$200; center, hand-carved canoe, marked, "Germany," with Indian and shooting companion, 10-1/2" long—$35; right, ceramic Indian match holder, stamped on the base, "Quality Guaranteed, Japan," 3-1/4" high—$25. (Privately owned)

Toy weaving looms with dolls, Navajo, 1940-1950. Left example has a round paper label on the base, "Made by American Indians"—$35; right, signed on the upright beam, "Lorraine Smith, Chinle, Arizona, 86503"—$65. Tallest is 10" high. (Privately owned)

Left, 1900 Plains Indian doll, beaded, hide clothing—$200; right, painted Plains hand drum, 1880s, hide stretched on wood, tied with sinew, 10" high, 9" diameter—$500. (Privately owned)

Grouping of three 1960s sand paintings—$20 each. The tallest is 9" high. (Privately owned)

Assorted miniature grouping of sewing baskets, pin cushion, and scissors holder; woven of splints and sweet grass, Mohawk—$150 for the grouping. Smallest is 1-1/8" high. (Privately owned)

Indian yarn or string holders with lids and braided rope handles, ca. 1910, probably Maine, splint and sweet grass, popular with tourists—$100 each, 7-3/4" high, 10" high. (Privately owned)

Dried animal skull with horns, 12" high x 12" wide, depicts "Kicking Bear—A Sioux apostle of the ghost dance religion." Artist signed "Gary Monsey, Okl., 1993"—$450. (Privately owned)

Contemporary limited-edition ceramics by Stan Padilla, 1994. Top left, "Little Bluebird's Lullaby," Iroquois, second edition—$200; top right, "Little Buffalo's Story," Black-foot—$200; bottom right, "Swift Beaver's Journey," Chip-pewa—$200; "Morning Star's Doll," Seminole—$100. (Privately owned)

Bookends: cast iron chiefs, silvered—$75 pair; cast iron painted and bronzed Indians, 3" high—$100 pair. (Privately owned)

Cast bronze buffalo, Austria, marble mount—$150; tired warrior cast bronze bookends, "The End of the Trail," 5-3/4" high—$125 pair. (Privately owned)

Framed Russell print, 1877, with inset feather and arrowhead—$250. (Privately owned)

Unusual two-view painting on panel board, Indian and erotic nude, signed "1939—Ed Magudes"—$500, 25" wide x 31" high. (Privately owned)

Detailed Indian chief painted on soft-tanned steer hide, New England, early 20th century, 36" wide x 40" long—$225. (Privately owned)

Contemporary oil painting, ca. 1960s, on canvas, signed "C. Emery," 30" high x 25" wide—$500. (Privately owned)

Five chiefs illustrated by James L. Vlasaty for M.A. Dono-hue & Co., Chicago, IL. Top, left to right, "Red Jacket," Seneca (1756-1830); "Dull Knife," Cheyenne (1828?-1879); "Yoholo-Micco," Creek (1790-1838); bottom, left to right, Chief Joseph, Nez Perce (1840-1904); and "Red Cloud," Sioux (1822-1909), 10" wide and 12" long—$10 each. (Privately owned)

Indian symbol postcard—$5. (Privately owned)

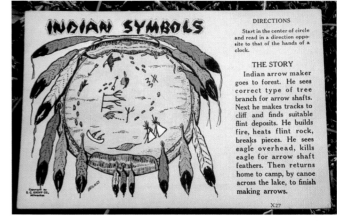

Indian symbol postcard—$5. (Privately owned)

Postcards. Top, Piegan Indian warrior—$6; middle, children, 1905—$5; "Miss Two Lances," Cheyenne—$5; "Hattie Tom," 1904, Chiricahua Apache—$6. Bottom row, Julia Buck and Family, Utes—$6; "Maha Boy," Omaha Indian—$5; and "Man-Going-Up-Hill," Araphoe—$5. (Privately owned)

Postcards. Top, left to right, Mad Bear, Chief "Bear Goes in the Woods," Chief "Yellow Hair" and Chief "Little White Cloud." Printed by Cummin's Wild West Indian Congress—$5 each. Bottom, left to right: silk, 1904—$6.50; Buffalo Bill's Wild West Show—$9; 1904 BBWWS—$9; Chief "Flat Iron," Sioux—$9. (Privately owned)

Postcards. Top, unusual card from the Nederland—$5; middle left, by Tuck, "Chief Not Afraid of Pawnee"—$6; right, "Pelone," Ute Brave—$6; bottom, an Eskimo Walrus Hunter, Alaska—$6. (Privately owned)

Postcards. From an American Indian Series—$10 each, by Raphael Tuck & Sons, England. Top, Cheyenne, Navajo and Sioux; bottom, Muscalero Apache. (Privately owned)

Grouping of eight postcards, top six— $5 each; bottom two—$9 each. Row one, left to right, Chief "Afraid of Eagle," Chief "Bear Goes in the Woods" and Chief "Black-hawk." Row two, Chief "Yellow Hair," Chief "Tall Crane" and Chief "Lone Wolf." Bottom row, Chief Wolf Robe, Cheyenne, 1903; and Chief Hollow Horn Bear, 1906. (Privately owned)

Postcards. Top left, Chief "White Eagle," Cherokee; right, a Seminole Indian brave and his wife on the Florida reservation; middle, Pueblo Indian women making pottery, 1951; bottom, Native Skookum Indian papooses, British Columbia, Canada, "Fair and Dry, Wet and Stormy"—all cards are $2 each. (Privately owned)

Postcards. Top left, Navajo women making a rug, 1946; top right, Ottawa Indian of Northern Michigan playing a Tom-Tom; bottom left, Indian Totem Poles, Thunderbird Park, Victoria, British Columbia, Canada; bottom right, Indian Village, St. Ignace, MI—$2 each. (Privately owned)

Postcards. Top, 1938 Greetings from the Southwest; middle, a cute "Honest Injun" saying; bottom, sign language for "Indian kill buffalo"—$3 each. (Privately owned)

Chapter 6

NATIVE AMERICAN HISTORY: UNITED STATES

1500: Spaniards were to teach the Indians Christianity and use their labor as "vassals of the crown." Many of Columbus's successors explored the Gulf Coast, Florida and Mexico.

1501: Inuits in Greenland, more than 50, are kidnapped by the Portuguese and taken to Lisbon.

1503: Trade is established between English fishermen off the Atlantic Coast and Indian tribes including the Abenakis, Passamaquoddy, Penobscots, Malacites and Micmacs.

1504: Amerigo Vespucci, a Florentine, on his second voyage proposes that this is a new world, America, is named after him.

1506-1518: French fishermen trade with the Huron and Iroquois in Canada along the St. Lawrence River.

1511: A debate is raised in the Spanish community as Father Antonio de Montesinos in a sermon asks "if Indians are men and have souls?"

1513: The Calusas a southwestern Florida tribe learn of Ponce de Leon's brutality and drive him off with 80 war canoes.

1515: *The Historia de las Indias* by Bartolome de Las Casas describes the cruelty of Spaniards toward the Arawaks.

1521: The Calusas resist Ponce de Leon's second expedition; Ponce de Leon dies from a poison dart to the thigh.

1523-1524: Accounts are given of Verrazano's Atlantic Coastal travels and trade with the Narragansetts, Delaware and Wampanoag.

1528: A group of 400 Spanish settlers led by Panfilo de Narvaez attempt to start a colony near Tampa, Florida. The Timcua Indians drive them off.

1534: Frenchman Jacques Cartier travels to the coast of Labrador and establishes friendly terms with the Micmic Indians.

1535: Jacques Cartier's second voyage to Quebec and Montreal leads him to Chief Donnacona, a St. Lawrence Iroquois. Their friendship brings about goods and furs exchanges. The chief's two sons go back to France.

1535-1541: Cartier learns the ways of the Iroquois and the Algonquin; brewing white cedar tea prevents vitamin C deficiency. Ten chiefs travel with Cartier to France; Chief Donnacona dies there.

1539: The Zuni kill Estevanico, sent ahead of Coronado as an inspector. De Soto destroys the Timcua of Florida, looting and taking men and women as slaves.

1540: De Soto reaches the Creeks in South Carolina and receives mica, corn and fresh-water pearls. He takes the niece of the chief with him to guard his way. De Soto crosses the Appalachian Mountains and discovers the Coosas. They wear elaborate feather headresses, build great temple mounds and arrange their homes geometrically. De Soto stays for one month. The Mobiles of Alabama fight the Spanish and lose. Thousands of Indians died. De Soto spends the winter in abandoned Chickasaw towns; recovers from his wounds. The Southwest is searched by Coronado to discover the "seven cities of gold." The Zuni of Arizona fight and are defeated. The Hopi pueblo of Awatovi comes in contact with the Spanish; they view the Grand Canyon.

Three variegated splint painted baskets, ca. 1840s, Eastern Algonkian. Top two have stamped designs, New England and New York State—$1,000 for the grouping. Bottom basket measures 11-1/2" high x 17-1/2" wide. (Privately owned)

Grouping, left to right, two red fox furs—$35 each; Northeast basket with handles, Mohegan, 1875-1900 in "Twist Weave" or "Porcupine Twist"— $125; corn meal sifter, hickory splint, Seneca, 18-1/2" diameter— $100; contemporary drum—$100; Navajo woven rug, ca. 1930— $100. (Privately owned)

Back row, left, Papago Arizona contemporary round tray, 8-1/2" diameter, Feather Stitch—$35; Papago basket from Sells, AZ, two-banded stepline design by Mary Tanacio at Topawa, created from coiled beargrass, bleached yucca leaves, willow shoots and brown yucca root, ca. 1920s, 3" high x 10" wide—$100. Bottom row, left, Papago, first half of the 20th century, "Feather Stitches"—$100; Hopi pottery bowl, 1925, signed "Namoki," white slip with red and black designs polychromed, 3" high x 5" wide—$150; right, Pima woven basket, 7" diameter—$100. (Privately owned)

Contemporary bow and arrows made in the traditional manner—$300. (Privately owned)

Contemporary painted tortoise-shell beaded stem rattle and pipe—$200. (Privately owned)

Contemporary painted buffalo jaw bone club—$85. (Privately owned)

1541-1542: Quigaltam, chief and spiritual head, of the Natchez nation meets De Soto. The chief is carried on a litter, has a flattened head and is tattooed over his body in red, black and blue designs.

1542: De Soto dies; his successor is Luis de Moscoso who travels as far as Texas, turns around and follows the Mississippi River to the Gulf of Mexico. Coronado is fooled by his Pawnee slave/guide; no cities of gold are found; back home in Spain he is tried for Indian cruelty and army mismanagement.

1542-1543: Cartier searches with no success for precious metals in Canada. Conditions between him and the Stadacona Iroquois deteriorate.

1543: De Soto meets with the Tonkawa in eastern Texas, then heads for the Mississippi River and the Gulf of Mexico. Natchez war canoes pursue the Spanish who escape.

1562: To escape persecution, French Huguenots occupy South Carolina.

1563: French artist, Jacques Le Moyne draws the South Carolina Indians.

1566: The Spanish invade the Calusa Indians; the young chief and 20 of his warriors are beheaded. The Calusa retaliate by burning their capital and abandoning the island. Survivors became, with the Creeks, the Seminoles of Florida.

1570: A Spanish mission is established on the Chesapeake Bay in Maryland by seven Jesuits; they are killed by Powhatans or residents.

1580: Disease and slavery raids wipe out dozens of Indian villages in Newfoundland.

1587: Corn is introduced to the English by the North Carolina Indians.

1590-1598: Mexican Spanish travel through the Rio Grande Valley; the governor of New Mexico is Juan de Onate. Groups are driven by the Apache and the Pueblo; in 1598 a colony is established at San Juan Pueblo.

1597: Georgia coastal Indians, the Guale, rebel against the Spanish missions.

1598: Juan de Zaldivar tries to have the Acoma submit to the Spanish crown; he is killed along with 800 Indians. New Mexico governor had women 12 to 25 indentured for 20 years at San Juan. Males over 12 had one foot chopped off. Later, governor Juan de Onate was tried for cruelty.

1600: New Mexico is colonized for Spain by Juan Onate; the Indians are "protected" in exchange for work and products. Apaches, Utes and Navajos are sold to silver mining camps in the south.

1603: Samuel de Champlain travels south to Cape Cod and makes contact with Algonquin and Iroquois tribes.

1604: A trade agreement takes place between the French and Canadian Micmac, giving the French rights in their provinces. Chief Membertou begins trade at Port Royal with the French.

1606: The Pueblo, Jemez and Navajo fight with the Spanish, take their horses and trade them.

1607: Powhatan or Chief Wahunsonacock ruled 30 tribes and aided the English at Jamestown, VA. John Smith's men were given game, fish and corn.

1608: John Smith asks Powhatan to submit to the English Crown. Champlain is greeted by the Iroquois nation. A French trading post is constructed at the former Iroquois village, Stadacona.

1609: As more settlers arrived war broke out between Powhatan and the English. The gentry did not wish to work and attempted to drive the Indians from their cleared fields and villages. Champlain helps the Montagnais of Canada and the Algonquins fight against the Mohawks giving them guns and powder. Henry Hudson trades furs in the Netherlands (New York) with the Lenape, Mohican, Munsee, Hackensack and the Manhattan. Catholic missions are created in Santa Fe; Navajo women and children are sold into slavery. The Huron travel to Quebec City to buy muskets from Jacques Cartier.

1610: Lord Delaware stays at Jamestown one year; named the Bay the Delaware and the Indians Delaware (Lenape).

1612: The Iroquois trade with the Dutch on the Hudson. Powhatan instructs the English in cultivating tobacco.

1613: As more settlers laid claims to lands in Jamestown for the growing of tobacco, Indian tempers flared; there was killing on both sides and prisoners. Pocahontas, the chief's daughter, was taken. The English offered to return her for all English prisoners. Upon the release, she stayed, took the name Rebecca and agreed to marry widower, John Rolfe. The French arm the Micmacs, fighting against the Beothuk, who have a bounty on their scalps.

1614: Pocahontas marries John Rolfe on April 5, 1614. John Smith refers to the northern Atlantic Coast as "New England." Squanto, also called "Tisquantum," is kidnapped along with 23 others by Captain Thomas Hunt. He is sold in a Spanish slave market, ransomed by monks, escapes to England and in 1619 returns to North America.

1615: Rebecca Rolfe gives birth to a son, Thomas. The Huron, numbering 30,000, welcomed Samuel de Champlain to Huronia, near Lake Simcoe.

1615-1649: Huron-French fur trading relations at their peak.

1616-1619: Smallpox destroys complete villages of New England Indians from Maine to Massachusetts.

1617: Pocahontas dies in England and is buried at Graveshead in an unmarked grave. Later her son returns to Virginia to become wealthy growing tobacco.

1618: Powhatan dies; his brother who is much more hostile, becomes the new leader. Opechancanough creates 25 years of dislike between the English and the Powhatan.

1619: A school is created for Indian children in Jamestown in an attempt to sway them to Christianity. Squanto visits his deserted village, Patuxet; meets with Chief Massasoit.

1620: Pilgrims land at Plymouth on December 21 aboard the *Mayflower*.

1621: Wampanoag chief, Massasoit, formed a peace agreement with the Pilgrims, using Squanto to translate.

1621: New Mexico ranchers are given permission to use Pueblo men on horseback.

1621-1660: Over 40,000 colonists arrive in the Massachusetts Bay Colony. Exclusive use of land and private property were not terms that the Indians understood.

1622: Powhatan uprising, the burning of Jamestown, 350 colonists are killed. Friends to the Powhatan, the Chickaminy were almost destroyed by the English.

1623: False English-Powhatan peace conference; Indians are poisoned and shot. Peace came in 1632 with massive colonial expansion; the Powhatans were reduced in population from 30,000 to 2,000.

Contemporary large tortoise shell rattle with feathers and beading—$150. (Privately owned)

Left to right, top, double-spout jar, signed "R.L. Natseway Leguna '84," molded, polychromed—$75; Hopi, 1925 painted bowl, signed "Namoki"—$190. Front left, signed "Yepa-Jemez," double wedding jar—$50; right, Acoma vase, New Mexico, Thunderbird decor, signed "Acoma NM-CC"—$50. (Privately owned)

Miniatures, left to right, Seminole doll, 2"—$25; beading loom, 4"—$25. (Privately owned)

Contemporary dart game made by the author from straw, corn cobs, feathers and corn shocks—$50. (Privately owned)

Color plate, "Seven Long Nights And Day He Sat There," from The Story of Hiawatha, 1910, by M.L. Kirk—$75 for the book. (Privately owned)

"SEVEN LONG DAYS AND NIGHTS HE SAT THERE"—Page 293

Color plate, "And Each Figure Had A Meaning," from The Story of Hiawatha, 1910, by M.L. Kirk— $75 for the book. (Privately owned)

"AND EACH FIGURE HAD A MEANING"—Page 236

1624: Fort Orange erected at Albany by the Dutch West India Company.

1626: The island of Manhattan is bought from the Shinnecock Indians for 60 Dutch guilders, about $24.

1629-1633: Spanish missions use forced labor to build churches at the Hopi, Zuni and Acoma pueblos.

1632: English settlers use Indians as slaves on their tobacco plantations. Brief peace exists between the Chickahominy and the Pamunkey Indians in central Virginia.

1633: The Zuni revolted, killing the Spanish soldiers and two Catholic missionaries.

1633: Government of Massachusetts Colony is centralized to deal with Indian problems.

1633-1635: Smallpox travels through New Netherlands, New England and New France colonies; 10,000 Huron die.

1635: Beaver Wars begin between the Iroquois and the Huron.

1636: Roger Williams founds Rhode Island due to Massachusetts Bay Colony treatment of the Indians. In Providence, Church and State become separate.

1636-1637: Pequot War, May 26, 1637, Captain John Mason and 200 Mohegan and Narragansett set fire to the Pequot fort killing 700 men, women and children.

1636-1640: Iroquois and Huron Wars in the St. Lawrence area.

1637: The Ute become powerful with the acquisition of the horse.

1638: English Puritans take most of the Quinnipiacs' land with an agreement that leaves only 1,200 acres for a reservation.

1639: Taos Indians leave New Mexico and travel with Spanish horses to Kansas. Here they introduce the animal to the southern Plains Indians, the Kiowa, Comanche and Wichita.

1640: Dakota bands as a result of dispute left northern Minnesota and migrated to the Great Plains. Ursuline nuns in Canada taught the Hurons and Northeast Indians embroidery and European florals as part of their beadwork.

1641: Five Iroquois Nations attempt to make peace with the French and negotiate with the Huron.

1642: Roger William's Algonquin-English dictionary is published in London making it the first Native American dictionary. Montreal is founded by the French. Lord Calvert's Maryland settlers defeat the Susquehannocks.

1643: The Susquehannocks with the help of Sweden defeated Lord Calvert.

1643-1701: Iroquois Wars.

1644: Second Powhatan uprising in Virginia.

1646: John Eliot translated the Bible into Algonquin trying to convert Massachusetts Indians to Christianity.

1649: The Iroquois defeat the Huron, combining the forces of the Mohawks and the Senecas.

1650: Zuni Mountain Apaches war against Spain. The Iroquois massacre the Nipissing near Lake Nipissing, Ontario.

1654: The Iroquois expand in the Great Lakes with trade wars attacking the Chippewa, Illinois, Ottawa, Shawnee, Cheyenne and the Huron. The Michigan Peninsula is almost uninhabited.

1655: Ojibwa attack the Iroquois in Michigan, near Sault Ste. Marie. The Timcua Rebellion in Florida and the end of the nation.

1656: Jesuit mission is established by the French at Onondaga, NY. In two years an epidemic had killed numerous adults and 500 children. The Iroquois wipe out the Erie tribe in the Lakes area.

1658: The Mohawks destroy the Onondaga mission.

1659: Measles kills 10,000 Florida Indians.

1659-1660: The French trade furs in the Hudson Bay area using the name, Rupert's Land Company; trade with the Cree Indians and also intermarry.

1661: The Chippewa were pushed west by the French and the Iroquois. They invaded Minnesota Sioux territory. Later the Sioux moved west to the Plains. Sioux dialects include: Santee, Yankton and Teton. Subgroups of the Teton Sioux are Hunkpapa, Oglala, Sans Arc, Blackfoot, Two Kettle, Brule and Miniconjou. Spanish missions on the Savannah River are attacked by Georgia Indians and abandoned. The Spanish raid underground kivas and burn hundreds of religious objects and kachina masks, outlaw dance and religion. Massasoit dies. His two sons assume leadership; Metacomet and Wamsutta, the elder who becomes the sachem. John Eliot's Bible published in America.

1662: Wamsutta dies; Metacomet takes over organizing a general uprising to include the Nausets, Pamets, Narragansetts, Sakonets and Nipmucks.

1664: English supply the Iroquois confederacy with weapons in order to trade with French allied interior Indians. English hire the Mohawks to fight the Esopus by the Hudson River. Spanish issue laws preventing Apache/Pueblo trading.

1666: Tionontoguen in New York destroyed by the French. Mohawk villages burned by De Tracy.

1669: John Eliot's "Praying Indians" in eastern Massachusetts, at Natick, join in an attack against the Mohawks in the west; the mission is a failure.

1671: French fur trading post competes with England's Hudson Bay Company processing furs.

1675-1676: King Philip's War; 52 of 90 towns in Rhode Island and Massachusetts were attacked by Metacomet, 12 were destroyed. His coalition against the expanding colonists included the Nipmucks, Mohegans, Podunks, Narragansetts and Wampanoags. The Indians were slaughtered, imprisoned or sold into slavery. Metacomet was beheaded and displayed in Plymouth. Bacon's Rebellion in western Virginia was between land-hungry colonists and Nanticoke and Susquehannock villages.

1680: Pueblo villages rebelled in New Mexico on August 10, 1680. All evidence of Spain was destroyed, records, rosaries, the language and the peach tree. Four-hundred Spanish were killed and 21 priests.

1680: Westos Indians are destroyed by the Shawnee and South Carolina inhabitants.

1680-1684: Coastal Georgia Indians, the Guale and the Yamasee rebel against the Spanish.

1682: Mary Rowlandson, Deerfield, MA, publishes her account of Indian captivity.

1682-1683: William Penn is permitted to create a colony at present day Philadelphia by an agreement signed with the Lenape Indians.

1687: Four Seneca villages in New York are destroyed by the French and Western Indians. Iroquois massacre the Miami Indians near Chicago, IL.

Color plate, "Dead He Lay There In The Sunset," from The Story of Hiawatha, 1910, by M.L. Kirk—$75 for the book. (Privately owned)

Color plate, "Take My Bait, Oh King Of Fishes," from The Story of Hiawatha, 1910, by M.L. Kirk—$75 for the book. (Privately owned)

Walnut-framed Navajo dye chart by Betty Yazzie—$150. Shown are Alder bark, Snakeweed, Gamble Oak bark, Sage Brush, Purple Bee plant, Holly berries, brown onion skin and red onion skin. In the center is portion of a miniature weaving. (Privately owned)

Framed, steel-engraved and colored "Order of Red Man Certificate," borders show a variety of Indian scenes, dated 1928, 27" high x 23" wide—$250. (Privately owned)

A leather teepee and eight contemporary dolls, plus two clay deer figures in the foreground. Teepee—$20, dolls—$10-$20 each, figurines—$5 each. (Privately owned)

Twelve tobacco silks, Tokio cigarettes, stitched together and framed, 12" high x 16" wide—$250. Illustrated top from left to right, Red Thunder, Chief Joseph, Big Razor, Young Whirlwind, Crow's Breast and Lean Wolf. Bottom, left to right, Noon Day, Keokuk, Red Bird, Black Eye, Clam Fish and Keokuk's Son. A most unusual example, ca. 1910. (Privately owned)

1687-1697: King William's Wars occur between the French, English and Indian allies for control of North American lands. The Iroquois went with the English; the French had the Algonquins on their side.

1691: Traveling along the East Coast, Jacques Le Tort's group makes contact with 40 Indian groups. English who marry Indians or Blacks are banned from Virginia.

1692: Santa Fe becomes New Mexico's capital as the Spanish conquer the Pueblo Indians.

1692-1696: Spain's military under Diego de Vargas is given permission to take over the Pueblos; of the pre-revolt Rio Grande villages, only 16 remained of 60.

1695: In New Mexico and Arizona the Pima revolt against Spain.

1700: Migration to the Plains begins. Hopis massacre all the males in the Awatovi village by setting fire to the kivas as they were preparing for religious ceremonies. This showed the strong will by the Hopi to resist control by Spain.

1701: Iroquois Wars end. Peace councils took place at Albany, NY; Onondaga, NY; and Montreal, Canada. A final council was held in Montreal where 20 tribes appeared. A policy of neutrality was established between the French and the British; Iroquois and Ottawa could also travel in peace. Fort Pontchartrain is founded by the French at Detroit under Antoine de Cadillac. The Iroquois become neutral to the English and the French. The Susquehannocks of Pennsylvania are accorded a special relationship with William Penn.

1703-1704: A French mission is created near Utica, IL, the home of the Illinois confederacy.

1704: Spanish missions are raided by the English; the Creek and the Cherokee as allies attack the Guale of Georgia.

1708: Yamasee mission Indians, about 12,000, living in the Carolinas are seized by the English and sold into West Indies slavery.

1710: Four Mohawk leaders go to London to meet Queene Anne and have their portraits painted. The Treaty at Conestoga is signed between Pennsylvania and the Iroquois League.

1712: Tuscarora Wars in North Carolina are fought with English slave traders; the Tuscarora leave for New York to become the sixth nation of the Iroquois confederacy.

1712-1736: Fox Wars commence.

1713: Maliseet and Micmac refuse to recognize their homelands as being English. Canadian lands were transferred from the French to the English in the Treaty of Utrecht.

1715: Queen Anne, Powhatan tribal leader, speaks to the Virginia legislature about alcohol, surveying policies and the payment of an annual tribute. The fee is abolished when Anne agrees to send her son to William and Mary. War in Georgia, called the Yamasee War, challenges British slavers against the Creek and the Yamasee. Delaware Indians move into the western part of Pennsylvania and the Ohio Valley.

1722: The Tuscarora officially join the Iroquois confederacy and the force becomes known as the Six Nations of the Iroquois League; the number of chiefs was limited to 49.

1724-1729: Two-hundred French killed on the Natchez plantation; raids by the French destroy the Natchez nation. Great Sun, their scared chief, along with 480 are sold into Caribbean slavery.

1730: The French kill 400 Fox and sell 500 into slavery.

1734: The Fox and the Sauk in the battle of Butte des Morts defeat the French.

1737: Thousands of Lenape Indians are forced from Pennsylvania by the "Walking Purchase," "as far as a man can go in a day and a half." Thomas Penn, son of William Penn, found the signed treaty.

1738: The Mandan of North Dakota are visited by Gaultier de la Verendrye.

1742: The Pennsylvania Walking Purchase is enforced by the Iroquois. Great Lakes Indians begin trading with the British.

1747: Huron leader Orontony (Nicholas) rose against the French traders in Michigan.

1749: Ohio colonial settlements built.

1750: Moor's Indian Charity school established in Connecticut, later moved to Hanover, NH; called Dartmouth College. The Ohio Company of Virginia opens the rich lands of the Ohio Valley for development.

1752: Virginia makes a treaty at Ambridge, PA, with the local Ohio tribes. The French and the Ottawa fight in Ohio and defeat the Miami Indians, on the British side.

1753: Pennsylvania traders are expelled by the French from the Ohio Valley. George Washington, a young surveyor, is sent to Ohio to enforce the Virginia claim. French allied with Indians defeat him.

1753: Benjamin Franklin meets at Carlisle, PA, with Ohio Indians regarding a treaty; a wampum belt is presented to the Indians. This forms the nucleus for creating later documents to establish unity in the colonies.

1754: Benjamin Franklin drafts the Albany Plan of Union, at the outset of the fourth French and Indian War. This document formed the basis of the Articles of Confederation in 1777 and the U.S. Constitution in 1789.

1754-1763: French and Indian Wars in America. The opening battle between the British and the French was over control of the Ohio Valley.

1755: Mohawk, Molly Brant, marries Sir William Johnson, English Superintendent of Indian affairs. Battle of Lake George; the French are defeated; Johnson is wounded and healed at Saratoga Springs. The French defeat the British at Fort Duquesne.

1758: Delawares leave Pennsylvania to settle in eastern Ohio. The British recapture Fort Duquesne and call it Fort Pitt.

1759: Indians in Pennsylvania and New York are divided over the continued alliance with the French.

1760: Standing Turkey, Kanagagot, chief of the Cherokees, allies with the British against the French and Indian tribes in Tennessee, Virginia and Kentucky.

1760: The Plains Indians acquire the horse.

1760-1763: Neolin, a Delaware Indian prophet in Ohio had a vision of the Old Northwest with no Europeans present. Pontiac, the Ottawa chief used this message to mobilize against the new British rule.

1762: Benjamin Franklin publishes 13 Indian treaties made during the 1736-1762 era.

1763: The smallpox virus is spread by Sir Jeffrey Amherst through infected blankets.

1765: Land-hungry settlers in Pennsylvania scalp 20 Susquehannocks, 14 who were in jail; known as the Paxton raid.

1766: Pontiac and 40 chiefs make peace with the British.

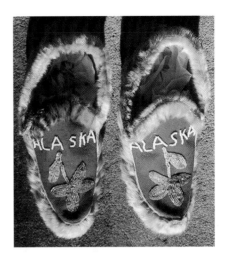

Size 10 sealskin moccasins, ca. 1940s, floral beading and "Alaska" sewn on felt—$100. (Privately owned)

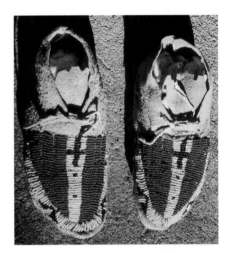

Child's beaded moccasins on hide—$450, 6-1/2" long. (Privately owned)

Wooden plaque carved by a German prisoner of war at Fort Riley, near Junction City, KS, around 1940s, patterned after Chief Pontiac—$200. Measures 8-1/2" x 7". (Privately owned)

Unusual formed oval basket with braided two piece handle, attributed to the Siletz, Western Oregon, 12" high x 8" across, finely woven—$500. (Privately owned)

Soundly constructed splint burden basket, 19" high x 13-1/2" across, back side conforms to being worn against the shoulders, ca. 1890, Northeast area, probably Maine—$225. (Privately owned)

Navajo hand-woven rug, ca. 1920-1930, 67" long x 39" wide, four colors, light and dark brown, tan and white—$400. (Privately owned)

Henry Brackenridge from Pennsylvania published information about the Indian mounds near the Ohio and Scioto Rivers.

1766-1774: Indian concerns mount concerning hostilities between the French, British and the colonists. In Pennsylvania there were bounties such as, $130 for a boy or woman, $134 for a scalp of dead Indian and $150 for each male Indian over 10 years of age.

1769: Daniel Boone born in Pennsylvania journeyed from Virginia to Kentucky opening the Wilderness Road; the Shawnees captured him taking his foods and gear since he was trespassing on Indian grounds. He was released and settlers still continued to inhabit lands owned by the Shawnee and Cherokee. Mission San Diego is founded by the Spanish in California; this is the first of 21 missions. Over 300 Indian groups were destroyed in southern California by the Spanish mission system.

1773: Kentucky border wars continue between colonists and settlers. Indian hunting grounds of the Delaware, Shawnee and Cherokee are trespassed. Chief John Logan, Cayuga and his Shawnee wife are murdered.

1774: The First Continental Congress appoints a Committee on Indian Affairs to negotiate terms. The Yuma in Arizona resist Salvador Palma. The boundary between the English and Crown lands extends into Ohio; known as the Quebec Act. Lord Dunmore's War pits 3,000 militia against the Shawnee and Cornstalk, their leader.

1775: Northern, Southern and Middle departments of Indian affairs are created by the Second Continental Congress. They are headed by Benjamin Franklin, James Wilson and Patrick Henry. The Six Nations with 65 counselors met in German Flats, NY, to create a treaty of neutrality.

1776: San Juan Capistrano, a Spanish mission, has an Indian population of 785.

1777: Under a flag of truce, Cornstalk is murdered at Fort Randolph. Washington's starving troops are aided at Valley Forge, PA, by the Delaware, Tuscarora and Oneida Indians. The Iroquois Six Nations divide: Mohawks join the British; neutral are the Seneca and the Onondaga; and siding with the colonists the Oneida and Tuscarora.

1778: The Delaware (Turtle people) sign a peace treaty with the U.S. at Fort Pitt; representatives may be sent to Congress.

1779: General John Sullivan and 4,000 troops attack the Iroquois confederacy in western New York. Iroquois capital, Onondaga, is destroyed by the U.S. forces and Oneida Indians. Only the federal government may transfer ownership of Indian lands. George Rogers Clark discovers a temple mound, the city of Cahokia, at the jointure of the Mississippi and Missouri Rivers.

1780: The Spanish branch out their Indian missions in California.

1780-1782: Smallpox spreads through the Great Plains.

1781: The Battle of Yorktown and Cornwallis' surrender.

1783: Iroquois confederacy dissolved.

1784: Fort Stanwix Treaty between the U.S. and Six Iroquois Nations.

1785: Surveyed townships, 36 sections of 640 acres each, at $1 an acre took more Indian lands; called The Ordinance of 1785. The Treaty of Fort McIntosh gives lands in Pennsylvania, Ohio and Tennessee to the U.S.

1787: Congress passes the Northwest Ordinance.

1788: Kentucky grounds are given to settlers by the Iroquois.

1789: The War Department takes over Indian affairs.

1789-1850: The U.S. government takes 450 million acres of Indian land.

1790: Blue Jacket and Little Turtle defeat General Harmar's army in the Northwest Territory.

1799: Fascination commences as visitors return from the Ohio Valley showing Indian artifacts and speaking about the earthwork mounds.

1790: Trade and Intercourse Act enacted by Congress places trade under federal control.

1791: Little Turtle, Blue Jacket and 14 other tribes defeat General St. Clair; one of the worst losses by the U.S. Army. A total of 623 soldiers/civilians were killed.

1793: $1 million given by Congress to avenge St. Clair's defeat; the Legion of the U.S. was to be formed.

1794: Battle of Fallen Timbers takes place in a field where trees had been blown over by a tornado. Gen. "Mad Anthony" Wayne is victorious over Little Turtle and other Indian tribes. An agreement is made by the Tuscarora, Oneida and Stockbridge Indians in support of Indian education.

1795: Greenville Treaty of Peace signed by 1,100 western confederated tribes represented by chiefs; the document was on parchment and measured 7 feet in length and 3 feet wide.

1797: New York Senecas sell western New York and northwestern Pennsylvania. To explore ruins becomes the goal of the Philadelphia American Philosophical Society.

1799: A large Indian village was uncovered near Nashville, TN, by Andrew Jackson's law partner. The Longhouse religion established through a vision by Handsome Lake stated that natives should live in peace with the U.S., but remain Iroquois.

1802: Enraged, the Tlingit Indians destroy Sitka, AK. Seminole leader, Osceola is born. Sale of liquor to Indians, through the Trade and Intercourse Act, is enacted.

1805-1806: Sacajawea guides the Lewis and Clark expedition; she is diplomat, guide, interpreter and translator.

1805: The Tlingits destroy a second Russian fur post, at Yakutat.

1806-1809: Tecumseh, as a Shawnee warrior, becomes highly respected as an orator and spokesman. "Whiskey Treaty" at Fort Wayne, IN, gives lands away in Ohio and Indiana for 8 cents an acre. The legitimacy of the treaty questioned by the Indians.

1810: Tecumseh delivers address at Vincennes, IN, on August12, claiming "since made miserable by the white people who are never contented but always encroaching…"

1811: Tecumseh allies the Creek of Florida and Georgia. Battle of Tippecanoe shows William Henry Harrison's power over the Shawnee.

1812: Creek Civil War in Florida and Georgia.

1813: Tecumseh defeats the Americans and Fort Detroit surrenders. He forms an alliance with the Fox, Sauk, Sioux, Winnebago, Chippewa, Wyandot, Delaware, Shawnee, Kickapoo and Potawatomi. The Battle of River Thames and the death of Tecumseh. Over 350 killed by the Upper Creeks (Red Sticks) at Fort Mims in Alabama. Tennessee militia enter villages of Seminoles in northern Florida.

1814: Andrew Jackson kills 1,000 Creeks at the Battle of Horseshoe Bend, to retaliate for the attack on Fort Mims; 20

Grouping of dolls: left, 9" high, hand stitched, leather face with beading and yarn hair, tanned suede body, beaded pants, shirt and moccasins, ornate beaded necklace, probably Niagara Falls area—$300; center, all original signed "Armand Marseille, 370, A.M. 8/OX. D.E.P. Made in Germany," buckskin clothes with fringes and beading—$225; right, cornhusk doll, 12" high, hand-stitched dress with black velvet undergarment, beaded around the fringe, on the pants and on the moccasins, original tag "Made by Canadian Indians," 1930s—$100. (Privately owned)

Two fine pairs of Plains dolls, Sioux, ornately beaded; left, 11" high, buckskin clothing and horsehair wigs—$1,000 for the pair; right, cloth outfits, beautiful beading, yarn hair—$750 for the pair; both pairs date from the 1880s. (Privately owned)

Eskimo, painted wooden-faced doll with wooden harpoon, dressed in rabbit hood, sealskin outfit trimmed in beaver, two seal skins at the base of the doll, mounted on an old board, 10" high—$225. (Privately owned)

Eskimo walrus stomach skin drum, round wooden form with nails and handles, of recent manufacturer, rawhide and skin lashing, St. Lawrence Island, AK. (Bowers Museum Collections, photo by A.J. Labbe)

Eskimo roll or kit of tools: fish skin roll with pouch to hold tools with linear skin-appliquéd design embroidered in colored thread. (Bowers Museum Collections, photo by A.J. Labbe)

Eskimo purse, St. Lawrence Island, AK, caribou skin with cotton lining, fringed opening, strap with six bear claws as ornaments. (Bowers Museum Collections, photo by A.J. Labbe)

million acres are ceded by the Creek.

1815: Choctaw help the Americans win the Battle of New Orleans.

1817: Georgia Cherokee lands are exchanged for Arkansas Territory.

1817-1818: First Seminole War; as a youth Osceola fights Andrew Jackson.

1818: Josiah Francis, Creek leader is tricked onto an American gunboat and executed.

1823: Settlement established by the Oneida Indians at Green Bay, WI. The Office of Indian Affairs fall under the U.S. War Department.

1825: McIntosh Creek Treaty dismissed as illegal by President John Quincy Adams.

1827: Cherokee chief, Path Killer dies.

1828: John Ross becomes the new chief of the Cherokee. Sequoyah publishes the Cherokee newspaper, the *Phoenix*; columns were in English and Cherokee.

1829: Gold is discovered on Cherokee lands; the Georgia legislature creates laws forbidding Cherokees to mine gold, hold political assemblies or testify against whites. In Washington, John Ross protests treaty violations.

1830: President Jackson signs the Indian Removal Act. The Treaty of Dancing Rabbit Creek and the removal of Choctaw.

1831: The Cherokee Nation sues Georgia in the U.S. Supreme Court.

1832: In the suit Worcester v. Georgia, Chief Justice Marshall rules for the white missionary on behalf of the Cherokee. Black Hawk's War. Creeks surrender Alabama and move to Oklahoma.

1833: A biography of Black Hawk is written by Antoine LeClaire. A lottery is held by the state of Georgia to sell off land and property.

1834-1835: New Echota Treaty sells off Cherokee lands for $5 million. John Ridge, his son and nephew, are assassinated in Oklahoma by the Cherokee in 1839 in retribution for his trip to Washington.

1834: Thousands of Chumash Indians in California are set free by the Spanish mission.

1835-1842: Second Seminole War; $50 million appropriated by the U.S. government.

1836: Cherokee walk to Oklahoma from Georgia; the migration included 16,000 and took six months.

1837: Payments for lands ceded or sold are stopped by Congress.

1837-1838: North Dakota Mandans are reduced from 10,000 to 130 due to an epidemic of smallpox. Chickasaw leave Alabama and Mississippi.

1842: Seneca Indians moved to reservations.

1846-1868: Apache Wars in New Mexico; fought by Red Sleeves and Cochise against miners and the U.S. Army.

1849: Indian Service becomes part of the Interior Department.

1849-1850: 130 Pomo men, women and children are massacred in California.

1851: First Treaty of Fort Laramie. Fort Defiance constructed in Arizona to control Navajo "wild tribes."

1852: Quechan (Yuma) Indians revolt in southern Arizona as U.S. troops build Fort Yuma.

1854: Gadsden Purchase gives the U.S. lands in New Mexico, Arizona and southern California. The Missouri Treaty signed by the Omaha Indians gave the U.S. 43 million acres in Kansas and Nebraska.

1855-1858: Third Seminole War.

1857: The Senecas buy back reservation lands from the Ogden Land Company.

1860: Navajo 1,000 strong, led by Manuelito, attack Fort Defiance. This marked the beginning of the "total war" policy against the Navajos.

1862: Apache resist the Arizona state militia.

1862-1864: Starving Santee Sioux attack white settlements in Minnesota; more than 1,000 settlers were killed. The leader, Little Crow, and 37 warriors were hanged in a mass execution in Mankato, MN. It was the largest public hanging in the history of the U.S.

1862-1863: Apache/Navajo Wars.

1863: Apache leader, Mangas Colorada, killed at Fort McLane.

1863-1864: War against the Navajo led by Kit Carson. Over 8,000 Navajo and Mescalero Apache were marched 350 miles from Fort Defiance to Bosque Redondo.

1864: Sand Creek Massacre on November 29 by the Reverend John Chivington, 700 troops and four howitzers of the Third Colorado Cavalry. Gold is discovered in Montana opens Teton Sioux lands to prospectors and brings about war under Red Cloud and Spotted Tail.

1865: War begins on the northern Plains following the Sand Creek Massacre. Parties of Sioux, Arapaho and Cheyenne raided the North and South Platte Rivers. They frustrated the U.S. army as an elusive enemy.

1866: A peace council was called at Fort Laramie attended by Red Cloud and other Sioux leaders; learning about a chain of forts to be built from Wyoming to Montana, the Indians leave and the Bozeman Trail again becomes unsafe.

1867: The Northern Pacific Railroad advances into Sioux territory.

1868: Chief Red Cloud signs the Fort Laramie Treaty; the U.S. does not keep the terms of the treaty. Black Kettle and his wife are killed by Custer, even though they support a white flag. Sherman becomes commander in chief of U.S. forces in the West.

1870: President Grant gives control of Indian agencies to Christian missionary denominations. $100,000 is provided for American Indian education. At Fort Berthold in Dakota Territory, the Mandan, Arikara and Gros Ventre give up claims to all their lands.

1871: Congress decides not to have additional treaties with the Indian nations.

1872-1874: The buffalo are slaughtered on the Plains.

1874: The 1868 Fort Laramie Treaty is violated when groups headed by Custer hunt for gold in the Black Hills and discover it.

1875: Sitting Bull becomes the chief of the Teton Sioux. The Black Hills gold rush begins.

1876: Custer and 225 soldiers are killed at the Battle of Little Bighorn. The only survivor is a horse named "Comanche."

1876-1886: Apache Wars.

1877: Sioux resistance broken, many groups return to reservations. Crazy Horse surrenders and is killed; Sitting Bull takes his

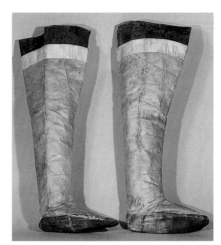

Mukluks, Eskimo, St. Lawrence Island, AK, light tan seal skin, white cuff, brown seal fur on the inner boot, knee high, waterproof. (Bowers Museum Collections, photo by A.J. Labbe)

Ovoidal wooden bowl or fat storage pan, Eskimo, St. Lawrence Island, AK; two pieces, one for the base and the other for the side. The base is recessed and the sides are bound together with very thin strips of bark. The side is bound to the base with nails. (Bowers Museum Collections, photo by A.J. Labbe)

Yukon Territory near the Mackenzie Eskimo, tall lidded storage basket, 16-1/2" diameter, 18-1/2" high, coiled construction using natural grasses, grass sewn, umbricated geometric design from strips of bird skin taken from the legs of birds and woven into the basket. (Bowers Museum Collections, photo by A.J. Labbe)

Tlinkit storage basket with rattle top, 7-7/16" diameter, plain 2-element-Z-twined weave, false embroidery decoration in dyed orange and yellow grasses, commercial dyes, although yellow was accomplished by steeping in moss grass solution, spruce root and maiden hair fern stems. Design on the lid and the body combines the wave pattern and the brown bear footprint; designs occurred during the 1800s and continue to be popular. Lid's center has a "fern frond" swirl, being indicative of the young fern leaves as they uncurl in the spring. A space was formed in the lid for seeds or pebbles which rattle when shaken. (Bowers Museum Collections, photo by A.J. Labbe)

Prince Rupert, British Columbia, Makah covered bottle, 8-15/16" high, 2-1/2" diameter, twined, warp twisted from cedar bark, weft from squaw grass, known as bird-cage weave. The dyed grass ornamentation shows seven bands of varying width in black, orange, brown and red, each colored band containing a different design in contrasting color. (Bowers Museum Collections, photo by A.J. Labbe)

Hunkpapa Sioux to Canada. Chief Joseph makes his way with 750 across Oregon, Idaho, Wyoming and Montana. He surrenders to General Miles.

1878: Hampton Institute, Virginia is expanded to educate Indians. Shoshoni chief, Washakie, accepts a silver saddle from President Ulysses S. Grant, due to cooperating with the U.S. Santanta, Kiowa Orator of the Plains, falls to his death from a hospital prison window in Huntsville, TX.

1879: Carlisle Indian School established at Carlisle, PA.

1881: Sitting Bull crosses the Canadian border with his group and is taken to Standing Rock Reservation. Sitting Bull also appears for five years in Buffalo Bill Cody Wild West Show.

1882: Executive order by President Chester Arthur makes 4,000 acres of northern Arizona into reservation for the Hopi.

1883: Sitting Bull invited to Bismarck, ND, for ceremonies opening the transcontinental Northern Pacific Railroad.

1885: Indian police units established at 48 Indian agencies by the Bureau of Indian Affairs.

1886: Geronimo and his "army" of 24 surrender to be taken to Fort Marion in Florida.

1887: The Dawes Act dissolves tribal landholdings.

1889: Omaha Indian, Susan La Flesche, is the first Native American physician. The Ghost Dance is revived by Wovoka, a Paiute holy man in Nevada.

1889-1890: Oklahoma land rush.

1890: Sitting Bull returns to the Standing Rock Reservation; he, his son and six body guards are killed. Massacre of the Sioux at Wounded Knee. Indian population at 237,196.

1892: Geronimo and his band are taken to Mount Vernon Barracks, AL.

1894: Geronimo and survivors are transported to Fort Sill, OK.

1901: Geronimo rides in the inaugural parade for Roosevelt.

1902: Territory of Oklahoma established; Five Civilized Tribes dissolved.

1904: Sun Dance among Plain Indians is outlawed; the Sioux are given lands in South Dakota.

1906: Edward Curtis begins photographing Indian tribes in the Northwest and the West, financially supported by J.P. Morgan. More Indian lands made available through Congress and the Allotment Act.

1907: Francis Leupp becomes Indian affairs commissioner as a friend of Theodore Roosevelt.

1910: More than 30 reservations in the West are opened to allotment.

1912: The Roosevelt Dam in Arizona is built with the help of Apaches. They were chained at night to prevent them from running away.

1917: Draft registration for all male Indians begins; more than 10,000 enlisted. Crow reservation lands, 5,000 acres, is used for growing sugar beets. Woodrow Wilson appoints Cato Sells to be commissioner of Indian affairs. As part of their religion the Native American Church of Oklahoma stated their right to use peyote.

1918: Bill introduced in Congress to outlaw peyote use by Indians; the bill is defeated.

1918-1919: Influenza epidemic sweeps reservations and schools in Arizona, New Mexico and the Rocky Mountain states; thousands die. Indians serving in the Armed Forces become citizens.

1920: Indian populations begin to increase.

1922: Oil is discovered on the Navajo reservation; false business dealings lead to the Teapot Dome scandal. The first Pueblo All Confederation Council is formed to defeat a bill that would give non-Indians Pueblo water and lands. Negotiation of water rights on the Colorado River form the means to build the Boulder Dam.

1924: Indian Citizenship Act makes American Indians citizens. Pueblo Lands Act; John Collier becomes the voice of Indian reform.

1926: Native Americans ask that a presidential commission review Indian policies.

1928: The Meriam Report over three years learned about the status of Indians; it began Indian policy reform.

1930: Kidnapping of Navajo children is investigated by the U.S. Senate.

1932-1936: Under the stock reduction policy 250,000 Navajo sheep and goats are killed by federal agents.

1932: John Neidardt interviews and publishes the life of Oglala Sioux holy man, Black Elk. *Black Elk Speaks* begins in the 1860s up to 1889.

1933: John Collier receives $6 million to begin the Indian Emergency Conservation Work Program. Some form of work was begun on 33 reservations.

1934: Worst drought in U.S. history; known as the Dust Bowl. Valuable topsoil was blown away. The Indian New Deal creates tribal governments with rights and responsibilities and answering to the federal government.

1935: Tribes vote concerning the Indian Reorganization Act: 181 accept; 77 vote it down.

1936: Oliver La Farge traveled to the Hopi reservation to help with forming a constitution; 90% of eligible voters stayed home. Even so, the government created a two-part faction with a tribal council and priests. Native Alaskan peoples are aided through the Native Reorganization Act in setting up corporations.

1937: Navajo tribal council formed.

1938: Indian Lands Mining Act passed with the right to issue 10-year leases.

1939: The All-Pueblo Council in New Mexico seeks the right to vote in state elections.

1941-1945: Native American men are required to register for the draft. In World War II over 24,000 served; others worked in the defense industries bringing the total to over 70,000.

1941: Felix Cohen publishes his *Handbook of Federal Indian Law*.

1942: The "Navajo codetalkers" were an elite Navajo group who used Navajo words to communicate in the Pacific. The Japanese never broke the code. Some 420 Navajo served. Japanese prisoners were placed in Arizona on lands taken from the Mohave and Pima. Some 900,000 acres were used in Alaska for Japanese internment, gun ranges, air bases and nuclear sites. Six Iroquois Nations declare war on the Axis powers. The Seminole Nation v. U.S., is won by the Seminole, with regard to failure to pay trust moneys.

1944: National Congress of American Indians is brought about by Salish Indian D'Arch McNickle and over 100 tribal reservation leaders.

1945: Ira Hayes, a Pima of Arizona, becomes one of five soldiers raising the U.S. flag on Iwo Jima. "New Deal" ends with a policy toward termination.

1946: National Indian Claims Court set up. The most acclaimed law firm in the nation to handle tribal claims becomes Wilkinson, Clagun and Barker. Mining companies seek title to 20 billion tons of coal on Hopi and Navajo reservations. Bureau of Land Management is formed.

Attributed to the Yokuts, Central California, bottle neck basket, coiled fiber, split willow design, rattlesnake in red and black, lightning edge with three remaining quail tufts, 4-3/16" diameter, 6-3/16" depth. (Bowers Museum Collections, photo by A.J. Labbe)

Yokut basket, bowl coiled, foundation willow or sumac root, sewing root of slouth grass, 4-1/16" high, 11-7/8" rim diameter. Two bands of modified rattlesnake design with row of swastikas between; the black is from fern stem and the red from red bud. (Bowers Museum Collections, photo by A.J. Labbe)

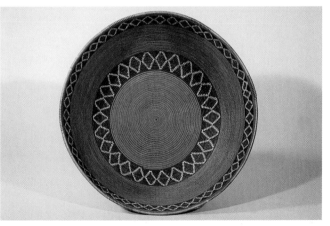

Deep Yokut bowl, collected about 1870, very rare, two encircling bands of connected diamonds in dark red, outlined with undyed quills in a black ground, 6-15/16" high, 12-3/8" diameter. (Bowers Museum Collections, photo by A.J. Labbe)

Yokut bowl-shaped basket, 6-7/16" diameter, 9-7/8" depth, coiled, diamond-stylized rattlesnake motif, two wide bands in typical colors, red bud diamonds in a field of lighter colored swamp grass and a border of black fern stem, coiled fiber and split willow. (Bowers Museum Collection)

Boat-shaped Yokut basket, 13-5/8" long, 10-7/8" wide, split willow fiber, rattlesnake design in red and black, a single row of human figures, quail tufted edge. (Bowers Museum Collection)

Yokut shoulder basket, "Tulare bottle-neck," young willow sprouts served as foundation, fern roots and red bud bark make up the design; two rows of human figures are symbolic of a ritualistic dance, 11-7/8" diameter, 6-15/16" high, top diameter is 4-11/16". (Bowers Museum Collection)

1947: The government completes surveys of minerals on reservations: they include gas, oil, coal, uranium. Felix Cohen rules on the minerals on Hopi and Navajo reservations. Both parties own equal rights. Dams destroy salmon sites and flood the Fort Berthold, Standing Rock Sioux and Cheyenne River Reservations.

1948: Arizona Indians are given the right to vote.

1949: The Hoover Commission proposed integration of Indians into American life and terminate responsibility for Indian affairs.

1950: Dillon Meyer becomes head of Indian Affairs. The Sun Dance is practiced openly by the Sioux. The Navajo Hopi Rehabilitation Act becomes a test case for urbanization and termination.

1951: Uranium is found on Navajo reservations in Arizona and New Mexico. John Boyden was chosen as Hopi tribal lawyer.

1953-1962: The official American Indian policy is termination. Under this practice, tribes lost federal services and protection, paid taxes, sold lands and provided for education and health services. During the Kennedy administration, this policy was outlawed.

1953: Senator Arthur Watkins from Utah set out to get rid of the reservation system and other programs and services. Tribes targeted were the Klamath from Oregon, the Chippewas of North Dakota, the Flatheads of Montana, the Menominees of Wisconsin, and the Potawatomis of Nebraska and Kansas. The philosophy was and still is, to mainstream.

1954: Menominee Termination Act; other acts are introduced to speed termination of many tribes.

1955: Termination slowed with Democrats in the House and Senate.

1956-1958: Senator Barry Goldwater from Arizona proposes Bill S.231 to decide mineral rights on Black Mesa. The Hopi were to sue the Navajo to gain a clear title. The bill was defeated in 1956 and 1957 and passed in 1958.

1957: The right of eminent domain is tried in upstate New York on Tuscarora reservations. The Seneca lose 10,000 acres of reservation lands with the Kinzua Dam.

1958: Lands of Spanish origin in California are terminated. The Ku Klux Klan threaten the Lumbees of North Carolina. The Indians drive them off with shotguns. Florida Miccosukee go against the Army Corps of Engineers to reclaim portions of the Everglades. A $1 billion federal project is attempting to return the river to its original site to save the Everglades. Tuscarora given $13 million for lands taken by the New York Power Authority.

1959: Natives of Alaska sought 300 million acres of land.

1961: Kinzua Dam finished. Flooding destroys Cornplanter's place of burial and Seneca lands in New York. National Indian Youth Council founded. The American Indian National Council met in Chicago to discuss termination and its threat to Indian well-being. President Kennedy appointed Philleo Nash commissioner of Indian affairs under Stewart Udall of Arizona, Secretary of the Interior. Net fishing (as opposed to hook-and-line fishing) comes to a head in Washington State. The state police arrest Nisqualli Indians for using nets. This was a beginning for national media attention.

1962: Indians in New Mexico are permitted to vote. The Institute of American Indian Art is founded in Santa Fe. In the suit of the Hopi and the Navajo, both tribes had "joint, equal and undivided rights" to 1.8 million acres. The Hopi had rights to District Six.

1963: After 30 years Arizona received a larger share of waters coming from the Colorado River. Fishing with nets in the State of Washington is ruled illegal.

1964: Historical Society of the American Indian is created in California. The Office of Economic Opportunity directed grants to tribal governments.

1965: Alaska Federated Natives is created. Thirty-three thousand California Natives receive $900 each in compensation for lands given up.

1966: Hopi/Navajo councils sign agreements with Kennecott Copper and Peabody Coal on Joined Use Land.

1968: *House Made of Dawn* by N. Scott Momaday, Kiowa, receives the Pulitzer Prize. American Indian Movement established in Minneapolis. The Akwesasne Mohawk Reserve blocks the International Bridge joining Canada and the U.S. to protest the paying of custom taxes and border duties.

1969-1971: Alcatraz Island is inhabited by many Indian tribes as they seek to gain "surplus land" from the U.S.

1969: Vine Deloria, a Sioux, publishes *Custer Died for Your Sins*.

1970: Nevada Paiutes sue the Interior Department when they drain Pyramid Lake. The 48,000 acre Blue Lake watershed is returned to the Taos and the Taos Land Bill gives them perpetual trust of the area. BIA offices throughout the country are occupied to draw attention to Indian rights, protections and abuses. Two-hundred Iroquois meet in Geneva, NY, to discuss a plan where they can regain powers lost to state and federal governments. Mount Rushmore in the Black Hills is reclaimed by 50 Indians. American Indian Movement boards *Mayflower II* at Plymouth to declare Thanksgiving a day for mourning. Mohave Generating Station opens in Nevada run by reservation coal. President Nixon brings to an end the termination policy and creates the Indian self-determination policy.

1971: Alaska Native Claims Settlement Act awards 44 million acres and $962,000 for violating native land rights. Native American Rights Fund gives legal advice to tribes. Five Civilized Tribes are permitted to elect directly their own chiefs.

1972: Organizer of fishing rights movement murdered in Tacoma, WA. ATM Caravan travels from San Francisco to Washington and occupies Washington, DC, BIA offices. Paiutes win their suit concerning Pyramid Lake and unlawful water drainage.

1973: President Nixon rejects the Twenty Points on Indian rights. Over 2,000 Indians go to Pine Ridge and occupy the Wounded Knee site for 71 days.

1974: Forty Indian nations create the International Treaty Council. Mohawks protest at Eagle Bay in New York State. Women of All Red Nations is founded. Coal lease canceled in favor of the Northern Cheyenne living in Montana and Wyoming. Hopi Land Settlement Act relocates 12,000 Navajo living over coal deposits; becomes the largest group relocated since the 1800s.

1975: As a tribute in agreements made with George Washington in 1776, the Passamaquoddy of Maine have returned national forests. Violence at Pine Ridge, SD, drawing attention to the uranium in the area and the dangers of the nuclear industry. Leonard Peltier jailed with two consecutive life terms; one AIM member died, two FBI agents were killed.

Basket attributed to the Yokut culture; this coiled bottle-necked form brings together several features: the jar neck from the broad flat shoulder, the use of the diamond pattern, which is used along with other elements. Red bud is used for the diamond, swamp grass for the light background and black fern stems for the border. The insertion of quail top knot feathers around the edge of the shoulder were a feature of Yokut baskets used in ceremonial or mortuary rites. (Bowers Museum Collection)

Yokut shaman's hat, basketry with raven feathers and eagle down inserted vertically into basketry and down feathers inserted horizontally at the rim, 13" high, 7-7/8" diameter at the rim. The leather cover on the bottom has leather chin straps. A costume worn by Tache Youts during rainmaking and other ceremonies. Used in scenes enacted by the banks of the Kern River, 1954, in a film supervised by Frank Latta. (Bowers Museum Collection)

An interesting coiled, boat-shaped "dance" basket, variations of the rattlesnake pattern in bands at the top and bottom. Between are men and women figures holding hands, possibly representing participation in dance rituals. Use of human figures in Yokut basketry dates before 1875. Executed designs are in alternating colors of red bud and black fern stem. Colors are reversed in the two diamond patterns. Ticking on the rim may have come from neighboring tribes east of Yokut territory, 16-1/4" long, 12-1/4" wide, 5" high. (Bowers Museum Collection)

According to Craig Bates, Yosemite's National Park Curator, this twined basket woven of grass and completely covered with trade beads in yellow, blue and white, was made by the Achomawi or Atougawi. The basket weave is plain, 2-element-Z-twining with overlay stitches in alternating bands visible on the inside. The trade beads are in geometrics sewn on a cloth backing, rather than woven into the twined stitches, 5-1/2" diameter, 3-3/4" high. (Bowers Museum Collection)

1975: Council of Energy Resource Tribes formed to protect 25 reservations containing mineral supplies.

1979: Radioactive water, 100 million gallons, released into the Rio Puerco at Church Rock, NM. This was the largest U.S. nuclear accident and occurred on July 16. The cleanup still continues. Indian religion is protected as the American Indian Religious Freedom Act becomes law. Piscataway chief, Turkey Tayac, is buried on the banks of Mount Vernon opposite Mount Vernon. William Janklow becomes governor of South Dakota and abolishes the Department of Environmental Protection. Its duties fell under the Department of Natural Resources. The Black Hills Alliance in South Dakota warns people about the nuclear mining dangers. Archaeological Resources Protection Act is passed. Navajo miners and families get lung cancer from uranium.

1980: Native American population reaches 1.5 million.

1982: President Reagan celebrates National Navajo Codetalkers Day. Jim Thorpe's Olympic medals are returned.

1985: Wilma Mankiller becomes Cherokee chief of the tribe in Oklahoma, the first woman in modern times; the council consists of 15 members.

1986: Deadline for Navajo removal from Hopi/Navajo Joint Use Lands. Foxwoods High Stakes Bingo and Resort Casino opening in Connecticut by the Mashantucket Pequot tribe with bingo.

1987: Ben Nighthorse Campbell, Northern Cheyenne, is elected to U.S. Congress.

1989: Congress establishes as part of the Smithsonian, a National Museum of the American Indian in New York.

1990: The Native American Graves Protection and Repatriation Act gives federal funds to universities and museums. Supreme Court ruling notes that states may outlaw Native American religious practices, including peyote. Stewart Udall represents Navajo uranium miners seeking compensation. Over 1,000 applied, about 300 got awards. Mohawk protests at the expansion of a golf course on burial grounds close to Oklahoma, Quebec.

1992: Foxwoods Casino opens in February. Columbus Quincentennial celebrated with the second voyage of the *Santa Maria*, *Nina* and the *Pinta* into New York's harbor.

1994: Over 50 tribes are approached by the federal government offering multi-million-dollar contracts to establish nuclear waste storage sites. The Mescalero Apache are the only ones to sign. New Mexico's governor opposed the move. A Native American group also opposes the Mescalero decision. Elder Navajo and chairwoman, Roberta Blackgoat, traveled to the UN in New York and Switzerland to present the human rights case for the Navajos.

Pomo "treasure basket" with clam shell beads, Northern California, coiled with about 24 stitches in red bud per inch, the clam shell disc beads had a monetary value to the Pomo similar to "wampum" of Native Americans in Northeastern U.S. The weaver decorated this basket with some of her wealth, 6-1/2" diameter, 2-1/4" high. (Bowers Museum Collection)

Matthew Coon Come, Cree, receives the Goldman Environmental Prize in San Francisco, after 15 years of fighting the James Bay Hydro Quebec project.

1996: Peabody Coal Company loses its suit with a Navajo group made up of 500 from the Black Mesa; their permanent permit is denied until they comply with safety standards. BIA can not account for $2.4 billion. Chief Joseph Interpretive Center being built in the Wallowa Valley in Oregon.

1997: The Cheyennes and Arapahos gave the Democratic National Committee $107,000 from their welfare fund for medi- cines and winter heating fuel. In turn, they seek 7,500 acres, the grounds of defunct Fort Reno. The issue goes back to the infa- mous Sand Creek Massacre in 1864 and the Battle of the Washita shortly after the Civil War. Actually, if they were to seek all the lands that the U.S. government promised, it would amount to 51.2 million acres.

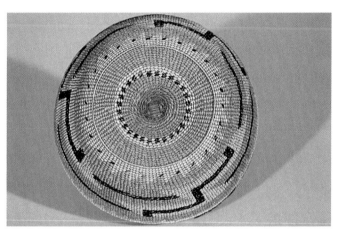

Hupa squaw cap basket, Russian River, Sonoma County, CA, twined warp of willow rods, weft root of sedge, white stems of cercis occidentalis; the figures are done in red bud or brown splints of cercis, the ends of warp stems are cut off at the upper edge. (Bowers Museum Collections, photo by A.J. Labbe)

Paiute oval basket, ca. 1960, designs in red and black fibers, willow, yucca root and sumac; made by Minnie Brown, 9-1/2" long, 5-1/2" wide. (Bowers Museum Collection)

Ladies' Huppa basket cap, Northern California, 3-1/4" high, 7-7/16" diameter, tan and brown design; maiden hair fern stem form the dark design, crown cap has brown circle with five designs. The rest of the cap has a design of three brown double-parallelogram shapes with tan-Z design in each. (Bowers Museum Collections, photo by A.J. Labbe)

Brown bottle covered with alternating brown and yellow weaving in spiral design to shoul- der of the bottle, neck has three small and two large bands of brown with yellow in between, a portion of the bottle shows at the top, 11-3/8" high, 3-7/16" diameter, Shasta, Northern California. (Bowers Museum Collections, photo by A.J. Labbe)

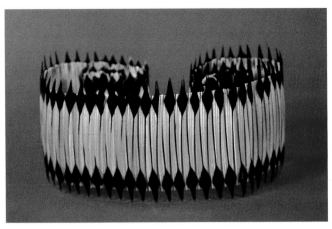

Feathered headband, Northern California cultures, late 19th/early 20th century, quills, red shafted flicker feathers and fiber, 4" high, 49-1/2" long. (Bowers Museum Collection)

Mission basket, possibly Central Valley, California, reminiscent of Tulare work, 2" high, 8-7/16" diameter, interlocking radiating stars which also serve as diamonds, alternating yellow and black central designs. (Bowers Museum Collections, photo by A.J. Labbe)

Mission storage basket, counterclockwise start, various shades of juncus, woven into a stylized butterfly design, interspersed with geometric star-like patterns in black, Southern California, height 5-15/16", diameter 9-11/16". (Bowers Museum Collections, photo by A.J. Labbe)

Mission storage basket, Southern California, very finely coiled "rattlesnake" design encircling the upper portion. Further decoration is a four-petaled bottom flower and triangular motifs dispersed below the shoulder of the basket. Since earliest times, weavers have made rattlesnake patterns; during the 1890-1940 period numerous weavers among the Mission Indians used this pattern. (Bowers Museum Collection)

Tulare basket bowl, Southern California, 11-7/8" diameter, 5-15/16" high, foundation consists of a bundle of stems of yellow grass (Epicampes rigens). The black is the root of the fern, the red is obtained from the red bud, gathered after the fall rains when the bark is red, central and outer rattlesnake designs. (Bowers Museum Collections, photo by A.J. Labbe)

Shoeshine coiled bottleneck basket, Central and Southern California, design of alternating man and woman around the center (four men and four women); four smaller figures of women on the flange of the basket. Arrow points and crosses are included in the design, 3-7/16" rim diameter, 5-3/16" high. (Bowers Museum Collection)

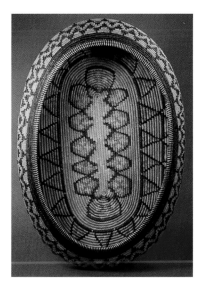

Coiled basket with geometric design, Cahuilla Culture, Southern California, early to mid 20th century, sumac, natural and dyed juncus, on a grass foundation, 20-7/8" long, 14-9/16" wide, 5" high. (Bowers Museum Collection)

Diegueno mission basket tray with flaring sides, Southern California, juncus weft over a grass bundle foundation, coiled. The design is composed of a central rosette with radiating spurs, 1-5/8" high, 11-7/8" deep. (Bowers Museum Collections, photo by A.J. Labbe)

Ceremonial carved disc, undetermined age, uncovered in a plowed field on the Cole ranch in the early 20th century, Orange County, Southern California. The object is reminiscent of the Southern California Indian girl's puberty ceremonial sand-painting. The notches on the steatite at the top form a butterfly pattern, a common symbol of metamorphosis, as well as fertility. The number of notches would indicate a monthly cycle. (Bowers Museum Collection)

Rare cog stone, brown limestone, deep rounded grooves are cut approximately equidistant across the edge, ridges unaltered, not round at the edge of the grooves, Orange County, California, 3-1/2" diameter, 1-1/2" thick. (Bowers Museum Collections, photo by A.J. Labbe)

Greenish cog stone disk, both faces concave, cogs made by cutting 16 rounded grooves approximately equidistant across the edge, Orange County, California. (Bowers Museum Collections, photo by A.J. Labbe)

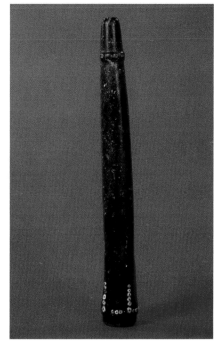

Steatite pipe, Canalino Culture, ca. 1600, Southern California, decorated with clamshell beads inlay at the drilled bowl, 12-1/16" long. (Bowers Museum Collection)

Steatite carved whale, one piece, a figurative zoomorphic effigy depicting a whale with raised dorsal fin and flattened tail, incised eyes and mouth in smiling expression, late Canalino Culture to that of modern origin, possibly 1600, 2-1/2" high, 3-15/16" long, 7-3/16" diameter. (Bowers Museum Collection)

Coiled serpent with incised diamonds, possibly Canalino Indian Culture, South Coastal California, ca. 1000-1850, steatite and shell. This carving may be a representation of the Milky Way, which was rendered as a diamondback rattlesnake, 8-13/16" long, 7-1/8" wide. (Bowers Museum Collection)

Polished steatite pelican stone, Canalino Culture, 1600, 5-7/16" high, 2-15/16" wide. (Bowers Museum Collection)

Chumash twined water bottle, interior and outer rim sealed with pine pitch to make it waterproof. Plain 2-element-Z-twined and strengthened at intervals with 3-element-Z-twining, found in the Cuyama Valley, Santa Barbara County, California, typical of the region. It is thought that this bottle was "ritually killed" by cutting holes in the bottom edge and at the neck, rendering it useless. (Bowers Museum Collections, photo by A.J. Labbe)

Steatite fish effigy pipe with inlaid shell, 14" long, Chumash Culture, Santa Barbara County, Southern California, ca. 1000-1750. (Bowers Museum Collection)

Steatite carved dolphin, one piece, Canalino Culture, Southern California, ca. 1600, figurative zoomorphic effigy depicting a dolphin with raised dorsal fin, flattened tail, bottle-nose snout, inset with white clamshell beads for eyes, 3" high, 7-3/16" long. (Bowers Museum Collection)

Pima coiled basket constructed of a tulle foundation with stitches in willow and devil's claw, typical braided rim, Arizona, 5-15/16" high, 15-1/8" diameter. The design depicts the "turtle back" a traditional motif, seen by observing the concentric rectangle forms. Such examples were sometimes used in winnowing grain and for catching the ground wheat that was made into pinole and tortillas. (Bowers Museum Collections, photo by A.J. Labbe)

Apache wood and leather cradleboard with beading in black, yellow, green, blue and white. A dressed doll with hair is attached to the board, there is also a beaded necklace and headband, 13-7/8" long. This object was collected by a doctor in the late 1800s working for the army at Fort Wachucka. (Bowers Museum Collection)

Native American Apache basket, Southwest, 3-15/16" high, 16-13/16" diameter, constructed from willow using the coiling method. Shown are four figures in three groups, and three figures in one group, plus a geometric center design. (Bowers Museum Collections, photo by A.J. Labbe)

Yavapai Western Apache coiled basket on three-rod foundation. Made of (possibly) willow and devil's claw, design consists of a band of T-shaped elements at the rim, below is a fret-like geometric radiating a flora pattern at the bottom of the basket. The rim is in devil's claw as is the solid center. (Bowers Museum Collections, photo by A.J. Labbe)

Apache bowl, 1890-1910, dark center with lightening bolt designs coming from it, light and dark brown triangles checkerboard the rim, collected in the 1880s by an army doctor working at Fort Wachucka. (Bowers Museum Collections, photo by A.J. Labbe)

Apache olla basket, 10-7/8" high, depicting several sections with animal and geometric designs, woven in dark and light brown. (Bowers Museum Collections, photo by A.J. Labbe)

Apache basket dish with design of diamonds, animal figures, triangles and a star in the center, 1890-1910, 15-7/8" diameter. (Bowers Museum Collections, photo by A.J. Labbe)

Anasazi ladle, Kayenta Branch, ca. 1200-1300, black-on-orange decor with handle, end perforated for hanging, fired clay. The central motif is an abstract "swastika," two of the arms terminate in key-shaped "cloud" symbols, which interlock with hatched serrated elements, lightning as a negative design, remaining design of unknown significance. (Bowers Museum Collections, photo by A.J. Labbe)

Anasazi, Mesa Verde black-on-white mug, 3-5/8" high, 3-5/8" diameter, ca. 1200-1300, exterior design only with framing bands at top and bottom. The design consists of interlocking coils (this is an early form of the wind symbol), both solid and dotted, rim ticked, handle decorated with dotted vertical bands. (Bowers Museum Collections, photo by A. J. Labbe)

Anasazi Tularosa clay ladle, black-on-white, hollow handle has four small holes used for safety in the firing process. Possibly ca. 1100-1200. Negative-design lightning symbols are formed by the interaction of the hatched geometric elements and the highly stylized solid line "swastika-like" element. (Bowers Museum Collections, photo by A.J. Labbe)

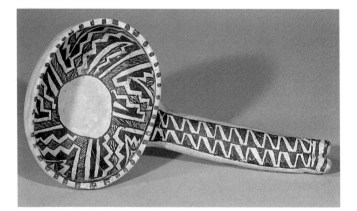

Anasazi ladle with bowl and handle, black-on-white, ca. 1200, 10" long, 5-1/4" wide. "Dazzler" geometrics are composed of serrated "cloud" elements in hatched and solid and cross-hatched lines in interlocking fashion, the handle is decorated with interlocking triangular elements. (Bowers Museum Collections, photo by A.J. Labbe)

Basketmakers' wooden ladle, 200 B.C. to 200 A.D., precursors of the Anasazi-Pueblo, found near Grants, NM, 6" long, 2" high, 5" wide. (Bowers Museum Collections, photo by A.J. Labbe)

152

Early 20th century Acoma, NM, ceramic jar, polychromed in black and white, base red, 9-7/8" high, 13-7/8" diameter, A geometric design incorporates stepped or terraced "clouds" and curvilinear "wind" symbols in solid and hatched line. This design is inspired by prehistoric Tularosa and Roosevelt black-on-white geometric compositions found around 1200 in New Mexico and Arizona. Hachured geometrics are opposed to solid geometrics of similar but complementary forms. Overall the composition represents interacting paired opposites and connotes fertility and dynamism. (Bowers Museum Collections, photo by A.J. Labbe)

Handmade ceramic vessel, potted and painted by Lucy Lewis in 1981 at the Bowers Museum during a ceramic workshop conducted by Lucy and her family, donated by the artist, 4-15/16" high, 20-1/16" wide. This Acoma example has an overall creamy background and interior, brown double-banded rim, four deer figures occupy the main body in brown, each stag is white-rumped and displays the heart-line motif with orange tip. (Bowers Museum Collection)

Acoma Pueblo polychromed shoulder jar, 15-3/8" high, 9-3/16" diameter, very busy geometrics in orange, white and black. Reputed to have won first prize at the International Exposition, held in 1915 in San Francisco. (Bowers Museum Collection)

Painted olla with repeating geometric design, Acoma Pueblo Culture, Acoma, NM, early 20th century, baked ceramic with applied slip and paint, 12" high, 14" diameter. (Bowers Museum Collection)

Polychromed painted jar with geometric birds, by Fannie Nampeyo, Hopi, First Mesa, Northeastern Arizona, late 20th century, baked clay, slip and paint, 7-1/2" high, 7" diameter. (Bowers Museum Collection)

Hopi polychromed jar entitled "Butterfly Maiden," 6" high, by Tom Polacca, Hopi, First Mesa, Northeastern Arizona, late 20th century, carved and baked clay, slip, paint and inlaid turquoise beads. (Bowers Museum Collection)

Elva Nampeyo, Hopi, First Mesa, polychromed jar with stylized geometric wing design, late 20th century, baked clay,
slip and paint, 6-1/4" high. (Bowers Museum Collection)

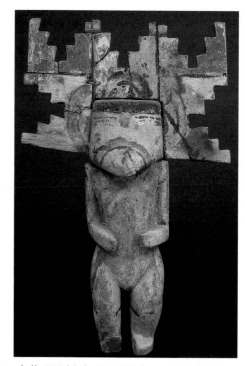

Kachina doll, 13" high, Hopi Culture, Northeastern
Arizona, ca. 1890, cottonwood, paint and string, done in
the Shalaka mana-style; the identity of the carving is to be
questioned. (Bowers Museum Collection)

Fetish jar, Zuni Culture, New Mexico, late 19th/mid 20th
century, baked ceramic, bone, antler, turquoise, coral
shell, rawhide, serpentine, feathers and other fetishes.
Jars such as this were sometimes buried, accounting for
the fine patination on this specimen. A small hole at the
base of the vessel is for ceremonially feeding the fetish
placed inside the vessel. (Bowers Museum Collection)

Hair roach, Northern
Plains, 11-3/8" long,
with two pieces of
leather thong 14"
and 17" long. This
head ornament was
created from dyed
deer hair and porcu-
pine; the animal
hairs are woven with
thread into a mat
base with strings to
be tied under the
wearer's chin and
around the neck.
(Bowers Museum
Collection)

Ogalala Western Sioux, Lakota ash wood pipe and Catlinite pipestone, ca. 1844, very important since it was
personally owned by Sitting Bull, Chief of the Dakotas. It
was given to Doctor Mortimer Jesuru of Douglas, WY, in
1884, then it was obtained by Ray Billingsley of Villa Park.
The ash stem has a twisting grooved pattern quite
common in 19th century pipes, interesting effigy figures
on the bowl. (Bowers Museum Collection)

Beaded hat with
floral design,
Iroquois, New York,
ca. 1849, velvet,
glass beads sewn
with thread,
purchased in 1849
by James P.
Thurston, from an
Iroquois. (Bowers
Museum Collection)

A GLOSSARY OF NATIVE AMERICAN TERMS

Aatsosni: A clan of the Navajo, means "narrow gorge."

Ababco: Sub-tribe of the Algonquins with lands on the south bank of the Choptank River, MD.

Abayca: Tequesta village in southern Florida, noted by Ponce de Leon in 1512.

Aberginian: Early Massachusetts settlers used this term to describe area Indians.

Abihka: Creek town, on the Coosa River, AL.

Abikudshi: Abihka Indians resided here and spoke the Chickasaw dialect. An early Creek town near the Coosa River, Talladega County, AL.

Abiquiu: Pueblo founded in 1747 by the Spanish. Raided and abandoned on several occasions. The town's name was changed in 1765 to Santos Tomas, located in New Mexico.

Abnaki: Algonquin tribe in Maine visited by Champlain in 1604. He noted bark huts near the Penobscot River.

Accomac: A town in Virginia. Also a tribe of the Virginia Confederacy. Their tribal identity was lost after 1812.

Acconoc: Powhatan village in 1608 located in New Kent County, VA.

Accoondews: Means large blueberries in Powhatan.

Acela: Small Indian village in central Florida visited by De Sota in 1539.

Achillimo: Chumashan village in Santa Barbara County, CA.

Achois: Southern California Indian village, became the mission of San Fernando on September 8, 1797.

Achougoula: Choctaw meaning pipe; known as the pipe people, nine villages in 1699.

Acoma Pueblo: "People of the white rock," known for their pottery. The oldest inhabited settlement in the U.S. Sixty miles west of the Rio Grande, Valencia County, NM. The Acoma raised corn, melons and flocks of turkeys.

Acoti: "Birth place of Montezuma," Indian site west of Taos in New Mexico.

Actinea: Plant used by the Navajo to create yellow green dye.

Adai: Members of the Caddo confederacy who had a contraband trail, which went between Spanish and French provinces.

Adario: Tionontate chief who made a treaty with the French to attack the Iroquois. With his war party on the way, he heard that the French were making peace with the Iroquois. Adario ambushed the envoys and set the Iroquois free. Later, the Iroquois attacked Montreal, killing hundreds of settlers. In 1701, Adario died in Montreal and was buried with honors by the French.

Adirondack: Mohawk meaning "they eat trees"; one of the Algonquin tribes that lived north of the St. Lawrence River.

Adobe: Sun-dried brick made with mud and straw, 18 inches long by 5 by 8 inches.

Adoeette: Kiowa chief, known as "Big Tree," who lived in Oklahoma and made raids into Texas. Captured and served at the Fort Sill Penitentiary; later released to become a Christian.

Adzes: A wood cutting tool used especially by the Pacific Northwest Indians. Constructed from copper, shell, bone and stone.

Aepjin: Dutch meaning "little ape," and the name of the resident chief, of an Indian village, Rensselaer County, NY.

Afsinimins: Powhatan word for walnut.

Agaihtikara: A tribe numbering 1,500 Indians, ruled by Chief Oderie, active around 1866, known as "fish eaters."

Agawam: "A place to cure fish," sites existed in the early 1600s. Areas included Ipswich, MA, also Springfield and Wareham.

Aguacay: An important salt manufacturing village along the Washita River, AK.

Ahapopka: Seminole Indian town, north central Florida.

Ahone: Meant God and used by the Virginia Powhatan Indians.

Ahosulga: Seminole town in Florida.

Ahpewk: Virginia Indian word meaning feathers.

Ahqwohhooc: Drum in the Virginia Indian language.

Akasguy: Extinct tribe who lived near the Brazos River, TX. Clothing was of bison hair adorned with bird feathers.

Alafiers: Seminole town; a tribe led by Chief Alligator.

Algonkian: A term used to describe rocks found in the Lake Superior region; also the same territory where the Algonquin tribes lived.

Algonkin: Indians who formed a close alliance with the French; scattered when attacked by the Iroquois. This small tribe lived east of the present city of Ottawa, Canada.

Algonquin: Tribes that were agricultural and sedentary. Their lodges were oval and constructed from birch bark. Others were made from saplings and twigs and logs. Famous leaders included Philip, Pontiac, Tecumseh, Powhatan and Opechancanough. This family occupied more territory than any other in North America.

Alki: Word found on the seal of the state of Washington, means "in the future."

Alle: Occupied by the Piros in 1589, a pueblo near Salinas, NM.

Allegheny: Iroquois reservation in the State of New York.

Alouko: Seminole town, Wakulla County, FL.

Altar: Both simply constructed and also on occasions complex. Could be springs, a pile of rocks or an animal skull. Some altars pointed north, south, east and west. Indians would pray for favorable weather, good hunting, good crops, etc.

Alum: Used by the Navajo during the dyeing process.

American Horse: Oglala Sioux chief, fought with Sitting Bull in the Sioux war.

Amerind: Suggested in 1899 by an American lexicographer to mean the races of man that lived in the New World before the Europeans arrived.

Amkonnmg: Means poisonous black cherry blossom, Powhatan Indian word.

Analco: Ancient pueblo of the Tewa, next to the San Miguel chapel, now Santa Fe, NM.

Anchor stones: Smooth stones with a groove to which a rope was attached and used to anchor Indian boats.

Andesite: Light gray to black rock found in the west around volcanoes. Used for making utensils and implements.

Apache: Lived on the plains of New Mexico and west Texas, warlike, raided both Indians and whites. Skilled at making baskets. Divided into numerous clans. Led by Nana, Victorio, Cochise and Geronimo.

Apokan: Powhatan Indian word meaning tobacco pipe.

Arapaho: Plains tribe of the Algonquin family, divided into the Northern and Southern Arapaho, the Atsina, the "rock men" and the "big lodge pole people."

Archaeology: The scientific study of ancient man revealed through digs.

Architecture: Types of building materials and construction: skin tents, adobes, wooden houses, cliff dwellers, also those homes fabricated from bark.

Aridian: Arts and works of the southern Arizona Indians.

Arrow: Constructed from a variety of materials to include hard and light woods, feathers, sinew and arrow shaft. The parts include: the head, shaft, foreshaft, shaftment, feathering and the neck. Some arrows had "blood grooves" or "lightning marks."

Arrowhead: Points usually chipped from flint; other materials include wood, bone, antlers, shell, iron and copper. Measure less than 2 inches long; spearheads were longer. Some points are leaf-shaped, others barbed to inflict jagged wounds.

Artifact: Manufactured works of man; a term used by archaeologists.

Ashes of juniper: A Navajo dye which was mixed with water and strained. Green needles were burned to an ash.

Ashkanena: Band of Crow Indians, means "Blackfoot lodges."

Aspinet: Leader of the Nauset, well known to the Plymouth colonists. In the winter of 1622, he and his tribe brought corn and beans to the starving.

Asqweowan: Means arrow in Powhatan.

Assahampehooke: The term for lobster in Powhatan.

Assiniboin: Large Siouan tribe who lived in the Lake Superior and Lake Winnipeg areas to the Lake of the Woods. Bison was the main portion of their diet. They dried and pounded meat (pemmican) and bartered with the whites.

Assumption: A mission established in 1728, located near

Detroit.

Assuti: A Nez Perce band who joined with Chief Joseph in the Nez Perce war of 1877.

Athapascan: A widely known linguistic Indian family, considered to be the largest in North America.

Atlatl: A device which assists in throwing a spear. The thrower has added leverage using this short stick which has a cup in one end into which the spear end is placed.

Attomoys: Powhatan for dog.

Attucks: Crispus Attucks, part Black and part Indian. The first person killed in the Boston massacre on March 5, 1770. His mother was an Indian; historians say that this battle opened the American Revolution.

Awatobi: A pueblo of the Hopi on a mesa 9 miles southeast of Walpi in northeastern Arizona.

Awl: A tool used to make holes and perforations. Used mainly in sewing, also for etching, scratching and in pottery making. Made from turkey and bear bones, antlers, wood, bone, splinters of flint, agave, thorns and cactus needles.

Axes: Vary from an ounce to 30 pounds, usually from one to six pounds. Made from granite, sandstone and slate. Generally one of two grooves were cut through the thickest portion of the ax. The haft was attached with sinew or rawhide. The Indians sought the iron axes brought by the white man.

Aztec National Monument: Pueblo ruins a few miles from Aztec, NM, on U.S. 550. Here the Anasazi people lived around 1,100 A.D.

Backhook: The Hook tribe lived around 1700 along the Pee Dee River in South Carolina.

Baking stone: Usually soapstone, rectangular, about an inch thick and a foot long. The hole in the center permits the baker to move it out of the fire. Its function could also be to lower into boiling liquids. Found in southern California and also used by the Pueblos.

Balcony house: A 25-room cliff dwelling in Mesa Verde, southern Colorado.

Ball playing: Played in California by eight or 10 men; also hundreds on occasion participated. Ceremonies and feasts were held before the game. The ball was made from deerskin stuffed with hair and moss; rackets were also used. The game became popular with whites and is now known as lacrosse.

Banner stones: "Butterfly stones," made of copper, hematite, clay, slate, usually having a double blade with a hole in the center. Possible uses: hung around the neck, used as a ceremonial weapon, fastened to the headdress.

Bannock: A Shoshonean tribe who lived in western Wyoming and Southern Idaho.

Baptiste Jean Baptiste: Christianized Indian, chief of the Iroquois.

Bark: Used by American Indians for smoking, covering houses, making beds, boxes and baskets, it was eaten and spruce and hemlock were made into cakes by Pacific and Southwestern tribes. Dyes were made, bark was also used as padding, torches and ropes.

Basal grinding: A method of grinding where the base of a stone tool is formed to prevent it from cutting the binding.

Basketry: Many uses and types; practiced by American Indians. Roots, fibers of plants, tree bark, feathers and other materials. Designs were copied from nature, dyes were secured from plants and minerals.

Batni: Site of the first pueblo built by the Hopi, Tusayan, northeastern Arizona. A sacred location for special offerings by the Hopi Snake People. A name given to a gourd in which sacred ceremonial water was carried.

Baton: A ceremonial staff of authority carried by a chief or shaman.

Bayberry: Used in New England for making candles. The berries were collected and boiled in water; wax floated to the surface and was skimmed. Also known as "wax myrtle," popular with the early New England settlers.

Bayogoula: Muskhogean who lived several miles from the mouth of the Mississippi River; also known as "bayou people."

Beads: Made from bone, minerals, bird beads, clay, seeds, shells, wood, teeth. The settlers brought glass beads as a big item of trade. Wampum was used in the northeast; the white and purple portions were used, the latter being more valued.

Bee plant: Used as a dye by the Navajo Indians; from the Rock-

ies.

Bells: Metal bells were brought by the whites as a trade object. Tribes made bells from clay and copper. The Southern states used copper bells, the material probably came from Central America and Mexico.

Beothuk: Indians of the Newfoundland area who painted themselves with red clay.

Bethlehem: An important center of Indian conversion, founded in 1740 in Pennsylvania by Moravians.

Bible: The Bible was first translated into the language of the Massachusetts Indians by John Eliot in 1661, completed in 1663. Later, the Bible was translated numerous times to fit the needs of a variety of tribes and missionaries.

Big Bill: Paiute chief, joined Mormon John D. Lee on September 11, 1857 in the Mountain Meadow massacre, southwestern Utah.

Big Jim: Grandson of Tecumseh, born in Texas in 1834, full-blooded Shawnee. Caught smallpox in Mexico and died in 1900.

Bird stones: Stones made to resemble birds, found in Ohio. Possibly used in ceremonies in connection with women's marriage and pregnancy.

Bison: Described by Europeans in 1530, also called buffalo. Caught and killed in tree traps, driven off cliffs, circled by fire and hunted with bows and arrows and spears. The whole tribe hunted in the summer. A valuable source of clothing, food and other essentials. Whites reduced them to less than 1,000 by 1890.

Bitterball: Sacred plant to the Navajo, used for dye and medicine.

Black Beaver: Interpreter between the whites and the Kiowa, Wichita and Comanche; also a guide and scout.

Black drink: Known as "Carolina Tea," made from the Ilex cassine leaf. Contains caffeine; popular with the Catawba Indians in South Carolina.

Black Hawk (1767-1838): Sac tribal leader who formed a confederation of Indian tribes to protest numerous dubious U.S. treaties. Joined the British in the War of 1812. In the Treaty of 1804, surrendered all the tribal lands east of the Mississippi.

Black Indians: Had a darker color than the general Indians who traded with the Dutch along the Schuylkill River in New York.

Blacksnake: Chief of the Seneca Indians, fought with the Americans in the battle of Fort George on August 17, 1813.

Black Tortoise: Mythical Indian tribe supposed to live in the Mississippi Valley area.

Blank: Any artifact roughly shaped but not yet completed.

Blankets: Designs were woven into the blankets, some were trimmed with feathers and fur. Used by the Indians as a hanging, rug, as a body covering, door covering, partition, sunshade, for babies and to carry food. Vital to the Indian way of life. In 1831, a blanket factory was established in Buffalo, NY, creating "Mackinaw blankets." The Spanish brought the sheep to the Southwest and the Navaho soon learned the value of wool.

Blount Indians: A Seminole Indian tribe, moving from Florida to Alabama and then to Polk County, TX, in 1870.

Boats: Numerous types: birch bark, popular in the Northeast; dugouts made from burned-out tree trunks and those with animal skins.

Boat stones: Found east of the Mississippi, considered to be charms worn around the neck.

Bone: Taken from many animals and used as fish hooks, musical instruments and other objects. Leg bones were used to create flutes.

Bosomworth: Mary Bosomworth, Creek Indian, interpreter to Governor Oglethorpe, Georgia. Married the Reverend Thomas Bosomworth; also known as Mary Musgrove and Mary Mathews as a result of two previous marriages.

Boxes: Made by sedentary and those tribes that lived in wooded areas. These include Northwest Coast Indians who made cedar boxes; those on the East Coast who used birch bark; California Indians who fabricated round wooden cases to hold feathers. Plains Indians relied upon animal hides and their containers are known as parfleches.

Broken Arm: Chief of the Winnebago, also called Spotted Arm.

Brule: Sub-tribe of the Teton, division of the Dakotas. Known by Lewis and Clark in 1804. They lived along the Missouri River from the White to the Teton Rivers.

Bruneau Shoshoni: A band who lived along the Bruneau Creek, in the southeast portion of Idaho.

Buckongahelas: Chief of the Delaware Indians who lived in

Ohio. Fought first with the English, but in 1794 changed sides and joined the Americans. Signed treaties at Vincennes, IN, in 1804; Fort Wayne, IN, in 1803; and Greenville, OH, in 1795.

Buena Vista: "Good view," a name given to prehistoric pueblo in Graham County, southeastern Arizona, on the Gila River.

Buli: Butterfly clan of the Hopi Indians.

Bullroarer: A sacred instrument associated with wind, rain, thunder, and lightning. Constructed of pine and fir, especially a tree struck by lightning. Also called a whizzer, rhombus or lightning stick. A rectangular stick of wood from 6 inches to 2 feet long with a cord attached. The slats in the wood make a sound similar to the wind, thunder and lightning as the object is twirled above the head.

Bureau of American Ethnology: Organized in 1879, founded by Major J.W. Powell. Deals with the study of specific cultures.

Busk: A celebration by the Creeks called the "green corn dance." Done annually and lasting from four to eight days. A period of cleaning and forgiveness, which gave new moral and physical life to all. Even new clothing was created. Special foods were eaten and the drinks caused one to regurgitate as a cleansing process. New fires had four logs pointing to four cardinal points.

Butterfly stones: Also called banner stones.

Byengeahtein: A Nanticoke village, Lancaster County, PA.

Cache: A deposit of implements from flint or other stones. Generally located in the Atlantic States or in the Mississippi Valley. Archaeologists discover large accumulations at burial sites.

Caching: The hiding of supplies when they all could not be carried. Articles were buried and the spot concealed with a fire, sand, rocks, hollow trees and water.

Caddo: A confederacy of tribes who lived along the Red River in the states of Arkansas, Louisiana and Texas. Visited by La Salle in 1687.

Cahokia mound: Prehistoric mound 998 feet by 721 feet by 99 feet high. Also called Monk's mound, located 6 miles from St. Louis, MO. There are some 45 smaller mounds in the area.

California Indians: Includes three large groups, the Shosgonean, the Yuman and the Athapascan, plus 18 smaller divisions. Acorns were an important food source, only the Yuman farmed. Some tribes include Maidu, Yuma, Yokut, Miwok, Chumash and Pomo. Sometimes California Indians are called Mission Indians.

Calumet: A "peace pipe" and a "war pipe." The stem is decorated with feathers and carvings; both public and sacred pipe were used. Pipes were smoked by both the friend and the foe to determine peace and war. Carvings and feathers often showed intentions before the ceremonies commenced.

Calusa: An important tribe living in southern Florida on Lake Okeechobee. They attacked Ponce de Leon in 1513 with 80 canoes; the battled lasted all day and the Spanish withdrew. The tribe killed all enemies, made human sacrifices and had much gold taken from Spanish wrecks.

Camp circles: When camping, the tribe would camp in a large circle. Each member had a location to set their tent; most of the property was owned by women. Concentric circles of three or four lines were used as a guarding device. Camps extended a quarter of a mile, each organization in the camp had a special place in the circle.

Canada: Used by early writers to discuss Indians who lived north of the St. Lawrence River.

Canadasaga: Seneca Indian town near Geneva, NY; in 1732, most of the tribe died of smallpox.

Canajoharie: An important Mohawk village located along the Mohawk River in New York.

Canarsee: One of 13 tribes that lived on Long Island, NY. All Long Island tribes paid tribute to the Iroquois. Brooklyn is situated on land formerly owned by the Canarsee Indians.

Caneadea: Old Seneca village, in Allegheny County, NY. The most southern Seneca town; the departure point for war parties traveling south and west.

Cannibalism: The practice of eating human flesh either as part of a ceremony and during starvation periods. The heart, bone marrow and brains were eaten. Prisoners as part of their torture were made to eat their own flesh. Tribes that ate human flesh were the Northwest Coast Indians, Kiowa, Sioux, Cree, Foxes, Iroquois, Micmac, Caddo and Chippewa.

Canonicus: Chief of the Narraganset Indians who challenged the colonists in 1622. Later he made friends with Roger Williams and signed over land.

Canopus: Chief of the Wappinger Indians, New York.

Cantico: Dutch and English term for dance, lively gathering or a noisy ceremony of the Indians. Also spelled: antico, kantico, kanticoy, kinticka and kantikanti.

Cape Fear Indians: Lived near the mouth of Cape Fear River, NC. The English started a settlement here in 1661 and took some Indian children to England for schooling; the Indians drove them away because of their dislike.

Carlisle School: The first non-reservation school in the U.S., located in Carlisle, PA; opened on November 1, 1879. James Francis Thorpe entered this school in 1907 and was coached by Pop Warner. He played professional baseball and football and won gold medals in both the pentathlon and the decathlon in the 1912 Olympic Games in Stockholm, Sweden. Born in Prague, OK, on May 28, 1886, of mixed Indian and white parents, the King of Sweden called him "the greatest athlete in the world." He is buried in Jim Thorpe, PA.

Casa Blanca: Spanish meaning "white house," and a name given to the Laguan pueblo, Valencia County, NM; the Pima village along the Gila River, AZ; and a ruined pueblo, Canyon de Chelly, northeastern Arizona.

Casa Grande National Monument: A large pueblo built by the Salado in the 14th century.

Catahecassa: Born about 1740, strong Shawnee chief, fought the whites; defeated by General Anthony Wayne. Turned into a staunch supporter of the whites.

Catalpa: An ornamental tree, known as the bean and candle tree.

Catatoga: Cherokee settlement, Macon County, NC.

Catawba: Located in South Carolina, an important Siouan tribe; in the early days they were very warlike and were devastated by smallpox. In 1841, South Carolina "bought" all of their reservation but one square mile. They know pottery making and cattle raising.

Catawba grape: A cultivated northern fox grape, named for Major Catherine's Town: Seneca Indian village, Catherine, NY, named for a woman captured by the Indians who became a power in the tribe.

Catholic: First full-blooded Indian, Negahnquet, to become a Roman Catholic Priest.

Catlinite: Red claystone found in Minnesota, used for making beautiful pipe bowls. Named for George Catlin, famous traveler and accomplished Indian painter. The quarries were considered sacred so even enemies could come there without fear to renew their pipestone supplies, for fabricating ceremonial pipes.

Catskill: Division of the Munsee tribes.

Caughnawaga: Seat of the Mohawk tribe, New York; here Jesuits maintained St. Pierre mission. The town was raided and destroyed by the French in 1693.

Cayuga: One of the five nations of the Iroquois who lived along the shores of the Cayuga Lake, NY. Some of the tribe moved to Ohio after the Revolution.

Cayuse: A tribe who lived in Washington and Oregon. In 1855, the Cayuse adopted a treaty and formed the Umatilla Reservation. Wars and smallpox caused the decline and extinction of pure-blooded Cayuse.

Cayuse pony: A well known term in the northwest U.S.; named for the Cayuse Indians who caught and bred wild horses.

Cazazhita: Dakota Indian division under Chief Shonka; the names means "bad or broken arrows."

Cebolleta: A 1746 Navajo settlement under Father Juan M. Menchero, Valencia County, NM. In 1747, the Navajo moved away because of their dislike of a sedentary life.

Cedar: Powhatan Indian word for tree.

Celt: Chisel and ungrooved ax blades, made of stone, varying in weight up to 20 pounds. Some wedge shapes are polished, other are not. The origin of the name is uncertain.

Cement: A variety of adhesives used by American Indian tribes to include: the boiled ends of deer antlers in Virginia, bitumen used by the southern Arizona and California groups, plus mesquite gum, greasewood and evergreen pitch used hot.

Chaco Canyon: A National Park, northwest New Mexico, 60 miles from Thoreau, NM, on U.S. 66. A large concentration of Anasazi pueblo ruins and restored kivas (underground chambers).

Chamizo: Shrub plant grown on the mesas, used for the creation of light yellow dye by the Navajo.

Channel flake: A long spall or flake which is chipped the length of the spear point or arrow, forming a groove.

Chaouacha: A small tribe who after the Natchez war came under the suspicion of the French. The French used Blacks to attack the tribe, since the two races would not band together.

Chartierstown: A Shawnee village, occupied up to 1748 on the Ohio River, Pennsylvania. The town was named for an Indian half-breed, Peter Chartier.

Chattanooga: Cherokee name for the point along the Tennessee River where the present city is situated.

Chaui: Confederacy of the Pawnee who lived in Nebraska.

Chaunis Temoatan: A 1586 Virginia Indian village known for its salt making.

Chautauqua: Seneca for "one has taken out fish here," now known for the Scientific and Literary Circle founded in 1878 by Bishop Vincent of the Methodist Episcopal Church.

Chebacco: A type of fishing boat used in Massachusetts and Newfoundland; also called "tobacco boats" and "pink sterns."

Chechawkose: Chief of the Potawatomi, lived on the south side of the Tippecanoe River, IN.

Cheeshateaumuck: New England Indian who graduated from Harvard in 1666.

Chekilli: Principal chief of the Creek confederacy in 1733 in Georgia, visited England in 1735.

Cherokee: Iroquoian family, formerly held southern Virginia, North and South Carolina, Georgia and Ohio.

Chettrokettle: An important pueblo of the Chaco Canyon Group, located in New Mexico, known as the "rain pueblo."

Cheyenne: Important tribe of the Plains group, part of the Algonquin family. Their name means to "speak a strange language." The tribes before 1700 are said to have lived in Minnesota along the Mississippi. Some lived along the Missouri River and made pottery and farmed. After being driven to the plains they became hunters of the bison. They fought closely with the Comanche, Kiowa and the Sioux. One of their greatest tribal ceremonies was the sun dance.

Chicago: Chief of the Illinois Indians; a site on the southern portion of Lake Michigan called by the Sauk, Fox and Kickapoo.

Chickahominy: Important Virginia tribe of the Powhatan confederacy. The name means "hominy people," or "coarse pounded corn people."

Chickamauga: Cherokee band that aided the English in the Revolution.

Chickasaw: Related to the Choctaw, an important Muskhogean tribe who lived along the Yazoo, Tallahatchie and Mississippi Rivers.

Chief: The political head with certain rights and obligations. The Iroquois and the Creeks had the most complex governments and there was no head chief as such. Chieftainship could be inherited through the mother.

Chinook: Northwest tribe who lived at the mouth of the Columbia River, OR. Great canoe makers, gathered wild rice, practiced cannibalism, built bark houses and had little contact with whites.

Chippewa: One of the largest tribes north of Mexico.

Chippewa Princess: Daughter to Nanawonggabe, chief of the Chippewa, who lived near Lake Superior. She was the only female permitted to wear warrior's clothes and participate in warfare ceremonies.

Chiricahua: An Apache division.

Chisro: Hopi "snow bunting clan."

Chitola: Zuni "Rattlesnake Clan."

Choctaw: Tribe with flattened heads, accomplished by continually placing a board on the child's head from birth on. Noted for their agriculture and lived in large towns.

Chorruco: Texas coastal tribe; Cabeza de Vaca lived with the tribe for six years.

Chosro: Hopi "Bluebird Clan."

Chua: Hopi "Rattlesnake Clan."

Chukai: Mud clan of the Hopi Indians.

Chumashan: Santa Barbara Indians, great fishermen, grew to dislike the Spanish and disposed of mission authority in 1824. Skilled with canoes in the open sea, made canoes of planks, caulked.

Chunkey: A man's game played in the Mississippi area. Played with a stone disk and a stick with an end crook. The disk was rolled, then the stick was thrown to stop the disk from rolling. The object was to have the disk stop in the crooked end of the stick. Disks are also termed "chunkey stones" and discoidal stones.

Clan: A division within a tribe with rights and privileges. These were granted, earned or inherited. Descent is traced through the female and the gentile name is usually an outstanding feature of an animal.

Clear Lake Indians: Pomo Indians who lived along the shore of Clear Lake in northern California.

Cliff dwellings: Houses built high on the sides of a cliff; used as natural rock shelters and cliffs. Located mostly in Utah, Arizona, Colorado and New Mexico. Food was grown on top of the mesa and in the canyons. Water came from springs and hollow places in the rocks.

Cliff Palace: Well preserved 146-room cliff dwelling in Walnut Canyon, Mesa Verde, CO.

Cliff rose: Evergreen twigs used by the Navajo to create golden dye.

Clothing: The amount of clothing depended upon the climate. Deerskin, hides of moose, mountain sheep, elk and bison and the pelts of rabbits and birds were used. The Northwest Coastal Indians used the bark of the cedar tree. Adornments included beads, shells, scalp locks, claws of animals, feathers and the quills of the porcupine.

Clubs: Many varieties were in use. There were ceremonial which were well decorated, those used for driving stakes, pounding pemmican and the warfare type which could be held or thrown.

Cochise: Well known Apache chief who in 1861 went under a flag of truce to deny part in the abduction of a white child. The commanding officer did not hold up his part of the bargain and hung the chiefs because they would not confess. Cochise escaped and fought the American troops for 10 years. He was defeated in September 1871. His son, Taza, became chief.

Comanche: The southern branch of the Shoshonean group who lived on the plains. Generally friendly to Americans, bitter enemies to Texans who took their best hunting grounds. They fought the Texans for 40 years; now reside on a reservation in Oklahoma.

Conchoidal: Chipped surfaces made up of concave and convex parts.

Conestoga wagon: Made in Conestoga, PA, and pulled by six to eight horses. This large covered wagon carried freight and passengers West from about 1850. The ends were higher than the middle. Tops were red, bottoms blue. Wheels were broad and spoked, the roof was white canvas.

Confederation: A group or political organization where two or more tribes banded together for defense or offense.

Connewango: A village of Seneca near Warren, PA.

Coonti: Plant used by the Florida Seminoles to make flour used in baking bread. Also spelled koontie and kunti.

Copper: Originally the ore was used as found and pounded into shapes. Later it was pounded into tablets, celts, bracelets and blades. Used by the tribes of the Lake Superior area, originating with and used widely in the Ohio region.

Cornplanter: John O'Bail, well known Seneca chief, born about 1732 at Conewaugus, NY. The State of Pennsylvania gave him a pension and a land grant.

Corn pone: A small round flat bread made from sweet potatoes, sugar and herbs, also from a variety of corn, seeds and eggs.

Corrugated pottery: Designs created in the pottery from the coiling.

Cotton: Indians of the lower Mississippi Valley used cotton blankets, believed by De Soto's troops to have been brought from the Hopi in Arizona and New Mexico.

Coups: A French-Canadian term for victory. Indian tribes had many coups: killing an enemy, scalping, touching a dead enemy and stealing the enemy's horse. The number of coups earned created an Indian's rank.

Cradle: An Indian board made in a variety of ways depending upon materials in the locality. Babies were laced into the cradle and carried for about one year. Cradles were handed down in the family and were considered sacred. Some were carried, hung from the back, the side of the horse or leaned against the house. Notches indicated how many children were in the family. Cradles were lined with cedar bark, soft animal skins, moss and down from birds.

Crazy Horse: A bold and daring chief of the Oglala Sioux. He got his name when a wild horse dashed through his camp when he was born or when his father, a holy man, watched him fight against the enemy. He killed his first buffalo when he was 12 and had his own horse. In raids he was skilled at decoy tactics. The Black Hills

Gold Rush of 1876 brought miners, speculators and General George Cook's army of 1,300 to face Crazy Horse's 1,200 force. Cook withdrew with heavy losses. The famous Battle of the Little Bighorn started on June 25, 1876, and ended the same day with all soldiers dead including General George A. Custer. Crazy Horse was arrested and killed at Fort Robinson on September 5, 1877.

Cree: Algonquin, stock, an important tribe of the Canadian area.

Creeks: The largest group of Muskhogeans, allies to the English in 1703, hostile to Spaniards in Florida. Defeated by General Jackson in the Creek War in 1813. The English gave them their name due to the many streams and creeks in the area.

Crook's Commission: Treaty made in 1887 by a government commission with the Sioux in Dakota; the Indians agreed to give up half their land.

Crow: Known as the "bird people," they were a wandering tribe, formerly along the Missouri River and then moved to the Rocky Mountains.

Crow Dog: Chief of the Oglala Sioux, who shot and killed Spotted Tail on the reservation in 1881. Tried and sentenced to hang, the Supreme Court ruled that they had no control over crimes committed on the reservations. Thus, he was released.

Cueva pintada: A "painted cave," 25 miles from Santa Fe, NM, known for its cave paintings and pictographs.

Curly Head: Chief of the Mississippi Chippewa.

Cussewago: Seneca village, 1750, later used for the building of Fort Le Boeuf, now Waterford, PA.

Cuttatawomen: Two tribes of Powhatan Indians that had villages of the same name; reported by Captain John Smith.

Dakota: The largest division of the Siouan family; their name means "allies," "ladders" or "enemies." Reported to be the top both physically and mentally of the Western tribes.

Davis, John: Creek Indian taken prisoner as a small boy. He translated and was an active worker with missionaries.

Deflector: A slab of rock or other material used in a fireplace or a kiva, to control the fire.

Dekanawida: Iroquois prophet and statesman who helped found the federation of the Five Nations.

Delaware: Important confederacy of the Algonquin. They called themselves Lenape, which meant "real men." The whites and the Iroquois forced them to move to Indiana, Wyoming and Ohio.

Deposit: An accumulation of rock and debris laid down by the action of the elements. Artifacts can be dated when the action and the resulting layers are measured.

Deseronto: Mohawk chief, also called "John Mohawk," fought in the Revolution in 1777.

Diatom: Microscopic algae found in rock which tells of climate changes in the past ages.

Didzedigozhiih: Bark and roots of small trees used by the Navajo for a purple dye.

Diffusion: The process by which a culture spreads to another culture.

Digger: Used for every tribe that had roots as a main portion of their diet.

Dighton rock: An 11 by 5 foot rock found near the Taunton River, MA; one surface was covered with difficult inscriptions like pictographs.

Directional colors: The Hopi use a variety of colors on kachinas to indicate the direction he has come: red (south or southeast); yellow (north or northwest); blue-green (west or southwest); white (east or northeast); black (the underworld). Colors may also be dots, stripes or solid forms.

Disconformity: Where a lower bed is eroded away and the upper bed of a different material, is deposited on the eroded area.

Dishes: Fabricated from stone, bark, clay and wood depending upon the available materials and the kind of food to be eaten.

Dlohazihih: A plant called Mormon tea, used by the Navajo.

Dolores: A mission also called San Francisco de Assisi, started on October 9, 1776.

Drills: Constructed from hard materials, stone, bone and wood. Used to bore objects. Both hand-held and hands/knees drills were used. There were simple and complicated drills (bow drill).

Dry painting: Known as sand painting, done by the Navajo as part of a special ceremony. Colored sands were ground from various sandstones.

Dsah: A basin sagebrush, used by the Navajo for medicine and to make light green dye.

Dull Knife: Cheyenne chief, signer of the Fort Laramie treaty in 1868.

Dyes: Accomplished by using grapes, sumac, bloodroot, roots, lichens, pokeberries and other material available.

Eagle: A sacred bird and the basis for many ceremonies. The feathers are used in rattles, war bonnets, shields, pipes, prayer sticks and baskets. Clipping, coloring and special additions to the feather formed a system of ranks and deeds. A young Indian would set an underground trap, bait it, hide in it and cover himself over with twigs, leaves and branches. Once an eagle attempted to get the bait, the Indian would try for the bird and as many feathers as he could grab. He was then honored and called a brave. Proper credentials are required and the provenance essential to own eagle feather. Technically, only Native Americans are permitted to own them since they are part of their heritage.

Earth lodge: A house made partially underground, especially the Osage, Pawnee, Omaha and Ponca. A large circle 30 to 60 feet was on the ground and then dug out to 3 or 4 feet. A roof was built in all directions, leaving a 3-foot hole in the center as a smoke hole. The building was laced and covered with grasses. This in turn was covered with sod. The roof was pounded to make it hard and waterproof. A long entrance was constructed facing east. A skin was used at the door. The lodge on the outside was about 7 feet. Several families could live here. Skins divided the house and also created warmth. Logs served to support the roof.

Eastman, Charles A.: Well known physician and author, his father was "Many Lightnings," a Sioux. Eastman graduated from Dartmouth in 1887. His books include: *Red Hunters, Indian Boyhood* and *The Animal People*. In 1891 he married Elaine Goodale, they had six children.

Ehartsar: One of four divisions of the Crow Indians.

Eliot Bible: The first printing and translation of the Bible into American Indian language.

Emistesigo: Chief of the Upper Creeks, over 6-feet tall, died in battle at the age of 30.

English: First contacts with the American Indians were friendly. Then the Indians were taken advantage of, the Church tried to get rid of "the accursed seed of Canaan." Colleges were started such as William and Mary, Dartmouth and Harvard to educate the American Indians. Harvard's charter stated: "the education of the English and Indian youth in knowledge and Godliness." Dartmouth's charter is part stated: "for the education and instruction of youths of the Indian tribes in this land." The English also influenced by intermarriage, the introduction of tools, farm implements, weapons and trade beads.

Enmegahbowh: An ordained minister, Reverend John Johnson, Methodist, born in the Ottawa tribe, adopted by the Chippewa and educated at the Methodist Missionary School, Jacksonville, IL.

Ensenore: Chief of the Wingandacoa of North Carolina.

Erie: Large tribe of Iroquoian Indians located from the Ohio River to the Genesee River, along Lake Erie and the Allegheny River.

Eskimo: "Raw meat eaters," the Inuit and Yupik speaking peoples who live along the Arctic Rim in North American and Asia.

Esquipomgole: A mixture of tobacco, sumac leaves and the inner bark of the dogwood. An Algonquin word to mean "what is mixed." Also called kinnikinnick.

Etaa: "Turtle clan" of the Zuni Indians, New Mexico.

Ethics: Early settlers did not understand the Indians, therefore, there was much difficulty. Indians had strong ethical codes for themselves and expected all to follow them.

Ethnology: The scientific study of a culture.

Family: All tribes had rules and regulations regarding position, rank and property. Rules of families concerned prisoners, death, births, marriage and adoption.

Farmer's Brother: Born about 1719, chief of the Seneca. He fought at Fort George, NY, when he was over 80 years of age.

Fast: To do without food or water for a specific period. This was spiritual and occult things could happen while fasting. Puberty and special war parties were two occasions when this happened.

Fauna: Past and present animal life in an area.

Feasts: Preceded by an offering to the points on the compass. Held for the opening of a big hunt or as a political tool.

Fermentation: This was rare when done on purpose. Tiswin, a type of beer was made by the Apache. Corn was soaked until it sprouted, then it was dried and ground. Then it was soaked again in a warm location until it fermented.

Fetish: An object that is carried in a small corded bag. The fetish is kept secret by the owner and it is a means to secure help from spirits. It may be feathers, bone, wood, part of an object, all intended to help its owner.

Fort Ancient: In Warren County, OH, along the Little Miami River, 6 to 19 feet high and 18,712 feet around.

Four Creek Tribes: Tribes of the Yokuts that lived along four streams that ran into the Tulare Lake, CA.

Fox: Clan of the red fox, Algonquin tribe; the French identified them while out hunting, so the tribe became the Foxes. Had a primitive society, were warlike and lived in Wisconsin.

French: Did a big business with the Algonquin tribes. Learned the Indian languages and came to understand their life.

Friedenshuetten: Converted Indian village along the Susquehanna River a few miles below Wyalusing, PA.

Fuller, William: Hereditary chief of the Miwuk Indians, California. He was the last of his tribe to speak the native language; the now-extinct language was recorded by Columbia University before Chief Fuller died.

Furniture: Simple, beds made of skins which were laid over a slat frame. Bed posts are driven into the ground, stools were constructed of clay, stone and wood.

Fur trading: Single trappers were to be feared since they wished to work along and exterminate the Indian. Hudson Bay and Missouri Fur Company and others worked with the Indians. Tribes also banded together for food and furs, alliances often lasted years.

Galena: Lead ore in bright cubical shapes found in Missouri and Illinois. Used for ceremonial purposes, placed on the altars and in the mounds.

Gall: Chief of the Hunkpapa Teton Sioux, assisted Sitting Bull in the battle of Little Bighorn, June 25, 1876. In 1889, he became a judge in Indian Court on the Standing Rock Reservation.

Gambel's oak: Tree bark used by the Navajo to make a dull brown dye.

Games: Two kinds were played, games of chance and games of skill. Games of chance were participated in with pebbles, sticks, etc. Some games were played during certain seasons; sometimes the entire tribe participated.

Ganahadi: A Tlingit division who lived in British Columbia. Their groups settled at Klawak, Yakutat, Chilkat, Taku and Tongas.

Garakonthie: Chief of the Onondaga, died in 1676.

G'asdah bee gah: A plant known as the owl's claw, used by the Navajo for creating yellow dye.

Gelelemend: Strong Delaware chief, also known as Killbuck, baptized as William Henry. Friendly toward the whites, promoted peace. White men attacked the tribe in 1782, killing all but the chief, who swam to safety. He joined the Moravian Indians of Pennsylvania and died in January 1811.

German: Germans had an influence on the Indians among the Eskimo, the Delawares, the Iroquois in Pennsylvania and New York and in South Carolina among the Cherokee.

Geronimo: Chiricahua Apache, born in 1834 near the headwaters of the Gila River, New Mexico. Fought against General George H. Crook in the Sierre Madre Mountains.

Ghost dance: Originated with the Paviotso in Nevada about 1888. The religion was begun by a Paiute Indian, Wovoka, a medicine man. Sick with fever, an eclipse occurred and Wovoka had a spiritual revelation from God. The revelation said that the Indians would be restored to their natural heritage; thus the tribe must practice songs and ceremonies. The dance was accomplished by the men and women without musical instruments; hands were held and all walked in a large circle.

Gold: Nuggets were found and used by the Mexican Indians, they did not melt or hammer them into shapes. Florida Indians also had gold and it was believed that it came from Spanish ships that wrecked on Florida's coast as they journeyed back to Spain from Mexico.

Gorgets: Simple ornaments hung from the neck or suspended from the ears. They were worn for their beauty.

Goshgoshunk: Three village settlement occupied by Seneca, Munsee and Delaware, located in Venango County, PA. In 1768 it became a Moravian mission.

Gouges: Stone tools of the northern Indians, look like a shoe horn, believed to be used in harvesting sap from maple trees. The sap ran down and out the stone groove.

Gourds: Many species were raised for food and seeds. Dried shells were fabricated into spoons, bowls, dippers, masks, rattles and other ornaments. Gourds were bound while growing to create interesting shapes.

Grand Saux: Name given to the Plains and Dakotas Indians; used to differentiate these groups from the Sioux living in the eastern woodlands.

Ground lichen: Used by the Navajo to make light orange dye.

Guachoya: Village on the west bank of the Mississippi; site where De Soto died, May 21, 1542.

Gun: A variety of pistols and rifles were used by the Indians. Some were taken from the enemy, others were purchased. Types include Colt, Springfield, Spencer, Remington and Winchester. The wooden rifle stocks were often adorned with brass nail designs.

Ha'altsedih: Navajo for wild walnut tree; the nuts and leaves were boiled in water to make a dark brown dye.

Haida: Northwest Coast Indians, grouped with the Tlingit and Tsimshian. Created large totems, cedar canoes, fine wooden houses.

Haiglar: Known as King Haiglar by the English, chief of the Catawba Indians, South Carolina. Killed by the Shawnee in 1762.

Hair: All forms were employed as a textile by the Indians of North America: bison, elk, moose, mountain sheep, dog, human, rabbit and beaver.

Hair forms: Hair-do styles varied with the tribe. Pawnee wore their hair short with a stiff scalp lock in the center, stiffened with fat and paint. "Roaching" was popular with many eastern tribes. Dakotas parted their hair in the middle and braided the long strands wrapping them in cloth and skins. Idaho tribes wore their hair loose, such as the Nez Perces. Southwest men wore bangs and a knot in the back. The Hopi women wore whorls over each ear which signified the squash blossom and marriage, then the braids were plain. In the Southwest, hair was washed in soap from the yucca root.

Half Chief: Seneca chief, born 1700. He died at the home of John Harris in 1754, at the present site of Harrisburg, PA.

Hammerstones: Used by tribes to drive tent stakes, as weapons, etc. Some were grooved with a handle fastened to them, others were hand held.

Hanging Maw: Chief of the Cherokee Indians; his name means "his stomach hangs down."

Hano: Intermarried with the Hopi and the easternmost pueblo of the Tusayan in northeastern Arizona.

Harris, Mary: The wife of Eagle Feather, a white girl the chief had taken prisoner. Eagle Feather's other wife was Newcomer.

Hatchet: Considered a tool for use around the camp, however, it was employed as a club or tomahawk on occasion. Stone was replaced by iron hatchets.

Hatchures: A design on pottery, that is, closely aligned parallel lines.

Haza'aleehtsoh: Navajo term for wild celery used to create light yellow dye.

Hematite: Oxide of iron, known as red ochre, used by the Indians for paint.

Hiawatha: Hereditary name and title of the chieftainship of the turtle clan of Mohawk Indians. Considered to be one of the founders of the Confederation of the Five Nations of the Iroquois. Longfellow's poem made his name famous, although the facts are not accurate.

Hickory Indians: A small tribe of Indians who lived near Lancaster, PA.

Hillis Hadjo: Leader and prophet of the Florida Seminoles.

Hishkowits: Known as Harvey Whiteshield, interpreter for the Southern Cheyenne. Also worked on a dictionary of the Cheyenne Indian language. Born in 1876 in Oklahoma.

Hobnuts: A root used by the Algonquin Indians which grew in swamps.

Hobomok: Chief of the Wampanoag of Plymouth, MA. Friend of the English, also became a Christian.

Hogan: Navajo-type house made from logs, planks and using either sod, clay or adobe bricks for filler. The roof was covered with hide and the structure had eight sides.

Holatamico: "Billy Bowlegs," one of the last chiefs of the Seminoles in Florida. He and his tribe moved to a western reservation in

1858.

Hominy: Food made from corn which is soaked in water and wood ashes to remove the kernel shell. Then it is cooked with meat or fish, now known as "hominy grits."

Hook stone: Made from soft stone sometimes soapstone, 1 to 5 inches long, shaped like a small letter "l."

Hopi: First visited by the Spanish in 1540. A large and powerful tribe in the northeastern portion of Arizona. Their name means "the peaceful ones, all peaceful."

Horizon: The level or stratum of a particular culture.

Hornotlimed: Seminole chief, active in the Seminole War in 1817, also called "Old Red Stick."

Horse: Brought to the Indians by Spanish explorers. Coronado brought the horse to the Plains Indians in 1541. Antonio de Espejo brought the horse to the Hopi in 1583. The Iroquois received the horse in the early 17th century. This animal was exceedingly important to the Indians, especially to pull things, for transportation and in times of war, plus buffalo raids.

Huma: Choctaw tribe from Louisiana around 1699. These "red people" due to war and disease became extinct.

Humbo: Used in New Hampshire, closely related to Chippewan and Algonquin, meaning to boil the sap of the maple tree to create maple syrup.

Hunting: Done for food and to secure hides for clothing. Animals were hunted while they slept or at night, such as birds. Clams were harvested by hand. Arrows, stones and spears proved effective, along with snares, traps and pits. Fresh water fish were drugged and caught using walnut root bark.

Hwoshntxyeeli binesd'a': The prickly pear cactus used by the Navajo for food and rose colored dye.

Iebathu: White corn clan of the pueblo home, Isleta, NM.

Iechur: Yellow corn clan of the Tigua of the pueblo, Isleta, NM.

Iefeu: Red corn clan of the Tigua of the pueblo, Isleta, NM.

Ieshur: Blue corn clan, Tigua pueblo, Isleta, NM.

Illinois: A confederacy of the Algonquin; formerly lived in Illinois, Wisconsin, Iowa and portions of Missouri.

Illinois nut: The nuts from pecan trees used for food and highly incised to scratch or cut into the surface on pottery.

Indian: The name first used by Columbus in February, 1493; he believed his destination reached was India. Today the term is all inclusive to mean all Indians.

Indian events: Powwows and Indian ceremonials held throughout the U.S., especially during the summer and the fall.

Indian reservations: Plentiful and shown on maps especially those at AAA in their states tour books. Many can be toured where arts and crafts may be observed. Stores are open for purchases and pictures may be taken.

Indian Rights Association: Formed December 15, 1882, in Philadelphia to promote education and civil rights for Indians.

Intrusive: An article discovered in a layer or stratum which differs from that in which it is usually discovered. Thus, it was not originally deposited there.

Iowa: Southwestern tribes of the Sioux, originally from Winnebago stock. In 1824, they ceded all Missouri lands, moved to Kansas and later to Oklahoma.

Ironwood: Also called ma'iidaa' and g'iishzniniih, a Navajo term to describe the plant, used for ceremonies. The plant produces blue berries that can be turned into a gray dye.

Iroquoian family: Made up of numerous tribes, a linguistic group. Highly organized, with a strong government and military. A complex social set-up, women voted, owned land and houses.

Iroquois Indians: The Five Nations composed of the Onondaga, Seneca, Mohawk, Oneida and Cayuga. Later they were called the "Six Nations" when the Tuscarora were added.

Jacal: A house built from wood and adobe. Poles are set at intervals in rows and then plastered with mud and bricks.

Jacobs: Delaware chief who fought against General Braddock's army and also along the Pennsylvania settlements. The Indians and their leader were wiped out by Colonel John Armstrong at Kittanning, PA, on September 8, 1756.

Japazaws: Powhatan Indian chief who talked Pocahontas into boarding an English ship in 1611. She was then held hostage so that her father Powhatan would behave in the English's favor.

Jennesedaga: Former Seneca village located on the Allegheny River, near Warren, PA. Well known chief, Cornplanter, lived here in

1816.

Jet: Velvet black coal used by various Indians to make jewelry, small figures and also ground to make face paint. Known in Colorado, New Mexico and Ohio.

Jicara: Spanish for a small gourd or Indian basket.

Jolly, John: Cherokee Chief known as adopted father to General Samuel Houston.

Joseph: Name given to a fine Nez Perces Chief by missionaries. He and his people roamed Idaho and then by the treaty of 1863 were forced to move to northeastern Oregon. Chief Joseph died on September 21, 1904 on the Colville Reservation in Washington. Joseph possessed remarkable military skill defeating superior U.S. forces and with his tribe were only miles from the Canadian border, when they found themselves outnumbered by cavalry, howitzer cannons and Gatlin guns. The exhausted leader gave his moving and dramatic speech on this occasion, October 5, 1877.

Junaluska: Chief of the Cherokee who fought with General Jackson in the Creek Wars of 1813-1814.

Kachina: Sacred Hopi Indian dancers of the southwest. Small antique and contemporary Kachina dancers are available at shows, markets, etc., carved elaborately of wood and colorfully dressed in skins and feathers and also painted. Most new examples range in size from about 6 inches to several feet; they are signed and dated by the artist.

Kaigwu: The oldest division of the Kiowa Indians from which Kiowa is derived. This group was entrusted with the medicine tipi.

Kamaiakan: Yakima Chief who led his people to a three-year war concerning removal to reservations. He was beaten in 1858 at Four Lakes on the southern branch of the Spokane River. Kamaiakan crossed the border to Canada and lived there.

Kanakuk: Kickapoo Indian Chief who lived in Illinois, died of smallpox in 1852.

Kanapima: Known also by his Christian name, Augustin Hammelin Jr., Chief of the Ottawa tribe. Sent to a Catholic Seminary in Cincinnati at an early age and then to Rome to study. Deaths in the family forced him to return and he aided in making a treaty with the government in 1835.

Kanhanghton: Delaware Indian village on the Chemung River, Bradford County, PA, destroyed by the Iroquois in 1764 since they were friendly with the whites.

Karankawa: A small tribe along the Texas coast who fished in the sea and got food on the chase. They practiced head flattening and ate human flesh like other Texas tribes. Exterminated in an attack by Juan Nepomuceno Cortina in 1858.

Karok: California Indians who lived along the Klamath River and did not make canoes from redwood, but instead purchased them from their neighbors.

Kasihta: Creek town along the Chattahoochee River, Georgia, who were visited by De Soto in 1540. The people thought they were descended from the Sun.

Kaskaskia: Peoria tribes meaning "he scrapes it off by means of a tool," who lived in the Illinois confederacy. They were visited by Marquette in 1673 and this was their first contact with whites.

Katamoonchink: A Delaware village in Chester County, PA.

Katimin: The village of Karok along the Klamath River about one mile from the Salmon River. The Karok thought this location was the center of the earth and it was very sacred to them. Yearly ceremonies took place there and the town was burned by whites in 1852.

Katzimo: A mesa about three miles northwest of Acoma. It was considered to have a historic past. A story claimed that during a storm the mesa broke away, was cut off from the world and the people perished. Archaeological research has proven that an ancient peoples lived here, proving the Acoma story correct.

Kaynaguhti: Apache band known as the "people at the mouth of the canyon," they were part of the Fort Apache Agency, Arizona.

Kecoughtan: Small group of the Powhatan confederacy, lived in the James River area, near Elizabeth City, VA, about 1607.

Kennebunker: An English word combined with Algonquin, meaning "at the long water," also used by Maine logging men to mean a type of clothing bag, especially useful in winter. Derived from the Kennebunk River, ME.

Keokuk: Leader of the Sauk, he was a guest keeper and entertained at tribal expense. After the Black Hawk War he was made chief. He died in 1848 in Kansas, he is buried in Keokuk, IA, and there is a bronze bust to his memory in Washington, D.C.

Kickapoo: First visited by Allouez in 1667; they took part in the plan to burn Fort Detroit in 1712. Numerous Kickapoo fought with Tecumseh and Black Hawk.

Kickapoo: Prophet (1785-1852), also known as Kenekuk. He had a vision to create a moral and religious community; it drew from the Kickapoo religion, Catholic and Protestant. His statement including agriculture/farming communities, be friends with the U.S. settlers, develop a religious and moral community and preserve their lands and their identity. He and his people were removed from Illinois to Kansas in 1833.

Kicking Bear: Nephew to Sitting Bull and fought with him at Big Horn and Rosebud. He was the apostle for the Ghost Dance and believed that their dead would arise, the hunting lands and the buffalo would return and white men would leave. He taught his people that the dance would repel the white man's bullets. On January 15, 1891, surrounded at White Clay Creek, Kicking Bear gave up his rifle to General Miles.

Kicking Bird: Kiowa Chief, established the first school for his tribe in 1873.

Killed pottery: Pottery broken during a ceremony to remind others of the individuals death. By breaking the pottery it was believed that the spirit of the person would be released and could travel.

Killhag: A wooden trap, derived from the Algonquin, used in Maine and other New England states.

Kinbinyol: The whirlwind pueblo, northwestern New Mexico, located in the Chaco Canyon.

Kingep: The largest and most important tribal division of the Kiowa.

King Philip: Second son of Massasoit, the English knew him as Philip of Pokanoket. He plotted for nine years and formed a confederacy and war broke out in 1675. King Philip was killed in Rhode Island on August 12, 1676.

Kintpuash: Captain Jack, leader in the Modoc War 1872 to 1873. Subchief of the Modocs who lived between Oregon and California. His 80 men surrendered to 1,056 regular army on May 22, 1873.

Kiowa: Located in Montana at the head of the Missouri River and along the North Platte River. They did not make a treaty with the whites until 1837.

Kitchen middens: Shell heaps, refuse piles found along streams and large bodies of water. Mounds may be several acres.

Kittanning: Important village on the Allegheny River, Armstrong County, PA. Composed of Iroquois, Delaware and Caughnawago, destroyed by Pennsylvania settlers in 1756.

Kitteaumut: Christian Indian settlement, 1674, in the southern part of the Plymouth County, MA.

Kiva: Hopi underground chamber for special ceremonies. Women are not permitted to enter. A kiva is entered from the top by a ladder. Some villages, depending upon size, had many kivas. Kivas were discovered in Arizona, Utah, New Mexico and Colorado.

Klondike: A corruption of the Athapascan dialect; the correct spelling is "Thron Duick," a river in northwestern Canada, the name suggests gold, riches, fortune, especially after the gold rush days of 1898.

Knife: Made from various materials: the teeth of beaver, bear and others; bone, stone, wood, shells, antlers and metals. Used both as a war weapon and in crafts. Often decorated with beads.

Korusi: A Patwin group formerly living in Colusa County, CA. Their creation story of the earth involved a giant turtle who dove to the bottom of the sea and brought back land to create mountains.

Kuato: A Kiowa division who in 1780 battled with the Sioux and were wiped out. They had planned to retreat but their chief said if they did they would not be accepted into the hereafter.

Kwahari: Comanche division who roamed the Staked Texas Plains, called "antelopes," they surrendered in 1874.

Labrets: Ornaments worn through the lips, first noticed by Spain's explorer Cabeza de Vaca when visiting Texas. Creations from shell, bone, stone and wood.

Lackawanna: A type of coal, also the name of a Susquehanna River tributary in Pennsylvania. The name is derived from the Lenape and/or Delaware dialect, meaning "a stream forks."

Lackawaxen: Lenape for "the forked road," given to two villages in Delaware, one in Northampton and one in Wayne County, PA.

La Flesche: Former chief of the Omaha, his full name was Francis La Flesche, married Rosa Bourassa, a Chippewa, in 1906.

Lake Indians: A term to designate the Indians who resided around the Great Lakes regions.

Laminations: Several fine layers of sand or clay deposited in an area to form beds. Measured and used for dating.

Lance: A long wooden pole with a sharp shaft attached. Used in both hunting and war. The hunting specimen had a shorter shaft and a heavier and broader head. War lances were light and had long shafts. Popular with the Plains Indians, often used while on horseback.

Languages: American Indian languages have a great variety of structures and phonetics. At one time there were over 1,000.

Lappawinze: Delaware Chief, signer of the Treaty of 1737 at Philadelphia. This agreement was known as the "walking purchase." Pennsylvania's governor ordered a road built inland, he then hired a trained runner to go the distance. Originally the agreement was from the Neshaming Creek to as far as a man could walk in 1-1/2 days.

Larkspur: Sacred to the Navajo, used in special ceremonies.

Lassik: Chief of this people who lived along the Eel River near the Mad River headwaters, California. The Athapascan people lived in conical houses structured from tree bark. Their dialect was like the Hupa, they constructed twined baskets and hunted the deer until the animal dropped exhausted.

Huron: Chief, signed the Greenville, Ohio, treaty in August 1795. Because of his help and friendship to the whites, they erected a monument to him in 1888.

Lehigh: Delaware dialect, "fork in the river," named for the County and a tributary of the Delaware River, PA.

Leschi: Chief of the Nisqualli and the Yakima, he led over 1,000 men on an attack of Seattle, WA, on January 29, 1856. A warship in the harbor drove them off; Leschi was captured by his own men for a reward, condemned and hanged on February 19, 1857.

Limonite: Brown oxide of iron, called yellow ochre, used for paint.

Lincoln, Abraham: During his presidency Lincoln met with a great number of Indian dignitaries. He was also known to have pardoned some Indians from hanging.

Little Crow: Former chief of the Sioux, Little Crow was his father and Little Thunder his grandfather. He and his people were removed to a reservation. On August 18, 1862 they rose up against the whites on a 200-mile front.

Little Raven: Former chief of the Arapaho, first signer for the Southern Arapaho at the treaty of Fort Wise, CO, on February 18, 1861.

Little Thunder: Chief of the Brule Sioux, 6 feet 6 inches tall. Commanded the battle of the Grattan massacre near Fort Laramie, WY, when Chief Singing Bear was killed in 1854.

Little Turtle: Chief of the Miami of Indiana; credited with the defeat of General Harmar on the Miami River in the battle of October, 1790.

Logan: Iroquois Chief, born in Shamokin, PA, about 1725. Also known as a Cayuga chief and as Mingo.

Lone Wolf: Kiowa Chief, one of nine who signed the 1867 agreement at Medicine Lodge, KS. His son was killed by the whites, he became hostile and fought until 1875. He was captured and sent to prison in Fort Marion, FL.

Long Sioux: Chief of the Dakota bands; roamed Montana in 1872. Lowrey, John: Known as Colonel Lowrey, Chief of the Cherokee, fought with General Andrew Jackson.

Maccarib: Algonquin derivation to describe northern deer and caribou.

MacIntosh, Chilly: Former chief of the Creek Indians, killed by half-breed Indian, Chief Menewa. His death was ordered since he had transferred land to the whites.

MacIntosh, William: Lower Creeks Chief, leader in the battle of Horseshoe Bend, AL, where nearly 1,000 men were killed. He helped the whites and gave them land, consequently the council of the tribe sentenced him to die. On May 1, 1825, warriors carried out the sentence.

Mackinaw: Famous trading post between Lakes Michigan and Huron. The name means "big turtle," a species of lake trout, a heavy blanket and a large flat barge.

Mad Bear Anderson: Iroquois lawyer who in 1959 led a group of Indians to Washington demanding to see President Eisenhower to present a grievance; they were turned away.

Madokawando: Penobscot Chief in 1630, made war on the whites in 1691, attacked the village of York, ME, killing 77. His one daughter was wife to Baron Castine.

Magnus: Chief of the Narragansett Indians, she was one of six chiefs in the area. Killed by the English in a swamp battle in Warwick, RI, in 1676.

Mahala mats: Designates the "squaw, or the squaw's rug in California.

Mahican: A large tribe that lived near the Hudson River in New York State. The Dutch termed them River Indians and the French addressed them as "Loups" or "Wolf people." In 1730, a large group moved along the Susquehanna River in Pennsylvania; later they went to Ohio and lost their identity.

Mahtoiowa: Brule Teton Sioux Chief who defended an Indian who killed a white man. Lieutenant Grattan demanded that Mahtoiowa turn over the guilty party. The chief pointed out the tipi and Lieutenant Grattan had one of his soldiers fire a howitzer into the tipi. Many were killed and the rest of the Indians attack the troops, killing all of them.

Maize: A derivation of grass, a cereal plant, from the mountains of Peru. Indian Corn was used and highly developed at the time the whites began settling. Corn was prepared numerous ways and also turned into "corn flakes."

Mangas Coloradas: Well known Apache Chief, called "red sleeves." Born in 1797, he died in 1863 while trying to escape from Fort McLane. Copper miners were killed to avenge the killing of some Apaches, who were invited to dinner by the whites and then killed. Coloradas was whipped by a group of miners and released. He formed an alliance with Cochise and attacked California troops in southern Arizona at Apache Pass.

Manhattan: The Island was purchased from the Wappinger confederacy by Peter Minuit a Dutchman, for 60 guilders' worth of articles. Manhattan means "island of hills," and the main village of the Manhattan Indians was near Yonkers. Villages on the island were for fishing and hunting.

Maninose: Soft-shell clams found along the eastern coast of the U.S.

Mano: Describes a grinding stone used in grinding grain.

Many Horses: Piegan Chief, Missouri area. He owned more horses than his entire tribe. Many war parties were against the Crows and the Atsina, in an effort to get more horses.

Maple sugar: Syrup and sugar making were learned from the Canadian Iroquois, upper New York and New England tribes. The word "sugar bush" is French; little has changed in collecting and preparing since early Indian days.

Massachusetts: Important Algonquin tribe that lived in the Massachusetts Bay area; the tribe almost became extinct in 1620 due to a plague. The word means "at the great hill."

Massassoit: Main Chief of the Wampanoag, Bristol, RI. A friend to the English, he passed away in 1662; King Philip, his son, was a famous fighter against the English.

Mazakutemani: Chief of the Sisseton Sioux, friendly to whites. About 1855, he became a Christian; he signed the Traverse des Sioux, July 1851, and treaties in Washington, June 19, 1858. He died about 1880.

Menatonon: Algonquin chief, 1585-1586, helped inform Ralph Layne about the new country; Layne had been directed by Sir Walter Raleigh.

Mesa Grande: Small village of the Diegueno in the western portion of San Diego County, CA. Later the name was given to the Mission Tule River Indian Reservation.

Mesa Verde: A National Park off U.S. 160 near Cortez, CO. Here lived the Anasazi people, circa 300 to 1,300 A.D. There are great cliff houses, kivas and a fine museum.

Mescaleros: Apache tribe who formerly lived from Pecos, NM, to the Rio Grande River. Their name is Spanish since the tribe ate mescal, an agave cactus.

Metals: Metals were used by the Indians before the whites arrived. Most prevalent was copper, followed by gold, silver and iron ores. Metals were often hammered into shapes. Copper artifacts have been unearthed in Ohio, Wisconsin, Alabama and other state mounds.

Metate: Spanish for "hand," where a device grinds corn or grains for flour. A flat stone with a depression in the center is used along with a flat or round grinding stone. A circular and rubbing motion between the rocks causes the grains to be broken down.

Metea: Famous Potawatomi Chief, one of the leaders of a massacre at the Chicago garrison. Active at the Chicago Council in 1821 and at the Wabash Treaty framed in 1826.

Metis: French-speaking people of the Northwest used this term to mean half-white and half-Indian, commonly "half-breed." The word is derived from Latin meaning "to mix."

Miami: "People who live on the peninsula," met first by Frenchman Perrot in 1668, when they lived in Wisconsin along the Fox River. Their power traveled to Detroit and Chicago; they traveled by land and the men were skilled at tattooing.

Miantonomo: Chief of the Narragansett who helped the English against the Pequot. The English did not trust him and tried several times to convict him of crimes. Finally he was captured and turned over to the English at Hartford; he was sentenced to die and killed by enemy chief, Uncas. His burial site is honored with a monument placed there in 1841.

Micmac: Algonquin who lived along the Great Lakes; supposedly the first Indians seen by Europeans. Three Indians were taken back to England by Sebastian Cabot in 1497.

Milky Wash Ruins: A prehistoric village located nine miles from the Petrified Forest, AZ. Ruins show stove-like altars.

Milly: Daughter of a Seminole Chief, Milly Hado saved the life of an American called McKrimmon. She begged for his life, even agreeing to give her own life. McKrimmon was sold to the Spanish. Later Milly and her tribe were taken by Americans; it was McKrimmon who came to her aid. The two became husband and wife.

Mingo: In Colonial times it meant "Chief." In Algonquin it is defined as "treacherous." It also is used to describe a detached band of Iroquois who left their main villages before 1750.

Minnehaha: The name was first used in Mrs. Mary Eastman's book, *Life and Legends of the Sioux*, 1849. Minnehaha is from the Teton Sioux dialect and means "water laughing."

Mishcup: From the Algonquin to mean a little fish such as a porgy or bream. The meaning "close together" describes the scales of this small fish.

Mission Indians: These California Indians came under 21 Spanish missions founded between 1769 and 1823. Franciscan fathers owned the land and herds of sheep, but both were put into trust for the Indians.

Missions: Established early by the Spanish and the French; Roman Catholic religion. In 1642 the first Protestant mission became a reality, established by Mayhew and Eliot in Massachusetts. Other denominations also participated.

Missouri: Indians consisting of Oto, Iowa and Missouri. The word means "Great muddy," and by the 1850s tribes left for Nebraska. Later they were broken up and "removed" to Oklahoma.

Mixed-bloods: A name assigned to Indians who mix with whites and raise a family; thus they are no longer pure-blooded.

Moccasin: Shapes and designs of this important article of clothing vary considerably from one tribe to another. The skin that remained predominate was deer skin often adorned in designs created with porcupine quills, beads, shells and buttons. Colors and designs have symbolic meanings and aid in identifying the tribe. Plains tribes wore a hard sole and a soft upper. Woodland Indians wore an entirely soft moccasin. Tribes in southeastern Texas and Northwest Coast Indians often went barefoot. "Moccason" is the former way of spelling moccasin.

Mocho: Prominent Texas Apache Chief, meaning "the cropped one," which refers to an ear he lost in a fight. Several Spanish plots failed to kill him.

Mocuck: A birch bark container to store maple syrup.

Mogg: Abnaki Chief in Maine, converted to Christianity. A Colonel Westbrook attacked and burned the village in 1722. The English killed many of the Indians. John Greenleaf Whittier wrote about Mogg in the poem "Mogg Megone."

Mohave: A large tribe of Yumans living along the Colorado River. They constructed rafts of reeds tied with bundles. The people also tattooed.

Mohawk: The most eastern of the Iroquoian confederacy. The Dutch carried on large amounts of trade and by securing firearms they became powerful against the Munsee and the Delawares. Main Mohawk villages were around Lake Mohawk, New York state.

Mohock: Early colonists used this term to mean a tough person or a present day mugger or gangster.

Monk's Mound: A large Ohio mound in an area where Trappist monks lived.

Montezuma: Known as Carlos Montezuma; Apache, born about 1866 near Mazatzal Mountains in southern Arizona. Taken prisoner in 1871 by the Pima. Sold to Mr. C. Gentile, an Italian native prospecting in Arizona. Gentile took Montezuma to Chicago where he attended the University of Illinois and the Chicago Medical School. Starting in 1890 he served the Shoshone Reservation, North Dakota. He departed the Indian service, returned to Chicago and taught at the College of Physicians and Surgeons, 1907.

Moosehead Indians: Penobscot who reside near and around Moosehead.

Moraine: An accumulation of rock and other material deposited by a glacier at its end.

Mortar: Used in a variety of forms by all Indians. Structured of wood, bone and stone. A flat or hollow rock was used as a container and another rock was used as a press upon and grind the grain in between. The plain or carved grinding device is often referred to in combination, as a mortar and pestle. Hollow and shallow places on boulders were used to grind corn, acorns, beans, etc. Wooden mortars were used by the New York Iroquois. Rawhide basins were popular with the Plains Indians and stone types were employed in the southwest.

Mosaics: Bits of shell, bone and others fastened with pitch and asphaltum to handles and ceremonial objects.

Moss: Used by Indians to make cradles for their babies. Added warmth came from deerskin and rabbit hair. Early settlers also used this popular method with their young children.

Mounds: Unusual formations created by prehistoric Indians. There are effigy mounds in Wisconsin, serpents in Ohio and birds in Georgia. Formations may be stone or a mix with fine dirt and stones. Heights range from 3 to 6 feet and are from 100 to 600 feet long.

Moytoy: Cherokee Chief in Tennessee. Pledged his people to the English and King George; later the two became bitter enemies.

Mugg: Arosaguntacook Chief who fought against the English in 1675. The site was Scarboro, ME; Mugg was later taken prisoner and brought to Boston. After his release he attacked Black Point and was killed on May 16, 1677.

Muller: Similar to a mortar, the Indians placed grain between two flat stones and rubbed them back and forth to procure grain.

Munsee: One of three Delaware divisions who formerly lived in New York, New Jersey and Pennsylvania. Also spelled Munsi, the main village was in Minisink, Sussex County, NJ.

Muruam: A Texas tribe that was baptized at missions in San Antonio, TX, at the beginning of the 18th century.

Music: An important aspect of Indian life; ceremonies were all performed accompanied with music. There were vocals and a variety of rhythms. Instruments included drums, flutes of pottery and wood, rattles, bone, whistles and notched sticks were rubbed together. Some tribes had musical bows. Clans used special officers to create and transmit songs correctly.

Muskeg: A "grassy bog," swamp or marsh; used by the Chippewa, "muskig," and also in the Kickapoo language "maskyag." Also noted along the Canadian border and by the Great Lakes Indians.

Mystic: Means "great tidal river." Mystic, CT, so named to the high incidents of tides in the area.

Nacheninga: Iowa Chief, "no heart of fear," and his son by the same name was painted by George Catlin when the Indian visited Washington, DC. The painting is in the collection of the National Museum, Washington, DC.

Nagonub: Chippewa Indian, born 1815, a favorite with the white ladies, had his portrait painted by J.0. Lewis but it was destroyed in a Washington, DC, fire in 1865.

Nahche: The second son of Cochise, "the mischievous one," he led raids on early settlements in New Mexico and Arizona. Captured by General Miles and placed in the Fort Sill prison, Oklahoma.

Nahpope: Black Hawk warrior who fought against the Americans at Wisconsin Heights; his portrait was painted by Catlin.

Nain: A 1757 Moravian mission built near Bethlehem, PA; used to convert Delawares, abandoned in 1763, moved to Philadelphia.

Nakasinena: Arapaho division living around Colorado Springs; their name means "the sagebrush people," and they claimed to be the mother tribe of the Arapahos.

Nakaydi: White Mountain Apaches, mostly captured Mexicans

and their descendants. The people walked with their toes out.

Namaycush: Trout found in the Great Lakes, also called Mackinaw trout.

Names: Often changed during their lifetime, governed by birth circumstances, puberty, warfare, retirement. Some names were inherited, others came about through a dream, others were taken for revenge. Christian names were also popular; much is often lost in the meaning when a name is translated.

Nanabozho: A great spirit who shaped the earth and the beings on it. Flint and fire were provided by Nanabozho who lived in the "Ice Country" of the far north.

Nanepashemet: Nipmuc Indian Chief, Middlesex County, MA. Killed in 1619 his widow assumed his station and was called sachem or Squaw chief.

Nanikypusson: Shawnee Chief signed a peace treaty in Ohio; Sir William Johnson was the signer for the British.

Nanticoke: Algonquin tribe who lived near the Nanticoke River in Maryland. In 1748 after difficulties with the early settlers, they moved north along the Susquehanna River joining the New York State Iroquois.

Nanuntenoo: Narraganset Chief, fought against the English, captured and taken to Stonington, CT. Here he was killed by the English, decapitated and his head was sent to the city fathers of Hartford.

Napeshneeduta: Sioux and Dakota Indian baptized and accepted into the Christian church. He was given the name Joseph Napeshnee, was married several times, recovered from fever in 1862, turned against his own people and fought with whites.

Narraganset: A leading Algonquin tribe in Rhode Island who lived away from other tribes and only suffered few smallpox losses. They lost power when over 1,000 men were killed near Kingston, RI.

Nasheakusk: The eldest son of Black Hawk, "loud thunder," his portrait was done by Samuel M. Brookes and is the property of the State Historical Society, Madison, WI.

Nashobah: A village of Christian Indians living near Littleton, MA.

Nassauaketon: One of the four divisions of the Ottawa, Michigan and northern Wisconsin. The name means "forked river people."

Nation: Used to describe the Five Civilized Tribes Cherokee, Creek, Chickasaw, Choctaw and Oklahoma.

National Indian Association: Organized in 1879 by interested whites to prevent "encroachments of the white people on the Indian." They published a paper called *The Indian's Friend*.

Nattahattawants: A Christian Indian chief who resided near what is now Concord, MA. Selling large plots of land to the whites, he received "six lengths of beads, a waistcoat and a pair of pants." His son, John Tahattawan led the "praying Indians," Nashobah, MA.

Nauhaught: Christian Indian, Massachusetts, known as Elisha. Deacon of an Indian church, Yarmouth, MA. Remembered in John Greenleaf Whittier's poem, "Nauhaught the Deacon."

Navajo: Warlike Athapascan tribe that lived in Arizona and New Mexico. Beaten by Colonel "Kit" Carson who attacked in 1863, killing most of their sheep so that they would be starved into submission. The Navajo made peace with the U.S. and acknowledged their rule on September 9, 1849.

Navajo tea: A plant used by the Navajo to make orange dye.

Neamathla: Seminole Chief who signed a treaty on September 18, 1823, giving the Americans 5 million acres of land. Most of the Seminoles did not agree with Neamathla, so he departed and joined the Creeks.

Needle: Created from bone, wood and spines from the cactus and locus tree. Iron needle came about through the settlers; human hair, horsehair and plant fibers were used for thread.

Negahnquet: First full-blooded U.S. Indian to become an ordained Catholic Priest. A Potawatomi Indian, he entered Catholic mission school given by the Benedictine Monks at Sacred Heart Mission, Oklahoma. He later studied in Rome, returning home and ordained in 1903 he worked among the Indians in a religious manner.

Negro slaves: Bought to the U.S. beginning in 1501 since they seemed stronger and easier to control than Indian slaves.

Negwagon: Well known Ottawa Chief who lived in Michigan. Lost a son in the War of 1812, adopted Austin E. Wing as his new son. English spotted the American flag flying in his camp and he was ordered to take it down. Then he wrapped the flag about him, took out his tomahawk and commented: "Englishmen, Negwagon is a friend of the Americans. He has but one heart and one flag; if you take one you must take the other." He and his family visited Detroit by canoe after the war, an American flag flew from the stern.

Neokautah: Winnebago Chief whose village was situated at Neenah, WI.

Neolithic: Generally accepted as the period when man raised crops, made pottery and domesticated animals.

Neron: Onondaga Chief of the Iroquois. He had burned over 80 prisoners and killed 60 with his own hands.

Nererahhe: Peace Chief of the Shawnee. Present at the meeting of the Six Nations, April, 1774 in New York.

Nescopeck: An Indian village in Luzerne County, PA, formerly occupied by the Iroquois, Delawares and the Shawnee.

Neshaw: The name for eel found along the Massachusetts coast.

Neswage: This Delaware Chief was attacked by the Sioux in 1841 in Dallas County, ID; all but one was killed. Then over 500 Fox and Sauk attacked the Sioux war party and killed all of them.

Netop: English greeting meaning "friend," "be my woman" and "comrade."

Neutrals: A neutral division of the Iroquois in the wars between the Hurons and the Iroquois. They lived near Seneca Lake, NY.

Newspapers: The first printed newspaper in North American Indian language was the *Cherokee Phoenix*, February 21, 1828; it was both in English and Cherokee. A semi-monthly paper in the Shawnee language called the *Shawnee Sun* came out March 1, 1835.

Nez Perces: This name was given to these Indians since they pierced their noses and inserted ornaments. Most of the time, they were friendly with whites.

Nikikouek: The Chippewa "otter people" who lived along Lake Huron and enjoyed fishing and hunting.

Nimham: Wappinger Indian Chief who lived along the Hudson River. In 1762, he traveled to England to plead for land claims. He got favorable replies but the Revolution stopped his claim. Fighting with the Americans at the Kingsbridge Battle on August 3, 1778, he was killed.

Ninivois: Potawatomi Chief of the Fox who fought with Pontiac at the siege of Detroit in 1763.

Nipinichsen: Village of Manhattan Indians on the east bank of the Hudson River, New York.

Nissowaquet: Ottawa Chief; his sister married Charles de Langlade of Wisconsin. Her name was Domitilde.

Nocake: An early Indian food adapted by the settlers, consisting of parched corn meal eaten with a little water.

Norse: Scandinavian explorers occupied the coast of Labrador and parts of Nova Scotia between 985 A.D. up through 1500. Possibly the Indians learned how to construct log houses from these early groups.

Notched plates: Found in Mississippi, Ohio, Alabama and other Gulf States, possibly for the grinding of paint pigments. Some stone plates have intricate bird and snake designs.

Nottoway: An Iroquoian tribe who lived in the southeastern part of Virginia. The Nottoway River gets its name from the tribe.

Nut-stone: Found in Ohio and other locations, this type is also known as cupstones. The stones are round with hollow depressions; they may have been used to crack nuts, mix paints, create drill handles or used as fire stones.

Obsidian: Black volcanic glass used by Indians to make bladed spear points and arrowheads. Since it is not usually discovered east of the Rocky Mountains, specimens outside of the area must have been secured through trade.

Occom, Samson: Christian Mohegan Indian who preached in Suffolk County, Long Island, NY, and wrote several hymns, one is "Now the Shades of Night are Gone." Also known as "pious Mohegan," he lived near New London, CT.

Ochionagueras: Christian Onondaga Chief who in 1654 was given the name Jean Baptiste.

Oconostota: Former Cherokee Chief, friends with the English and then changed over to the French.

Oglala: One main division of the Teton Sioux who lived in South Dakota. Famous leaders included Crazy Horse and Sitting Bull. This group was the terror of the west.

Okafalaya: One of three divisions of the Choctaw in the lower Mississippi.

Okisko: Weapemeoc Chief who gave Sir Walter Raleigh infor-

mation about the surrounding area. Although pledged to English rule, he was accused of treachery and plotting to massacre settlers.

Omaha: A main tribe of the Siouan family, means "against the current or wind." The treaty of March 16, 1854, gave all of their land west of the Missouri to the government. In 1802 smallpox reduced their numbers to less than 300. Their homes were of earth and sod, except when they traveled and then they were skin tents.

Onagatano: A location in the mountains where the Apalachee were said to have found gold in the 16th century.

Onasakenrat: Mohawk Chief who translated the Bible and other religious pieces into his native tongue.

One-seeded juniper: A plant used by the Navajo to create an orange-brown dye that serves as a chemical to color fabrics.

Ootun: Cheese or milk products that curdled; a Powhatan word.

Opechancanough: Powhatan Chief in Virginia who captured Captain John Smith. After his release, Powhatan went to his brother's camp Opechancanough, grabbed him and took him away for ransom. Set free, Opechancanough planned to attack Jamestown and did so on March 22, 1622.

Oraibi: "Rock place," largest village of the Hopi, northeastern Arizona.

Oratamin: Hackensack Chief, early 17th century.

Osage: Western division of the Sioux living in Illinois, Kansas and Missouri. First met by Marquette, a white, in 1673.

Osceola: Seminole Chief, born in 1803, who fought with the Americans for many years and was captured by American General Jesup when he came under a flag of truce to talk. Jailed at Fort Moultrie, he died there in January 1838.

Oshkosh: "Hoof or toe," Menominee Chief, fought with the English and helped to capture Fort Mackinaw, MI, from the American army in July 1812. Chief Oshkosh was painted by Samuel M. Brookes; the painting is at the State Historical Society in Wisconsin.

Ossahinta: Onondaga Chief from 1830-1846, belonged to the turtle clan; he was sometimes known as "Captain Frost."

Osunkhirhine: Abnaki Indian called Pierre Paul Osunkhirhine, he did much to translate the Bible and other important religious materials into the Penobscot dialects. Books that he wrote were signed "Wzokhiilan," the best translation that he could provide.

Oswego tea: Used by the Indians and settlers for its medicinal value.

Otherday, John: Wahpeton Sioux Christian Indian who married a white woman; he died of tuberculosis in 1871.

Otsiquette, Peter: Chief of the Oneidas and signer of the 1788 treaty.

Ottawa: Met by Champlain in 1615; woodland tribes whose name means "to barter or trade with others." Lived around the Great Lakes and in Canada.

Ouray (1820-1880): Chief of the Uncimpahgre Utes, Colorado. He was noted as a dangerous and cunning warrior; he also negotiated treaties with the U.S. and in 1863 gave all the lands east of the Continental Divide. Ouray and eight other Utes visited Washington in 1872 in an attempt to stop miners from trespassing, the Utes were pressured into giving 4 million acres for $25,000 per year. Ouray received an additional $1,000 annuity.

Oxidization: The change that occurs when objects are exposed to air, heat, cold, dampness, etc. It can be noted on pottery and metal; copper changes from a warm reddish color to a green and iron from gray to reddish brown.

Pack strap: Also called a burden strap or a tump line. The strap was around the forehead and extended over the back; employed by New England Indians to carry packs.

Paddle and anvil: A pottery technique where the paddle assists in making the object smooth and the anvil inside helps the pottery to keep its shape.

Painting: A popular process during both peaceful and war times. The body, horses and all types of objects were decorated. Paints were from a variety of materials: colored sand, charcoal, plants, minerals and even blood.

Paleolithic: The age of man where he was occupied with hunting, not farming. Stone articles were created by percussion.

Pamacocack: Powhatan settlement along the Potomac River, 30 miles from Alexandria, VA. Captain John Smith visited there in 1608.

Pani: A name given by Indians and early settlers to any Indian who became a slave, especially the Pawnee.

Panisee: A shaman or medicine man, used in the Northeastern

U.S.

Papago: The "bean people," of the arid and desert lands, south of Tucson, AZ, and Mexico.

Parched Corn Indians: "Civilized" Indians who still do many old things of their people, also farmers.

Parfleche: A tough rawhide bag or box with the hair removed. Often well painted and decorated and used to carry a great variety. Made by the Plains Indians and the Rocky Mountain Indians.

Parker, Eli Samuel: New York Seneca and mixed blood of the Wolf clan. Studied in the public schools, became a civil engineer. Joined General Ulysses S. Grant at the start of the Civil War, fought with Grant at Vicksburg. Assistant Adjutant General in 1863, later Grant's secretary. Parker wrote in his own hand the terms of surrender signed by Grant and Lee which ended the Civil War. Commissioner of Indian Affairs in 1869; died in Fairfield, CT, August 21, 1895.

Pashipaho: Sauk Chief, signed the treaty which gave Sauk lands in Illinois and Wisconsin to the whites.

Patina: A crust or oxidized film that is formed on buried and exposed objects. Also called patination, yields a very desirable glow and aesthetically adds to the object's value. The object should not be polished, scraped, dipped, sanded and so forth.

Pawnee: "Horn people" for the way they fixed their hair, also "men of men," since they were often used as slaves by other Indian tribes in the area. The Pawnee never declared war on the U.S.

Paxinos: Shawnee and Minisink Chief who fought with the Mohawk against the French in 1680. Friendly with Moravian missionaries his wife converted.

Peag: Massachusetts for wampum; white and purple beads made from shells. The Indian word is wampanpeag.

Pearls: Pearls appeared in Ohio mounds and the Gulf Coast Indians used pearls to decorate and for burials. De Soto dug up numerous Indian graves to secure the buried pearls.

Pecos: One of the largest pueblos in New Mexico; Jemez who lived here were met by Spanish explorer Coronado in 1540.

Pemmican: Deer meat dried over a fire or by the sun, then pounded with one part melted fat mixed in. Dried berries were also added and the mixture was packed in skin bags where it would keep up to five years. Buffalo and moose meat also used.

Penobscot Abnaki: people who still live in Maine on land that was theirs during early settlement days.

Pequot: Algonquin Connecticut tribe considered one of the most dangerous of the New England area. The name means "the destroyers."

Percussion flaking: A delicate and skillful process used to shape stone articles by tapping and hammering with another stone or heavy bone.

Persimmon: Used to make beer in the south, also mixed, cooked and dried with other foods. John Smith commented: "It draws a man's mouth awry with much torment!"

Peyote: "Caterpillar" in Spanish, also "mescal" by whites. The dried cactus "buttons" were dried and eaten during special ceremonies, creating dreams and hallucinations. Mostly in the Gulf States and northwest of the Rocky Mountains.

Philadelphia: "The City of Brotherly Love," named for the Biblical city in Asia minor was founded by William Penn in his 1682 treaty with the Indians. The Delaware village of Shackamaxon was near Philadelphia.

Piasa: To the Chippewa a large bird, the thunderbird.

Pick: Constructed of stone the Indian pick cut stone and wood and was used as a chisel, adz and celt.

Pictograph: A form of picture writing, a means of communication. Found on the sides of cliffs, cave walls, wood, shells, hides and humans. Simple features are included and the drawings may depict real or supernatural beings/objects. Some pictographs may be colored; they are found throughout the world.

Pierced tablets: Similar to banner stones; flat plates several inches long with a drilled hole or two through the edge.

Pieskaret, Simon: St. Lawrence Algonquin Chief; he became a Catholic in 1641, killed by the Iroquois in 1647.

Pillagers: Advanced guard of the Chippewa who entered Sioux country to become established there.

Pima: People in the southern part of Arizona; they did not take the scalps as they thought the enemy evil and would not touch them after they were dead.

Pinedrop: A Navajo plant used in its entirety to make dull brown dye.

Pipe: Various Indian forms; some were long, others shaped like a pipe, others for ceremonies only, like the calumet. Pipes were made during the Colonial Period in Europe and became trade items; many had inlays of other metals, initials, carving, beads.

Pipsissewa: Indian plant used to remove gall stones. Beer was also made with the addition of yeast, sugar and ginger root.

Pitchlynn, Peter Perkins: Choctaw Chief, of mixed blood, born January 30, 1806. Attended school to read, would not sign a fraudulent treaty or shake hands with General Jackson. Charles Dickens wrote about him after they met in 1842. He fought for the North during the Civil War while his sons fought for the South. He was a Mason, Indian agent and member of the Lutheran Church in Washington, DC. He died January 17, 1881, and is buried in the Congressional Cemetery.

Pizhiki: Chippewa Chief of Wisconsin, signer of many treaties, called "Buffalo" by the whites.

Plummets: Indian objects used a net sinkers, charms and for ceremonial purposes. Egg-shaped, sometimes drilled and grooved. Made of wood, copper and stone.

Pocahontas: Mrs. John Rolfe, Lady Rebecca and Matoaka. The Powhatan Indian woman who is said to have saved Captain John Smith's life. Then Smith left for England in 1609 and Pocahontas boarded an English ship to Jamestown in 1612, where she was ransomed by her father, the chief. Here she met John Rolfe in April, 1613, and they were married. She became a Christian and traveled to England in 1616. In March, 1617, she caught smallpox and died on ship. Thomas Rolfe, her one son, returned to Virginia and became wealthy. He had one daughter. Her burial was in St. George's Church, Gravesend.

Poison: Tribes employed poisons for hunting, warfare and in special ceremonies. Poisons stupefied fish and decayed substances and the juices of the yucca stopped invader and created infections.

Pokagon: One of the last full-blooded Potawatomi Chiefs. Attended Oberlin College, Ohio; became a Catholic; was active at the 1893 Chicago World's Fair; was an author and a poet; and got a claim of $150,000 from the government for the Potawatomi in Michigan.

Pokeloken: Indian term used by whites to indicate a swamp.

Poke weed: Also called Indian poke; a plant used by Indians to make a red dye.

Polychrome Pottery: Decorated surfaces beautifully rendered with three or more surface colors.

Pontiac: Ottawa Chief born about 1720 in Ohio. He agreed to give Detroit to the British and Major Robert Rogers to save attacks on his tribe. Because of harsh treatment, he got all the tribes north of the Ohio River together. They attacked all the British posts on the Great Lakes. Eight of 10 forts were seized, except Fort Pitt and Fort Detroit.

Poquosin: Means a "dismal swamp" or lands flooded at certain times.

Porgy: A North Atlantic fish: bream, poghaden, pogie, pogy and pin fish.

Porter, Pleasant: One of the last Creek Chiefs of Oklahoma, a Christian, fought on the side of the South during the Civil War.

Potlatch: A ceremony, "giving away" everything including slaves, houses, hides, canoes, etc. The giver then expected the receiver to do him one better.

Powwow: Get-togethers by Indians to talk, especially political. Also a time for medicine and possible witchcraft.

Praying Indians: Describes Indians who became Christians of one faith or another.

Pressure flaking: Objects are shaped from stone with the use of pressure against the surface.

Property: That which a person wore was their own; crops, fields, canoes belonged to the tribe; names belonged to the clan; sacred objects belonged to guardians, etc.

Prophet: Also known as Wabokieshiek, born in 1794 in Prophetstown, IL. As direct advisor to Black Hawk, he was blamed for the Black Hawk War. He was placed in irons and taken to Jefferson Barracks, MO, in 1832. He was later moved to a Kansas reservation where he died in 1841. Paintings of the Prophet were done by R.M. Sully and George Catlin.

Pueblo: Spanish word for village, especially those in Arizona and New Mexico. The Zuni, Hopi and Tewa are Indian descendants of prehistoric Indians that lived in the area for 1,500 years.

Pung: A sled or toboggan created from split pieces of wood which are fastened together.

Punkie: "Living ashes," a Lenape term applied to a sandfly which like an ash burns when it bites.

Pyrite: Crystals of iron pyrite were used to create a fire when they were struck against a rock to yield sparks.

Queen Anne: Pamunkey woman Chief after her husband Totopotomoi was killed. The battle was Bacon's Rebellion in 1675. She and her people were promised a reward, but she waited 20 years and then pleaded again with her son. A silver crown with the words "Queen of Pamunkey" was created, but she died in 1715 and never got to enjoy the result. The Society for the Preservation of Virginia Antiquities, Richmond, VA, received the "crown."

Querecho: Pueblo name for the Apache who hunted bison on the plains of New Mexico and Texas.

Quillwork: An early form of decorating before the use of beads. A very time-consuming and precise art using the quills of the porcupine and of birds. The art was accomplished throughout the U.S. in all areas except the southern plains and California. The quills varying in length and circumference and were dyed with berry juices. Quills had to be flattened in the mouth between the teeth. They were also softened with hot water and flattened with rocks. This type of collectible art was laced into moccasins, shirts, pipe bags and others.

Quinney, John: A Mohegan who assisted in the translation of prayers into the tribe's language. Joseph, one of his sons, was the deacon of a Stockbridge, NY, church (1817).

Quinney, John W.: Former Stockbridge Indian Chief, born 1797; a chief in Wisconsin from 1852 until his death in 1855. A painting of Quinney was presented to the State Historical Society, Madison, WI.

Quiver: The case used to hold and carry arrows. Its size was determined by the length of the bow and arrows. In Canada and the Rockies, deerskin was popular; the Pacific coast areas made quivers of cedar; skins of the otter, coyote and mountain lion were also used.

Quoddy: A term applied to a type of herring caught off Maine's coast; also, fishing boats known as quoddy boats.

Race: Indians had names for the various white sects that they came in contact with: "white skin," "big knife," "he who makes axes," "hairy mouths," "his eyes stick out," "big knife, long knife." The English were "coat men," French were "builders of wooden ships," the Germans and Dutch "those who talk ya ya," the blacks "black face," and the Chinese were "pig tail."

Rain-in-the-Face: Had seven wives, Sioux Chief born along the Cheyenne River in North Dakota. While in a fight as a boy, his face was cut; the blood and war paint streaked and others said he looked "rained upon." Renamed, his name was confirmed. He fought in numerous battles and most notable with Sitting Bull at Little Big Horn. Rumor has it that Rain-in-the-Face killed General Custer.

Rattles: Part of the music ritual to include ceremonies and witchcraft. Made from the beaks of birds, pods, seeds, tortoiseshells, hooves of animals and the dried scrotum of various animals.

Rawhide: Dried and stretched skins of animals that are fleshed and de-haired. Suitable in strips for tying and fastening, drum heads, etc. Shrinkage was part of the process; the parfleche was of rawhide.

Red Bird: Winnebago Chief, friend to settlers of Prairie du Chien, WI.

Red Cloud: Oglala Teton Sioux Chief, born 1822 near the Platte River, NE. He fought to maintain lands needed for a food supply for his people and prevented a road being built through Montana.

Red Jacket: Seneca Indian born 1756 at Canoga, NY, fought with the British during the Revolution and got his name from the red jacket that he wore. New ones were furnished by the British. In 1824 a mission on the reservation was removed due to a New York law. Red Jacket's dislike was revealed when he commented: "Because they do us no good. If they are not useful to the white people why do they send them to the Indians, why do not they keep them home?... these men know that we do not understand their religion, we cannot read their book, they tell different stories about what it contains."

Red Men: The idea began in Philadelphia around 1772 by a society called "The Sons of Tammany." Mr. James Byrn's home was their meeting place. The organization did charitable acts and the organization came to be known as. Improved Order of Red Men.

Roman Nose: Himoiyoqis war Chief, also known as Cheyenne and "Roman Nose," due to the shape of his nose.

Rubberplant: Used by the Navajo to make a bright yellow dye,

its meaning is "eared owl's foot."

Red mud: Southwest Indians collected the muddy runoff after a rain and used it as a dyestuff.

Red Thunder: Yanktonai Sioux Chief; fought at Fort Meigs and Sandusky, OH.

Renville, Gabriel: The last chief of the Sisseton Sioux, friend to the whites.

Reservations: Established by the U.S. government to control the Indians in the early days and remove him/her from their native habitat. The reservations were not always the best lands and Indian feelings were not taken into consideration.

Retouch: To rework or fix a broken point or turn the article into something else.

Robinson, Alexander: Potawatomi Chief who made peace between the Indians and the settlers. He was interpreter for General Lewis Cass during treaty formations at Prairie du Chien, WI, July 29, 1829.

Russia: Around 1741, Russian traders landed in Alaska and Canada. Siberian natives and American Eskimo were hostile to the Russians. Those that got through were met by hostile French and Spanish traders plus well armed Haida and Tlingit tribes. Russians owned small parcels of land in the area to raise foods for their traders.

Russian thistle: The entire plant was used by the Navajo to make dull green dye.

Sabeata: Jumano Christian Indian Chief asked the Texas Governor for protection against the Apache and for a mission for his people.

Sacagawea: A Shoshonean woman who traveled with Lewis and Clark west. She was captured by the Hidatsa of North Dakota at 14. Acting as an interpreter, she got horses to cross the mountains. She gave birth to a son on the trip. There is a brass tablet on her grave in Cheyenne, WY, and a bronze statue erected to her honor in Portland, OR.

Sacrifice: The Indian religion was a way to appease the spirits, "sacrifice" was accomplished using a pipe and tobacco, throwing objects into a fire; leaving rocks at certain locations, giving self inflicted wounds during the Sun Dance, cutting off joints to please the gods. Early settlers often did not understand the ceremony and too many times, meat roasting became human sacrificial flesh.

Samoset: One of the chiefs who came to the Pilgrims in 1620 and introduced them to Massasoit. A deal was struck in July, 1625, between the Indians giving the English 12,000 acres of land. Samoset died in 1653 and is buried near Round Pond in Bristol, ME; his name means "he who walks over much."

Samp: A type of mush made with beaten corn which has been cooked. It was important for both Indians and colonists.

San Antonio: Former Tigua settlement; several Spanish missions were established in the area. One was called the San Antonio de Valero, better known as the Alamo. The battle between the Texans and the Mexican soldiers took place here on March 6, 1836.

Sandal: A low cut shoe fastened by an ankle strap; worn mainly by the desert peoples, some in California and a few in the Gulf area.

San Diego: The first Spanish mission established in California on July 16, 1769. Indians in the area were of Yuman stock; those who came within reach of the mission were Dieguenos.

Sand painting: The same as dry painting.

Sandwich: Massachusetts town known for its early glass making; in 1685, this village was Nauset and Wampanoag Indians.

Santa Barbara: The tenth Franciscan mission founded in 1782 in California.

Sapohanikan: Delaware trade center, Hoboken, NJ. Furs and other items were taken to New York City from this point.

Saratoga: Mohawk village, "where the ashes float," there were famous mineral springs here. Also a name given to the "Saratoga Trunk" one with a large rounded top. George Crumb, an American Indian chef at Moon's Lake House, created the crisp brown "Saratoga chips" which became one of America's favorite between-meals snacks.

Satanta: Kiowa Chief born in 1830, known as "Orator of the Plains." Was one who signed the Medicine Lodge Treaty of 1867 which forced his people to live on a reservation. Taken prisoner by General Custer, he committed suicide in prison on October 11, 1878.

Scalps: Taken by a very few tribes in the early days. Many whites started the practice and encouraged it by offering up to $50 per scalp.

The Iroquois practiced it. The other governments including England, Spain, France and Holland also encouraged it as a means of counting. Scalps were taken from the back crown of the head and often cut from the person while they were still alive. Scalps were braided and knotted, sometimes dyed. As the settlers spread, so did the practice of scalping.

Scraper: Known by their particular use: side scraper, bottom scraper, etc. The device was used to scrap woods, hides and bone.

Scrub Oak: Navajo used the (galls), fungi and insect parasites found on this oak to create a golden dye.

Scuppernong: A white grape used to create table wine by Captain John Smith.

Sego: The root of this lily was used as food by the Indians of Utah.

Seminole: Muskhogean mixture of Creeks, Upper Creeks and Yuchi. The name means "peninsula people." The first Seminole war began in 1817. The treaty of 1823 was to have the people move from Florida in three years. Osceola, in 1835, started the second Seminole war which lasted for eight years. Those who stayed in the Everglades never made peace with the government.

Sequoia: Also spelled Sequoya, this Cherokee was born in Taskigi, TN, about 1760. He developed the Cherokee alphabet in 1821 which assisted his people with reading and writing. The redwoods of California were named after him by the government.

Setangya: Kiowa Chief and medicine man, also known as Satank. Signer of the Medicine Lodge Treaty in 1867. He went to Texas to get the bones of his son who had died there. In Texas, he attacked several wagon trains and bragged about it a year later in Oklahoma. He was arrested and sent to trial in Texas. Setangya drew a knife and a guard shot and killed him. He is interred in the military cemetery, Fort Sill, OK.

Shakehand: Yankton Sioux Chief who met in 1804 with Lewis and Clark.

Shamokin: Means "horns are plenty," and one of the largest Pennsylvania Lenape settlements. Located near the Susquehanna River forks, near Sunbury, Northumberland County.

Shawnee: Lived in Pennsylvania, Ohio, Tennessee and South Carolina. Their enemies were the Catawbas of the Carolinas.

Sherd: Also shard, meaning a piece of pottery found at a site.

Shield: Most were used for ceremonial purposes, especially the plains and southern Indians. Not common with eastern and woodland types.

Shipaulovi: Pueblos had to be abandoned due to the hordes of mosquitoes on the Middle Mesa of the Tusayan, northeastern Arizona.

Shoe: Powhatan Indian word is chapant.

Short Bull: Brule Sioux Chief, born 1845 in Nevada, became a Christian, took part in the Ghost Dance and thought of himself as the Messiah.

Shoshoni: A group who lived in Wyoming, Idaho and Nevada. Known as the "grass people," they relied on the bison and the horse.

Signals: Indians could use signs to show trouble, the enemy, friendship, fresh game. Such devices as a tomahawk in a tree to show the way, smoke signals, dust thrown into the air, fires that were lit in a visible area. Indians also walked or rode in circles and zigzagged when riding.

Sign language: Gestures were used as a system of communication between tribes having different languages, used chiefly by the plains Indians.

Silverwork: At the time of discovery, silver was not in use by the Mexican Indians. The craft was learned from Spanish explorers; now the Indians of the southwest excel and create outstanding works of art.

Sinew: The portion of the animal known as the tendon. It is taken from the backbone of the bison, deer and other larger animals. After pounding and drying, sinew was used for sewing; ropes and fish lines were twisted and braided from sinew.

Single-flowered actinea: Leaves, flowers and stems of this plant were used by the Navajo to create yellow dye.

Sitting Bull: Hunkpapa Teton Sioux Chief and leader, born 1834 in South Dakota. His name as a boy was Jumping Badger. His prediction of victory over Custer and carrying out the mission successfully gave him great honor. While trying to be rescued from prison on December 15, 1890, two Indian Police by the names of Bullhead and Tomahawk killed him.

Skookum Indian Dolls: Stereotyped Indian couples with baby, their eyes looking to the left, rare when looking to the right. Composition heads, sharp noses, closed mouths, braided wigs stitched down the center. Both adults wear flannel blankets, leather or plastic shoes and beaded necklaces. The bodies are stuffed cloth; paper labels are attached to the feet: "SKOOKUM/(Bully Good)/Indian/USA," designed by Mary McAboy, Missoula, MT; manufactured by H.H. Tammen Co., Los Angeles, CA; distributed by Arrow Novelty Co., New York City; circa 1920-1930.

Sleeping Wolf: Five chiefs were known by this name; the second Kiowa Chief went to Washington in 1872.

Sleepy Eyes: Sisseton Sioux Chief around 1822. A type of pottery and stoneware decorated with the profile of this famous Indian; made by the Western Stoneware Co., and others.

Slip: A thin coating of colored clay used to patch, cast, decorate or bond one object to another.

Smallpox: An acute contagious disease caused by the pox virus with skin eruptions, pustules, sloughing and scars.

Smoking: A practice well established by the Indians who smoked tobacco mixed with other plants. Done mainly at ceremonies and special occasions. Tobacco use spread to Europe and Asia. At one time, children in English schools were encouraged to smoke as an effective means against the plague.

Snake Dance: Held every two years by the Hopi of Arizona. The ceremony is associated with rainmaking and begins eight days before the public view it. The dance and the pageantry end with the snakes, who are carried in the mouth. After songs and special rites, the snakes are released to go and seek rain and then return. The tribe has both feasting and games.

Sofk: Corn meal food, ground, placed in hot water, cooled, then water is added that has been dripped through wood ashes. To this thick mix are added ground nuts and bone marrow.

Spade stone: Also called "ceremonial," an artifact found in mounds, they resemble shovel or spade blades.

Spall: A small chip or flake broken from a larger rock or mineral.

Spanish influence: Introduced chickens, goats, pigs, sheep and the horse. Silversmithing was taught and improved and some customs were abolished. The Spanish went deep into Indian country in their quest for gold. The Spanish also influenced the Indians with their missionary work.

Spemicslawba: Shawnee Chief, also known by James Logan. Taken prisoner as a child by General Logan. He later became a captain and fought for the Americans in the War of 1812.

Spirit Walker: Wahpeton Sioux Chief born around 1795 near Lacquiparle, Minnesota. A Christian who fought against the Sioux in 1862.

Spoons: Created from the horns of sheep, pottery, wood, shell and gourds. They were much larger than present day utensils.

Spotted Arm: Winnebago Chief, born 1772; his name was derived from the fact that he had a bad arm wound and painted it to look like a fresh wound, also called Broken Arm.

Squantersquah: Early spelling for squash and used by the Indians for food, utensils and rattles.

Squaw: A universal term to mean woman.

Standing Bear: Ponca Chief who lived in Nebraska. Taken to Kansas, they were asked to select a reservation site, but refused and walked 500 miles to their old village. Standing Bear and his people were arrested; in the new climate there was much sickness. Chief Standing Bear traveled the country telling about harsh treatment.

Steatite: A soft stone referred to as soapstone.

Stilts: A game played by the Hopi and the Shoshone children.

Stogie: Conestoga, PA, an Iroquois town, known for its short, hand-made cigars and Conestoga Wagons.

Struck by the Ree: Head Yankton Sioux Chief in Yankton, South Dakota. When he was born, Lewis and Clark were in the village and after seeing the baby wrapped it in the American flag. Years later the chief took great pride in this incident and was strong friends with the whites.

Succotash: A mixture of green corn from the cob, beans, milk and a form of meat, usually bear.

Sun Dance: Plains Indians ceremony performed in the summer, lasting for eight days. There was smoking, fasting and the completion of rites. Self-torture and penance were the main objects. Pegs were inserted through the skin of the chest, the Indians were raised from the floor or pulled with their bodies on the pegs. They were to eventually break their flesh and set themselves free. The Kiowa did not practice self-torture and missionaries and the government frowned on the practice.

Susquehanna: A 1608 Iroquoian town located near the lower Susquehanna River. Also spelled "Sasquesahannocks," by Captain John Smith. This tribe was friends to the early settlers and even assisted them in battles. Some historians have said that this is the most beautiful and melodic word in the Indian language.

Sweat lodge: Universal for the tribes north of Mexico. A small, rounded house was structured from sod, sticks or hide. Each of the individuals or one individual placed water on hot rocks inside to create steam. After a specified time, the person would plunge into cold water or snow. The lodge was intended to purify and cure disease. There were special lodge rituals.

Taimah: Fox tribe lower Chief of the Thunder Clan, signer of a treaty at Washington with the Foxes and the Sauk in 1824.

Tamaha: Mdewankanton Sioux Chief about 1775; he lost one eye when he was young, known as "One Eye" by the English, fought on the American side in the War of 1812, always wore a stove pipe hat.

Tamaque: Delaware Chief who caused Pennsylvania settlers great trouble. Sided with the English, then switched to the French. After 1764 he was influenced by Moravian missionaries and became a Christian.

Tammany: Famous Delaware Chief, the whites liked him to the extent that legends were told about him. Also called St. Tammany and the Patron Saint of America. The Tammany Society of New York became part of the Democratic Party.

Tarapins: Also terrapin, tulpa, turebe and terebins. A variety of American turtles living in both fresh and brackish water. Used by the Indians for food. The shells were cherished as hand and ankle rattles.

Tavibo: Paiute Chief and medicine man. He had a vision while the whites pushed his people out of their land: both the whites and the Indians would be swallowed by a giant earthquake; only the Indian would return to the land of plenty. Many hopefuls followed his teachings from Oregon, Idaho and Nevada.

Tecumseh: Shawnee Chief born near the Mad River a few miles from Springfield, OH. Tecumseh tried to organize all the Indians from Ohio to Florida to resist the whites and their habit of taking land.

Tenskwatawa (1778-1837): Means "open door," Shawnee Prophet, brother to Tecumseh. He lost the sight in his left eye as the result of a hunting accident. His message was to return to traditions, avoid European intermarriage and stay away from foreigners. He claimed that he could cure sickness and prevent death. Indiana governor William Henry Harrison challenged him to "cause the sun to stand still" and "the moon to change its course." Tenskwatawa predicted the total eclipse of the sun on June 16, 1806. Thousands of Indians joined his ranks in belief. He was interviewed by George Catlin in 1832 and had his picture painted. Prophetstown was founded by Tecumseh and Tenskwatawa and many Indians lived there. Tecumseh left on a trip in 1811 and his brother took charge. He was advised not to confront Harrison's troops but was drawn into the Battle of Tippecanoe in November 1811. He magic did not work that day, the Indians were soundly defeated and the prophet lost all of his influence.

Terrace: A geological step-like formation created when a stream or river cuts through land and exposes various earth layers, thus steps and terraces are formed.

Teton: Western prairie division of the Dakotas and the Sioux; the word means people.

Thayendanegea: Well known Mohawk Chief, through his mother's remarriage he became known as Joseph Brant. He married and joined the Episcopal Church and fought for the English in the Pontiac War of 1763. His sister Molly married Sir William Johnson, a British official. Joseph Brant convinced General George Washington, future U.S. president, to send an army into Iroquois country and the mission was a success. He was also commissioned in 1775 as a colonel in the British army due to his skills in diplomacy. At retirement the English gave him a pension and a large tract along the Grand River, Ontario. He also translated the Bible into Mohawk.

Thunderbird: Believed to be the cause for thunder and lightning, when a great bird flaps his wings. When hit by lightning, you are said to possess mystical powers. Thunder is a fight between the thunderbird and a giant serpent.

Tioga: Former Iroquois village near Athens, PA; it was the central area for tribes traveling north and south.

Tipi: The Sioux word for dwelling or house; Plains Indians made cone-shaped houses from bison skins and decorated them on the exterior. It required 10 or more skins and some 20 or more long and slender cedar poles, depending upon the size of the family. The hides were tied at the top and fastened around the framework. Tops were left open to let out smoke from the fire, the entrance was covered with a flap and sleeping was on mats around the wall.

Tippecanoe: The name means "at the place of the buffalo fish," and the phrase "Tippecanoe and Tyler Too" comes from the battle where William Henry Harrison defeated the Indians. During the presidential election the cry was used against Tyler.

Tomahawk: Used freely to mean club, ax, war club, hammer or a pipe which could be smoked and also used as an ax. With some exceptions, this tool with a handle could be used to chop wood, drive stakes into the ground or become a weapon.

Tomau: Menominee Chief acted as a scout and guide for Zebulon Pike.

Tomochichi: Creek Chief, appeared in Georgia in 1733 at the colony founded by Oglethorpe.

Travois: Consisted of poles tied to either side of a dog or horse with the ends dragging on the ground. Sometimes a small hut constructed from branches carried a small child. For the most part, provisions and the tipi hides were fastened between the poles. These sulkies without wheels were in use from 1540.

Treaties: The U.S. government claimed complete sovereignty over the Indians, but treated them like foreigners. Hundreds of signed treaties were broken, time and time again and Indian promises for the most part were never fulfilled. There was a grand movement by the government to "terminate" the Indian with the hope that they would eventually become extinct. Congress established the Indian Claims Commission in 1946 to terminate American Indian treaty rights; they gave the Indian tribes five years to file land claims. Much is yet to be done through activist movements, publications, organizations, legislation and self-determination.

Tribe: A large or small group of individuals bound together in a permanent body and having a unified purpose.

Tuckahoe: Known as floating arum Virginia truffle and Virginia Wakerobin, it served as a food in the form of a fungus and a root.

Twilling: A diagonal weave brought about when the woof threads are carried over one and under two of the warp threads.

Unaduti: Former Cherokee Chief the son of Reverend Jesse Bushyhead, a Baptist minister. In 1849, he traveled west to the gold rush and remained there until 1868.

Utchowig: A 1608 Erie village on the Susquehanna River, PA.

Ute: Large and important division of the Shoshonean tribes formerly living in Utah, Colorado and extending down into New Mexico. A warlike people, they did not practice farming.

Varves: Glacial deposits found in pairs, the upper shows clay and the lower sand. This process occurs each summer by the melting of the glacier. It is possible to date an area by counting the layers.

Vppeinfaman: A glue or gum used by Virginia Indians to secure their arrowheads to the shaft.

Waban: Nipmucs Chief, the first in Massachusetts to be converted to Christianity.

Wabanaquot: Chippewa Chief who became chief after his father's death, was a Christian Indian; his name means "White Cloud."

Wafford, James D.: Cherokee, born 1806, Clarksville, GA, attended school and became employed for the Bureau of Ethnology (the science that deals with the division of mankind into races and origins).

Wampum: A medium of exchange between the Indians and the settlers. Belts from wampum conveyed the idea of togetherness and peace or war could be arranged through this belt. The beads were from the hard clam and the whelk, found along coastal areas. The beads 1/4-inch long were either purple or white.

Washakie: Shoshoni Chief of the Wyoming tribe who disappeared for almost two months when 70 young men tried to get rid of him as chief. He reappeared at the council meeting with six scalps that he had taken and reestablished himself as chief. He died on February 20, 1900 and was buried with military honors at Fort Washakie, WY.

White Indians: A term used in various portions of the country to describe Indians who were white, had beards and dressed like Europeans.

White Swan: Crow scout under General Custer at the battle of Little Bighorn. A wound received in 1876 with the Sioux made him a cripple until death. His site of burial is the National Cemetery, Custer Battlefield, Montana.

Wigwam: Known by a variety of terms: wetu, witu, wetuom and wekuwomut. The term describes an Algonquin house or dwelling in the northeastern portion of the U.S. Constructed from bark and sticks, it is domed shaped, a hole at the top permits the smoke to go out. Wigwams vary greatly from tipis.

Wigwassing: Used by New England settlers to describe Indians hunting with a torch at night for eels.

Wild rice: Found in the Great Lakes area, gathered by hand as the canoe floated through the shallows. Indian women would bend the grain heads over into the canoe and hit them with a stick, thus collecting in woven baskets the rough grains.

Williams, Eleazar: In later life he claimed to be the Lost Dauphin of France. There is a painting in the State Historical Society at Madison, WI. He was born near Lake George, NY, about 1788; the son of a Christianized Indian, all 13 children attended the Catholic Church.

Winema: Also called Toby Riddle, woman Modocs Chief, born about 1842, married a miner named Frank Riddle and became an interpreter for the government.

Winnemucca: Paiute woman born in Nevada around 1844. Her full name was Sarah Winnemucca Hopkins; she was an interpreter and taught Indian school at the Vancouver Barracks in Washington. She secured land for an Indian school which she established near Lovelock, NV.

Woock: Powhatan Indian word for the roe of the sturgeon.

Wovoka: Originated the Ghost Dance, Paiute medicine man, also known as Jack Wilson.

Xalibu: Micmac word for reindeer or caribou.

Xinesi: Name assigned to the head of the ceremonies, a religious leader.

Yahuskin: Former tribe of the Shoshonean who lived in Oregon.

Yamasee: Former tribe who lived along the Georgia coast down into Florida. The Spanish in 1570 tried to bring them into slave labor. The tribe revolted and in 1687 went to South Carolina and lived under English rule. The "Yamasee stroke" came into being due to their skill with a canoe.

Yanegua: Former Cherokee Chief, also called Big Bear.

Yanktonai: Important tribe of the Dakotas in Minnesota and the Dakotas.

Yellow Thunder: Winnebago Chief, born about 1774. Signed a treaty to remove his tribe to a reservation in eight months. Through a misunderstanding, the chief thought the time was eight years and the chief was placed in chains. He was painted by S.D. Coates and the piece is in the State Historical Society, Madison, WI.

Yoholo-Micco: Georgia Creeks Chief, fought with General Jackson against the Creeks in 1813.

Yonaguska: Prominent Cherokee Chief who lived in North Carolina. A strong leader, at 60 became a prophet, led his people against removal and alcohol. Suspicious of missionaries, he noted on having the Bible read to him: "It's a good book, but it's strange that the white people are not better, having had it so long." Also called Drowning Bear.

Yuman: Wore little or no clothing, their living conditions had to do with their poor lands. These people lived in the southwestern part of California and around the Gulf of California. They made rafts of bundles of grass tied together to cross the water.

Zanckone: Virginia Indian term meaning to sneeze.

Zuni: Well known pueblo, Valencia County, AZ. The name was adapted from the Keresan and the meaning has been lost. It is supposed to be one of the seven lost cities of Cibola, for which the Spanish explorers were searching. The first Zuni mission was established in 1629.

DIRECTORY OF SOURCES

Acoma Pueblo: Rt. 23, Acoma, NM

Acoma Reservation (traditional and contemporary pottery): San Fidel, NM

Adobe Artes (jewelry, pottery, kachinas, fetishes, painting, baskets): 192 E. Main St., Huntington, Long Island, NY

Adobe East (Kachinas): 445 Springfield Ave., Summit, NJ

Alaska State Museum: Wittier Street, Juneau, AK

Ale-Chin Him-Dak Museum: Maricopa, AZ

American Indian Contemporary Arts: 685 Market St., San Francisco, CA

American Museum of Natural History: New York, NY

Ancient Traditions Gallery: 1010 Nicollet Mall, Minneapolis, MN

Apache Cultural Center: Fort Apache, AZ

Arizona Historical Society: Tucson, AZ

Arizona State Museum: Tucson, AZ

Autry Museum of Western Heritage: 4700 Western Heritage Way, Los Angeles, CA

Aztec Ruins National Monument: 1 mile north of Aztec, NM

Brooklyn Museum: New York, NY

Buffalo Bill Historical Center: Cody, WY

C.M. Russell Museum: Great Falls, MT

Cameron Trading Post: Cameron, AZ

Canyon Records: 4143 N. 16th St., Phoenix, AZ

Carnegie Museum: Pittsburgh, PA

Choctaw Trading Post: P.O. Box 76443, Oklahoma City, OK

Cibecue Trading Company: 31 N. Cromwell Rd., Cibecue, AZ

Coghlan Art (Pacific Northwest Coast): 26168 58th Ave., Aldergrove, British Columbia, Canada

Colorado River Indian Tribes Museum: Rt. 1, Parker, AZ

Colorado Springs Fine Arts Center: 30 W. Dale St., Colorado Springs, CO

Colorado State Historical Society: Denver, CO

Cowboy Artists of American Museum: 1550 Bandera Hwy., Kerrville, TX

Craig Dan Goseyun Studio: Rt. 2, Santa Fe, NM

Cranbrook Institute of Science: Bloomfield Hills, MI

Crow Canyon Archaeological Center: 23390 County Road K, Cortez, CO

Denver Art Museum: 100 W. 14th Ave., Parkway Denver, CO

Eagle Plume's (Fine Arts of the American Indian): Highway 7, Allenspark, CO

Eiteljorg Museum of American Indian and Western Art: 500 W. Washington St., Indianapolis, IN

Ernest Thompson Furniture: 4531 Osuna NE, Albuquerque, NM

Favell Museum: 125 W. Main St., Klamath Falls, OR

Felix Vigil Studio: Jemez Pueblo, NM

Five Civilized Tribes Museum: Agency Hill, Honor Heights Dr., Muskagee, OK

Flathead Indian Museum, Trading Post and Art Gallery: St. Ignatius, MT

Four Winds Gallery: 5512 Walnut St., Shadyside, Pittsburgh, PA

Gila River Arts and Crafts Center: Sacaton, AZ

Glenn Green Galleries (sculpture, paintings, drawings): 50 E. San Francisco St., Santa Fe, NM

Havasupai Tribal Museum: Supai, AZ

The Heard Museum, Shop and Bookstore: 22 East Monte Vista Rd., Phoenix, AZ

Hermon Adams Studio: 1030 Sandretto Dr., Prescott, AZ

High Desert Museum: Bend, OR

Hoer's Indian Shop: 9440 N. Highway 89A, Sedona, AZ

HooHoogam Ki Museum (Pima-Maricopa Indian Community): Rt. 1, Scottsdale, AZ

Hopi Cultural Center Museum and Arts and Crafts Guild: Second Mesa, AZ

Hudson Museum University of Maine: Orono, ME

Idyllwild Arts Summer Program: P.O. Box 38, Idyllwild, CA

Indian Center Museum of the Mid-America All-Indian Center: Wichita, KS

Indian Hills Trading Company and Indian Art Gallery: 1681 Harbor Rd., Petoskey, MI

Institute of American Indian Arts Museum: Cathedral Pl., Santa Fe, NM

Intertribal Trading Post: Oakland, CA

Iroquois Indian Museum: Howes Cava, NY

Jim Bob Tinsley Museum: 20 W. Jordan St., Brevard, NC

Joslyn Art Museum: Omaha, NE

The Kalbab Shops: 284143 N. Campbell, Tucson, AZ

Kansas State Museum: Topeka, KS

Kerr Museum: Poteau, OK

Kit Carson Home and Museum: East Kit Carson Ave., Taos, NM

Bruce LaFountain: Old Santa Fe Trail, Rt. 19, Santa Fe, NM

Linden-Museum: Stuttgart, Germany

Lovena Ohl Gallery: 4251 N. Marshall Way, Scottsdale, AZ

Many Hands Gallery: 301 Highway 179, Sedona, AZ

Margaret Patricio Arts and Crafts: Sells, AZ

Maslak McLeod (Inuit, Native, Canadian art): 607 Old Santa Fe Trail, Santa Fe, NM

Maxwell Museum of Anthropology: University of New Mexico, University Boulevard, Albuquerque, NM

Mazatzal Casino Gift Shop: Payson, AZ

Mesa Verde National Park: off Rt. 160, 10 miles East of Cortez, CO

Milwaukee Public Museum: Milwaukee, WI

Minnesota Historical Society: St. Paul, MN

Montana Historical Society: Helena, MT

The Montclair Art Museum: 3 S. Mountain Ave., Montclair, NJ

Museum of Fine Arts: On the Plaza, Santa Fe, NM

Museum of Indian Arts and Culture: 708710 Camino Lejo, Santa Fe, NM

Museum of Indian Heritage: 6040 DeLong Rd., Indianapolis, IN

Museum of Natural History: Chicago, IL

Museum of Northern Arizona: Rt. 4, Flagstaff, AZ

Museum of Primitive Art: New York, NY

Museum of the Cherokee Indian: Rt. 441, Cherokee, NC

Museum of the Horse: Ruidoso Downs, NM

Museum of the Great Plains: Lawton, OK

Museum of the Plains Indian and Crafts Center: Browning, MT

National Cowboy Hall of Fame: 1700 N.E. 63rd St., Oklahoma City, OK

National Museum of the American Indian: Heye Center, One Bowling Green, New York, NY

National Museum of the American Indian: Smithsonian Institute, Washington, DC

National Museum of Canada: Ottawa, Canada

Native American Preparatory School (9th and 10th grade and gifted): P.O. Box 160, Rowe, NM

Native Indian Community House: 708 Broadway, New York, NY

Native Naturals (antlers, bones, claws, feet, hides, jaws, skulls, tails and teeth): Staten Island, NY

Navajo Arts and Crafts Enterprise: Window Rock, AZ

Navajo Gallery: R.C. Gorman Works, 210 Ledoux St., Taos, NM

Nebraska Historical Society: Lincoln, NE

Nevada Historical Society: Reno, NV

New York State Museum: Albany, NY

Nez Perce National Historical Park: Visitor's Center, Spalding, ID

Niman Fine Art: 125 Lincoln Ave., Ste. 116, Santa Fe, NM

Northern Plains Indian Craft Association: Billings, MT

The Old Territorial Shop: 7220 E. Main, Scottsdale, AZ

One Nation Gallery: 108A Civic Plaza Dr,. Taos, NM

Orca Art Gallery: 300 W. Grand Ave., Chicago, IL

Peabody Museum: Salem, MA

The Philbrook Museum of Art: 2727 S. Rockford Rd., Tulsa, OK

Phoenix Art Museum: 1625 N. Central Ave., Phoenix, AZ

Phoenix Fine Art: 401 Front Ave., Suite. U-2 Coeur d' Alene, ID

Pipestone Indian Shrine Association: Pipestone, MN

Wendy Ponca (Osage artist): 453 Cerrillos Rd., Santa Fe, NM

Pueblo Grande Museum: 4619 E. Washington St., Phoenix, AZ

Quechan Museum: Yuma, AZ

Quintana Galleries: 139 N.W. Second Ave., Portland, OR

Rabbit Studio (original paintings): 231 S. Taylor, Pryor, OK

Rattlesnake and Star: 209 N. Presa, San Antonio, TX

Remington Art Museum: 303 Washington St., Ogdensburg, NY

River Gallery: Bluff View Art District, 400 E. Second St., Chattanooga, TN

Robinson Museum: Pierre, SD

Rochester Museum of Arts and Science: Rochester, NY

Rockwell Gallery (Remington bronzes, paintings, drawings, pastels, Winchester rifles, Colt pistols, Navajo Indian rugs): West Market Street, Corning, NY

Rogues Gallery: P.O. Box 418, Hulett, WY

Roy Rogers and Dale Evans Museum: 15650 Seneca Rd., Victorville, CA

Royal Ontario Museum: Toronto, Canada

St. Joseph Museum: St. Joseph, MO

Sakiestewa Textiles, (Ancient Blanket Series): P.O. Box 9337, Santa Fe, NM

Sam English Gallery: 2031 Mountain Road NW, Bldg. C, Ste. 2., Old Town, Albuquerque, NM

San Carlos Apache Cultural Center: Peridot, AZ

San Diego Museum of Man: 1350 El Prado, Balboa Park, San Diego, CA

San Juan Southern Paiute Yingup Weavers Association: Tuba City, AZ

Schenectady County Historical Society: 32 Washington Ave., Schenectady, NY

Scottsdale Center: 7380 E. 2nd St., Scottsdale, AZ

Seminole Cultural Center: 5221 Orient Rd., Tampa, FL

Sioux City Public Museum: Sioux City, IA

Sioux Indian Museum: Rapid City, SD

Southern Plains Indian Museum: Highway 62 East, Anadarko, OK

Southwest Museum: 234 Museum Dr., Los Angeles, CA

Southwest Studio Connection (contemporary Southwestern and Native American fine arts, jewelry and apparel) 65 Main St., Southampton, NY

State Historical Society of Wisconsin: Madison, WI

Stattliche Museen zu Berlin, Museum fur Volkerkunde: Berlin, Germany

Herbert Taylor (Navajo jeweler): 17483 E. Jackrabbit Rd., Mayer, AZ

Tecumseh's Frontier Trading Post (handmade buckskin clothing, weapons, etc.): 140 W. Yellowstone Ave., Cody, WY

Tex Ritter Museum: 30 W. Panola, Carthage, TX

Third Canyon Gallery: 1512 Larimer St., Denver, CO

Thomas Gilcrease Museum: 1400 Gilcrease Museum Rd., Tulsa, OK

Totem Bight State Park: off Tongaa Highway, north of Ketchikan, AK

Robert Dale Tsosie: Rt. 1, Espanola, NM

Buddy Tubinaghtewa (Hopi carvings and paintings): P.O. Box 34321, Phoenix, AZ

Ubersee Museum: Bremen, Germany

University of Pennsylvania Museum: Philadelphia, PA

Western Accessories Trading Corp. (sterling silver, genuine turquoise, black onyx): P.O. Box 1036, Lewisburg, TN

West Reading Museum: West Reading, PA

Wheelwright Museum of the American Indian: 704 Camino Lejo, Santa Fe, NM

Wild Wings (Native American replicas): P.O. Box 451, Lake City, MN

Tandy Young: Choctaw, President Native America Travel Service and Tourism Center

Zion Natural History Association: Fredonia, AZ

BIBLIOGRAPHY

Adair, John, *The Navajo and Pueblo-Silversmiths*. Norman, OK: University of Oklahoma Press, 1944.

Anderson, Gilbert and Kerbow, *American Indian Auction Price Guides*. Vol. 1 and 2, Beowulf Fine Art Ltd., Houston, TX: 1992, 1993.

Andrews, Ralph W., *Indians As the Westerners Saw Them*. Seattle, WA: Superior Publishing Company, 1962.

Appleton, Le Roy, *Indian Art of the Americas*. New York: Charles Scribner's Sons, 1950.

Arnold, David L., "Pueblo Artistry in Clay," *National Geographic*, November 1982.

Bahti, Tom, *Southwestern Indian Arts and Crafts*. Flagstaff, AZ: KC Publications, 1970.

Bahti, Tom. *Southwestern Indian Tribes*. Las Vegas, NV: KC Publications, 1971.

Barbeau, Charles Marius. "Totem Poles," *Bulletin of the National Museum of Canada*, No. 119, 2 volumes. Ottawa, Canada, 1930.

Barnard, Edward S., editor, *Story of the Great American West*, Pleasantville, NY: The Reader's Digest Association, 1977.

Bass, Athea, *The Arapaho Way: A Memoir of an Indian Boyhood*. New York: Clarkson N. Potter, 1966.

Beebe, Lucius and Charles Clegg, *The American West*. New York: E.P. Dutton, 1955.

Bennett, Edna Mae and John F., *Turquoise Jewelry of the Indians of the Southwest*. Colorado: Turquoise Books, 1973.

Birket-Smith, Kaj, *The Eskimos*. New York: E.P. Dutton, 1936.

Bleeker, Sonia, *The Sioux Indians: Hunters and Warriors of the Plains*. New York: William Morrow and Company, 1962.

Blevins, Winfred, *Dictionary of the American West*. New York: Facts On File, 1993.

Bourie, Steve, *American Casino Guide*. Dania, FL: Casino vacations, 1997.

Bourke, John G., "Medicine-Men of the Apache," *Ninth Annual Report of the American Ethnology*. Washington, DC: Smithsonian Institution, 1892.

Brady, Cyrus Townsend, *Indian Fights and Fighters*. Lincoln, NE: University of Nebraska Press, 1971.

Branch, E. Douglas, *The Hunting of Buffalo*. Lincoln, NE: University of Nebraska Press, 1962.

Brose, Davis S., James A. Brown and David W. Penney, *Ancient Art of the American Woodland Indians*. New York: Harry Abrams, 1985.

Brown, Dee, *The American West*. New York: Touchstone, 1995.

Brown, Mark H. and W.R. Felton, *The Frontier Years*. New York: Bramhall House, 1955.

Burbank, E.A., *Burbank Among the Indians*. Caldwell, ID: Caxton Printers, 1946.

Buttree, Julia M., *The Rhythm of the Redman*. New York: Ronald Press Company, 1930.

Campbell, David, editor, *Native American Arts and Folklore*. New York: Crescent Books, 1993.

Catlin, George, *Letter and Notes on the Manners, Customs and Conditions of the North American Indian*. New York: Dover Publications, 1973.

Champagne, Duane, *Native American Portrait of the Peoples*. Detroit, MI: Visible Ink Press, 1994.

Ciment, James, *Encyclopedia of the North American Indian*. New York: Scholastic Reference, 1996.

Collier, John, *Patterns and Ceremonials of the Indians of the Southwest*. New York: Dover, 1995.

Colton, Harold S., *Hopi Kachina Dolls*. Albuquerque, NM: University of New Mexico Press, 1959.

Cronyn, George W., editor. *American Indian Poetry*. New York: Fawcett Columbine, 1991.

Cunningham, Robert E., *Indian Territory*. Norman, OK: University of Oklahoma Press, 1957.

Davis, Robert T., *Native Arts of the Pacific Northwest*. Stanford, CA: Stanford University Press, 1949.

Dallas, Sandra, "Triumph on a Loom," *Americana*, June 1988, pp. 54-57.

Densmore, Frances, *How Indians Use Wild Plants for Food, Medicine and Crafts*. New York: Dover Publications, 1974.

Dixon, Joseph E., *The Vanishing Race*. New York: Doubleday, Page and Company, 1913.

Dockstader, Frederick J., *Weaving Arts of the North American Indian*. New York: Harper Collins, 1993.

Douglas, F.H., *Indian Culture Areas in the United States*. Denver, CO: Denver Art Museum, 1950.

Drew, Lisa, "A Feast Fit For Eagles," *National Wildlife*, December-/January 1966, pp. 46-49.

Driggs, Howard R., *The Old West Speaks*. Englewood Cliffs, NJ: Prentice-Hall, 1956.

Driver, Harold E., *Indians of North America*. Chicago, IL: University of Chicago Press, 1961.

Drucker, Philip, *Indians of the Northwest Coast*, Handbook Series No. 10, *American Museum of Natural History*. New York: McGraw-Hill, 1955.

Dunning's American Indian Auction Catalogue, Sunday, October 27, 1996, Elgin, IL.

Durrell, Pat, "Collecting Trade Beads." *The Indian Trader*, October 1987, pp. 4-5.

"Eagle," *Compton's Encyclopedia*, 1988, Vol. 7, p. 2.

Elliott, Mark, "Basic Techniques in Beading and Material Techniques of Beadwork," *The Indian Trader*, October 1987, pp. 14-15.

Erdrich, Louise, *Love Medicine*. New York: Holt, Rinehart and Winston, 1984.

Farb, Peter. *Man's Rise To Civilization*. New York: E.P. Dutton and Company, 1968.

Farley, Ronnie, *Women of the Native Struggle*. New York: Orion Books, 1993.

Feder, Norman, *American Indian Art*. New York: Harry N. Abrams, 1965.

Flaherty, Thomas H., *The Spirit World*. Morristown, NJ: Time-Life Books, 1993.

Forbes, Jack D., *The Indian in America's Past*. Englewood Cliffs, NJ: Prentice-Hall, 1966.

Frank, Larry, "Indian Silver Jewelry of the Southwest," 1868-1930. Boston: New York Graphic Society, 1978.

Fronval, George and Daniel Dubois, *Indian Signals and Sign Language*. New York: Wing Books, 1985.

Gard, Wayne, *The Great Buffalo Hunt*. Lincoln, NE: University of Nebraska Press, 1959.

Gill, Spenser, *Pottery Treasures*. Portland, OR: Graphic Arts Center Publishing Company, 1976.

Glass, Paul, *Songs and Stories of the North American Indians*. New York: Grosset and Dunlap, 1968.

Gragg, Rod, *The Old West Quiz and Fact Book*. New York: Promontory Books, 1993.

Graham, Frank Jr., "Winged Victory," *Audubon*, July-August 1994, pp. 36-49.

Grier, James W., "Our American Eagle," *Wild Bird*, August 1996, pp. 26-29.

Hassrick, Royal B., *North American Indians*. London, England: Octopus Books, 1974.

Hayes, Allan and John Blom, *Southwestern Pottery*. Hong Kong, South Sea International Press, 1996.

Hill, Norbert S. Jr., editor, *Words of Power*. Golden, CO: Fulcrum Publishing, 1994.

Hothem, Lar., *North American Indian Artifacts*. Florence, AL: Books Americana, 1994.

Hunt, David, editor, *Native Indian Wild Game, Fish & Wild Foods Cookbook*, Castle Books, Edison, NJ, 1992.

Hunt, Norman Bancroft, *Warriors Warfare and the Native American Indian*, London, England: Salamander Books, 1995.

Hutchens, Alma R., *A Handbook of Native American Herbs*. Boston: Shambhala Publications, 1992.

Hyde, John, "A Celebration of Flight," *Wild Bird*, November 1992, pp. 30-33.

Jacka, Jerry, "The Miracle of Hopi Corn," *Arizona Highways*, January 1978, pp. 3-15.

Jacka, Jerry and Spencer Gill, *Pottery Treasures*. Portland, OR: Graphic Arts Center Publishing Company, 1976.

James, George Wharton, *Indian Basketry*. New York: Dover Publications, 1972.

Johnson, Frederick. Editor, *Man in Northeastern North America*. Andover, MA, Phillips Academy, 1946.

Josephy, Alvin M. Jr., *The American Heritage of America*. New York: Alfred A. Knopf, 1968.

Ketchum, William C. Jr., *Collecting the West*. New York: Crown Publishers, 1993.

Kidwell, Clara Sue and Richard W. Hill Sr., *Treasures of the National Museum of the American Indian*. New York: Abbeyville Press, 1996.

Korn, Jerry, editor, *The Indians*. New York: Time-Life Books, 1976.

Kroeber, A.L., *Handbook of the Indians of California*. New York: Dover Publications, 1976.

La Barre, Weston, *The Peyote Cult*. New Haven, CT: Yale University Press, 1938.

La Farge, Oliver, *A Pictorial History of the American Indian*. New York: Crown Publishers, 1951.

Lamb, E. Wendell and Lawrence W. Schultz, *Indian Lore*. Winona Lake, IN: Light and Life Press, 1964.

Lemmon, Robert, *Our Amazing Birds*. New York: Doubleday and Company, 1952.

Looney, Ralph and Bruce Dale, "The Navajo Nation Looks Ahead," *National Geographic*, December 1972.

Lowie, Robert H., *Indians of the Plains*. New York: McGraw-Hill, 1957.

Mails, Thomas E., *The Mystic Warriors of the Plains*. New York: Barnes and Noble, 1991.

Mason, Otis Tufton, *American Indian Basketry*. New York: Dover Publications, 1988.

Mather, Christine, *Native America Arts, Traditions and Celebrations*. New York: Clarkson Potter, 1990.

Maxwell, James A., editor, *America's Fascinating Indian Heritage*. Pleasantville, NY: The Reader's Digest Association, 1978.

McCracken, Harold, *George Catlin and the Old Frontier*. New York: Bonanza Books, 1959.

McGuire, J.D., "Pipes and Smoking Customs of the American Aborigines," *Annual Report of the United States National Museum for 1897*, pp. 351-645.

McLain, Gary, *The Indian Way*. Santa Fe, NM: John Muir Publications, 1990.

Meadows, Kenneth, *Earth Medicine*. Rockport, MA: Element Books, 1996.

Meadowcroft, Enid Lamonte, *The Story of Crazy Horse*. New York: Grosset and Dunlap, 1954.

Means, Russell and Marvin J. Wolf, Where *White Men Fear to Tread*. New York: St. Martin's Press, 1995.

Miles, Charles and Pierre Bovis, *American Indian and Eskimo Basketry*. New York: Bonanza, 1969.

Minor, Nono and Marz Minor, *The American Indian Craft Book*. Lincoln, NE: University of Nebraska Press, 1978.

Morgan, Lewis Henry, *The League of the Iroquois*. North Dighton, MA: JG Press, 1995.

Morphet, Tom, "Valley of the Eagles," *Wild Bird*, November 1995, pp. 54-57.

Murdock, David, *North American Indian*. New York: Alfred A. Knopf, 1995.

Native American Wisdom, Philadelphia: Running Press, 1994.

Native Peoples Magazine: A variety of issues.

Naylor, Marcia, editor, *Authentic Indian Designs*. New York: Dover Publications, 1971.

Nies, Judith, *Native American History*. New York: Ballantine Books, 1996.

Parker, Arthur C., *The Indian How Book*. New York: Dover Publications, 1975.

Penney, David W., *Art of the American Indian Frontier*. Seattle, WA: University of Washington Press, 1992.

Powell, Peter J., *Sweet Medicine*. Norman, OK: University of Oklahoma Press, 1969.

Quimby, George Irving, *Indian Culture and European Trade Goods*. Madison, WI: University of Wisconsin Press, 1966.

Raphael, Ralph B., *The Book of American Indians*. Greenwich, CT: Fawcett Publications, 1953.

Reno, Dawn E., *Native American Collectibles*. New York: Avon Books, 1994.

Roe, Frank Gilbert, *The Indian and the Horse*. Norman, OK: University of Oklahoma Press, 1955.

Ruoff, A. LaVonne Brown, *Indians of North America: Literatures of the American Indian*. New York: Chelsea House, 1991.

Sell, Henry Blackman and Victor Weybright, *Buffalo Bill and the West*. New York: Oxford University Press, 1955.

Seton, Julia M., *American Indian Arts*. New York: The Ronald Press, 1962.

Sommer, Robin Langley, *Native American Art*. New York: Smithmark Publishers, 1994.

Spicer, Edward H., editor, *Perspectives in American Indian Culture Change*. Chicago, IL: University of Chicago Press, 1961.

"State Name," *Compton's Encyclopedia*. Chicago, IL: 24 volumes, 1988.

Steer, Diana, *Native American Women*. New York: Barnes and Noble, 1996.

Stirling, Matthew W., *Indians of the Americas*. Washington, DC: The National Geographic Society, 1961.

Stokes, Winston, *The Story of Hiawatha*. New York: Frederick A. Stokes Company, 1910.

Storm, Hyemeyohsts, *Seven Arrows*. New York: Ballantine Books, 1972.

Stoutenburgh, John Jr., *Dictionary of the American Indian*. New York: Philosophical Library, 1960.

Tanner, Clara Lee, *Indian Baskets of the Southwest*. Tucson, AZ: University of Arizona Press, 1983.

Taylor, Colin F., editorial consultant, *Native American Arts and Crafts*. New York: Smithmark Publishers, 1995.

Taylor, Colin F., *Native American Life*. New York: Smithmark, 1996.

Terres, John K., *How Birds Fly*. Mechanicsburg, PA: Stackpole Books, 1994.

Thomas, D.H., *The Southwestern Indian Detours*. Phoenix, AZ: Hunter Publishing Company, 1978.

Tibbles, Thomas Henry, *Buckskin and Blanket Days*. Garden City, NY: Doubleday and Company, 1957.

Tschopik, Harry Jr., *Indians of North America*. New York: American Museum of Natural History, 1952.

Turnbaugh, Sarah and William, *Indian Baskets*. West Chester, PA: Schiffer Publishing, 1986.

Underhill, Ruth, *Red Man's America*. Chicago, IL: University of Chicago Press, 1956.

Vidler, Virginia, *Sugar-bush Antiques*. Cranbury, NJ: A.S. Barnes and Company, 1979.

Waldman, Carl and Molly Braun, *Word Dance*. New York: Facts on File, 1994.

Walter, Anna Lee, *The Spirit of Native America*. San Francisco, CA: Chronicle Books, 1989.

Walker, Bryce, *Through Indian Eyes*. Pleasantville, NY: The Reader's Digest Association, 1995.

Washburn, Wilcomb E., *The Indians in America*. New York: Harper and Row, 1975.

Weatherford, Jack, *Native Roots*. New York; Fawcett Columbine, 1991.

White, Jon Manchip, *Everyday Life of the North American Indian*. New York: Indian Head Books, 1993.

Whiteford, Andrew Hunter, *North American Indian Arts*. New York: Golden Press, 1983.

Wissler, Clark, *Indians of the United States*. Garden City, NY: Doubleday and Company, 1949.

Wolfe, Gus, "Weathering the Storm," *Wild Bird*, November 1992, pp. 34-35.

INDEX ◄

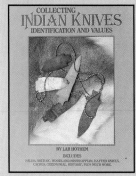
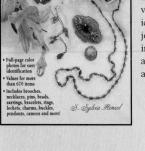
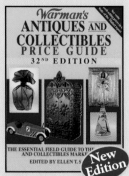

'With *The Fever*, Megan Abbott has created a mesmerizing, modern portrait of teenage life today: brutal crushes, competing allegiances and first-bloom sensuality, all magnified by the rush and crush of technology. *The Fever* holds true to its title: it's dark, disturbing, strangely beautiful and utterly unshakeable'

Gillian Flynn, author of *Gone Girl*

'Right now America's best novelists are women, and Megan Abbott is up there at the top'

Lee Child, author of the Jack Reacher series

'Megan Abbott is an extraordinary writer'

Nick Hornby, *The Believer*

'If the phenomenon that led to the Salem Witch trials were to revisit the world today, it might very well look like the scenario in Megan Abbott's engrossing, disturbing, panic attack of a novel, *The Fever*. In a time when suicide and pregnancy pacts can go viral, this story of mass hysteria in a high school is not only completely plausible – it's impossible to put down'

Jodi Picoult, author of *The Storyteller*

'The lives of teenage girls are dangerous, beautiful things in Abbott's stunning seventh novel . . . Abbott expertly withholds just enough information to slowly ratchet up the suspense until the reader is as breathless as Deenie at the arrival of each new text message or cryptic phone call and the school vibrates with half-formed theories and speculations . . . Nothing should be taken at face value in this jealousy- and hormone-soaked world except that Abbott is certainly our very best guide'

Kirkus (starred review)

THE FEVER

Megan Abbott is an award-winning author of noir fiction including *Queenpin* and *Bury Me Deep* (nominated for the 2010 Edgar Award and the *Los Angeles Times* Book Prize). Her novel *The End of Everything* was a 2011 Richard and Judy selection and *Dare Me* was shortlisted for the CWA Steel Dagger 2012 and was a 2013 Specsavers Crime Thriller Bookclub selection. *Dare Me* is soon to be a major motion picture. Born in the Detroit area, Megan now lives in Queens, New York City.

THE
FEVER

MEGAN ABBOTT

PICADOR

First published 2014 by Little, Brown and Company,
Hachette Book Group, New York

First published in the UK in paperback 2014 by Picador

This edition first published 2015 by Picador,
an imprint of Pan Macmillan
20 New Wharf Road, London N1 9RR
Associated companies throughout the world
www.panmacmillan.com

ISBN 978-1-4472-2633-8

1 3 5 7 9 8 6 4 2

A CIP catalogue record for this book is available from the British Library.

Printed and bound by CPI Group (UK) Ltd, Croydon, CR0 4YY

For my brother, Josh Abbott

In all disorder [there is] a secret order.

Carl Jung

THE FEVER

Before

The first time, you can't believe how much it hurts."

Deenie's legs are shaking, but she tries to hide it, pushing her knees together, her hands hot on her thighs.

Six other girls are waiting. A few have done it before, but most are like Deenie.

"I heard you might want to throw up even," one says. "I knew a girl who passed out. They had to stop in the middle."

"It just kind of burns," says another. "You're sore for a few days. They say by the third time, you don't even feel it."

I'm next, Deenie thinks, *a few minutes and it'll be me.*

If only she'd gotten it over with a year ago. But she'd heard about how much it hurt and no one else had done it yet, at least not anyone she knew.

Now she's one of the last ones.

When Lise comes out, her face puckered, holding on to her stomach, she won't say a word, just sits there with her hand over her mouth.

"It's nothing to be scared of," Gabby says, looking at Deenie. "I'm not afraid."

And she takes Deenie's hand and grips it, fingers digging into palm, their clasped hands pressing down so Deenie's legs stop shaking, so she feels okay.

"We're in it together," Gabby adds, making Deenie look in her eyes, black and unflinching.

"Right," Deenie says, nodding. "How bad can it be?"

The door opens.

"Deenie Nash," a voice calls out.

Four minutes later, her thigh stinging, she's done. It's over.

Walking back out, shoes catching on the carpet, legs heavy as iron, she feels light-headed, a little drunk.

All the girls look at her, Gabby's face grave and expectant.

"It's nothing," Deenie says, grinning. "It's just . . . nothing."

1

At first, Lise's desk chair just seemed to be rocking. Deenie's eyes were on it, watching the motion. The rocking of it made her feel a little sick. It reminded her of something.

She wondered if Lise was nervous about the quiz.

The night before, Deenie had prepared a long time, bringing her laptop under her covers, lying there for hours, staring at equations.

She wasn't sure it was studying, exactly, but it made her feel better, her eyes dry from screen glare, fingers tapping her lower lip. There was an uncomfortable smell from somewhere in her clothes, musky and foreign. She wanted to shower, but her dad might hear and wonder.

Two hours before, she'd been at work, dropping dough balls in a machine and punching them out into square pans slick with oil. Lise and Gabby had come by and ordered the fat pizza sticks, even though Deenie warned them not to. Showed them the plastic tub of melted butter that sat all day by the hot ovens. Showed them how the oven workers stroked the sticks with the butter from that tub and how it looked like soap or old cheese.

As they left, oil-bottomed paper sacks in their hands, she

wished she were going with them, wherever they were going. She was glad to see them together. Gabby and Lise were Deenie's best friends but never really seemed easy with just each other.

By the ovens, Sean Lurie clocked in late. Wielding his long iron grippers like swords, he started teasing her. About the fancy-girl arc of her hand when she'd grab a dough ball, like she was holding a kitten. The way, he said, her tongue stuck out slightly when she stretched the dough.

"Like my little sister," he teased, "with her Play-Doh."

He was a senior at Star-of-the-Sea, shaggy black hair, very tall. He never wore his hat, much less the hairnet, and he had a way of smiling lopsided that made her tie her apron strings tighter, made her adjust her cap.

The heat from the ovens made his skin glow.

She didn't even mind all the sweat. The sweat was part of it.

Like her brother after hockey, his dark hair wet and face sheened over—she'd tease him about it, but it was a look of aliveness you wanted to be around.

How it happened that two hours later she was in Sean Lurie's car, and a half hour after that they were parked on Montrose, deep in Binnorie Woods, she couldn't say for sure.

She always heard you looked different, after.

But only the first time, said Gabby, who'd done it just twice herself. *To make you remember it, I guess.* Deenie had wondered how you could ever forget.

You look in the mirror after, Gabby said, *and it's not even you.*

Except Deenie had never really believed it. It seemed like one of those things they told you to make you wait forever for something everyone else was doing anyway. They didn't want you to be part of the club.

And yet, looking in the bathroom mirror after she got home, she'd realized Gabby was right.

It was partly the eyes—something narrow there, something less bright—but mostly it was the mouth, which looked tender, bruised, and now forever open.

Her hands hooked on the sink ledge, her eyes resting on her dad's aftershave in the deep green bottle, the same kind he'd used all her life. He'd been on a date too, she realized.

Then, remembering: she hadn't really been on a date.

Now, in class, all these thoughts thudding around, it was hard to concentrate, and even harder given the rocking in Lise's chair, her whole desk vibrating.

"Lise," Mrs. Chalmers called out. "You're bothering everyone else."

"It's happening, it's happening" came a low snarl from Lise's delicate pink mouth. "Uh-uh-uh."

Her hands flying up, she grabbed her throat, her body jolting to one side.

Then, in one swoop—as if one of the football players had taken his meaty forearm and hurled it—her desk overturned, clattering to the floor.

And with it Lise. Her head twisting, slamming into the tiles, her bright red face turned up, mouth teeming with froth.

"Lise," sighed Mrs. Chalmers, too far in front to see. "What is your problem?"

★   ★   ★

Standing at his locker, late for class, Eli Nash looked at the text for a long time, and at the photo that had come with it. A girl's bare midriff.

7

Eli, for you xxxx!

He didn't recognize the number.

It wasn't the first time he'd gotten one of these, but they always surprised him. He tried to imagine what she was thinking, this faceless girl. Purple nails touching the tops of her panties, purple too, with large white polka dots.

He had no idea who it was.

Did she want him to text her back, invite her over? To sneak her into his bedroom and nudge her shaky, pliant legs apart until he was through?

A few times he'd done just that. Told them to come by, smuggled them to his room. The last one, a sophomore everyone called Shawty, cried after.

She admitted to drinking four beers before she came on account of nervousness, and even still, had she put her legs where she should? Should she have made more noise?

Secretly, he'd wished she'd made less noise.

Since then, he could only ever think about his sister, one wall away. And how he hoped Deenie never did things like this. With guys like him.

So now, when he got these texts, he didn't reply.

Except sometimes he felt kind of lonely.

The night before, his friends at a party, he'd stayed home. He imagined maybe a family night of bad TV and board games moldy from the basement. But Deenie wasn't around, and his dad had his own plans.

"Who is she?" he'd asked, seeing his father wearing his date sweater, the charcoal V-neck of a serious man.

"A nice woman, very smart," he said. "I hope I can keep up."

"You will," Eli said. His dad was the smartest teacher in the school and the smartest guy Eli knew.

After one of those times sneaking a girl out of his room, Eli had gotten caught, sort of. In the upstairs hallway, his dad nearly bumped into her as she hitched her tank-top strap up her shoulder. He'd looked at Eli and then at the girl and she'd looked at him and smiled like the prom queen she was.

"Hey, Mr. Nash," she cheeped. "Guess what? I got an eighty-five in Chem Two this year."

"Great, Britt," he said, his eyes not focusing on hers. "I always knew you could do better. Glad to hear you're doing me proud."

After, Eli shut his door and turned his music as loud as he could and hoped his dad wouldn't come talk to him.

He never did.

★   ★   ★

Dryden was the cloudiest city in the state, the sky white for much of the year and the rest of the time a kind of molten gray broken up by bright bolts of mysterious sun.

Tom Nash had lived here for twenty years, had moved with Georgia the summer after they'd finished their teaching certificates, and she'd gotten a job starting up the district's new special-education office.

Like many long-term transplants, he had the uncomplicated pride of a self-proclaimed native, but with the renewing wonder a native never has.

In the deep white empty of February when his students would get that morose look, their faces slightly green like the moss that lined all their basements, he'd tell them that Dryden was special. That he had grown up in Yuma, Arizona, the sunniest city in the United States, and that he'd never really looked up until he went away to summer camp and realized the sky was there after all and filled with mystery.

9

For Dryden kids, of course, there was no mystery to any of it. They didn't realize how much it had shaped them, how it had let them retain, long past childhood fairy tales, the opportunity to experience forces beyond their understanding. The way weather tumbled through the town, striking it with hail, lightning, sudden bursts of both clouds and sun, like no other place Tom had ever been. Some days, the winter wind moving fast across the lake's warm waters, the sun unaccountably piercing everything, students came to school, faces slicked in ice, looking stunned and radiant. As if saying: *I'm sixteen and bored and indifferent to life, but my eyes are suddenly open, for a second, to this.*

The first year he and Georgia lived here, Dryden had been this puzzle to them both. Coming home at night, the haze of the streetlamps, shaking off the damp, they would look around, their once-copper skin gleaming white, and marvel over it.

Pregnant with Eli and her body changing already, giving her this unearthly beauty, Georgia decided Dryden wasn't a real place at all but some misty idea of a town. A suburban Brigadoon, she called it.

Eventually—though it felt like suddenly to him—something changed.

One afternoon two years ago, he came home and found her at the dining-room table drinking scotch from a jam jar.

Living here, she said, *is like living at the bottom of an old man's shoe.*

Then she looked at him as if hoping he could say something to make it not feel true.

But he couldn't think of a thing to say.

It wasn't long after that he found out about the affair, a year along by then, and that she was pregnant. She miscarried three days later and he took her to the hospital, the blood slipping down her leg, her hands tight on him.

Now he saw her maybe four times a year. She'd moved all the way to Merrivale, where Eli and Deenie spent one weekend a month and a full ten days each summer, after which they came back tan and blooming and consumed by guilt the moment they saw him.

In his middle-of-the-night bad thoughts, he now felt sure he'd never really understood his wife, or any woman maybe.

Whenever he thought he understood Deenie, she seemed to change.

Dad, I don't listen to that kind of music.

Dad, I never go to the mall anymore.

Lately, even her face looked different, her baby-doll mouth gone. The daddy's girl who used to climb his leg, face turned up to his. Who sat in his leather reading chair for hours, head bent over his own childhood books on Greek mythology, then Tudor kings, anything.

"I'm taking the bus," she'd said that very morning, halfway out the door, those spindle legs of hers swiveling in her sneakers.

"I can drive you," he'd said. "You're so early."

Deenie hadn't beaten him to breakfast since she was ten, back when she was trying to be grown-up and would make him toaster waffles, with extra syrup he'd be tugging from the roof of his mouth all day.

Eli off to hockey practice at six a.m., Tom liked these drives alone with Deenie, the only time he could peek into the murky teen-girl-ness in her head. And get occasional smiles from her, make bad jokes about her music.

A few times, after dates like the one he'd had the night before—a substitute teacher divorced three months who'd spent most of dinner talking about her dying cat—driving to school with Deenie was the thing that roused him from bed in the morning.

But not this morning.

"I have a test to study for," she'd said, not even turning her head as she pushed through the door.

Sometimes, during those same bleak middle-of-the-nights, he held secret fears he never said aloud. Demons had come in the dark, come with the famous Dryden fog that rolled through the town, and taken possession of his lovely, smart, kindhearted wife. And next they'd come for his daughter too.

2

Deenie couldn't get the look on Lise's face out of her head.

Her eyes had shot open seconds after she fell.

"Why am I here?" she whispered, blinking ferociously, back arched on the floor, her legs turned in funny ways, her skirt flown up to her waist, and Mrs. Chalmers shouting in the hallway for help.

It had taken two boys and Mr. Banasiak from across the hall to get her to her feet.

Deenie watched them steer her down the hall, her head resting on Billy Gaughan's linebacker shoulder, her long hair thick with floor dust.

"Deenie, no," Mrs. Chalmers said, taking her firmly by the shoulders. "You stay here."

But Deenie didn't want to stay. Didn't want to join the thrusting clutches of girls whispering behind their lockers, the boys watching Lise turn the corner, her skirt hitched high in the back, her legs bare despite the cold weather, the neon flare of her underpants.

After, ducking into the girls' room, Deenie saw she was still bleeding a little from the night before. When she walked it felt weird, like parts of her insides had shifted. She could never have ridden to school with her dad. What if he saw? She felt like everyone could see. That they knew what she'd done.

As it was happening, it had hurt a lot, and then a sharp look of surprise on Sean Lurie's face when he realized. When she couldn't hide what she was, and wasn't, what she had clearly never done before—thinking of it made her cover her face now, her hand cold and one pinkie shaking.

You should have told me, he'd said.

Told you what.

Swinging open the lavatory door, she began walking quickly down the teeming hall.

"Deenie, I heard something." It was Gabby, sneaking up behind her in her sparkled low-riders. They never made any noise. "About you."

Gabby's face seemed filled with fresh knowledge, but there was no way she could know. Sean Lurie went to Star-of-the-Sea. People couldn't know.

"Did you hear what just happened to Lise?" Deenie countered, pivoting to look at her. "I was there. I saw it."

Gabby's eyebrows lifted and she held her books to her chest.

"What do you mean? What do you mean?" she repeated. "Tell me everything."

At first they wouldn't let her into the nurse's office.

"Deenie, her mother isn't even here yet," snipped Mrs. Harris, the head of something called facilities operations.

"My dad asked me to check on her," Deenie lied, Gabby nodding next to her.

The ruse worked, though not for Gabby, who, lacking my-father-is-a-teacher privileges, was dispatched immediately to second period.

"Find out everything," Gabby whispered as Mrs. Harris waved her out.

The nurse's office door was ajar and Deenie could hear Lise calling her name. Everyone could hear, teachers stopping at their mailboxes.

"Deenie," Lise cried out. "What did I do? Did I do something? Who saw?"

Peering in the open door, Deenie saw Lise keeling over on the exam table, her lips ribboned with drying froth, one shoe hanging from her foot. She wasn't wearing any tights, her legs goose-quilled and whiter than the paper sheet.

"She...she bit me." Nurse Tammy was holding her own forearm, which looked wet. She hadn't been working there long, and rumor was, a senior athlete with a sore knee had scored two Tylenol with codeines from her on her very first day.

"Deenie!" Head whipping around, Lise gripped the table edge beneath her thighs, and Nurse Tammy rushed forward, trying to help her.

"Deenie," she repeated. "What happened to me? Is everyone talking about it? Did they see what I did?"

Outside the nurse's office, Mrs. Harris was arguing with someone about something, the assistant principal's stern jock voice joining in.

"No one saw," Deenie said. "No way. Are you okay?"

But Lise couldn't seem to focus, her hands doing some kind of strange wobbling thing in front of her, like she was conducting an invisible concert.

"I...I..." she stuttered, her eyes panicked. "Are they laughing at me?"

Deenie wanted to say something reassuring. Lise's mother,

vaguely hysterical under the best of circumstances, would be here any second, and she wanted to help while she could.

"No one's laughing. Everyone saw your Hello Kitty undies, though," Deenie tried, smiling. "Watch the boys come now."

As Deenie walked out, a coolness began to sink into her. The feeling that something was wrong with Lise, but the wrongness was large and without reference. She'd seen Lise with a hangover, with mono. She'd seen girlfriends throw up behind the loading dock after football games and faint in gym class, their bodies loaded with diet pills and cigarettes. She'd seen Gabby black out in the girls' room after she gave blood. But those times never felt like this.

Lying on the floor, her mouth open, tongue lolling, Lise hadn't seemed like a girl at all.

It must have been a trick of the light, she told herself.

But looking down at Lise, lips stretched wide, Deenie thought, for one second, that she saw something hanging inside Lise's mouth, something black, like a bat flapping.

★   ★   ★

"Mr. Nash," piped Brooke Campos, "can I go to the nurse's office? I'm feeling upset."

"What are you upset about, Brooke," Tom replied. There was fidgeting in a dozen seats. Something had happened, and he could see everyone was looking for an advantage in it.

"It's about Lise. I saw it go down and it's a lot to take in."

Two jocks in the back stifled braying laughs. They seemed to go to class solely in the hopes of hearing accidental (or were they?) double entendres from girls like Brooke, girls eternally tanned and bursting from T-shirts so tight they inched up their stomachs all day.

"What about Lise?" Tom asked, setting his chalk down. He'd known Lise Daniels since she was ten years old and first started coming to the house, hovering around Deenie, following her from room to room. Sometimes he swore he could hear her panting like a puppy. That was back when she was a chubby little elfin girl, before that robin's-breast belly of hers disappeared, and, seemingly overnight, she became overwhelmingly pretty, with big fawn eyes, her mouth forever open.

He never really had a sense of her, knew only that she played the flute, had perpetually skinned knees from soccer, and appeared ever out of place alongside his own brilliant, complicated little girl and her even more complicated friend Gabby.

Four years ago, Gabby's father, blasted on cocaine, had taken a claw hammer to his wife's Acura. When Gabby's mother tried to stop him, his hammer caught her on the downswing, tearing a hole clean through her face and down her throat.

Gabby's mother recovered, though now all the kids at the community college where she taught called her Scarface behind her back.

Her father had served a seven-month sentence and was now selling real estate in the next county and making occasional, un-welcome reappearances.

In the school's hallways, Tom could see it: Gabby carried the glamour of experience, like a dark queen with a bloody train trailing behind her.

It was hard to fathom girls like that walking the same corridors as girls like Brooke Campos, thumbs callused from incessant texting, or even girls like downy-cheeked Lise.

"Mr. Nash," Brooke said, rolling the tip of her pen around in her mouth like it hurt to think about, "it's so traumatic."

He tried again. "So what is it that happened to Lise?"

"She had a grand male in Algebra Two," Brooke announced, eyes popping.

The jocks broke into a fresh round of laughter.

"A grand mal?" he asked, squinting. "A seizure?"

Up front, antic grade-grubber Jaymie Hurwich squirmed painfully in her seat, hand raised.

"It's true, Mr. Nash," she told him. "I didn't see it, but I heard her mouth was frothing like a dog's. I had a dog that happened to once." She paused. "Mr. Nash, he died."

A hard knock in his chest in spite of himself, he looked at Brooke, at all of them.

He was trying to think of something to say.

"So . . ." Brooke said, rising tentatively in her seat, "can I see the nurse now?"

After second period, he found Deenie buried in her locker nearly to her waist, hunting for something.

"Honey, what happened with Lise?" he asked, hand on her back.

She turned slowly, one arm still rooted inside.

"I don't know, Dad."

For a second, she wouldn't look up at him, her eyes darting at the passing kids.

"But you saw it?"

"Dad," she said, giving him that look that had made his chest ache since she was four years old. "I don't want to talk now."

Now meaning here: *Not at school, Da-ad.*

Meaning he had to just let her go, watch her dark ponytail swinging down the hall, head dipped furtively, that red hoodie hunching up her neck, helping her hide.

3

Eli Nash was supposed to be in class. Practice had ended a long time ago, but he was still circling the rink behind the school. No sound except the faint hum of its refrigeration coils.

Looking up, he could see Gabby Bishop in the library. Back facing him, she was pressed against the windowpane like one of those butterflies under glass.

Deenie and Gabby and Lise. The Trio Grande. Always huddled together, whispering, a kind of closeness that interested him. He wondered what it might be like. He never wanted to huddle with his friends, though he guessed in a way he did it all the time, playing hockey.

Sometimes it was annoying. The way the three of them would be like this little knot in the house. He could hear them through the wall at night, laughing.

Lately, Lise and Gabby didn't seem to come over as much, or maybe he'd just stopped noticing. But it always felt weird when girls were laughing together and you didn't know why. Sometimes it was like they knew all these things he didn't.

Other times he wondered if they knew anything at all.

They didn't know about guys, as far as he could tell. At least not the things he wished his sister knew. He would catch her looking at Ryan Denning or that guy who won Battle of the Bands.

That dreamy expression she wore, her face showing everything she was feeling. Imagining big love and romance, he guessed. But she didn't realize what they saw, looking back at her: a girl, lips slightly parted, her head tilted hungrily. What they saw was *I'm ready. Let's go.*

"Nash," a voice rang out.

Eli looked up and saw A.J., the team captain, baseball cap low to cover his cigarette.

"Bro," he said, "you missed it. I got an eyeful of Lise Daniels's pretty white ass this morning." He tilted his head toward the school. "Come on. Who knows what's next?"

Eli felt the cold in his lungs, the ache of it. It felt good out here, and just looking at A.J. made him tired. All the effort, hat brim angled, jacket open. Smirk.

"Nah," he said. "Not yet."

A.J. grinned. "I feel you," he said.

Eli nodded, pushing off on his skates, gliding backward.

"Say hi to your sister for me," A.J. shouted.

Turning his head, Eli felt his skate catch a fallen branch.

★　★　★

The library was quiet, a glass-walled hothouse overlooking a narrow creek dense with mud.

Deenie found Gabby behind the gray bank of computers along the far wall. She was sitting on the floor, knees bent, her sneakers pressed against the tall reference volumes on the lowest shelf.

As always, she was bookended by two girls.

To her right crouched thick-braced Kim Court, in her usual pose, whispering in Gabby's ear.

And to her left sat Skye Osbourne, her blond hair spanning the musty world atlases behind her. Lately, Skye was always around, that web of hair, her long mantis sleeves.

All three looked up when they saw Deenie.

"What did you hear?" Gabby asked, fingers tapping on her lip.

"Nothing," Deenie said, sliding down to the floor next to Kim.

She wished it were just her and Gabby. No one else to hear them and they could talk about Lise alone.

This was their favorite place to meet. It always felt hidden, forgotten. The gold-lettered *World Book* encyclopedias from the 1980s. The smell of old glue and crumbling paper, the industrial carpet burning her palms.

It reminded her of what you did when you were a little girl, making little burrows and hideaways. Like boys did with forts. Eli and his friend, stacking sofa cushions, pretending to be sharp-shooters. With girls, you didn't call them forts, though it was the same.

This was the place Deenie and Gabby first really spoke, fresh-man year, both of them hiding back here, heads ducked over identical books (something about angels, back when that was all they read). They'd snuck looks at each other, smiled.

"Did you see her before school?" Deenie asked Gabby.

"No, I was late," Gabby said. "Skye couldn't find her purse."

"Is she pregnant?" whispered Kim, her tongue thrust between her wired teeth.

"Lise?" Deenie said. "No. Of course not."

"Pregnant people faint all the time," Kim said, tugging her tights up her legs, inching as close to Gabby as she could without landing in her lap.

"She's not pregnant," Deenie said. Then, turning to Gabby: "Her mom came and took her home."

Gabby nodded, looking down at her hands, clasped over her

notebook. Deenie knew she wished they were alone too. Ever since that first week of school freshman year, it had been hard to find Gabby alone—at least at school, where girls hung from her like tassels.

"How can we go to class when this is going on?" Kim said. "We should go to her house."

"Have you ever even been to Lise's house?" Deenie said. Kim and Lise occupied starkly opposite poles in a group of friends. A year younger, filled with hard sophomore ambition, Kim was eager to spread herself wide, offering car rides, expensive eye shadow swiped from her mother, free gift cards from her job at the mall. She was the kind of girl you end up being friends with just because. The opposite of Lise, whom Deenie had known since third grade, whom she traded clothes, even underwear, with. Three days ago even helping her unwedge a crooked tampon, Lise laughing the whole time, wiggling her pelvis to assist.

That was how she knew Lise wasn't pregnant. That, and other reasons, like that Lise was still a virgin, mostly.

"The point is," Deenie said, "they're not going to just let us leave school."

"Maybe it was an allergic reaction," Skye said, tufting her hair against her cheek thoughtfully. "Don't you get those?"

Everyone looked at Kim, who was in fact allergic to everything, a special page in the school safety manual devoted to her. Nuts, eggs, wheat, yeast, shellfish, even some kinds of paper.

"I don't think that was it," Kim said, unwilling to share her special status. Then, swiveling closer to Gabby, eyes widening, "Oh God, maybe it's something to do with that one guy."

Deenie paused. "What guy?"

"You know," Kim said, dropping her chin, lowering her voice. "Don't you know?" Her lips were shining, like when she had her sister's car, waving the keys at everyone like they changed every-thing. "Didn't she tell you?"

"There's no guy," Deenie said. "So stop making stuff up."

Boy crazy, that's what Ms. Enright, the English teacher, called Lise. But who could blame her? No guy had ever looked at Lise until suddenly they all did. Last summer, she wore a white bathing suit hooked with bamboo rings to the big Fourth of July barbecue and someone's older brother, who was in college, started calling her La Lise and even e-mailed her a song he wrote about her and her Lise-a-licious bikini.

Lise's mother would never have let her go out with him, but it set something off among the other boys and a fever in Lise, who suddenly decided that all boys were a-mazing, every one.

After that, Lise had vowed she'd never get that baby fat back, and every morning she'd chew on parsley or drink swampy green shakes out of her Dryden Wind & Strings thermos. It was the only way, because her mom made her finish a full glass of buttermilk at night, which, no matter what her mom said, she was sure was full of fat. *Maybe she wants me to be fat,* Lise said, *because she always makes monkey bread too and she knows I can't stop eating it.*

"You must've heard," Kim said, looking to Gabby, then Skye, who didn't even seem to be listening, her fingers running along the lacy hem of her many-tiered skirt, vintage and baroque.

Gabby shook her head. "Lise didn't have a boyfriend," she said, looking at Deenie.

"Okay," Kim said, smiling enigmatically. "But I didn't say he was her *boyfriend.*"

"What would a guy have to do with her fainting anyway?" Deenie asked. "She's not pregnant."

"It could be a lot of things that aren't pregnant," Skye said, gaze still resting on her hair, webbed between her ringed fingers.

"Like what?" Kim asked, squirming onto her knees with fresh vigor.

"I knew this girl who got this thing from this guy once, an older guy, a club promoter," Skye said. "He had a big house on the lake and he gave her all this great red-string Thai stick. He leaves for the Philippines, she wakes up with trich. That's a sexual parasite. It crawls inside you." She reached down for her bag, tangled with fringe. "So."

No one said anything for a moment. Skye was somehow to be trusted in these matters. It was part of her mystique. That white-blond hair and thrift-store peacoat, the slave bracelets and green vinyl cowboy boots. Sunny, the artist aunt she lived with but whom Deenie had never seen and who let Skye's ex-boyfriend sleep over, even though he was supposedly twenty-six years old, though no one had ever actually seen him either. The rumor was he'd been one of her aunt's students, even her boyfriend. After they broke up, Skye wore his coat, a long leather *Shaft* duster, to school every day until a hard winter rain shredded it.

"Well, maybe it doesn't have anything to do with guys," Kim said, facing them again, twisting her lips. "Maybe she's just sick."

Deenie picked up her phone and began typing.

eye roll, she texted Gabby, whose phone burbled immediately.

Gabby looked at her phone, grinned. Kim looked at both of them questioningly.

Nobody said anything, Kim's eyes darting back and forth between them.

"Well," Kim said, rising, tugging again at her tights, the ones just like Gabby's favorite pair, silver striped, "I got stuff to do."

"See ya," Deenie said, and they all watched until she was gone.

Nestling next to Gabby, Deenie let her head knock against hers.

Skye stood up, grabbing her purse, and Deenie's chest lifted in anticipation. At last, she'd have Gabby alone.

But then Gabby rose too, looping her arm in Skye's to gain footing.

"Bye, Deenie," Skye said, already turning away.

"See you, Deenie," Gabby said, smiling apologetically. "Next semester I hope we get the same lunch period."

"Yeah," said Deenie, watching them walk away, their hair—Gabby's dark to Skye's bone-white—swinging in sync, their matching metallic tights. Those two leaving together again. Which happened a lot lately, like last week at the lake, and other times. Leaving together and leaving Deenie alone.

★   ★   ★

"Nash, get your ass to class."

Coach Haller's face was always red, a tomato with a crew cut. Eli's dad said he looked like every coach he'd ever known.

"Yes, sir," Eli said, rising from the locker-room bench. He had that crazy cold-hot feeling from the practice drills in the makeshift rink outside, the hot shower after, the school always blasting with forced heat that groaned through the building.

He'd been staring a long time at the picture on his phone, the girl in the purple underwear. Something about it.

And then there was the other thing. Something he'd overheard that morning, about his sister. Someone seeing her get into a car last night, with some guy. And then there was A.J., that smirk of his.

All of that and looking at the purple panties on his phone, the girl's skin shining like girls' skin always seemed to. He began to feel a little queasy.

Sometimes he wished he didn't have a sister, though he loved Deenie and still remembered the feeling he had when he caught that kid Ethan pushing her off the swing set in the school yard in fifth grade. And how time seemed to speed up until he was shoving the kid into the fence and tearing his jacket. The admiring look his sister gave him after, the way his parents pretended to be mad at him but he could tell they weren't.

These days, it was pretty different. There'd be those moments he was forced to think about her not just as Deenie but as the girl whose slender tank tops hung over the shower curtain. Like bright streamers, like the flair the cheerleaders threw at games.

Sometimes he wished he didn't have a sister.

★   ★   ★

"Tell me again what Lise said," Gabby said when they caught each other between classes. "When you saw her."

"She wanted to know what happened to her," Deenie said. "She was really scared."

She couldn't remember any more than that, it had happened so fast. And now Kim's grimy insinuations, and Skye and her deadpan cool, were laid over her own bad feelings. She couldn't think. She just kept picturing Lise's face, the way her bare legs jerked when she went down.

"We should go check on her," Gabby said, scratching her palm. "See how she's doing."

"Leave school?"

"Yes."

"We'll get busted," Deenie said. "You will." Gabby had earned two detentions in the last month, one for smoking clove cigarettes in the kiln room and one for wandering off school property, sneaking to Skye's house, just a few blocks away.

"You, then. You won't get in trouble," Gabby said. "Your dad would understand."

"I'm not sure," Deenie said, but she knew she would go. Gabby was right. Someone had to see.

The bus ride was quick, and no one saw her.

Lise lived with her mom in a duplex on Easter Way. Despite all these years of being friends with her, Deenie had spent little time there.

"My mom doesn't like me to make lots of noise," Lise always said. Though they had never been noisy girls. At her own house, they spent most of their time watching movies and lying on Deenie's bed, listening to music and talking about how someday they'd travel through Africa or hand-feed stingrays in Bora Bora or ride Arabian horses in some desert, somewhere.

But Lise's mom usually preferred Lise to be at home with her, especially lately, when her daughter seemed to look more and more like she herself looked in her old modeling scrapbooks, posing in the Spiegel catalog and at trade shows, gold-shellacked hair and breasts like globes.

"Yes, she's a lovely woman," Deenie's dad had said when Lise once suggested he date her mother. "Lovely."

He said it very politely, like the time Deenie showed him the two-piece bathing suit her mom had bought her last summer. After, Deenie hid it in the back of the drawer and never wore it.

"Mr. Nash, I think she'd be so happy if she found a boyfriend," Lise had added, watching Mr. Nash as he focused intently on their English muffins, the toaster buzzing red beneath him.

"Lise," Deenie said later, "you can barely stand her. Why should my dad have to?"

27

As soon as the words came out, she regretted them.

But Lise had just sighed, winsomely, her pretty face crumpling a little.

"I just wish she had something to do. Other than watch my Facebook page."

Walking the three blocks from the bus stop, Deenie knew this was the right thing to do.

By the time she reached the front door, though, it felt like a big mistake. Except she'd promised Gabby, and, anyway, it looked like no one was home.

A long minute passed after she'd rung the bell.

She felt a grim thickness in the front of her head, a feeling of knowing something very important without knowing what it really meant. It reminded her of the day her mom decided to move out. The stillness in the morning, the house keys sitting in the middle of the kitchen table.

Her dad had spent hours shoveling the driveway, the front walk. She hadn't thought he'd ever come back inside.

Suddenly, the front door swung open. It was an older woman, her short white hair closely cropped, coat half open, purse slipping from her arm.

Deenie was pretty sure it was Lise's grandmother, but friends' grandmothers all kind of looked alike.

"Oh!" the woman said, startled. "Honey, what are you doing here?"

"I came to see how Lise was," Deenie said. "I was there when she—"

"She's not here," the woman blurted, her hands shaking wildly, car keys tight in red fingers. "They took her to the hospital. I'm going there now."

Behind her, the coffee table was overturned and a rug askew. There was a sharp smell of vomit.

"What happened?" Deenie said, her voice high. "Where's Lise?"

The car keys seemed to spring from the woman's hands, clattering onto the cement porch. They both bent down to grab them. Deenie could hear the woman's hard, hurried breaths. She grabbed the keys from Deenie's hands and inhaled deeply.

"Sweetie," she said, hands on Deenie's shoulders like she was seven, "go back to school, okay?"

Before Deenie could say what she wanted to—*Can I come too? I need to come too*—the woman was running down the steps and to her car, its door hanging open.

Deenie looked back into the living room. A slick of vomit, a torn latex glove. Imagined Lise lying there, head knocking against the floor.

Lise on the classroom floor, eyes black.

Deenie now feeling her own knees shaking, like she hadn't eaten anything. The sense, again, of a bigness to the day that was more than she could ever want.

Lise.

You spend a long time waiting for life to start—her past year or two filled with all these firsts, everything new and terrifying and significant—and then it does start and you realize it isn't what you'd expected, or asked for.

4

Standing in front of his students, his butane lighters on, Tom couldn't get anyone's attention, not even Nat Dubow's, who loved to demonstrate every day how much he knew, who shot videos of himself doing chemistry experiments in a laboratory in his parents' garage and then posted the videos on the web under the name Nat Du-Wow. Despite Nat's constant urging—he'd planted his open laptop on Tom's desk one day, tail wagging—Tom always claimed he was too busy at the moment to watch, sorry. One night at home, though, he looked up an episode and was surprised to see four hundred comments posted and more than twelve hundred thumbs-up. All of it made him feel unbearably old.

But even Nat was distracted today, talking about epilepsy and electrical currents and auras.

"Mr. Nash, what if it was a tonic-clonic?" he burst out, voice breaking. "It can damage your brain forever."

"Nat," he said, "let's focus, okay?"

But Tom was having trouble focusing too. He'd even walked down the aisles summoning all his best jokes, teasing Bailey Lu about the doodles on her hand, which usually made her blush and giggle.

Nothing worked, and Bailey could only stare at her hands in distress, her inky palms sweat-smeared.

Clearly, and he felt it himself, it wasn't the kind of day one of Mr. Nash's awesome gummy-bear-and-potassium-chlorate or Mentos-and-Diet-Coke demonstrations would become the talk of the school.

So he surrendered, gave them a pop quiz, and gazed out the window while they moaned and protested, their hysteria giving way to cries of injustice and the cruelty of teachers.

Meanwhile, he thought about Lise, and what it must be like for her mother, worrying. Sheila Daniels worried constantly anyway: about school trips to the falls, vaccines, the sound of hydraulic drills by the water wells.

And he reminded himself it was likely nothing. Girls fainted, kids fainted, fevers could do things to them, stress too. Some of these girls never seemed to eat, floating through the hallways like wraiths, drooping under the bleachers during gym. There wasn't much he hadn't seen in twenty years of high-school teaching.

After fourth period, Tom walked outside to the wind-slapping corner by the practice rink.

The new French teacher with the tattoo on her nape was leaning against a heating duct, smoking.

The first time he'd met her, he tried to imagine how he would have felt as a high-school kid if he'd had a slinky thirty-year-old French teacher with leather boots and a tattoo of a peacock feather snaking around her neck.

He wondered why Eli didn't take French.

"Bad habits," she said, grinning, and he started a little.

She gestured to her cigarette. He smiled.

"There are worse ones," he said.

"Like what?" she said, still grinning.

"Crack?" he ventured. "High-fructose corn syrup?"

"Come on," she said, offering him the gold pack in her ringed hand. "Don't make me the provocateur."

Just then, his cell phone tingled to life.

Deenie, the screen flashed, the picture of her in the sock-monkey hat she used to wear.

"Hey, Deen," he answered.

"Dad," she said, her voice sounding very far away.

"What's wrong, honey? Where are you?"

"Dad, can you come get me? Can you take me to the hospital?"

He spotted her standing in front of the Danielses' duplex, head-phones on, jumping a little in the cold.

Her parka, those skinny legs—she looked for all the world like she had at eleven years old.

Noticing her bluing ankles, he could imagine what Georgia would say. He only hoped she'd taken the bus to Lise's and not gotten a ride with an older student, some boy. Sometimes Tom found it hard to believe he was in charge.

He wanted to ask what made her think it was okay to leave school like that, but he didn't. The truth was, he was always glad when she asked for a favor because she almost never did.

"Hey," he said, "get in."

Just like her brother, she didn't seem to get in the car so much as tumble into it, like it was a disappearing space she had to hurry in and out of.

Headphones on, not quite looking him in the eye.

"So," he said, turning the steering wheel as he backed up, "to St. Ann's?"

She nodded, leaning her head against the glass.

He was used to teen sullenness, even though Deenie's sullenness was only occasional and never sour. But this felt like something else.

He wondered how bad it had been for her, seeing Lise. What had she seen?

"Are you going to tell me what's going on?" he asked.

"Did they say anything at school?" she asked. Tom could hear a screeching from her headphones. "About Lise?"

"I didn't wait," he said. "I just left. Carl took my fifth period."

Pushing her headphones from her ears, she looked at him.

Her face seeming to wilt, flower-like, before his eyes.

"Dad," she said softly. "I think something really bad's happening."

He looked at her, nodded, pressed the gas harder.

"Okay," he said, hand on her forearm. "One step at a time."

"My daughter is her best friend. She was there when Lise fainted. You can't tell me anything?"

The admitting nurse, glasses smeary, hair slipping from its clip, sighed and shook her head.

"You're not family, sir."

He looked at her, saw the weariness set on her, the feeling around her of fluorescence and confusion, a surly man with a mustache shouting at her from his chair about the president and single-payer health care.

"I know," he said. "I'm sorry." He gave the slightest of smiles, the one Georgia used to call the Charmer and eventually called the Croc, and set his palms lightly on the counter. "I'm being a pain in the ass. It's just, my little girl over there..."

He let the nurse's eyes wander over. He imagined how Deenie looked to her, her parka sleeves too long, her brother's old trapper hat slipping from her brown hair.

"...she got spooked seeing her friend faint," he said. "Now she's just scared out of her mind. I promised I'd find out something."

The nurse wouldn't give him a smile in return, but she did let her gaze float down to the computer screen.

"What's the girl's last name again? Daniels?"

He nodded.

She typed a moment, then her face tightened.

★ ★ ★

Standing by the dusty halogen lamp in the corner of the waiting room, Deenie was watching her father talk to the nurse when the corridor doors swung open wildly.

A middle-aged woman bucked past them, a frizz of blond hair, her bright down coat flapping.

"Oh God," she said, spotting Deenie. "Oh, honey."

It was Lise's mom.

Rushing toward Deenie, she seemed to envelop her in the coat's puffy squares.

"My baby," she said, pushing herself against Deenie, a gust of perfume and sweat. "You should see what they've done to my baby."

At first, it was like on television.

On TV, this was when you find out your friend is dead. Her face punched through a windshield in a drunk-driving accident. Strangled by her jealous boyfriend. Locked in a cage by a man she met on the Internet.

Even though it didn't seem real, Deenie found herself wanting to do what they did on TV, maybe sink to her knees, the camera overhead swirling away from her, the music cueing up.

But then a doctor arrived to talk to Mrs. Daniels.

And hearing him, it became real.

"Deenie," her dad was saying, "it's okay."

He was holding on to her shoulder, which was shaking. She felt her whole body shaking and wondered: *Is this how it felt for Lise?*

"We're very lucky she was here when it happened," the doctor was saying to Mrs. Daniels. "You did the right thing calling 911. Every second counted. A cardiac event of this kind at home..."

"Her heart stopped," Mrs. Daniels said, her face damp, mascara ashed across her left cheekbone. "I could feel it in my hands."

Seconds later, Mrs. Daniels and the doctor disappeared behind the swinging doors, and her dad kept trying to explain things to her.

"Lise had a seizure at home," he said, "a bad one. And her mom called an ambulance. When she got there, something happened to her heart, but they were able to stabilize her. They're taking good care of her."

Deenie nodded and nodded, but all she could think was she wished he weren't there with her. All the smiling-at-nurses in the world wouldn't get her behind those doors to see Lise. If her dad were gone she could find a way to get back there. She and Gabby always found ways to get places: behind the tall fences at the shuttered train depot, into that room in the school's basement where they kept old VCRs so they could watch a mildewed cassette of *Romeo + Juliet* during Back to School Night.

"We can wait," he said, "if you want."

"Okay."

"Let me just drive over to the school and set it up with my classes. And tell Eli."

Deenie nodded.

"Are you going to be okay here, by yourself?"

"I am, Dad," she said, keeping her voice even, steady. "I have to stay."

Sitting in one of the metal chairs, as far from the angry man with the droopy mustache as possible, she tried to text Gabby but couldn't think what to say.

Then she saw a couple, the woman with a crying toddler in green overalls sobbing at her hip. They were talking to a doctor and nurse in front of the same double doors Lise's mom had exited.

Behind them, somewhere inside the belly of St. Ann's, was Lise.

She couldn't believe no one saw her walk in, but then many times she felt invisible. At school, the mall, she could feel people walk right through her. Sometimes, with boys, she realized they could see straight behind her head, to blond-lashed Lise, to long-legged Gabby, to anyone else but her.

★   ★   ★

His leg shook a little on the gas. He was thinking about Deenie in that waiting room with the growling man with the coffee-damp mustache and who knew what new arrivals. Down-river bikers with meth mouths, suburban predators prowling for teenage girls.

Lately, when he read the crime-beat section of the paper, he'd begun to feel his once-gentle town, their little Brigadoon, was teeming with endless threats imperiling his children.

He could hear Georgia's voice buzzing in his head.

So you left her there? You couldn't just call the school? Call our son?

Sometimes it felt like parenting amounted to a series of questionable decisions, one after another.

At least his version of it.

It was just before lunch and the corridors were swollen with students, dozens of hunch-hooded sweatshirts, the boys shoving one another into lockers while the girls glided by in low-tops, skirts, and three layers of tights, their smiles nervous and intricate. Tom spent half his day feeling sorry for girls.

His phone vibrating, he thought it might be Deenie, but the minute he moved past the front entryway, the screen went black, his signal lost.

When he stepped out again, he couldn't get it back.

He waited at Eli's locker, and waited, and then the second bell rang, and everyone scattered, backpacks like cockroach shells.

There was a slight ripple in his chest. *Where is Eli, anyway?* As if Eli were as reliable as an elevator and not his shaggy, perennially late son.

He'll be here any second, he told himself, but a nagging fear came from nowhere: *What if, what if?*

Rounding the corner, he spotted his son's blaring-blue hockey jersey.

There he was, standing in front of his calculus class, shoving folded papers into a textbook.

Tall and carefree and more handsome than any son of his had a right to be. And late as ever, for everything. It was hard to explain the relief he felt.

"Dad?" Eli said, looking up, surprised. "Dad, why are you smiling?"

5

Walking through the cafeteria, Eli Nash was thinking about Lise, whom he'd known since she was bucktoothed and round as a tennis ball. She'd grown into the teeth, but not all the way, and the overbite made her look older, like her new body did, like everything did. She'd been one of those baby-fatted girls who laughed too loudly, covering their mouths, squealing. Then, at some point, overnight, she'd done something, or God had, because she was so pretty it sometimes hurt to look at her.

It felt like, whatever happened now, Lise was maybe gone. That maybe it'd be like his friend Rufus, who'd hit his head on the practice rink last year and who seemed okay but never laughed at anyone's jokes anymore and sometimes couldn't smell his food.

"Eli," his dad had said, finding him before calculus. Wearing a funny smile like the one he'd have after Eli had had a rough game, a cut over his eye, a stick across the face. "Can you do something for me?"

He said of course he would.

Right away, he spotted Gabby in the cafeteria's far corner, where she always sat, usually with his sister, their heads together as if planning a heist.

Gabby was the one all the girls puppy-dogged after at school, the kind other girls thought was "gorgeous" and guys didn't get at all. Or they got something, which made them nervous. Made him nervous.

All the stuff that had gone down with her family, it seemed to give Gabby this thick glaze, like the old tables in the library that shone golden-like, with dark whorls, but when you got close and touched them, they felt like plastic, like nothing. All they did was push splinters into your hand.

Eli didn't much like sitting in the library either.

She was spinning a can of soda between her palms, that girl Skye lurking behind her, the one with all the bracelets and heavy skirts, the one who got suspended once for coming to health class with a copy of the *Kama Sutra,* which she said was her aunt Sunny's, as if it were something everyone had at home, like the dictionary.

"Gabby," he said, tapping her shoulder.

Gabby's head whipped around and she looked at him, eyes wide.

"Oh!" she said. "Eli. You scared me."

Skye was looking at him, her eyes narrow, and Eli removed his fingers quickly from Gabby's shoulder.

"Sorry," he said. "Can I talk to you for a second?" He looked at Skye. "Alone?"

"Okay," Gabby said, slowly. "Sure."

They walked over to one of the far tables. Gabby was almost as tall as he was and had a big heap of hair on top of her head, like Skye and so many of the other girls seemed to be copying. Sometimes they'd put their hair in heavy braids they'd wrap across their heads and he didn't get it but figured it was a fashion thing beyond his grasp.

"Deenie's at the hospital," he said as they sat down, "with Lise. Something happened to Lise. I figured you might not know."

"I didn't," she said, shaking her head.

Three tables behind, Eli could see still Skye, her ringed fingers clawed around her phone, head bowed, typing something.

"I mean, I didn't know Deenie was at the hospital," Gabby said. "Or that Lise was."

He didn't think he'd ever sat so close to Gabby, her skin pale and that serious expression she always wore. He had the sense of so many things going on behind that face.

"Yeah," Eli said. "They had to call an ambulance, I guess. She's there now."

Gabby's phone buzzed slightly on the table. They both looked at it.

"So, what happened? Is it..." Gabby started. "Is it mono again?"

Eli paused, licking his lips.

"I don't think so," he said.

★   ★   ★

Once she got behind the double doors, Deenie had no idea how to find Lise. There was a feeling to the place like in the basement at school, where they held classes for a while when enrollment ran too high. A furnacey smell and uncertain buzzing and whirring sounds. Turning the corners, the floor sloping, you felt like you were going down into something no one knew about, had forgotten about.

At the end of the first long hallway she could see an old man sitting in a wheelchair, his white hair tufted high like a cartoon bird. He was wearing a very nice robe, quilted, like in an old movie. She wondered who'd bought it for him and where that person was now.

The man's head kept drifting from side to side, his mouth open in a kind of perpetual, silent panic. *How did this happen? Why am I here?*

"Hi," she said as she approached, surprising herself.

He looked up with a start, his swampy green eyes trying to focus on her.

"Not another one?" he said, his voice small and wavery. "Are you another one?"

One hand lifted forward from his silken lap.

She smiled uneasily, not knowing what else to do.

"Okay, well," she said, and kept walking.

Maybe that's what it's like when you're old, she thought. Always more young people, a parade of them going by. *Here's another one.*

"I hope it will be okay," he said, his voice rising as she passed. "I hope."

Far down the hall now, her head feeling hot, she turned to look back at him.

"I . . . I . . ." he was saying, his voice like a creak.

She started to smile at him but saw his face—from this distance a white smudge—and stopped.

It took five minutes, and no one questioned her or even seemed to notice.

Rushing as if with purpose, she spotted Mrs. Daniels's turquoise coat in an open doorway, hovering just inside the threshold, Lise's grandmother beside her.

Walking in, she saw the hospital bed webbed with wires, a sickly sac hanging in one corner like a trapped mite. It reminded her of Skye once telling them that you should put cobwebs on wounds, that it stopped blood.

"Deenie," Mrs. Daniels cried out. "Look at our Lisey."

The puff of both women's winter coats, the sputtering monitor, a nurse suddenly coming behind her, and Mrs. Daniels sobbing to breathlessness—Deenie pushed past it all to try to get closer to Lise. Like people did in the movies, she would push past everything. She would not be stopped.

But when she got to the foot of Lise's bed, she halted.

All she could see was a violet blur and something that looked like a dent down the middle of Lise's delicate forehead.

"What happened," Deenie said, a statement more than a question. "What's wrong with her."

"She hit her head on the coffee table," the grandmother said. As if that were the problem. As if the purple gape on Lise's brow were the problem here. Were why they were all here.

Though it kind of felt that way to Deenie too because there it was. A broken mirror where the pieces didn't line up. Splitting Lise's face in two. Changing it.

"That's not Lise," Deenie said, the words falling from her mouth.

Everyone looked at her, Mrs. Daniels's chin shaking.

But it felt true.

The nurse took Deenie's arm roughly.

"They always look different," the nurse said. "She's very weak. You need to leave."

Mrs. Daniels made a moaning sound, tugging on her mother's coat front.

"But are you sure it's her?" Deenie asked as the nurse walked her to the door. "Mrs. Daniels, are you sure that's Lise?"

6

Pulling into the hospital lot, Tom found his daughter standing out front, pogo-ing on the sidewalk to keep warm.

She climbed inside the car.

"Dad, I don't want to be there anymore, okay?"

"Sure," he said. "No one likes hospitals."

Her chin kept jogging up and down, but she wouldn't look at him.

"I don't like it there," she said. "I really don't."

"I know," he said, watching her scroll through text messages. One after another, they arrived, her phone sputtering in her hand.

She hadn't met his eyes once.

"Deenie," he said, "I think I should just take you home."

"I think..." she started, then set her phone on her lap. "I want to go back to school, Dad."

There was an energy on her that worried him, like right before she left for her mom's place each month. Sometimes it felt like she spent hours putting things in and taking things out of her backpack. Blue sweater in, blue sweater out, *Invisible Man* in, then out, biting her lip and staring upward. *What is it I need, what is missing.*

"A lot's happening," he tried again. "We can go home. Watch a movie. I'll heat up those frozen turnovers. Those fat apple ones you love. Your favorite Saturday-night special."

"When I was twelve," she said, like that was a million years ago. It had been their weekly ritual. She liked to watch teen movies from the '80s and make fun of their hair but by the end she would tear up when the tomboy with the wrong clothes danced with the prom king under pink balloons and scattered lights. It turned out he'd missed the perfect girl, right in front of him all along.

"I just want to be at school," she said, softly.

He guessed there might be something soothing about the noise and routine of school. Except she didn't know yet that the school didn't feel routine right now.

"Okay," he said, after a pause. "If you're sure."

His mind was full of ideas, ways to comfort her, all of them wrong.

"But Deenie," he said.

"Yeah, Dad."

"It's going to be okay," he said. The eternal parent lie, a hustle.

She seemed to hear him but not really hear him.

"I don't think it was even her," she said, a tremble to her voice.

"Was who? Did you *see* her, Deenie? At the hospital?"

She nodded, her fingerless gloves reaching up to her face.

"Just for a second. But I don't think that was Lise," she repeated, shaking her head.

"Baby," he said, slowing the car down. He wondered what she'd seen. How bad Lise looked. "It was her."

"I mean, none of it was Lise," she said, eyes on the traffic as they approached the school. "In class this morning too. Watching her. She looked so weird. So angry."

Her voice speeding up, like her mother's did when she got excited. Trying to help him see something.

"Like she was mad at me," she went on. "Even though I knew she wasn't. But it was like she was. She looked so mad."

"Why would she be mad at you, Deenie?" he said, stopping the car too long at the blinking red, someone honking. "She wasn't. You had nothing to do with this."

She looked at him, her eyes dark and stricken, like she'd been hit.

★ ★ ★

It just wasn't a day for going to class.

It was nearly sixth period and, so far, Eli had made it only to French II—he never missed it, spent all forty-two minutes with his eyes anchored to the soft swell of Ms. Loll's chest. The way she pushed her hair up off her neck when she got frustrated, her dark nails on that swirling tattoo.

He never missed French.

But the idea of going to history, of sitting in class with everyone gripped in the talk of Lise Daniels and her rabid-dog routine and his sister seeing it—it all knotted inside him.

He didn't like to imagine what Deenie must have been feeling to ditch school, which wasn't something she ever did. She was the kind of girl who burst into tears when her fourth-grade teacher called her Life Sciences folder "unkempt."

So he found himself back behind the school, where the equipment manager kept the rusting bins of rubber balls, hockey pucks, and helmets.

The air heavy with Sani Sport and ammonia and old sweat, it reminded him of the smell when he'd put his skates on the radiator after a game, scorching them to dryness. As cold as it was, he could still smell it, and it soothed him.

He was sitting on the railing of the loading ramp when he heard a skitter, then the shush of a heavy skirt.

"You want some?" a crackly voice said.

He turned and saw that Skye girl again, leaning against the brick wall, a beret tugged over her masses of blond hair.

She was holding a brown cigarette in her hand, a sweet scent wafting from her, mixed with girl smells like hairspray and powder.

"What?" he said, stalling for time, watching her walk closer to him, her vinyl boots glossy and damp.

She waved the cigarette at him.

He wasn't sure what it was, but it didn't smell like pot. He wouldn't have wanted it if it was. It affected his play. A few times, though, he'd smoked at night, at a party, then picked up his skates, headed to the community rink. Coach had given him a key and he could go after closing, the ice strewn with shavings from the night's free-skate, the hard cuts from a pickup game. He could go as slow as he wanted.

He'd spin circuits, the gliding settling him, the feeling in his chest and the black sky through the tall windows.

Sometimes he felt like it was the only time he truly breathed. It reminded him of being six and his mom first taking him out on the ice, kneeling down to hold his quaking ankles with her purple mittens, stiff with snow.

"It's all-natural," Skye said, returning the cigarette to her mouth. Her lavender lips. "I don't believe in putting bad things inside me. It's musk root. It helps you achieve balance."

"My balance is good," he said, the smell of her cigarette drifting toward him again. Spicy, cloying. He kind of liked it but didn't want to. "But thanks."

"I heard Deenie went to the hospital," she said. "And that Lise's mom's freaking out and that Lise almost died."

Everyone knew things so fast, phones like constant pulses under the skin.

"I don't really know," he said. "You'd have to ask her."

She nodded, then seemed to shudder a little, her na[...]ders bending in like a bird's.

"It's funny how you never think about your heart," she said.

"What?"

"About your real heart," she said. "Not when you're young like us. I heard her heart stopped for a minute. I never thought about my heart before. Have you?"

Eli didn't say anything but slid off the ramp. Looking at her hands, he saw they were shaking, and he wondered for a second if she was going to be sick.

"It's funny," she said, "because it's almost like I *felt it* before it happened. I've known Lise awhile. We used to share bunks at sleepaway camp. She has a very strong energy, don't you think?"

"I don't know," he said, heading toward the door, the blast of heat from inside.

"This morning I was waiting for Lise at her locker. I had my hand on the locker door and it was so freaky. I felt this energy shoot up my body."

She lifted her free hand and fluttered it from her waist to her neck.

He watched her.

"Like a little jolt. Right to the center of me."

She let her hand, blue from the cold, drift down to her stomach and rest, the dark-red tassels of her scarf hanging there.

"But that's how I am," she said. "My aunt says I was born with dark circles on my feet, like a tortoiseshell. Which means I feel things very deeply."

★   ★   ★

There was only one period left and suddenly Deenie couldn't remember where she was supposed to be.

She'd thought school would be easier, busier. She was trying to get the picture of Lise out of her head. The angry crack down her face. Lise was never angry at anyone. Even when she should be.

But now Deenie wished she were at home instead, sitting on the sunken L-shaped sofa watching movies with her dad, her fingers greased with puff pastry.

And so she walked aimlessly, the sound of her squeaking sneakers loud in her ears. A haunted feeling to go with the hauntedness of the day.

It wasn't until Mrs. Zwada, frosted hair like a corona, called out to her from the biology lab that she realized that was where she was supposed to be.

For a moment, Deenie just stood in the doorway, the room filled with gaping faces. The penetrating gaze of Brooke Campos, her useless lab partner who never did the write-ups and refused to touch the fetal pig.

"Honey, I think you should sit down," Mrs. Zwada said, her brightly lacquered face softer than Deenie had ever seen it. "You can just sit and listen."

"No," Deenie said, backing up a little.

Everyone in the class seemed to be looking at her, all their faces like one big face.

"I'm sorry," she said. "I have to find Gabby."

She began to edge into the hall, but Mrs. Zwada's expression swiftly hardened into its usual rictus.

"There's going to be some order to this day," she said, grabbing Deenie by the shoulder and ushering her inside.

So Deenie sat and listened to all the talk of mitosis, watched the squirming cells on the PowerPoint. The hard forks of splitting DNA, or something.

A few minutes before class ended, Brooke Campos poked her in the neck from behind.

Leaning forward, breath sugared with kettle corn, she whispered in Deenie's ear.

"I heard something about you. And a guy."

The bell rang, the class clattered to life, and Brooke rose to her feet.

Looking down at Deenie, she grinned. "But I don't believe it."

"What?" Deenie said, looking up at her, her face hot. "What?"

Her winter hat yanked over her long hair, hair nearly to her waist, Gabby was standing at her locker. Again, with Skye.

Until last fall, Deenie never really knew Skye, even though she'd been in classes with her since seventh grade. Skye was never in school choir, yearbook, French club, plays. She never helped decorate the homecoming float.

But she became Gabby's friend in that way that can happen, because the girl with the cool boots always finds the girl with the occasional slash of pink in her hair. The two of them like a pair of exotic birds dipping over the school's water fountains—you knew they would find each other. And, about a year ago, they had.

At first, Gabby told Deenie she liked to spend time at Skye's house because her aunt was never home and you could just hang out, listen to music, drink the fogged jugs of Chablis in the fridge or a stewed-fruit concoction her uncle used to make in the basement and called prison wine.

But Deenie knew it was more than that. Saw the way they'd exchange looks, how Gabby would come to school wearing Skye's catbird ring. She worried Gabby maybe shared things with Skye, personal things, like about her dad. Things she'd only ever shared with Deenie.

It's like you with Lise, Gabby once said. *You guys have this thing.* Which Deenie guessed was true because she'd known Lise forever and Gabby only since middle school, and Lise was part of her growing up and Gabby was part of everything newer, more exciting. And everything to come.

"Deenie," Gabby called out. "What happened?"

"It was bad," Deenie said. And then stopped. You couldn't talk about it the way you'd talk about a pop quiz or shin splints from gym. Your words had to show how big it was.

"What's wrong with her?" Gabby asked.

"Did you talk to her?" Skye asked.

"Talk to her? No. You don't get it. She's..."

Skye looked at her. They both were looking at her, both so tall and heavy-haired and clustered close. Waiting.

She didn't know how to talk about it, about what she'd seen. *Her face, it wasn't hers. It wasn't her. It was two pieces that didn't go together and neither of them was Lise.*

"Something happened," she finally said. "To her heart."

"Is she going to be okay?" Gabby asked, her chin shaking. "Is she, Deenie?"

Deenie didn't know what to say. Her mouth opened and nothing came out.

★   ★   ★

"We haven't been able to find out much," Principal Crowder said to Tom. "The hospital won't release information without her mother's permission, but Mrs. Daniels hasn't returned our calls. Understandable, of course."

"Right," Tom said, recalling the way Sheila Daniels had looked in the waiting room. He'd tried phoning her twice, thinking that's what one did. "If I can help..."

A teacher for nearly two decades, Tom still felt vaguely un-comfortable in the principal's office. Even though the principal—Ben Crowder, a shiny-faced former "curricular specialist" from the state education department—was only a few years older. Once, he'd flagged Tom down at a local gas station as he struggled to remove the frozen fuel cap from the tank of his Volkswagen.

Help a brother out? he'd asked, a desperate gleam in his eye.

"I've talked to all Miss Daniels's teachers," Crowder said, tap-ping his fountain pen on the desk, "but I wanted to talk to you too. I heard you left campus to see her."

"Yes," he said, noticing his phone was flashing with that red zigzag of a missed call, something that always snagged at his nerves. "My daughter's best friends with her. But I guess I know about as much as you. It was a pretty chaotic scene."

"We followed all the procedures on our end," Crowder said. "But apparently things took a turn when she got home. Some kind of arrhythmia brought on by a seizure. Of course, there's already rumors."

"Rumors?"

"I wondered if you'd heard anything."

"No," Tom said. "Like what?"

But Crowder only leaned back in his chair and sighed.

"What a thing. I've only met the mother once, at a school-board meeting last fall. She seemed like a...cautious woman. The anxious type. So this has to be especially challenging."

"Well," Tom said, his fingers resting on his phone, "I guess all we can do is wait. I'm sure we'll know more soon."

"Right," Crowder said, tapping his pen on the legal pad in front of him. "That's right."

From the entrance of the breezeway, Tom watched the throngs of woolly-hatted kids and pink-necked seniors pushing their way out of the school and over to the parking lot, the slightly rusting bus-stop sign quaking in the hard wind.

He sent Eli a quick text, hoped he'd get it.

Can you take D home and bring car back before yr practice?

He wanted to take her home himself, but he had detention duty.

And there was the missed call: **Lara Bishop**.

Gabby's mom.

"Lara," he said, "how are you?"

It seemed like a silly question, but he didn't know what she'd heard about Lise. And he'd never felt particularly at ease with her. She had a look about her, a wariness, a watchfulness. He'd once heard the phrase *cop eyes,* and when he looked at Lara Bishop he thought maybe that's what cop eyes looked like. Or maybe it was just that he knew what she'd been through.

Maybe, really, it was the way he looked at her.

"Tom," she said, in that low voice of hers, always barely above a whisper, "how scary. I got a message from Sheila. I don't even know her very well. I called back, but I just got voice mail."

"Maybe an allergic reaction?" Tom said. "Maybe epilepsy?" It was the first time all day he'd speculated out loud. It felt like a relief.

"She sounded kind of...off," she said. "But how else would she sound, right? She kept saying her daughter was the healthiest girl in the world and hadn't done anything to deserve this."

"People say all kinds of things," Tom said, but he felt a slight twinge behind his left eye. He was remembering Sheila from that school-board meeting now. Going on and on about vaccinations and autism. She had had some kind of petition.

"Is Deenie doing okay?" she said. "Did she talk to her mom?"

Tom paused for a second, realizing he had no idea.

"Everything's been happening so fast," he said, feeling a burr of irritation he couldn't identify.

"Of course," Lara replied quickly. "I haven't even had a chance to talk to Gabby. I'm heading over there now to get her."

"I'm sure everything's going to be fine," he found himself saying for what seemed to be the hundredth time that day. Each time, he felt like he made it worse.

"Well," she sighed, and Tom thought he could hear the click in her throat, a vestige from the tracheostomy after the accident. (The *accident*—is that what you called a claw hammer to the face?) She always wore a thin pearl choker to try to cover the scar, two curved lines, like an eye. Every time Tom had ever seen her, she'd put her fingertips to her throat at least once. Sometimes he saw Gabby do it too. That scar was so small compared to the one on her face, but she tried to cover that too, with a swoop of her dark red hair.

"Well," he said, offering a faint laugh—the nervous laughter worried parents share when they realize, jointly, there's nothing they can do. *You can't stop them, you can only try to keep the lines of communication open.* "I hear anything, I'll call you."

"Thanks, Tom," she said, the rasp there. "This stuff happens— you just want to *see* them, you know?"

53

★   ★   ★

Walking from the west faculty lot, hoping her brother's unprecedented offer would wait, Deenie hunted for Gabby.

Amid the crush of pink-puffer freshmen, she found her by the front circle, talking on her phone, her eyes covered by large green sunglasses.

"Hey, girl," Deenie said. "Wanna ride?"

"Hey, girl," Gabby said, shoving her phone in her pocket. "My mom's on her way. She heard about everything."

"Too bad. Eli offered. He must've gotten hit in the head with a puck today."

"That is too bad," Gabby said, smiling a little. And they were both quiet for a second.

"I still can't believe it," Gabby said. "About Lise."

They spotted Mrs. Bishop's car, the only black one, like a carpenter ant.

"Yeah," Deenie said. "Maybe...maybe the two of us could go to the hospital later, if—"

"I can't go back there," Gabby said quickly.

At first, Deenie wasn't sure what she meant. But seeing Gabby's mother pull up, she realized what it was. It'd been four years since Gabby's dad did what he did, which wasn't a long time, really. Four years since she and her mother were rolled into the emergency room of St. Ann's. That was the last time anything big had happened in Dryden. A thought fluttered through her head: *What are the odds that the two biggest things ever to happen here happen to my two best friends?*

"I'm sorry," Gabby said. "Am I a bad friend?"

"No," Deenie said, pushing a smile through her frozen face. "I get it."

Gabby tried for a smile too, but there was something under it, heavy and broody. You could feel it under your skin. In so many ways, knowing Gabby was like brushing up against something meaningful, pained, and grand. Before her, the only time Deenie had ever felt it was that time she was ten and the whole family went to the Cave of the Winds, which Deenie had read about in a book. Enfolded between a wall of rock and the falls, Deenie had held her mom's hand and felt the water and the winds and the cataracts mix. "A mysterious and indelible experience," the book had said, and that's how it felt. A thing that marked you. Like Gabby's history marked her, had marked her mother.

"Gabby, she's going to be okay," Deenie said. "Lise is."

Opening the car door to a blast of heat, Gabby turned and faced Deenie. "Definitely," she said. "She's our Lise."

Deenie watched as Gabby slid into the car, her sparkling low-tops, her knit ballet tights bright and jaunty, a day begun in a different place.

"Bye, Mrs. Bishop," Deenie said.

"Take care of yourself, Deenie," Gabby's mom said, waving a gloved hand, her sunglasses larger than Gabby's even, almost covering her whole face.

★   ★   ★

DETENTION CANCELED, Tom wrote on the sign, slapping it on the classroom door. It felt like a day for executive decisions.

He didn't know what he'd been thinking, leaving Deenie alone at the house after everything that had happened. And what if she decided to go to the hospital again?

Walking into the lot, he saw Eli had already returned his car, angled rather dramatically and nearly touching the French teacher's perky Vespa. Tomato red.

Seated behind the wheel, he made the call before he could stop and plan it out. Didn't want to always be readying himself to talk to her. Two years, it should be easier.

"Hey, Georgia."

He told her everything as quickly as he could, hearing her gasp, her voice rushing forward.

"Oh, Tom," she said, and it was like no time had passed. *Georgia, Eli fell off his bike, jammed his finger in gym, split his forehead on the ice.* Her hand on his. *Oh, Tom.*

"I thought you should know," he said.

There was a pause. He could hear her breathing. "I can't believe it. Little Lise."

And there it was: the immediate gloom in her voice, almost like resignation. *Life is so goddamned hard.* Near the end, she'd sounded like that a lot.

"I'm sure she's going to be okay," he said. "And Deenie's doing fine."

"Now all I can do is picture the girls in the backyard," she said. "Lise with her little potbelly, running through the sprinkler in her two-piece."

Tom felt his face warm. Last summer, Lise in a two-piece. From across the town pool, from behind, he'd mistaken her for one of Deenie's swim instructors. Carla, the graduate student in kinesiology who always teased him about needing a haircut.

"I thought probably you knew already," he said, his voice suddenly louder than he meant. "That Deenie'd called you."

"No." The drop in her voice gave him a second of shameful pleasure.

It had been a lousy thing for him to say. Deenie almost never called her.

"Bad reception at the school," he said quickly. "You remember. The hospital too."

"Right. God, that town," she said, as if she had never lived here at all.

Turning the radio loud, listening to some frenzied music Eli had left for him, Tom drove home along Dryden Lake. There were other routes, faster ones, but he liked it.

He remembered swimming in it when they'd first moved here, before all the stories came out. He loved the way it shimmered darkly. It looked alien, an otherworldly lagoon.

Even then, there was talk of designating it a dead lake, the worst phrase he'd ever heard. At some point, people started calling it that, overrun by plants and no fish to be found, and the department of health coming all the time to take water samples.

It was almost ten years ago when the little boy died there, his body seizing up and his lungs filling with furred water. It was the asthma attack that killed him and the boy should never have been swimming alone, but it didn't matter. After, the city threw up high sheet fences and ominous skull–and–crossbones signs. Eli used to have nightmares about the boy. All the kids did. *It could happen to me, Dad. What if it's me?*

But for years, Georgia still liked to swim there at night when it was very warm. Sometimes, he would go too, if the kids were asleep. They felt like bad parents, sneaking out at night, driving the mile and a half, laughing guiltily in the car.

It was something.

The blue–green algal blooms effloresced at night. Georgia loved them, said they were like velvet pillows under her feet. He remembered grabbing her soft ankle in the water, radioactive white.

After a while, he stopped going. Or she stopped inviting him. He wasn't sure which came first.

One night, she came home, her face deathly pale and her mouth black inside. She told him the algae was like she'd never seen it, a lush green carpet, and she couldn't stop swimming, even when it started to hurt her eyes, thicken in her throat.

All night she threw up, her body icy and shaking, and by five a.m., he finally stopped listening to her refusals, gathered her in his arms, and drove her to the emergency room. They kept her for a few hours, fed her a charcoal slurry that made her mouth blacker still. She'd be fine in a day.

"I can't breathe," she kept saying. "I can't breathe."

* * *

Hey—U ok? Just saying . . .

That's what the text said, but Deenie didn't recognize the number.

She'd inherited Eli's old phone and often got texts meant for him. One night, that senior girl who always talked about ballet and wore leotards and jeans to school texted twenty-four times. One of the texts had said—Deenie never forgot it—**my pussy aches for u.** It had to have been the worst thing she'd ever read. She'd read it over and over before deleting it.

Except this didn't seem like one of those texts.

Who r u? Deenie typed back but stopped before she hit SEND.

She leaned back on her bed. The house felt quiet, peaceful.

Downstairs, Dad and Eli were watching TV. Something loud and somehow soothing on ESPN Classic. The constant hum of the household for ten years.

It was nine thirty, and she wanted to stay off the computer. Red pop-ups in the bottom corner of her laptop.

The worst was the picture of Lise everyone was posting. Someone must have taken it with a phone right after it happened. A blurred shot of Lise's bare legs, a rake of hair across her face, that made Deenie almost cry.

There seemed no stopping all the texts jangling from her phone. People she barely knew but who knew she was friends with Lise.

Kim C says she heard Lise was on Pill was she

Why did everything have to be about sex, she wondered. Didn't it make a lot more sense that it was something else? Like in sixth grade when Kim Court ate the frozen Drumstick and Mrs. Rosen had to inject her with the EpiPen in front of everyone. After, everyone called her EpiGirl or, worse, Nutz Girl, and since then no one could eat nuts anywhere at all.

Have u heard of toxik shok? tampax can kill u

Then came crazy thoughts, like what if, trying to help Lise dislodge that crooked tampon a few days before, she'd done something wrong? What if it was her fault?

She kept thinking about what Gabby had said: *Am I a bad friend?*

That morning, Deenie hadn't even met Lise at her locker. She hadn't wanted to see her. Her head still muggy with thoughts of the night before, of Sean Lurie, she wasn't ready to tell. And Lise would see her, and would just *know*.

Tugging off her tights and jeans, she took a long bath, pushing her hand down on her pelvis until it burned.

She still felt funny down there, like things weren't right.

When you thought about your body, about how much of it you couldn't even see, it was no wonder it could all go wrong. All those tender nerves, sudden pulses. Who knew.

Right now, she couldn't even picture Sean Lurie's face.

She remembered, though, the oven grit under his fingernails, the grunt from his mouth, the rough shudder, jerking her back and forth beneath him so she thought something had gone wrong. And then the soft sigh, like everything was good at last.

It made her head hurt, and she put it all away in a high corner of her thoughts, where she wouldn't have to look at it for a while.

After the bath, she sprawled on her bed and opened her history book and read about ancient Egypt.

Mr. Mendel had told them that Cleopatra may have been a virgin when she smuggled herself in a hemp sack to meet Julius Caesar. Giving herself to him was pivotal to her rise to power.

The book explained how Cleopatra first enticed Mark Antony by dropping one of her pearl earrings into a wine goblet. As it dissolved, she swallowed while he watched.

Deenie read the passage three times, trying to imagine it. She wasn't sure why it was sexy, but it was. She could picture the pearly rind on the queen's lips.

In class, Skye said she'd read something online about how Cleopatra used diaphragms made of wool and honey, and a paste of salt, mouse droppings, honey, and resin for a morning-after pill, both of which seemed maybe worse than being pregnant.

Deenie wondered how it all came to pass, the virgin–turned–seductress–turned–sorceress of her own body.

She thought for a second about the snap of the condom Sean Lurie had used and she covered her face with her book, squeezing her eyes tight until she forced it out of her head.

By ten o'clock, she'd read all forty of the assigned pages, plus ten extra.

At some point, she could hear Eli in his room, his phone and computer making their noises, Eli clearing his throat.

Once, a few weeks ago, she'd heard a girl's voice in there and wondered if it was porn on the computer until she could tell it wasn't. She heard the voice say Eli's name. *E-liiii.*

She'd turned her music as loud as she could, held her hands to her ears, even sang to herself, eyes clamped shut. She hoped he heard her fling off her Ked so hard it hit the wall. She hoped he remembered she was here.

Tonight, though, the house was hushed. She was so glad for it she didn't even feel bad about not calling her mom back. And when her dad knocked good night and said he loved her, she made sure he heard her reply.

"Me too. Thanks, Dad."

At midnight, she felt her phone throb under her hand.

The picture of Gabby from when she had that magenta streak in her hair.

"Hey, girl."

"Hey, girl," Gabby said, a slur to her voice. "I just fell asleep. I dreamed it was tomorrow and she was back. Lise. She was laughing at us."

"Laughing at us?" Deenie said. She wondered if Gabby was still sleeping. She sounded funny, like her tongue was stuck to the roof of her mouth. "Why?"

"I don't know. It was a dream," Gabby said. "When I woke up, I thought maybe something happened. Maybe she called you."

Deenie paused, wondering how Gabby could ever think that. But Gabby hadn't been to the hospital. Hadn't seen Lise, seen her mom. Hadn't heard all that talk about the heart, Lise's heart. Deenie pictured it now, like a bruised plum in her mom's hand.

"No," Deenie said, carefully. "I don't think it's going to be that quick."

"I know," Gabby said, her voice sludgy and strange. "Listen, I'll see you tomorrow, Deenie."

"Okay," Deenie said. She wanted to say something more, but she couldn't guess what it would be. Then she remembered something. "Gabby, what was the rumor?"

There was a pause and for a second she thought Gabby had fallen asleep.

"What?" she finally said.

"This morning, before everything, you said you heard something about me."

"I did?" she said, voice faraway. "I don't remember that at all."

7

When he woke up, Eli thought for a second that he was on the ice. Felt his feet in his skates, legs pushing down, grinding the blades hard. His chest cold and full. This happened sometimes.

It was still dark when he left the house for practice. It always was, and he never minded.

He rode his bike through the town, swooping under the traffic lights, counting the number of times the red signals would blink and no one would be there to stop.

It took him a long time to remember everything that happened the day before.

Morning practice felt like part of the dream and he woke up after, in the locker-room shower, his legs loosening and the heat gusting around him, his body finally stopping and his mind slowly rousing. Remembering all the things he'd forgotten.

★ ★ ★

"Principal Crowder's having a very bad time," Mrs. Harris whispered to Tom as he strolled through the administration office. "He can't get any information on Lise Daniels, and parents keep calling."

"Well," he said, reaching for his mail, "I'm sure Crowder's state of mind isn't a big concern for Lise's mom."

"Of course not," Mrs. Harris said. "But it would help us to know. To calm everyone down. When something happens in front of students . . ."

Tom nodded. He was looking at an interoffice memo: *Spring Will Spring (Soon!): A Morning Concert. All Faculty Expected to Attend.*

"So this is still happening today?" he asked. A picture came to him of Lise, rosebud lips perched on her silver flute, at the last recital, at every recital since fifth grade. She used to practice on a plastic water bottle. *You pretend like you're spitting a watermelon seed,* he once heard her tell Deenie, and they both giggled. All the talk of tonguing and fingering and the two girls laughing without even knowing why. These days, they didn't laugh about any of that—a thought that made Tom nervous to ponder.

"Of course," Mrs. Harris said. Everything with her was *Of course* and *Of course not.* "They've been practicing for weeks."

Tom looked at the concert flyer, the graphic of the drunken music note swimming through flower petals.

Driving Deenie to school that morning, he'd felt the exhaustion on her, and a watchfulness. The waiting—which felt like it could end in a second or never, like waiting for all things out of your hands—seemed so weighty on her, her body so tiny next to him, her shoulders sunken.

Maybe a distraction was what she needed, what everyone needed.

★   ★   ★

"So you still have to play?" Deenie asked. "Without Lise?"

They were in the frigid girls' room, the high window always

propped open. It was as if the school thought girls gave off so much heat and pungency that constant ventilation was required.

"I guess," Gabby said from behind a stall. She was changing from her jeans into her long performance skirt. "I think they want to do it."

"They should do it," Kim Court said, appearing from a corner stall. Kim again, like a bad penny. "For Lise. To send good thoughts to her."

Combing her fingers through her hair, Deenie didn't say anything.

"Deenie," Gabby said, her voice echoey from behind the door, "do you ever feel like something bad is about to happen, but you don't know what?"

"What do you mean?" Deenie said. Bad things, for her, were always a gruesome surprise.

"I bet Lise never guessed what would happen to her," Kim said, shaking her head. "Whatever happened to her."

"Maybe she did," Deenie said, always wanting to disagree with Kim. "Like when you're about to get your period, or when Lise got mono that time. The whole week before, she kept saying her neck felt thick."

"Yeah," Gabby said. Her voice sounded funny, like on the phone last night. Slow and soupy. "I felt a little like that this morning. Last night. My head felt so heavy."

Deenie turned and faced Gabby's stall, but she couldn't think of anything to say.

"I know just what you mean," Kim said, nodding fervently, as if Gabby could see her. "I feel funny too." She leaned toward the mirror, examining herself. "My teeth even hurt."

Deenie watched her. Kim's big tusks crowding her mouth. Guys called her the Horse, her braces elaborate, like the inside of your phone if you break it. Deenie wished she could feel sorry for her, but Kim made it impossible.

"We'll get good news today," Deenie said. "Our girl's strong."

"It's so messed up," Kim said, standing in front of Gabby's stall to make sure she could hear. "Lise should be on that stage with you today, Gabby."

Gabby opened the stall so quickly she almost hit Kim in the face.

Her performance shirt bright white, the hem of her dark skirt swirling at her feet, she was holding her vibrating phone open in her palm, staring at the flashing screen.

No one said anything for a second, Kim squirming a little.

Then Deenie's phone chirped, and less than a second later, Kim's squawked.

The texts seemed to come from three or four friends at the same time.

Lise's mom won't let any visitors & hospital called in s.o. from public health!!

nurse tammy reported something abt Lise—what IS happening?!!

Health dept people here now—WTF?

"Health department?" Kim said. "Why..."

Gabby curled her fingers around her phone and looked at Deenie.

Kim was saying something else, but Deenie wasn't listening.

★   ★   ★

When Tom walked into first period that morning, the students were arrayed in little clumps of speculation. The back corner, the windowsill, the deep resin lab sinks. Bowed over their phones, a pinwheel of purple, pink, mesh, leopard, all their slick cases.

"Phones off and out of sight," he said. "Let's go."

Herding them through the hallways took a long time, all the last-minute stops at lockers, and a notebook slipped from sweaty hands, careering down the stairwell and making everyone jump.

But once they arrived, everything changed.

The solemnity of the auditorium always did something to students. Lights dimmed, you couldn't see the water-stained ceiling, didn't notice the squeaking risers. The darkened space, all the guffaws and giggles brought low, to hushes and the odd screech. The stage lit a soft purple. The formal way student musicians always sat, their eyes locked on their easels or on Mr. Timmins, the sweaty, loose-shirttailed music teacher.

There was the feeling of something important about to occur, made all the more important by the circumstances of the day before. It all felt a little like church.

Instead of promoting a tentative freshman to Lise's second chair, Mr. Timmins had decided, in some gesture of something, to do without, leaving Lise's folding chair conspicuously empty. Its black metal base seemed to catch all the light on the stage. You couldn't take your eyes off it.

The music began, the dirge-y strain of "Scarborough Fair," which felt anything but springlike. Tom only hoped this number had been planned all along and wasn't a hasty replacement in honor of Lise. *She's in the hospital, for God's sake,* he thought, *she's not dead.*

Eyes wandering, he saw Eli standing in the back by himself, looking at his phone. A pair of long-necked freshman girls in front of him kept wiggling in their seats, trying to catch his attention. The kid could not manage it better if he was trying, Tom thought. The less interested he was, the harder they tried, their faces red and stimulated.

Up front, he spotted Deenie, her ponytail slipping loose, seated beside Skye Osbourne, with her great swoop of platinum hair. He'd never known Skye to show up for any school event, mandatory or otherwise. The drama of the day seemed to take all comers.

He imagined Deenie's eyes were mostly on the empty chair, but maybe also on Gabby, the cello between her legs, a dramatic skirt of violet lace, a floodlight at her feet.

Maybe it was the lights but her cheekbones looked touched with violet too. Her grave face and dark hair, the sound of the music, the captured angst of the students—so ready for angst anyway and now with the ripest of occasions—it made everything feel even more heightened.

He felt a stirring in his chest, and looking at Deenie, her slight neck arched up, he wanted to put his hands on her shoulders and promise her something.

★   ★   ★

Deenie liked being in the auditorium, like the bottom of a deep coat pocket, the warm hollow at the center of the quilt on the sofa in the den.

There had only been a few moments for her to think about the texts, the idea of the health department—what was a health department, anyway? What exactly did it do?—on the premises, investigating something. She wondered if they would want to talk to her. She'd been a witness, after all.

She pictured Nurse Tammy, her face struck with alarm, forearm wet with Lise's spit. Lise, face a vivid red, like she'd been painted. Deenie had been a witness, but she wasn't sure what she'd been a witness to.

"Can I sit here?"

Deenie looked up and, squinting, saw Skye through the spotlights, a blaze of white.

"Okay," Deenie said, pulling her bag from the cushion. "You never come to things."

Slinking into the seat, she shrugged. "Mr. Banasiak hooked me. And I was worried about Gabby. She's not feeling good."

Deenie looked at her, about to ask her what she meant, but then the lights dimmed again and the music rose up and she shook it loose from her head, turning to face the stage.

At first, she could only watch Lise's empty chair.

But then "The Sound of Silence" began and she looked over at Gabby, who was staring off to one side of the stage, waiting to play.

When her cue came, Gabby lifted her white hand and it fluttered across the cello like a bird as her bow dipped and turned, the other hand bouncing and snapping against its neck.

Her eyes were focused straight ahead, into the back of the auditorium, into nothing.

★   ★   ★

Eli looked up suddenly from his phone, a shiver between his shoulder blades.

The music was so bleak and he'd been trying not to listen, but when he saw Gabby on the stage, she looked so focused, so intent.

Most times when he skated he felt like that, like there was no one else on the ice.

The only sound, the puck clinking on the post, thunking against the boards.

He would fix his eyes like hers were fixed. He would look toward the net with such intensity nothing could stop him from getting what he wanted.

★ ★ ★

Tom wasn't sure of the moment Gabby's neck started to dip back because at first it felt like part of the performance, her knotted brow, her hand vibrating on the slender fingerboard, everything.

It started with her chin, then her whole jaw.

He watched as Gabby's face started to tremble, and then, the way the light hit, it was like her face itself was bending.

Her chair skidded loudly, her neck thrown back so far that, in the darkness, it looked like her head had disappeared.

For one terrifying instant, gone.

The cello still tight between her clenched legs, she lifted herself upright again, her face flushed.

Mr. Timmins had dropped his baton and was moving toward her, and Tom saw Deenie jump to her feet in the front row.

★ ★ ★

It's the same thing, Deenie thought, feeling herself rise, it's happening again. It's the same thing, the same time, the same everything.

She felt her legs hurtle up the steps, the stage lights hot on her.

Her dad seemed to be behind her in an instant, hands on her shoulders.

Mr. Timmins was leaning over Gabby, still in her chair, her legs twisted around its legs, its rubber feet clacking on the stage floor.

She was holding on to the cello and smiling oddly.

"I'm sorry," she said, her face like a flame. "I'm sorry."

★ ★ ★

Tom had one hand on his daughter as the other band members, instruments in hand, were closing in on Gabby.

Gasps, brass clattering on the floor, one girl tripping over herself, nearly teetering off the foot of the stage.

"Back everyone," Tom said, arms out. "Stand back."

Without thinking, he pushed Deenie back too.

Somewhere, a camera flashed, then another. Girls with their phones tucked in their long velvet skirts.

"Stop that!" shouted Mr. Timmins. "Phones away!"

"Gabby, honey," Tom said, leaning down in front of her. "Are you okay?"

There was a film over her eyes, like she might be about to cry.

Then her neck seemed to jolt back with such force he expected to hear a pop, her body surrendering to thunderous motion, every limb shuddering and her torso slumping to the right.

He and Mr. Timmins gripped her, locking her between their arms, Mr. Timmins trying to take the cello from her.

"I'm okay," she said, dropping the cello at last, hand over her mouth.

"Dad," Tom heard a voice behind him say. "Dad."

8

Standing in the back, Eli had been the one who'd called 911.

Four minutes later, the back doors flew open and he showed the paramedics where to go.

"Oh, man," the taller one said, rubbing his winter-red face. "Another one?"

Onstage, Mr. Timmins was kneeling over Gabby, who was looking up at him, her hands around her own neck like she was trying to hold it straight.

All of them had their hands over their mouths, watching.

"Goddamn it, Jeremy."

Eli watched as his dad grabbed a phone from one of the boys' hands.

"I'm sorry," Gabby kept saying, her voice inexplicably loud, carrying through the space. "Did that happen? I just got confused. Are we in school?"

The cello kept getting knocked around, wobbling and quaking like it was a live thing.

"Can you breathe, miss?" the paramedic asked.

"What," Gabby said, her voice high and puzzled. "Yes."

"Let's get everyone out of here," the tall one said, motioning to Mr. Timmins to help. "Clear this area. Give her some room."

They couldn't wrest the bow from Gabby's hand.

Tiptoeing, Deenie kept trying to see over the bear-shouldered paramedics, who were trying to snap an oxygen mask on Gabby's face.

"I don't need to go anywhere," she was saying, her fingers crooked over the mask, pushing it away. Her eyes landed on Deenie. "Deenie, I *don't*."

"I know," Deenie said, nodding, her neck thrusting almost as hard as Gabby's had. It hurt to look at.

"I just felt dizzy or something."

"But just to be safe," Deenie said. "Okay, G?"

★ ★ ★

Tom sat Deenie down in the car, windows shut tight. He asked her to breathe slowly. He was trying to explain something he couldn't explain.

"... and as soon as we can reach out to Gabby's mom, we will. They'll do some tests. It's just better if you stay here. With me."

"Why couldn't we go to the hospital?" Deenie said. "Gabby wanted me to."

Tom wasn't so sure about that. When Lara Bishop arrived, soon after the EMS, Gabby's embarrassment seemed heavy and tortured. She couldn't even look her mother in the eye.

"She didn't faint," Deenie said. "But her body. What was happening to her body?"

The pensive look on Deenie's face, like when she was small. Finding a cat drowned in the ditch by the mailbox. He didn't know how long she'd been staring at it, her brother next to her touching it gently with a stick, hoping to nudge it to life. That night she'd had nightmares, her mouth was filled with mud. He'd tried to explain it to her, how accidents happen but we really are safe. But there was, already, the sense that nothing he said touched what was really bothering her, which was the realization that you can't stop bad things from happening to other people, other things. And that would be hard forever. He'd never quite gotten used to it himself.

"And what does it all have to do with the health department?" she asked.

"They're just making sure everything's okay," he said.

Of course, he had no idea. When he'd learned about their visit, just before first period, he hadn't liked the sound of it.

"It was the nurse," Bill Banasiak told him. "She blew the whistle."

The new nurse, the peaked blond one whose name Tom could never remember, had called her supervisor at the hospital about a bite on her arm from Lise. Embarrassed, she hadn't told anyone at first. But now she was worried. What if there was some kind of virus at the school? One of those new kinds?

"Not the sort of talk you want to have at a school," Banasiak said, shaking his head.

Especially not coming from the nurse, Tom thought.

But he didn't tell Deenie any of this.

"I'm sure we'll know more soon," he told her now, realizing he'd said the same thing ten times about Lise. "Okay?"

"Dad," she said, looking down at his phone resting on the gear panel, "can we call Lise's mom again?"

"Sure," he said finally. "I'll call in a little bit."

"How about now?" she asked.

"Not right now, okay?"

Deenie nodded tiredly. For a second, she looked very old to him, the rhythmic chin wobble of his own grandmother.

But when she turned back to him, her chin had steadied. Tugging her jacket collar from her neck, she said, "But you will?"

"I will," he said. Then, "You feel up to class?"

Part of it seemed ridiculous to him, to have his daughter sit and listen to a lecture about the Panama Canal, but he couldn't think what else to do with her.

For a moment, only a moment, he wished Georgia were there. Georgia, at least the Georgia from before, would have canceled her own appointments, left work, and hijacked Deenie for a soothing schedule of girl time. Or their version of girl time: buying stacks of magazines and tall coffee drinks and curling on the den sofa together. Or something. She seemed to know how to do those things. Until she didn't.

"I can't get away," she had started saying the year before she left. "I'm sorry, Tom. I can't get away." That's how she would put it, as if home were "away." This was when she was spending an hour a day at the Seven Swallows Inn on Beam Road with her co-worker lover (What else could you call him? Married himself, with three kids, cat, dog, hamster). She confessed to this and everything, far more than he'd ever wanted to know, including how ashamed she was of keeping spare underwear in her desk drawer. And how she was "very—mostly—sure" that this coworker lover wasn't responsible for the pregnancy, and thus not for the ugly miscarriage, nine days of bleeding and sorrow. That was something else she had Tom to thank for, he guessed.

Later, after she was gone, he found himself driving to the Seven Swallows, sitting in the parking lot for hours, going through the bank statements, the separation agreement, divorce papers, filling in squares with a ballpoint pen, gaze returning again and again to the sign out front: CLEAN COMFORT HERE. He wanted to keep everything in his head all at once.

"I can go to class," Deenie was saying now, her hand on his arm. "Dad, I can."

Tom looked at her, saw her eyes fixed on him, searching. Like she had seen something on his face. Something that worried her.

"It's okay, Dad," she said, firmly. "I'll be fine."

"Sheila," he said. "Tom Nash. Just leaving another message to see if there's anything I can do. Call me, okay? If I can be any help. Deenie sends her love to you and Lise both. We all do."

He thought of Deenie inside the school, wondering, worrying.

An uneasy thought came to him: If she doesn't find out something, what if she takes off for the hospital again?

So he had another idea.

"Billing, can I help you?"

"Hey, is this Diane? This is Tom. Tom Nash."

The harried voice on the other end eased into something soft, breathy.

"Tom. Well, well. I was hoping you'd call. I'd given up a little."

He cleared his throat. "I'd been meaning to. I had a great time. It's been a crazy couple weeks."

"Eight weeks." She laughed.

He'd met her at the post office, on the longest line either had ever seen. She'd told him her son was trying out for junior hockey and Eli was his idol. She didn't want her boy to play because she worked at the hospital and saw all the players come in with faces dented by flying pucks, teeth knocked out, cracked cheekbones, and, once, a blade to the neck. But what could you do, he loved it.

Tom said he understood.

She'd given him her number and they had dinner at someplace Tom couldn't quite remember. Maybe it was Italian. He'd meant to call again. A second date always felt like an announcement at his age. And he never felt ready for the announcement.

"Eight weeks, really? I'm sorry. But I've been meaning to and now I have a reason, a good excuse."

"You didn't need an excuse."

"Okay, but here it is."

It turned out all he had to do was say Lise's name.

"Oh, that girl."

There was a pause on Diane's end, and Tom wasn't sure what to make of it. It wasn't a large hospital, but still, he was surprised she knew who he meant.

"Yeah," Tom said. "We were over there yesterday, but they didn't know much then."

He heard a momentary clicking sound. "Let's see what I can find," she said.

Her lack of hesitation in breaking HIPAA regulations and various laws was a relief. He felt a kick of revived interest in her, followed by wanting to kick himself.

"She's still not conscious," she said. "She's stabilized, though. And they're doing diagnostics. I can't tell you exactly."

"Oh," Tom said. It seemed like a long time to be unconscious. Unless *not conscious* was code for "coma."

"But the mother is a real problem," she said, her voice quickening a little. "Everyone's talking about it. First, she blamed the paramedics. Claimed they'd dropped her. They don't do that, Tom. Then she blamed the ER doctor. Now she seems to have darker theories."

"Darker theories?"

"I don't know. Crazy stuff she probably got off the Internet."

"Ah."

"We're hoping she doesn't find out about the other one."

"Gabby Bishop," Tom said quietly.

"You know her too?"

"I do." Part of him was expecting her to say Gabby was also un-conscious. That maybe something had happened to her heart too.

"Jesus, sorry, Tom," she said. "But they're not the same. It's not the same thing. That's not a cardiac situation."

He could tell she was the kind of woman who told men what they wanted to hear. That didn't strike him as a bad thing, even though he knew it should.

"I saw it happen," he said. "It looked like a seizure."

"Well, they haven't even admitted her. They're doing tests."

"Diagnostics?"

"Yes," she said gently.

"Thanks a lot," he said, "for all this."

Then a lilt returned to her voice. "You know you left your dog-gie bag in my fridge. I gave you two days to call, then I ate all that peach cobbler myself."

* * *

Standing in the corner of one of the bathroom stalls, Deenie was trying to slow her breath.

Stop, she told herself. You're not one of those hysterical girls. You're not Jaymie Hurwich, who started sobbing in gym class and had to be walked to the nurse's office for hyperventilation. Jaymie, who went to the nurse's office for hyperventilation at least once a month, upset about a test grade, fighting with her boyfriend, grounded by her dad.

Kim Court said she'd seen Skye huddled by herself on the load-ing dock. "I didn't think Skye got upset," she'd said. "Did you?"

And Deenie's phone kept flashing with texts, one after another.

What is HAPPENING?
Gabby has it too!
Did u see her face??

And pictures of Gabby. Even videos someone took with the phone. A gruesome one of Gabby's head rearing back, her neck thick and purple under the lights.

And all Deenie could think of was Gabby and Lise in hospital beds, side by side, their arms connected to an elaborate blinking web of cords, tubes.

Both their heads somehow purple and split, their mouths open.

If it happens to both your best friends, the next one must be you. If it happens to both your best friends, it must be you.

But it wasn't the same. Gabby hadn't fainted, had never even fallen, exactly, never hit her head or bit anyone. Never had that look Lise had, like an animal trapped.

Gabby had only looked confused, lost, mortified. Which was how everyone looked some of the time, every day.

The door to the girls' room swung open.

"It was just like with my cat, I'm telling you," Brooke Campos was saying loudly. "Do they know if she was sleeping in a room with a bat? Or was around a sick bat? That's how it happens. We found one in our garage, hanging right over the cat bed. We had to have Mr. Mittens destroyed."

Deenie opened the stall door to see Brooke with a clump of senior girls, all waving their lip-gloss wands, passing them from one to another—watermelon crush, scarlet bloom.

"So you're saying they both just happened to get bit by bats?" one of the seniors said.

"It was probably the same bat," Brooke said, a little defensively.

The stall next to Deenie opened and Skye appeared. Deenie hadn't even known she was in there, those long crocheted skirts of hers, one layered over the other, muffling her movements.

"Hey," she said, nodding to Deenie.

And she started unhooking all her exotic bracelets to wash her hands, her fingers moving gracefully over the fasteners. It was strangely hypnotic.

"Hey," Deenie said, thinking about what Kim had said about seeing Skye curled up on the loading dock. She looked at Skye's face, hunting for a sign: red eyes, swollen face. But you could never see much through all the hair.

"I mean, think about it. What if they slept in the same place?" Brooke said, blotting her mouth with a paper towel. "Gabby and Lise."

"A place compromised by bats?" the same senior girl said, hand on hip.

"You can say what you want," Brooke said, digging her heels in. "I just know what it looked like. Her mouth was foaming and her tongue went like this."

Leaning into the mirror, she stuck her tongue violently to one corner of her mouth.

"That's not what happened," Deenie said, watching her. "You don't know what you're talking about."

"I heard Nurse Tammy got bit," Brooke added, ignoring Deenie. "Lise *bit* her. And she has big teeth."

"A vampire walks among us," whistled one of the girls, hooking her fingers under her mouth like fangs.

"So, Brooke, are you saying Lise bit Gabby too?" Deenie said, looking at Skye, trying to get some help. "Or that she just licked her?"

Brooke shook her head pityingly. "I know she's your friend. Both of them. But."

"There's bats down by the lake," Skye said quietly, looking in the mirror, lifting her hair from her brow.

Deenie looked at Skye, shaking her hands dry.

"If it were rabies, they would have known right away," the most sensible senior girl asserted. "That's not hard to figure out."

Tugging loose three paper towels, Deenie rubbed her hands roughly, until they turned red.

"We'd be lucky if it was rabies," Skye said, twirling her bracelets back down her wet wrists. "They have a shot for that."

"So what are you saying it is?" the senior girl said, eyeing Skye, trying to up-and-down look at her, but Skye was not the type to be chastened by that.

Shrugging lightly, she shook a cigarette loose from somewhere in the folds of her skirt. "I don't know," she said. "I'm just thinking about the lake."

Deenie looked at her.

The senior shook her head dismissively. "No one goes in the lake anyway."

"No." Skye nodded, letting her eyes skate across Deenie's face, and keep going. "They never do."

★   ★   ★

Like after all school disruptions, there was a window during which you could do anything, and Eli took advantage, finding a corner in the back of the auditorium as teachers corralled the remaining students.

But soon enough, Assistant Principal Hawk—his real name, maybe—took Eli's shoulder in his talon grip and marched him to earth science.

No one was paying any attention to poor Mr. Yates talking about natural-gas extraction. Everyone in school had seen what happened to Gabby.

One girl, breathless, announced that Gabby's mother had arrived and that "her scar looked bigger than ever!"

"Let's try to keep our focus on the subject at hand," Mr. Yates said, straining.

"Mr. Yates, maybe it's the drilling!" Bailey Lu exclaimed, her palm slapping her desk. "My mom says it's poisoning us!"

Slipping in his earbuds, Eli stared out the window at the practice rink, bright with cut ice.

He wondered if it was one of those superflus and was glad he and Deenie had had all those shots the month before, their arms thick and throbbing. Or maybe it was a girl thing, one of those mysteries, like the way the moon affected them, or like in some of the videos he'd seen online that, mostly, he wished he hadn't.

But it didn't matter what it was. It was going to be bad for his sister, who loved Gabby even more than she loved Lise. Who talked so much, always in a hushed voice, about the Thing That Happened to Gabby, about her cokehead father, who liked to show up at school every so often, begging to see his daughter. *Maybe you should have thought about that before you picked up the claw hammer,* Eli always thought.

The truth was, he didn't know Gabby very well, just as the tall, pale-faced girl all the other girls copied, her clothes, the streaks she'd put in her hair then dye away again, the way she spray-painted her cello case silver.

He did remember being surprised last fall when she started hanging out with Tyler Nagy, a hockey player from Star-of-the-Sea. Eli had never liked him, the way he was always talking about the screeching girls who came to all the games, the fourteen-year-old he said wanted him to do things to her with the taped end of his stick.

The only time Eli'd ever really spent with Gabby was when Deenie was a freshman and Gabby had stayed with them for a few weeks. Her mother was having a "hard time," which had something to do with all the empty wine bottles in her recycling bin and not being able to get out of bed, but no one ever told him the rest. It was soon after their own mom had moved out, and it seemed like having Gabby there was good for Deenie too, who'd spent hours reading by herself in her room back then.

As far as he could tell, Gabby never really slept. More than once, he'd spotted her hiding on the sofa in the den, watching TV in the middle of the night. Hour after hour of the same show where they dressed middle-aged women in new outfits, dyeing all their hair the same shiny red.

His dad told him he kept finding gum wrappers, dozens of them, trapped in the folds of the quilt.

One night, not long before she went home, he found her in the basement, lying on the Ping-Pong table, crying.

Girls—at least, the girls he knew, not his sister but other girls—always seemed to be crying.

But Gabby's crying was different, felt wild and broken and hurt his chest to hear.

Drumming his fingers on the Ping-Pong table until it vibrated, he tried to talk to her, to make her feel better, but the things that worked on Deenie—recounting graphic hockey injuries, popping his shoulder blade, trying to rap—didn't seem right.

Finally, he had an idea. Took a chance. Pulled one of the Ping-Pong rackets from under her left thigh, reached to the floor for the ball.

"Come on, little girl," he said, pointing to the other racket. "Show me what you got."

The grin that cracked—with tortured slowness—across her face stunned and rallied him.

They played for forty-five minutes, flicking and top-spinning and crushing that hollow ball, until they woke up everyone in the house.

★   ★   ★

I'm just thinking about the lake.

Deenie couldn't believe Skye had said it. In front of all those girls. In front of Brooke Campos, who stopped talking only while texting and usually not then.

At the final bell, Deenie found her at her locker.

"Skye, why did you mention the lake?"

"What do you mean?"

"It doesn't have anything to do with any of this," Deenie whispered. "So why bring it up?"

Skye looked at her, shrugged. Skye was always shrugging.

"I don't think," she said, closing her locker door, "we really know what this has to do with."

They weren't supposed to go into the lake. No one was. School trips, Girl Scout outings, science class, you might go and look at it, stand behind the orange mesh fences.

Every spring and at the end of the summer, the lake would give over to acid green. It was called "the bloom" and Deenie's fifth-grade teacher warned them, pointing to the iridescent water, that it meant it was filled with bacteria and hidden species. With a stick, he would poke one of the large blades of algae that washed up on the shoreline. One year, during a conservation project for Girl Scouts, they found a dead dog on one of the banks, its fur neon, mouth hanging open, tongue bright like a highlighter pen.

When she was very young, she believed the slumber-party tales about it, that a teenage couple had gone skinny-dipping and drowned, their mouths clogged with loam, bodies seen glowing on the shoreline from miles away. Or that swimming in it gave you miscarriages or took away your ovaries and you'd be barren for life. Or the worst one, that a little boy had died in the lake and his cries could still be heard on summer nights.

A few years ago, long after it had been closed, Eli said he saw a girl swimming in it, coming out of the water in a bikini, laughing at her frightened boyfriend, seaweed snaking around her. He said she looked like a mermaid. Deenie always pictured it like in one of those books of mythology she used to love, a girl rising from the foam gritted with pearls, mussels, the glitter of the sea.

"It looks beautiful," her mom had said once when they were driving by at night, its waters opaline. "It *is* beautiful. But it makes people sick."

To Deenie, it was one of many interesting things that adults said would kill you: Easter lilies, jellyfish, copperhead snakes with their diamond heads, tails bright as sulfur. Don't touch, don't taste, don't get too close.

And then, last week.

It had been Lise's idea to go to the lake, to go in the water. She'd stood in it, waving at them, her tights stripped off, her legs white as the moon.

★   ★   ★

It was nine o'clock and Tom wasn't sure where the day had gone, other than to ragged places, again.

Deenie was hunched over the kitchen island, eating cereal for dinner.

Outside, Eli was slamming a tennis ball against the garage door with his practice stick. Sometimes it was hard to remember his son without that stick in his hand, cocked over his shoulder. Even watching TV, he'd have it propped on his knee. It seemed to have happened sometime during early high school, when the other parts of Eli, the boy who liked camping and books about shipwrecks and expeditions and looking for arrowheads in Binnorie Woods after a heavy rain, had drifted away, or been swallowed whole.

His phone rang: Lara Bishop.

"Tom, thanks for your message."

"Of course," he said. "How's Gabby?"

"We're home. They were going to keep her overnight, but she seemed to be doing okay. And she hates that place so much. So here we are."

"I'm glad to hear it," he said. "Really glad."

He could feel Deenie's stare, her hand gripping her own phone.

"Well," she said, and there was a pause. "I guess I just wanted you to know. And, you know, to check in. See what you might have ... I don't know."

"I understand," he said, but he wasn't sure what she was suggesting.

"I mean, we don't know what this *is*," she said.

"No," he said, eyes on Deenie. "But I don't know anything. You mean about Lise?" He wasn't going to tell her what Medical Biller Diane had said.

"Or if maybe ... Gabby's dad didn't call you, did he?"

"Charlie? No. No."

"I was worried he might have found out. From the school maybe. I don't want Gabby to have to deal with him right now."

"Of course not." But what he was thinking was, Weren't they obligated to notify him? He was still her dad.

"Thanks. It's just ..." And her voice trailed away.

"And if he had called," he added, though he wasn't sure why, "I wouldn't have told him anything."

"Thank you, Tom." He could hear the relief in her voice. It all felt oddly intimate, in that parents-in-shared-crisis way. Lightning hitting the Little League batting cage. Mall security agreeing not to call the police. Those "whew" moments fellow parents share.

After he hung up, he wondered how he would feel if he were Charlie Bishop. He would never, ever do what Charlie had done, even if it had been an accident. Once, before everything, they'd been teammates for a pickup baseball game, had cheered each other on, played darts after and drank shots of tequila with beer backs.

That was just a few weeks before the accident and it made Tom sick to think about now. How much he'd liked Charlie. How Charlie had slapped him on the back and said he knew just how hard marriage could be.

★   ★   ★

The minute her phone rang, Deenie began running upstairs to her room.

"Gabby—"

"Hey, girl," Gabby said.

"Are you okay, what—"

"Hey, girl," she repeated.

"Hey, girl," Deenie replied, slowing her words down, almost grinning. "What'd they say at the hospital?"

She leaned back on her bed, feeling the soft thunk of her pillow.

"They did all these tests," Gabby said. "They made me count and say who the last two presidents were. They gave me a tall drink of something that was like those candy orange peanuts that taste like banana. If you put a bag of those in a blender with gravel and old milk."

"Yum, girl."

Gabby snickered a little. "Then they strapped a mask on me and rolled me into this thing that was like the worst tanning bed ever. Everything smelled. Then they did this other thing where they put these little puckers all over my head and I had to lie there for twenty minutes while they shot electricity through my body." She laughed. "It was awesome."

"It sounds awesome," Deenie said, forcing a laugh. "So."

"So."

"What is it? What happened to you?"

"They don't know," she said. "They even made me talk to a headshrinker. She asked if I was under stress. She told my mom that sometimes this happens. Like maybe I was upset and my body just freaked out."

"Oh," Deenie said.

"I asked her if she meant 'stress' like having your dad tear a hole through your mom's face."

Deenie felt her chest tighten, but Gabby was laughing, tiredly.

"So they don't think it's like with Lise?"

"I just need to relax," Gabby said, not really answering, a funny bump in her voice. "I guess maybe if I light some geranium candles and take a bath, like the doctors used to tell my mom when she couldn't breathe in the grocery store or the mall."

It was interesting to think about, the slender filaments between the worry in your head, or the squeeze in your chest, and the rest of your body, your whole body and everything in it.

Lise, the summer before, had lost thirteen pounds in less than two weeks after something had happened at the town pool with a boy she liked. She'd thought he liked her, and maybe he did, but then suddenly he didn't anymore.

She and Lise and Gabby had devoted endless hours to imagining him as Lise's boyfriend and then to hating him and the girl with the keyhole bikini they'd spotted walking with him by the snack bar. Deenie was sure he'd be at the center of their thoughts forever. But right now she couldn't summon his name.

Since then, there'd been so many boys they'd speculated about. Boys who liked them and then didn't. Or maybe a boy they didn't like until the boy liked someone else.

But Lise said the boy at the pool was worth it. Running her fingers over her stomach, she called it the Mike Meister diet.

Mike Meister, that was his name. Always a new boy, even last week, Lise at the lake, whispering about one in Deenie's ear. How could you believe any of it was real?

Lise, her head, her body, her flighty, fitful heart, were like one thing, and always changing.

But it was different with Gabby. Deenie knew all her beats and rhythms, had seen her through everything with her dad, her mom, her bad breakup. And this was not the way stresses played themselves out on her body. Everything stayed inside, her body folding in on itself.

"Well," Deenie said. "You're home now. That's good."

"I guess everyone was talking about it," Gabby said. "The whole school saw."

Deenie didn't say anything. She was thinking of Gabby on that stage, the way her body jerked like a pull-string toy. Like a body never moves, not a real body of someone you know.

"Deenie," she said. "Say something."

"What did it feel like?" Deenie blurted, her face feeling hotter on the pillow.

Gabby paused. Then her voice dropped low, like she was right there beside her. "There was this shadow," she said. "I could see it from the corner of my eye, but I wasn't supposed to look at it."

Deenie felt her hand go around her own neck.

"If I turned my head to look," Gabby continued, "something really scary would happen. So I couldn't look. I didn't dare look."

Deenie pictured it. That smile on Gabby's face after, when everyone surrounded her on the stage. Like something painted on her face. A red-moon curve.

"I didn't look, Deenie," Gabby whispered. "But it happened anyway."

I'm okay, she'd said. *I really am. I'm fine.*

That smile, not a real thing but something set there, to promise you something, to give you a white lie.

★   ★   ★

He waited until he couldn't hear the hum of her voice anymore through the floor. Then he knocked on Deenie's door.

"Hey, honey," he said, poking his head in.

"Hey," Deenie said, cross-legged on her bed.

As ever, her bed like a towering nest, always at least two or three books tufted in its folds. Deenie never fell asleep without a book or her phone in her hands. Probably both. When Georgia used to make her clean, Deenie would hoist the bedding over her head, shaking all the books, folders, handouts onto the carpet.

"They told her it might be stress," Deenie said. "Like you said."

Walking toward her, his foot caught on her white Pizza House shirt, ruched in the quilt where it hit the floor.

"Well," he said, picking up the shirt, sprayed with flour and forever damp, "when things like this happen, they can really knock around your body."

"I guess," she said, watching him closely. He wondered if he wasn't supposed to pick up her things. He tossed the shirt onto the bed lightly.

"What about you?" he asked. "What do you think?"

"I don't know," she said. "That doesn't seem like Gabby to me."

"I know, Deenie," he said. "We just gotta wait and see."

He sat down at the foot of the bed. She looked expectant, like she wanted something from him, but he had no idea what. He'd seen that look a hundred times before, from her and from her mother.

Then, nodding, she fumbled for her headphones, and he could feel her retreating, her face turning cloudy and inscrutable.

"Dad," she said, sliding the headphones on, "maybe I shouldn't go to work on Saturday. With everything that's going on."

He looked at her.

"I think maybe I just want to be home."

He didn't know what to say, her eyes big and baffling as ever, so he said yes.

★ ★ ★

The minute her dad left the room, Deenie wanted to jump up and throw the shirt in the laundry basket. She didn't know why she hadn't already.

But she didn't want to touch it or look at it.

It reminded her of the car, and Sean Lurie, the shirt wedged beneath her on the seat.

And then all the other things she didn't want to think about.

Lise's face. The lake. Everything.

There was too much already, without thinking about that.

9

Just after six in the morning, Eli stepped into the dark garage, slung his gear bag over the front handlebars of his bike.

As the garage door shuddered open, he saw something move outside, in the driveway.

For a drowsy moment, he thought it might be a deer, like he sometimes saw on the road at night if he rode far out of town, into the thick of Binnorie Woods.

But then he heard a voice, high and quavery, and knew it was a girl.

He ducked under the half-raised garage door and peered out.

All he could see was a powder-blue coat with a furred hood, a frill of blond hair nearly white under the porch light.

"Who's there?" Eli asked, squinting into the misted driveway.

With a tug, she pulled the hood from her head.

Except it wasn't a girl. It was Lise Daniels's mom, the neighbors' floodlight hot across her.

"Eli?" she called out, hand visored over her eyes. "Is that Eli?"

"It's me," he said.

He'd seen her at the house dozens of times to pick up Lise, had seen her at school events, hands always tugging Lise's ponytail tighter, always calling after her, telling her to call, to hurry, to be on time, to watch out, to be careful. But Eli wasn't sure she'd ever said a word to him in his life. He knew he'd never said a word to her.

"Eli," she said, loudly now. "Tell your father I'm sorry I haven't called him back."

The halo of her hair, the pink crimp of her mouth. It was weird with moms, how you could see the faces of their daughters trapped in their own faces. Mrs. Daniels's body was larger, her shoulders round and her cheeks too, but somewhere in there, the neat prettiness of Lise lay half buried.

"Okay. Mrs. Daniels, are you okay?" he asked, and she moved closer to him, coming out from under the flat glare of the floodlight. "Did something happen at the hospital?"

For a moment, the vision of Lise fluttered before him, twirling in her turquoise tights, skirt billowing as she bounded up the school steps.

"I'm not supposed to talk about it," she said. "I've been advised not to speak to anyone associated with the school, and your father is a school employee."

He wondered how long she'd been standing out here. He thought of her looking up at the second-floor windows, waiting for a light to go on. Once, back when he played JV, he spotted a girl doing that after one of his games. A freshman on her bike, one sneaker flipping the pedal around, gazing up at his bedroom window. Until then, he hadn't thought girls did those things. When he'd waved, she jumped back on her seat and rode away.

"Oh, Eli," Mrs. Daniels said, shaking her head hard, her hood shaking too. "You're going to hear things. But I'm telling *you*."

"Maybe you should come inside," Eli tried, the wheels of his bike retreating from her as if on their own. "I can wake Dad up. I bet he'd want to talk."

But she shook her head harder, shook that pale nimbus of hair. "There's no time for that. But I need you to pass along an important message. You know I've always thought of Deenie as a daughter."

She was moving close to him, as if to ensure they were quiet, though her voice wasn't quiet but blaring.

"What does this have to do with Deenie?"

"Oh, Eli," she said, nearly gasping. "It has to do with all of them. All of them. Don't you see? It's just begun."

Before he could say anything, before she could get any closer to him, he heard the door into the garage pop open behind him.

"Eli, who are you—"

"Dad," Eli said, relieved, waving him over. "Lise's mom is here."

"My Lise," she said, not even acknowledging Eli's dad, her eyes, crepey and sweat-slicked, fixed on Eli. "It's already over for her. Now all we can do is hope. But it's not too late for the others."

Arm darting out, her red hand clasped him. "What if we can stop it?"

"Sheila," his dad said, walking toward her. "Did something happen?" He reached out to touch her shoulder gently, but the move startled her. She tripped, stumbling into Eli.

He tried to steady her, feeling her cold cheek pressed into his shoulder, a musky smell coming from her.

"Sheila," his dad was saying, more firmly now.

"Oh, Tom," she said, whirling around. "I need to tell you about Deenie."

"What about Deenie?" Eli thought he heard a hitch in his father's voice.

"They want us to believe they're helping our girls. They're killing our girls. It's a kind of murder. A careless murder."

"Sheila, why don't you come inside?" his dad said in that calm-down voice that used to drive his mom crazy. "Let's sit down and—"

"I can't do that, Tom," she said, her voice turning into a moan. "Our girls. I remember when I took Lise and Deenie shopping for their first bras. I remember showing them how to adjust the training straps. Those little pink ribbons."

"Sheila, I—"

"Who would ever have thought in a few years we'd be poisoning them?"

His dad was saying something, but Eli wasn't listening, couldn't stop looking at her, her mouth like a slash.

As if sensing his stare, she turned to Eli again.

"The things we do to our girls because of you."

Eli felt his hands wet on his bike handles.

"Me?"

Something was turning in her face, like a Halloween mask from the inside.

"The dangers our girls suffer at your hands," she said. "We know and we'll do anything to protect them. To inoculate them. *Anything.*"

"Sheila, have you slept at all?" His dad put his arm on Eli's shoulder, gave him a look. "Let's get you some coffee and—"

She shook her head, eyes pink and large and trained on Eli.

"No one made *you* shoot yourself full of poison," she said, voice rising high.

She pointed her finger at Eli, below his waist.

"All of you," she said, eyes now on Eli's dad. "Spreading your se-men anywhere you want. That's the poison. Your semen is poison."

"Sheila, Sheila..."

"Don't say I didn't do what I could." She turned and started walking away. "I hope it's not too late."

★   ★   ★

It had been a night of blurry, jumbled sleep. Deenie woke with a vague memory of dreaming she was at the Pizza House, standing in front of the creaking dough machine, Sean Lurie coming out slowly from behind the ovens, looking at her, head cocked, grin crooked.

What? she'd said. *What is it?*

It's you, he said, standing in front of the blazing oven.

And she'd stepped back from the machine suddenly, the airy dough passing between her hands, soft like a bird breast.

It fell to the bleached floor, flour atomizing up.

Hands slick with oil, and Sean's eyes on them. On her hands.

And she looking down at them, seeing them glazed not with oil but with green sludge, the green glowing, the lights flickering off.

Deenie stood at the kitchen island, phone in hand.

Mom wont let me go to school tday, Gabby's text read. **Sorry, DD.**

After everything Gabby had been through, she was still worried about Deenie having to navigate the day without her. Because these were things they maneuvered together—school, divorces, faraway parents who wanted things. Boys.

The side door slammed and her dad came into the kitchen, shoving the morning paper into his book bag.

Something in the heave of morning air made her remember.

"Dad," she said, "did you hear something earlier? A noise."

Vaguely, she remembered looking out her window, expecting a barn owl screeching.

He turned toward the coffeepot.

"Mrs. Daniels came by this morning," he said. "She couldn't stay long, but Lise is doing okay. No change, but nothing's happened."

"Why didn't you wake me up?"

"There wasn't time," he said, lifting his cup to his face. "She couldn't stay. She had to go back."

"But can we go over there now?"

"No," he said, quickly.

Deenie looked at him, the way he held his coffee cup over his mouth when he spoke.

"I mean," he added, "we'll see."

Outside, it was bitter cold, the sky onion white.

Eli came with them on the drive to school, which never happened.

Riding together, it felt like long ago, fighting in the backseat until Dad would have to stop the car and make one of them sit up front.

She felt a wave of nostalgia, even for the times he kicked her and tore holes in her tights with his skates.

"Eli Nash, skipping practice. I bet you broke Coach Haller's heart," Deenie said, looking at her brother in the backseat, legs astride, the taped knob white with baby powder, like Wayne Gretzky's. But he wouldn't look at her.

"I bet they didn't even have practice without you," she tried again. "I bet they all took their helmets off in your honor. I bet they hung black streamers over the rink and cried."

"I overslept," he said, facing the window. He didn't look annoyed. He didn't even seem to be listening to her.

She waited a moment, for something, then turned back around. The sky looked so lonely.

The car turned, and there was the lake.

"Deenie," her dad said, so suddenly his voice startled her, "Lise and Gabby haven't been in the lake lately, have they?"

★   ★   ★

He regretted it the moment he said it, and a hundred times more when he saw her body stiffen.

Wrung out from scant sleep, he wasn't sure his mind was quite his own. All of Sheila's ravings, he hadn't quite pieced them together, but he could guess. It had something to do with vaccinations, a predatory attorney, the teeming Internet. She needed an explanation, badly, and he couldn't blame her.

Driving, though, he couldn't shake the feeling of something, some idea.

Then his eyes had landed on the lake, its impossible phosphorescence, even in the bitter cold, still half frozen over, the algae beneath like a sneaking promise. Remembering Georgia, her mouth ringed black that night years ago. She said she'd dreamed she put her own fingers down her throat, all the way down, and felt something like the soft lake floor there, mossy and wet and tainted.

She was never the same after that, he'd decided. Though he also knew that wasn't true. She hadn't been the same before that. No one was ever the same, except him.

So, his head still muddled, he'd found himself asking Deenie that ridiculous question about the lake, no better than Sheila's speculations.

He could see her whole body seize up.

"We're not allowed in the lake," she replied, which wasn't really an answer. "Why are you asking me that?"

"No reason," he said. "I guess I'm just getting ready for today's rumors."

"Sometimes kids go in anyway," Eli said from the backseat. "I've seen it."

Deenie turned around to face him. "Like you, you mean. You and me."

"What?"

"We used to go in it, before. We used to swim in it, remember?"

"That's right," Tom said. "We used to take you."

When they were little, long before the boy drowned. Tom had a memory of pushing the corner of a towel in Eli's ear, hoping it wouldn't be another infection, that milky white drip down his neck. Why did he ever let them in that lake, even then?

He could hear Eli twisting his stick left and right. "But something happened to it. It doesn't even seem like the same lake. And it smells like the bottom of the funkiest pair of skates in the locker room."

"You mean yours?" Deenie said, like they were ten and twelve again, except there was a roughness in their voices Tom didn't like.

And Deenie's chin was shaking.

Tom could see it shaking.

He found himself watching it with exaggerated closeness, until she noticed him and stared back, her face locking into stillness.

"Dad!" she said. "You missed it. You missed the turn. It was back there."

You're a careless person, Georgia once said to him. He didn't even remember why. He didn't remember anything. She was always coming out of the water to say things, her mouth black.

★ ★ ★

@hospital did they ask u abt lake, Deenie texted Gabby. She was standing by the window in the second-floor girls' room, the best place in the school to get reception. But it still wouldn't go through.

It had been a week ago. Deenie and Gabby and Lise and Skye all in Lise's mother's Dodge with the screeching heater and the perennial smell of hand lotion. Lise said the steering wheel always felt damp with it.

As they drove along the lake, Skye told them she'd seen two guys in the water the week before, the first flicker of spring and their speakers blaring music from open car doors. One had a tattoo that began on his chest and disappeared beneath his jeans.

"Maybe they're there now," Lise had said, leaning forward eagerly, laughing. Boy crazy.

They all knew they wouldn't be, really, and they weren't. It was just the lake in front of them, its surface skimmed bright green.

And soon enough they were all in the water, just barely, ankle-deep, then a little more, all their tights squirreled away on the bank.

Wading deeper, Lise pulled her skirt high, and her legs were so long and skinny, with the keyhole between her thighs like a model.

You couldn't help but look.

She had a moon shape on her inner thigh that Deenie had never seen before. Later, Lise would say it happened when she lost weight, a stretch mark that wouldn't go away.

And then Gabby and Skye left, their calves slick with the water, thick as pea soup.

With Gabby gone, everything was less interesting, but it was easier. It was like before. Those days of just Deenie and Lise, and Deenie let herself settle into the sugar-soft of Lise's voice, and how easy she was and the water so delicious and Lise with stories to tell.

Now, remembering it, standing at the bathroom mirror, Deenie looked at herself.

Had the water done something? *Did it do something to me?* she wondered. *Do I look different?*

Then she remembered asking herself that question before, two days ago. How could you even tell, the way things kept happening to you, maybe leaving their marks in ways you couldn't even see.

She walked to her locker and opened it, stood there.

If she had to sit through first period, she thought she might explode.

"K.C.," she called out, spotting a familiar glint of braces in her locker-door mirror. "You have your car?"

Kim Court moved closer, smiling, nodding. Shaking her keys.

Gabby lived ten twisty miles from the school, an A-frame like an arrowhead snug in the Binnorie Woods. There was no regular bus route and the house was always hard to find. Deenie's dad had picked her up there countless times but sometimes he still got lost, calling Gabby's mom, who would laugh softly and give him the same directions again. *No, that's a right at the yellow mailbox.*

Gabby said living out here made her mom feel safer, tucked away like a nest at the top of a tree. But whenever Deenie was in the house, with its creaking wood and big windows, she couldn't imagine feeling more exposed.

"I always wanted to see it," Kim whispered, leaning over the steering wheel, gazing at the roof, its edges weeping with purple ivy. "It's like a gingerbread house."

They stood on the porch, hopping in their sneakers to keep

warm. Kim in her rainbow-glittered ones, like the ones Gabby wore all last year.

It seemed to take a long time. Gabby's cat, Larue, watched them from the window with suspicious eyes.

Finally, Deenie saw a curtain twitch, and the door swung open.

"Hey." It was Skye, wrapped up in one of her fisherman's sweaters with the elbow torn through. "What's going on?"

"Hi," Deenie said, walking inside. She didn't want to show her disappointment that Skye was there again.

At some point, Deenie was going to have to get used to it. This new alliance.

After all, you could never be everything to one person.

Across the living room, Gabby was perched in the roll-arm chair. Larue hopped from the windowsill and stretched across her lap.

Kim's eyes were floating everywhere—at the helix of books stacked in one corner, *Closing the Circle—NOW!* on top, and up into the wooden eaves, dark enough for bats.

Gabby and her mom had lived here for two years, but it still looked temporary, the furniture for a different kind of house, modern and sleek, beneath the heavy wooden ceiling fan, the faded stained glass.

"Where's your mom?" Deenie asked.

"Sleeping," Gabby said, her fingers picking at her scalp. "Look how gross this is. I can't get the glue out."

"Glue?" Kim asked, using it as an excuse to hover over Gabby.

"From the EEG," Gabby said as Kim leaned over Gabby, peeking through her long locks.

"It smells," Kim said.

"It's toxic," Skye noted, gazing out the window behind the sofa. "So it smells."

Kim shrank back from Gabby's head, her fingers wiggling like she'd nearly touched a spider.

"I've been texting you," Deenie said. "Gabby."

Gabby turned and looked at her.

"My mom made me turn off my phone," she said. "And computer. Because of the pictures and stuff."

"Right," Deenie said. She hoped Gabby hadn't seen that video of her onstage. She'd heard it was on YouTube: "Cello Girl Possessed!"

"And Mrs. Daniels was calling me."

"Mrs. Daniels?" Deenie wondered if she'd showed up here too. "What for?"

"I don't know," Gabby said. "She wants us to come see her lawyer and some special doctor."

"So she thinks it's the same thing? What happened to Lise and what happened to you?"

"I guess." Gabby shrugged. "My mom says we shouldn't get involved."

"Sheila Daniels has a bad mojo happening," Skye said. "You can feel it coming off her. Maybe she doesn't want the truth. She just wants an answer."

"What do you know about it?" Deenie asked. "Do you even know Mrs. Daniels?"

"Not really," Skye said, walking to the sofa. "But maybe she's just not someone to be around right now. She's carrying a lot of pain."

"Tell them about the girl," Gabby said to Skye. "Skye was telling me this freaky story."

Deenie and Kim looked at Skye.

"Oh, just something I read online," she said. "This eleven-year-old girl a long time ago who got super, super sick. Her eyes sunk back in her head and she'd roll around on the floor. And her body started to do crazy things, like bending back on itself. So her parents called the doctor. And when he came, the girl opened her mouth and started pulling trash out of it."

"Trash, gross," Kim said.

"Not like our trash," Skye said. "Straw, gravel, chicken feathers, eggshells, pine needles, bones of little animals."

Kim's fingers touched her lips, eyes wide. "She was eating animals?"

"No," Skye said, shaking her head. "And she wasn't just throwing up things from her stomach. Because everything was always dry. The doctor could blow the feathers in his hand."

Kim gasped.

"Well, the Internet never lies," Deenie said, but then Skye loaded up the page on her phone. She showed them a picture, a girl with big haunted eyes, her mouth open. You couldn't really see anything, but her mouth looked gigantic, like a hole in the center of her face.

Gabby took the phone from Skye, stared at it, Larue spiraled on her lap, tail twirling.

"When the doctor put tongs down her throat," Skye added, "the girl spat out a cinder as big as a chestnut and so hot it burnt his hand."

Taking the phone back from Gabby, Skye showed them a picture of a stern-faced doctor, his hand out, a scythe–like scar in the center of his palm.

"What's a cinder?" Kim asked, teeth tugging at her lip. "Like a rock?"

"This is all very helpful," Deenie said. Gabby couldn't really want Skye here. She was only making it worse. Worse than even the pictures on the Internet. "Thanks, Skye."

"So then what happened?" Gabby asked, Larue's tail tickling her neck.

Skye shrugged. "I didn't read it all. Maybe they burned a bunch of people in the town square. That's what they usually do."

"No," Gabby said, "I mean to the girl. What happened to her?"

"Oh," Skye said. "I don't know. It doesn't say."

Deenie sat down on the roll-arm next to Gabby.

"Mrs. Daniels came to our house this morning," Deenie said.

Gabby looked up at her. "What for?"

"I don't know," Deenie said, realizing it herself.

Everyone was quiet for a moment.

Skye was kneeling on the sofa, looking out the window. Larue leaped from Gabby's lap and winnowed between Skye's calves and scuffed boot heels.

"Gabby, are you going back to the doctor today?" Kim asked.

"We're waiting and seeing," Gabby said, her fingers flying back to her scalp. "For some results or something. I can't think of what more they could do. Or ask. 'Have you visited a foreign country recently? Have you been camping? Could you be pregnant?'"

There was a banging sound from somewhere in the house.

"That's Mom," Gabby said, jumping to her feet. "She's probably not going to like you guys cutting."

Skye didn't move, so Deenie didn't either. She hadn't had a chance to talk to Gabby and she needed to before it was too late.

"Gabby," she asked abruptly, "did they ask you anything about the lake?"

"The lake?" Kim looked at Deenie, her face animating. "What about it?"

Deenie watched the back of Skye's head, which didn't move.

"We were there last week," Skye said. "Isn't that what you mean, Deenie?"

And then something happened.

Gabby's jaw jolted to the left, then jolted again and again.

Grabbing the chair arm, she pressed her face hard against the back cushion to try to stop it.

Kim was watching, her fingers to her mouth as Gabby's jaw slammed into the cushion over and over.

They were all watching.

"Don't tell my mom," Gabby cried out, her jaw popping like a firecracker. "Deenie, don't."

★   ★   ★

Sitting in the parking lot, Tom spread the newspaper across the steering wheel and read the article. He hadn't wanted to read it in front of Deenie and he didn't want to be seen reading it in school.

Mystery Illness Strikes Best Friends at High School

There was a large photo of Lise and Gabby, cropped. In the original version—slapped, milk-spattered, to Tom's refrigerator door the previous fall—Deenie stood beside Gabby. In the newspaper, only Deenie's hand remained, resting on Gabby's shoulder like a ghost's. The girls, tanned and triumphant during a trip to WaterWonders last fall. Lise bursting from a star-spangled halter top that, no matter how she shifted or twisted, always seemed to land one of its biggest stars in the center of a breast, a bull's-eye.

He'd taken the girls himself, with Eli as company, both pretending not to hear the high frenzy of the backseat, the girls talking the whole eighty-minute drive in a language impenetrable and self-delighted. On the ride back, their bodies chlorine-streaked to numbness, a torpor set in and he and Eli could watch the twilit horizon stretched across the windshield, and not say a word.

...Lise Daniels, 16, remains unconscious at St. Ann's Hospital. Doctors would not confirm a connection between her condition and that of her best friend and fellow orchestra member Gabrielle Bishop, also 16. Bishop was given an EEG, among other tests. An unnamed source tells the *Beacon* that the results were "in the normal range," suggesting no seizure had occurred...

Midway down the page was another photo inset. A creamy lavender brochure he recognized:

HPV AND YOUR DAUGHTER: VACCINATE TODAY, PROTECT HER FOREVER

Oh no, he thought. Here it is. What Sheila was raving about that morning. Alongside the photo came the subhead:

A Mother's Heartache Raises Serious Questions

...school and hospital officials have been tight-lipped. "It is not our role to speculate," Hospital Superintendent Bradford noted in an e-mail. "It's our job to get to the bottom of this and to see that these girls receive the best possible care."

This stance appears to carry little weight with Sheila Daniels, 43, mother of the first afflicted girl, who is still waiting for answers, especially about a controversial new vaccination that has had many parents nationwide crying foul...

There was a quote from Mindy Parker's father, Drew Parker, Esq., who was now speaking on Sheila Daniels's behalf.

"The situation has escalated beyond one mother's personal tragedy to a potential public health crisis," he said. "We can't rely on the public health department as our sole information source. After all, they were the ones who promoted this particular vaccination."

While officials at the health department had not returned calls at press time, one source there, speaking off the record, said the vaccine in question is "very safe. As safe as these things get."

Tom looked at the brochure inset again. *Protect her forever.* It had accompanied the letter all the parents in the school system had received the prior summer.

Parents of all rising sixth-grade girls are required to submit evidence of immunization or an opt-out notice, but all parents are strongly urged to vaccinate their daughters. The main cause of cervical cancer, HPV is easily transmitted via skin-to-skin contact during sexual activity. It is far more effective if girls get the vaccine before their first sexual contact. For your convenience, the department of health will conduct vaccinations on school grounds on the following dates...

So she'd done it, the whole series. Three boosters over six months. They sent text-message reminders. The final one had been just a few weeks ago.

He'd been glad for it, though he tried not to think about it for long. He knew his daughter would eventually have sex. That any day now she might find a boyfriend and then it was inevitable. That wasn't the part that bothered him. It was the peril out there. Infections, cancer, a havoc upon his sweet daughter's small, graceful little body. One she held so closely, so tightly. Even hugging her, he felt her smallness and delicacy.

She liked the high dive and played soccer and, in gym class or touch football with Eli and himself, was always bold and fearless. Skinned knees, bruised elbow, *I can play too*. But sometimes he wondered if that was by necessity, a girl living with two males, a girl who might rather be up in her room with Gabby, with Lise, or with her books, that endless pile of novels with limp-bodied girls on the cover. Girls in bathtubs, in dark woods. Girls underwater.

And when he touched her, he couldn't help but think: What happens when someone touches her someday and doesn't understand these things about her? That she was both fearless and fragile and could be hurt badly in ways he could not fix.

And now, with Lise and Gabby, he was more glad than ever that he'd done what he could to take care of her. Whatever theories Sheila Daniels held in her fevered head, the shots were not to blame.

Vaccines, like all great scientific discoveries, are counterintuitive. You must take the very thing you are protecting yourself against. So your body remembers it, knows how to fight it.

You have to do whatever you can to shield their bodies. And sometimes that means you have to expose them to the very thing you want to protect them from. Which is the most unfair thing in the world.

★   ★   ★

"Oh my God, Deenie, did you *see* her?" Kim said, tearing open a bag of gummy worms from a warm spot under her car's heat vent. "Did you see what happened to her face? That sound?"

Nerves, Gabby had insisted, laughing lurchingly. *Stress.*

And now, heading back to school, Deenie wished she hadn't gone in the first place. She was going to make it just in time for third period and she hadn't even gotten to talk to Gabby alone. And she wished she hadn't brought up the lake.

"And why doesn't she want her mom to know?" Kim asked, teeth tearing noisily at the green worm dangling from her braces.

"I don't know," Deenie said. "Turn left."

"Here," Kim said, handing Deenie her phone. "Find some music. I can't think and drive."

Deenie scrolled down the playlist mindlessly with her thumb.

"You know," Kim said, mind-reading, "that lake water is in everything. It's not just in the lake. If you know what I mean."

"Is that some kind of riddle?"

"Do you ever drink from the water fountains in the school?" Kim said. "It's the same stuff. And remember that day in gym, when we played soccer in the field and we all got that orange stuff on our shoes?"

Deenie looked at her thumbprint seared onto Kim's phone, set it down on the gear panel.

"No," Deenie said, "I wasn't there."

Deenie's own phone began humming on her thighs. It was another text from the number she didn't recognize.

if I have the wrong # u can tell me
Who r u, she started to type. Then stopped.

The thought came: *Could it be Sean Lurie?*

And then she pushed it away. Nearly shaking her head as if to shake the idea loose. She didn't have time to think about any of that.

"So," Kim said, looking at her from the corner of her eye. "You guys went in the lake?"

"We were just there," Deenie said. "We weren't doing anything."

"But did you get near the water?"

"No," Deenie lied.

"Huh. Well, *you're* okay, right?" she said, looking at Deenie, maybe squinting a little.

"Don't I look okay?" Deenie replied.

Kim looked at her for a moment longer, then turned her eyes back to the road, tugging at a gummy worm, letting it snap against her lip.

Deenie's phone burred again, a text from Gabby, who must've gotten her phone back.

Don't worry. we didn't put our face under water. we were never all the way in.

But Deenie had. Though Gabby didn't know it.

It'd been after she and Skye left, disappearing up the bank.

Leaning back, Lise kicked her legs, her breasts bobbling from her cotton bra.

Swim with me, Deenie, she said. *Let's do it, huh?*

And she'd found she wanted to. Cool as Gabby and Skye were, with ex-boyfriends and birth control and complicated hair, maybe Lise and Deenie were cool too. Maybe they were lawbreakers. Rebels.

So they swam, even putting their heads under.

Afterward, lying on the bank, Lise had told her the story, whispering it in her ear. About the thing she had done with the boy, that he had done to her, in the bushes by the school. And she just had to tell Deenie about it. And how it had felt.

Deenie hadn't been able to put it out of her head for days after. She guessed she hadn't put it out of her head yet.

★   ★   ★

All during class, every time he walked by the window, Tom saw it, from the corner of his eye. Amid all the hay-brown thatch of late winter, a flash of neon pink, just outside, by the tall hedges.

Soon, he found himself teaching from that corner, trying to get a better look.

It looked familiar and he couldn't figure out why.

After the bell, in nothing but shirtsleeves, his face flushed from the cold, he crept along outside his own classroom windows like some kind of peeper.

Right by the dense, snow-furred hedges, there was a crumpled pile and first he thought it was a winter scarf swirling around itself, but when he reached out, he felt the thick knit of a pair of girl's tights, Fair Isles like Georgia used to wear on winter mornings, long ago. Vivid pink with fat white snowflakes.

He thought about tugging the wool loose from the brambles, taking the tights to Lost and Found, but he didn't.

Just looking at them, how small they were, he didn't know what to do.

★　★　★

Is everything ok? Your sister won't call/text me back. MOM.
it's ok, Eli typed, she will.

He hoped she would. He could still remember Deenie's tight, red-faced anger at their mom, all through the divorce. The way it sometimes seemed her forehead would split open. It had settled into something quieter, less vivid. Something worse, like grooves sunk deep, unfixable. It had been so much harder for Deenie. All because their mom couldn't control herself, she said. Which is disgusting.

Thrusting his phone to the bottom of his backpack, he opened the door to the loading dock.

And there, once again, was Skye Osbourne, prowling up the ramp from the parking lot.

He was beginning to wonder if she lived out here. But he guessed she could wonder the same thing about him.

She smiled through a crest of smoke. It smelled like honey.

"Sometimes a girl's gotta get some fresh air," she said. "Or she might go crazy."

He dropped his backpack to the ground, climbed up on the railing.

There was a heaviness to the sky, the whisper of something wet in the air.

"Hey," she said, tugging a fraying scarf from her neck. "Feel how warm it's getting."

She dropped her bag and climbed up beside him.

"I heard Lise's mom came to see you."

"Who told you that?"

"Deenie."

"Really?" he said. He had the impression Deenie wasn't really friends with Skye. Friends of friends. Sometimes Eli felt like that's all he had. Friends of friends.

"What did she want?"

"I don't know. She was acting pretty crazy."

"Huh," Skye said. "Did she say stuff?"

All those layers of sweater and scarf, and beneath those, her legs, boots climbing to her midthigh. When she turned, her skirt whirled slowly, and, for a split second, he could see the inside of one of those thighs. Stark white through the skein of fishnets.

He watched her thigh. She watched him.

"Sort of," he said. All that came into his head was Mrs. Daniels saying *Spreading your semen anywhere you want*. "I don't remember."

She looked at him and he thought he saw a funny kind of smile there. He tried to imagine having sex with Skye, to picture her body underneath all those folds and seams. To picture her eyes rolling back, her skin flushed, her body giving way. He couldn't.

It made him feel relieved.

He didn't think he'd ever be interested in Skye, but he was glad girls like her existed. Ones who didn't need him to feel good, pretty, forgiven, safe.

★   ★   ★

There were marks on Lise's locker, like from a big claw.

"They didn't have her combination," Jaymie Hurwich told Deenie breathlessly. Class salutatorian and Most Self-Motivated Student, Jaymie said everything breathlessly. "The janitor opened it with a bolt cutter."

Deenie put her finger on the metal-scrape scar.

"They looked, but then they didn't touch anything," Jaymie said, hand on the large padlock hanging from it now. "You missed geo, Deenie. How come?"

Deenie didn't say anything. She knew exactly what was inside Lise's locker: packs of highlighters, wild-berry hand sanitizer, the dented thermos containing sludgy remnants of yesterday morning's health smoothie. What could they learn from that?

Then Jaymie told her the other news: a silver-haired woman in a pantsuit had been spotted in the nurse's office. No one knew whether Nurse Tammy had quit or been suspended or fired, but she was gone. And the silver-haired woman was maybe not even a nurse at all but someone important. The lanyard on her neck read *Dryden County Health*.

"Do you think they'll cancel midterms?" Jaymie asked.

Deenie didn't answer. She was reading the newspaper article that had been making the rounds, the paper greased to near silk by now.

The picture of Gabby and Lise, best friends forever.

Which was all she could see at first until Jaymie spread her hand like a spider over the photo of the lavender brochure.

"It could happen to any of us," Jaymie said gravely. "We all have it in us."

The first shots were six months ago.

HPV vaccines are more effective if administered before sexual debut.

That's what the department of health poster in the nurse's office said. Gabby had read it aloud, making wide eyes at Deenie until she'd laughed.

Debut. Take a bow after. Hold your applause till the end, please.

Freshman girls were now required to have it before enrolling.

Brooke Campos said most of the fifth-grade girls had already had it. "Sluts," Brooke had said, annoyed at being beaten by her eleven-year-old sister. "The little sluts."

And here they were, high-school juniors with condoms hurled at their feet wherever they turned, it seemed. And they hadn't gotten the shots.

"The human papillomavirus can infect you anywhere," Ms. Dyer, the health teacher, announced before the first round of shots in September, "and can cause everything from benign warts on the hands and feet to cancer of the cervix, anus, mouth, and throat."

A papilloma, she explained, grows outward like a projecting finger and looks like cauliflower.

Deenie didn't see how a finger could look like a cauliflower but, watching Ms. Dyer holding up her pinkie, she knew she didn't want either of them inside her.

And then Ms. Dyer said that HPV had been around forever, even in those fairy tales you read as a kid, when the witches and trolls have bumps on their faces and hands.

"Can't warts just be warts?" Brooke Campos asked, grimacing. "Let's not get crazy." Brooke was always the person in English class who complained that Ms. Enright was "reading too much into things."

"This isn't a joke," Ms. Dyer said. No one would ever assume anything Ms. Dyer said was a joke. Twenty-eight years old with a master's in female adolescent something, she paused before she answered any question, pushing her oversize blue-framed glasses higher on her nose thoughtfully. Deenie's dad said, with women like her, a sense of humor comes a few years later.

"See how wide this area is?" she said, holding a diagram of a cervix across her pelvis, making the girls in the front row flinch. "At your age, this is the area most vulnerable to invasion. It's utterly exposed. In a few years, it will retract. You'll be safer."

Lise whispered that it made her feel like her insides were on the outside and anyone could touch them.

"Until then," Ms. Dyer said, pointing to the sink handle on the lab unit, "you are as open as the mouth on that faucet."

Skye looked up for a moment from mild contemplation of her own fingers, bundled with rings—arrows, snakes, a silver seahorse.

"Ms. Dyer, I read something," she said. "Most people with HPV have issues with feeling grounded, with self-judgment, with their sexual energies."

"Where'd you read that, Skye?" Ms. Dyer asked, her fingers wrapped around the sink handle. Teachers never knew what to do with Skye, Ms. Dyer least of all. Whenever Skye spoke, Ms. Dyer tended to shift the weight on her feet back and forth until it made Deenie dizzy.

"Online," Skye replied. "It has to do with repression. Warts mean you're holding something back that needs to be released."

"Like what? Pus?" Deenie asked. Everything was always so easy for Skye, with her older boyfriends, the way her aunt bought her cool old-time lingerie from vintage shops, the strip of birth control pills she once unfurled for them like candy.

"No," Skye said. "Sexual hang-ups. Hiding your erotic powers. Fear. Secrets. You have to release all that."

"But how?" Lise peeped from behind Skye. "What are you supposed to do?"

Everyone started giggling except Lise, her face puzzled and reddening.

"Don't worry, Lise," Skye said, not even turning around to look at her. "You'll know just what to do."

The first round of shots, Deenie was surprised how little it hurt, and disappointed.

All the rumors were that it hurt more than any other vaccine, ever.

She remembered Jaymie Hurwich. It had taken her ten minutes because the nurse couldn't calm her down.

Finally, she told me to watch the ladybug on the window, Jaymie said after. *And I said, What window? By then she'd stuck it in.*

Back then, the prospect of her or Gabby or Lise having sex seemed remote. None of them had boyfriends and there had been the dramatic cautionary tale of a girl Deenie worked with at the Pizza House. The one who'd confided that she thought she was pregnant by the assistant manager at the ear-piercing booth at the mall. It turned out she wasn't pregnant but did have gonorrhea, which was disgusting to all of them in ten different ways, "starting with the name," Lise had said, shivering a little.

But the third booster round came after Gabby and Tyler Nagy. They'd had sex twice, but Gabby wasn't even sure it worked the first time, though she'd spent four summers at horse camp, so it was hard to know.

After the second time, Tyler broke up with her while she was still putting her jeans back on. "I should never have done it," Gabby said. "And now it's gone."

Around then, she'd started to spend lots of time with Skye, who sent Tyler a text message calling him an abuser of women. She told them there were secret codes embedded in the text and it was a hex. She shook the phone when she sent it, to increase the mayhem. And when Deenie thought about it now, it was then that Gabby and Skye's friendship was sealed.

Later, the brief reign of Gabby and Tyler—had it really only lasted a month?—became a sign to Deenie that there were entire dark corridors too awful to ponder. It wouldn't be that way for her, she decided. And she never would have dated anyone like Tyler, or any hockey player.

But it wasn't just Gabby. There was Lise, her body bursting with power and beauty, mere seconds away from a wealth of thrilling boyfriend possibilities, which would surely lead to romantic sex and never anything to feel bad about, ever.

Sexual debut. Sometimes it seemed to Deenie that high school was like a long game of And Then There Were None.

Every Monday, another girl's debut.

★   ★   ★

A sharp burst of screams erupted from inside the gym.

"Put your fingers in her mouth," someone was shouting, and A.J. and Scotty Tredwell were rushing down the hall, pulling Eli with them through the locker-room exit, following the noise.

The doors pitched wide, but all Eli could see was a band of girls' legs in all those colored tights like Gabby's, like the bright pegs in a game board, grouped so closely he couldn't see past them to whatever they were staring at on the floor.

Mrs. Darger, whistle jammed in her mouth, was shoving them aside like a pro lineman, and when the last clenched-face girl stumbled sideways, Eli spotted a pair of rainbow-colored sneakers twitching on the floor, heard the rapid sound of someone's head hitting hard wood, rat-a-tat-tat.

It was the red-haired girl, Kim someone, who used to trail after Gabby when she came to watch that jackass Nagy play. Laugh-filled braces, she'd flashed her shirt upward at him, but only as high as her white belly, freckle-sprayed. Once Gabby stopped coming to the games, Kim did too.

Suddenly there was a strong smell, a geyser of vomit from the girl's mouth, carrot-colored to match her hair.

"It's me," her voice came. "Oh no, it's me."

Eli had long gotten used to the screams of girls, their faces ruddy and ecstatic behind the throbbing Plexiglas.

You could never really distinguish them from the noise of everything else in the rink, the seashell roar under his helmet, the double-tap of a stick, the whistle shrieks, the sounds of his own breathing, ragged and focused.

But this wasn't the same anyway, the sound that came from the girl's—Kim Court's—mouth as she saw the paramedics arrive.

It wasn't a scream, really.

More like a howl, a moaning howl that reminded him of something he couldn't name. An animal dying, something.

When they sat her up, there was a spray of blood down the back of her shirt from where her head had hit the floor.

"You're okay," Mrs. Darger had said, her face a funny shade of green. "You just spooked yourself."

Like you might say if she had gotten hit in the head with a volleyball.

"What happened," someone whispered, and Eli could smell the vomit on the floor. One of the paramedics stepped on it, smearing it as he wheeled Kim Court away.

"She was standing and then she wasn't."

"That is so gross."

"She was standing next to me," someone said, "and she was saying, 'Why are you so gray?'"

★   ★   ★

There was a long message from Gabby, broken across seven, eight texts.

Standing outside the east breezeway, Deenie read them, one eye on her cell phone signal, her thumb pressing anxiously on the screen, *refresh-refresh-refresh,* for the next one.

I was scared he'd do this.

It was about Gabby's dad. Only he could make her like this.

She said he'd just showed up at the house, had learned what happened from Mrs. Daniels. Couldn't believe he had to hear it from a stranger on his voice mail. And wasn't that typical, Gabby said, because Mrs. Daniels was no stranger. Had in fact called the police on Mr. Bishop once, a year ago, when he'd come to pick up his daughter and driven right onto the front lawn, tearing out a porch light and insisting Gabby get in the car, now.

He went to hosp. looking for me, Gabby wrote. He just wants to show off. He doesn't care. He was yelling and mom wouldn't come from behind the dining rm table.

Then:

He started crying, big shock. Mom said what are you gonna do? Cry your whole life?

But Gabby's final text wasn't about her dad. It was short and the words seemed to flash at Deenie, her screen catching the sun's glare.

Also: I'm thinking about the lake. What if u r right. What if it was in the lake. What if it is in us.

Deenie looked at the words, which seemed to float before her eyes.

But I'm okay, she wanted to say, to type. But she just looked at the screen instead.

That was when she heard the funny pant, someone rushing up to her, the hall echoing with new noise.

Keith Barbour was charging down the hall with another senior boy, both their necks ringed by monster headphones.

"Did you hear?" he barked, shoving Deenie in the arm. "Kim Court's getting wheeled out on a gurney."

"Kim?" Deenie asked, her phone smacking the floor. "What happened?"

"You're all going down." The other boy laughed, beats thrumming through the open mouths of his headphones. "One by one."

★ ★ ★

The whole school had a rabid energy, like nothing would settle again.

And then, a few minutes before sixth period began, Eli showed up at Tom's classroom door.

Tom hadn't even had a chance to talk to him about what had happened that morning.

The dangers our girls suffer at your hands, Sheila Daniels had said to poor Eli. Eli, the sweetest boy in the world. *We know and we'll do anything to protect them. Anything.*

A woman who laid that charge at the feet of his son, a boy

121

who couldn't even enjoy the girls, their avid eyes always on him, seemed outrageously cruel.

"Dad," Eli said, face pale, one hand tight on the door frame. "I need to talk to you."

Tom stepped outside the classroom and Eli told him what he'd just seen, the redheaded sophomore on the gym floor.

"The one with all the braces," Eli said.

"That must be Kim Court," Tom said. "It sounds like Kim Court."

Kim had been in his class last semester. She was one of the ones always trailing behind Gabby and who seemed years younger than her, mouth thick with orthodontia, skittering in her tennis shoes, spinning in the hallways like a red top.

"She didn't look good," Eli said. His eyes were glazed and wouldn't quite meet Tom's.

"This is just crazy," Tom said. "I'll see what I can find out."

Eli didn't say anything.

The bell rang.

"Okay," Eli said, swinging his backpack up behind him.

Something in his face when he turned away made Tom pause. An expression he'd almost forgotten. Back when Eli was ten or eleven, that time when he stopped sleeping. Georgia would hear him moaning, go to his room, and find Eli sitting in the dark, his arms wrapped around his shins. He'd say his bones felt like they were popping. The doctor said it was growing pains, which Tom hadn't realized was a literal thing.

"Kids can become very emotional when they don't sleep," the doctor had told them. "It's natural."

The only thing that seemed to help was when Georgia rubbed his legs, which she would do for a half hour or more, coming back to their bed her hands slippery with vitamin oil.

Driving him to school in the morning in those days, Tom would watch him in the rearview mirror, eyes ringed gray. It was hard to see. This, his easy child, none of the sweeping emotions of his daughter, her warmth and sorrow both heavy things. He wasn't used to it on Eli.

"Dad," Eli had asked one morning, "what if you woke up one day and you were gone?"

"If you woke up and I was gone? That wouldn't ever happen, Eli."

"No, what if I woke up and I was gone."

Tom had looked at him in the backseat, his limbs growing so long, his face changing so fast you could almost watch it happen, and felt a fierce loss and didn't know why.

10

Eli sat, playing it and replaying it in his mind. The girl's head slapping the floor, the glare from all those braces, like a mouth full of tinfoil.

Horse. Now he remembered. That's what they called her.

Language lab should have started five minutes ago, but Ms. Chase, who gave out the peeling headphones, was nowhere to be found. Under the faded poster of the Eiffel Tower, A.J. and Stim, both in their jerseys, were sitting on top of their desks, speculating loudly that school would be canceled.

"They gotta do it now," A.J. said. "Quarantine. Lock your daughters up!"

"I'm telling you, it's some kind of mutant STD," Stim said, flapping the edge of the long gauze pad on his forearm, an acrid smell wafting from it. "I won't be hitting any of that. I'm sticking with Star-of-the-Sea girls."

"Oh, man, those girls *all* have STDs. They don't believe in condoms."

Eli looked longingly out the classroom door. Maybe he could just leave.

"Why don't you ask Nash?" Stim said, spinning the dials on the ancient analog tape deck. "He's the one who got a booty call from Mo McLoughlin after the Brother Rice game."

Maureen. The one who'd chugged hard cider on the way over and thrown up in his wastebasket after. So tiny, school gymnast, her fingernails looked like one of Deenie's old dolls', tiny as baby's teeth.

"I doubt Horse gets enough play to get a mutant STD," A.J. said, baring his teeth like a donkey, "or even a regular one."

"Speaking of, Nash," Stim said, still plucking at the gauze, "I saw your sister take off with her this morning."

"What do you mean?"

"Before everything. Your sister and K-Court were in a car, driving toward the woods."

A.J. smiled. "She's getting to be quite the little rebel, that sister of yours."

Eli placed his palm over his textbook, a different picture of the Eiffel Tower on it. *French in Action! L'Avenir Est à Vous,* it was called.

"It's evolution," Stim said. "With Lise Daniels and Gabby Bishop on the DL, somebody's gotta step up."

"Not even," A.J. said, shaking his head and laughing. "She's his sister, man."

Stim shoved a pencil under his gauze, scratching thoughtfully. "Did you see Lise in her bikini last summer? The top, it was just like triangles over her tits, and when she walked past... and sometimes the fabric, it'd kinda buckle. Man, I loved that suit."

"I think you should shut the fuck up," Eli said, throwing his bag down with a thud that made everyone in the lab look up. "I think it's time you do that."

Stim looked at him carefully.

Eyes darting between the two of them, A.J. seemed to be waiting for something, grinning a little.

Stim shrugged. "Lise isn't your sister, Nash," he said. "They're not all your sisters."

★ ★ ★

The teachers' lounge was the liveliest Tom had ever seen it, at least since Mr. Tomalla had been fired for taking photographs of female students' feet with his cell phone beneath his desk. He had posted them online and had twenty thousand hits, far more than Nat Dubow's YouTube science videos.

Everyone was waiting for Principal Crowder.

Laptops open, several teachers were hovering and gasping over photos of Lise and Gabby that had been posted online. A frightening snapshot of Lise's white thigh, her fingers locked around it. And one of Gabby, mid-seizure and curiously glamorous: jaw struck high, the auditorium's stage lights rendering her a pop singer, a movie star.

Tom didn't want to look, and didn't want to join in the tsk-tsking or the bemoaning of our social media–ridden culture.

Checking his e-mail at the communal workstation, he saw three messages from Georgia:

Why won't Deenie call me back? Is it true about Gabby?

What's happening?

Have D. call me ASAP, okay?

He told himself he would call her as soon as he could.

"A few other girls—I mean, has anyone else seen anything odd?" asked June Fisk, one of the scarved social-science teachers—there were three of them, and they liked to sit in the lounge and drink from their glass water bottles and talk about the decline of grammar, the rise of bullying, the dangers of fracking.

"Jaymie Hurwich," said Brad Crews, rapping his fingers on his business-math textbook. "She kept blinking through all of sixth period."

"What, she shouldn't be blinking?" Tom asked.

"That's not what I mean," Brad said, looking slightly dazed—though he always did, the father of six-month-old twin girls who seemed to have ravaged him. "It was constant. And really hard. She's an intense girl to begin with."

Everyone knew vaguely about Jaymie's family situation, a long-estranged mother with emotional problems of some unspecified nature, which meant everyone was easy on her even when she was hard on them, crying over A minuses, over class critiques.

"They're scared," said Erika Dyer, the health teacher, snapping her laptop shut loudly. Tom couldn't look at her now without thinking of her presentation to parents last year: *HPV and Your Daughter.*

"Maybe because they feel like everyone's watching them," she added, poking her glasses farther up the bridge of her nose. "Their own teachers, maybe."

"I couldn't concentrate," Brad said, wiping his face, staring down at his shoes. "It was...unsettling."

"Of course it was," piped up Liz somebody, who wasn't even a teacher but an ed student from the community college. "You feel like any one of them might fly from their chairs at any moment." Tom couldn't help but notice how hard Liz was blinking.

"The sympathy in this room is affecting," Erika said. "Truly."

"I have nothing but sympathy for Lise Daniels," June Fisk insisted. "And as if Gabby Bishop didn't have enough trouble. But how are we supposed to teach like this? Pretend like nothing is going on?"

Carl Brophy groaned loudly. "Teenage girls fidgeting, high-school students trying to get out of class. Clearly, it's a supervirus. Call the CDC. Alert the World Health Organization."

At that moment, Ben Crowder swung open the door, which felt like a relief, though the look on his face, gray and tight, reminded Tom of the final years of Ben's predecessor, who'd retired at age seventy, skin like wet paper.

"First, an update on Kimberly Court," he said. "Her doctor said it looks to him like a panic attack. And the parents, in this case, seem to understand that. They had trouble at her old school with a few boys who teased her. Some bullying. They say she's always been a high-strung girl."

It seemed a funny thing for parents to say about their own child under these circumstances. Even if they might think it.

"So they released her?" Erika asked.

"She's probably heading home as we speak," he said, nodding firmly.

"But you don't know?" June Fisk said.

"I've been on the phone with the superintendent," Crowder continued, ignoring her, "and spent the past hour talking to the health department. What's important is this: Do not speculate, especially with students or parents. If parents come to you with questions, please direct them to me or the superintendent. And, in particular, if you have any contact with Sheila Daniels, please alert us immediately."

There was much exchanging of looks, but Tom kept his eyes on Crowder, trying to read him. He wondered if Sheila Daniels planned to sue the school district along with the health department.

Fleetingly, he wondered if it was possible that she did know something none of the rest of them did. It wasn't a thought he wanted to hold on to.

"But this vaccine stuff she's talking about is everywhere now," Brad said. "I'm the parent coordinator and I have thirty-two e-mails about it in my inbox. What am I supposed to say to parents?"

Crowder took a deep breath, lifting his arms as if encouraging everyone to breathe with him.

"Our primary goal as educators," he said, his shirtsleeves furrowed with sweat, "needs to be containment of panic."

Erika Dyer, fingers still pushing those glasses up that dainty nose, hurried along next to him as they walked into the east corridor.

"Lise Daniels's mother called me," she whispered, not looking at him.

Tom felt like he had somehow been elected universal reassurer.

"Oh, don't worry," he said. "She's all over the place right now, and—"

"She told me I'd poisoned her daughter just as surely as the vaccine itself."

"She's just swinging wildly at anything. She came to my—"

"It's my job, you know?" she said, her voice trembling slightly. "To protect those girls. Girls like Lise. She came to my office just last week. I was trying to help her understand her body. The feelings she had. Things happening to her. And now..."

"These girls trust you. Sheila should be thanking you. And when she settles down, she'll realize you don't have any say in public-health policy for the school system."

Erika looked at him, fingers cradled around her ear in a way that reminded him of Deenie.

"She said as sure as if I'd held the poison syringe in my fingers, I had harmed her daughter."

"She's hysterical," he began, then paused a moment. "Hold on. Lise came to see you last week?"

She looked at him. "Yes."

Tom waited a second.

"Of course, whatever she said, that's private," she added.

"Of course," Tom said, a little embarrassed. What did it matter now?

But it felt like it might.

Erika looked at him, her right eyelid trembling behind her clever glasses.

"You can't let it get to you," he said. "None of it's your fault."

★   ★   ★

Maybe it's from the funky ooze out by football field after it rains

Touretts like my uncle Steve no one likes him lost IT job after

Deenie wanted to turn her phone off, to stop the texts nearly rattling her phone off the kitchen island.

But it might be Gabby.

Let's meet up, she'd texted Gabby an hour ago, to talk abt Kim & lake.

So she was left with bad thoughts.

One, two, three girls. The way it was moving, like the way pink eye or strep would tear through the school, a blazing red mouth swallowing them one by one, it didn't feel like a vaccine. It felt like a virus, a plague.

She clicked to the latest news article and read it while she ate dinner, toaster waffles that were still cold inside.

Of the two hundred and seven girls in the school, the article pointed out, more than half had been vaccinated.

In her head, she kept running numbers. More than a hundred girls had had the vaccine. But what were the odds that she would be friends with all three of the Girls. *The Girls.* The *Afflicted* Girls.

"Police and public-health officials," the article said, "are working together to determine commonalities among the girls: hobbies, medications, health histories, personal histories."

"Me," Deenie found herself saying out loud, washing her dinner plate, gluey with syrup, her fingers grating through it.

Lise to Gabby to Kim, and what did they all have in common?

They're friends with each other, sort of.

But how long before someone said, *All of them are friends with Deenie.*

Deenie is the thing they have in common.

It's Deenie.

"At that age, it's all about yourself," she'd overheard her mom say once. "You think the whole world spins around you."

Deenie had missed the context. All she knew was how it felt to hear that coming from her mom, the woman who'd overturned the family like a box of garage-sale toys to suit herself.

Maybe that's what this thinking was, her maternal inheritance. Something happened, anything, and it was all about *me, me, me.*

Her phone shot to life, buzzing across the counter.

The number flashing: **Kim C**.

Deenie grabbed for it.

"K.C., are you okay?"

"I can't talk long," came the choked whisper. "I'm not supposed to be on the phone."

"Why not? What happened?"

"I'm still at the hospital. They won't let me go."

"Why? They let Gabby go after. Are you . . ."

"I don't have time, Deenie. I just—look, I'm gonna have to tell them."

Deenie set down her fork, sticky in her hands. "Tell them what?"

"About the lake."

"Kim, you weren't at the lake. You don't know anything about it. You don't know what you're talking about."

"It might be why," she said. "It might be why it happened to me."

"Why *what* happened to you? Why you threw up in the gym? Someone throws up in gym every week."

Deenie knew it was mean to say. But what happened to Kim just didn't sound scary, like with Gabby or with Lise. At least not the way Keith Barbour had described it, twirling in a circle and gagging. And, privately, the thought had come to her: it's just Kim Court, anyway. Kim Court, who copied Gabby's tights, Gabby's shoes, lapped up everything Gabby ever said.

Kim didn't say anything, clearing her throat in a raw way that hurt Deenie to hear.

"You weren't even in the lake, Kim," Deenie added, dropping her plate in the sink, her right hand in the hot dishwater, swirling.

"But I was with Gabby. In her house. I touched her hair. You saw me."

"What?" Deenie asked, even as she remembered Kim's stubby fingers digging in Gabby's scalp, that dark swarm of Gabby hair threaded with glue from the plugs on her head. Frankenstein's creature.

"And—" She paused and Deenie could hear her breath coming faster. "And you."

"You didn't touch my hair," Deenie said, her hand stinging from the sink's hot water.

"We were together. You were in my car..."

Find some music. I can't think and drive.

"...and then it happened to me."

Deenie pictured her fingers rubbing along the playlist on Kim's phone.

"It's not fair..." Kim gasped. "I didn't do anything wrong."

"No one did," Deenie said, coolly.

"And how come..." Kim let the question trail off for a second. "I mean, how come everyone but you, Deenie?"

Deenie looked down at her hands, red and raw in the dishwater.

"What did the doctors say?" she asked.

"They don't know," Kim said, her voice dropping so low Deenie could barely hear it. "But I'm telling you: there was something inside me, and it was in my throat."

"Vomit, Kim," Deenie said roughly, her eyes stinging from the water.

"No, but that's why I threw up. Because I couldn't get it out. I couldn't stop it."

"Stop what?"

"The way it felt, the things I knew."

"Things you... What do you mean?"

"And it's *not* the vaccine, Deenie," she said, voice rising. "That's what I wanted to tell you. Don't listen to them about the vaccine!"

"Kim, what—"

Through the phone, Deenie could hear the crackling PA of the hospital, paging someone. She felt a click in her own throat but stopped herself from clearing it.

"I have to go," Kim said. "I can't explain it to you. It has to happen to you for you to understand."

★   ★   ★

Lying on his bed, three warm beers heavy inside him, Eli wished he'd just gone home after practice.

Instead, he'd followed A.J. to Brooke Campos's house. They were all freaked out about Kim Court and everything, though no one would admit it.

Brooke took them to the basement, where there was a broken fridge. Laid flat like a glossy white coffin, it was packed with skunked Yuengling abandoned after her dad's poker game. They sat on it and drank and talked about everything.

Brooke said she used to go to camp with a girl who'd had the shots and her heart had expanded to the size of a grapefruit and she died. She said she always felt sorry for how she'd treated that girl and for pushing her off the diving board that time and now it was too late.

Then Brooke started crying, her head thrown back, just like Gabby in all those pictures. Leaning first against A.J., then Eli, with a kind of breathless warmth, she cried, her fingers clinging to their shirtfronts. Eli left before things got too crazy. Even A.J. seemed upset, talking about his brother, who died of septic shock when A.J. was five.

You never knew how things would make you feel. The kinds of people who might feel things.

That's what he was thinking, lying on his bed, eyes on the spider cracks in the ceiling.

Reaching over, he grabbed his backpack, trying to shake his phone free. He hadn't looked at it in hours, afraid it'd be his mom again, texting about Deenie. He felt sorry for her, a little. And for himself.

Maybe he'd had four beers.

And the phone wouldn't shake loose.

Finally, lifting his torso woozily against his pillows, he turned the backpack inside out, scattering loose-leaf, handouts, practice schedules all over the bed and floor.

"Deenie," he said. "Can I come in?"

Through the door, he could hear her moving, thought he heard a sharp inhale, like she was deciding whether to answer.

"Okay," she said. "You can."

"You haven't seen my phone, have you?" he said, pushing the door open, surveying the room, the tangle of loose charger cords sprouting from the wall, jeans coiled at the foot of the bed, one long dust-streaked sock. And always the books, their covers creased, spines spread across the floor. He thought girls were supposed to be clean.

She was standing in the middle of the room, which surprised him. Her fingers were pinched red, latticed tight in the strings of her hoodie.

She stared at the knotted string ends in her hand for a second.

Then she looked up at him.

"Don't tell Dad," she said, voice so small.

"Tell Dad what?"

★ ★ ★

It was after seven o'clock, and Tom was sitting in the driveway looking at his house, holding his phone.

He'd just listened to another voice mail from Georgia: *Tom, maybe Deenie should stay with me. Maybe she'll be safer away from Dryden.*

And now, still not moving, not even taking the keys out of the ignition, he looked once more at the three texts from Deenie, asking if he'd heard anything about anything.

I'll tell you when I get home, he'd replied.

When r u coming home, she'd answered, more than two hours ago.

The meeting with Crowder had gone late, everyone with a great deal to say, and then talking to Erika and finally helping the French teacher—Kit was her name, he had to remember that— jump her scooter, stalled from the sudden damp in the air, the temperature rising twenty degrees or more since the day before in that weird way of Dryden.

"Isn't it something?" she'd said throatily, looking around, her cheekbones misted and her lipstick slightly smudged. "Like a fairy tale."

He'd said he knew just what she meant.

And she'd mentioned Eli's *magnifique* attendance, and Tom pretended he knew, even though he'd been sure Eli took Spanish.

Finally, they had talked about the image of Gabby posted everywhere, that curtain of hair, the theatrical arc of her neck, the inflamed cheeks.

"Like a ballerina," Kit said. "All the girls will want to steal that pose for their yearbook photos."

And now it was after seven, and he was still sitting in the car.

Did they tell u what is happening, Deenie's text read. **Do they know yet.**

Taking a breath, he picked up his phone one last time.

"Medical billing, Diane speaking."

"Diane," he said, "it's Tom. I wasn't sure you'd still be there."

"Tom," she said. "Well, I'm twelve-to-eight today."

"I'm sorry to keep calling," he said, sensing a tightness in her voice. "I was just wondering if you had any news."

There was a pause, then a sigh.

"Hey, I get it," she said. "If I had a daughter at that school, I'd want to know everything too. And a lot's been happening."

"A girl named Kim Court, she was there today, at the hospital, right?"

"Yes, she's here."

"Still? I thought they were sending her home. That it was just a panic attack."

"We have to keep her until she seems stable. After a seizure—"

"So it was a seizure?"

"No," she said, then lowered her voice. "I didn't mean that. But they have to rule out some things."

"Like what?"

"When teenagers come, and they're having hallucinations—"

"Hallucinations? I didn't know she was—"

"—we have to rule out drugs. Ecstasy, MDMA. There's a lot of ecstasy at that school."

"There is?"

"Or it could be the onset of schizophrenia."

"Jesus."

"Can I call you back?" she said suddenly.

"Sure."

A moment later, the phone rang.

"I'm calling from my cell," she whispered, a nervous titter in her voice, "from the ladies' room."

As if by magic, the smooth professional tone—professional biller, professional dater-slash-divorcée—was gone. She sounded suddenly younger, girlish.

"They wouldn't even let us leave for dinner because of the reporters out front," she was saying. "We're not supposed to be talking about any of this. They made us sign something."

"I'm putting you in a bad position," Tom said.

"I have a friend in ER," she said, words rushing, jumbling together. "She said the Court girl kept shoving her hand in her mouth. She got her whole fist in there. And when they put the restraints on, she started screaming that something was touching her from the inside."

"Touching her?"

"Well, people can say all kinds of things in that state. But they didn't find any drugs. I don't think."

Tom took a breath.

"How's Lise Daniels?"

A pause.

"I can't talk any more about her."

"What do you mean?"

"Listen, I just—" He heard the sound of another woman's voice, everything echoing, the rush of water. "I have to go."

"Right," he said. "I understand. It's just...when you have a daughter."

Her voice cracked a little. "Oh, Tom, I know. I wish..."

"No, I don't want to get you in any kind of trouble."

"It's just...Can I say something?" Whispering.

"Sure," he said, feeling a churning inside. There was a long pause, then the thud of a door.

"Tom. It feels crazy in here right now."

Tom could hear her breath catch.

"The mother, she walks the halls all night. That's what Patty, one of the nurses, told me. The mother walked by the nurses' station so many times last night, Patty thought she'd go crazy herself. She keeps telling them her daughter has been destroyed. That's the word she used. *Destroyed*. Like you do with an animal. After."

*   *   *

It didn't seem so bad to him. Nowhere near as bad as Deenie seemed to think.

Sitting down on the edge of her bed, Eli watched his sister bobbing from foot to foot, just like she had during countless past confidences, shared reports of dirty deeds, stolen candy, a pilfered beer, running a bike over Mom's violets. Except that was a long time ago. It hadn't happened in a long time.

When she'd first started talking, he'd been afraid. He'd had this squinting sense, lately, of something. That she was different, changed.

A month or so ago, he and his friends had gone to Pizza House for slices after a game and he'd seen her in the kitchen. Her cap pushed back, she was carrying cold trays of glistening dough rounds, and her face had a kind of pink to it, her hips turning to knock the freezer door shut.

I didn't spit on it, Deenie had promised, winking at him from behind the scarlet heat lamps.

He'd stood there, arrested. The pizza box hot in his hands.

She looked different than at school and especially at home, and she was acting differently. Moving differently.

He couldn't stop watching her, his friends all around him, loud and triumphant, their faces swathed with sweat.

Next to her, by the ovens, was that guy Sean, the one who used to play forward for Star-of-the-Sea. Once, Sean had asked him about Lise, wondered if Eli knew her. *Her tits look like sno-cones,* he'd said. *Beautiful sno-cones.*

And now Deenie stood before him, her body tight, the zipper on her hoodie pinching that tiny bird neck of hers, saying, "Don't tell Dad. Okay?"

But what she told him had nothing to do with what he'd noticed at the Pizza House, whatever that was. Or the other thing— the thing he'd almost forgotten. Someone at school saying he saw his sister getting into a car with some guy.

Instead, it was just some crazy story about the lake.

"But Eli, we put our feet in. Last week. What if it did something?"

He shook his head. "If it did something, you'd be sick too. And Skye Osbourne, she was with you, right? She'd be sick too."

"Maybe it affected us in different ways."

She looked at him. The look he'd seen since they were small, like camping, her pale face in the tent flap when he'd spook her, telling her there were bears out there, hidden in the green daze of Binnorie Woods.

"Deenie," he said, "it's not the lake."

"How do you know?"

He looked at her. It was one of those tricks his dad always pulled off. He used to watch him do it with Mom over and over. *I promise you, I promise you,* a smile, a coaxing shoulder rub, spinning her around like dancing, *everything will be okay.* Mom used to call it the Croc dance, to go with the Croc smile.

"The doctors would know, Deenie," he said, the thought coming to him just as he needed it. "They've been doing tests, right? For toxins and stuff. They'd pick that up."

"Oh," Deenie said. "Right."

He could see her shoulders relax a little. He was surprised how easy it was. Just like when they were little. Taking her hand and dragging her out of the tent, promising her there were no bears out there after all. They were safe.

"So you feel better?"

She nodded.

"Okay, then," he said, leaning back, feeling his body loosen, the beer bloom returning.

Except there was something wedged under him, Deenie's Pizza House shirt, stiff with old flour or whatever it was they made pizzas with.

"Jesus, Deenie, don't you ever wash your uniform?" he teased, fingering the shirt, feigning throwing it at her.

She didn't say anything, her hands once more gripping the ends of her drawstring. Tugging it back and forth. It was like it had lasted only a second, that brief spasm of relief.

Girls never stopped being mysterious, he thought, tossing the shirt to the floor.

Sinking back onto her pillow, he lay there for a moment, staring at her ceiling, wondering about his missing phone, or something.

11

Sitting at the kitchen table, Tom was trying hard to think of exactly nothing except the beer in front of him when he felt a hand on his shoulder.

His shoulder jerked, but it was just Deenie, her fingernails short and painted silver, like all the girls'.

"Dad," she said, "Gabby called. Can I borrow the car?"

She almost never asked. With only a learner's permit, she wasn't supposed to drive without an adult.

But it was the first thing she'd said to him since he came home and told her what Principal Crowder had said, or insisted. That everyone was working very hard to figure this thing out and that it was important not to get caught up in all the rumors. She'd given him a look that suggested what he knew to be true: he didn't really have any information at all.

So now, when she asked him for the car, something in him stirred, and, without even saying a word, he found himself sliding the keys across the table and dropping them into her palm, which closed over them instantly.

"Thanks, Dad," she said, grasping them so tight it hurt to look.

"But Deenie," he said, although she was already halfway to the door, "call your mom tonight, okay?"

She said she would.

★ ★ ★

It felt so warm outside, one of those weird nights when the temperature rises, making everything look strange and glowy.

Gabby's mom had taken pity on her and said she could go out for a while.

And, unaccountably, Deenie's dad had loaned her the car.

"The air," Gabby said, taking a few tight, sharp breaths. "Even the air hurts."

"It does?" To Deenie, it felt delicious. When she breathed, the warm seemed to swirl in her mouth. "At least your mom let you out."

Once they'd gotten a few miles from her house, Gabby, her face pale and puffy, said she didn't want to be in the car.

So they decided to walk through town, hands shoved in pockets and the sky a ghostly shade of violet.

For a few minutes, Deenie forgot everything.

No one was out, and there was a ghost-town feel, like no one knew winter was over, at least for the night, and the streets had a kind of fuzzy beauty, the air briny from four months of rock salt, the pavement spongy under Deenie's feet.

Across the street was the orange flare of the Pizza House. She wondered if Sean Lurie was at the ovens, grip in either hand, smiling.

"I can't believe Kim called you from the hospital," Gabby said. "I can't believe she's still there."

"Yeah," Deenie replied, shuttled out of her daydream. "They told my dad—they told all the teachers—that she's fine. It's stress."

"Do you believe it?" Gabby asked, leading them toward the misty blur of the elementary school, its bricks streaked with salt.

"I don't know," she said slowly. "I didn't see it. Eli said she just threw up."

"But, I mean, what Kim said to you. About it being something in the lake. Do you think it's true?"

"Kim was never in the lake," Deenie said, her new refrain.

They arrived at the square across from the school, its olden-times town pump splintered and gray. Back in fourth grade, their teacher said it was the spot where they whipped people centuries ago. For months afterward, every time they stood there, waiting for the bus, Deenie and Lise talked about it, pretended.

Lise, color high, howling upward, chubby arms wrapped around that old pump, *Forty lashes, forty lashes, no, kind sir!*

"She wasn't in the lake," Gabby said, her face hidden behind her hair, her sunken hat. "But maybe that's why she's not as sick as Lise. Why it isn't as bad for her."

"But why would Kim be sick at all?"

"Because," Gabby said, and then she said the thing they hadn't said, not aloud to each other, "because maybe it's inside us now. And she got it. From us."

Deenie felt something twitch at her temple. For a moment, she felt like she had when she saw Skye at Gabby's house. Like everything was tilting and she'd only just realized it, but it had been tilting slowly for a while.

"But nothing happened to me," she said. "I'm fine."

"Well," Gabby said, looking down as their feet dusted along the glistening grass of the square, "some people are just carriers. Maybe that's what you are."

Deenie looked at her.

"Like those boys with HPV," she added, still not meeting Deenie's eyes. "They never get sick. They just make everyone else sick."

Deenie couldn't get anything to come out of her mouth, and they kept walking, and Gabby wouldn't turn her head, and then they were in the darkened center of the square, under the old elm.

It didn't even sound like Gabby and she wondered where it all came from. *Carriers.* In its own way, it didn't feel different from what Skye had said, all her talk about bad energy.

"So maybe that's what you are," Gabby added.

And they kept walking. And as they did, Deenie's lungs started tightening. Pressing her palm on the cold of the tree trunk, she had to stop.

It turned out the air did hurt, and Gabby was right.

"I'm sorry," Gabby said, stopping too, her eyes burning under the lamppost. Watching Deenie. "I'm sorry."

★ ★ ★

When the phone rang, Tom was afraid it was Georgia again, asking why Deenie hadn't called. But it was Dave Hurwich, Jaymie's father, whose barking tone reminded Tom why he'd stopped coaching soccer.

"What kind of school endorses medical experimentation on its students?" Dave asked. "You're a man of science. I'm on the CDC website right now, Tom. I'm looking at the VAERS. Do you know what we're dealing with here with this vaccine?"

Tom sighed. There was no use talking epidemiology with Dave Hurwich, who always knew more about law than lawyers, more about cars than mechanics. And there was no use trying to explain the nuances of school-board recommendations versus forced government vaccinations of children.

A single dad, Dave prided himself on his parenting and on his daughter Jaymie's academic successes, which were due at least half the time to her ability to wear down all her teachers (*But I did the extra credit and I wrote twice as much and I never missed a class and I always contribute...*) as relentlessly as her dad. Whenever Tom began to lose his patience with either of them, he tried to remember the "family situation," Jaymie's out-of-the-picture mother—was it something to do with postpartum? The details were vague and it never felt appropriate to ask.

"It was a stressful day for all of us, Dave. How's Jaymie doing?"

"Let me tell you how she's doing," he said, a smacking sound like his tongue was dry from making phone calls all night. "She hasn't stopped blinking since she got home. It's like looking at a Christmas tree."

So why are you calling me? Tom wanted to ask. Except he got the feeling Mr. Hurwich was calling everyone, anyone.

"I've been reading all about that supposed vaccine. You're the chemistry teacher. You should know. It's loaded with aluminum and sodium borate. Do you know what that is? That's what they use to kill roaches. They treated my daughter like a roach. And yours."

"Dave, I'm sure your doctor—"

"That goddamned doctor doesn't know anything. He prescribed vitamins. None of them know anything."

There was a pause, a creaking sound.

"She says it's like a light flashing in the corner of her eye all the time. She's my little girl," Mr. Hurwich said, and all the hardness broke apart in an instant. "She doesn't even look the same."

Tom swallowed. "What do you mean?"

"I don't know," he said, voice cracking. "The way she looks at me. Something. It doesn't look like my daughter."

★   ★   ★

"Let's just drive, okay?" Gabby said. "Can we drive?"

And they both knew where they were going.

Looping back and forth along the lake, three, four times.

At first, they kept the windows shut tight.

Finally, the fifth time, Gabby opened hers, her hair slapping across the pane.

The raw smell from the water, like a presence. Something furred resting in your throat.

It reminded Deenie of something, some school-retreat middle-of-the-night story Brooke Campos had told Deenie and Lise and Kim Court about how, when she was thirteen, her big sister's boyfriend had offered her ten dollars to "taste something she'd never tasted."

Clutching her throat as she told it, Brooke almost cried and couldn't finish the story. It was all anyone could talk about for weeks. Kim kept asking everyone, *But did she? Did she do it?* And nobody knew. They'd never gotten to hear the end.

"I should go home," Gabby said, looking down at her phone in her lap. "My mom's called twice."

"Does she know you're with me?" Deenie asked. *Carriers. Maybe that's what you are.* "She'd let you be with *me?*"

"Of course," Gabby said. "What—"

Before she could say more, Gabby's phone lit up: **Skye.**

But Gabby didn't answer, just stared at it.

And then a text followed.

"What is it?" Deenie said, trying to sound even.

"She said there was a story on the news. About something happening at the hospital."

"With Lise? Is she okay?"

"I don't know," Gabby said, staring at her phone. "But I better go home."

"Gabby," Deenie said, turning the wheel hard, "we have to go there now."

"No, Deenie," Gabby said, her voice rushing up over the radio, the wind charging from the window.

But Deenie decided she didn't care and she was the one driving anyway and the hospital was only a few miles up the road, lit like a torch.

Lise. Lise.

"You don't have to go inside, Gabby," Deenie said, voice surprisingly hard. "But I am."

Deenie was driving very fast, the stoplights shuddering above them and her foot pumping the gas.

"She's all alone," Deenie said. "And we don't know what's happened."

Gabby looked at her, chin tight, like wires pulled taut and hooked behind her ears. Like the ventriloquist's dummy that used to perform at the mall, Deenie thought, then felt bad about it.

"Okay," Gabby said, as if she had a choice. "I'll go."

The white steeple of the hospital's clock tower gleaming, Deenie was walking Gabby, directing her in a way that felt unfamiliar and powerful.

But it wouldn't be like before, wouldn't be so easy.

As soon as they walked in, a lady in a gold-buttoned suit jacket at the welcome desk recognized Gabby.

"Oh no," she said, rising to her feet. "Not again. Let me page the ER."

The alarm on her face stopped both girls.

"We're okay," Gabby said. "We're here to see Lise."

"Oh no," she repeated, shaking her head, "that's not possible."

★   ★   ★

So they sat in the parking lot, three spots behind Mrs. Daniels's wind-battered Dodge.

They had the idea that if she came out, she might let them see Lise.

"Maybe she sleeps there," Gabby said. "Maybe she never comes out."

"She has to come out," Deenie said, flipping the radio dial, trying to find news. "Something's happening in there."

She wondered if Gabby was thinking about the night her mother was wheeled in on a gurney. The way Deenie heard it, the hammer prongs almost severed an artery and Gabby had had to hold the hammer in place until the paramedics came or her mom would have died.

Deenie didn't know if it was true, but she always remembered the one detail Gabby had told her, that the sound coming from her mom reminded her of those slide whistles they'd give out at Fun Palace when they were kids.

Bad things happen and then they're over, but where do they go? Deenie wondered, watching Gabby. Are they ours forever, leeching under our skin?

She didn't even see the woman approach the car, and when the rapping on the window came, her body leaped to life.

★　★　★

Still thinking about Dave Hurwich's call, Tom was finishing his beer and considering a second, was half ready to ask his son to join him, when his phone rang again: **Lara Bishop.**

"Tom, sorry to call so late. Is Gabby there?" she said, voice raspy and anxious.

"Lara," Tom said, phone slipping slightly from his hand. "No. Deenie's not home either. Has it been that long?"

He looked at the clock over the stove and was surprised to see it was nearly eleven.

He didn't really know where the hours had gone, a stack of week-old tests on his lap, watching a documentary about people dying on Mount Everest along with Eli, whose eyes had a boozy luster, his long limbs heavy. There was a feeling of warmth about Eli, his peculiar brand of gloomy nostalgia ("Hey, Dad, remember that time you took us to Indian Cave and we found those frozen bones with hair?").

"I keep calling Gabby," Lara said, "and she won't pick up. Can you call Deenie?"

"Of course." And he felt a surge of shame in his chest. The girls dropping like dainty flies at school, their limbs like bendy straws, their bodies collapsing, and he gives his daughter car keys and sends her out into the great dark nettles of Dryden with the girl who had violently collapsed in front of the whole school only the day before.

What made him think he could forget for an hour with his daughter out there, somewhere?

"Dad," Deenie answered, almost before Tom heard the call go through. "I'm coming home. I am."

"Are you okay? What happened?"

"We went to the hospital." Gulping, hectic. He thought he could hear someone in the background crying. "I think something happened."

* * *

At first Deenie thought she was hallucinating, that gigantic face at the car window, neck crooked down, hair like soft butter. A woman she recognized, something heavy in her hand like a metal flashlight, using it to tap on the glass.

"Deenie," Gabby was saying, next to her, "Deenie, don't."

There was an insignia on the flashlight, the numeral seven, with a lightning bolt like a superhero's, and she realized it wasn't a flashlight. It was a microphone.

"Don't open the window, Deenie!" Gabby said. "Don't talk to her!"

But Deenie had already pushed the window button, the woman's lips turning into a smile.

That's when she realized who the woman was. The lady from TV, the one who had emceed the big school fund-raiser to not quite pay for the new football field that never got built.

"Hey, I'm Katie," she said, her voice bell-clear. "Are you a friend of Lise Daniels?"

Deenie didn't say anything.

"Can you come out and talk for a second?" the woman said. Then, craning down, she peered at Gabby, who quickly turned away, her neck twisted.

"You're the second," the woman said, pointing with the microphone at Gabby. "You're Girl Two."

A few minutes later, they were all standing by the car.

"Gabby," Deenie had whispered, "it's the only way we'll find out."

A man with a large camera hoisted over his shoulder appeared from nowhere, but the TV woman handed him the microphone and waved him away.

That was when Deenie noticed a truck and two vans with satellites like giant teacup saucers had pulled in behind them.

She looked at the TV woman, her hair crisp but eye makeup blurred in the mist.

"We got a tip from the Danielses' lawyer," she said, wiping her face with the back of her hand. "He's friendly that way. He's going to give us some camera time. He's got a statement to issue."

Deenie felt her chest pinch. "Something happened to Lise?"

"No. Not yet." She shook her head, her eyes as white as pearls under the parking-lot lights. "The mother is trying to move her to the medical center all the way down in Mercy-Starr Clark. Looks like she's going to be suing. Suing everybody."

"Suing for what?" Deenie said. "Over the vaccine?"

"You bet. We heard the state health department people were here today, someone from the DA's office, cops, who knows what's next."

There was a slamming of doors somewhere and the camera guy, his face concealed behind the great black box slung on his shoulder, was suddenly there again.

"Now?" the TV woman asked him.

He nodded.

"Wait," Deenie said. "But do you know about Lise, about how she is?"

The camera light went on and the woman's worn face sprang magically to life.

"Well, you two probably know more than anyone," she said, her voice newly smooth, buttery as her hair. "How about we just talk a few minutes. Have you ever been on TV?"

"No," Deenie said. "I—"

"Not you," the woman said. "Her."

Deenie turned to Gabby, who was facing the car.

"No," Deenie said, watching Gabby's body, wire-tight, her elbows clamped to her sides. It looked like she was trying to hold herself together, to keep herself from blowing apart.

The front doors of the hospital opened loudly and all the lights seemed to go on everywhere.

★　★　★

Listening to Rick Jeanneret's cracking voice on ESPN Classic, Eli was thinking again about what Deenie had said about going into the lake. In some ways, what she'd told him *was* like the thing he'd noticed about her at the Pizza House that night, or other nights, other things. Because the Deenie he knew wasn't the kind to break rules, take chances.

The lake was the last place he'd want to go. The smell, even from the car, felt wrong. It reminded him of the basement of their house.

Back when Deenie was in middle school, she was always having sleepovers. All that girly thumping and trills on the other side of his bedroom wall confused and annoyed and stirred him, so he'd sneak down to the basement and page through a mildewed 1985 *Playboy* he'd found under the laundry chute. The pictures were startling and beautiful, but he always felt ashamed after, standing at the laundry sink where his mom scrubbed his uniform.

And through the chute, he could still hear the girls, two floors above. The basement's drop ceiling porous and seeming to breathe. After a long rain, it smelled just like the lake.

Once, a senior girl from Star-of-the-Sea tried to get him to climb the safety fence, but he said no. Wiggling out of her halter dress, she said, her tongue between her teeth, *It's okay. We can always skinny-dip right in your car. Who needs water?*

"You're the luckiest mother I ever knew," A.J. said when Eli told him about it. "Screw that pretty face of yours."

Lying there, Eli fumbled for his phone before remembering it wasn't there.

★　★　★

"Dad," Deenie said, answering her phone. "I'm coming home. I am."

"You better be," her dad said in a tone he rarely used.

The car thudding along the road, the spatter of light rain, she and Gabby didn't say anything for a mile or two.

Finally, Gabby spoke. "They're going to want to bring me back in again, aren't they? They're going to want to talk to me again."

Deenie looked at her, passing headlights flashing across her face, and saw something pulsing there, from her temple to her jaw.

"I don't know."

It hurt to look at her, the way she was holding her body so tightly, her arms rigid at her sides, a girl made of wood. "Maybe not."

When they entered Binnorie Woods, Deenie's heart started to slow down a little. No streetlights and the car dark, it was like being under your covers, your sleeping bag at camp. She'd always liked that feeling, and the smell of cedar coming through the vents.

"Maybe," Deenie said, "this means Lise is doing better. If they can move her she must be doing better."

Gabby nodded lightly, her head canting to one side.

"You know what I thought," she said quietly, "when the reporter came over, you know what I thought she was going to tell us?"

"What?"

"That Lise was dead."

★   ★   ★

"It's okay, Lara. She's driving Gabby home to you right now."

"Thank God. Tom, have you seen some of these pictures? And videos?"

"I saw a few," Tom said, thinking of that striking one of Gabby. "Wait, videos?"

"There's a video of Kim Court. Some kid must've taken it while it was happening. It's all over. It's on the news now."

Tom grabbed the remote from Eli.

There, on Channel 7, was a grainy YouTube video of Kim Court, body twitching on the gym floor.

The screen crawl read: *Mysterious Outbreak: Parents' Rush to Vaccinate to Blame?*

And then, hands gripping her own neck, a blur of vomit, head thrown so far back you could only see the glint of her braces. The piano-tinkling score from *The Exorcist* played.

"Lara," he said. "Turn off the TV."

★ ★ ★

They were deep into the woods now and Deenie couldn't remember the way. Gabby had to keep saying, softly, *Right, right, left here. Left.*

"Deenie, remember what Kim told us in the library," Gabby said, resting her head on the window. "About Lise having a boyfriend?"

Deenie looked at her, not even remembering for a moment.

"In the library. Kim told us something about Lise and some guy."

"Why would Kim Court know anything about Lise? Gabby, why are we talking about this now—"

"I think it might be true."

Gabby faced the window and Deenie could hear a faint rattling: Gabby's head against the glass.

"No," Deenie said. "It's not true."

Technically, it was not. There was the thing Lise had told her at the lake, the thing she'd done with the boy. But that boy was not Lise's boyfriend, not at all.

"Deenie, I've heard it from other people. I thought she might have told you. Sometimes she tells you things she doesn't tell me."

"No," Deenie said.

"Because lately, Skye and me, we've been noticing Lise has been kind of secretive. Like maybe she was hiding something. When I took her to the Pizza House the other night, I tried to talk to her, but—"

"Skye?" Deenie barked, so loud she surprised herself. "Skye doesn't know a goddamn thing about Lise. Why would you listen to her? Lise wasn't hiding anything." Taking a breath, she tried to calm herself. Then added, "No one's hiding anything, Gabby."

Gabby nodded, the worst, most thoughtless kind of nod Deenie could imagine.

Then she turned and faced Deenie. "I just remembered what I heard about you," Gabby said. "The other day."

Deenie looked over at her, the car swerving slightly. "What?"

"That you were in a car with some guy. You never told me that."

Deenie faced the road again. "Because it's not true. It was probably Eli."

"Stop!" Gabby shouted, her voice suddenly loud, Deenie nearly jumping in her seat, words rushing to her head, flooding her mouth without emerging.

"My house," Gabby said, one hand dropping on Deenie's arm, the other pointing to driveway.

Deenie turned the wheel.

The house blazing with lights, Mrs. Bishop was running out, her legs and feet bare, the headlights making her scar look red, alive.

Any anger on her face seemed to break to pieces the minute her daughter stepped from the car.

Backing out, Deenie watched as Gabby slumped into her

mother's arms wearily, a veteran home from battle. Mrs. Bishop folding her in her arms in such a mom way. In a way that made Deenie blink.

★   ★   ★

Face drawn, hair half caught in her rubber band, his daughter looked half and twice her age at the same time.

Nearly midnight, on either side of the kitchen island, Deenie told him about the hospital.

"And so the reporter said Mrs. Daniels is trying to move Lise to the medical center."

"That probably means she's stable," he said. "So that's something."

Her mouth twisted, dubious, like Georgia somehow, that was the echo, and the way her shirt was riding up and her arm stretching tiredly and with dismissal.

"I'm going to bed," she said.

"Did you call your mom?" he said, holding out his hand for the car keys. A gesture stolen, he was sure, from his own father, a century ago.

"No," she said. "I didn't have time."

"Deenie," he said. "You were gone for hours."

"The reporter wanted us to talk on camera," she said. "She wouldn't leave us alone. But we wouldn't do it."

He sighed. "How did Gabby seem?"

He watched her try to pull the rubber band from her hair, her eyes down, and he wanted to reach over and help her untangle it, but her body looked so closed off, a tooth clamp.

"I don't know, Dad."

He found his hand reaching out to her anyway, and the flinch that came was sudden, terrible.

★   ★   ★

Trying to push herself, hard, into sleep, Deenie felt her toes cramp painfully, a pang in them she had to rub away, tangled under her own sheets, breathing hard until it stopped again.

Then her phone hissed: **Skye**.

She could have sworn she'd turned it off.

U still ok, right?

Yes, Deenie typed. She never got texts from Skye and she almost wondered if she had fallen asleep.

U saw Gabby tonite?

Yeah. Why?

We need to protect each other, came Skye's reply. **We R surrounded by bad energy.**

Staring at the words blinking hard at her, almost spasming, she had a sick feeling in her stomach and turned the phone off.

What made Skye think she could text her? Because they were the only ones left? Skye's words always felt cryptic. *Shake it off,* she told herself. *Don't let her get under your skin.*

And she grabbed for the bottle of antihistamine left over from the flu and drank three plastic cups.

Somewhere in the gluey Nyquil haze, the vision came of standing in the lake with Lise the week before, stomping their feet in the emerald thick of the water.

On the shoreline were Skye's hard-jeaned boys with the disappearing tattoos. They whistled at Lise, fingers hooked in their mouths.

Let's do it, Lise whispered in her ear, her tongue showing between her teeth. *Let's go in.*

When she woke up, in the purple of four a.m., she could still hear Lise's voice in her ear, high as a little girl's.

We went behind those tall bushes. He took my tights off first. It was so cold, but his hands . . .

Who was it? Deenie had asked, kept asking.

Then, finally, Lise whispered the boy's name, and Deenie was surprised.

Really? Him?

And Lise's smile filled with teeth, a giggle up her throat.

Like something inside opening, she said as they sprawled on the shoreline, feet tangled in seaweed tickling up their legs, *and then opening something else.*

Don't tell anyone, she made Deenie promise. *They'll think I'm a slut.*

No, they won't, Deenie said. Though you could never be sure.

I told him not to do what he was doing. That it was disgusting. I don't know why I thought that, but I did. We put our mouths down there with boys, but . . . but he was down there and everything happened.

But she said his hands were cool, like a doctor's. And that made it seem okay. And soon enough she was so hot, a burning down there, and his mouth cool too, and the way, like—and she was so embarrassed to say it, to have even thought of it—like a flute, the flutter tongue. The move it takes so long to learn.

I don't know, she said, her fingers curled over her mouth like eating a candy. *I don't know.* And then she said the thing about how it was like an opening, an opening, and forever opening.

She never even knew before what it meant to see stars.

That was all she could say. Deenie wanted her to say more.

Since it was a boy she knew, she wanted to picture it.

Is it disgusting? Lise asked, but she was smiling as she said it, face red. *Was it bad?*

Deenie didn't say anything. Their legs slimy from the water.

Deenie, she said, *am I bad?*

No, Deenie said. *Not you, Lise.*

Never you.

12

It was maybe five, the light looked like five, but without his phone, Eli had no idea.

There was a freedom in it.

It was warmer than in months, as if the temperature had risen during the night, and the bike ride through town felt delirious and wonderful.

His hand kept reaching for his pocket, the phantom buzz.

But nothing.

Maybe he'd never have a phone again.

He was nearly to school before he remembered everything from the night before, all the beer and ruminations and sinking to drunken sleep on the floor of the den, carpet burn on his face.

When he walked in the locker room, everything was unusually quiet. No clattering sticks or ripping tape or the low din of players rousing themselves to life.

But he could hear something, the tinny sound of someone's computer speakers, a soft voice and panting.

" . . . my tongue is tingling, like, all the time. If you could see . . ."

He knew this was going to mean another speech from Coach about how important it was not to degrade women's bodies with pornography because what if they were your mothers, or your sisters.

" . . . something in my throat. And it's getting bigger . . ."

When he reached the last bank of lockers, he saw seven, eight players huddled around Mark Pulaski's laptop, transfixed. A.J. was grinning and shaking his head. A.J. was always grinning and shaking his head.

"Get a load, Nash. Get a fucking load of this."

There was a stutter and hiss as the video began again.

It was the latest girl, that Kim girl, glowing from the light of her own phone screen.

Panting noisily, like her tongue was too big for her mouth, she couldn't seem to quite catch her breath. Her face looked wet, her eyes ringed vampire-brown and her mouth slickly red.

It was dark all around her, but you could see the green fluorescence of some light somewhere, the hospital corridor.

And she was talking straight into the camera, her phone.

Her words slow and dreamlike.

"Hey, everybody, I know you're all probably worried about me and I wanted to let you know how I'm doing since it happened."

Breathing, breathing.

"I'm still at the hospital. They won't let me go."

Her fingers reached up to that glossy mouth.

"My tongue is tingling, like, all the time, and this side feels like it's got a lot of pressure and it's hard to keep my eye open on this side. It feels like this side of my face is slipping from me. Like it'll slip right off."

She started clearing her throat, and once she started it was like she couldn't stop.

"But most of all it's here," she said, clawing at her neck. "It feels like there's something in my throat. And it's getting bigger."

A scraping sound came from her mouth as she pushed her face closer to the camera, the lens distorting everything, fish-eyeing her.

When she opened her mouth, those teeth, enormous and iron-girded, were blue.

"I'm sure you're hearing lots of things. About what's happening. Let me tell you: No one here wants to know the truth. That's why they won't let me go."

Suddenly, as if she'd heard something, a muffled sound too fast to recognize, Kim flinched, her eyes jumping to her left, pupils gleaming.

There was a long, long pause, her face palsied. Eli felt something even in his own chest: *What did she hear? See?*

Then her face turned slowly to the camera again, her throat a death rattle.

"But there's other girls out there. And they have it. Maybe ones you can't even tell. Who knows how many of us?"

"I know it by heart," A.J. said, leaping onto one of the benches. "Brooke and her sister were watching it all night."

"'There's other girlth out there,'" he slurred, his tongue hanging from the corner of his mouth. "'Who knowth how many of us?'"

Eli looked back at the screen, Kim's face caught. Beneath, there were 624 likes and dozens of comments: *oh, kim, be strong! kim, i've been feeling weird too, did u faint when you got the shot? Young lady: this is demonic possession. You can read about it in the New Testament. The solution is to find a True Man of God who can cast the demon out. Receiving Christ can cure you. Blessings to you and your family!*

Eli fixed his eyes on the screen. It reminded him, in some ob-scure way, of those girls at the games, the younger ones who came in groups and banded behind the Plexiglas, bap-bap-bapping with open palms or the bottoms of their fists, their mouths sprung wide, their tongues between their teeth. *Me. Me. Me.*

"I don't..." Eli started. "Is she wearing makeup?" He was try-ing to figure something out.

"Maybe she'll get her own reality show," A.J. said. *"Kim's Wrecked World. My Toxic Sweet Sixteen."*

"And she didn't say anything about the shots," Eli said, just re-alizing it. "About the vaccine."

Mark Pulaski turned around to face Eli.

"You think she's faking it?" he said, his voice breaking. "Did you see her? My sister got her first shot last week. She woke up from a nap yesterday and couldn't turn her head. She's fucking eleven years old."

Eli looked at him, not knowing what to say.

"Just because your sister's bouncing around the school while all her friends are fucking dying, man. Your sister..." Mark's voice trailed off. "Jesus, man."

Eli watched Mark for a second, and everyone else watched Eli. He felt A.J.'s fist tap his shoulder.

"I'm sorry," Eli said. "Sorry, man."

He turned back to the computer screen, the big arrow over Kim's face, trembling.

★   ★   ★

Her backpack on her lap, Deenie talked to him the entire ride to school.

For the first miles, Tom let himself enjoy it. It felt almost like before, maybe a few years ago, when she always seemed to be bursting with giddy, nervous animation. *Dad, Dad, wait, listen, Dad, listen.* Telling him about a book, a science project.

But all the itchy squirming in her seat now, it was like she was trying to rally herself to get through the day to come. Or else she just needed to keep talking because she was afraid of not talking. He wondered if she felt guilty for the night before, for staying out late with the car.

"Dad," she said finally, after seven solid minutes about the algebra quiz, the rancid grilled cheese in the cafeteria, the stink of Eli's gym bag, "what do you think will happen today?"

He looked at the road, the steam from the streets, the crazy heat wave that had landed, the temperatures rising above sixty degrees, and tried to think of something to say.

The school felt anarchic inside, like the time Paul Lozelle let a pair of chickens loose in the cafeteria, a prank that had been musty when Tom was in high school.

Everywhere he looked, there were long bands of girls in their colored minis and tights, ropes of them, like the friendship bracelets that covered their arms, their faces tense and watchful. And the boys, in their own swells of confusion and bravado, stood apart, almost like in middle school, elementary school. Like they were suddenly afraid to get too close. Though maybe that was how they always were and he'd never noticed.

The teachers, in turn, were either spring-loaded, grasping their dry-erase markers like emergency flares, or slouched against doorways, filled with louche contempt.

Walking toward his classroom, its familiar formaldehyde smell, he tried to imagine how any of them were going to make it to three o'clock without spontaneously combusting.

A free first period, he spent a half hour in the dark auditorium, drinking coffee and watching one of the custodians trying to buff away the scratch marks the EMS gurney had left on the stage.

He couldn't stop himself from walking past Deenie's ancient civ class. She was in the back, so he had to move very close to the door to see her, but there she was, pen in mouth, brow tightly triangled.

It was when he finally stopped by the teachers' lounge to check his e-mail that he saw June Fisk and her chubby-cheeked teacher's aide gaping at the monitor, their mouths open.

On the screen, Kim Court's blue-lit face.

"It's not the only one," June said, rolling a chair toward him. "I've heard there's another one. Maybe more."

Tom watched it three times, silently.

He thought of Deenie sitting in that classroom and wondered if she'd watched it too, and what she'd thought.

★   ★   ★

Back to hospital today for more tests, Gabby's text read.

It felt a little like the days the orchestra went to regionals—no Lise, no Gabby at school. Except now there weren't even people like Kim, or Jaymie Hurwich, who would quiz Deenie before a test, her fingers always on her tablet, her flying-flash-cards app, her virtual periodic table.

And Skye was nowhere in sight.

Deenie wondered if she and Gabby were hidden away at Skye's parentless house, playing music or reading tarot or whatever they did together. All their private conversations.

Maybe it was for the best that Gabby wasn't there. It felt easier somehow.

★   ★   ★

Not having a phone at school didn't matter at all. You couldn't get reception most places, and you weren't supposed to use it anyway.

But what Eli liked about it was that when someone asked him, "Why didn't you text me back? Didn't you hear about the plan?" he could say, "Sorry, I lost my phone."

Except for the tickling sense in the back of his brain that there was something to it, that he might be missing something that mattered.

Like he'd felt after his mom left. All those days he'd walk past his parents' bedroom and still smell her smell, like those shiny orange soap bars she used.

Since then, his clothes had never felt the same, not soft like before, and no one ever slapped the kitchen table when they laughed hard, and all the blue flowers by the side door were gone. They smelled like grape candy.

He wondered if Deenie, who never seemed to miss anything about their mom, ever missed any of those things. After she moved out, two days after Christmas, Deenie piled her gifts into a trash bag and threw it down the basement stairs. For months, they were down there, the bag striped with mold.

The sound of the second bell jarred him and he was surprised to see the halls were empty, except for one freshman girl at the far end, leaning against the blasted brick.

One arm hanging to her side, she was breathing loudly, just like Kim Court in the video.

"Hey," he called out.

Her head flew up, scraping against the brick.

"Are you okay?" he asked.

She didn't move.

He started walking toward her, but before he'd taken three

steps, she scurried away, off into some freshman-girl hiding place.

Sliding on his headphones, he began walking to fourth period.

As he approached the classroom, he saw another girl lurking, but this one didn't seem sickly or afraid.

It was Skye Osbourne, wearing a long scarf the same color as her mouth, like those dark figs that hung from the tree by the practice rink every fall, the ones that split under your skates.

And this time it felt like she was looking for him.

"Ditch with me," she said, nodding her head toward the double doors.

He stopped, headphones still on.

"Why?"

"Because," she said, a slanting smile. "I'm pretty."

Funnily, Eli wasn't sure Skye was pretty.

If he saw her without all that hair, which looked like it'd been stripped from a corncob and massed thick, and without all the things she draped over and on top of herself, the scarves and snake rings and coiling bracelets, he wondered if he'd recognize her at all.

"What's the point of here," she added, waving something in her hand, a joint, a white Bic.

What's the point of here, he thought, looking at that fig mouth of hers.

Pushing through the doors swinging behind her, he stepped outside. The air felt hard, good.

★   ★   ★

There was a low rumble everywhere, even coming from his own classroom. The drum of confusion, skidding sneakers, a girl's lone yelp, a teacher trying to be heard.

He turned the corner and that's when he saw them.

A long line, like the one to get your school ID photo taken, your yearbook portrait. To get your shots.

Except they were all girls. Ten, twelve, he guessed, close to twenty wrapped around the hallway in groups and individually. Drooping against lockers, slumped on the floor, their legs flung out, doll-like, one in the middle of the corridor, spinning like a flower child.

Danielle Schultz, her right arm swinging like a baton every third second, synced to her own loud breaths.

Brandi Carruthers, junior-class treasurer and weekend pageant queen, her face streaked with a kind of gray sweat.

Two freshman girls who looked all of eleven grappling each other in that way very young girls do, as if the whole world were conspiring to ravage them.

"Pins and needles, pins and needles," stallion-legged track star Tricia Lawson was saying, over and over again, rubbing her long limbs.

Even strapping Brooke Campos was there, tan as ever in her buttercup-yellow tank top, but holding her pelvis in a way that made Tom look away.

The line hooked down one hall and then bottlenecked at the administration office.

Inside, Mrs. Harris, a swath of hair matted to her forehead, was hoarsely calling for quiet, the nurse's office door shut tight.

"He's not here," she whispered to Tom, nodding toward Crowder's office.

"Oh?"

Leaning closer, smelling of Pall Malls and desperation, she added, "He had a seven a.m. meeting at Gem Donuts with the superintendent. He must still be with him."

The door opened and Tom glimpsed two nurses and a badged woman from the health department, the back of her hand resting on her forehead and something unsettling in her eyes. Like a medic on his first day in-country.

Mrs. Harris tapped Tom's shoulder.

"They want to talk to you," she said.

"Who?"

"Are you Tom Nash?" the health department woman said, approaching him. "You were next on my list."

"Your list?"

"We'd like to speak to your daughter."

★   ★   ★

Standing in the breezeway, Deenie watched both the videos back to back on Julie Drew's smeary phone.

First there was Kim, her face sparkly with makeup.

Kim. Kim, a chilly voice inside her said, *this is the best thing that ever happened to you, isn't it?*

All your hard preening and social ambition has finally paid off. Forever craving attention, always the one dying to know the secret you don't, to have the gossip first, waving it like a peacock fan. And to use that gossip as her golden ticket to the inner circle, or its starry center: Gabby.

Except. Except the Kim on YouTube didn't quite seem like that Kim.

In spite of the makeup, the dramatic way she'd tilted the camera to hide her braces, there was something that felt very, intensely real about the Kim on the screen.

The fear hovering in her eyes.

And that moment when she looked off camera, as if she'd heard something.

The way her body had been loose and liquid and then, in an instant, turned stiff.

She seemed to be looking intently at something for a moment. Whatever it was, it made her stop everything, her face frozen, her red mouth open, those glistening night eyes of hers.

The video had had 850 views since it had been posted, at two in the morning.

But then there was the second video, Jaymie Hurwich, who hadn't come to school that day.

Jaymie, Deenie's number-one study pal, who never, ever missed school, who once came even with strep because of a geometry test. Who came even the day after her sister overdosed on ecstasy at college.

Behind her the baby blue of her bedroom, the zebra lampshade by her bed, Jaymie was talking, and moving.

Blinking hard, so hard it hurt to look at it.

And incessantly stroking her hair. First with her left hand, then her right. Smoothing it over and over, her fingers moving as though playing a harp.

The video header read: *DON'T MAKE MY MISTAKE!*

"I'm Jaymie. I'm sixteen and I live with my dad and I go to Dryden High and I love school and my friends and playing softball. I pretty much have a great life."

Blinking rapidly, she let out a long sigh, tugging the fallen strap on her tank top.

"And I'm here to talk about the shots that changed my life forever."

Deenie took the phone from Julie's hand, pulling it closer.

"I've never done this before," Jaymie was saying. "But I don't know how else to deal with what's happening! Two weeks ago, I had my first HPV shot..."

171

Her fingers wiggled as if plucking her imaginary harp.

"I was okay for a few days. Then all this started happening," she said, her hand twitching, like she wanted to stop stroking her hair but her hand wouldn't let her.

"I kept quiet about it. But now I know I'm not the only one. You probably heard about Lise Daniels."

Blinking, blinking like an LED. Deenie felt her own eyes twitching.

"So my dad saw what was happening to me. He went and looked it all up and found out about the shots. About what they did to us. He got so scared. I've never seen him so scared."

She looked down, shaking her head, her fingers still wiggling in the air in front of her mouth, then grabbing at her hair, tearing at it.

"The doctor told us it was stress. There's no way that's true. There was nothing wrong in my life. I had the best grades in my class. I studied all the time. My dad treated me like a princess. My life was perfect. Until I got the shots."

Suddenly, her eyes snapped shut, then shuddered open, as if she'd startled herself. Her hand flew to her mouth, sparkle nail polish flashing, her head jerking hard three times, then her eyes rolled back in their sockets.

A beat, then Jamie's eyes landed on the camera again.

Her eyes wide with alarm.

"There was nothing wrong," she said, breathless now. "Everything was perfect. There was nothing wrong."

Shaking her head, looking down. Voice breaking.

"I don't feel like myself anymore."

When it was over, Julie Drew wanted to watch both videos again. She said she'd heard there were more to watch, "*lots* more." And she said this morning Jaymie's dad had parked himself in front of some congressman's district office and refused to leave until he got "some satisfaction."

But I have nothing to do with Jaymie Hurwich, Deenie thought, walking to next period, her head fogged. *All I ever did was study sometimes with her. We never shared anything. This one is nothing to me.*

For thirty seconds, she felt a swell of relief.

But then both videos began playing again in her head, those slumber-party voices.

My life was perfect, Jaymie had said. *Until I got the shots.*

Her head so filled with thoughts of the lake, Deenie had barely let her mind rest on the vaccine. Could that really be it?

It was the thing they'd shared, all of them.

The same lilac-walled clinic, side by side in the tandem seating, the laminated chair arms locked together.

One by one, going into the little room behind the lilac-painted door.

Slow deep breaths, and don't watch it go in. That was everyone's warning.

They'd all talked about it for days, the first time.

After that, no one talked about it much. But now Deenie could remember how it burned and that was all, and how part of her felt a little sad when the burning went away.

How could all this be about those little shots?

It had to be something else. A thing you didn't know you were waiting for.

Like something inside opening, and then opening something else.

The second bell rang, and she was going to be late.

Turning the corner fast, she nearly ran into the three of them, gloves on, clustered around Lise's locker, its door swung open.

There was a man holding Lise's gym uniform, wilted as a lily pad, and her thermos, its lip stained green from her morning health shakes.

The woman next to him, in a blue parka, was carrying a large bag with smaller bags inside.

The third person was Assistant Principal Hawk, his arms folded, missing the usual disdainful curl of the lip, the tan creases in his forehead thicker than Deenie had ever seen them.

"Is this yours?" the man said, pointing to Deenie's locker. She could see what looked like the hard corner of Lise's "purrfect cat" binder cutting into the bag's bottom.

"Hey, that's Lise's private stuff," she said, unsure where the defiance in her voice came from, the Hawk standing right there.

"That's her," Hawk told the others.

She drew her book bag close to her chest.

"She's the one," he added.

★   ★   ★

They were lying on the bed of Coach Haller's pickup truck, Skye on her stomach, legs waving in the air, the bottoms of her boot heels slicked with grass.

Eli took a long drag, his first since the summer before, that long family trip to WaterWonders. After the marathon car ride—Gabby and Lise and Deenie, high on sugar and new bathing suits, babbling in the backseat the whole time—his dad took pity on him, giving him thirty dollars and letting him wander alone. He met the guy operating the Tadpole Hole who shared his joint, teased him by saying some girl was watching him. "That one's in love with you, bro," he'd said, but the girl turned out just to be Gabby.

That joint had felt weak, easy, but this one was different. Skye said it wasn't pot but the leaves from a plant used by Cherokees and other tribes. If you smoked it before bed, you would have lucid dreams.

"It clears away darkness," she said. "And banishes negative energy."

That sounded okay, and he took a long drag, closing his eyes.

Something passed suddenly, wind rustling above them, and Skye was showing him her bare back, her sweater pulled all the way up so he could see her twisting spine.

"When I was little," she said, "my uncle called me the Rattler. He said it looked like a rattlesnake."

Leaning down, Eli gave it a long look, the pale skin, bra Mountain Dew–green, that pearly white canal from her neck to the waist of her skirt. The swooping curve of the spine, an *S* for Skye.

All right there, for him.

What was he waiting for? Why didn't he set his hand there, flat on the center of that sloping spine?

Her skin would probably feel cool, like a smooth stone.

"When I was eleven they gave me the forward-bending test," she said, looking over her shoulder at him, sharp shoulder blade arching. "Did you never have one of those?"

"No."

"I guess it's only for girls."

Looking at her faint grin, he found himself speculating about figs. Sometimes he'd see one crushed open by the ice rink, its insides filled with dead wasps.

"He's an artist," she was saying. "My uncle. He took out his paints and painted up my spine. A diamondback coiling with my coil."

Coiling with my coil.

He was listening to her in a way, the joint working on him like warm hands. But he was wondering about something. Like what was stopping him from putting his hand on that skin of hers, displayed just for him.

"He told me to never be ashamed," she said. "That it was beautiful."

Looking at her, he could almost see the painted serpent squirming on her skin, ready to turn, mouth open.

He started thinking something about her uncle, but the thought drifted away before it could take hold.

"He kept rattlers in the old rabbit hutch. Did you know that baby rattlers have this tiny little button on the tip of their tail? It doesn't make any sound. It feels like velvet. I've touched it."

She turned on her side but kept the sweater hitched high. He could see the bottom edges of her green bra, half moons. But he didn't feel what he'd normally feel. It was like looking at a painting.

"They lose it when they shed their first skin," she said, her fingertips grazing her stomach. "After that, they grow the hard rattle. The one that makes all the noise. It doesn't sound so much like a rattle. It's softer than that. More like this."

She lifted her fingers over those dark lips of hers and made a sound.

To him it sounded like locusts deep in Binnorie Woods.

He didn't know how long they had been lying there, his head going to places, like that time he fell in practice and his cheek split open and his mom had to pick him up in the middle of the day.

Sitting in his mom's front seat, his skates on the floor in front of him, feeling the soft tickle of something, a pair of women's underpants, ice-blue, on the floor of the car.

He would never forget the look on her face. His mom's face.

Did that really happen? It did. Both of them sat there as if it hadn't, the entire drive home, the dull thud of the car over the wet streets.

He never told anyone, they never spoke about it, and six months later, two days after Christmas, she'd moved out. Sometimes he could still feel it on his ankles, the sneaking sense that something had gone wrong and it was right there and it was touching you, rustling against you all the time even if you didn't look.

Then, through the fog of his head, Skye spoke.

"Have you gone to see her?"

"Who?"

"Lise."

"Lise," he said, her name sounding funny in his mouth. A picture of her coming to him, that pudgy Lise with her shirt always lifting above her belly.

"I heard she might be talking now. I wondered if she'd talked to you."

"Me?" he said. "Why would she talk to me?"

"Oh," she said, and he turned his head to her, her face suddenly so close, and the smell of something rotten from that dark berried mouth. It was like that fig, he thought. With something inside you didn't expect. "I heard some things. Maybe I was wrong."

"What did you hear?"

"I don't know. Something sexy. About you two."

"What?" He started to prop himself up on his elbows, one of them tugging on her long hair.

She didn't move, her stomach still bare, her fingers dancing along it. "That you two were doing something. Before school."

"What do you mean, doing something?"

"By the practice rink, behind the bushes. You and Lise. You were both lying on the grass and you were taking off her tights. They said."

Those bushes, he knew them, their toothed leaves, thick-veined, and the seed pods laced with thorns. They grew wild and it was a place you could drink beer or do things.

"No way," he said, shaking his head, shaking the image of Lise, bare-legged, her skirt hitched high, from his thoughts. "Lise, she's a sister to me."

"Oh," she said, fingertips making circles just above the waist of her skirt. Wider and wider circles.

"A sister," he repeated.

He looked at her. There was something scratching again, in the corner above his eye, like those metal probes at the dentist clawing at your teeth.

"Who told you that?" he asked, his voice lifting to a new place. He didn't sound like himself. "Who's 'they'?"

Skye looked over at him, and in his head he could see the wasps.

"Listen," he said, grabbing for his bag. "I gotta get to class."

★   ★   ★

"Mr. Nash, we'd like to talk to your daughter."

She said she was Sue Brennan, deputy public-health commissioner.

"About what?"

They were sitting in Principal Crowder's vacant office.

Her bra strap was sliding down her shoulder and her hair looked dirty. She was wearing latex gloves. Her wrists were red.

"We're trying to trace as closely as possible Lise Daniels's movements prior to the attack."

"But why? You've got a public-health crisis here and—"

"We're looking into whether she may have come into contact with or been exposed to something."

"You think it might be something toxic?" Tom asked.

"Mr. Nash, we'd really just like to talk to your daughter." She folded her hands, then seemed to realize she still had the gloves on. Looked at them, not sure what to do.

"So you're talking to everybody?"

"We know Deenie was one of the last people with Lise before the event."

Tom looked at her, squinted. "So was a class full of other kids. A school full of people. Are you talking to everyone?"

"There's many parties involved, and we're pursuing all avenues."

"Who's the 'we' here?"

"You have nothing to be concerned about."

She was giving him a blank face. Like the woman at a car-rental desk, or an airline check-in. *Calm down, sir.*

"I have nothing to be concerned about?" Tom said. "Pardon me, but have you looked around you? Do you see what's happening here?"

"Mr. Nash," she said as she finally stripped the gloves from her hands, ashed with powder and trembling slightly. "We need to find out everything about Lise. About all these girls."

He leaned back in his chair.

"Why now, why three days later? Why weren't you talking to Deenie before? Do you have some new information?"

She crimped her file folders in her hand.

"Mr. Nash, I would think it would be important to you. To try to help our investigation. Don't you want to understand what's happening to these girls? What if your daughter was next?"

"She won't be," he said, his voice suddenly hard.

She looked at him, paused. "No?"

"I know my daughter," he said, rising. He had no idea what he was talking about. What did it have to do with knowing his daughter? And was his answer, precisely, true?

"Of course you do," she said, glancing at her phone. "Anyway, it looks like they may have already gotten what they need from her."

* * *

They took her to the music room, empty except for a pair of orchestra stands on the floor. Deenie wondered which girl's raging spasm had knocked them down, emptying the room, which now smelled of fresh bleach.

"Did something happen to Lise?" she asked. "Something else?"

The woman in the parka shook her head. The man with Lise's uniform had left. So had Assistant Principal Hawk.

"We're trying to get some information about what Lise was doing before she got sick," the woman said. "Since you're pals, maybe you can help."

There were no chairs, so they sat on either end of Mr. Timmins's coffee-ringed desk.

"I don't know anything about that," Deenie said. "She was in class, and she jumped up and then she fell down."

"Did you see her before class?"

"No."

"Did you usually see her before class?"

"Not really," Deenie lied. She didn't want to explain that she hadn't gone to Lise's locker like she usually did. That she hadn't wanted to talk about what had happened with Sean Lurie. And she'd been worried Lise might see her and just know.

"And did Lise use any drugs that you know about?"

"What? No!"

"It's okay. No one's in trouble. Not even the occasional joint?"

"No," Deenie said, shaking her head.

"Is it possible Lise had been experimenting with someone else?" the woman asked. "Did you have the sense Lise didn't tell you everything?"

"She told me everything," Deenie said coolly. "She tells me everything."

"And that day... had you talked on the phone? Exchanged texts?"

"No, but that doesn't mean anything," Deenie replied, which was sort of a weird response and she wasn't even sure what she meant by it.

"I'm sure it doesn't," the woman said. "And how about Lise and boys?"

Deenie felt her body seize slightly, her shoulders clenching hard, a string pulled in the center of her, tight, and her dad's voice seemed to rise up from inside her, though it was really from the hallway, loud and meaningful.

★   ★   ★

"They wouldn't let me go home," Brooke Campos whispered to Eli, across the aisle. "The sub nurse is a class-A bitch."

Eli looked over at her. Beneath the desk, her jeans were unsnapped, her brown pelvis exposed.

"It hurts so bad," she said, rubbing her stomach. "They said it was stress. *Stress* seems to mean 'everything.'"

It might have been the smartest thing Brooke Campos ever said.

"You should go home," Eli said.

She pressed her fingertips on her pelvic bones, jutting from her low-slung jeans.

"It's like something's burning inside me."

"Miss Campos, Mr. Nash," called out Mr. Banasiak from under the blue haze of his PowerPoint presentation.

Looking up, they waited for him to say more, but that seemed to be the sum of it.

The lights dimmed and Eli watched Brooke, shifting in her seat.

"Brooke," he whispered. "Did you ever hear anything about me and Lise?"

"What?" she said, her teeth bright white against her tan skin, teeth sunk into her lips. Like a bronzed beaver, he thought.

"Any stories, about us?"

"No," she said, slowly. Then added, "Well, yeah. I mean, I heard stuff about Lise. But it doesn't have to do with you."

"Who does it have to do with?"

"Some guy from another school. A hockey player."

★   ★   ★

"Mr. Nash, there's nothing cloak-and-dagger about this," Sue Brennan was calling out, still far behind him. "I've told you where she—"

Later, Tom wouldn't even remember walking, or running, he guessed it was, from the catch in his breath, the wet feeling around his shirt collar, the thump in his chest when he finally arrived in the music room.

His hand rattling loudly on the locked doorknob, he could see Deenie inside, eyes large through the door pane.

Some woman in a dark parka hovering over her like a crow.

"Open this goddamned door," he heard himself say, a voice distinctly his father's rather than his own.

The parka woman turned, a flash of recognition on her face, as if she knew him.

She was saying things, telling him to calm down.

Suddenly, all he could think of was Sheila Daniels's face under the garage-door light, her mouth open, braying.

The door opened, the parka woman saying things to him, and Deenie behind her saying, "It's okay, Dad. I promise."

Before they left school, Principal Crowder caught Tom, made some kind of assurances as they stood at Deenie's locker, Deenie sliding on her jacket.

"You should have been present when they spoke to her, obviously," he said. "Things are just happening very quickly right now."

Tom didn't say anything, grabbing Deenie's book bag, slamming her locker door.

"And, Tom," Crowder added, "I know I can count on you at the PTA meeting tonight."

"PTA meeting?" he asked, stopping himself from tugging up Deenie's jacket zipper as if she were five.

"Didn't you get the announcements? There's an emergency meeting," Crowder said, eyes darting back and forth between them. "We need you there."

"I'll be there," Tom said. "But why tonight?"

"Didn't you hear?" Crowder looked at Deenie, hesitating. "Can we speak alone for a second?"

Crowder's face, up close, sweat-varnished, as they stood in front of his computer in his office, Deenie waiting outside anxiously.

"It's all over the news," Crowder said. "It's on CNN."

Leaning over, he unpaused the video flickering there.

It was Kim Court again.

"I saw this," Tom said.

"No. This is a new one."

On the screen, Kim looked even more haggard now, her face lit green, her mouth open.

"Don't believe the lies!" she said in that lisping, tongue-rasping voice. "I won't keep silent anymore. This isn't about some stupid vaccine. Because guess what, everyone? I never had the shot. I'm allergic and I couldn't get the shot.

"So listen! Listen!"

Leaning closer.

"Whatever's happening to us, it's bigger than any shot."

Voice scurrying up her throat, eyes rolling back.

"It's bigger than everything."

Driving home with Deenie, he took the shortcut through the back roads, skipping the lake.

"It wasn't anything, sweetie," he said. "Just another of those videos."

"Okay," Deenie said.

"So tonight, I just want you to stay home and stay off the computer. And the TV," he said. Which was ridiculous, but it must have been a sign of how crazy he was acting that Deenie just nodded. "And no more talking to anybody without me there, okay? Anybody."

Deenie nodded.

He hadn't ever wanted to be one of the hysterical parents, the handwringers, the finger-pointers. But wasn't this different? It felt different in every way.

"And you're sure all they asked you was if you had seen Lise that morning?"

Deenie nodded, eyes turning to the window.

They drove in silence for a moment.

"But Dad," Deenie said, abruptly, "who was that woman, anyway? The one in the big parka?"

"What do you mean?"

"She didn't have the health department thing around her neck. Who was she?"

"She didn't identify herself?" Tom couldn't believe he hadn't asked.

His phone trilled on the gear panel between them. Missed calls: **Georgia, Georgia, Georgia.**

"I don't remember," Deenie said. "There's so many people at the school now."

"I'm just glad I found you," he said.

She looked at him, and he guessed he wanted a smile or something, but she was staring at his phone, her mother's name flashing.

13

From her bedroom window, Deenie could see her dad standing in the backyard, smoking, which she hadn't seen him do ever, except in the browning snapshots in the photo albums in the hall closet, the ones with the pages tacky to touch, the binding peeled and cracked like everything from the 1980s.

He was leaning against the house, so hidden he was nearly under a corner gutter downspout.

His head turned and she jumped back. She couldn't bear the thought that he'd see her seeing him.

She was afraid to look at her phone. There was something on it. A text Julie Drew had sent, with a new YouTube link.

What if it was Skye? Then she'd be the only one left from the lake.

But she knew it wasn't going to be Skye. Skye would never record a video of herself for the world. Not Skye, who hardly ever let anyone inside her house because her aunt had tinnitus. Not Skye, who told everyone she didn't even have a Social Security number because that was like being in prison, or a concentration camp. *You have to be in charge of your own numbers,* she said. *You can't let them put a number on you.*

But more so this:

Something in her said nothing could ever happen to Skye. She didn't have that thing Lise had, Gabby had, even Kim and Jaymie had. That softness, that tenderness. Easy to bruise.

But then again, Deenie thought, *I guess I don't have it either.*

★   ★   ★

Eli held back Brooke's long hair, twined it in his hand, as she leaned over, bent at the waist.

The noise she made, low and guttural, didn't even sound like a girl's, sounded like the noises players made at the rink, stick in the gut, a wrister off the groin.

"Do you want me to get the nurse?" Eli asked, one hand on her shoulder, twig-brown but cold and goose-bumped in his hand.

"I don't think so," she whispered, looking down at her feet. "I thought I was going to throw up. But I didn't."

It was a funny thing to say, as if he hadn't just seen her do it, his hands still in her hair as she righted herself.

She leaned against the wall, her face slick with saliva, her tank top riding up like a crumpled daffodil.

She was staring out the breezeway's glass panels, fogged from the humidity.

Pointing at the tall hedges, her face whitened, her hands covering her mouth.

"That's where. Right there," Brooke said. "Last week. I saw Lise walking out from behind the bushes with some guy. I've seen him before, but I don't know his name. She was sliding her skirt around so it faced front."

Eli couldn't imagine Lise doing what Brooke was suggesting. Anywhere. Much less in the bushes by school. He was sure it couldn't be true.

"I guess I wasn't the only one to see," she said, eyes on the glass as if she were still seeing it.

187

"Wait," he said. "Why would anyone think it was me?"

"I don't know. He looked like you a little. And he was wearing one of those red interscholastic jackets like you sometimes wear."

Eli didn't say anything, but she shrugged as if he had.

"Lise Daniels," she said, eyes narrowing. "All the sudden she was so goddamned pretty. Some of us have been pretty forever."

It was like she was talking to no one, or to the whole world.

"No one cares if you've always been pretty," she said, palm stretched flat against the glass. "It's the same old news. But if all the sudden you're beautiful, you can do anything. That's what she must've thought, anyway."

Eli looked at her.

When he saw her expression, he thought she was going to get sick again, but then he realized she'd just heard herself. Heard aloud, for the first time, what had been in her head, maybe for a long time.

★   ★   ★

"Listen!" Kim Court shouted on the video. "Whatever's happening to us, it's bigger than any shot. It's bigger than everything."

The clip, which Deenie found on both CNN and Fox News, was only twenty seconds long, edited for the single revelation.

As the headline read, "Afflicted Girl Warns: It's Bigger than Any Vaccine!"

Deenie searched around for Kim's own YouTube channel and found a longer version.

Seven minutes long, with a staggering twenty thousand viewings, including thumbs-up (654) and thumbs-down (245) ratings.

It began with Kim muttering, like the words were sticky in her mouth.

"I told them not to put the glue in my hair," she was saying.

The light was so dim that everything looked brown, murky, and her eyes, amid the haze, looked like black holes.

"Because that's what they did to Gabby and I touched it."

Her fingers were on her throat, and the voice like a gurgle, like she was underwater.

"If I sound weird," Kim said, "it's only because my tongue is so big and my mouth is so small. They're giving me drugs. But if they want to help me, why did they put glue in my hair?"

For a painful moment, Kim seemed to have to gasp for breath. Then she breathed deep, a scraping noise lifting from her.

"I know I was dreaming," she continued. "They said I was. But it was so real. The man with tornado legs. I always dreamed about him, since I was little. And Gabby too! She was pulling seaweed from her throat. The stones that were her eyes. She found Lise down there."

Her eyes suddenly darted to one side, like before, the whites glowing.

Then a light went on somewhere and Kim's hands dropped from her throat, skin bright and raw. Clawed.

She faced the camera again.

"And I heard Deenie Nash is here now too.

"I heard her talking last night. I knew she had to be here."

Kim's eyes burning, the knowing look there as she said:

"Deenie's the one."

Her finger pressing until it turned white, Deenie shut off the phone.

★　★　★

"The parents of Kimberly Court confirmed through their family doctor that, due to an allergy to a component of the vaccine, their daughter never received the HPV shot," the newscaster announced.

Tom had never thought it was the vaccine, never believed it.

But he had the sudden sense, as his phone filled with voice mails from parents, and texts, and e-mails, that everything had become much, much worse.

Now that the definable horror, the specific one, had been eliminated, a pit had opened up beneath them. Beneath all these parents. All parents.

If not that, what?

He picked up his phone.

"Hi, you've reached Diane in Billing. Please leave a message."

Her voice cool, professional, friendly.

He left a message with no confidence she would ever call back.

Then remembering what Deenie had said.

Dad, who was that woman, anyway?

The woman in the parka, who could she have been? CDC? He didn't think so. Sometimes on TV, CDC officials wore uniforms. She didn't even have an ID badge.

And there was something else about her. Her stance. The way one leg was behind her, her hips angled, knees slightly bent.

Like a cop.

★   ★   ★

Straight-backed, Deenie sat on her bed, thinking about Kim Court, guessing who had watched the video, knowing it was everyone, everyone in the world maybe. All wondering what Kim meant when she said, "Deenie's the one."

And the even crazier part: *Deenie Nash is here now too. I heard her talking last night. I knew she had to be here.*

Like there might be another version of herself out there, in the hospital, with Lise.

Once, Skye told them about a cousin who could astrally project himself. He used to visit her at night and she thought she was dreaming until he asked her once, *When did you get the new pajamas, the blue ones with the rainbows?*

Part of her wished she could do that. She tried to imagine what Lise looked like now, if she looked different, better, something. But then the picture came to her, that mottled buckling in the middle of her forehead.

She turned to face her bedside table. Behind the empty Kleenex box, the gumball desk lamp, there was a picture frame draped in electric-blue Mardi Gras beads. Middle-school graduation, she and Lise, cheek to cheek, cap tassels pressed into open mouths. The old Lise. Lise with a forehead scraped with acne, Lise with a snuggle of flesh around her beaming face.

But it was hard to picture the Lise of now, or of last week at least. The Lise who poked her head around Deenie's locker every morning to say hello, except on the morning it happened, when Deenie never went to her locker. Because of what she'd done with Sean Lurie.

The only Lise she could picture anymore was the one convulsing on the classroom floor. The surprise in her eyes.

It was like the surprise in Sean's eyes. That instant he'd realized the truth about Deenie, knew her secret, or thought he did.

Lise and Sean, their matching stuttered-open expressions.

They weren't the same thing, except maybe they were: *You didn't tell me. You should have told me. You didn't tell me it was going to be like this. You should've told me. Deenie, why didn't you tell me.*

191

Or maybe it was like the look in her own eyes, Sean pressed hard against her. A look she herself never got to see: *I didn't know it was this. If someone had told me it was this. If.*

She didn't remember turning the phone back on.

"Mom," she said, the phone shaking in her shaking hand. Had she really pressed her mother's name? "Mom, can you come here?"

★   ★   ★

The phone was ringing.

Not Tom's phone, not anyone's phone. The landline, which almost never rang except right before Election Day, which sat on a table in the hallway like a blistered antique.

"Is this Deenie Nash's dad?"

"Yes," Tom answered.

"Um, can you let Deenie know she doesn't have to come in tomorrow?"

"What?" Tom said, then realized it must be someone at the Pizza House. "Oh, okay. I'll have her call you if she doesn't plan on coming."

There was a brief pause. "No, I mean, Deenie should just take the night off. And Sunday too, okay?"

"What do you mean?"

Another pause.

"We're just being careful, sir."

"So you're closed for business?" Tom said, trying to keep his voice steady. "Who's going to be working?"

"We just don't need Deenie," the man said. "That's all."

"Listen, none of this has anything to do with Deenie," he said. "Though your concern for my daughter's health, since I'm sure that's what this really is, is admirable."

Phones rang in the background, pots clattering, for several seconds before the man spoke again.

"Look, I'm sorry, Mr. Nash, but none of us really know what this has to do with."

"Where did you get this idea? What made you think my daughter—"

"Sir, I don't think anything. I just know I got a call about when she'd last worked a shift. And I hear things. I live here too, you know."

Tom hung up.

Laptop open, he watched the Kim Court video again. The whole video. Filled with gaping eyes and throat clutching and then the worst part. The crazy talk about Deenie being in the hospital too. About Deenie being "the one."

It was the ramblings of a confused, overwrought girl.

The vaccine theory hadn't made sense. Nor had the elaborate theories about bats and toxins. But most of all, the notion that his daughter might be some kind of Typhoid Mary scything her way through Dryden.

He remembered watching a documentary about her on public television.

Her peach ice cream was highly regarded and often requested—that's what they said about Mary, a cook for the wealthy, a carrier who infected dozens of families.

He pictured Deenie at the Pizza House, hands blotted with flour, grinning at him from the back, the steel dough roller rattling before her dainty frame.

The PTA meeting was in a half hour, and he wanted to get there early.

★   ★   ★

"I'm so glad to hear your voice, baby," Deenie's mom kept saying, had said three, four times.

"I didn't feel like talking. A lot's been going on."

"Deenie," she said, "I'm so sorry you're going through all this alone."

"I'm not alone," Deenie said, all the urgency she'd felt when she'd first called draining away and something else, older and warier, taking its place.

"No, I know," her mom said quickly. "I'm just sorry you're going through it without me."

Deenie grabbed for the Mardi Gras beads, rolling them between her fingers, trying to listen, or not listen.

"I keep hearing all these conflicting things," her mom said, her voice filling the silence. "The vaccine. All those antivaccine people. I remember when you all had your measles shots in fifth grade. Your dad trying to explain to everyone how vaccines work. I bet that's what he's doing now."

Deenie didn't say anything.

"And the congressman keeps talking about the lake."

"What about the lake?" Deenie said, her spine stiffening.

"I always wondered about that lake. That smell."

Deenie felt her hand cover her mouth.

"It used to be so beautiful," her mom was saying, "and then it changed."

"Mom."

"Is it still thick like that, like a bright green carpet on top? Does it still smell like animal fur?"

"Are you coming, Mom?" Deenie blurted, her jaw shaking.

"No" came the reply just as quickly.

The pause that followed felt endless, Deenie's hand aching from squeezing the phone so hard.

"Come stay here, baby," her mom said, voice speeding up. "I'll get in the car right now. I'll pick you up by midnight. You can stay here until—"

"No, Mom. No!" Her voice rising, that shrill tone only her mom could bring out of her, all those months and months after the separation, slowly understanding what her mother had done.

"Deenie, it's not safe for you there," she said. "They don't know what it is."

"Dad takes care of me."

"I can take care of you. Deenie, I always—"

"You were never good for anything," Deenie said. "Except ruining everything."

★   ★   ★

Eli's eyes scanned the team showcase.

Glancing at the clock on the wall, he noticed it was almost seven. It had been hours since that smoke with Skye, hours spent on the thawing practice rink that seemed to pass in an instant.

There was a lot of noise echoing from the gym. They were setting up for something. It seemed a bad time to hold a game, a college fair.

He stopped at last year's trophy, a gold-dipped puck presented by the mayor, dusty ribbons, the team photo, sticks slanted in perfect symmetry.

And the big photo from last year's interscholastic banquet.

There were other players from Dryden, and from Brother Rice, Star-of-the-Sea.

He was thinking of what Brooke had said, about the boy with Lise.

In the picture, everyone wore the same dark blue blazers, the same button-down shirts and shiny loafers, the same ironic grins.

They all looked like him.

★   ★   ★

Her head hot and her room smaller than ever, and Deenie couldn't believe she'd called her mom, hated herself for it.

Her phone kept ringing, but she didn't want to turn it off because it might be Gabby.

She was remembering, again, the hundred muffled conversations in her parents' bedroom and doors slamming and her mother crying in the basement, echoing up the laundry chute. She couldn't figure any of it out at first and then finally one night she'd heard it, her dad's voice high and strange through the walls. *Couldn't keep your legs together couldn't stop yourself look what you've done look what happened.*

The next morning, they sat Deenie and Eli down at the dining-room table and she told them she was leaving, a roller bag upright between her knees.

The entire time, Deenie's eyes were trained on her dad sitting there next to her mother, not saying a word, head down, thumbnail gouging a notch in the table.

★   ★   ★

Tom wasn't sure at first where the sound was coming from, or what it was.

But then he moved toward the kitchen and heard the distinctive chugging of the washing machine.

He walked down the rickety steps, thick with layers of old paint.

Deenie didn't seem to hear him at first, the washer grinding to a halt. Quickly, almost furtively, she jerked the lid open, lifting her Pizza House shirt from the depths of the old Maytag.

He watched as she held up the shirt to the lightbulb hanging above.

As she pressed her face against it.

"Deenie," he called out, standing at the foot of the basement stairs.

"Yeah, Dad," her voice came, a hitch in it. She didn't turn around but pulled the shirt from her face, slapped it onto the lid.

It was dark down there, he couldn't quite see, but it felt private. Not illicit, just private.

"You okay?"

"Yeah."

"You said you didn't want to work tomorrow, right?"

"Yeah," she said, still not turning her head. "It just doesn't seem right to go to work. With everything happening."

Her hands were tight on the shirt, red and wet.

14

From the rain-whisked parking lot, Tom could see the gym burning bright as a game night.

Streaking past him, a Channel 7 News van, its antenna corded like a peppermint twist.

In the distance, he could see Dave Hurwich having a heated discussion with a woman in a yellow slicker and matching hat, a container of some kind in her arms.

Walking faster, Tom passed a trench-coated reporter standing at the foot of the building's front steps, a camera light illuminating his face as he spoke:

"Though school officials claim the purpose of this hastily scheduled meeting is to address all parental concerns, it is hard not to see a connection to tonight's revelation."

Another reporter ten feet away, fingers to earpiece:

"If Miss Court never received the much-discussed vaccination, many parents are saying that calls into question the most pervasive theory for the outbreak."

The reporter held the microphone out to a woman in a purple anorak beside him. Tom vaguely recalled her from Parents' Night.

"The vaccine was a red herring," the woman said sternly, leaning over the microphone. "So where does that leave us now? It could be anything. That's just not acceptable!"

Tom kept walking.

A small group was gathered at the school's front door. At the center, a man with headphones and a Channel 4 baseball cap was talking to Assistant Principal Hawk.

"This is a public meeting, isn't it?"

"This isn't a school-board meeting," Hawk said, his face bone-white and wet, his Dryden Stallions baseball cap soaked through. "This meeting was called by the parent-teacher association. We need to respect their privacy."

"But you're a public school, aren't you? What makes you think—"

Tom hurried past, ducking his head, nearly tripping over the long licorice cords snaking from the van.

"Is that the Nash girl's father?" he heard someone say.

He didn't stop. He just kept going.

★ ★ ★

Her mom left two long messages that Deenie let play as the phone rested on the counter and she ate her cereal.

She turned the radio louder so she could hear even less.

It shouldn't have been a surprise that her mom wouldn't come. It wasn't a surprise.

In the past two years, she hadn't spent more than ten minutes in the house, more than an hour in Dryden. When she picked them up, she waited in the car as if there were police tape draped across the entryway.

Sometimes, peeking under the sun visor, her mom would look up at it like it was haunted.

Deenie threw the rest of her cereal into the sink and opened the refrigerator, considered a bottle of beer nestled in the back corner. She had only had maybe ten beers in her life, but it seemed like what you did, what one did in a situation like this. As if there had ever been a situation like this.

The news report came on with that plunky news music.

... called by Sheila Daniels, mother of Lise Daniels, and her attorney, possibly to discuss attempts to move her daughter to the medical center at Mercy-Starr Clark. The press conference will be held on hospital grounds at ten o'clock tonight, after the school's PTA meeting is expected to end. The hospital denies the story, asserting that any such event on their property requires permission to assemble and they have received no such request.

Deenie sat back down, thinking of the hospital, of being in the parking lot the night before, the closest she'd been to the thing that was happening. It was happening there. With Lise.

And then hearing Kim Court's voice, her eyes muddy ringed.

Deenie Nash is here now too ... I knew she had to be here. Deenie's the one.

She picked up her phone, trying Gabby again.

"Deenie, I don't want to talk." Gabby's voice sounded soft and sludgy, like when she had strep, her tongue furred white.

"But what happened today? Weren't you going to the hospital for more tests?"

"Yeah. I'm home now."

"What did they do to you?"

"I don't know, Deenie. More blood, gross stuff. More head-shrinking. I don't want to talk about it."

Deenie paused. She pictured Gabby like a ball rolled tight and there was nothing she could do to unpeel her arms from her legs, unfurl her head from her chest.

"Is Skye with you?" Deenie asked, then felt embarrassed.

"What? No."

"Did you see the videos?" Deenie tried again. "Kim Court?"

"No," she said. "No, I'm not watching anything. My mom said I couldn't watch anything. Deenie, I don't want to talk about it. Okay? Please."

But Deenie couldn't stop herself, her voice pushing forward.

"Gabby, we have to do something. What if we went to the hospital? Maybe, with everything going on, we could try to see Lise now—"

"No" came Gabby's voice, loud and urgent. "I'm never, ever going back there. What is wrong with you, Deenie? What do you think is going to happen if you go? That Lise is dying to see you so much she'll come out of the coma?"

Deenie didn't say anything for a second.

"Coma?" she said at last. "What do you mean, 'coma'? I thought she was just unconscious."

There was no sound on the other end.

Then a vague clicking, like a tongue across the roof of the mouth.

"Deenie," Gabby said finally, "people aren't just unconscious for four days."

"But we don't know...she may be conscious now. We don't know."

There was a muffled sound, but Deenie couldn't hear what it was, her forehead wet and tingling. She felt so far away from Gabby. Like with everything lately, even before this, all Gabby's adventures with Skye. The only other time she remembered feeling that way was a few years ago. That time Gabby stayed with them for almost two weeks. Every night, Deenie tried to get her to talk and she wouldn't. A few times, though, she heard Eli talking to her downstairs and Gabby laughing, and it had to be Gabby but didn't sound like her laugh, or like Gabby.

Which was funny to think of now, because those weeks Gabby stayed with them seemed to be the thing that had made them best friends. After that, they were closer than ever.

"Deenie." Gabby's voice returned, a whisper. "What is it you're trying to do?"

Click, click, and Deenie felt her own lips, tongue. Was the sound coming from her own mouth?

"Deenie," Gabby said, "we're all sick here."

Ten minutes later, her coat on, she was ready to go.

If I text him, she thought, *he'll say no.*

Tearing a page from her spiral notebook, she wrote a note.

* * *

The minute Tom walked inside the school, he felt it.

It was loud, louder than any school event he could remember.

The pitchy clamor of nervous parents finding other nervous parents to be even more nervous together.

A flurry of shouts at the door as the sole security guard tried to keep another reporter or producer from entering through the loading dock.

The screeching of gym risers pushed down the hallway, veering hard into the rattling lockers, sending a rolling garbage can careering into the wall.

Two sets of parents shouting at each other, something about a fender bender in the parking lot, and one of the fathers inexplicably crying, humiliating tears of frustration he tried to hide behind his shirtsleeve.

At the gym's double doors, the fleecy-haired student-council president stood as sentry, a name tag slapped across his navy blazer: PATRICK.

"I don't have any information. But don't worry," the boy said, his voice cracking, to the mother speaking fervently to him, her glasses crooked and fogged. "They're gonna explain everything."

He couldn't remember ever seeing the gym so full.

Principal Crowder himself, shirtsleeves rolled up like a junior senator, was directing a letter-jacketed student-council type in how to push open the high windows with the extension pole.

If it hadn't been so hot already, the air outside so preternaturally mild and the school holding all the furnaced breath of months of winter, then maybe the two hundred or more parents packed so tightly would not have radiated so much heat.

The air thick with it, the high windows wisped with condensation, Tom walked through, pushing past the straining masses, the gym starting to feel like some kind of torpid hothouse or sweatshop, the creaking hold of an ancient ship.

And they were all there.

A *This Is Your Life* of parents, current, recent, long past (what was Constance Keith doing there, both her rambunctious, teeth-flashing, hells-yeah daughters and her Adderall-dealing son long gone to state schools, possibly state prison?).

There were the earnest parents, notepads and pens out, clasping copies of news articles printed from the Internet in their shaking hands.

And there were the ones wearing vaguely stunned expressions, the same ones who could never quite believe their children were failing chemistry, had scorched their lab partners' hair while swinging burners like flamethrowers, had referred to other classmates as "pass-around pussies."

And there were the ones, fewer than usual, with their eyes fixed on their phones, just like during Back to School Night, concerts, graduations, their faces veiled now so you couldn't be sure if they were merely biding their time, reviewing the news reports, poised to pounce on the school officials, or if their thoughts were elsewhere (on work, on Scrabble, the Tetris slink).

Standing room only, like a rock concert, and Tom tried to avoid them all, finding a corner by the boys' locker-room doors, against the vaguely damp wall mats smelling strongly of mildew, spit, boys.

Through the aluminum crossbars, fifteen feet away, he could see Lara Bishop in her own hideout, chewing gum with the vigor of a former smoker.

He worked a long time to catch her eye and finally she nodded back, a half smile filled with knowingness. Sometimes she reminded him of one of those world-weary actresses in old movies, the ones who looked knocked around but instead of making them harder, it seemed to make them more generous-spirited.

"You're hiding too," a voice beside him said.

It was the French teacher, Kit, walking toward him, sliding off a tiny leather jacket, tomato red, like her Vespa.

Where did this woman come from? he wondered. And where had she been when he was single? Then he remembered he was single.

A sudden screech from the mike system made her wince, smiling, her shoulders pushing together in a way that reminded him, unnervingly, of Gabby, Lise, Deenie.

"If I can have your attention..."

Principal Crowder began, papers rolled in his hand, pen behind his ear. A cartoonist's drawing of an important person. First, he introduced the murderers' row of officials standing at his side. Deputy Commissioner Sue Brennan, next to the superintendent in his usual taupe suit, then a silver-haired woman introduced as the hospital's "chief information officer," flanked by an unidentified man in a three-piece suit, fingers tight around his cell phone.

And poor Mark Tierney, the PTA chair and a pediatrician, his face crimped and flushed, like a man caught in the middle of a rope pull.

"Thank you for coming tonight," the superintendent began. "Concerned parents are involved parents, and involved parents make our district strong. The safety and well-being of our students is our utmost priority. We are working closely with the affected students, their parents, and health officials to gather all the facts. We ask the community to respect the privacy of the families involved as we progress and that any questions you may have be addressed to Principal Crowder directly."

It was a marvelous string of sentences containing no information at all.

All eyes turned over to Crowder, who momentarily flashed his toothy grin, as if forgetting the occasion.

"Thank you all for coming. While privacy laws prevent us from getting into specifics, we want to be clear that all girls have received or are receiving appropriate medical attention. The headline here is that there's no evidence—and Mrs. Tomlinson from the hospital can back me up here—suggesting we are dealing with a contagious threat of any kind."

The silver-haired hospital woman stiffened visibly, locking eyes with Crowder. It was like watching a couple of battery men at a ball game, still working out their signals. Crowder caught her signal, only a little late.

"But the investigation is ongoing," Crowder said, eyes dropping down to a folded sheet of paper in his hands. "Essentially, what we're trying to do here is walk the cat backward. The district and health officials are working together, trying to determine any commonalities the girls share that might explain their conditions."

"Here's a commonality," someone shouted from the throng. "They all attend *this* school."

There it was. It hadn't taken long, but it almost felt like a relief to get it over with, to have someone start.

Tom could feel the pressure in the gym release momentarily around him and, in seconds, build up again, random parents straining to move forward, others waving for the student with the microphone. The buzz of two dozen or more conversations vibrating louder.

Crowder cleared this throat. "I was getting to that. The department of health is preparing to conduct a full review of the premises, and the deputy commissioner can tell you about that now. I know she's happy to answer any questions."

Sue Brennan stepped forward to the mike stand, teetering ever so slightly on her heels.

Tom focused closely on her, this woman who had spoken so inscrutably, so evasively, it seemed to him now, about his daughter.

"After Ms. Bishop's incident, our staff reached out to officials at the state department of health, including the environmental health and communicable diseases divisions. They're helping us review all available medical tests and sharing epidemiologic, clinical, and environmental data. Several of you have asked about autoimmune conditions, like PANDAS, but none of the girls have recently had strep. We've ruled out many standard infections—*E. coli,* staph. Also neurological infections—encephalitis, meningitis, late-stage syphilis."

You could feel the frenzy in the gym ramp up more and more with each word. Listing all these possibilities, even to dismiss them, seemed like a bad idea. The word *syphilis* felt like a fever in Tom's own brain.

"But it's important to note," she continued, "infections don't discriminate. If this were an infection, we'd see more people affected and not just young girls. But the process is ongoing. The main thing we need is your patience."

"Why would we trust you now?" a voice bellowed from within the body of the twitching crowd. "Any of you? You're the ones who pushed your poison down our girls' throats."

Tom moved forward a few steps, closer to Kit now, and saw it was Dave Hurwich, a tankard of coffee in his hand, a sheaf of curling papers under his arm.

"Lined them up like concentration-camp victims," he added, rising to his feet as the student-council rep with the portable microphone ran toward him.

"Sir," Sue Brennan began, "if you are referring to the HPV vaccine—"

"Principal Crowder, why did you give it to them?" a woman up front called out, voice shaking. "I'm not against shots, but this isn't like the measles. My daughters can't catch HPV in school. Why did you make it mandatory, given all the risks?"

"Mrs. Dunn," Crowder said, stepping forward quickly, "the vaccine was not mandatory. But HPV *is* a virus. No, you can't catch it from a doorknob, but—"

"Are you going to allow sex in the halls next?" someone shouted. "Because that's the only way they could catch it at school."

Dripping with sweat now, the mounting anxiety in the gym crackling loudly in Tom's ears, Tom shifted a few feet, hoping for more space, more room to breathe.

It was an odd thing, to disagree with everything everyone was saying but at the same time share the dread behind it.

"When are you going to admit we're likely dealing with a hot-lot situation here?" It was Dave Hurwich again, shouting and waving papers in his hand. "You've been playing Russian roulette with our daughters!"

"Sir, if you're referring to rumors that there may have been a bad batch of the HPV vaccine, that's highly unlikely," Sue Brennan replied, her voice just starting to break as she tried to be heard. "Vaccine lots contain thousands of doses. If that were the problem, we'd be facing a citywide or even regional crisis."

Hot lot, bad batches—this was the first Tom had heard about any of it. He felt negligent, wondered if he should at least have been reading up on all this instead of just waiting for someone to tell him what went wrong.

"I wonder what guys like Dave Hurwich did before the Internet," Kit whispered, rubbing the back of her neck, the peacock-feather tattoo flaring. "Don't you sometimes wish you could have a school without parents?"

Tom looked at her and she seemed to catch herself, her eyebrows lifting in mild alarm. "I mean parents like that," she added, nodding toward the rising noise up front.

"Why are we even talking about the vaccine?" a woman shouted. "We know the Court girl didn't get it. That's all been a costly distraction."

There was a low roar of approval from all corners of the gym.

"That's true," Sue Brennan began, her voice nearly drowned out by the noise. "Kimberly Court did not receive the vaccine. Due to a yeast allergy, she—"

"The Court girl's the one speaking the truth here," the same woman interrupted. "Didn't you hear her video?"

"Are you a reporter?" a male voice barked from somewhere. "I've never seen you before!"

The woman stood now, and Tom recognized her: Mary Lu, Bailey's mother. A member of the Dryden Land Trust, of Energy

Watch, of Safe Dryden. Tom had signed dozens of her petitions, had once even let her sucker him into a phone bank about pesticide drift.

"My daughter attends this school," Mary Lu was shouting at the man, voice breaking. "And I have as much right as you to—"

Dozens of voices reared up across the gym, shouts and yeas and boos.

"Can we please keep some kind of order here, please?" Crowder was saying, another screech from the sound system as he tried to drag the microphone stand to himself.

A few yards away from Tom, Carl Brophy, the physics teacher, waved his hand vigorously until the student-council kid found him with the microphone.

"Excuse me," he rasped. "What about the obvious explanation? That this isn't something coming from outside but from inside these girls' heads?"

"Hear, hear," an exhausted-looking man in front agreed loudly but somehow wearily from his seat. "As a doctor, I'm pretty skeptical of any epidemiological event that affects only girls—"

A billow of hisses, claps, and shouts swept through the gym.

Tom glanced over Kit's shoulder but could no longer see Lara Bishop.

"It only affects girls because they were the ones shot up with poison," Dave Hurwich said, face surging with blood.

"—and from what I've heard, the affected girls have troubled home lives," the doctor continued. "Girls without fathers in their lives, broken homes. Emotional issues."

A great ribbon of noise seemed to unfurl across the gym, and in the row closest to Tom, a woman leaped to her feet.

"What does that have to do with my Tricia?" she said, nearly bounding forward, looking like she wanted to shake the doctor, any of them, by the lapels. "Until yesterday, she was always a happy, normal girl!"

"Mrs. Lawson—" Principal Crowder tried, stepping toward her.

"Ma'am," the doctor said, "I don't know your daughter, but do *you*?"

More shouts and jeers.

"How does a divorce or whatever explain why her head turned to one side so far I thought it might spin," Mrs. Lawson cried out, her voice splintering. "She said it felt like her skin was burning off. I wanted to call a priest."

She snatched the microphone from the white-faced student-council rep and turned to the audience.

"Tricia hasn't had any trauma," she announced, seemingly to everyone, the microphone piercing with feedback. "She's a varsity athlete. She's a beautiful girl. She never did anything wrong."

"Jaymie was just happy, going along," Dave Hurwich said, rising beside her, voice breaking, touching the woman's shoulder gently. "She was as happy as can be."

At just that moment, there was a loud snap from one of the high windows: its rusty prop rod had slipped loose.

Suddenly, a spray of rainwater shot forth and landed, sizzling, on the audio speakers, which fizzled and crackled.

"Be careful!" Tom called out as several sparks flew, a group of parents jumping back.

The room burst into a new level of noise and confusion, the speakers popping and squealing, a sense of cascading panic.

The superintendent hijacked the portable microphone from the student-council boy himself.

"Everyone stand away from the equipment," he said. "Can we all just try to stay on point here?"

"But you're not listening!" shouted Mary Lu. "This school district spends a king's ransom on refrigerating a goddamn ice rink, but when it comes to protecting our—"

"Mrs. Lu, we've received your e-mails and—"

"You keep talking about what might be *inside* the girls," she said, stepping forward, sneakers squeaking on the wet wood. "What about what's *inside* the school. In the walls. Under the floors."

Tom looked down at his feet, at the splintery shellacked floor. It didn't seem any more likely a cause than the vaccine, or at least not much more, but even he could feel the hysteria. All the things Georgia used to say. About this town, this rotting place.

"The school passed all prior air- and water-quality inspections," Sue Brennan said, her face looking slicker now under the lights.

"Isn't it true that the school is heated by those natural-gas wells just a few hundred feet away?" Mary said, shouting even louder now, voice gaining confidence. "And that those tanks have leaked onto the football field? Some trees died. You walk through it and your ankles are covered with black powder. Wasn't the school told to dig up the affected soil?"

The stir was loud and immediate, the floorboards seeming to thrum, the gathered sense of gathering something.

"That powder is just common grass smut," called out Crowder, but without the microphone he could barely be heard, except for the word *smut*. "We sprayed—"

"It's important to note," Sue Brennan interrupted, talking over him rapidly, "just like infections, environmental causes do not discriminate. If the cause were environmental, we would see a wide range of people affected, not just these few girls."

The cavernous space seemed to explode with diffuse panic:

hollers and howls, countless arms raised above heads, fingers pointing like lightning bolts.

Up front, Julie Drew's mother was keeling as if about to swoon from the heat and terror.

"Get her some water!" someone called out, inciting a new spasm of shoving bodies and tumult.

More and more, Tom sensed that if he stayed a moment longer, he would start to feel it too. Feel this sense that nothing could protect his daughter from anything because everything was out to doom her. To annihilate her.

Looking over Kit's shiny head, he searched once more for Lara Bishop. She was definitely gone.

In her place, a pair of oblivious students were making out with long, ravenous stretches of tongue, as if none of these dangers could ever befall them. The cluelessness he wished for all of them, amid this.

Looking past them, through the crossbars of the bleachers, he saw a woman with a long dark braid who looked familiar.

It took a moment, but as she turned to talk to the man next to her, something in the stiffness and purpose of the way her body moved triggered his memory.

The woman in the parka. The one in the classroom questioning Deenie.

She wasn't wearing the parka anymore, just a dark raincoat.

And the man she was talking to was a uniformed cop.

"Isn't it enough that our lake is forever polluted by who knows what sins of the past?" Mary Lu was shouting, her voice strong and searing.

But everything else fell away for Tom. Because it seemed suddenly, palpably clear that his daughter had been talking to the police that afternoon and didn't know it.

The woman and the cop started walking swiftly toward the back exit.

Placing his hand on Kit's shoulder—her body jumping from it—he moved past her and walked quickly toward the pair, disappearing behind the heavy exit doors.

"Hey," Tom called out. "Hey, stop!"

★   ★   ★

There was a thud from the school's east breezeway, something hitting the glass.

A light arced across the floor.

Eli walked slowly toward it, the same spot he and Brooke had stood a few hours ago.

That's where, she'd said, pointing to the bushes. *Right there.*

Outside, there was a blur of movement, the strobing of flashlights.

From the dim corridor, just before the breach into the breezeway, he peered through the glass.

Three figures in dark jackets, caps. Light blue plastic gloves like at the hospital.

One of them was lifting something off the ground with a stick. A bit of pink fabric, spattered with mud.

Another was holding a shovel, its tip grass-stained.

A camera flashed and Eli jumped back, as if they were looking for him.

And that made him think of something.

He couldn't be sure if he'd have thought of it sooner if he hadn't smoked with Skye, or if he wouldn't have thought of it at all.

Walking briskly now, he returned to the trophy case. The banquet picture.

The shaggy-haired kid next to him.

"You two are sporting quite the hockey flows," the photographer had said to them both. "You think you're Guy Lafleur or something?"

The forward from Star-of-the-Sea, Sean.

The one who worked with Deenie.

Sean. Sean Lurie.

★   ★   ★

The night air like a wet hand over his mouth, Tom pushed through the doors, caught sight of the woman and the uniformed cop walking purposefully ahead of him, across the parking lot.

Running now, the fierceness in his chest nearly took his breath away, reminded him of when the kids were little, those moments you'd realize how vulnerable they were. A decade ago, that visit to DC, he'd made Deenie hold his hand everywhere, made her walk on the inside of the sidewalk, her rampart against chaos, against pain.

"Stop!" he called out again, chest clutching.

Both of them swiveled around.

"What were you talking to my daughter about?" He panted, hand to chest.

"Excuse me," the woman said, blinking.

"My daughter, today. You locked her in a room." His voice sounded rough and unfamiliar to him.

She squinted, then appeared to recognize him. "Mr. Nash," she said, "I tried to tell you this afternoon, those were standard questions. The room was not locked."

The officer next to her stepped forward slightly, his hands at his waist.

"You didn't say you were a cop," Tom said. "That's what you are, isn't it?"

"Detective Kurtz," she said. "And I did identify myself. All we were doing was gathering information."

"What do you have to do with any of this?" Tom said. "It doesn't make sense."

"Sir, can you keep your voice down?" she said, but all he could see was the woman, the flat line of her mouth, and the way everything felt wet and close and she was not giving him anything.

"We're here to help you," she said, "all of you."

"How does interrogating my daughter help anybody?" He couldn't stop his voice from sounding loud, ragged. The way they were looking at him, standing so still it made him feel like he was lurching.

"We were not interrogating your daughter, Mr. Nash," she said. "Do you have a reason to believe we might be?"

"You *know* something," Tom insisted, not answering the question. "Why aren't you telling us what you—"

"Now I remember," the uniformed cop interrupted. "How are you, Mr. Nash?"

Tom pivoted. "What? Do I know you?"

Both of them so infuriatingly calm, their hands at their waists, their feet planted, watching him.

"I was there that time your wife called us," the cop said. "That fistfight between you and that fellow in the district parking lot."

The back doors to the school now rattling open and shut, Tom felt the push of people exiting, gusts of heat and wet insulation and rage, and his chest corded tight.

"Hope things are easier now," the cop added.

Tom stared at him, his glistening rain-cap cover and fogged glasses.

"That was a long time ago," Tom said, breathing carefully, "and that wasn't how it happened."

It wasn't a fistfight, or any kind of fight. There'd been some shoving, like you might see at a ball game, a barbecue, or a bar after one too many beers.

He couldn't believe the officer remembered.

Georgia, he never understood why she'd gotten so upset, that look on her face and crying. They hadn't even put cuffs on him.

And he hadn't known until now that she was the one who'd called the police.

"Mr. Nash," the detective said. "You should go home now, be with your daughter."

Later, he would try to understand what happened next, what tore through him, the words seeming to come from some hidden well inside him, bottomless and newly ruptured.

"Do you have a daughter? Did either of you ever have a daughter?" he said, his voice shredding. "Because if you did, you'd know why I have to ask you these questions, why I had to chase you out here, why I have to not care what you or anyone thinks. I have to do something, don't I?"

Moving closer and closer to her.

"I have to do it, raise her, protect her. And no one ever tells you what it means. To hurl your kid out into this world. And no one ever warns you about the real dangers. Not dangers like this."

His hand, his pointing finger, a hard jab, perilously close to the woman's chest before he stopped himself, the officer stepping forward fast.

Moving back, hands in the air, and saying, "Did you ever look out in that dark and fucked-up world out there and think, How do I let my daughter out into that? And how do I stop her? And the things you can't stop because you're . . . because—"

"Mr. Nash," the detective started, voice firm, arm out, but Tom

could barely hear her, people everywhere now, noise and confusion, and the car lights coming up, "don't make us—"

But both their radios began clicking then and the uniformed
cop whispered something in her ear.

From the edge of the parking lot, from the tall hedges that crept
along the breezeway, another officer emerged and headed toward
them carrying a plastic bag in either gloved hand, his face wet and
forearms streaked green.

"Mr. Nash," the detective said, moving to block his view, turning her eyes hard on the officers, "Mr. Nash, you need to leave..."

Her eyes suddenly avid, anxious, desperate.

15

Sean Lurie. Sean Lurie.

The sound of Eli's tires thumping the name.

Maybe it was the strange crystal dewiness in the air.

But probably it was because the streets were empty, carless, noiseless.

All the sound sucked out of the world.

He had that feeling he'd get, flying down the wing with the puck, and you know you can't look back, but someone's behind you, someone's catching up. You can tell by the sound of his skates shredding that ice.

And the quick double-tap of a stick, and someone's open and you have to decide: Do I turn my head or do I just send the puck over?

Except, in some way, he was both players. Part of him was charging ahead and the other part saying, *Don't miss it, don't miss it.*

From a half mile away, he could see the glow from the Pizza House sign.

The hardest-working 510 square feet in Dryden! read the cartoon bubble over the mustachioed man on the storefront sign, his chef's hat tall and tilting.

The whole window seemed to radiate orange.

Skidding to a halt out front, he looked inside.

A gum-chewing boy, face ablaze with acne, stared back at him from the carryout counter.

"Is Sean here?" Eli asked, walking inside, the bell ringing.

★   ★   ★

Driving home the quick way, skipping the lake, the sky like wine on wood, Tom turned the radio loud, Eli's clamorous hip-hop. Anything to make noise.

Listen, I'm not the bad guy here. That's what the man had said. Georgia's lover.

He'd said it, shoulders hunched into a hapless shrug, to Tom in the parking lot of the Community School District 17 building.

Tom in the car on the way to the hospital, Georgia next to him, her knees tucked against her chest, sobbing. *It couldn't be his, he's nothing at all.* As if that should make him feel better.

This man. The man with whom his wife spent all those hours at Seven Swallows Inn. The man with whom she'd been so careless that maybe she'd even gotten herself pregnant by him, despite her promises at the time (*It's not his. I swear to God*).

Tom couldn't even remember driving to Georgia's building, couldn't remember how long he'd waited before he saw the man.

The man who actually raised his briefcase in the air as if to say, *Who, me?*

In the face of that, who would not have done what Tom did, thrusting his arms out and shoving him, the briefcase falling, spinning like a top on the ice-gruffed concrete.

He could still picture Georgia tapping on the second-floor window, pounding maybe, mouthing, *Stop, stop.*

A shove back, another shove, the man slipping, his elbow cracking. The blood seeping through the arm of his coat, spider-webbing the ice.

Tom could hardly believe it when the police came.

Could hardly believe that the raging man with the scarlet face in the car's side mirror was him.

It wasn't him.

The uniformed officer who thought he'd remembered him was wrong.

That wasn't me.

Except it was.

Now, less than seven minutes from home, Tom saw it.

In front of him, the bar's sign winked: TUDGE'S PUB.

He turned the wheel, hard.

The air inside felt cool, artificial, the vague scent of Freon, wood soap, and popcorn. The sulfuric tug from the gold-foil can of Bar Keepers Friend just behind the tap handles.

He couldn't remember the last time he'd been in a bar, a true bar with creaking floors and varnished wood yellow with smoke, with glowing bottles of forgotten liquors (Haig & Haig Five Star, Ronrico rum, green Chartreuse) arrayed pipe-organ style, a long clouded mirror behind them.

Where friends meet, the cursive letters announced, half-mooned over the crested center where the cash register sat. Above it, a pair of hockey sticks crossed.

He'd forgotten all of it. The comforting feel of a nearly empty bar, the bartender's expectant eyes, the red vinyl stools like cherries, the soft black in the middle, where the bar itself met the back tables, the jukebox and its sizzling promise.

That great soft black, like lifting the bedcovers, inviting you in.

"Whiskey, on the rocks," he said, sliding onto a stool, even letting his fingers curl under the wood ridge, shellacked with oil, grime, pleasure.

It seemed only appropriate to order a real drink, even though he could scarcely remember what he liked and hoped it was this.

Why, he asked himself, taking his first biting sip, *did I ever stop going to bars?*

And just when he thought the relief couldn't be greater or more vivid, the jukebox hummed to life. A song he couldn't identify but that had surely been tattooed on his heart, something from twenty years ago, his college dorm room, a car at night with a girl, a sleeping porch.

"Ohh," he said, not realizing until he heard himself that he'd said it out loud.

Swiveling on his bar stool, he turned and saw a woman standing in front of the electric juke. And she was looking straight at him.

"Tom Nash," she said.

"Lara Bishop." He smiled.

★   ★   ★

All the lights from all the news trucks, it felt to Deenie like a Hollywood premiere.

The hospital's front steps were swarmed over with people, cameramen, women like the TV woman from the night before, panty hose and business-suited, waiting.

Dozens of bright-colored suits, the slick Action News and Eyewitness News seals on the cameras, all under the mounted lights, everything rotating, snapping, and flicking.

From a distance, it looked like one moving thing, like when you peer into a microscope. Like when her dad used to show her gliding bacteria, swaying filaments like ribbons. It made her stomach squirm but it was also oddly beautiful.

Exiting the bus with all the night-shift nurses and orderlies, Deenie had no plan, but something about the way no one spoke, their hands wrapped tightly around their travel mugs, told her no regular rules applied right now.

It gave her a sense she could do anything. No one was looking at her.

The hospital staff, heads down, moved quickly to the back entrance where two security guards stood, hands on belts like soldiers.

It felt as if a presidential helicopter might appear in the sky and land on the front steps.

Nothing had ever happened here, until it did.

"It hasn't started yet."

Deenie didn't see the woman until she was right next to her.

She was wearing a yellow raincoat and matching hat that shone under the parking lot lights. In her arms she held a large Tupperware container.

"Oh," Deenie said. "I'm not here for that."

"Do you know what this is?" the woman said, holding out the container, something orange settled at its bottom.

"No," Deenie said, trying to figure out if she knew the woman, her face dark under the hat brim.

"A fungus," the woman said, lifting it so Deenie could see. "It comes during warm, damp springs after hard winters."

Deenie squinted at it. It looked like the Tang her grandparents used to keep in the kitchen cupboard.

"I think maybe it's just rust," Deenie said.

"All rusts are parasites," the woman said, nodding. "They need a living host."

Deenie tugged at the wool of her jacket on her neck. "Where did you get it?"

"From the shore of the lake."

There was something scraping up Deenie's throat, a word, a sound.

"The lake water's in everything. So this," the woman said, gazing into the bottom of the container, "could be in all of us."

She looked back at Deenie, one long strand of rain sliding from the brim of her hat.

"But it's definitely in those girls," she said. "The girls at the school."

The woman lifted the container up in the air so the parking lot light hit it, making it glow.

Suspended in the liquid were a few grass blades, hovering. Sticking to them, the smallest of spores, or something.

"It affects the brain," the woman was saying.

It did look, to Deenie, like something.

But who could tell, with the mist-scattered light and the pearly sheen of the Tupperware.

"What does it do?" Deenie said. "If it's in you."

"Spasms, convulsions," she said. "Some people feel like they're burning inside."

The shimmering spores reminded her of the MagiQuarium she'd had as a kid, the dark wonders inside, the hatching and un-hatching. The spinning and seizing of dying things, a briny trail at the bottom of the tank. The sea monkeys that, Eli told her with horror, mate for days at a time. Stuck together, twisting as if trying to strangle each other.

Eyes fixed on them, Deenie felt her mouth go dry. *Inside. Inside a girl.*

"How . . . how does it affect the brain?"

"That's the next stage. Visual disturbances. Hallucinations. Seizures."

"Oh," Deenie said.

The woman turned the bright orb in her hands, catching the light so it looked almost on fire.

Then she said, "It makes you lose your mind."

★   ★   ★

"Your sister's not working tonight," Sean Lurie said from the back ovens, behind the warming station.

"I know," Eli said. "I'm not here to see her. I'm here for you."

"For me?" He grinned, pushing his hair off his brow. "Well, I'm working now, dude."

"Take a break," Eli said, glancing around at the deserted store, the barren warming shelf under the cone lamps.

Sean looked at him for what seemed like a long time.

It was almost as if he knew why Eli was there.

"Out back," Sean said, very quietly. "Meet me out in the back."

The alley had a dank cat smell, but the parking-lot light gave everything a sparkly look that Eli found hypnotic, like the rink after it'd been sheared to glass.

And the longer he stood there, the more he thought maybe the smell was coming from him, the salty tang of his hockey gear, which seemed to leach into his skin.

He waited three minutes until he realized Sean wasn't coming out.

"Dude," the ruddy kid at the counter said, "he's gone."

Running outside, Eli caught sight of Sean across the street, the blare of his red interscholastic jacket in front of a rusted Firebird.

Spotting Eli, Sean fumbled with his keys, which fell onto the street, then down the storm drain.

"You never were very fast," Eli said, slowing down to a stride. "You just knew how to hook and not get caught."

★　　★　　★

"I don't see what's funny about it," Lara Bishop said, wiping a slick of cream from the corner of her mouth.

"No, it's not funny," Tom said. "I just haven't seen a grown-up drink a white Russian since 1978. I think that was what my dad used to seduce the neighbor women."

"Well," Lara said, tilting her glass side to side, "I haven't had anything to drink in so long, I figured it'd be best to have something I'd never want two of."

"I know what you mean," Tom said.

"But it turns out," she continued, that whisper of a smile, "I was wrong."

Tom smiled, waving for the bartender. "Two more, please?"

He tried not to let his eyes fix on his phone, silent and gleaming on the bar top.

"Bad taste in drinks, bad taste in men," she said, winking.

"Bottoms up," Tom said, clinking his glass with hers.

They finished just as the second round arrived.

"So," Lara said, "did you stay till the bitter end?"

One of them had to bring it up eventually, though he was sorry for it. And then felt guilty for feeling sorry for it.

"Long past when I should have," he said, flicking his phone on the bar, like the pointer on a board game. Like spin the bottle.

"I figured I'd duck out," she said, looking at her own phone, "before Goody Osbourne took the stand."

Tom smiled, surprised. He wasn't sure what to say.

"And how's Deenie doing?"

"Well," Tom said, then added, "under the circumstances." Eyes back on his phone, he said, "Georgia would kill me if she knew I was here."

"Well," Lara said, tilting her head and leaning back a little. "She's not here, is she?"

"She is definitely not here," Tom admitted.

"Besides, look at me."

Somehow, he found himself taking it literally, his eyes resting on hers, her fingers touching her necklace delicately. In the dim bar light, he couldn't see the scar, but he could feel it. It was an odd sensation he couldn't quite name.

"And, anyway," she said, "it's good they're together."

"Who?"

"The girls. Gabby had me drop her at your place on the way to the meeting. I couldn't leave her at the house alone." She looked at him. "Didn't you know?"

"No," Tom said, a little embarrassed but also relieved for Deenie. "So."

And her smile, under the light of the peeling Tiffany, was so warm, so inviting.

"So," she repeated.

★   ★   ★

"So, tell me. Are you one of the girls?"

The woman was gaping at Deenie from under her trickling rain hat.

Deenie felt her head jerk. "No. No, I'm not."

"Are you sure?"

"I'm sure," Deenie said, wiping the mist from her eyes.

And it was then that she finally recognized the woman.

She had seen her many times at the public library, sitting in the stacks. Kids used to make fun of her, the way she'd tear off scraps of pink Post-its and mark pages of books no one had looked in for years.

Then one day she saw Jaymie Hurwich talking to the woman and someone told her it was Jaymie's mom, which couldn't be true, because Jaymie's mom lived in Florida, everyone knew. No one had ever seen her.

She was just piecing this all together when it began.

Tire thuds, a swirl of headlights from opposite directions, the long coil of reporters tightening around the neck of the hospital's stone steps.

With alarming swiftness, the woman fled Deenie's side, dashing across the parking lot, the Tupperware cradled in front of her, pressed against her slicker.

But Deenie didn't move.

Moving seemed unsafe, with her head muddled and her throat plugged with humid air and with whatever it was in that container, which felt, suddenly and powerfully, like the thing inside her.

A thing twitching, haired, squirming, fatal.

Before she could let those thoughts take hold, she heard a crackle of static in the distance, saw the pair of security guards bolting toward the front of the hospital, radios to their mouths.

Her eyes returned to the employee entrance. Unmanned.

It felt like it can in a dream sometimes, where you know the door is there just for you. Maybe it wasn't even there until you needed it.

Once inside, the doors shushing behind her, Deenie found herself in some white corner of the hospital she didn't know.

Briskly, she walked through a series of random rooms, one with laundry bins, another with fleets of flower vases on long racks, a tangle of brittle petals in each.

Soon enough she found the Critical Care sign, its long red arrow stretched along the wall.

She walked with purpose, head down, and it was easy because there were jumbles of people everywhere, everything rolling, the clicking casters of IV stands, gurneys, trolleys.

Once, she caught sight of a girl she recognized, a freshman abandoned in a wheelchair, her head dropping to her chest then jerking up again.

The girl's hand was in her mouth, like she was trying to swallow her fist. Lise always could do it, her bones soft like a baby's.

Another corner and everything started to look familiar. The cartoon Band-Aid figure on the bulletin board, the big red lips on the *Shhh . . . Silent Hospitals Help Healing* sign. And posters with dire warnings.

> *It May Be a Spider Bite.*
> *Would You Put Her at Risk?*
> *You Don't Have to Be Next.*

All the posters she must have passed on Tuesday without noticing. Now they felt pointed, urgent, damning.

Turning the last corner, she heard the radio first.

Another security guard, his back to Deenie, stood at the nurses' station talking to a woman with hair hoisted back into a large clip, hand clenched at her side, her face kneaded red.

It was Mrs. Daniels, forty feet away, and no place to hide.

Head turning slightly, her eyes rested directly on Deenie.

For a split second, Deenie thought the guard would turn his head to follow Mrs. Daniels's gaze.

But then Mrs. Daniels's mouth opened, and she was saying something to him.

The guard started nodding.

And Mrs. Daniels kept talking, sliding her phone into the pocket of her coat.

It was like she knew Deenie was there.

Knew and was letting it happen.

"You can't!"

It was Lise's grandmother, standing in front of a room, an empty plastic water bottle clutched to her chest.

The collar of her shirt was gray, her neat white hair now flat like a wet otter's. Deenie wondered if she had even left the hospital since Tuesday. Her eyes, her skin had the look of someone who had not seen the sun in a long time.

"You can't!" she said again.

Deenie didn't say anything, only nodded, walking past her, into the blue swallow of the room.

★   ★   ★

The swaying way she'd been sitting, the bloom on her face, it had been Tom's idea to make sure Lara got home safely, driving behind her through the black fen of Binnorie Woods.

Walking her to her front door, he'd hit his head on a porch eave, and now he was on her living-room sofa, ice pack to his forehead, water tickling his face.

"But Gabby's dad liked to drink it with peppermint," Lara said, grabbing for a sofa cushion. "Rumple Minze. Which isn't a white Russian anymore. Do you know what it is? A cocaine lady."

"Never a subtle fellow, that ex of yours."

Leaning back, she looked at him, the whisper of a smile amplifying.

"You know, he always liked you."

"Charlie?"

As surprised as he was to find himself sitting, so closely, with Lara Bishop on her sofa in her cozy matchbox of a house, he was even more surprised to watch as, scar blazing up her neck, she began reminiscing about the man who'd put it there.

"Yeah." Then she smiled a little, as if remembering something. Shook her head. "But he always thought you were a secret tomcat."

"What?"

"Well, he said it wouldn't surprise him. He saw you once with somebody. Or something."

"No," Tom said, setting the ice pack down. "He didn't."

She looked at him.

"But that was the thing about him," she said, after a pause. "That was always the thing."

He had no idea what she meant, but he was glad she'd changed the subject.

She tucked her legs under herself, one shoe falling to the floor, her face newly grave.

"You think I'm a terrible mother, right?" she said.

"God, no," he blurted. "What are you talking about?"

"It's not that I'm not terrified," she said. "Just not about those things."

"I know," he said, though again he wasn't sure he did.

"At the hospital, Gabby said they kept asking her about drugs," Lara said, "and she said, 'Mom, like I would ever do *that* stuff.' I was so relieved I almost burst into tears." She paused. "I mean, I *loved* drugs at her age."

She looked at him expectantly, but his thoughts had sling-shotted. "Who asked her about drugs? The doctors? Lara, did the police talk to her?"

Lara nodded. "There was someone from the police there. What did they call her? Public health and safety liaison? But the girls just kept coming in. The looks on their faces."

His thoughts blurred back to earlier in the day, to watching the girls in line at the nurse's office. The eerie feeling of something unstoppable, feeding on itself.

"She hated being back in that hospital. All this is making her crazy. I heard her up all night, pacing the house."

"I'm sure it's brought back a lot of bad stuff."

"It's funny," she said, "when you think there's a whole other kid you'd have had if you hadn't done all the things you did to them."

"But you didn't do anything to her," Tom said, leaning forward. "It wasn't you."

She smiled, a smile filled with things he couldn't hold on to.

"You've protected her, you . . ." he started, but the words felt too heavy in his mouth and she didn't seem to be listening exactly, reaching down to the floor to seize the bottle of whatever they were drinking.

He couldn't help but notice the way her shirt pulled, the delicate skin there, a bristle of black lace.

"You know what else is funny?" she said, pouring a little into her glass. "Last week I was worried about what she was up to with boys. Doesn't that seem silly now?"

"No. *That* is something that never feels silly."

She covered her face, embarrassed. "Can I tell you? I found something on her phone."

He felt himself leaning forward.

"I can't believe I'm telling you."

"What?" he said. "Sext—sexts?" The word fumbled from his mouth and she laughed, poking him with her bare foot.

It shouldn't have been funny, but it was because it didn't feel remotely possible. Gabby with her serious face and her cool-girl acumen, her silver-sprayed cello case and her meant-for-college-guys gravitas.

"Sort of," she said, looking at him from behind the hand still covering her blushing face. "A picture. Of her in her underwear."

Tom felt himself go red now. "Well, girls, they . . ."

"I never saw such lingerie. The most alarming purple thong. You couldn't see her face, so I told myself, That's not her. But if it wasn't her, why was it on her phone?"

"I don't know," Tom said, and he couldn't quite separate out all the complicated feelings, the uncomfortable idea of Gabby in a thong, even the word *thong* in the context of a friend of his daughter's.

And then here, Lara Bishop, the top button of her blouse having slid open and the way her body kept squirming girlishly and the way her face and neck bloomed with drunkenness. The way it made that scar look even darker, more striking, a red plume, and he wanted more than anything to touch it.

His head thick and mazy with whiskey and liquors unknown, he couldn't stop himself, reaching toward her. She nearly jumped but didn't stop him, her eyes wide and puzzled and not stopping him.

He put his fingers to it, the scar. Touched the soft fold, which felt warm, like a pulse point, like he was somehow touching her heart, or his.

"I'm sorry," he said, starting to pull his hand back but then feeling her hand grip his wrist, holding it in place.

There was a long, puzzling moment when neither spoke.

"Everyone's sorry," she said, smiling faintly. "The whole world's sorry."

And he could feel the goose bumps on her skin and wondered when was the last time he'd felt that.

Charlie Bishop had been right about something. Tom had had chances, many chances. There were women, other teachers, even a friend of Georgia's who sometimes called after she'd been drinking, told him how lonely she was and that she knew he was too. But he'd never done anything about it.

Hell, he'd had a hundred chances, but he'd never done what Georgia had done. Even though he bet he'd had twice the opportunity.

A few kisses, sure. One with the guidance counselor behind the sugar maple at the faculty picnic, high on foamy keg beer. Five years later, he could still taste the caramel malt on her tongue.

But he'd always stopped himself, and Georgia hadn't. She just did what she wanted and now she treated him, all of them, like they were the blight. That house, its residents, they were the thing. The affliction. The scourge.

"Your eyes," Lara Bishop was saying to him, her skin like a living thing, "are so sad."

* * *

It was like a doll, a rubber doll, or a vinyl one puffed with air.

Deenie couldn't see most of Lise's face, directed toward the window.

Only the round slope of the cheek.

A bulbous head, the sloping brow of a baby or a cartoon character.

Deep down, she must have thought Lise would look like Lise

again, or at least like the girl from the other day everyone said was Lise. The Lise with the dent in the center of her forehead.

But this wasn't either girl, or any girl.

She moved closer, because she could. Because this wasn't Lise. Clearly Lise had been moved to another room, or had left the hospital entirely. And been replaced with this.

Or maybe was in the bathroom, in her monkey pajamas, and would pop out any second and say, *Here I am, Deenie. Here I am.*

Like her outgoing voice-mail message:

"It's Lise! . . . Leave me a message or I'll *die!*"

As it was, without seeing her face, without Lise's strawberry-cream skin and marble-blue eyes and the flash of her teeth laughing—well, it looked less like Lise than anyone, or anything, in the world.

Except.

Except, getting closer, there was the scent of something. Beneath the tubes and wires and the pulp of her ruined face, she caught a scent as distinctive as a thumbprint. A smell of Lise that Deenie couldn't name or define but that was Lise as sure as that butter curl of an ear.

"Lise," Deenie heard herself crying out.

And slowly, slowly, she made her way around the bed.

If I can see her face, she thought, *I will know. I will know something.*

The head so round and enormous, purpled through like the largest birthmark ever, spreading from the center of her face up to her scalp.

The scalp half shorn, tiny baby hairs like soft chick feathers blowing, the gusting air from all the machines.

And, finally, reaching the far side of the bed, too dark to see anything at first, but then something glowing there.

Lise's eyes, open.

Open and wandering, like those plastic wiggly eyes on puppets. Her mouth a wet rag. A tube snaking in and a violet lattice around it and the puff of her lower cheeks, and it was like something was inside the cavity. Or many things, packed tightly there, like a toy stuffed with sawdust.

It reminded Deenie of the girl Skye had told them about.

The one with the mouth filled with cinders, eggshell pieces, the tiny bones of animals. The things no one would want but that were inside of her.

That girl must have swallowed them, all of them, Deenie realized, her head light with the revelation. She'd swallowed all of them. And now they were hers.

Deenie heard a noise, a loud noise, a loud *oooh,* which had come from her own mouth, from somewhere inside her.

Because there was Lise, one wet eye suddenly on Deenie, its lid pitching higher, as if stuck there.

And Deenie's own mouth opening, as if a cinder would fall from it, moss clumps, leaf smut, grass blades powdered with spores.

"I didn't mean to, Lise," she said. "Don't be angry. I didn't mean it."

★　★　★

"And you think it was me?" Sean said, his face grimy from bending over the storm drain, holding up his phone for the light. "With Lise Daniels?"

"I don't know," Eli said, sitting on the curb. "We look a little alike, I guess. And you asked me about her once."

"Why do you care?" Sean said, sitting beside Eli, kicking his car tire ruefully.

"If people think it was me with her..." But Eli didn't know how to finish the sentence. The truth was, he wasn't sure why he cared, but the knot in his chest felt tighter and tighter. The sense he was circling something, drilling in.

Sean sighed, leaning back, his elbows on the sidewalk.

"We didn't . . . we were just messing around. We didn't fuck."

Eli nodded. He couldn't say he'd never thought of Lise like that. But he'd always pushed it away. There were other girls. Girls his sister didn't share clothes with, tell secrets to, keep secrets for.

"I'd see her around. I tried asking her out, but her mom's not cool. She wouldn't let her out of her sight. Dropped her off at school, picked her up. So I asked her if I could come before school and we could hang out. She was afraid someone would see us. We found this place behind these big bushes."

"People saw you anyway," Eli said.

"We didn't fuck," Sean said again. "We just messed around. She'd never done anything. She kept laughing and covering her face."

He paused, a far-off look in his eyes.

"It was funny," he said. "She wasn't like I thought. She was so . . . young." He said the last word softly, confusion on his face.

Eli didn't say anything. Picking up a shorn branch end, he poked into the grate beneath him, spotting the glint of Sean's car keys.

"Anyway, it was only a few times. Last week, I guess, and Tuesday. Was that the day she got sick?"

"Yeah."

"She seemed fine," Sean said, shaking his head. "There was nothing wrong with her."

Eli nodded.

"Except," Sean said, scratching the back of his neck. "This weird thing happened."

★ ★ ★

"This way," Lara whispered.

His elbow caught a hard corner as they stumbled to her bedroom.

The crisp smell of night air and pine needles, and the quilt? comforter? on the bed was the softest thing he'd ever felt.

There was the crashing sound, a water pitcher, and a muffled laugh and her hands on his belt buckle.

The sinking sense of future regret hurtled away the instant he saw her tug off her shirt with such vigor a button popped, skittering across the floor.

His hand seemed to hit the warm flesh of her stomach the minute the sound came, the bray of guitar so loud he thought a band had kicked up in the living room.

"My kids," he blurted.

"What?" she whispered, hand on the tongue of his belt.

"My phone," he said. "It's for me."

★ ★ ★

"I didn't mean it," Deenie said, looking down at her hands, not looking at Lise, that open eye. "But you didn't like him, exactly. He wasn't your boyfriend."

She kept starting to say Sean Lurie's name, but it only came out as a lispy hiss.

"And it was after work and we were in his car. I don't know why I did it, Lise. But I just had to."

Which was true. In his car, all the breathing and hands and power of it. Like her body had known something her head never would. Nothing could have stopped her.

Not even knowing Sean was the boy who'd taken off Lise's tights the week before.

And guess who it is, Deenie? That's what Lise had said at the lake, wriggling closer, her fingers over her mouth. *Guess who the guy is. It's Sean. Sean Lurie.*

Waving the milfoil under her chin, throwing her head back, telling her the thing Sean had done to her and how it made her feel.

Hearing it made something inside Deenie twitch, her whole body wanting to squirm. Her face red and hot, like watching a movie with her dad and suddenly there's a scene you don't want to watch with your dad.

That night, though, trying to sleep, all she could think about was how it might feel to have Sean Lurie put his hands there, his mouth.

Watching him at the pizza ovens Monday night, all she could think of was what Lise had told her.

When he offered to drive her home, it felt like it was meant to be.

She never thought of Lise once.

So she didn't meet Lise at her locker the next morning.

In fact, the next time Deenie saw her, Lise was jumping from her desk chair, falling to the floor.

And now here Lise was, or the thing that had been Lise, lying under the cage of wires.

"I'm sorry," Deenie said. "For everything. It's all my fault."

Which couldn't be true, but felt utterly true.

And that's when she saw it. The way Lise's eye gaped, an oily egg rolling.

"Lise?" Deenie said, nearly yelped.

And a sound coming, like a high whistle.

She's saying something, Deenie thought, *inside.*

Like that comic book Eli loved as a kid, *The Count of Monte Cristo,* the corpse with living eyes.

His face is like marble, Eli would read aloud, scaring her, *but from it burned a rage that could not be contained.*

Lithe and cherry-lipped, the real Lise was locked inside this dented and bloated thing, this blow-up toy, but what she was saying inside was *You, you, you.*

And now here she was, her right eye large and gaping and staring at her.

As if she were saying, *Deenie, how could you? He wasn't my boyfriend, but he was mine. I told you and then you had to have him too. And now look what happened. What you've done.*

★ ★ ★

Eli couldn't figure out what it all meant, but he knew it meant something.

"All the sudden she got really nervous," Sean explained. "She said she lost her backpack. No, wait. She said she thought someone took it."

Listening, thinking, Eli felt the branch hit something inside the street grate, heard a jingle.

"She kept saying, *Someone's watching, I know it.* Finally, she just jumped up. She didn't have time to put her tights back on. She jumped up like she saw a ghost."

Eli felt for the key ring, caught it with the branch.

"You..." Sean said, watching Eli delicately lift the key ring up through the iron spokes, "you don't think it has anything to do with what...happened to her? To all of them?"

"I don't know," Eli said, the keys hanging from the twig. "Did you take them all out by the bushes?"

"No," Sean said, looking suddenly very tired, shaking his head. "I didn't."

With a clean move, like the faintest of wrist shots, Eli flicked the branch back over the grate, Sean's keys falling soundlessly down the bottomless sewer.

Sean started to say something but stopped.

"Sorry," Eli said, then rose to his feet and began walking away.

"Hey," Sean called out. "By the way, how's your sister? She's okay, right?"

"Yeah, she's fine."

"I've been texting her, but she won't text me back."

Eli stopped and looked at him. "Why are you texting my sister?"

Sean stood, shaking his head, not looking at Eli. "I heard she wasn't working this weekend. Just wondering."

Eli looked at him. Slowly nodded.

★ ★ ★

"You have to leave," Lise's grandmother rasped from the doorway. "They're coming. People are coming."

"I am," Deenie said, walking out. "I'm sorry. But she . . . she was looking at me."

"I know you love our Lise," she said, not even seeming to hear Deenie. "But things have gotten bad today."

"Bad?"

"That other girl upset her!" she whispered, holding Deenie's arm. "I could just tell. A grandmother knows."

"What other girl?"

"The one who came earlier."

"Gabby?" Deenie asked. "She didn't tell me she—"

"No, some girl with hair white as a witch," she said. "She was in there and we didn't even know how she got in."

Deenie felt her flesh tingle.

"And when she came out, she was crying, like an animal. Her whole body. Have you ever seen a snake sidewinding? That's what it looked like."

Deenie didn't say anything, just nodded. She didn't know what it was about, but she knew it was very wrong.

Lise's grandmother leaned closer, so close Deenie could smell her medicinal moisturizer.

"Who was she?" she asked. "Tell me."

"Her name is Skye," Deenie said. "And you shouldn't let her back in."

★   ★   ★

No one was home and the house had that spooky feel it always had when the weather changed suddenly. The squeaking and wheezing of floorboards, the walls inhaling and exhaling like a sleeping giant.

Eli read Deenie's note on the kitchen table, the wild lope of her handwriting.

Turning on the TV loud, he collapsed on the sofa.

He was trying to think through everything, but before he knew it, he was asleep.

It couldn't have been more than ten minutes, but everything felt different when he woke up, with a jolt. A noise in the house, in the basement.

It must have been a dream, but it wasn't like any dream he'd had, at least not since he was a kid when he'd run a high fever and go to all kinds of places in his head—the South Pole, Madripoor, Mutant Town, as vivid as comics, as life, but more so—and wake up feeling as though he finally understood everything.

In the dream, whatever it was, he was still on the couch,

but Skye Osbourne was with him, her arms hidden in her long sweater, which was like tendrils, and the light came and he could see through it to her breasts, her nipples like gold coins.

One hand, tiny and clawed, suddenly appeared through the bottom of her sleeve and she was holding his phone, as though it had never been lost.

Climbing on top of him, she wrapped her legs tight, waving his phone in front of his face, the picture there. The faceless girl with the purple nails and purple panties.

"You should delete it," she said, craning her neck down, her breasts swinging. He'd never known her breasts were so large. "What if she dies? Then she's on your phone forever."

"Who? Who's the girl? Is it—"

"Maybe it's your fault," she said. "The camera stole her soul."

Her hair falling onto his face as she arched her neck, as she looked at the photo glimmering in her own hand.

"Look," she said. "You can see her heart."

16

When's the next bus?" Deenie asked a pair of hospital employees smoking out back. "I'm in a hurry."

"Where you going, honey?" one asked, a lady with pouched eyes and a lab coat under her puffer.

"Over by the high school."

"I'm leaving. I'll take you," she said, throwing her cigarette to the ground.

On the way, the woman talked without stopping.

She told Deenie how the pharmacy had never had a day like this, the dispenser beeping ceaselessly, the premixed IVs gone by four o'clock, a tech fainting and splitting her scalp, four girls an hour admitted at first, double that by the time she left.

"I saw you and I thought, *Not another one.* All day, each of you acting crazier than the last."

"I was visiting a friend."

Mind racing, somersaulting, Deenie was trying to piece it all together: Why was Skye visiting Lise? What did it all mean?

The woman glanced over at her in a way that made Deenie's eye twitch.

"A girl came in to visit her sister, and ten minutes later she was spinning around on the floor. We can't get this tiger by the tail. Your eye always do that?"

"I'm okay," Deenie said. "What happened at the press conference?"

The woman kept looking at her, "They canceled it," she said. "Everything's changed."

"What do you mean? What happened?" Deenie felt her eye throbbing, wanted to put her finger to it, make it stop.

"Because of the police investigation."

"What?"

"They found something in the girl's locker. The first girl."

Deenie thought of the people digging through Lise's locker, their gloved hands on Lise's gym uniform, her thermos, her binder.

"What did they find?"

"Look, I can't talk about it," the woman said, eyes returning to the road. "They made us sign all these papers."

The feeling came over Deenie like a rush of water to the mouth, rimy and overflowing.

Please tell me, she tried to say, but her mouth wouldn't do what it was supposed to, and the woman looked at her as if deciding something.

"I don't really know, honey," she said. "But I heard they think someone gave her something that made her sick. Very sick."

Deenie sat for a moment, thinking.

"Like a roofie?" she asked, remembering from health class.

"No. We check for that right away."

"So...so that's what happened to everyone? To the other girls too?"

"No. Their tox screens came back negative."

"But that doesn't make any sense," Deenie said, twitching, the vein at her temple like a wriggling worm, her hand jerking up, trying to hide it. "It can't be just Lise."

At that moment, the road rose and the school loomed on the horizon.

"You can stop right here," Deenie said, pointing hurriedly to the nearest corner.

"I can't leave you," the woman said, squinting out the window, the empty parking lot. "It's not safe."

Deenie looked at her. Then it was like she'd touched a frayed plug. She felt something like sparks, her head jerking against the car window.

She looked at her hands, which tingled.

"Honey, you . . ." the woman started, her eyes leaping to Deenie.

"My dad teaches here. He's inside waiting for me," Deenie said, gritting her teeth to make the shaking stop, which only made it worse. She reached for the door handle. "Stop the car. Let me out now, please."

The woman slowed the car to a stop, looking down the empty street.

"I don't see anyone . . ." she began, but before she could say more, Deenie felt her shoulders vault forward, jaw percussing.

Swinging open the door, she jumped out of the car. And then she ran.

★　★　★

It was a little click-click sound and seemed to be coming from below.

Standing at the top of the basement stairs, Eli wondered if it was the dryer, or if it was a raccoon, like once before. For months after, Deenie wouldn't go down there without singing loudly or raking one of Eli's old hockey sticks across the rail.

"Deenie?" Eli called out. "Dad?"

"No," a voice came, throaty, cautious.

Three steps down, he stopped.

She was sitting on the Ping-Pong table, purple rain boots dangling off the edge.

At first he could barely see her face, long hair catching the light and her face tucked behind it.

But then she turned, and he saw her eyes widen, heard the smallest gasp.

"Gabby," he said, walking down the remaining steps.

"I'm sorry for coming in," she said quickly. "Did I scare you?"

"No," he said. "No problem."

"It was raining," she added. Under the lightbulb, her hair glistened from within its deep pockets. All the girls loved Gabby's hair, but Eli always thought it looked so heavy, so complicated, like one of those leathery cocoons you stare into at the science center.

"I had a key from before," she said.

"Good thing," he said. "I was wondering what happened."

"What do you mean?" she said, clasping her phone between her palms.

"To you and Deenie. Where is she?"

Gabby just looked at him.

"Deenie left a note that she was with you," Eli said, walking over to the Ping-Pong table.

She said something, but with her voice so soft and the furnace kicking up, he couldn't hear, so he moved closer.

"No. I was just trying to find her," she said, almost leaning back from him, as if he were standing too close. "I came here to find her. I really need to see her."

There was the smell on her of something, something in her hair that reminded him of his dad's classroom.

He must have made some small gesture because she said, "They put glue in, for the EEG."

"No, I—" he began.

"I can't get it out," she said, touching it. "Witch hazel, aspirin crushed in water, nail polish remover. I tried everything. Maybe I'll just cut it all off."

"Don't cut it off," he said, smiling.

She didn't say anything, looking down at her phone. He was a little sick, thinking of Gabby in the house while he was having that dream. Skye and her golden nipples and grinding hips.

"I guess they're all still at the meeting at the school," he said, eager to make conversation, to get the noise out of his head. "Things were crazy over there. I saw them digging around outside."

Her eyes lifted. "Saw who?"

Eli shrugged. "I don't know." He thought about it. The dark coats and the blue plastic gloves. The one with a rain cover stretching over his hat brim. "The cops, I think." And then, fitting pieces together in his head, he added, "By the breezeway. By those big bushes. I guess it had to do with Lise being back there."

"What do you mean?" Her eyes back down on her phone.

He didn't want to tell her, but he was trying to see what the pieces meant.

"Lise," he said, his brain churning, attempting to make sense of it. "She was back there. With a guy. Screwing around, I don't know. What I don't get is why the police . . ."

He stopped.

The look on her face, the way it seemed to collapse upon itself, to wither inside that cocoon of hair. He was the biggest jerk in the world. No one wanted to hear stuff like that about her friend.

"Wait, stop," she said, shaking her head so forcefully it startled him. "I don't understand. Why are you telling me?"

"I'm sorry," he said. What if she was having another seizure, or whatever that thing was? "I shouldn't have said anything. I only found out because there was a mistake. People thought it was me back there with Lise. People were saying it was me."

Her head shot up.

"What?"

"But it wasn't me. I'd never—well, it wasn't me."

"It *was* you," she said, looking at him, eyes black and obscure.

"You heard that too, huh?" He hoped Deenie hadn't. "No way, ever. This guy just looks like me, sort of. This guy, Sean, from the Pizza House."

"It *was* you," she repeated, louder now.

"No," he said, looking at her. "But it doesn't matter. I'm sure it has nothing to do with all this. I'm sure—"

And something seemed to snap hard in her face, like a rubber band stretched too far.

"Oh, Eli, no. Look what happened, and now," she said, her voice going loose, like someone slipping under anesthesia, like when he watched his teammate get his arm rebroken after a game. "Lise. Lise is going to die."

"Hey," he said, gently. "No, she's not."

Her hands gripped the table beneath her.

"She is. She is."

He put his hand on her arm, hot to the touch.

She breathed in fast, shuddering.

"I better go," she said, pressing her body against him for the most fleeting moment, so close he could feel the swell of her breasts, the heat of her breath on his neck.

Before he could say anything, she slid off the table, her jacket dragging behind her as she raced up the stairs.

"Hey," he called out. "How..."

But she was gone.

Stuck with the landline, it took him several minutes and a few tries to figure out his dad's cell number.

He could hear Gabby on the front porch, talking into her phone.

After six long rings, his dad answered, "Deenie?" His voice breathless and sharp.

"Dad," Eli said. "Deenie's not here. I don't know where she is."

"She and Gabby must have gone out." It sounded like his dad was even panting a little.

"No, Gabby's here, Dad. She's been waiting for her. She doesn't know where Deenie is either."

There was a pause. Eli thought he heard music in the background.

"Dad," he asked, "where are *you?*"

"Okay, I'm going to find her. I'm going to look for her. I'll call you."

*   *   *

Trying to buckle his half-undone belt with one hand, Tom called Deenie. There was no answer.

On the edge of the bed, Lara was talking to Gabby on her own phone. A lock of hair drooping forward, she spoke in low mothering tones.

"I'm not mad at you, Gabby, but...okay, it's okay..."

Walking into the hallway, he decided to call Eli back.

Just as his call went through, almost in the same instant, he heard the electronic bleat of a ringtone from another room.

Then came the recognition. That ringtone—the shriek of a goal horn. It was Eli's phone. In the Bishop house.

Following the sound, he stopped at the doorway to what had to be Gabby's room.

He could feel Lara behind him now. "What the...?"

"That's Eli's phone. Why would..."

Lara's eyes darted around the room. In seconds, she was kneeling over Gabby's laundry hamper, hands rustling through the clothes.

When she rose with Eli's familiar Calgary-red phone in her hand, Tom hung up.

"I don't know," she said, shaking her head.

For several minutes, they stood over the hamper, pushing buttons on the phone, popping the dying battery in and out. It didn't matter. The screen was blank. No call history other than Tom's own call moments before, no contacts, no texts. The phone was immaculate.

★   ★   ★

There wasn't any time to think, just a few minutes, Deenie walking swiftly, a block over to Revello Way.

For a panicked moment, Deenie wasn't sure she'd recognize it. She'd only been to Skye's house a few times, and never inside.

But then she spotted the glint of the gold-rimmed sundial on the front lawn.

It was a ranch house, a rambling one that hooked over a sharp incline on one side. There was the whispery sound of chimes in every window—capiz, bamboo, glinting crystal—and the creaking of its eaves, heavy with old leaves.

It felt too late to knock on the door, but it didn't matter because she saw a light on in the garage.

Making her way up the drive, she caught a flash of white.

T-shirt, bare legs, and the distinct white flare of Skye's hair.

Her back to Deenie, she was completely still, shoulders bent.

Like a picture Deenie once saw of a white cobra, its hood spread.

Girls like Skye, she would never understand. Girls who got away with ditching school and never doing any homework, who could have twenty-six-year-old boyfriends and be able to explain what fisting was and why anyone would enjoy it and had aunts who gave them copies of the *Kama Sutra* and who made everything seem easy and adult and anyone who found it all confusing and maybe scary was just a kid, just a little kid.

Girls who, despite never having been your real friend at all, felt it was okay to visit your oldest friend's bedside and lurk there in that Skye way, like a living ghost, a cobra-hooded witch.

"Skye," Deenie called out softly, wet sneakers grinding up the gravel drive. "Skye."

But Skye didn't move or even flinch, shoulders bony under her thin shirt. Her head down.

Approaching, Deenie finally saw what Skye was standing in front of, a wet-wood hutch on stilts, its front traps open.

"Skye," she hissed, "it's Deenie."

But still her head wouldn't turn, her shoulders hunched, her white figure ghostlike, and a tiny noise of something chewing, gnawing.

"Skye?"

★   ★   ★

Through the window, Eli could see Gabby on the front porch.

At first, he thought she was still on the phone, but then he saw she was writing something in one of her notebooks, writing faster than he'd ever seen anyone write.

He walked through the house, his head starting to feel things again, and badly. Everything seemed to be coming undone, like the ceiling corners, swollen with rain. *The house,* his mom used to say, *is weeping.*

Passing headlights flashed across the front windows and he looked out to the front porch to see Gabby was gone.

★   ★   ★

The drive back through Binnorie Woods seemed to take forever, twisting down one veiny road after another, while Tom tried to will himself sober. To reckon with the snarl in his head, which included a sneaking sense of relief.

He'd promised to bring Gabby back, had insisted Lara shouldn't drive. And now, the road doing odd, shimmery things, he was pretty sure he shouldn't be driving either.

"I know what it is," Lara had said as he was halfway out the door, still buttoning his shirt with one hand, the other hand crushed over his car keys.

"What?"

"Everything happening," she said, standing in the hard light of the entryway. Saying it quietly, barely a whisper.

He froze, waited.

"It's what we put in the ground," she said. "And in the walls. The lake, the air. And the vaccines we give them. The food, the water, the things we say, the things we do. All of it, straight into their sturdy little bodies. Because even if it isn't any of these things, it *could* be. Because all we do from the minute they're born is put them at risk."

He felt his keys cut into his fingers.

"We put them at risk just by having them," he blurted, not even knowing what he meant. Touched by her words, frightened by them. "And the hazards never stop."

She paused, looking at him. A chill on his neck, he felt as though she could see everything.

"Well," she said softly, her hand in her hair. "We're all at risk."

And she'd slipped back into the house, closing the door.

Now, in his car, he rolled down the windows all the way, tried to breathe. He couldn't really breathe.

He could still smell her on his shirt and hands and mouth, feel her mysterious energy. Warm and unsettling.

In the strangest way, it reminded him of Georgia.

This is why I don't drink, he thought, because a hundred things he'd shut in shoeboxes and hidden in closet tops cast themselves down again.

Like how he'd wanted to grind that guy's face into the icy parking lot.

How he'd called Georgia ugly names, said things in front of Deenie and Eli.

Once he'd even pointed out the guy to Eli at the grocery store. Said, *There he is, that's what your mother did it all for. That loser in the orange tie.*

And that other time. Opening all Georgia's dresser drawers, Deenie in the doorway, balling up his wife's lingerie, her panties, throwing them at Georgia. Wanting to stuff them in her mouth. Stopping himself. He stopped himself.

But that was a short period of time, a long time ago.

How do you get over it? he'd asked Lara Bishop before he left. *Over what happened to you?*

But she just smiled like it was a stupid question, or at least the wrong one.

★   ★   ★

The streak of her white T-shirt, the hunch of her back, head dipped low, the stillness of her.

"Skye," Deenie said, louder now, the smell of sawdust, ammonia, fur everywhere. "Skye, turn around."

And Skye's head turned slowly, as if she'd barely heard, earbuds dropping to her collarbones.

Her face cool and expressionless and so pale it was near translucent.

"Deenie," she said, her skinny arms inside the open door of the hutch, stroking something. A cherry-eyed rabbit with long ears.

"This is Crow Jane," she said. "Meet Crow Jane."

Deenie stopped short as Skye lifted the animal, its plush fur like the purple foot charm Deenie used to hang on her backpack when she was little.

"His mother tried to eat him," Skye said, fingering a pellet into the rabbit's mouth. "It happens sometimes. When they get scared or confused. Or by accident. Or if they think something's wrong with the baby."

"Why are you out here this late?" Deenie asked, even though she was the one out at midnight, in Skye's backyard.

Skye shrugged.

There was a smell that reminded her of the time the lawn mower sparked and burned up one side of the front lawn.

"What..." Deenie began, and it seemed to happen at that same second, the sharp twinge in Deenie's neck, her head bobbing, and Skye saying, "Are you okay, Deenie?"

Something in Skye's calm made her feel crazy, her neck and jaw throbbing.

"Why were you in Lise's hospital room?" Deenie asked, almost a bark. "What would you be doing there?"

Staring at her, Skye lifted the rabbit to her chest, rubbing its body.

"You've been there too, right?" she asked, her fingers nestled in the fur, stroking it with her thin fingers. "I guess the same as you."

"You were never friends with her," Deenie said, voice shaking now. "Not like me."

Something was shifting in Skye's eyes. "No one can be as close to anyone as you, is that it?"

"What does that mean?"

Skye didn't answer, taking Crow Jane by the cowl and setting her, a little roughly, back into the soggy hutch.

A wind gusted up and the smell, sooty and sweet, came strong from beyond the hutch.

"Were you burning something?" Deenie asked, the smell thick in her mouth.

Walking past the hutch, Deenie felt the ground soft with ash.

Skye shrugged. "My aunt does it. We have lots of weeds."

The school's bell tower chimed midnight, an ancient clang, heavy with rust and lime.

Both their heads turned.

That was when Deenie saw.

Through the dark of Skye's zigzagging backyard, the knotted brush, there it was. Its familiar gloomy limestone, veined with soot.

"You can see the school from here," Deenie said.

Something was coming together in her head, sharp fragments, thin as ice, assembling, sliding into place.

"Not really," Skye said. "Until they cut back those trees after the ice storm."

Deenie walked across the yard, straight toward the greening black of trees in the rear.

"Is this the way you get to school? You walk this back way?"

She thought she could hear Skye's breath catch. Heard the hook of the latch on the hutch and then Skye moving behind her, toward her.

"Sometimes."

Deenie walked to the far corner. From there, a few muddy steps and it was a clean path along the long row of hedges that ran up to the breezeway on the east side of the school.

We went behind those tall bushes, she could hear Lise saying now, her legs covered with milfoil. *He took my tights off first.*

"Did you see Lise back there, Skye?"

"Lise?" Skye's eyes narrowed to slits, and Deenie knew she was close to something.

"You saw, didn't you? What Lise did."

Skye looked at Deenie.

"Sure," she said, her voice changed. "I saw. I guess Gabby finally told you. I know Lise wouldn't."

"Gabby?"

"I saw it all," Skye continued. "You should've seen the things your brother was doing to her."

Deenie felt something crack and twist at her temple.

"What? What did you say?"

"Your brother going down on your Lise. Lise's leg twitching like a dog's."

Deenie felt her neck stiffen to wood, her hand leaping to it. She couldn't stop it, or Skye. Why Skye would say—

"She seemed to love it," Skye said, jaw out, her lips white. "She didn't care who saw. Your brother didn't either."

"You shut the fuck up. You don't know what you're talking about. It wasn't my brother," Deenie said. "Stop saying that. It wasn't him."

Skye's hand was at her mouth.

"Skye," Deenie said, voice creaky and high, "did you do something to Lise?"

"She did it to herself."

★   ★   ★

FOR ELI

The note was folded and stuck in the space between the storm door and the wooden one.

It was hard to read, the letters smeared and only the muzzy glare of the porch light. But once he started, he couldn't stop to go inside.

Eli:

The first time I met you, back when Deenie and me were just freshmen, you wore a shirt with a dinosaur on it and you were practicing wrist shots against the garage. You smiled at me and waved and said if I ever had a bad day I should try it, and you showed me the dents your stick made in the door. You put your fingers in them. Deenie kept saying, let's go inside. I couldn't move, I felt it already.

Every time I go by the garage, tonight even, I put my hand over those dents. My fingers fit in all the grooves.

The first time Deenie asked me to sleep over, I ran into you in the hall upstairs. You said you liked my Tupac T-shirt (for the longest time after I wore it every time I might see you). I could smell the beers on you. I couldn't breathe. I stood in the bathroom and held the sink edge. I knew I'd love you forever.

I could tell you a 100 stories like that and you wouldn't remember any of them. If you didn't remember the Ping-Pong, I might die.

That time we went to WaterWonders, I followed you all day. I told Lise and Deenie I got lost. I decided it was going to be the day I told you. But then I saw you talking to that disgusting girl in the white jeans, and I lost my nerve. What if I <u>had</u> done it. What if I had. Wouldn't it be something if you loved me too. If all along you were waiting too.

(Even just now, in the basement, it seemed like you were going to kiss me except my hair smelled so bad. I could feel it. Were you?)

I only went out with Tyler because he was on the team so I could go to the games and watch you. I only ever watched you. I thought I could make him feel like you in my head. I couldn't. And I couldn't make it go away. And sometimes I was sure you felt something. (Did you?) It's what I lived for.

So I have your phone, but I can't tell you how I got it. I had to get rid of the picture I sent you. I was sure you knew it was me, but I guess you didn't. (Except that awful, awful feeling I keep pushing away: you did know it was me and never said anything at all.)

I should have thrown the phone out. I couldn't even turn it off. Having it the past two days, it was like being connected to you. It kept me strong. I even charged it once, held it in my hand like it was part of you. I can't believe I just told you that. I hate myself so much.

I keep thinking about when Deenie finds out. She thinks I need her but she's the one who needs me. I make her feel more interesting. Your sister's a really good person. But she doesn't know me at all. I *hide myself from her. I would never want her to know. Now I guess she'll know everything.*

I have another friend who gets what I'm really like, and I get her. She scares me. Did you ever see yourself times ten in another person and want to cover your eyes?

I believed her when she said it was you with Lise by the bushes. It was the worst moment in my life, worse even than the other. It wasn't supposed to happen like it did. It was just supposed to embarrass her. I thought it would just make her look bad, make her head crazy a while. Maybe I wanted her to have to feel crazy for a little while.

Lise is beautiful and there is nothing dark and messy in her. Nothing bad ever happened to her that I ever heard of except her dad dying when she was a baby. She's unmarked. No one asks to be marked up. And nothing was hard for her ever. And then she got to have you too. Or that's what I thought. Now I have to fix things.

I wanted to play Ping-Pong with you forever. Would you have let me.

I'm just so in love with you. I just can't stop being in love with you.

This is the first letter I ever wrote.

xx Gabby

★   ★   ★

"Your daughter couldn't be here, sir," the nurse told him. "Visiting hours ended at nine."

"I know," Tom said, "but I think she might be."

Where else would she be? he thought. Not at home, not at Gabby's—there was no other place.

"Sir, we have a lot going on in here right now."

"I know, I do. I promise, I'm not being a jerk. I think she might have gone to see Lise Daniels. Can you at least let me—"

"Sir, have you been drinking?"

"Listen, can you page Sheila Daniels for me? She'll vouch for me," he said, though he had no idea if she would. "I promise."

The nurse looked at him blankly.

Nurses are like cops, he thought. You can't hide anything.

But then he remembered he had nothing, really, to hide.

Together, they sat on pastel chairs in the Critical Care waiting room.

The slump of Sheila's body, so different from the Sheila of the other morning, or most of the times he saw her, always running on nerves and worry. Now there was a zombie sedation about her that made her easier to talk to, but much sadder.

Her hands, chapped, were folded in her lap, the nails lined red.

"Deenie was here," Sheila said, the smell on her like a live presence. "I saw her. I think I did. The pills they gave me..."

"When?"

"An hour ago, maybe. I don't know. My mom saw her too."

"Do you know where she—"

"You know, I've only been home once. For an hour. The coffee table was still tipped over. I keep thinking about that coffee table." She looked at him, eyes yellowed. "That's what did it, in the end."

Something ghastly turned inside him. "In the end? Sheila, is Lise..."

But she shook her head, over and over. "Nothing's changed. Except everything. I don't understand. Tom, who would hurt my girl?"

"Sheila, I don't... what's happened?"

"I told them Lisey doesn't use drugs," she said. "Is Deenie a drug user now?"

"Deenie? No."

"That's what I told them."

"The police?" he asked, though he knew. "And they were asking about Deenie?"

"All day I've been talking to them," she said.

"Detectives? A woman with a ponytail—"

"They found something in Lise's thermos," she said, taking a crumpled piece of paper from her pocket, reading from it. *"Datura stramonium."*

Tom looked at the paper, a printout from the web. With a picture of a white flower like a pinwheel, smooth with toothed leaves.

D. stramonium—*Jimsonweed; thorn apple; Jamestown weed (Family: Nightshade). A foul-smelling herb that forms bushes up to five feet tall. Its stems fork into leafy branches, each leaf with a single, erect flower.*

For centuries, Datura has been used as an herbal medicine. It is also a potent hallucinogen and deliriant that can generate powerful visions. Legend has it that Cleopatra used the extract as a love potion in her seduction of Caesar.

Low recreational doses are usually absorbed through smoking the plant's leaves. It can, however, prove fatally toxic in only slightly higher amounts, and reckless use can result in hospitalization and even death. Amnesia of the poisoning event is common.

Late signs/fatal reactions: convulsions, cardiovascular weakening, coma.

Tom tried to concentrate on the words, but the noise in his head wouldn't let him.

"Jimsonweed. Someone gave her this?" he said. "Someone gave this to all these girls?"

"They gave it to Lise," Sheila said, swallowing loudly, the paper shaking in her hand. "They couldn't find it in the other girls."

"Do they know why? And what about..." There were too many questions and she wasn't listening anyway.

She looked down at the printout, turning it over, showing him the drawing of the plant's chemical composition.

Looking up, she smiled vaguely, her voice rising and pushing the words out: "Blind as a bat, mad as a hatter..."

"Red as a beet," continued Tom, an old memory, cramming for a long-ago exam, rising up in him, "hot as a hare, dry as a bone, and the—"

"—heart runs alone," she finished. "The doctor told me that's how they memorize it in med school. The symptoms. Toxic something. I forgot to write that part down."

"Poisoned," he said. "She was poisoned."

"The heart runs alone," she repeated, turning from the paper to Tom. "Isn't that horrible?" Then, looking up at him. "Or beautiful?"

★   ★   ★

"Skye," Deenie whispered loudly, moving closer. "What did you *do?*"

"Why would I tell you?" she said, arm lifting to the dark boughs of the tree above her. "What did you ever care about me? The only one who ever cared is Gabby."

"Gabby cares about Lise," Deenie said. *"What did you do, Skye?"*

And that's when Skye's mouth started its clicking sound again.

"I can't believe you never knew," she said. "About Gabby."

"What does Gabby..." But already something was happening, a feeling.

"About Gabby," Skye said. "About how fucking much she loves your brother."

"What..." Deenie started, but she couldn't make the words come. Because there it was, some private song she knew from far back in a cobwebby corner of her head. A song so faint she'd barely heard it, but now, the sound turned up, she couldn't muffle it anymore.

Gabby, who always walked so fast by his bedroom door. Gabby standing beside her at the washing machine, her hand on Eli's T-shirt. Her fingers. Deenie wanted to look away. A dozen times like that. The way her body battened tight when he came in the room. The way her face...

This song, she'd heard it so low and quiet so long, she never really heard it at all.

"She could never tell you," Skye said. "She knew you wouldn't understand, or help her. But she had me."

Deenie felt something drag up her spine. Turning, she said, each word slow and raking up her throat, "Had you for... what? *What did you do, Skye?*"

And, stepping farther back under the black canopy of the tree, Skye seemed to draw herself into herself, a small white flower.

There, hidden, her voice low and forceful and insistent, almost a chant, she told Deenie a story, the way only Skye would tell it.

Of how she and Gabby became friends, true friends, because they both knew how to keep secrets. How one night last year, Skye caught her hiding in the tall trees by the school, watching Eli Nash skating by himself on the practice rink. She was so embarrassed, and Skye said she shouldn't be and invited Gabby to her house to do the love tarot.

They sat for hours and Gabby told Skye she'd loved Eli since the day she met him, and he was all she thought about. And that she loved Deenie but that she'd mostly become friends with her because of Eli, whom she loved so much she wanted to die.

It never stopped, the feeling, and watching him with all those girls, once or twice hearing them in Deenie's house, was almost too much for Gabby to bear. Sometimes she even thought that if it weren't for Deenie...

But Skye had told her it didn't matter. That was how guys were, trapped for years in the mindless mojo of lust. And together they cast love spells from the Internet, mixing honey, oils, and leaves with things—hair, pens, stick wax, a roll of grip tape—stolen from Eli's backpack, his house.

Once, they used a dove heart Skye's cat carried in from the backyard.

Once, they used menstrual blood.

And then one day it happened, or they thought it did.

I saw him in the hallway, Gabby said, *and you should have seen it, the way he looked at me. I know it worked. I know it.*

To bind it, Skye cautioned, they would have to send him a picture. If it stays on his phone for twelve days, the spell will work. And Gabby said she'd do it. She was not afraid.

But the spell didn't work in time. Or it worked the wrong way. It worked for Lise.

Because one morning, a week ago, Skye was walking to school, late, head full of bad dreams like always, and she saw it all. Saw the secret. Behind the bushes. Lise and Eli Nash.

She told Gabby what she'd seen. And Gabby could think of nothing else: *I want to die,* she told Skye. *I'm dying now.*

The next day, they'd all gone to the lake.

Gabby was so angry, she couldn't even look at Lise. Lise showing off her body in the water. And that spot on the inside of her thigh, like a moon, a kiss, a witch's mark. The whole time, Gabby kept whispering to Skye, *She stole him from me.*

And so Skye promised to reverse it. And she knew just how.

Sulfur, honey, and dried jimson flowers from the bushes out back, the kind that bloomed at night. They're called love-will. She'd found it in a book. A spell to scare a faithless lover into repentance.

She made the mixture and gave it to Gabby and Gabby put it in Lise's thermos. It was important that Gabby do it herself. It was the only way the spell would work.

And they couldn't be responsible for what happened. In fact, didn't Lise's reaction show that it was Lise who was a faithless lover? Was holding some bad energy inside that needed to be released?

Deenie listened and listened and finally broke in.

"But you gave Lise . . . sulfur?"

"Jimson. It runs wild back here. If you dry the leaves and smoke them, you can have visions," Skye said, stepping back even farther under the heavy branches, only her mouth and chin visible now. "But it only makes visible a darkness that's already there. Maybe eating it like that . . ."

She looked at Deenie, her voice like a pulse in Deenie's brain. "Maybe you bring the darkness inside you. Maybe Lise has it inside her now."

Deenie felt herself sinking, her hand reaching out for the tree beside her, knuckles pressing into its hard bark.

"They'll find it," Deenie said, huskily. "They're finding everything."

"I burned it all," she said, head tilting toward the dredged ashes mixing with the sawdust by the rabbit hutch. That smell Deenie had caught, now nearly gone. "The plants were so beautiful. It's all done."

Pressing her hand to her chest, Deenie tried to get a breath that wouldn't come.

"I'm going to tell," she whispered.

"It doesn't matter to me."

A wind came and Skye's head dipped down from the tree's shadow and Deenie saw her face, hair blown back. Her face bare and clean as she'd never seen it. She looked small and dangerous.

"Skye," she said, softly, "Lise is going to die."

There was a pause. Deenie couldn't look at her, her face so naked, her eyes like hard green marbles.

"I'm not sorry, Deenie," Skye was saying. "And you shouldn't be. We don't owe anybody anything."

Deenie couldn't imagine anything less true. The hardest part was how much we owed everyone.

"You poisoned her," Deenie said, feeling her neck throb from its seizing bursts, her body aching from it. "You poisoned everybody."

"No," Skye said. "She was the only one."

Deenie looked at her, trying to puzzle it all out, including the long, fevered lurches of her own body, heart. How was it possible?

"And it's not poison," Skye said, stepping forward, so close to Deenie she could smell the sawdust, the ashes. "Your brother had some, he smoked some today and he didn't get sick."

Deenie lifted her head, eyes on Skye, the white smear of her face. It seemed to happen instantaneously, her body moving fast across the lawn.

★   ★   ★

"Sheila Daniels, please return to ICU."

The crackle from the ancient PA system.

"Maybe she's awake," Tom said, rising, helping Sheila to her feet.

Her body bobbled between his forearms, her hair slipping from its clip, he grabbed for one shoulder to try to keep her upright.

"I'll come with you," he said. "You..."

But she had pulled away from him and charged through the double doors with surprising suddenness and strength.

All Sheila Daniels's constant, exhausting vigilance over the years looked different now. It made you wonder if, in some obscure way, she had known what was coming and spent all her days raising the ramparts, doing whatever she could to forestall it, or at least pre-pare for it.

Except what, or who, had she been protecting Lise from? He couldn't imagine why anyone in the world would want to hurt that sweet girl.

And now he was bounding through the front doors, not stopping to think where he could find Deenie, just knowing he would.

His phone started ringing just as he reached his car.

"Hello?" he answered, not even looking.

"I can't breathe. I can't breathe and I..."

And it was Deenie's voice, one he hadn't heard in a thousand years, and she was saying things, frantically, breathlessly, but with the sound of everything in the world roaring in his ear, he could only hear "Daddy."

★   ★   ★

It was five miles or more, even if she found the right shortcuts, iron spreading through her chest as she ran.

There was no guessing about it, but a picture kept coming: Eli's head hitting the ice, like she'd once seen happen at a practice, his

267

helmet shorn off, two teeth knocked out. Deenie had been there, felt her heart stop.

And her mom running onto the ice, arms around him in seconds. Scrambling to find both teeth. Deenie watched as she foisted them back in Eli's open mouth. And he was fine. Because Eli was always fine, wasn't he?

Running faster, breathing harder, her face slicked from the damp, her sneakers nearly twisting off her feet, she pressed her phone against her ear.

Her dad was telling her to slow down, to breathe.

"Where's Eli," she said and it wasn't her voice now but her voice in an old home video, long-ago Christmas mornings, a canoe trip, the time she first rode a bike and fell elbow first onto the sidewalk. "Daddy, he's poisoned."

* * *

A two-liter nestled between his legs, Eli held Gabby's letter in his hand.

He was drinking fast, trying to wake up, to shake off the final dregs of the smoke, to understand what he'd read and what it meant.

There were revelations tumbling through his head—so many moments that looked different now, how he'd read them all wrong—but he pushed them aside for the moment because of the sickly urgency he felt. *Now I have to fix things,* she'd written, a sentence that had a sense of purpose. And finality.

He picked up the kitchen phone again, realized he didn't have her number.

Pulling his laptop out of his bag, he e-mailed Gabby, the first time he ever had.

Gabby, call me. come back.

Then he sat for a second, waiting, hoping.

All those times with Gabby, her stern and mysterious face. To matter so much to someone you hardly thought about. To care so much about someone who maybe didn't even wonder about you, or check in much to see if you were okay because that person wasn't thinking about you, not really, and maybe had moved far away, three hours or something, just far enough to be able to put you out of her mind whenever she wanted.

The phone rang.

"Eli, it's Dad."

"Hey," Eli said. "Gabby left. And this thing happened. I don't know—"

"Are you okay, Eli?" his dad said, his voice even more breathless than before. "Are you all right?"

"Yeah, Dad, but Gab—"

"We'll be right there, okay? Don't—just sit still, okay? Just don't do anything."

"What?" Eli said, but all he heard was the smack of tires on a wet road, then a click.

★　　★　　★

She saw the car, the only car in the world, the streets desolate and haunted, like a town during a plague.

"Deenie," her dad was shouting from the rolled-down window.

And the car nearly jumped the curb, spraying her with gathered water.

"You were supposed to go to Eli," she shouted, holding her trapper hat on her head, heavy with rain.

"Deenie," he said, "get in."

269

She stood for a second, looking at her father, his face red and fevered, hands gripping the wheel.

She felt so sorry for him.

* * *

Eli kept trying to tell them he was okay, but they wouldn't listen.

Knees up in the backseat, Deenie had her head buried in her arms, and he thought she might be crying.

Dad drove faster than Eli had ever seen anyone drive, faster even than A.J. drag-racing by the old wire factory outside of town.

"Did you drink something?" his dad kept asking. "Did someone give you something? How about in your thermos?"

"What? No. I don't have a thermos," he said. "I'm okay, Dad."

"You're not," Deenie said from the back. "You think you are, but you're not."

The hospital was there, lit so brightly it hurt his eyes, the parking lot like the school's before a big game.

Their headlights skated across a pair of girls, maybe ten or eleven, in flannel pajamas, their mother with an arm around each of them, rushing them inside. They both wore big slippers—lobsters and bunny rabbits—oozing with gray rain, so heavy they could barely lift their feet.

Time shuttered to a stop as Eli watched them, their faces blue in the light, looking at the windshield, at him. He squinted and saw they were older than they'd first looked. The one with the bunny slippers he recognized as the sophomore girl everyone called Shawty, the one who'd snuck into his bedroom months ago, the one who'd cried when it was over, worried she'd done it all wrong. After, she'd stayed in the bathroom a long time. When she came out, her face was bright with pain.

Girls changed after, he thought. Before, she'd been texting him all the time, pulling her shirt up at games, saying all the things she wanted to do to him, flashing that thong at him.

And then after. But it changed for him after too. Growing up felt like a series of bewildering afters.

And now here she was, hair scraped back from her baby face, and she had stopped, and she was looking at him.

Recognizing him, remembering things. A hard wince sweeping across that soft face.

And he wasn't sure what her real name was.

Then came the girl's mother's burly arm covering her face, hoisting her along, and the girl was gone, lost behind the hospital's sliding doors.

"Deenie," Eli said, turning around to face his sister, "did Gabby find you? Did you talk to her?"

And she just shook her head, eyes wide and startled, mouth fixed.

"Because I have to show you something. You need to see something."

Reaching into his jeans pocket, he pulled out the note, damp in his hands.

★   ★   ★

A blurry half hour after he'd left, Tom was back in the hospital waiting room, this time with Eli and Deenie.

Eli, glassy-eyed, an arm around his sister, her face colorless, mouth slightly open.

He hadn't been able to get anything coherent from Deenie.

Like when she was little and would lose her breath and all he could do was say it would be okay, everything would be okay.

I can't breathe. I can't breathe.

271

Now, his heart still jamming against his chest, he tried to settle himself. He needed to be ready for anything.

There was something about seeing Eli, his hand on his sister's arm, saying things in her ear, that was beginning to work on him.

To calm him.

To make his breaths come slow, to let him stand back and see them both.

★   ★   ★

When her dad went up to the reception window, Deenie turned to Eli. He had something in his hand and kept trying to show it to her.

It was a piece of paper, like a wet leaf, and she recognized Gabby's tight scrawl.

She read in what felt like slow motion, each word shuddering a moment before locking into focus.

The first time I met you, back when Deenie and me were just freshmen, you wore a shirt with a dinosaur on it.

The things Skye said, they were true.

She thinks I need her but she's the one who needs me. I make her feel more interesting.

She read it and thought of everything that had ever happened with her and Gabby, and all the things she'd held tight to her own chest. About her part of the story, about Sean Lurie. And how neither Gabby nor Skye would ever find out.

Why should she tell them?

Your sister's a really good person, Gabby had written. *But she doesn't know me at all.*

Maybe we don't really know anybody, Deenie thought. *And maybe nobody knows us.*

* * *

The nurse was crazily beautiful, like a nurse in a porno movie, and Eli thought he must still be high, all these hours later.

Her breasts seemed to brush up against him every time she moved, checking his eyes, his pulse. Asking him a series of questions and then asking again.

Fifteen minutes before, he'd peed into a cup, handed it to her.

"Nothing here," she said now, looking at the results. It seemed impossibly fast.

"I haven't done any drugs," he said. "I don't use drugs."

He wondered if his dad, standing just a few feet away, was also noticing how beautiful the nurse was. But his dad didn't seem to notice anything, his eyes set on Eli, his gaze intent.

Another nurse, her scrubs dark with sweat, rolled a cart past them, the wheels screeching.

"I just don't know how we get out of this," she was saying to the beautiful nurse. "I've never seen anything like this."

There was a frenzy around him, a constant whir that didn't seem to touch him. Or his nurse, her voice tut-tutting, the fine gold cross around her neck, hanging between the tops of her breasts.

And then, as she bent the arm of a light above him, he saw she wasn't really crazily beautiful and was a lot older than he thought, but there was a tenderness and efficiency to her that made him feel like everything would be okay.

"We'll still take some blood but—" Just then a crash came, followed by the yelp of a girl's voice, the skidding of sneakers on the floor.

"Some help here!" a voice rose, deep and urgent.

"I'll be back," the nurse said to Eli's dad, putting her hands on his shoulders to direct him to a narrow waiting area crushed with parents. "Sit tight."

His dad just stood there, watching the unshaven men with pajama tops under their open coats, women wearing slipper boots, one father weeping into his lap.

"Eli," his dad was saying, "I have to make a call, okay?"

No one was looking.

Eli was the only male and that made it easier. No one was looking, so he started walking, exploring.

Hearing a dozen conversations, voices pinched and frightened.

"...and her throw-up looked like coffee grounds. I heard that means..."

"...explains why she's been this way for so long. All those ADD meds. Maybe this is why..."

"...all these clots when I was doing the laundry. And I asked her and she started crying..."

"...and heavy-metal poisoning, or mold? She kept saying everything smelled like meat. And then she'd throw up again."

"...like I was floating, and a darkness was closing in on me."

He had been sitting on a small chair, all the exam tables taken, when he spotted, under one of those rolling privacy screens, a pair of soggy bunny slippers.

And then the slippers started to move.

He saw her, the sophomore girl, walking toward the swinging doors.

And he couldn't sit there anymore.

And no one stopped him.

A man in scrubs, his forehead wet, clipboard in hand, called out to him as he passed a nursing station.

"That's my sister," Eli lied, rushing past the man, who started to say something and then stopped.

★   ★   ★

"I think he's fine. I don't know. They think he's fine."

"Oh, Tom," Georgia said, "what's happened?"

And he didn't know how to begin to answer that question.

He'd planned on telling her everything he knew, but it felt like so many enigmatic scraps, and all of it depended on her being here, on her knowing the teen-girl complexities of Deenie's friendships, of the extraordinary *something* that had overtaken all these girls and everyone in their lives. How did you explain any of that?

He could tell her about finding Eli's phone, and they could try to figure it all out, but he didn't know how to tell her without explaining why he'd been with Lara Bishop at midnight.

"I was always afraid something could happen to Eli on the ice," Georgia said. "That's the thing that kept me up nights."

"Georgia," he said suddenly, "why aren't you here?"

"Because," she said, "I'd only make it worse."

Then she told him she'd tried three times. Gotten in her car, driven nearly all the way to Dryden, three hours, before turning around and driving back. Now she was in the parking lot of a 7-Eleven twelve miles from her apartment.

"Drinking a can of beer," she said. "Genny Cream. Which I haven't done since I was twenty."

And he laughed, and she laughed.

And everything felt mysterious and lonely and half forgotten.

He could hear her laugh in the center of his brain and he thought, *That's not her laugh. I don't recognize that laugh at all.*

★   ★   ★

275

Eli lost sight of the sophomore girl quickly.

But down a long hallway in Critical Care, he found what he was looking for.

It was the quietest spot in the entire hospital, a building smaller than their school, which it seemed to be trying to contain right now, its walls swelling and straining.

The doors are always open in hospitals, which seemed funny to him, but he was glad.

Because there she was.

Lise Daniels.

* * *

It felt like she'd been alone in the waiting room a long time, her thoughts scattering everywhere, jumping to her feet whenever either set of doors opened.

But then Deenie's phone rang, and time seemed to stop entirely.

Gabby, the screen read.

She walked swiftly outside, into the back parking lot to a place hidden by a pair of drooping trees, and answered.

"Hey, girl."

"Hey, girl."

And a pause that felt electric before Gabby spoke again.

"So I'm waiting for my mom. I told them I wanted my mom here before I tell them."

"Where are you?"

"I'm at the police station," she said, voice hoarse and faint. "I walked for an hour and when I got there, I knew I would do it."

"But Gabby, listen to me —"

"Don't hate me, Deenie, okay? Whatever you hear."

"Gabby, I know what happened. I talked to Skye. It was Skye."

"No," Gabby said, with finality. The voice of someone who had decided many things, and now that she'd decided, she was done. *I won't see my dad, I won't talk to him. I'm done with him forever.* "It was me, Deenie. It was me. And I'm not going to tell them about her. You have to promise me you won't either."

"I won't promise! Listen to me, Gabby," she said again, trying to forget the things Skye had said, about Gabby not caring about Deenie, about how Deenie was in the way. "You wouldn't have done it without Skye. It's all her fault."

Then Gabby said the thing Deenie hoped she wouldn't say, never guessed she would.

"When I put the leaves in the thermos, I didn't know what would happen. I didn't care."

And Deenie could hear it, that click-click-click on the other end, Gabby's jaw like one of those old wind-up toys, a spinning monkey slapping cymbals. Deenie could practically see her shaking.

Then, as if Gabby had wedged her hand under her jaw to hold it in place, the words came fast and Deenie tried to hold on to them.

"Deenie, if Eli didn't love me, why would he have been so nice to me and played Ping-Pong with me and that time he gave me a ride on his handlebars? Why would he have treated me like I was special? Not like those hockey groupies, not like girls like Britt Olsen or those girls from Star-of-the-Sea or that slutty sophomore Michelle. But then I heard about Lise and the bushes by school."

There was a long, raspy gulp, like Gabby couldn't get air in. And when she started again, Deenie could feel everything falling apart for her. Gabby had many things to say, none of which could help her explain any of it.

"And the more Skye kept talking," she said, "the more it seemed right. It was supposed to be *me,* Deenie. He was supposed to love *me*. But we did the love spell wrong. And Skye told me what she saw. It was like a loop in my head. And he was pulling down her tights, that's what Skye said. Thinking of his hands on that... that-that-that *skin* of hers when it was supposed to be me."

The way she said it, *that skin of hers,* her voice shaking with anger and disgust, Deenie had the sudden feeling she'd had with Skye. For a fleeting second, she thought it was all a trick, some black art, and it was Skye on the other end of the phone, casting a spell.

"After, Skye said we shouldn't feel bad. She said it's what was supposed to happen. It's how the universe works. Lise's bad energy came back on her. Skye said when she looked at Lise, she saw a black mark, an aura. Just like the mark on Lise's thigh, it was a warning."

Deenie thought of it now, of Lise and the stretch mark on her thigh. And how the fevered mind of her fevered friend might believe anything.

But also, somewhere inside, it felt the smallest bit true. That the stretch mark was a kind of witch's mark, the blot on Lise's body that reminded you of what she had been—a plump, awkward girl—before the lithesome beauty took her place. It was a kind of witchcraft, that transformation.

"But Deenie, I *did* feel bad. It was like it was meant to happen. The bad thing you're waiting for, the thing you might do someday. And then you've done the thing, and there's no going back."

Once, after Deenie said something unbelievably awful to her mom, using a word she'd never even said aloud, shouting it so loud her throat hurt, her mom looked at her and said, *Deenie, someday it's going to happen to you. You're going to do something you never thought you would. And then you'll see, and then you'll know.*

I hope, she'd added, *it's not for a long time.*

"But at the school concert," Deenie said suddenly, remembering Gabby, her cello bow pitching, face scarlet. "Was that all fake?"

"No! I can't make my jaw stop," Gabby said, her voice cracking and a long, low sob. "I can't make my head right. It's like it's everything about me now. It's inside me and everywhere. It was always in me. I couldn't stop myself."

There was a long pause. Then Gabby whispered, "Deenie, I couldn't stop myself. I had to do it. Can you understand?"

Deenie felt her mouth go dry, her head throbbing. "Yes," she said. "Yes."

The clicks started again, and an awful rattle, and Deenie felt the phone hot on her face, beep-beep-beep, her cheek pressed against the keyboard.

Then, suddenly, Gabby's voice came again, low and strange.

"And now he'll never love me," Gabby said. "Now it'll never be me."

Deenie slowly lowered the phone from her ear.

"Deenie, did Eli read my letter? Did he say anything about me?"

★　　★　　★

At first Eli couldn't see her past the wires tentacled over her, the room blue and lonely.

There was just a swoop of a girl's cheek, and a flossy pile of hair, everything blue in the blue light.

And there was something resting in the middle of Lise's head. Something dark. Like in a fairy tale, a black cat perched, a swirl of smoke.

But then he remembered something Deenie had said, about a fall.

She made it sound gruesome, but it wasn't so bad.

Maybe it was because Lise's eyes were so pretty, shining and looking directly at him.

Following him as he walked toward the bed.

Gentle and soft, like Lise. And the light from the open door falling on her, giving her a funny kind of radiance.

Her mouth slightly opening, lips pale but full.

Eyes seeming to smile, at him.

"Do you see?" came the softest of whispers.

And it was Mrs. Daniels behind him, and she was smiling, like watching Lise play "Für Elise" on her flute.

"Do you see?" Mrs. Daniels whispered, her hand gentle on Eli's back. "She came back."

★   ★   ★

Alone in the waiting room, Deenie sat, her phone gripped in her hand.

Everything that day at the lake, just a week ago, started to look different.

The way Gabby looked at Lise, her long legs, like milk glass, thighs so narrow you could see between, like a keyhole.

How Gabby and Skye had stood next to each other, their ankles flecked green from the lake's creamy surface, and Gabby whispered something in Skye's ear, and Deenie had that feeling that she'd had so often in recent months: They are sharing something without me, they are talking about me, Gabby doesn't love me anymore.

And then Gabby wanted to leave, even though Lise was driving.

I can take you, Lise promised, but they were already walking away, their legs greened, never looking back.

And Skye said the lake had bad energy, arms folded, eyes on Lise.

Was that when Skye got the idea? Or had she and Gabby already decided by then?

It felt now like they had. Like it had already been too late.

Deenie wondered how it had felt for Lise, sharing her secret about Sean. Waiting for Skye and Gabby to leave to tell her. Wanting it to be theirs. A thing together. She couldn't know what might happen. How different it might have been had she told all of them.

Deenie thought about what Skye had said, that the whole time, Gabby was so angry she couldn't even look at Lise. Couldn't bear Lise showing off her body in the water. And whispering to Skye, *She stole him from me.*

That day, Lise had been more beautiful than she'd ever been before, her lashes iridescent and her face with an almost unearthly glow. Her body, Deenie guessed, felt her own in a way it only can when you've made it yourself.

Lise did give off a strong energy that day, but not like Skye meant.

And Deenie, she'd said, *Don't tell Gabby. Gabby's weird about this stuff.*

Deenie, you're my best friend.

Deenie, I didn't do anything wrong, right?

Deenie, am I bad?

Deenie, I hope you get to feel it. I hope it feels like that for you.

It was something powerful, and everyone wanted it.

17

It felt great, her hands on the wheel.

Lise almost never got to drive, but that day she got lucky and her mom let her drive the Dodge because she was at the ophthalmologist, getting drops in her eyes.

Gabby had been sad all day, like she was a lot. You would only find out later it was because her dad had called or it was the anniversary of something bad with Tyler Nagy.

"She won't even talk," Deenie whispered to her. "Let's try to cheer her up."

So they went for a drive, windows down and Gabby's favorite music and Big Gulps it took two hands to hold. The warmest day in months.

They saw Deenie's brother in the parking lot and Lise beeped her horn at him. Sometimes she wondered if Deenie knew how good-looking Eli was, if sisters could tell. Lise liked to watch him on the practice rink, his hair flying and the faraway look in his eyes. Her mom always said teenage boys only cared about one thing, but watching Eli, you just knew it wasn't true.

On the drive, Gabby and Skye didn't say a word the whole time, but she and Deenie sang loudly to the radio. It was fun.

As they drove past the lake, Skye started telling them this thing that had happened last week. She saw two guys wading in the lake, drinking beers, their car doors open and speakers gushing wild music that made her want to dance.

"They were sexy," Skye said. "One had a tattoo of a gold panther. It went down his whole body, from his neck down below his waist, into his jeans. I wonder where it ended."

Lise could picture the tattoo and the guy. In her head, his shirt was worn denim and he had aviator sunglasses and a wicked smile. And the panther, its gleaming haunches stretched along his torso, the panther's teeth disappearing below his golden hip bone.

"Maybe they're there now," Deenie said, laughing.

And Lise wondered about it, her stomach doing that funny kind of thing, like when Ryan Denning helped her with her fetal-pig dissection, seated on high stools and him reaching for the blunt probe, his hand brushing her lap.

"Let's stop and go in," she suggested, jumping forward in her seat, pressing against the steering wheel. "Let's go now."

So they did, hopping the orange safety fences. The guys with the car and the tattoo weren't there, except it almost felt like they were, the lake glittering with borrowed glamour.

"Maybe they'll show up later," Lise said, running down the bank, nearly sliding on the mud, which spattered up her legs. "Maybe they'll see us from the road."

Gabby and Skye were so quiet. Skye lit a clove cigarette and squinted down at Lise. She was saying something to Gabby, but Lise couldn't hear. They were always whispering to each other.

They were no fun and Lise felt high on all the sugar and soda and was trying to rouse Gabby and she tugged off her tights.

The water looked eerily lovely, like the kind of sparkling lake you'd see in a picture book, unicorns dipping their heads and cloudbursts overhead.

Waving up at the others lined up on the shore, she promised the water felt almost warm and like velvet under your feet and they had to come. It was true. Except it was freezing.

She pulled her skirt higher and spun.

"What's that?" Skye asked, pointing her cigarette at Lise, at her legs.

"Nothing," Lise said, and felt her face go hot.

She knew what Skye meant, the mark on her thigh, a pink crescent. It was from losing all that weight, a tiny stretch mark she put cocoa butter on every night, wishing it away.

"You're just stalling," Deenie shouted at Skye, and Lise smiled. "You're scared."

Deenie hated Skye.

And soon enough Deenie was yanking her jeans up to her knees and wading in too. And Lise was so grateful. Deenie was still hers.

"C'mon, Gabby," Deenie shouted, her jeans already soaked to the thigh. "It only hurts for a second."

And finally Gabby reached down and pulled off her tights, and then of course Skye did too, cigarette somehow still between her fingers, thin as a burnt match.

The water felt soft and globby, like sherbet, but smelled strongly of something Lise had never smelled before.

It was only a minute before Gabby said she was catching hypothermia and the lake was dirty and was making her head hurt. And then Skye said her head hurt too and the lake had a bad aura and you were asking for trouble being in it.

The boy who drowned here, she said, *can't you feel him? He was in the water for days. Do you know what happens? Your body turns to soap.*

And they all looked down in the water as if they would see the boy.

But Deenie said that was kid's stuff, and she scooped up a handful, foam bubbling, and flicked it toward them. That was when Lise knew Deenie was annoyed, or even mad, like she always was when Gabby was being secretive with Skye, which was all the time lately.

It never mattered much to Lise because she'd never felt as close to Gabby as Deenie did. Deenie, who'd never really gotten over the surprise that someone as cool as Gabby Bishop wanted to be her friend. For her part, Lise had realized a long time ago that the way to keep Deenie would be to let her love Gabby just this much.

Skye was the weirdest girl Lise had ever known. Once, a long time ago, in middle school, they'd been to the same sleepaway camp and Skye had the bunk above her. One night she came down the ladder, her legs snaking around it, and asked Lise if she wanted to see something.

Taking a deep breath, she lifted her nightshirt and showed Lise all these marks, like rosy ridges, on her arms all the way up to her shoulder. She said she'd made them herself, with a Bic lighter, and it had taken a long time. And now they were like the husk, the hard shell. Like finding a beetle or a mollusk shell at the lake, the rattle pods in Binnorie Woods. You shake and it's hollow. The thing inside died. You couldn't do anything to it anymore.

The cabin quiet and dark and Skye breathing hard, her arms outstretched, Lise hadn't known what to say, barely knew this girl. What did you say to something like that? And the next day, Skye wouldn't look at her, and then after that they never talked about it again.

She wondered if Skye remembered it.

"I can't do this," Gabby said suddenly. Her face looked green from the water.

Nodding to Skye, she began walking back to shore, her sweater heavy with water, trailing behind her.

"Come on, Gabby," Deenie said, calling out after her.

Lise bent over and lifted a long stretch of seaweed, draping it around Deenie's neck, like a mermaid's boa.

And Deenie smiled and flicked its edges up and pushed Lise, but when they both turned around again, Gabby and Skye were walking up the bank, their legs stained green.

"Are they going?" Lise asked, looking at Deenie.

Her long sweater sleeves weeping lake water, Skye offered a slow wave.

Gabby didn't even turn around, walking slowly up the slope, the damp edges of her skirt in her hands like petticoats.

"But Lise drove us," Deenie called out.

Except they kept walking, their heavy hair and long-legged elegance, and it was hard not to feel five years old.

So she said, "Swim with me, Deenie," backing up so the frigid water reached the bottom of her pelvis, the green water swimming between her thighs. "Let's do it, huh?"

After a moment, Deenie stopped looking back for Gabby and they stripped off their sweaters and waded in their tank tops and bras, Lise's skirt billowing like a white flower and Deenie's jeans accordioned on the shore.

And then Deenie even put her head under, came up with her hair black and inky.

At first, Lise wouldn't do it. She didn't want to and kept picturing that drowned boy, under the pearling water. *Was he there now? Would he curl his tiny fingers around her toe?*

But then Deenie grabbed her neck from behind and dunked her, and the icy water came so fast she almost couldn't breathe.

Under the surface, her ears hurt so bad she felt like someone had punched an iron rod in them.

But then the pressure broke and it was incredible, her head rushing with the feeling.

And while she was under, she knew it was time to tell Deenie, her best friend.

About the boy, almost as handsome as Eli Nash himself, but without the faraway eyes. The boy who'd looked right at her, rolling her tights down over her legs.

To whisper in Deenie's ear the wonderful thing that was happening and how it felt. She wanted to share it with her.

18

Sitting in his car in the school parking lot, Tom couldn't quite bring himself to go inside.

His gaze fixed on the breezeway beyond. All the hedges had been torn away, shorn stumps remaining, a stray evidence bag, a twirl of police tape. The orange streaks of herbicide dye.

He'd spent the day before driving Deenie the three hours to Merrivale, then turning around and driving home. It was the first time he'd seen Georgia's place, which was cozy and filled with light and fresh air. Deenie insisted on staying only two days, had a history test on Wednesday, had forgotten to bring her books. In fact, maybe she'd stay just overnight.

Eli had come too, had helped with the driving. Deenie kept watching him from the corner of her eye.

At the hospital, they'd tested his blood, even his hair, used enormous machines and tested the electrical activity of his heart. But whatever Eli had smoked with Skye Osbourne, they couldn't find anything dangerous in his body.

"There's nothing inside him," the doctor said. "Whatever it was, it's gone."

Eli told them the smoke had been for something called lucid dreaming.

"Did it work?" Tom asked.

Eli had paused, then said no.

The sharp bark of an engine stirred him to life. Looking out his car window, he saw the French teacher hopping off her Vespa and smiling at him, red-lipped.

"Open that window," she said. "Or invite me in."

He clicked the power locks and watched her glide around the car and climb inside.

Rubbing her hands together, she told him she couldn't take her eyes off the news.

"Gabby Bishop, Jesus," she said. "I never even had her in a class, but I knew about her. The way she'd walk down the hall, girls circling her like little magpies. All that hair and drama."

"Yeah," he said, just to say something.

Her hands dropping to her lap, she sighed. "It's all so freaky. All the other ones who got sick—I sent two to the nurse myself. So they must have gotten some of that jimson stuff, right? They must have smoked it too, like at a party?"

"I don't think so," Tom said. "I don't think they took anything."

She nodded and they sat silently for a moment.

"I remember when I was a sophomore in high school," she said. "There was this girl, the coolest girl in school. Laia Noone. Even her name was cool. She had a tattoo on her stomach: *I've seen love die.* In tenth grade!" She laughed. "All I wanted was to be like her."

"And now you're the coolest girl in school."

"You don't know the half of it," she said. Then she lowered her jacket zipper and, using two fingers, separated the space between a pair of blouse buttons, baring the smallest triangle of flesh. He could see only the middle words—*seen love*—but was sure the rest was there too.

"And so," Tom said, "marked for life."

"That's what high school does."

"And everything else," he said, smiling.

She smiled back, like he knew she would.

"It's funny the things you think of now," she said, yanking the zipper back up. "I remember last year once, Jaymie Hurwich crying in my classroom after school. She said there was something wrong with her mom's brain and it'd started when her mom was sixteen and now *she* was sixteen and what if something happened to her. She said her dad was always looking at her, like he was watching for signs."

Tom was surprised, but then everything surprised him now.

A hundred thoughts started floating in and out of his head, but none cohered.

"It's going to be hard for all of them," she said. "Everyone'll be looking at them. Like they're these damaged girls."

They sat for a minute.

"But not Deenie," she said, smiling. "Thank goodness. No one will be looking at her."

Tom looked at her. Nodded.

Troubling Questions Linger after Mystery Illness

Six weeks after Dryden High School faced a seeming health crisis among female students following the poisoning of a classmate, local health officials are still struggling to identify the cause.

At least 18 students were treated for symptoms ranging from facial and body tics to hallucinations and even temporary paralysis, but the case began with Lise Daniels, 16, who experienced a seizure following ingestion of dangerous jimsonweed placed in her thermos by a fellow student (see sidebar, "Student Faces Sentence after Plea Deal").

No jimsonweed was detected in any of the other afflicted girls, and health department officials have been unable to find any organic causes for individual cases or any connections among them.

Reports emerged this week that the department is now consulting with experts who specialize in "mass psychogenic illness," a condition in which physical symptoms that are psychological in origin emerge in a group, spreading from one person to the next. "It's not a copycat situation and no one's faking anything," clarified Dr. Robert Murray from the State Psychiatric Institute. "These girls had no control over their symptoms. Which can be terrifying."

Such outbreaks tend to occur within groups experiencing emotional stress and anxiety. "That's likely the scenario here," Dr. Murray said, adding he hadn't interviewed any of the girls so could not speak to their individual circumstances.

At least one parent, David Hurwich, 42, does not accept the diagnosis, and he may not be alone. Last night at a school-board meeting, several parents noted, off the record, that they continue to believe that the real cause is being ignored or covered up, citing ongoing concerns about air and water safety. "Time will tell," said Mr. Hurwich. "But I know my daughter. And that was not her."

Questions also remain for Miss Daniels, who was released from the hospital two weeks ago. Dr. April Fine, chair of psychiatry at Mercy-Starr Clark, warns that what the long-term side effects will be are unclear.

"This girl not only suffered significant physical trauma, she is also the victim of a crime," Dr. Fine said. "The real impact may not be felt for some time, and may emerge when least expected. In some ways, she's a ticking time bomb."

It was one of those painfully lovely late-spring mornings, the kind only Dryden could conjure.

The same obscure meteorology that produced the awesome ferocity of winters kept the lake unusually warm and made for cloudless skies. Only a few popcorn cumuli broke up the brilliant blue that hurt your eyes. It was called the oasis effect.

Waiting for the coffeemaker, or Deenie's sneakers on the stairs, Tom didn't know what to do with himself. He'd stopped reading the newspaper, listening to the news. None of it seemed to explain anything. That morning, though, he hadn't been able to stop himself. *Mass psychogenic illness.* There was a term for it, or so the article claimed.

The main story was about Gabby, who would be sentenced on Friday.

Every day, he thought about calling Lara Bishop, but she hadn't returned his other calls.

That night with her had come to feel like a murky dream, erotic and strange—the enigmatic beauty of it, her scar pulling from her neck, her voice in his ear—and best tucked in a far corner.

It was still hard to imagine. Gabby, the girl he was used to seeing at his kitchen table or nestled on his sofa with Deenie, their hands crackling in potato chip bags. The sushi-pattern pajamas she wore when she slept over. Hair hanging in her face over a morning cereal bowl.

Some days, he felt like she could almost be his own daughter.

Except that wasn't really true. She'd always felt grander, graver. Embossed with the gold stamp of Experience. Something adultlike about her, different. But in the end she was both different and not, burdened by both a girl's crush and a dense gnarl over her heart.

Or maybe he was wrong.

The coffee was ready.

"Deenie," he called out. "Let's go."

The second pot, and stronger. He'd been up awhile, had been lying awake in bed when he heard the click-click of Eli's hockey stick on the kitchen floor as he left the house for practice.

It was strange to think of his son now, after all this. The object of such intense feeling. Lady-killer. Heartbreaker. This was the boy for whom a girl had nearly killed, nearly died. Little Eli, who watched six consecutive hours of ESPN Classic, ate over the kitchen sink, and, despite having had at least one female visitor to his bedroom, never seemed to quite lock eyes with any girl, any woman. Except Deenie, and sometimes Georgia, though Tom hadn't seen them together in so long.

Whenever he looked at Eli now, he tried to find it, as if the answer might lie in some deeper enchantment a father couldn't see.

The skittering on the stairs startled him.

"We'll be late," Deenie said, running in, her hair brushed hard into a tight ponytail. "We better go."

In the car, she was quiet, folding and unfolding a new scarf, pale green like a lily pad. She'd brought it back after visiting Georgia, another visit cut short.

The day she returned, he found her in the basement, holding her pizza shirt up to the light, an errant grease stain still lurking.

"She never had a good reason," she'd said, "for not coming. When everything was happening."

"Deenie, she offered to come and get you. That's the same thing," he said, even though he knew it wasn't, exactly.

Dropping the shirt into the dryer, she looked at him, the longest look he could remember her ever giving.

"You would have come," she said at last.

"Yeah," he said, "but I wouldn't have known what to say. I would have—"

"But you would have come," she repeated.

And it was true, and it was something.

The car rattled as he made the turn onto the lake route, the trees giving way to a swath of cloudless sky.

And then he remembered what today was. Lise Daniels's first day back at school.

"Dad," Deenie said, turning the radio up as she spoke, rising a little in her seat. "The sky hurts my eyes."

★   ★   ★

Lying in bed before dawn, Deenie had heard Eli slip down the hall, the hushed drag of his stick bag against the carpet.

She wondered if Lise was up too. Maybe, over on Easter Way, Lise was nervously combing her hair, covering the violet zag in the center of her forehead, like a lightning bolt.

Or maybe she was doing what Deenie was doing, reading the news article on her phone:

The 16-year-old girl at the center of Dryden's poisoning case faces sentencing today.

They never printed her name, always called her "the girl." It made it seem like it could be anybody, any girl who was sixteen, in their midst.

The article said it would probably be probation, some community service. But it would remain on her record forever, just like they always say about everything you're never supposed to do.

A few weeks ago, Deenie had gotten a long letter from Gabby. It wasn't about Lise or Skye or even Eli. It was about the things she was learning, and how different she felt. She was changing, she said. But she didn't say what the changes were. Only that they were *big* and *important*.

There would always be things she'd never understand about Gabby. And that was the hardest part. That there would be mysteries impenetrable.

Had Gabby herself even known what she wanted, her fingers tucking Skye's poison down into the bottom of Lise's thermos, the same thermos that helped make Lise sylphlike and beautiful, her body so lovely and ready for wonder?

And then there was what Deenie herself had done. With Sean

Lurie. And how different it was, and how the same. *I want it too. I want what she has too. Why can't I get that too?*

Everyone wanted to be like Gabby. Her bright tights, the streak in her hair, the big glasses she wore when she read in class. Kim Court and Jaymie Hurwich, even Brooke Campos. Everyone.

Deenie wondered where all that frantic energy would go now. Did it just disappear, or did it go someplace else? She wondered about it for herself.

But Gabby was gone and probably wouldn't ever be back in their school. Probably she would move away, no matter what happened.

So where did all of it go, the things she felt for her?

Because, to her, it was Deenie-Gabby-Lise, snuggled together in sleeping bags, behind the bookshelves in the library, on the soccer field, in the auditorium.

Lise was still there. Today, her first day back at school.

She'd survived poisoning, which led to a seizure, which led to a cardiac event, which led to a fall, which led to blunt trauma to the head.

Everyone called her the Miracle Girl.

Deenie's dad called her Rasputin.

She said she didn't remember anything about that day, not even the drive to school that morning with her mom. The doctors told her that would happen, and she said she was glad, but it was hard for her to believe about Gabby, and she wasn't sure she ever would.

"What about the hospital?" Deenie asked her later. "Me visiting you?"

"No," Lise said. Deenie pictured herself at the foot of Lise's bed, trying to tell her about Sean Lurie. *And we were in his car. And he . . . or I. Me. It was me.* Lise's gleaming eye. The whistle from her white mouth.

The Fever

But Lise didn't remember any of that, either. And the first time Deenie visited her at home, she tried again. A twice-told confession.

"No," Lise interrupted, shaking her head, her hair oddly changed, a darker blond and not the same texture where it grew back, the center of her scalp where the dent terminated. "No, no. I don't want to talk about any of it. If I talk about any of it, my mouth fills up."

"Your mouth?"

"My chest, everything. I don't know, Deenie," she said, breathless. "Just stop."

And Deenie's dad told her that there could be emotional stuff for a long time, that it was a kind of trauma, and that Deenie shouldn't take it personally.

The word *trauma* seemed to cover a lot, a whole world of things, and it was the word they'd always used for Gabby, before what happened to Lise. To Gabby and Lise.

But it wasn't only Lise's hair—nothing was the same. Even her walk, the jut of her hip, the weight of her feet on her bedroom rug.

And most of all, it was something in her eyes, like when Lise first collapsed to the classroom floor that day, like something black, like a bat flapping.

* * *

Every morning, Eli woke from the same dream. Of riding in the passenger seat of a car and feeling something catch around his ankle, soft, light as air. Reaching down, he never found it.

Sometimes, he felt it when he was awake, in class, or even during a game, sweeping down the rink and feeling, even through his thick hockey socks, the boot of the skate, something both delicate and tight there on his ankle, grappling for him.

297

He tried not to think much about Gabby.

In a funny way, he was angry, and he didn't like the feeling. He'd always tried, very hard, not to feel mad at anybody, ever.

But there was someone he thought about more than Gabby, every time he walked by the double doors leading to the loading dock. Other times.

The night after Lise woke up, he and Deenie had stayed up late, sneaking beers from the fridge and talking. She told him about Skye, about everything. Or at least everything enough.

He could tell Deenie thought Skye was a monster.

But Gabby won't tell on her. It's all Skye's fault but Gabby won't tell. So now I can't.

He didn't point out that she didn't have to do what Gabby said. She could do whatever she wanted.

Instead, he just nodded, and nodded, and teased her about slurring her *s*'s.

And then she said, *I think Skye told me she gave you the jimson to get rid of me. And then she could run away. She knew I would have to find you.*

And he thought that part was probably true.

Then they watched *Meatballs* on cable, which their dad always loved, and Deenie fell asleep and snored just a little.

It was the best night ever.

And they hadn't talked about any of it since.

Stepping out onto the practice rink, he looked off into the backfield, the ground shorn of all its foliage, and the smell of ashes always now.

His skates hitting the ice, just starting to soften, he thought of Skye out there somewhere.

He'd heard her uncle had contacted the police, saying Skye had called him, collect, but he was already on probation and couldn't risk any trouble with the law. And besides, he was worried about her out there. She was just a kid.

Sometimes Eli thought he spotted her, a white flash in the corner of his eye.

No one had seen her since Deenie left her in her backyard the night Gabby confessed. The police were looking for her as part of the presentencing, were unsure of her role, if any, in what Gabby had done. They were following rumors, mostly.

Skye was a rumor now, a whiff of smoke drifting.

Now he thought he kind of understood what she meant about energies, the way they can be passed to you, can live in you even when you don't know it, until it's revealed to you. She was wrong about Lise. She didn't have any dark energy, or any powerful energy. Everyone else did, but not Lise.

When he got his phone back, he thought of Skye taking it, slipping it from his backpack as they sat on the loading dock. He wondered how long she'd had it before she gave it to Gabby.

Did she look at it, did she somehow see into him?

It was like his dream, Skye's thighs locked tight around him as he lay still. And her mouth opened and he could see inside, and . . .

There was a witchiness to her that was terrifying. And there was something else. Part of him wished he had put his hand on her back that day, on that twisted spine of hers, which she'd offered to him, asked of him.

But those were early-morning, predawn thoughts, out on the ice, dreaming.

★　★　★

The early spring had meant everything arrived early: the school grounds bursting with red shoots, the lawns thick with creeping phlox, other things he couldn't name.

Tom held the school door open for Deenie, her arms heavy with that monstrous book bag of hers.

The building smelled so different now. They had gone through the entire facility, the dropped ceilings in the basement, every stretch of the HVAC system. Scooped out every hidden cavity, scraped matter from each crease and furrow.

And they found many things.

Deep in the upper and lower corners of the old school they found pipes, fans, dampers, ducts coated with prehistoric sediments, gypsum board and ceiling tiles furred with mold, lead paint over older lead paint. PCBs in the caulk, the fluorescent lighting ballasts, the transformers that powered the school. Radon, mercury, arsenic in the water pipes, on the wood of the track hurdles, in the modular chairs, tables. The only thing they didn't find, other than, maybe, uranium, was asbestos. Everyone got rid of that a decade ago.

Trace amounts of a dozen or more things, most of which they'd removed over Easter break. The rest to be removed over the summer.

None of it, officials pointed out, had anything to do with what happened.

Because even if it isn't any of these things, it could *be,* Lara Bishop had said.

We put them at risk just by having them. And the hazards never stop.

But now, everything just smelled like nothing.

You wouldn't have thought nothing would have a smell.

"It's time, Dad," Deenie said, pointing to the old mounted clock, its brass casings stripped of green and newly shining.

"Right," he said, reaching down to hand her the new scarf, which had drifted to the floor. "Have a good day, D."

"Okay," she said, smiling a little, a half smile that was new to him. Wise and wary and not a girl's smile at all.

And he watched her walk all the way down the corridor, head lowered, hoodie half up her neck.

Each time her sneaker took a swivel on the bright polished floor, he felt his heart lurch.

★   ★   ★

There were only sixty seconds before the second bell, but everything seemed to slow down.

Shutting her locker, she put her hand on Lise's door, wondered where she was.

Walking through the halls, she saw all the girls with legs bare now, even though it was still too cold. A few of the boys were even wearing shorts.

She'd worked only one shift with Sean Lurie since everything happened.

He hadn't looked at her once, just took the order tickets, his nails greased. He was even wearing his cap, first time ever, so she couldn't see his eyes.

She didn't want to look at him anyway.

That night, a text came, the same unknown number as before. But this time, he said who he was:

Hey, u, Sean here. Sorry, k? we cool?
We cool, she'd typed back.

Then, somehow, they were never on the schedule again at the same time.

But he didn't go to Dryden High, so it was like it never even happened. She'd never told anyone other than Lise, and Lise didn't remember, so maybe it hadn't happened.

Except she could still feel all of it, but that was okay.

Turning the corner into the east wing, the breezeway unusually warm, the sun pounding on the glass, she saw Brooke Campos,

301

laughing loudly at something a boy had said, her mouth like a shark's.

All those girls, she wondered what they felt now. No one said anything, really. No one talked about the girls who'd been so sick.

Except for one of them, Kim Court, who'd transferred to Star-of-the-Sea after staying a long, long time in the hospital. Her videos were the only ones still online, and once in a while, the address still stored in her browser, Deenie would start typing and the video would come up, and there was Kim, talking about the man with tornado legs, about Gabby pulling seaweed from her throat, about Deenie being in the hospital, about Deenie being the one.

"Are you ready, Deenie?" It was Jaymie Hurwich, books clasped to her chest. "It's time."

And Deenie nodded.

The classroom door was open, and there was Lise, seated at her desk. The same spot she'd been in nearly seven weeks before, her legs tangled beneath her. Her chin tilted, looking out the window.

It was Lise, but it wasn't.

And Lise smiled at her, sort of. And Deenie sat down, and the bell rang, and everything shuttled back into place.

She'd never thought it would, that the fever would break. But the Lise who returned didn't seem like the same Lise. There were all these different Lises and none of them was Deenie's.

Looking out the window too, following Lise's gaze, Deenie saw the hedges, shorn to the ground.

And she could see through to the other wing, and there was Dad, charcoal sweater and handsome, talking to the French teacher again, showing her something on his phone. Giving her the smallest of smiles, the one her mom used to call the Croc.

All the trees and foliage had been torn away during the investigation, the remediation. Bushes razed, the earth seemingly shaken to its core. You could see everything now, if you wanted.

And though homeroom had begun, Eli was out there, outside, jacket off, on the practice rink, skating.

It was almost like fall, branches strewn across the thawing ice. Prickly globes split, seeds spilling, white petals pulped, spores that split red onto ice.

Each turn, graceful and lithe and hypnotic, she watched as his blades ran over every one.

Acknowledgments

There are not thanks enough to offer the incredible Reagan Arthur, nor Michael Pietsch and the magnificent, creative, and generous-spirited Little, Brown team, especially Theresa Giacopasi, Miriam Parker, Sarah J. Murphy, and Peggy Freudenthal. I'm honored to work among them all.

Immense gratitude is also owed to Paul Baggaley, Kate Harvey, Sophie Jonathan and Emma Bravo at Picador UK, and to Angharad Kowal, Maja Nikolic, and Bakara Wintner at Writers House and Sylvie Rabineau and Jill Gillett at RWSG. Thanks also to James Lavish and Vicki Pettersson, for an invaluable assist.

And foremost to Dan Conaway, without whom, in all ways.

My debt to the following just grows and grows: Phil & Patti Abbott; Josh, Julie & Kevin Abbott; Jeff, Ruth & Steve Nase; and the one and only Alison Quinn. And, as ever, thanks to Darcy Lockman, Kiki Wilkinson, and, of course, to the FLs. This year, I'm particularly grateful to the good folks of Oxford, Mississippi, including Jack Pendarvis, Theresa Starkey, and Ace Atkins.

And, as writer and reader both, I'm certain the greatest debt is owed to booksellers everywhere.

picador.com

blog
videos
interviews
extracts